28.

The Pageant Of World History

The Pageant Of World History

GERALD LEINWAND

Allyn and Bacon, Inc.

Boston · Rockleigh, N.J. · Atlanta · Dallas · San Jose
London · Sydney · Toronto

About the Author

Gerald Leinwand received his B.A., M.S., and Ph.D. degrees from New York University, and an M.A. from Columbia University. He is President of Western Oregon State College in Monmouth, Oregon. He was Professor of Education and Dean of the School of Education of the Bernard M. Baruch College of the City University of New York. Dr. Leinwand has taught world history on television, and for many years was a teacher in junior and senior high schools. He has written *The American Constitution: Tutor-text; Teaching History and Social Studies in Secondary Schools.* He is also author-editor of the paperback series *Problems of American Society.*

Edited and Designed by Cover to Cover, Inc.
  New York, New York

Publisher's Staff
  Design Coordinator: Beverly Fell
  Preparation Services Coordinator: Martha E. Ballentine
  Buyer: Linda Jackson

Cover Photo: John Martucci
Maps and Charts: Pictograph Corporation

Library of Congress Catalog Card No. 82-70154

Printed in the United States of America
  2 3 4 5 6 7 8 9 91 90 89 88 87 86 85 84 83

PREFACE

The world has changed greatly in the twenty-five years since *The Pageant of World History* was first published. During that time the text has gone through many revisions. It has had the benefit of the view of students and teachers who have used it and who have indicated what they liked and what they wanted changed. These ideas have found their way into this, the latest revision of *The Pageant of World History*.

The text gives a chronological examination of Western and non-Western history. The facts of world history are clearly stated so that students can draw major generalizations. The choice and presentation of world history have been carefully adjusted to the limitations of class time and to a controlled reading level.

Many special features of this revision engage students in the discovery of history and help to organize their learning. At the beginning of each chapter is a "Chapter Focus" which indicates the themes and sections of the chapter. At the end of each section are "Check in Here" questions which help students conceptualize and recall what was read. Phonetic spellings throughout aid in the pronunciation of difficult names. Biographies discuss prominent people in history. Time lines enable students to place specific events in historical context and to compare Western and non-Western cultures. A full-color map program with caption questions closely relates text and chapter content. At the end of each chapter are chapter summaries, questions which help students master the fundamentals, and a "You Are the Historian" activity which gives students an opportunity to analyze various kinds of data and draw their own conclusions. Chapter and unit research activities provide imaginative topics for work in depth to supplement the text. A comprehensive glossary and index are additional tools for students' use.

It is the constant aim of *The Pageant of World History* to present in their cause-and-effect relationships the major historical events from the ancient past to the present.

CONTENTS

UNIT IV The Dominance of Europe

UNIT VI Toward Global Peace 592

BIOGRAPHIES

MAPS

If the future is to be built on a foundation of past and present achievement, we must gain an understanding of world history to fulfill our responsibilities tomorrow.

NOTES TO THE STUDENT

The Pageant of World History has features that will make it easier to understand what you are reading.

Italicized Words

Some words are central to understanding the lesson. These words are *italicized* to make you aware of their importance. Many of them appear as "Terms to Understand" at the end of the chapter.

Phoneticized Words

The names of major people and places are spelled phonetically. The pronunciation of each word appears in brackets just after the word. The key below will help you to read the pronunciations.

a	hat, cap	i	it, pin	p	paper, cup	v	very, save
ā	age, face	ī	ice, live	r	run, try	w	will, woman
ä	father, far			s	say, yes	y	young, yet
		j	jam, enjoy	sh	she, rush	z	zero, breeze
b	bad, rob	k	kind, seek	t	tell, it	zh	measure, seizure
ch	child, much	l	land, coal	th	thin, both		
d	did, red	m	me, am	ᴛH	then, smooth	ə	represents:
		n	no, in				a in about
e	let, best	ng	long, bring	u	cup, butter		e in taken
ē	equal, be			ù	full, put		i in pencil
ėr	term, learn	o	hot, rock	ü	rule, move		o in lemon
		ō	open, go				u in circus
f	fat, if	ô	order, all				
g	go, bag	oi	oil, voice				
h	he, how	ou	house, out				

From Thorndike-Barnhart Intermediate Dictionary by E.L. Thorndike and Clarence L. Barnhart. Copyright © 1974 Scott, Foresman and Company. Reprinted by permission.

Prologue:
In Search of History

Archaeologists dig in Nippur, Iraq to find evidence of how people lived in ancient history.

The American historian and journalist Theodore White got his first introduction to newspaper work as a teenager when he sold newspapers on the streets of Boston. He would cry, *"Globe, Post, Herald, and Record* here! Papers?" Each morning White would scan the newspapers to find exciting headlines to shout, ones he thought would sell papers. Those headlines are now history. Years later, White wrote a book called *In Search of History.* The title of this Prologue is borrowed from that book.

Today's newspapers cover events all over the world. The lives of people in India, Africa, Europe, and China, the world's oil supply, the election of a pope, the launching of a space shuttle, and changes in governments are all reported in newspapers. Some or all of these events may influence your life. Headlines in today's newspapers are tomorrow's history. If you understand what is happening in today's world you will be better prepared for the future. In a similar way, learning about the past will help you understand the headlines that are being made today.

History

History is a record of what human beings have done on earth. This definition is useful, but it is not really a complete one. The English scholar Edward Hallet Carr has described history as "an unending dialogue [conversation] between the present and the past." What Mr. Carr

1

means is that the past and present are connected. We learn about ourselves by studying the past. To find out about the past we examine its records. These may be written or unwritten. They may be the stone tools that primitive people left behind. They may be bones, fossils, decayed ruins, or the great stone monuments that have withstood the passage of time. Or, the records may be written ones, such as laws, diaries, and business records. Indeed, any written document, including your history notebook, has value as a historical record.

Our knowledge of history is often incomplete. Some records have been lost or destroyed. Others have been deliberately changed so that the truth may never be known. For these reasons some people describe history as "bunk" and others describe it as "lies people have agreed upon." Can we accept these views of history? Although there are problems in the study of history, we must recognize that the study of history is a difficult and unending search to find the facts and to interpret them. And, rightly or wrongly, we interpret the past by the standards of the present. Studying and interpreting the past creates the dialogue about which Carr wrote.

The Value of History

History has value for the lessons it teaches. A society that does not study the past may repeat its mistakes. History has value for the light it sheds on the present. It helps us understand our problems better. It gives us a picture of how we have become what we are. History gives us a sense of belonging. We are members of the human community whose past is our past and whose future we will share. The past tells us that we are human beings whose lives depend on the contributions of human beings who came before us.

The *Pageant of World History* is concerned with every part of the globe. You will study world politics, world wars, and rulers who sought to dominate the entire world. You will learn about world cultures through their art, music, architecture, and literature. You will also study their scientific and technological progress. Unless you know the history of other lands, you cannot fully understand the history of your own. A study of world history will help you understand points of view and values that are different from your own. Because human beings have not always understood each other's points of view and values, the history of the world has too often been the story of conflict.

The Social Sciences

When people go to work or to school, or visit a friend, or go to a party, they take part in social events. Social events have to do with people. The *social sciences*, in simplest terms, may be said to be about society and people. The social sciences include the study of government, economics, geography, history, sociology, anthropology, and psychology.

The social science that studies the system of laws by which people live is called *government*. The social science called *economics* examines the ways in which people make a living. *Geography* is the study of the earth and the relationship of people to the earth. *History* is primarily concerned with the events and people of the past.

The social sciences that explore the ways people act and the reasons for their behavior are called the *behavioral sciences*. These include sociology, anthropology, and psychology. *Sociology* is the study of how people live in communities and the kinds of groups they form. *Anthropology* is the study of the origin of

A hunter is portrayed in this prehistoric rock painting found in Algeria.

human beings and their cultural development. Along with *statistics* (the collection and classification of numerical data) and *archaeology* (the study of early human remains), these subjects are all useful to the historian. They help the historian see the whole story more thoroughly than would otherwise be possible.

**How We Find Out
What Happened in the Past**

To find out about the past, historians use many different resources and reference materials. They use *primary* sources and *secondary* sources. A primary source is a document, record, or written account by someone who took part in an event. It is a firsthand account that comes directly from the past. Of course, the further back one goes in history, the more difficult it is to find primary sources. Some examples of primary sources are diaries, letters, acts of Congress, presidential speeches, and even parking tickets and laundry stubs.

Secondary sources are written some time after an event has taken place and by a person who was not an eyewitness. Secondary sources may or may not be based on primary sources. A textbook is an example of a secondary source. Someone using a secondary source in research would not rely entirely on it for information. He or she would also consult other kinds of sources, primary as well as secondary.

Both primary and secondary sources are valuable to historians. They must both be judged for accuracy and for their importance to the topic being researched. And sometimes primary and secondary sources disagree. In baseball the umpire tells when a given play is safe or out. The umpire makes the final decision, with little or no room for disagreement. In history there is no umpire to tell when something is accurate or inaccurate. There is tremendous room for disagreement. There may also be many different interpretations of the evidence. The historian, therefore, must study

Three examples of early calendars: (top) Egyptian; (center) Cretan; (bottom) Aztec.

many facts and make careful conclusions based on them. Then too, different historians using identical materials may reach different conclusions.

Researching and interpreting history is a challenging and complicated task. Throughout this text you will be given an opportunity to be a historian. You will find both primary and secondary sources. They should be studied as a historian would study them. You should try to interpret them in light of the evidence they present and then you should discuss your views with the class.

How Historians Determine When Something Happened

One problem a historian has is determining *when* something happened. This is more difficult than it sounds. Today, most people use the same calendar (although Muslims and Jews use their own calendars for religious purposes). But this was not always so. The ancient Egyptian, Babylonian, Greek, and Roman calendars were different from the one we use. A calendar may be based upon the moon's revolution around the earth or on the earth's revolution about the sun. Our calendar is based upon the earth's revolution around the sun and is called a *solar* calendar. In the Middle Ages, instruments were developed that measured exactly how long the earth's revolution takes. Errors in the solar calendar were shown. In 1582, Pope Gregory ordered changes in the Roman calendar to correct the errors. The *New Style* calendar, as it was called, was adopted by Catholic countries. Non-Catholic countries adopted it more slowly. England did not adopt the New Style calendar until 1752, and Russia did not adopt it until the Russian Revolution of 1917. Different dating systems in calendars make it hard for the historian to determine when something actually happened.

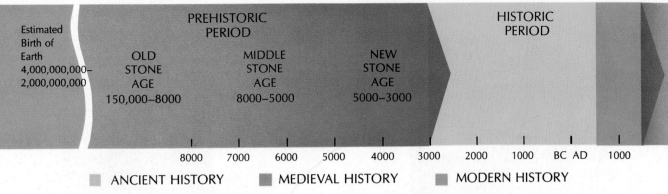

	PREHISTORIC PERIOD			HISTORIC PERIOD	

Estimated Birth of Earth 4,000,000,000– 2,000,000,000

OLD STONE AGE 150,000–8000

MIDDLE STONE AGE 8000–5000

NEW STONE AGE 5000–3000

8000   7000   6000   5000   4000   3000   2000   1000   BC   AD   1000

ANCIENT HISTORY   MEDIEVAL HISTORY   MODERN HISTORY

What is the difference between prehistoric time and historic time?

If a document has a date on it, that will help place it in time. The wise historian knows that the date may be in error. Have you ever written the wrong date on an assignment paper or on a letter to a friend? If that letter became a significant primary source in history, the date could confuse a historian trying to determine a series of events. Sometimes, the date on a document may have been deliberately falsified for some purpose. If a date is incorrect and the historian accepts it as accurate, she or he will be making an error in fact or judgment. Then our understanding of the past will not be correct. A historian may try to date a document by studying different writing and printing styles. A historian may determine the age of a document by the kind of paper and ink used. Sometimes clues in the document itself give a good indication of when it was written. For example, a document might refer to an event that happened sometime after the date on the document.

The letters *B.C.* in historical dates mean the time before Christ was born. The letters *A.D.* refer to the time after the birth of Christ (taken from the Latin *Anno Domini* meaning the year of our Lord).

As historians go further back in time, science comes to their aid. Radio-carbon dating may be used to give useful dates for the development of primitive people.

Through what is known as *Carbon-14* dating, scientists can determine how much Carbon-14 has decayed in the object being examined. The greater the decay, the older the object. Carbon dating is not perfect. It cannot be used in determining the age of stone tools, or pieces of pottery. It is good for dating *organic* remains (e.g., bones, teeth, hair). But it cannot give reliable dating beyond 40,000 years. New dating devices have been developed. They help the archaeologist and anthropologist as well as the historian. For example, the use of amino acids can date very old organic remains, and radioactive methods can give us reliable dates of ancient pottery.

The period during which people kept written records of their accomplishments is called the *historic* period. It includes the last 5,000 years. The period for which there are no written records (the millions of years before 3000 B.C.) is called the *prehistoric* period.

Because the prehistoric period lasted so long, it has been divided into the *Old, Middle,* and *New Stone Ages*. It is difficult to place beginning or ending dates on these periods. Many scientists believe that the Old Stone Age lasted two million years. It ended around 8000 B.C. It was the longest of the three periods. The Middle Stone Age was the shortest (8000 B.C.–5000 B.C.). It ended about the time some written records began to appear.

Archaeologists at work: Left: An archaeologist carefully reconstructs an ancient pot discovered near the Dead Sea in the Middle East. Right: At a site along the Alaskan pipeline, an archaeologist digs the soil for evidence of early life. Finding out about the past can be difficult and, at times, tedious, but the reward is the excitement of discovery.

The New Stone Age began about 5000 B.C. It led to the Bronze and Iron Ages when humankind learned to use metals, especially bronze and iron. The end of the prehistoric period and the beginning of written history vary from one part of the world to another. The change from the prehistoric period is still going on in some parts of the world. There are some people today who live essentially the way some of our ancestors did in prehistoric times.

What Early People Contributed to the Prehistoric Period

According to scholars of the Bible, humankind was created in the image of God. Some authorities believe that people developed from one or at most a small number of common ancestors. Which of these views is correct has yet to

become absolutely clear. The search for evidence of the human existence continues to interest scholars of both viewpoints.

Early remains of people were found in Java, an island off the coast of southeast Asia. Another group of remains was found in Peking, China. These sites, Java [jä′vä] and Peking [pā king′], gave their names to the groups of people who lived there in prehistoric times. No tools were found with the bones in Java. But in a cave in Peking, China, some simple tools were found along with a human skeleton. These tools were mostly rocks and sticks and stones that fit into the hands of Peking people. It was only later that these people learned how to make more complex tools for themselves.

Java and Peking people began to wander the earth. They advanced in technology when they learned to make axes.

An important milestone in the development of these early people was the invention of fire. Fire kept enemies, especially wild animals, away at night. Fire kept early humans warm, as well as enabling them to cook their food.

Neanderthals [nē an'dər thôlz'] (about 50,000 B.C.–40,000 B.C., according to scientists) were among the first people to live successfully in colder climates. They hunted giant animals such as the wooly rhinoceros, musk ox, mammoth, cave bear, and reindeer. Neanderthal people began to settle along paths animals tended to use. They thus had an easily available source of meat. Their need to wander in order to hunt was reduced. When people were able to stay in one place, settled communities began.

The Neanderthals were among the earliest to care for their sick and wounded. They took care of the elderly members of their group and had rituals for burying the dead. Thus, they probably thought about the meaning of life and death.

About 40,000 years ago, the scientists tell us the Neanderthals disappeared. No one knows why. They were replaced by a group of people known as the Cro-Magnon [krō mag'nən]. These people were named after the location in southern France where their remains were found. Perhaps the Cro-Magnons had a throwing spear that destroyed the Neanderthals. Another theory is that the Neanderthals were not killed off at all. Instead, they changed physically to the point where they could not be distinguished from the Cro-Magnons.

The bodies of Neanderthals and Cro-Magnons were very similar. Cro-Magnons advanced far more rapidly in technology. The Cro-Magnons made stone, bone, and wood tools. Stone tools were polished. Bones were made into fishhooks and harpoons; this made possible a new source of food: fish.

Neanderthals lived mostly in caves. Cro-Magnons moved from caves and began to build shelters. The dome-shaped huts of Pygmies, Bushmen, Australian Aborigines, and Mongolians are similar to the homes invented by the Cro-Magnons. The dome-shaped home is probably the earliest and most common form of housing throughout the world. Buckminster Fuller, the twentieth-century architect, designed a geodesic dome. He was inspired partly by the dome-shaped shelters of Cro-Magnon people.

For many years the remains at Java and Peking were believed to be the earliest known to history. In the 1970s, human remains were found in East Africa, at Olduvai Gorge [ōl dü vä gôrj] in Tanzania and in Ethiopia. They were discovered by anthropologists Drs. Louis and Mary Leakey [lē'kē]. Further work in Africa was done by their son Richard Leakey.

Since the discoveries of the Leakeys the four-million-year-old remains of a female were discovered by Dr. Donald Johanson. They show that humans may be much older than was once believed. These discoveries also suggested, but did not prove, that human beings may have originated in Africa. However, in 1979, anthropologists discovered jawbones in Burma believed to date back at least ten million years.

The search for history has two directions. The search goes on by those who examine humankind's remote past. It continues with those who study today's civilizations. You are about to start a search for history.

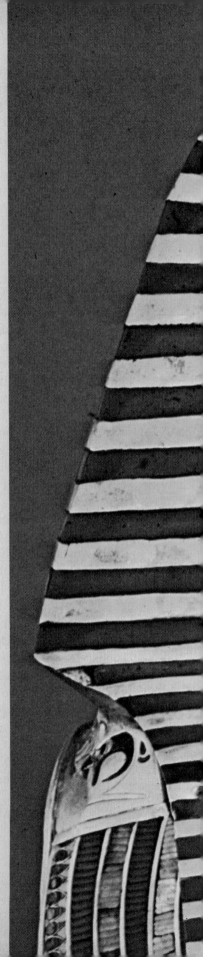

UNIT

I

Discovering the Cradles of Civilization

Funeral mask of Tutankhamen

8

Copy of a wall painting from the Tomb of Menna, c. 1420 B.C.

In the Cradle of the Middle East: The Gifts of the Nile, the Tigris, and the Euphrates

We are all interested in firsts. We like to know who the first person was to fly an airplane, when human beings first walked on the moon, when the first railroad was built. What were some of your "famous firsts"?

Remember the day you entered school for the first time, or the first time you made the school team, or won your first school prize? These events make a lasting impression on us. They are important times in growing up.

Historians, too, are often concerned with famous firsts. They want to know which nations were the first to find new lands or the first to build stable, lasting societies. Yet historical firsts are not always easy to find.

Historians cannot be sure which civilization developed first. However, they know that many ancient civilizations were born in the Middle East. The Middle East is the region where Europe, Asia, and Africa meet. This area has been called the cradle, or birthplace, of civilization. In other parts of the world, the Chinese and Indian civilizations grew. As historians studied North and South America, they found still more cradles of civilization. It is clear to us now that there were several beginning points of civilization rather than just one.

We begin our study of ancient history with Egypt. The Egyptians were one of the first people to make their country strong and united.

HOW ANCIENT EGYPT BUILT A CIVILIZATION

Why Egypt Was Called the Gift of the Nile

Egypt was called the "gift of the Nile" by the Greek historian Herodotus. The Nile River rises in east central Africa, and flows northward through Egypt. It made ancient Egypt's high level of civilization possible. Most Egyptians made their homes in the valley along the banks of the river. When the Nile River overflowed, as it did each year, it left fertile soil. The soil was used for farming. In Egypt, there is little rainfall. The flooding of the river every year is still of great importance. It makes growing food and other products possible.

The Nile Valley had fertile soil and sunny weather. It attracted settlers. Travel by river was easy and cheap. The Nile became a highway for travel and trade. The northern and southern parts of ancient Egypt joined and grew into a rich, strong, and united nation. This union took place at the very dawn of history and lasted for centuries.

How the Egyptian Mystery Was Solved

Egypt is a very old country. Except for the pyramids, little was known about Egypt for hundreds of years. One reason for this was that no one had ever been able to read Egyptian *hieroglyphics*, [hī′ər ə glif′iks], or picture writing.

In 1799, the French leader Napoleon invaded Egypt. A group of his soldiers found the ancient Egyptian temples at Luxor [luk′sôr] and Karnak [kär′nak]. Their most important discovery, however, was the *Rosetta* [rō zet′ə] *Stone,* which turned out to be the key to Egyptian writing. On the stone were Greek letters and Egyptian hieroglyphics. A French scholar, Jean Champollion [shän pô lyôn'], used his knowledge of Greek to figure out the hieroglyphics on the Rosetta Stone. He unlocked the mystery of Egyptian writing. He opened the way for the study of Egyptian history.

How Ancient Egypt's History Is Divided

By 2850 B.C., Lower Egypt (where the Nile Delta empties into the Mediterranean) and Upper Egypt (the Nile River Valley) were joined into one country. It was ruled by Pharaoh Menes [mē'nēz]. *Pharaoh* [fer'ō] was the Egyptian word for king. The nation's capital was at Memphis [mem'fis], near modern Cairo [kī'rō]. There Menes started a *dynasty* [dī'nəs tē], or family of rulers. From the days of Menes to about 300 B.C., there were thirty dynasties.

Historians have divided Egyptian history into three time periods. The first is called the *Old Kingdom,* or the Age of Pyramids. During this time (2615–1991 B.C.) the great pyramids were built by the pharaohs. The *Sphinx* [sfingks] was also built about then. The Sphinx is a massive stone statue with the head of a human attached to the body of a lion. Today, people come from far and wide to ride up the Nile River. They look with wonder at the pyramids in Giza and at the Sphinx.

A section of the Nile River Valley in Egypt. Very little rain falls in Egypt. Why then is the Nile River Valley a fertile area?

By the sixth dynasty the power of the pharaohs began to lessen. Nobles and priests became more powerful than the rulers. This was the beginning of the second period of Egyptian history. This period (1991–1570 B.C.) is called the *Middle Kingdom,* or the Age of the Nobles. During this time, Egypt remained united. However, it was not as strong as it had been during the Old Kingdom. The local nobles had a great deal of freedom. They took few orders from the pharaohs. The pharaohs moved the capital from Memphis to Thebes [thēbz]. On the outskirts of the city of Thebes, they built more pyramids. They also began the temples at Luxor and Karnak. They constructed large irrigation works. These were used to bring thousands of acres of land under cultivation. Crops could be grown on this land.

About 1800 B.C., the Hyksos [hik′sōs] came on horseback and invaded Egypt. They were a warlike people from the northeast. Fighting against an enemy on horses was new to the Egyptians, and they were easily defeated by the Hyksos. For about 200 years—to 1570 B.C.— the Hyksos ruled. Then the Egyptians learned the art of war on horseback and the Egyptians drove the Hyksos out.

The third period of Egyptian history (1570–332 B.C.) is called the *New Kingdom,* or the Age of Empire. The Egyptians looked for and found new lands to conquer. At this time Ethiopia, Palestine, and Syria became part of the Egyptian empire.

Three of the outstanding pharaohs of the New Kingdom were Queen Hatshepsut [hat shep′süt] (1503–1482 B.C.), Thutmose III [thüt mōs] (1504–1450 B.C.), and Ramses II [ram′sēz] (1304–1237 B.C.). Queen Hatshepsut reigned for many years. She ruled wisely, and the Egyptians prospered. The queen had *obelisks* [äb′ə lisks] built at Karnak. Obelisks

Ancient Egypt About 1450 B.C.

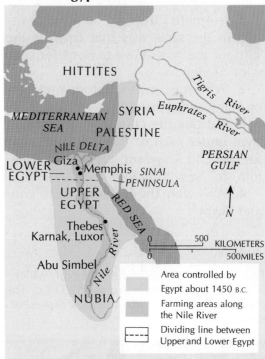

Farming in ancient Egypt took place along the Nile River.
- Into what body of water does the Nile River flow?
- Was the ancient city of Memphis in Upper Egypt or Lower Egypt?

are stone pillars built in honor of the sun. She also had a magnificent tomb built where her body might rest after death. Thutmose III was a great conqueror. He extended the Egyptian empire to the Euphrates River and made Syria a part of the empire. Ramses II won fame for fighting the warlike Hittites, although he eventually made peace with them. Ramses built many magnificent buildings, including the temple at Abu-Simbel [ä′bü′sim′bel]. His rule was noted for its luxury.

After 1150 B.C., the tables turned. Instead of being the conqueror, Egypt became the conquered. In 525 B.C., Egypt fell under the power of Persia. Egypt would not again be free until A.D. 1936.

13

Check in Here

1. Is America the "gift" of the Mississippi in the same way that Egypt is the "gift" of the Nile? Give reasons for your point of view.
2. Why was Egypt's history a mystery for many centuries?
3. Indicate the chief characteristic of Egypt under each of the following periods: (a) Old Kingdom; (b) Middle Kingdom; (c) New Kingdom.
4. Why were the Hyksos able to conquer Egypt?

The Temple of Abu-Simbel in Egypt, which was built by Ramses II around 1200 B.C. The giant figures carved into the rock represent Ramses II.

THE GOVERNMENT AND PEOPLE OF ANCIENT EGYPT

How Egypt Was Ruled

Egyptian government began as early as 3400 B.C. During the Old Kingdom the pharaoh governed from the capital at Memphis. The pharaoh's power and authority were complete and unquestioned. The pharaoh was a landlord, and all nobles rented their estates from him or her. The pharaoh was also considered a god and was believed to have divine powers. As well as being king or queen, the pharaoh was the high priest of the Egyptian people. With these powers, the pharaohs could rule a united country. They could build a strong army and extend their rule over other countries.

The pharaoh was served by a huge group of people. Today we would call these people government workers. The *vizir* [vi zir'] was an appointed prime minister. It was the vizir's job to see to it that the pharaoh's laws were carried out. *Scribes* [skrībz] kept the records of the nation. They knew how much had been spent at war, how many workers were building the pyramids, and how much the pyramids cost. The scribes recorded who owed taxes and how much. Egyptians lived their lives in the class into which they were born. Some scribes, however, could climb upward in the government. They were valued for their writing, a rare skill among Egyptians.

The pharaohs were very powerful during the Old Kingdom. During the Middle Kingdom and during the New Kingdom their powers grew less and less. This happened partly as a result of jealousy among the nobles. The nobles wanted more land and power. Although they were eventually driven out of Egypt, the Hyksos also weakened the pharaohs. The power of the pharaohs never really returned to what it had been during the

Old Kingdom. When the New Kingdom came to an end, the Egyptian pharaohs were mostly figureheads. That is, although the pharaoh still ruled, the priests, viziers, and scribes had more power.

How Religion Influenced the People

The Greek historian Herodotus wrote that the Egyptians were "the most religious of peoples." Religion was a part of everyday life. The pharaohs had great power because people believed they were gods. Egyptians also believed that many gods influenced the economy of the nation. They thought that the flooding of the Nile, the health of animals, the size of the harvest, and success in battle were in the hands of the gods.

Egyptians prayed to many gods. They considered animals such as the bull, the cat, and the crocodile to be holy. The two chief gods were Amon-Ra [ä′mən rä′] and Osiris [ō sī′ ris]. Amon-Ra was believed to be the sun god and the lord of the universe. As Egypt grew in strength, the worship of Amon-Ra spread to the lands that Egypt conquered. Egypt started, but never completed, the road that led to *monotheism* [mon′ə thē iz′əm], or the worship of a single god.

Osiris was the god of the underworld. Legends about him involve the idea of immortality (living forever in another world). Osiris was the god that made possible a peaceful afterlife. At first it was believed that only pharaohs had an afterlife. Later, everyone, animals as well as people, were thought to enjoy an afterlife. The Egyptian *Book of the Dead* contains the major ideas found in the Egyptian religion.

Amenhotep III [ä′mən hō′tep] (1407–1379 B.C.) encouraged the worship of Amon-Ra as the one god of the Egyp-

Amenhotep IV. He changed his name to Ikhnaton because of his religious beliefs. How did this king want to change Egyptian religion?

tians. His son, Amenhotep IV (1379–1362 B.C.) went even further. He tried to force Egypt to become a monotheistic nation. He changed Amon-Ra's name to Aton [ä′tən]. He called Aton "the sole god, beside whom there is no other." Amenhotep changed his own name to Ikhnaton [ik nä′tən]. He insisted that Aton was a god of kindness, love, and mercy. He wanted all Egyptians to worship one god. Ikhnaton ordered that names and pictures of Amon-Ra and other gods be destroyed. He tried to make religious reforms, but this did not please those who favored the old ways. The new religion went against the whole Egyptian way of life. When Ikhnaton died his religious reforms died with him.

Tutankhamen [tüt'ängk ä'mən] (1361–1351 B.C.) tried hard to return the nation to the worship of Amon-Ra. To do this, he gave great gifts to the priests of Amon-Ra, and dedicated the magnificent temples of Karnak and Luxor to Amon-Ra. Egypt turned away from monotheism.

Egyptians believed that a person's spirit lived on in the body after death. They, therefore, tried to preserve the bodies of the dead. Pharaohs wanted to make sure that their spirits were safe after death. They built great stone *pyramids.* These were elaborate tombs in which the pharaohs were buried with their treasures. The walls of the pyramids were covered with pictures and hieroglyphics. The story of the pharaoh's great and good deeds was told in the pictures and hieroglyphics. Thanks to this custom, the walls of the pyramids tell the story of ancient Egypt.

In 1922, an English archaeologist, Howard Carter, discovered the tomb of Tutankhamen. Tutankhamen's treasures provided valuable information about art and life in ancient Egypt. In 1978, the Cairo Museum allowed the treasures to go on display throughout the United States. Thousands of people saw them.

How People Live in Ancient Egypt

Organization of Society: In ancient Egypt it was difficult for the children of a poor family to rise above their class. To move from one class to another was difficult, if not impossible. Most people lived and died in the class in which they were born. Nobles, government officials, and religious leaders lived in luxury. However, most of the people were poor. Thousands of slaves were used to build pyramids, canals, temples, and other buildings.

Role of Women: In ancient Egypt, men had more power than women. However, women were allowed to own land. Women could give their land to their sons and daughters when they died. The position of women was higher in Egypt than it was in many other ancient lands. In some ancient countries women were treated as slaves.

Role of Children: Children and family life were important in ancient Egypt. Children of the middle and upper classes went to school where they were taught by priests. Children of lower classes were taught by their parents. Lower-class boys learned trades or farming from their fathers. Upper-class boys learned to write. Some became scribes. In schools discipline was strict, and the priests or teachers were stern. Would you like to go to a school where it was said, "The youth has a back and attends when he is beaten . . ."? Girls of both the upper and lower classes learned to run a household. The care and education of upper-class children were shared responsibilities. These children were raised by the family, the priests, and the pharaohs.

Farming: Most people in ancient Egypt were farmers. Farming was totally dependent upon the overflowing of the Nile. The yearly flooding of the river made the land fertile. All the land was owned by the pharaoh. Any crops left over after paying taxes belonged to the farmer. The Egyptian farmer grew wheat, barley, and other grains, vegetables, and different kinds of fruit, including dates. Flax was grown for linen and marsh reeds were harvested for *papyrus* [pə pī' rəs]. This was the writing material used by Egyptians. Farm animals included cattle, sheep, goats, and pigs; the donkey and the ox were beasts of burden. The horse was unknown to Egypt before 1700 B.C., and the camel was not used in Egypt until 525 B.C.

Manufacturing: Manufacturing in

Egypt developed over many centuries. Egyptians learned to mix tin and copper to make bronze. This they used in making weapons and tools. Egyptians made brick and cement, which were used in construction. They also knew how to blow glass and glaze pottery. Pottery was painted with beautiful colors. Egyptians carved wood and made fine furniture including chairs, beds, and cushions. They knew how to weave linen from flax. Fine jewelry, glass goblets, and glazed bowls were made in Egypt. These things were sold to other countries.

Trade: Some people earned a living by shipping and trading. Egyptian ships loaded with grain, glass, and cloth were a common sight. Traders sought amethyst, alabaster, granite, and a dark stone called diorite. Ebony, gold, ivory, ostrich feathers, leopard skins, and fragrant woods came from Nubia and the Sudan. These were countries to the south of Egypt. Turquoise, copper, and malachite were mined on the Sinai Peninsula. Products such as lapis lazuli, obsidian, olive oil, resins, wood, bronze, and tin came from Asia.

Egypt's Contributions to Civilization

Perhaps the greatest contribution of the early Egyptians was the writing system known as hieroglyphics. It was based on an alphabet of twenty-four signs. Each sign represented a basic consonant. There were no signs for vowels. The Egyptians were one of the first people to make a writing material. Writing was done as you already know, on papyrus, which was made from plants. Our word "paper" comes from the word "papyrus." The scribes wrote with a pen made from a pointed reed. They used ink made from vegetable gum.

Some of the most important gifts of Egypt to later civilizations were in the

An Egyptian wall painting combines painted figures and Egyptian writing. What is Egyptian writing called?

fields of mathematics, engineering, astronomy, and medicine. Egyptian numbers were clumsy to use. However, they were accurate. One stroke was made for 1; two strokes for 2; nine strokes for 9. A new sign was made for 10. There was no zero.

Egyptian engineering was based on a knowledge of mathematics. Some historians believe that Egyptian engineers developed the first ocean-going ships. The construction of the pyramids shows a knowledge of mathematical principles. For example, Egyptians knew how to use the square and the right angle. They knew how to use an inclined plane—and a lot of muscle—to pull, haul, and hoist the huge blocks of stone into place.

Egyptians learned to predict the flooding of the Nile every year from June to October. Egyptians learned that year after year, the flooding of the Nile came just after they could see the dog star, Sirius [sir'ē əs], in the early dawn. In this way, the Egyptians developed a sun calendar. The calendar was based on a year of 12 months. Each month had 30 days. Because this calendar was not strictly accurate, however, the Egyptians made an adjustment. They added five days to the year so that each year had 365 days. These were usually used for holidays of different kinds.

Egyptian medicine reached a high level. Famous Egyptian doctors were in demand in all parts of the ancient world. They knew about the function of the heart and how to heal wounds. They knew how to take the pulse, and studied the eyes of their patient for tell-tale signs of illness. Egyptian doctors developed many new medicines. One was castor oil.

Egyptians preserved the human body after death. They treated dead bodies with oil and spices and wrapped them in linen. This preparation required a high degree of medical skill. Their method of preserving the human body after death remains a secret.

Why Egypt Fell

Egyptian civilization made many contributions to history. Why then did that nation fail to remain a leader? One reason was that the pharaohs did not always use their power for the welfare of the people. They were too concerned with building pyramids and temples. They paid too much attention to winning new lands. Probably the most important reason for the fall of Egypt was the many costly wars it fought. All these things helped weaken Egyptian civilization.

Check in Here

1. Discuss the role of children in ancient Egypt. How was it different in the upper and lower classes?

2. Why did Ikhnaton's attempt to establish monotheism in Egypt fail?

3. Summarize life in ancient Egypt under each of these headings: (**a**) farming; (**b**) trading; (**c**) manufacturing.

4. Explain Egypt's contribution to civilization in each of the following areas: (**a**) writing; (**b**) medicine; (**c**) engineering.

5. Why do you think Egypt made important contributions in each of the above?

HOW CIVILIZATION DEVELOPED IN THE FERTILE CRESCENT

The Peoples of Mesopotamia

The *Fertile Crescent* is an area that begins in the valleys of the Tigris [tī'gris] and Euphrates [yü frā'tēz] rivers. It runs along the coast of the Mediterranean Sea as far as Egypt. The waters of the rivers make irrigation farming possible in this extremely dry land. The rivers are also routes for transportation and communication.

Between the two rivers a number of ancient civilizations were born, lived, and died. As the rich Nile River valley attracted settlers, so did the land between the Tigris and the Euphrates rivers. This region, a part of the Fertile Crescent, was called *Mesopotamia* [mes'ə pə tā'mē ə]. Today it is part of Iraq. Its history is one of the rise and fall of empires.

As early as 4000 B.C., people called the Sumerians [sü mer'ē ənz] settled in Mesopotamia. The Sumerians lived in small independent cities. They knew how to use the wheel and how to make tools and weapons of copper. They decorated objects with gold and silver and developed the earliest form of writing, which was called *cuneiform* [kyü nē'ə fôrm]. The Sumerians had no strong king to unite them. As a result, their cities were

Ancient Mesopotamia

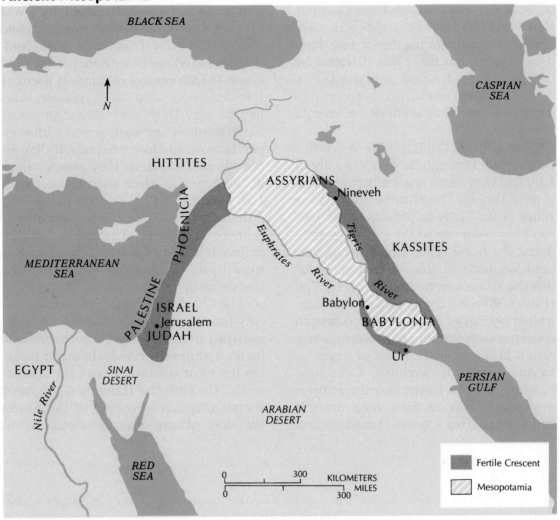

Mesopotamia was the site for many ancient empires.
- What two rivers dominated the Mesopotamian region? Into what body of water did they flow?
- Was Mesopotamia in the eastern or western part of the Fertile Crescent?

often at war with one another. These wars weakened the Sumerians. They were later conquered by their enemies.

About 2500 B.C., the great Sargon I [sär′gon] conquered the Sumerians. Sargon and his people came from the country of Akkad [ak′ad] in Mesopotamia. They were not as civilized as the Sumeri-

ans. They soon made Sumerian ways their own. Sargon united Akkad and Sumer into one big, strong, rich nation called the Kingdom of Sumer.

Sometime around 1800 B.C., Hammurabi [hä′mü rä′bē], the king of Babylonia [bab′ ə lō′nē ə], conquered the Kingdom of Sumer. Hammurabi built the mighty kingdom of Babylonia. The city of Babylon was its magnificent capital. Babylonia maintained its power over southern Mesopotamia for a few hundred years. It, in turn, was defeated by the Hittites, the Kassites, and the Assyrians. Babylonia would not become unified and powerful again until the seventh century B.C.

The Hittites [hit'ītz] were a warlike people who first appear in history about 2000 B.C. They came originally from what is now Turkey. The Hittites invaded the valley of the Tigris-Euphrates about 1600 B.C. They were one of the earliest people to use the horse. They made strong and hard weapons of iron, and because of this the Hittites were greatly feared. The Hittites invaded Syria, which was controlled by Egypt. At that time, Ikhnaton was busy with his religious reforms. As a result, Ikhnaton lost control of much of Egypt's northern territory. Continued fighting between Egypt and the Hittites over Syria went on for a long time. It ended when King Ramses II made peace.

The Hittites seem to have disappeared as a nation around 1200 B.C. Perhaps it was because the Hitties tried to rule lands and peoples very far from their homeland.

The Assyrians [ə sir'ē ənz], who lived about 483 kilometers (300 miles) north of Babylon, were also an aggressive, warlike people. They were almost unbeatable in battle. They were armed with copper, bronze, and iron weapons. Riding on horsedrawn chariots, they struck terror in the hearts of their enemies. Between 1100 B.C. and 612 B.C., they conquered Babylonia, Palestine, Syria, Phoenicia, Sumer, and Egypt. The great Assyrian empire fell in 612 B.C. when the Assyrians were badly defeated by the Chaldeans [kal dē'ənz].

The Chaldean Empire lasted only seventy-four years, from 612 to 538 B.C. During this period King Nebuchadnezzar [neb'ə kəd nez'ər] ruled. He made Babylon the most splendid city of the ancient world. He built the Hanging Gardens of Babylon, which were one of the Seven Wonders of the ancient world. Nebu-

An Assyrian horse-drawn chariot. The warlike Assyrians used such chariots in battles against their enemies. Who were some of the peoples they fought?

chadnezzar was the same king, however, who destroyed Jerusalem and made captives of the Hebrews.

Sumer, Babylon, Assyria, and Chaldea ruled over the land between the Tigris and the Euphrates rivers. Each country ruled and was defeated in turn. Each of these civilizations made contributions to world history. Historians feel that the contributions of the Babylonians (2100–1100 B.C.) were probably the greatest.

Check in Here

1. Why did early civilization develop in the Fertile Crescent?

2. Iron weapons and the use of the horse made the Hittites successful in war. Why?

3. Why were Sumerian cities often at war with one another? How did this weaken the Sumerians?

4. Summarize the role of each of the following in the ancient history of the land between the Tigris and the Euphrates: (a) Sumer; (b) Babylon; (c) Assyria; (d) Chaldea.

BABYLONIA'S CONTRIBUTIONS TO CIVILIZATION

What We Found Out About Ancient Babylonia

For many years the language of the Babylonians was not understood by scholars. Their writing is called cuneiform. Henry Rawlinson had studied Persian for many years. When Rawlinson served with the English army in Persia, he discovered some stories carved high up on a mountain cliff. The cliff is called the *Behistun* [bā′hi stün′] *Rock*. The stories were written in three languages. Two of these were written in Persian and Babylonian cunei-

form. Rawlinson risked his life many times to climb the mountain and read the writing. He painstakingly copied every letter in the stories. The stories told how the Persian ruler Darius the Great punished those who rebelled against him. Rawlinson used his knowledge of Persian to read the stories. He was able to work out the meaning of the Babylonian cuneiform. He thus made it possible for us to know more about the ancient and great land of Babylonia.

How the People of Babylonia Lived

Babylonia [bab′ə lō′nē ə], like Egypt, was ruled by a strong king. Class lines were clearly drawn between the rich and the poor. The scribes, who were educated, often became leading citizens. Most of the land was owned by the rich and was worked by slaves. The slaves were the most numerous group. They were the lowest class.

The Babylonians practiced *polytheism* [pol′ē thē iz′əm]—that is, they worshiped many gods. Babylonians prayed to statues representing nature gods. Among them were Marduk [mär′dük], god of the earth, and Anu [a′nü], god of the heavens. The Babylonians mixed superstition with religion. They used magic and believed that it would protect them from illness and evil spirits. The priests received gifts from the people who wanted to please the gods.

Women in Babylonia had many duties. The most important was bearing and bringing up children and looking after the family. In the course of their daily lives they were free to come and go in public the way men did. Women could own property. They could buy and sell property as they wished. They could leave what they owned to their children.

A sacred figure from Mesopotamia, around 2100 B.C. Cuneiform symbols decorate the lap of the statue.

utensils, and weapons. The Babylonian monarchs made strict rules about trade. There were also rules about prices. Merchants had to pay heavy taxes for the use of the canals, rivers, and roads.

Coins were not used in Babylonia. Instead, silver was weighed out to make purchases. Borrowing and lending were common practices. Loans were made in silver, and the amount of the loan was recorded by weight.

Babylonians operated their businesses efficiently. They kept careful records. Babylonians kept records of the contracts they made. They kept records of land which was bought and sold and partnerships that existed.

Some women owned shops; others became scribes. A number of girls, like some boys, were educated. Upperclass women had more rights than those of the lower class. Babylonian women had more privileges than women in Medieval Europe. (See page 194.)

The Babylonian Code of Laws

The Babylonians set down laws that helped to govern the people. Hammurabi is considered one of the greatest kings of Babylonia. He is better known for his *Code of Laws* than for his conquests. The Code of Laws was the first written effort to tell people all the laws they had to obey. A study of the code tells us something about the way the Babylonians lived. It also tells us how they were governed.

How People Made a Living in Babylonia

Most people in Babylonia made their living by farming. The water from the rivers was stored in open basins. It was then moved through canals and ditches to the fields. The people grew grains, fruits, nuts, and dates.

Business included manufacturing and trading. Cloth and clothing were made. Brick and metal were produced. These were used to make houses, household

The code was made up of 285 laws, which were listed under headings such as real estate, trade, and business. Many of the laws were fair and just. One feature of the code was the idea of an eye for an eye. This meant that the punishment should be equal to the crime. For example, if a house fell and killed the owner, the law said that the builder of the house had to die. If the owner's son was killed, then the son of the builder had to die. If a son beat his father, the son's fingers were to be cut off. What if a person was robbed, and the thief was not found? Then the city would repay the victim for the loss. This was also part of the code.

The principle of an eye for an eye held for those who were equal in rank, but not for those who were unequal. Thus, it was possible for a noble to be treated better than a slave. If a slave put out the eye of another slave, his or her eye was put out as punishment. What if a noble, however, put out the eye of a slave? Then the fine was thirty shekels of silver. If it were the eye of a free person, the fine was sixty shekels. The Hammurabi Code of Laws was harsh in some respects. But it was an early attempt to establish a fair code of laws by which everyone had to live.

What the Babylonians Contributed to Civilization

The Babylonians made many contributions to the learning of all peoples. They developed a system of writing. It was based on the cuneiform writing of the Sumerians. The Babylonians wrote on damp clay. They cut wedge-shaped marks into it with a sharp tool known as a *stylus* [stī′ləs]. After the surface had been written on, the damp tablets were dried. The tablets were placed in glass jars in libraries. They were grouped according to subject.

Language experts discovered that Babylonian language had more than 300 characters. Each character stood for a syllable. In Babylonian schools writing, mathematics, and religion were taught. If you think your books are heavy, just think of the clay tablets which Babylonian students carried each day.

Many Babylonians operated businesses. They kept records of sales, profits, and losses. To carry on their trade they had to know how to count. They had to add and subtract. Babylonians developed an advanced system of arithmetic

The Ishtar Gate was built as part of a temple for the god Ishtar. She was one of the most important Babylonian deities.

based on the unit of 60. Our number system is based on the unit of 10. The unit of 60 became the basis for telling time. The hour is divided into 60 minutes. Each minute is divided into 60 seconds. The circle of 360 degrees also comes from this counting unit.

The scientific world owes much to the Babylonians. They were interested in the stars and the heavens and studied the stars to foretell the future. Babylonians learned how to locate the paths of many of the planets. In most cases, the priests could predict eclipses of the moon. Our knowledge of the heavens is based in part on the observations and records of Babylonian astronomers.

As a result of their observations of space and time, Babylonians made a 12-month calendar. Their year had 354 days.

It takes the earth approximately 365¼ days to revolve around the sun. For this reason, a month was occasionally added to adjust the calendar to the movement of the earth.

The Egyptian (2615–332 B.C.) and Babylonian (3200–333 B.C.) civilizations existed at about the same time. These two countries traded with each other. They sent representatives to each other's monarchs. Babylonian civilization, however, was not as advanced as Egyptian civilization. Nevertheless, the Babylonians taught the foundations of arithmetic and science to the Greeks and the Romans. They passed on their legends and stories to the Hebrews.

Check in Here

1. Explain the similarities and differences between the work of Jean Champollion and Henry Rawlinson in helping us understand ancient civilizations.

2. What is the difference between the writing systems of Egypt and Babylonia?

3. What is the importance of Hammurabi's Code of Laws?

4. Describe the role of women in ancient Babylonia.

SMALL BUT IMPORTANT ANCIENT CIVILIZATIONS

What the Hebrews Brought to Civilization

Palestine [pal′i stīn′] was the land of the ancient Hebrews [hē′brūz]. Palestine was located between Egypt to the southwest and Mesopotamia to the northeast. Its western border was the coast of the Mediterranean Sea. Its eastern border was the Syrian desert. Palestine was not as large as either Egypt or Babylonia.

Nor was it located in a great river valley. However, enough rain fell to permit agriculture in some parts of the country. There was enough farmland to attract settlers. The Hebrews tilled the land and built canals to bring more water to the drier parts of the country. Unfortunately, there was much warfare over the years. Because of this, much farmland was laid waste.

Palestine was the biblical land of milk and honey. It played an important role in the history of the ancient world. Today, part of this land is the modern state of Israel. It was established by the descendants of the early Hebrews.

The Hebrews were a nomadic people from the desert. According to the Old Testament, there were twelve Hebrew tribes that wandered for years in search of a promised land. They settled in Palestine. Some Hebrews also settled in Egypt. Because the Egyptians feared the Hebrews, they made them slaves. The Hebrew leader Moses led the Hebrews from Egypt to Palestine. Under the rule of their early kings—Saul, David, and Solomon—the Hebrew nation prospered. Under King Solomon [sol′ə mən], it enjoyed great respect among the people of the Middle East.

The ancient Hebrews waged wars on other countries. They took prisoners and fought among themselves. King Solomon died about 900 B.C. Then Palestine split into two kingdoms. The Kingdom of Israel was formed in the north. The Kingdom of Judah was formed in the south. The Kingdom of Israel lasted for 250 years. Then it was destroyed by the Assyrians. The kingdom of Judah lasted for 400 years. However, during much of its history it was part of other empires. These were the empires of Assyria, Babylonia, and Persia.

The Hebrews are not remembered for their great buildings or beautiful palaces. Their great contribution to civilization

Moses before the burning bush.
From the twelfth century.

Moses (About 1200 B.C.)

Moses lived about 1200 years before Jesus. He was born in Egypt to Hebrew parents. The Old Testament tells the story of Moses' life. At the time of his birth the Hebrews were slaves of the pharaoh. The pharaoh ordered the deaths of all the first-born Hebrew males. For this reason Moses was hidden by his parents. He was then placed in an open basket and sent floating down a river. Moses was discovered by the pharaoh's daughter who adopted him.

The Bible tells us that Moses was brought up as a rich Egyptian nobleman. He grew up in the palace of the pharaoh, where he learned the arts of war. He became a military hero by leading an army against the Ethiopians. Moses could have lived a royal life and perhaps become pharaoh himself. However, when Moses learned of his origin, he became interested in the people called Hebrews. He saw an Egyptian guard beat a helpless Hebrew slave. In the Bible it is written that his anger grew so great that he killed the Egyptian. Because of this, Moses fled Egypt.

Moses was then forty years old. He was a lonely, homeless wanderer. In the Bible we read that Moses met the daughters of Jethro, a nomadic chief. They had brought their sheep to the well for water. When other shepherds tried to drive the daughters away, Moses defended them. They invited Moses to their father's tent. In time, Moses married one of Jethro's daughters.

The biblical story tells that Moses' life soon changed. While looking for a lost sheep, Moses had a vision of God in a burning bush. In this vision, God told him to free the Hebrews from slavery in Egypt. Moses returned to Egypt to lead his people to freedom. He wanted to find them a home.

The task of freeing the Hebrew slaves was not easy. The pharaoh blamed the Hebrews for the ten plagues. Moses demanded that the pharaoh, "Let my people go." The pharaoh listened and agreed. As soon as the Hebrews left the pharaoh sent his army after them. The Bible says that the Egyptian army drowned in the Red Sea.

For forty years Moses led the Hebrews through the desert. There, the Hebrews learned to live and work together. In the Bible we read that the Hebrews camped around the base of Mount Sinai [sī'nī], a mountain in the Sinai desert. Moses is said to have climbed the mountain. After forty days he came down. He brought with him two stone tablets on which were written the Ten Commandments. The Bible says that the commandments were given to Moses by God.

was the fulfillment of an idea. It was the idea of worshipping a single God. This idea, as we learned earlier in this chapter, is called monotheism. The Hebrews worshipped their God in simple ways. In other nations of that time, polytheism was practiced. The religion of the Hebrews presented a new idea to the world. The holy writings of the Hebrews included the Ten Commandments and the Old Testament. The Hebrew faith stressed belief in human kindness. It taught the importance of peace, and it pleaded for a moral society based on laws. These views influenced later faiths, including Christianity.

What the Phoenicians Brought to Civilization

The Egyptians and the Babylonians built great civilizations. However, it was the Phoenicians [fō nish′ənz] who spread the gifts of these civilizations. They were merchants, colonizers, and traders who carried Babylonian and Egyptian learning to other parts of the Mediterranean world. As seafaring merchants, the Phoenicians traded throughout the Mediterranean area and even ventured beyond the Straits of Gibraltar. They sailed as far as England and the west coast of Africa.

The Phoenicians traded mainly in crops and handicrafts. Their crafts people made such things as metal and glass ornaments, jewelry, vases, and weapons. The Phoenicians produced a purple dye. The color purple later became a symbol of royalty. Phoenician merchants became rich. They built great commercial cities such as Tyre [tīər] and important trading colonies such as Carthage.

As a result of their trading, the Phoenicians made contact with many different people. From these people the Phoenicians learned about the different civilizations in the Mediterranean world. The Phoenicians brought the learning of Egypt and Babylonia to Greece. From there it moved to Europe.

The Phoenicians developed an alphabet of twenty-two letters. Each letter stood for a single consonant sound. To this the Greeks added vowel sounds. This alphabet was an improvement over the Egyptian hieroglyphics. It was better than the Babylonian cuneiform because it was simpler. Later, the alphabet was changed by the Romans. It eventually became the one we use.

A Phoenician merchant galley. Phoenician traders spread the knowledge of the Babylonians and Egyptians to other cultures within the Mediterranean world.

What the Lydians and Persians Gave Us

North of the Fertile Crescent were two civilizations of importance, Lydia [lid′ē ə] and Persia [pür′zhə]. The Lydians (800–547 B.C.) established a system of coins. It was the first true money system in the ancient world. The Lydians were traders.

Phoenician Colonies and Trade Routes

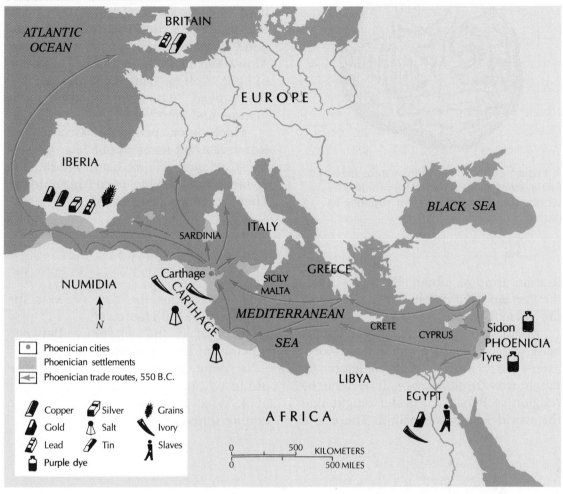

- Phoenicia was located on which coast of the Mediterranean Sea?
- What were three of the products Phoenician traders obtained from Iberia?

The use of money made trading much easier. *Barter* (the exchange of one product for another) was no longer necessary. Croesus [krē'səs], the king of Lydia, was supposed to be the richest king in the ancient world. His kingdom was conquered by Persia in the sixth century B.C.

Persia developed a very effective form of government. It controlled a vast empire. Under Darius I [də rī'əs] (550–486 B.C.), the Persian Empire included almost all of the civilized world. Persian kings had the power to do as they wished. However, they usually listened to their advisers. The advisers were members of the royal household.

The Persian Empire extended from India to the Mediterranean. It was divided into provinces, with each province governed in the king's name. The king allowed each province to keep its own customs. Sometimes provinces even kept their own leaders. People were generally happy under Persian rule. Until the

27

A Lydian coin. The Lydians established the first system of coinage in the ancient world. Why was this system superior to barter?

constant struggle between good and evil, light and darkness. Zoroaster believed that a person's duty was to fight for the good. In this struggle, people worshipped Ahura-Mazda [ä'hü rə maz'də], the god of light. "Tell me truly, O Ahura-Mazda," they prayed, "who determined the paths of suns and stars?"

Much later, people in Greece and Rome learned ideas about law, government, art, and science from Middle East civilizations. Greeks used those ideas. They expanded upon them.

Roman Empire, about 500 years later, the Persian government was the finest in the ancient world.

About 600 B.C., a Persian religious book was written by a man named Zoroaster [zôr'ō as'tər]. The religion he taught was *Zoroastrianism*. It became the religion of Persia. Zoroaster taught that the world is a battleground. There is a

Check in Here

1. What does the text say was the major gift of the Hebrews?
2. What is the difference between polytheism and monotheism?
3. What did the Phoenicians contribute to writing?
4. What probably made the Persian empire unusually successful?

REVIEWING THE BASICS

Early cradles of civilizations were often the product of river valleys. This was true for Egypt. It was also true for many of the nations that lived in the Fertile Crescent. Egypt is called the gift of the Nile. Every year the flooding of the Nile enabled the Egyptians to grow food and other products. The fertile soil of the Nile Valley attracted settlers. The Nile made it possible to unite the nation. By figuring out the writings on the Rosetta Stone, Champollion unlocked the mystery of ancient Egypt's history.

During the Old Kingdom, Egypt was ruled by a mighty pharaoh who governed from the capital at Memphis. During the Middle and New Kingdoms, the power of the pharaoh was not so great. The invasion of Hyksos caused a decline in the power of the Egyptian rulers. The Egyptians were a religious people who prayed to many gods. Amenhotep IV encouraged the worship of a single god, but this form of worship did not last long in Egypt. Hieroglyphics may be regarded as one of the greatest Egyptian contributions to civilization. Egyptian engineering skill is shown in the construction of the pyramids. Egyptians developed a calendar so that they would know when the Nile would flood.

The Babylonians developed a system of writing. Babylonia is best known for Hammurabi's Code of Laws. This was one of the first attempts to set laws down in writing. It was an attempt to be fair to all. The Hebrews worshipped one god. The Hebrew faith tried to make people more just and kind. The Lydians gave us a modern system of coinage. The Persians gave us a humane way of ruling an empire. The Phoenicians spread the civilizations of the Nile and Tigris and Euphrates river valleys to other peoples.

REVIEWING THE HIGHLIGHTS

People to Identify			
Jean Champollion	Ramses II	Darius I
Henry Rawlinson	Amenhotep III	Phoenicians
Nebuchadnezzar	Ikhnaton	Tutankhamen
Sargon I	Hammurabi	Howard Carter
Queen Hatshepsut	Zoroaster	Herodotus
Thutmose III	Moses	

Places to Locate			
Egypt	Fertile Crescent	Mesopotamia
Nile River	Tigris River	Palestine
Cairo	Euphrates River	Syria
Luxor	Chaldea	Babylon
Karnak	Turkey	

Terms to Understand			
"gift of the Nile"	Middle Kingdom	papyrus
Old Kingdom	New Kingdom	cuneiform
pharaoh	Amon-Ra	hieroglyphics
pyramid	Aton	monotheism
dynasty	Osiris	cradle
scribe	Rosetta Stone	of civilization
vizir	polytheism	Hittites
river valley	stylus	Sumerians
civilization	Hyksos	Assyrians
Hebrews	Behistun Rock	Chaldeans

1. Which area of the world is called the cradle of civilization? Why?
2. Is it more accurate to think of several cradles of civilization rather than just one? Why or why not?
3. Why is Egypt called "the gift of the Nile"?
4. Ancient Egyptian history is divided into three periods. Which one may be regarded as the height of Egyptian civilization? Explain why.
5. Who was Queen Hatshepsut? How would you describe her rule?
6. Describe the government of ancient Egypt.
7. How did the religious beliefs of the Egyptians strengthen the power of the pharaoh?
8. Which of Egypt's gifts to civilization do you consider most valuable? Why?
9. Why was Mesopotamia occupied by many nations?
10. What similarities and differences do you find between the religious beliefs of Babylonia and those of ancient Egypt?
11. Describe Hammurabi's Code of Law. Was this code a fair one? Give reasons.
12. Describe the Babylonian system of writing called cuneiform.
13. What were the Babylonian contributions to arithmetic, science, and law?
14. In what ways were the roles of women in ancient Egypt and Babylon similar?
15. What contributions did the Hebrews make to civilization?
16. Is the belief in one god (as opposed to a belief in many gods) a contribution to civilization? Why or why not?
17. Where is the area called the Fertile Crescent? Why was it given this name?
18. What was the major belief of Zoroastrianism?

THINGS TO DO

1. Prepare a conversation that might have taken place between each of the following individuals: (a) Tutankhamen and the museum director where Tutankhamen's treasures are on display; (b) Queen Hatshepsut and the following political figures: Margaret Thatcher, Indira Gandhi, Queen Elizabeth II; (c) Moses and a religious leader in your community.
2. Visit the Egyptian room of a leading nearby museum. Report to the class on what impressed you most.
3. Was Hammurabi's law code fair to all? Debate the issue.

The Tomb of Tutankhamen†

by Howard Carter

Slowly, desperately slowly it seemed to us as we watched, the remains of passage debris* that encumbered* the lower part of the doorway were removed, until at last we had the whole door clear before us. The decisive moment had arrived. With trembling hands I made a tiny breach* in the upper left-hand corner. Darkness and blank space, as far as an iron testing-rod could reach, showed that whatever lay beyond was empty, and not filled like the passage we had just cleared. Candle tests were applied as a precaution* against possible foul gases, and then, widening the hole a little, I inserted the candle and peered in . . . . At first I could see nothing, the hot air escaping from the chamber causing the candle flame to flicker, but presently, as my eyes grew accustomed to the light, details of the room within emerged slowly from the mist. . . . For the moment—an eternity it must have seemed to others standing by—I was struck dumb with amazement, and when Lord Carnarvon**, unable to stand the suspense any longer, inquired anxiously, "Can you see anything?" It was all I could do to get out the words, "Yes, wonderful things."

Vocabulary

debris—rubbish   breach—crack
encumbered—blocked   precaution—care taken beforehand

**Lord Carnarvon financed Howard Carter's archaeo-
logical expeditions to Egypt.

On the basis of your reading of the selection above, answer the questions that follow.

1. What is the author doing? How can you tell?
2. Why are his hands trembling?
3. Why is the author cautious before widening the hole?
4. His eyes grew used to the light and the details of the room became clear. What do you think he saw?
5. Might this be described as a primary or secondary source? Why?

†Howard Carter, *The Tomb of Tutankhamen* (New York; E. P. Dutton & Co. Inc., 1972), p. 35.

Detail from Greek vase, Attic period, 550–530 B.C.

The Gifts of Greece: Our Debt to Ancient Greece

Famous athletes are popular heroes in most countries. Each country has men and women who have brought glory to themselves and honor to their nations through their athletic skills. Organized athletic events encourage fair play and cooperation as well as competition. Their standards are designed to develop sound minds and bodies. Such standards were the foundation of the Olympic games. These games began many hundreds of years ago.

The first Olympic games were played in Greece in 776 B.C. The games were held every four years to celebrate religious and patriotic holidays. Only athletes who possessed great skill and good character were permitted to take part. Through the Olympic games the Greeks showed their values. They thought that physical fitness and mental and moral training were important. The Olympic games are one of the many contributions made by Greece to the world.

In his book *The Life of Greece,* the American historian Will Durant wrote: "There is nothing in Greek civilization that does not illuminate [shed light on] our own." Greek history sheds light on modern problems. Some of these modern problems are: How should people be ruled? How should leaders be trained? How should leaders be chosen and made to serve the people? Modern schools and gymnasiums (places where athletes train) had their beginnings in ancient Greece. So did geometry, history, biology, and hygiene.

THE ORIGINS OF ANCIENT GREECE

The Aegean Bridge

The islands of the Aegean [i jē'ən] Sea served as a cultural bridge over which the culture of the ancient Middle East moved to ancient Greece. The islands in the Aegean Sea were close to one another. A sailor could travel for days and not be far from land. The sea routes and ocean-going ships made it possible for different people and nations to keep in touch with one another. The sailors of Egypt, Phoenicia, and other countries sailed these waters. They carried the learning of the Middle East to the islands of the Aegean and to Greece. The island of Crete [krēt] was one of the important links in the bridge between the Middle East and Greece. Let us trace the spread of culture and learning from Crete to ancient Greece.

How We Found Out About the Civilization of Ancient Crete

From 1898 to 1935, Sir Arthur Evans, an English archaeologist, conducted *excavations,* or *digs,* on the island of Crete.

He found beautiful wall-paintings, pottery, and jewelry. He also found copper plumbing, bathrooms, and stairways. These showed that the people knew how to build practical things to make their lives easier. At digs at Cnossos [näs'əs], in central Crete, Sir Arthur Evans discovered extensive ruins. He called these ruins the Palace of Minos [mī'nəs]. King Minos was one of the rulers of the ancient civilization of Crete.

The civilization of Crete is called *Minoan* [min ō'ən], after King Minos. This civilization is divided into three main periods: Early Minoan (2700 B.C.–1900 B.C.), Middle Minoan (1900 B.C.–1600 B.C.), and Late Minoan (1600 B.C.–1100 B.C.). Minoan civilization probably reached its height from about 1300 to 1000 B.C.

The digs at Cnossos gave clues about a rich civilization. The people were creative and energetic. However, for many years scholars knew really very little about them. There was no Rosetta Stone or Behistun Rock to help archaeologists figure out the written Minoan language. Then, in 1900, Sir Arthur Evans found clay tablets with three different kinds of writing. One was made up entirely of *pictographs* (drawn pictures). Another appeared to be made up of pictographs and

Interior view of the restored Palace of Minos. Archaeologist Sir Arthur Evans found evidence of an advanced civilization at Cnossos, Crete. What were some of the clues he found?

other characters. He called this *Linear A.* The third system of writing, made up entirely of characters, he called *Linear B.*

Eventually, enough examples of Linear B were found to enable scholars to translate it. They used the skills of *cryptography* (inventing and breaking down secret codes). In this way, our knowledge of Minoan civilization grew. We have yet to learn to read Linear A and the picture writing. Nevertheless, because of Linear B we have a greater appreciation of how Minoan civilization developed. We can study how it influenced other cultures of the region.

At the height of its power, Crete probably ruled an empire that controlled the entire Aegean. Minoan traders carried their culture to the islands in the Aegean. They traveled to the Greek peninsula where they built new colonies. Minoan civilization declined rapidly, however, when it was attacked. It was plundered by invaders. Some of these invaders were ancestors of the ancient Greeks.

How and When Greek Civilization Began

Ancient Troy was another stopping place on the cultural bridge from the East to the West. Some of our knowledge about Troy comes from the stories related by the blind Greek poet Homer. He wrote the epic poems the *Iliad* [il'ē əd] and the *Odyssey* [od'i sē]. (An epic is a long, important story.) These epics were made up of stories and legends. The legends had been passed orally through the generations until Homer wrote them down.

The *Iliad* tells how Paris, a Trojan prince, stole the beautiful Helen. She was the wife of Menelaus [men'ə lā'əs], a legendary Greek king. The poem describes how the Greeks attacked Troy in revenge. According to the legend, the Greeks captured Troy with the Trojan Horse. This was a huge wooden horse filled with armed Greeks. The Greeks left the horse outside the city walls of Troy. Thinking it was a gift, the Trojans pulled the horse into the city. Once inside the city, the Greeks jumped out and opened the city gates to the Greek army. The ancient city of Troy fell and was captured.

Homer's other epic poem, the *Odyssey*, describes the long journey of Odysseus [ō dis'ē əs], king of Ithaca [ith'ə kə]. He traveled back from Troy to his home in Greece. After many years of wandering, Odysseus was reunited with his beloved wife, Penelope [pə nel'ə pē].

For many years, scholars did not believe that the city of Troy had ever existed. In the last half of the nineteenth century a German archaeologist, Heinrich Schliemann [shlē'män], made scientific explorations in the area described in the *Iliad*. After much searching and digging, he uncovered the ancient city of Troy. He proved that a fine civilization had once bloomed there.

Thanks to the work of Schliemann and others, we know a lot about Troy and a group of cities around Mycenae [mī sē'nē] in Greece. By 1400 B.C., they had a vigorous civilization. Archaeological evidence shows the influences of Crete.

The ancient Greeks are thought to have come from Central Europe. They probably belonged to shepherd tribes from the region of the Danube River in Europe. The tribes pushed south into the Aegean region between 1400 B.C. and 1100 B.C. They settled on the Greek peninsula. Eventually they moved onto the Aegean Islands and to Asia Minor.

The Ionians [ī ō'nē ənz] were the first Greeks to settle in central Greece and on the Aegean Islands. This tribe established the city of Athens, the most famous city in ancient Greece. Athens also had the most influence on the development of Western civilization.

The Achaeans [ə kē'ənz], another tribe, were perhaps the most important group and the most numerous. They conquered the civilizations they found on the Greek mainland, on Crete, and at Troy. The growth of Achaean culture began at Mycenae, on the mainland. It was the Achaeans that Homer wrote about in his poems. In 1100 B.C., the Achaeans were attacked by another tribe from Central Europe, the Dorians [dôr'ē ənz]. These tribes became known as *Hellenes* [hel'ēnz], or Greeks. They started what we know as the *Hellenic*, or Greek, civilization.

The history of ancient Greece may be divided into three major periods. The first is called the *Homeric Age,* or the Age of Kings. This lasted from about 1100 B.C. to 800 B.C. During the second period, from 800 B.C. to 600 B.C., the Greeks built colonies on many of the islands of the Aegean. The third period, from 600 B.C. to 400 B.C., was the period that may be called the *Golden Age* of ancient Greece. It is the Golden Age that you will read most about in this chapter. After 400 B.C. ancient Greece declined rapidly. It became part of the Macedonian empire of Alexander the Great.

During the Homeric Age, Greek civilization was in its early stages and in this period Greek city-states appeared. The geography of Greece influenced where the Greek tribes settled. It affected the contact they had with each other. Mountains and water divide the land area of the Greek peninsula into small living spaces. Although coastal plains and mountain valleys were several miles apart, these were the only places where the roving tribes could settle down to make a living. In these places they established settlements. Because of their geography the Greek-speaking people lived in isolated groups. Over a period of time they developed independent settlements. These Greek settlements are referred to as *city-states*.

The city-state was the basic unit of government in Greece. Each city-state had complete independence. Among the chief city-states were Athens [ath'ənz], Thebes [thēbz], Corinth [kôr'inth], and Sparta [spär'tə]. People swore allegiance to their city-state. When necessary, they fought for it. The city-states differed from one another. Ways in which people lived were different, and so were the forms of government that were established. In this section you will read about life in Sparta and Athens. Ways of life were very different in these city-states.

The geography of Greece influenced Greek history.
• Look at the map and explain why the geography of Greece gave rise to the development of isolated city-states.

Ancient Greece

1. How do the Olympics of ancient Greece resemble or differ from the modern Olympics?

2. Why are the islands in the Aegean called a "cultural bridge"?

3. Describe three characteristics of Minoan civilization.

4. Why did city-states develop?

A COMPARISON OF THE CITY-STATES OF ATHENS AND SPARTA

What It Was Like To Be a Spartan

Sparta was a city-state located on the southern part of the Greek peninsula. From the kind of life that developed in this city-state comes the word *spartan*. A spartan life is hard. It is one that denies many of the comforts of life. Self-denial and military discipline were Spartan ideals. During most of its history, Sparta was a military dictatorship. The entire economy and life of the city-state were geared to war.

Lycurgus [lī kėr'gəs] of Sparta was responsible for establishing the Spartan form of government. It was his main concern that Sparta be strong enough to defeat all its enemies. Spartan government was unusual in that it was headed by two hereditary kings. Although some kings were able, they had little real power. Political power in Sparta was held by the *Senate*. The Senate was made up of thirty elders. They were usually men above sixty years of age. All male citizens of thirty or above were members of the *Assembly*. Important matters were discussed and voted on in the Assembly. It is important to remember that in Sparta citizenship was limited to landowners.

Out of a population of about 375,000, only 10,000 males were citizens.

Real power in Sparta was held by five men called *ephors* [ef'ôrz], who were usually elderly men. These men were responsible for the day-to-day administration of the city. The ephors, in time, became more powerful than the kings. They commanded armies. They decided questions of law. They conducted affairs with other countries.

Sparta trained its sons and daughters to do without luxury. It expected them to live a tough and active life. Every healthy male citizen had to serve as a soldier. The highest form of devotion a Spartan could show was to fight his city's wars and to "return with his shield or on it."

Spartan youths were trained under a strict military system. From the age of seven they lived away from home. They were not under the influence of their parents. By the age of twenty they were fully trained soldiers. By age thirty they were eligible to take part in the government of Sparta.

The *helots* [hel'ots] were descendants of settlers who had been conquered by the Spartans. This group made up most of the Spartan population. They were serfs who tilled the land and produced the food for the Spartans. The rugged Spartans themselves were only a small part of the population.

Spartan women were educated mainly in the home. However, their lives were carefully regulated by the city-state. Education for Spartan women stressed the importance of motherhood. Spartan women were expected to take part in vigorous games and exercise. They were to prepare their bodies to give birth to healthy children. Men were expected to marry at age thirty and women at age twenty. It was a serious disgrace for men or women to be unmarried and not to have children.

Spartans ate simple meals at public tables. No one was allowed to eat in private or at home.

The position of women was higher in Sparta than it was in any other city-state of ancient Greece. Spartan women could inherit property. They could pass it on to their children. Women did not engage directly in warfare. However, they encouraged the men to go off to battle and to perform heroically in war. Spartan women were able to achieve power and control through their role in the economy. Nearly half the wealth of ancient Sparta was owned by them.

The Founders of Athenian Democracy

The city-state of Athens developed very differently from Sparta. Athens was the world's first democracy. Its government has been the source of many of our democratic ideals. Athenian democracy inspired those who founded American democracy. Athens too had leaders who helped it develop a democratic form of government. Important lawgivers contributed to the growth of democracy in Athens. Three of these were Draco [drā'ko], Solon [sō'lən], and Cleisthenes [klīs'thə nēz].

Around 620 B.C., Draco tried to bring about democratic reforms in Athens. He organized the laws by putting them down in a written code. The laws carried harsh penalties for those who broke them. Nevertheless, Draco's law code was significant. It let the people know exactly what the laws were. One important feature of Draco's code gave a person accused of murder the right to be tried. The accused had to be proven guilty before being punished. Draco helped Athens to develop a government based on written laws.

Solon was another person who helped to develop Athenian democracy. Solon was a leader in the government around 594 B.C. He had the power to make many changes. He made Draco's laws less harsh. He added economic and social reforms to the laws which helped the poor. In those days, a person who rented a farm and was unable to pay the rent was made a slave. Solon canceled all debts on land. He freed people who had become slaves because they owed money. He created a court for all citizens. All citizens were given the right to vote. Only men were citizens; women and slaves were not.

Solon's reforms gave more freedom to the lower classes. However, his changes did not go far enough. Freed slaves, poor landowners, and laborers were not satisfied. They wanted more power than they had. The wealthy classes were unhappy because some of their power had been taken away. By the time Solon left office (572 B.C.) he was not very popular.

A period of dictatorship followed. Then the third of Athens's democratic reformers, Cleisthenes, came to power. He was supported by the common people. He reorganized the social and military classes. In this way the power of various families was broken. He did away with the old system that permitted only nobles to become leaders in the government. Foreign-born freemen were made eligible for citizenship. As citizens they were allowed to take part in the government. Cleisthenes introduced *ostracism* [os′trə siz′əm] to protect the city from those who might be considered dangerous. This policy allowed citizens to vote to expel a person from the city. In this way, a person who tried to get too much power could be sent away.

The democracy of ancient Athens is often called *direct democracy*. That is, all citizens took part directly in government. They discussed and voted on the issues of the day. This tradition lives on in some small towns in the United States. There, citizens meet to decide how local problems should be solved.

The Acropolis of Athens with the Parthenon on the right. Many of the ancient Greek city-states grew around a high point or hill called an *acropolis*. Important temples were built on these hills to protect them from invaders. The Acropolis of Athens is the most famous example of this practice. The Athenians used the temples on the Acropolis primarily for religious ceremonies.

Athenian Democracy

Being a citizen in Athens meant more than voting. It also meant acting as a juror and holding office. Every citizen was expected to do his share as an office-holder. Since the term of officeholding was usually one year, many citizens were given a chance to serve their state.

Athenian democracy was not perfect. It was weak in many ways. The right to vote and to participate in the affairs of state was limited to citizens. The Athenian idea of citizenship was not the same as in the United States today. Anyone born in the United States is a citizen. Foreigners may become citizens. It was not that easy to gain citizenship in ancient Athens.

Citizenship in Athens was limited to men. Women and slaves could not become citizens. It was difficult and often impossible for foreigners to become citizens. Only a little more than half the adult male population were citizens. Taking part in government was limited to this small group. Slavery existed in ancient Athens. There was little opportunity for free speech. Democracy as we understand it in the United States today did not exist in Athens.

Check in Here

1. Identify three ways in which life in Sparta differed from life in Athens.
2. What is meant by the term *direct democracy*?
3. Indicate one democratic reform of each of the following: Draco, Solon, Cleisthenes.
4. In addition to voting, what were some of the other responsibilities of Athenian citizenship?

40

THE EFFECTS OF WAR ON ANCIENT GREECE

How the Persian Wars Challenged Athens

Democracies must always be alert to challenges that come from within and from outside the country. In the case of Athens, enemies came from both sides.

The challenge came first, in 492 B.C., from the Persian army. Under Darius I [də rī'əs], the army began attacking and defeating the Greek city-states one by one. Then, in 490 B.C., the Persian army stopped to rest on the Plains of Marathon [mar'ə thän']. Athenians, led by Miltiades [mil tī'ə dēs], made a surprise attack and defeated the Persians.

There is a sad story told about the victory at the Battle of Marathon. An Athenian athlete ran all the way from Marathon to Athens with the news. He arrived exhausted and announced the great victory. Then he collapsed and died. The marathon (a long-distance race) owes its name to this event in history.

Persia, however, did not give up the idea of conquering Greece. In 480 B.C., the Persian army under King Xerxes [zėrk'sēz], attacked the Greeks at Thermopylae [thər mop'ə lē]. The Greeks fought bravely; however, double-dealing brought them defeat. A Greek traitor showed the Persians a way to surround the Greek troops and defeat them. Then in later battles with the Persians, the Greeks were victors. They won a smashing naval victory at Salamis [sal'ə mis] (480 B.C.). The Persians left, never to return. Greece now had a chance to develop independently. It could lay the foundations for Western civilization.

Why the Greeks Fought Among Themselves

The victory over the Persians was largely due to Athens. During the period follow-

Greece and the Persian Empire About 480 B.C.

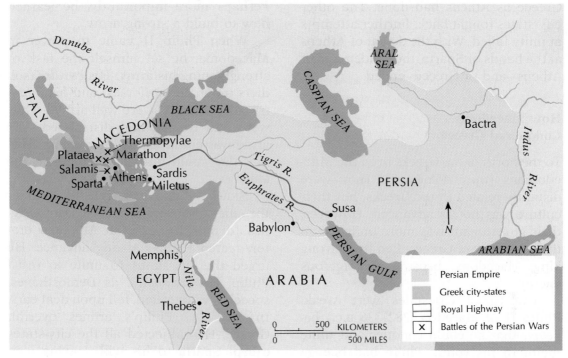

The Persian Empire was larger than any previously existing empire. In order to control this huge empire, Persian leaders built a famous road called the *Royal Highway.*

- The Royal Highway connected what two cities?
- What was the approximate distance traveled on the Royal Highway between these two cities?

ing the Persian Wars, Athens entered its Golden Age. It became the leader in Greek affairs among the city-states. Athenians feared another Persian invasion. They tried to build up their defenses. They rebuilt the long walls around the city. Pericles [per'ə klēz'] (490–429 B.C.), Athens greatest leader, tried to unite the Greek city-states into the Delian [dē'lē ən] League. This organization of city-states was to protect Greece from attack. Athens, the richest and most powerful city-state, gave most of the money and soldiers to the Delian League.

At first, the league worked well in unifying the city-states. As danger from the Persians passed, the city-states began to argue about their shares of the expense of protection. Athens, which paid the largest share, wanted the most power. It demanded obedience to its wishes. It tried to interfere in the affairs of the members of the league. Although Athens was democratically run at home, it tried to rule the other city-states as conquered cities.

Soon the city-states were fighting among themselves. Sparta thought that this was a good time to prove that it was the most important city-state in Greece. Sparta attacked Athens. A series of wars known as the Peloponnesian [pel'ə pə ne'shən] Wars (431–404 B.C.) began. Sparta was victorious.

Sparta tried to unify and dominate Greece as Athens had done. The other city-states fought back. Further attempts at unity failed. With the defeat of Athens at the hands of Sparta, the Golden Age of Athens—and of Greece—ended.

How Macedonia Conquered Greece

To the north of the Greeks lived the Macedonians [mas′i dō′nē ənz]. They were distantly related to the Greeks, but their culture was not as advanced. However, their government was more united than the city-states of Greece. Led by a strong king, Macedonia became a dangerous enemy.

The Greek city-states were weak. Philip II of Macedon (382–336 B.C.) believed that he could conquer and unite them. In his youth, Philip had been a hostage in Thebes [thēbz]. Thebes was then one of the most powerful city-states of Greece. While Philip was in Thebes, he learned something about Greek culture. Perhaps more importantly, he learned how to build a strong army.

When Philip II came to power in Macedonia, he set himself the task of strengthening his army. His *cavalry* (soldiers mounted on horses) and his *infantry* (foot soldiers) were well armed. They were well trained and disciplined. The army was equipped with a *catapult*. This machine could hurl large stones at the enemy.

Slowly, Philip was able to conquer the cities of northern Greece. Demosthenes [di mos′thə nēz′], an Athenian orator, feared Philip's steady advance. He urged the city-states to unite to resist Philip. His *philippics*, as Demosthenes' speeches were called, fell upon deaf ears. In 338 B.C., Philip's armies overran Greece. He subjected all the city-states except Sparta to his will. Having won Greece, Philip hoped to expand his conquests to Persia. His assassination, at a wedding in 336 B.C., brought his ambitions to an end.

How Alexander Started a New Culture

Philip's ambitions were realized by his twenty-one-year-old son, who became known as Alexander the Great. Alexander was a brilliant young man and a military genius. He had been taught by the Greek teacher Aristotle to admire culture. In 334 B.C., Alexander attacked and defeated Persia. Following this victory, he marched further eastward. He conquered what are now Afghanistan and northern India. These conquests combined the Eastern and Western worlds under one king. Alexander died in 323 B.C. at the age of thirty-two. He had lived a short but brilliant life. After his death, the empire that he built fell into three parts. Each part was ruled by one of Alexander's generals.

Philip II of Macedon on an ancient silver coin. Philip conquered almost all of the Greek city-states before his death. How did his son Alexander extend the empire that he began?

By the conquests of Alexander the Great, Greek civilization spread to the Eastern world. Alexander built great cities. His empire combined the cultures of the East and the West. This combination of Greek and Eastern culture was called *Hellenistic.* What were the characteristics of this Hellenistic culture? What were the contributions of some of its greatest thinkers? These will be explained later in this chapter.

Why the Achaean League Was Important

In Greece, an interesting experiment in government began about 280 B.C. It was known as the *Achaean League.* This was not an alliance or temporary association of city-states. It was, instead, a *federation.* A federation is a form of government. A number of smaller units agree to give up some powers to a stronger central government. In the Achaean League each city-state kept control of its own affairs. However, a central government had the power to levy taxes and to raise an army. The Achaean League did not last long. However, its main ideas were known to the leaders who founded the United States. Its organization might have had some influence on their ideas of government. The United States has a federation of fifty states. Each state is responsible for its own affairs under a strong central government.

An Indian miniature painting shows Alexander the Great being pulled from the sea, after observing underwater life.

Check in Here

1. What was the significance of the Persian Wars to (**a**) ancient Greece; (**b**) the development of Western civilization?

2. What were the causes of the Peloponnesian Wars?

3. Describe the conquests of each of these leaders: (**a**) Philip II of Macedon; (**b**) Alexander the Great?

4. How might the Achaean League have influenced the founders of the United States?

5. What was the difference between the Delian League and the Achaean Leagues?

The Empire of Alexander the Great About 323 B.C.

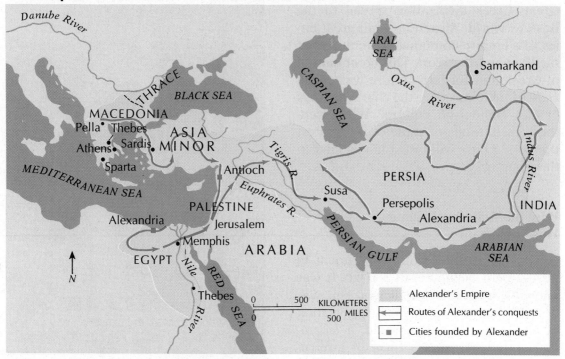

Alexander built new cities throughout his empire.
• What is the name of the city he built in Egypt?

A COMPARISON OF HELLENIC AND HELLENISTIC CIVILIZATIONS

The Part Religion Played in Ancient Greece

In the Hellenic, or Greek, civilization many gods were worshipped. Most of the gods—male and female—represented the forces of nature. The gods helped explain wind, rain, storms, birth, and death. The male gods included Zeus [züs], who was the ruler of all gods and humans. Poseidon [pō sīd'ən] was the ruler of the sea. Apollo [ə pol'ō] was the sun god, and Pluto [plü'tō] was the god of the lower world. Among the female gods was Demeter [di mē'tər], the god of agricul-

ture. Athena [ə thē'nə] was the god of wisdom, and Aphrodite [af'rə dī'tē] was the god of love. The great gods were thought to live on Mount Olympus, the highest peak in Greece. Human qualities were given to the gods. Greeks believed the gods—like human beings—made mistakes.

Religion played an important role in the daily life of ancient Greece. Religious ceremonies were elaborate and varied. They depended upon the god to be worshipped. In early days, human sacrifice was common. Later, the Greeks substituted animals in their sacrifices to the gods.

Superstition and religion were mixed. Greeks would never think of doing something important without first finding out whether or not the time chosen was a favorable one. To find out whether a favorable time had been selected, Greeks consulted an *oracle* [ôr′ə kl]. This was a female or male priest who was a source of wisdom and information. The Greeks believed the gods spoke to humans through oracles by signs or omens. The most famous oracle was the Delphic [del′fik] Oracle. She gave information to the government leaders regarding the right time to start wars, to pass laws, and to make treaties. The priests who served in the Greek temples had great influence.

How the Ancient Greeks Earned a Living

As in other places in the ancient world, most people in Greece were poor farmers. In Athens, however, even poor farmers (if they were citizens) could own their land. These farmers used simple tools and methods to grow cereals, figs, olives, and grapes.

Athens could not grow enough food for its own needs. It had to buy food from the other city-states. Thus, the citizens of Athens were interested in finding farmland. This led some people to move from Athens and some of the other Greek city-states to areas outside Greece. Some Greek farmers found land in Italy along the shores of the Mediterranean. They established colonies. Trade developed between these colonies and their parent city-states.

Business in ancient Greece centered around farming, manufacturing, and trading. Every city-state had its own system of coinage, weights and measures, and banking. Trade was a very important economic activity. Trade between city-states was undeveloped because land transportation was difficult. Commerce was generally carried on by sea. Shipping was less expensive and safer than land transportation. Manufacturers sold such items as weapons, clothing, and household utensils. Within the city-states, merchants sold their goods in street shops. These shops were opened to serve all who wanted to buy.

Minerals were found in certain parts of Greece. Silver, lead, zinc, and iron were found in the mountainous areas. Marble was plentiful and was used in buildings and in statues.

People worked at many trades. They built ships and houses. They made harnesses for horses, and they forged swords and shields for the warriors. Greeks were stone cutters, painters, fishmongers, bakers, millers, lyre tuners, and butchers. There were few machines. Small-scale factories were started to make fabric, armor, and pottery.

Athena, Greek god of wisdom. Religion played an important part in the daily lives of the Greeks. How did they think that their gods could help them?

Generally, the Greek wife was expected to maintain a home for her husband and children. She did not rule the household, her husband did. A wife did not even do the shopping for it. She made the clothing and bedding for the family and prepared its meals. However, the role of women varied among the city-states of ancient Greece. In Sparta, for example, the role of women in the economic life of the city-state was far greater than in ancient Athens. In Athens, women could not enter into contracts. They could not buy or sell anything. Women could not borrow money or sue in a court of law. When an Athenian woman's husband died, she did not inherit his property. Women had to be veiled when attending religious services.

While men spent their time in the *agora*, or market place, women spent their time in the women's quarters of the house.

By the middle of the fifth century B.C. Athenian women were beginning to complain about their station in life. In Aristophanes' play, "Lysistrata" [lis'i strä'tə], a woman asks, "What sensible thing are we women capable of doing? We do nothing but sit around. . . ." Gradually, the women of ancient Greece began to play more active parts in the culture of their communities.

The Social Classes in Ancient Greece

At the top rung of the social ladder were the citizens. In Athens, citizens made up

Ancient Greece and its Trade Routes

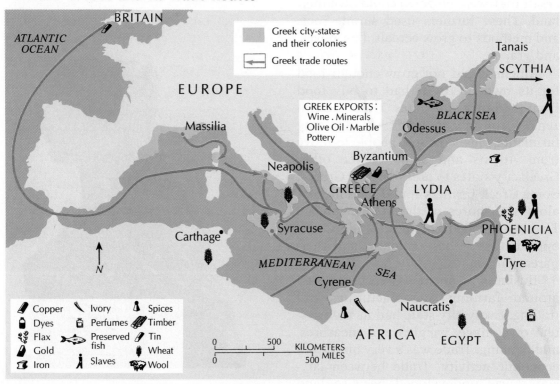

The Greek city-states were at the center of a vast trading network.
• List three products that Greece imported from other parts of the world.
• From what regions did Greece obtain slaves?

little more than half the male population. Just below them were the *metics* [mə'tiks], who were foreigners living in the cities. This group dominated the commercial life of the city. Shopkeepers, workers, merchants, and bankers were usually not citizens. Working for a living was considered undignified by the citizens of Athens. There was a small group of former slaves who had been made free. There was a very large group of slaves who did most of the work. In Athens the working group of slaves made up about 35 percent of the population. In other city-states the percentage of slaves was probably greater. For the most part, slaves were those who had been captured in war. Many had been teachers and professional people. They were often highly educated.

The people of ancient Greece lived very simply. Both clothing and shelter were plain. Their homes were made of sun-dried brick. On the whole, the homes had relatively little furniture.

In all Greek cities except Sparta, women had little voice in running the government. In 450 B.C. a leading Athenian woman, Aspasia [a spā'shə], opened a school for women. Many young women attended her classes. Both Pericles and Socrates are believed to have attended her discussions.

What We Know About Greek Art and Literature

Art, in the form of buildings, statues, and literature, is one of the lasting gifts of ancient Greece. Athens became the most beautiful city of the ancient world. On a hill in Athens was the *Acropolis* [ə krop'ə lis], where buildings were dedicated to religion and art. The *Parthenon* [pär'thə non'], the most beautiful building, had marble columns. These supported the roof and set a style of architecture that is used to this day. The types of columns most often used were known as Doric, Ionic, and Corinthian.

Sculpture was particularly well developed as an art form. Many of the ancient Greek statues have been preserved and

Examples of Greek Architecture

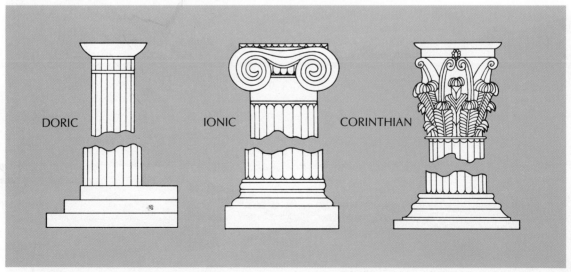

DORIC   IONIC   CORINTHIAN

The three orders, or styles, of Greek columns: Doric, Ionic, and Corinthian.

may be seen in museums. These sculptures are fine examples of the simplicity and beauty of Greek art.

Drama was an important form of Greek literature. Violence, death, humor, and comedy were the subjects of Greek plays. The tragedies of Aeschylus [es′kə ləs] and the comedies of Aristophanes [ar′i stof′ə nēz′] were very popular in ancient Greece.

Greek plays were performed in open-air theaters. The audience sat on stone seats without backs. The seats were not comfortable. Nevertheless, the theaters were crowded. The actors, who wore masks, and the chorus were always men. The audience often hissed the performers and performances they disliked. The female poet Sappho [saf′ō] composed some of the earliest and finest love poems that were ever written. Aeschylus, Sophocles [sof′ə klēz′], and Euripides [yü rip′i dēz′] were the great dramatists of Athens.

Greek Gifts to Learning

Three thinkers of ancient Greece were especially influential in philosophy and learning. They were Socrates [sok′rə tēz′], Plato [plā′tō], and Aristotle [ar′i stot′əl]. The earliest of these was Socrates (470–399 B.C.). He went about the city of Athens asking embarassing and difficult questions. He did this in order to point out evils in society. The Socratic method is one that teaches by asking thought-provoking questions.

Because Socrates left no writing, we have had to learn about him through the

The ancient Greek theater at Epidaurus. The plays of Aeschylus, Sophocles, and Euripides were staged in theaters like this one. How did Greek audiences react to a bad performance by an actor?

Socrates (470–399 B.C.)

Socrates was a man whose life we know only through the writings of others. Those who wrote about him either loved or hated him. It is difficult, therefore, to know what Socrates was really like. We do know that the Delphic oracle called Socrates "the wisest man in Greece."

It is believed that Socrates' father was a sculptor. As a young man Socrates followed his father's trade. He served with heroism in the Peloponnesian Wars. Later he married a woman named Xanthippe [zan tip'ē]. She had difficulty getting Socrates to support his family properly. Socrates was too busy being a philosopher to earn a decent living.

In a worn robe and sometimes without sandals, Socrates went about the marketplace of Athens. He raised questions about truth, justice, knowledge, and virtue. Socrates made many enemies in looking for the true meaning of these terms. He asked questions that made other people uncomfortable. People were forced to examine their beliefs. Socrates said that virtue and knowledge were the same. That is, people with knowledge are virtuous (good people). People of virtue, good people, have knowledge. Therefore, Socrates believed that no person knowingly acts wickedly. Would you agree or disagree with Socrates?

Socrates raised irritating questions. He laughed at the conventional wisdom of his time. He sought to teach virtue. Socrates clashed with what might be called the establishment of Athens. At his trial Socrates was sentenced to death for corrupting the youth. His friends begged him to escape. He refused because he did not want to break the laws of Athens. Instead, he drank the hemlock (poison) as the jury had ordered. Socrates killed himself, as an example to others. He felt that knowledge and virtue are worth pursuing, whatever the cost.

writings of Plato who was his admiring pupil. Socrates and Plato sought the meaning of truth and justice. They studied the meaning of life and how people should behave. Socrates believed that there was nothing as useful as knowledge. He thought that if people had knowledge, they could solve the problems that faced them. Socrates' methods and ideas irritated the older members of

Athenian society. He was condemned to death. Socrates is regarded as a martyr for the principle of free speech.

Of greater lasting influence, perhaps, was the work of Plato (427-347 B.C.). He is best known for his book *The Republic*. It is a record of conversations Socrates had with other Athenians. In *The Republic* Plato outlined a perfect society. The leaders would be philosophers because they were the wisest. Plato was not a great supporter of democracy. He thought that the important positions in a democracy were very often held by people who were not the best qualified. Plato feared that freedom in a democracy would not be used properly.

Plato planned what he thought was a perfect society. His pupil, Aristotle (384-322 B.C.), eagerly studied governments that had existed in the past. In his book, *Politics*, Aristotle pointed out some of the advantages and disadvantages of different forms of government. He made some suggestions for the improvement of government. Aristotle was a scientist as well as a philosopher. He was one of the first to believe that the earth is round.

The science of medicine was another gift of ancient Greece. Under Hippocrates [hi pok′rə tēz′] (460-377 B.C.) the practice of medicine gradually became more scientific. It became free of superstition. Medical records from this time show how a scientific attempt was made to treat disease. Hippocrates said that all diseases have natural causes; they were not caused by the gods. He raised the medical profession to a higher standing by insisting that certain medical rules be followed. One of these was that the doctor must not harm the patient. Today, doctors take the Hippocratic oath, which is based on the teachings of Hippocrates.

Herodotus [hə′räd ə təs] (484-428 B.C.) is often called the father of history. He traveled a great deal and was a careful observer. He visited the places about which he wrote and set down the ancient record of humankind. Some of his information was not accurate. He admitted that some of his stories were hearsay (information gotten from others). Herodotus wrote mainly about the Persian Wars. Thucydides [thü sid′ə dēz′], who lived some fifty years later, was a more exact historian. He is best known for his *History of the Peloponnesian Wars*.

Hellenistic Culture

Hellenistic culture, although mainly Greek, was greatly influenced by the culture of the East. The city of Alexandria in Egypt became the center of Hellenistic learning. Magnificent buildings and a tremendous library were built there. The lighthouse at the entrance to Alexandria harbor was one of the wonders of the world. At Antioch, in Syria, the streets were paved and lighted. The Colossus of Rhodes, built on the island of Rhodes, was a giant bronze statue of Apollo. It stood 105 feet high and was regarded as another wonder of the world. Buildings alone, however, do not tell the whole story of the spread of Hellenistic culture.

The scientists of the Hellenistic Age (323 B.C.-A.D. 14) developed much practical and useful knowledge. Archimedes [är′kə mē′dēz] was probably the greatest of the ancient scientists. He contributed to the development of modern inventions such as the steam engine. He also invented weapons of war such as the catapult. This machine could hurl rocks over great distances against an attacking army. Archimedes gave us a better understanding of the lever and the pulley.

Ptolemy [tol′ə mē] was an Egyptian scholar. He developed a theory which said that the heavenly bodies revolved around the earth. We know today that he was wrong. His theory, however, was accepted for over 1,500 years. Euclid [yü′klid] worked out the basic theorems of geometry. The geographer Eratosthenes [er'ə tos'thə nēz'], estimated the earth's circumference. He was only 314 kilometers (195 mi.) short of its actual measurements.

Hellenistic sculpture remains among the most beautiful in the world. The statue of the female god of love, the *Venus of Milo*, belongs to this Hellenistic period. Another example of fine Hellenistic sculpture is the famous *Laocoön* [lā äk'ō än']. This statue shows Laocoön and his two sons struggling with two sea serpents.

This sculpture of a boy leaning against a column is an example of the naturalistic style of Hellenistic sculpture.

Check in Here

1. Do you regard the ancient Greeks as a religious people? If your answer is yes, give two reasons why.

2. How were the roles of women in ancient Athens and Sparta different?

3. Name one difference between the modern American and ancient Athenian idea of citizenship.

4. Describe one major contribution that the ancient Greeks made to each of the following areas of knowledge: (**a**) art; (**b**) literature; (**c**) science.

REVIEWING THE BASICS

The most important gift of Greek civilization was, perhaps, the willingness of the Greeks to try new things. They experimented with a new form of government. They gave democracy a chance to grow and accepted new ideas. They tried to separate science from superstition. As a result, Greece made progress in arithmetic, geometry, zoology, astronomy, and trigonometry. Later progress was possible because of Greek contributions in these fields.

It was over the islands of the Aegean that the culture of the Middle East moved to ancient Greece. Ancient Troy and Crete were stepping stones from which the culture of the East came to be adopted by ancient Greece. Homer's epics the *Iliad* and the *Odyssey* are sources for much of our knowledge about the earliest Greeks. The Homeric period lasted from 1100 until 800 B.C. The Golden Age of Greece was the period between 600 B.C. and 400 B.C. After 400 B.C., a decline set in. Greece became part of the empire of Alexander the Great.

The basic unit of Greek society and government was the city-state. Each city-state developed somewhat differently. Sparta was a military state; Athens developed as a democracy. Many features of Athenian democracy have been adopted by modern governments, including the United States. Nevertheless, citizenship was limited in Athens. Slavery existed. Democracy, as we know it, did not exist.

In the Persian Wars, the Greeks held off the mighty Persian navy. In the Peloponnesian Wars between Athens and Sparta, Sparta was eventually victorious. Constant warfare weakened Greece. Greece was then conquered by Alexander. During the empire of Alexander, Hellenistic civilization developed. This was a combination of Greek (Hellenic) and Eastern culture. As Greek civilization declined, Rome's grew. That story follows.

REVIEWING THE HIGHLIGHTS

People to Identify			
Sir Arthur Evans	Philip II	Aristotle
Homer	Demosthenes	Hippocrates
Heinrich Schliemann	Alexander the Great	Herodotus
Draco	Aspasia	Thucydides
Solon	Aristophanes	Archimedes
Cleisthenes	Miltiades	Ptolemy
Darius I	Socrates	Euclid
King Xerxes	Sappho	Odysseus
Pericles	Plato	Lycurgus
		Eratosthenes

Places to Locate			
Aegean Sea	Athens	Thebes
Crete	Sparta	Alexandria
Cnossos	Marathon	Rhodes
Mycenae	Thermopylae	Macedonia
Troy	Salamis	Corinth

Terms to Understand			
direct democracy	ephors	Linear A
Homeric Age	Assembly	Linear B
Golden Age	Senate	Achaeans

ostracism	Hellenistic	Ionians
Delian League	metics	Dorians
city-state	Socratic method	Acropolis
Achaean League	Minoan	federation
Hellenic	helots	Macedonians
	Golden Age	

Events to Describe   Olympic Games   Persian Wars   Peloponnesian Wars

Mastering the Fundamentals

1. Why are the Aegean islands called a *cultural bridge?*
2. How did Sir Arthur Evans contribute to our knowledge of the civilization of Crete?
3. What did scholars learn about Minoan civilization after translating Linear B?
4. Explain how Schliemann's explorations contributed to our knowledge of Troy.
5. Was Athens a democracy? Why or why not?
6. What do we learn about ancient Greece from the epic poems of Homer?
7. Why was Solon unpopular despite his good work? Can you think of twentieth century leaders in similar positions?
8. List the weaknesses of Athenian democracy.
9. How does our idea of citizenship differ from that of ancient Greece?
10. How did the geography of Greece help or hurt the development of Greek civilization?
11. What was the purpose of the Delian League? Was it successful or not? Explain.
12. Who were the opposing sides in the Peloponnesian Wars? How do you account for the success of the victor?
13. What is meant by *Hellenistic culture?*
14. Describe how the Greeks mixed religion and superstition.
15. Was theater important to the ancient Greeks? How can you tell?
16. What did ancient Greece contribute to modern architecture?
17. How did the views of Plato differ from those of Aristotle?
18. Why was Socrates condemned to death?
19. How did the ancient Greeks contribute to the development of science?

THINGS TO DO

1. Hold a mock trial for Socrates. Decide what class members will be for or against Socrates. Pick the judge and jurors. Try to base your trial on research in the following areas: (a) Socrates' views; (b) his explanation of his views; (c) the objections to his views of the prominent people of Athens.

2. Prepare a map using papier-mâché to achieve a three-dimensional effect. Show the land and area over which Alexander ruled at the time of his death. Indicate on the map the major campaigns of Alexander.

3. Write a dialogue or conversation a woman of Athens and a woman of Sparta might have had. This kind of dramatization should highlight the different views of the women of these ancient city-states.

YOU ARE THE HISTORIAN

Read the selection that follows and answer the questions based on it.

And now, Athenians, I am not going to argue for my own sake, as you may think, but for yours, that you may not sin against the God by condemning me, who am his gift to you. For if you kill me, you will not easily find a successor to me, who, if I may use such a ludicrous* figure of speech, am sort of a gadfly given to the state by God; and the state is a great and noble steed* who is tardy* in his motions owing to his very size, and requires to be stirred into life. I am that gadfly which God has attached to the state; and all day long and in all places am always fastening upon you, arousing and persuading and reproaching* you. You will not easily find another like me, and therefore I would advise you to spare me.

Vocabulary
ludicrous—ridiculous *tardy*—slow
steed—horse *reproaching*—scolding

1. Where was the speaker when he made this speech? How can you tell?
2. Who do you think the speaker was? How can you tell?
3. What is a *gadfly*? (Use your dictionary.) Why does the speaker call himself a gadfly?
4. What rights did the speaker appear to want?
5. What effect do you think such a speech might have had on the listeners? Why?
6. What did the speaker ask of his listeners?
7. If you were among the listeners, would you grant the speaker his request? Why or why not?
8. Would you consider the source of this reading a primary or secondary one? Explain.
9. Is the problem presented in the speech still with us? How can you tell?
10. What is presented in the reading is only a portion of the speaker's remarks. Where would you find the remainder? How would you find them?

The Forum, Rome

Romans and Christians: Our Roman Heritage

If you or your family were to travel to Europe, one place you would surely visit is Rome. Rome was the home of an ancient civilization. It was the capital of the civilized world in ancient times. Within the city itself are the remains of the *Forum*, which was the business and lawmaking center of Rome. On the outskirts of the city stand portions of the *Colosseum* [kol'ə sē'əm]. There, Romans were entertained. The famous triumphal arches built to honor Roman emperors and to celebrate their victories also remain. Although now in decay, these ruins are powerful attractions for tourists and students of history.

Rome is also an historical center of Christianity, which is another reason for tourists to visit the

CHAPTER

3

city. There, one can see the *catacombs* [kat′ə kōmz′], underground chambers and tunnels where early Christians sometimes hid from the Romans. The early Christians buried their dead in the catacombs, too. It was in Rome that the Christians developed their new religious ideas, and a Roman emperor became the first ruler to adopt Christianity. Rome was responsible for the spread of new ideas in government and politics. It was also largely responsible for the spread of Christianity to the Western world.

THE ESTABLISHMENT OF THE ROMAN REPUBLIC

The Influence of Geography on Rome

Italy is a boot-shaped peninsula extending into the central Mediterranean Sea. It is a mountainous country with few natural resources. Yet, it provided the geographic setting in which a strong nation grew. About halfway down this peninsula, not far from the sea, on seven hills along the banks of the Tiber [tī′bər] River, the city of Rome was built.

About 1500 B.C., while the Greeks were building their city-states, primitive Italian tribes were building farm communities on the Italian peninsula. One of the tribes, the Latins [lat′ənz], united the people living on the seven hills to form the tiny city of Rome. By uniting, the tribes hoped to protect themselves from the Etruscans [i trus′kənz] in the north and the Samnites [sam′nītz] to the south.

The settlers of Rome took advantage of their good geographic position to become a powerful nation. Living on high ground, they could easily defend themselves from attack. Located near the center of Italy, the Romans became masters of that peninsula. And on the fertile Latin Plain, they grew crops to feed their people. Because these early Romans lived near the coast, they found it easy to expand into the entire Mediterranean region. A favorable geographic location made it possible for Rome to extend its rule over large parts of what we now call Europe, Africa, and the Middle East.

How Rome Conquered Italy

According to ancient stories, Rome was founded by Romulus [rom′ə ləs] and Remus [rē′məs], children of ancient gods. A jealous uncle, who wanted power for himself, put the twins in a wicker basket and threw it into the swift currents of the Tiber [tī′bər] River. Instead of sinking, the basket drifted ashore, and the twins were saved by a wolf who brought them up as her own. When the brothers grew up they killed their wicked uncle. They founded a city on the banks of the river from which they had been rescued. In time, Romulus killed his brother Remus and named the city (Rome) after himself.

Romans believed that their city was established in 753 B.C., and they dated their calendar from this date. The story of Romulus and Remus was cherished by the Romans as part of their history

A busy port stop on the Tiber River during the rule of Julius Caesar.

and traditions. Symbols of the wolf and the twin founders of Rome were placed upon Roman coins and official seals.

About 800 B.C., the early Romans (the Latins) were defeated by people called Etruscans. The Etruscans first settled to the north of the Romans and gradually conquered the city of Rome. They held back the advancing settlements of the Greeks in Italy. This gave the Romans time to become strong. The Etruscans showed the Romans how to use bronze and how to make better weapons. They taught the Romans the arts of war. By 500 B.C., the Romans proved that they had learned their lessons well. They drove out their former masters, the Etruscans, and established a republic.

How Rome Was Governed

Under the Etruscans, the Romans had been ruled by harsh kings. When independence was won, the Romans established a republican form of government. Although it was a republic, Rome was not a democracy. In the following paragraphs you will learn the difference between a republic and a democracy. Ancient Rome was a republic.

When Americans salute their flag and recite the Pledge of Allegiance, they swear their loyalty to "the Flag of the United States of America, and to the Republic for which it stands. . . ." A *republic* means a form of government in which elected representatives govern, as in the United States. The United States is also a democracy, since the people have the right to vote for their choice of parties and candidates.

The republic of Rome cannot be considered a democracy. The elected government leaders did not represent the total population. In the Roman Republic, the representatives who governed the people came only from the upper class. They were called *patricians* [pə trish'ənz]. At first, only patricians could hold office, and only they had an important voice in government affairs.

In the government of Rome, 300 patricians served for life in the Roman Senate. The Senate passed laws for the nation. The Senate was very powerful. But it shared some of its powers with an *Assembly of Centuries* and an *Assembly of Tribes*. The Assembly of Centuries, also made up of patricians, was responsible for military matters. The Assembly of Tribes was made up mostly of *plebeians* [plə bē'ənz]. The plebeians represented the thirty-five tribes into which the citizens of Rome were divided. As plebeians became more powerful, so too did the Assembly of Tribes.

The *magistrates*, that is, those who actually ran the Roman government, were at first drawn only from among the patricians. There were two *consuls* [kon'səlz] who served one-year terms. Since each consul had the power to *veto* (stop) the acts of the other, the two consuls had to agree before they could act. In time of war or some other emergency, the Senate replaced the two consuls with a *dictator*. The dictator was an official who could act with full power to make decisions quickly. This person's main purpose was to guide the government through any emergency. The government of Rome was also served by *praetors* [prā'tərz], or judges. They played an important part in interpreting the laws of Rome. *Censors* [sen'sərz] counted the people of Rome and determined how much in taxes, based on wealth, the people would pay.

Ten *tribunes* [trib'yünz], elected each year by the Assembly of Tribes, were plebeians and represented this group. With the power to override any act of any government official, they were able to protect the plebeians from the rich and powerful. Because of the veto, the plebeians were gradually able to increase their influence.

In 450 B.C., a code of laws, known as the *Twelve Tables*, was adopted. Carved in wood and placed in the Forum for all to see, the code applied to both patricians and plebeians. This helped create greater equality between the two groups. By 339 B.C., the plebeians had won the right to hold any public office. Plebeians also gained the right to marry patricians and to own more land. The Twelve Tables started Rome on its way toward making its greatest achievement—a body of fair laws and fair legal methods.

While reforms gave more rights to the plebeians, Rome was not a true democracy. This was because the small wealthy class continued to have the most powerful voice in the government. The patricians had, however, given up enough to insure the loyalty of the other classes. As a result of the reforms, Rome's government and people became strong enough to rule other lands.

How the Roman Army Was Organized

The expansion of Rome was made possible in part by the courage of the Roman soldiers. From the Etruscans, the Romans had learned how to make weapons of steel and of other metals. The Roman soldier was a fierce fighter. He had strong shields and armor, long swords, javelins for throwing, and spears for

A bas relief, or drawing carved into stone, shows a Roman ship bearing soldiers armed for battle.

thrusting. The Roman army, made up mainly of foot soldiers, fought best in close formations.

Early Roman armies were organized into *phalanxes* [fā'langk səz] of about 8,000 soldiers. The phalanx was subdivided into groups of a hundred known as *centuries.* After gaining some experience in battle with the large phalanx, the Romans decided to reorganize the army. They did away with the phalanx and divided the army into units made up of 3,600 men. These units were called *legions.* The legions were divided into groups of 60 to 120 men. These groups were called *maniples* [man'ə pəlz], a term that means "handful." This new organization was much more flexible in battle than the unwieldy phalanx.

Roman soldiers were not only tough and loyal, they were practical men who could survive during long marches. They knew how to sew and repair their own clothes and weapons. They could cook and knew how to build temporary roads, bridges, or boats as these were needed. Rarely was the Roman soldier taken by surprise. Moreover, Roman generals knew how to get the most out of the soldiers they commanded. The Greek historian Polybius [pə lib'ē əs], writing in the second century B.C., described the fate of a Roman soldier who fell asleep while on duty:

A court-martial composed of all the tribunes at once meets to try him, and if he is found guilty he is punished. . . . The tribune takes a cudgel [club] and just touches the condemned man with it, after which all in the camp beat or stone him, in most cases dispatching [killing] him in the camp itself. But even those who manage to escape are not saved thereby . . . for they are not allowed to return to their homes and none of the family would dare to receive such a man in his house. So that those who have once fallen into this misfortune are utterly ruined. . . .*

Those soldiers who have shown bravery in battle, however, are generously praised and more generously rewarded. Polybius tells us:

After a battle in which some of them have distinguished themselves, the general calls an assembly of the troops, and bringing forward those whom he considers to have displayed conspicuous valor [bravery], first of all speaks in laudatory [showing praise] terms of the courageous deeds of each . . . and afterwards distributes the following rewards. To the man who has wounded an enemy, a spear; to him who has slain and stripped an enemy, a cup. . . . To the first man to mount the wall at the assault on a city, he gives a crown of gold. . . .**

Thus were Roman soldiers punished and rewarded. They were organized into an army that conquered nearly all of the ancient world then known to Europeans.

Check in Here

1. How did Rome's geography contribute to its expansion?
2. Should a historian accept the story of Romulus and Remus as true? Were they the founders of Rome? Give reasons for your answer.

*Polybius, The Histories. Trans. W.R. Paton (Cambridge: Harvard University Press, Loeb Classical Library, 1967), Book VI, Chapter 37.

**Polybius, Book VIII, Chapter 39.

3. Why was Rome described as a *republic* but not a *democracy*?
4. How did the Twelve Tables help make Rome more democratic?
5. Why was the Roman army a powerful fighting force?

The Expansion of Rome on the Italian Peninsula

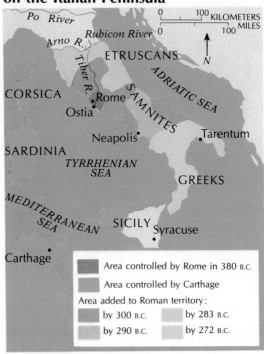

Roman power expanded from a small area in the west central region of the Italian peninsula.

- What people did the Romans conquer north of Rome? South of Rome?
- Who controlled the islands of Corsica and Sardinia and the western tip of Sicily?

THE NATURE OF THE ROMAN EMPIRE

How the Romans Created an Empire

The Romans, like the Greeks before them, were challenged by foreign powers. This happened not long after the plebeians helped make Rome more democratic. While the Roman government was becoming more democratic, it was also becoming more powerful. From 450 B.C. to 270 B.C., in a series of bitter wars with its neighbors (including the Gauls to the north, the Etruscans in the center, and the Samnites and Greeks in the south), Rome became ruler of the Italian peninsula.

Between 264 B.C. and 146 B.C., Rome and Carthage [kär'thij] fought three wars, known as the *Punic* [pyü'nik] *Wars.* These wars decided who would rule the Mediterranean. Carthage was founded in North Africa by the Phoenicians, who controlled the seas. Rome envied Carthage, and Carthage feared Rome. In one of the Punic Wars, Hannibal [han'ə bəl], a Carthaginian general, marched over the Alps and invaded northern Italy. The invasion was brilliantly carried out. However, Hannibal's victories proved only temporary. Hannibal was himself defeated by the Romans, and Carthage was completely destroyed. At the end of the hard-fought Punic Wars, Rome had won.

During a lull, or break, between the Punic Wars, Rome entered the Macedonian [mas'i dō'nē ən] Wars. These wars opened the way for the Roman conquest of the Middle East. The Romans defeated Philip V of Macedon. Greece and the Middle East came under Roman rule.

The Punic Wars established Roman power and rule in the Mediterranean area. Alexandria, Antioch, and Athens all bowed to the power of Rome. Through these wars Rome came into contact with Hellenistic culture, much of which it adopted and later passed on to us. The significance of the Punic Wars was that Rome, a republic, won over monarchies and dictatorships.

In time, Roman influence extended into Gaul [gôl] (now France and Germany), and Spain in Europe, Arabia and

A woodcut shows a battle between the Carthaginians and the Romans. Hannibal's troops used elephants to cross the Alps.

Egypt in the Middle East, and the northern edge of Africa. This large area was ruled from Rome, where trade and commerce grew and where people became prosperous.

Why Rome Became a Dictatorship

War brought power and glory to Rome. But it also brought death and destruction. While some Romans grew wealthy as a result of the Punic Wars, the majority of people suffered. Because they had slaves working for them, owners of large farms could sell their products at low prices. Small farmers could not afford to sell their products at low prices. They could not successfully compete with slave owners. As a result, many had to give up their farms. Unemployment mounted among the free laborers. The many wars waged by Rome made the gap between rich and poor even greater.

61

The Punic Wars, 264-146 B.C.

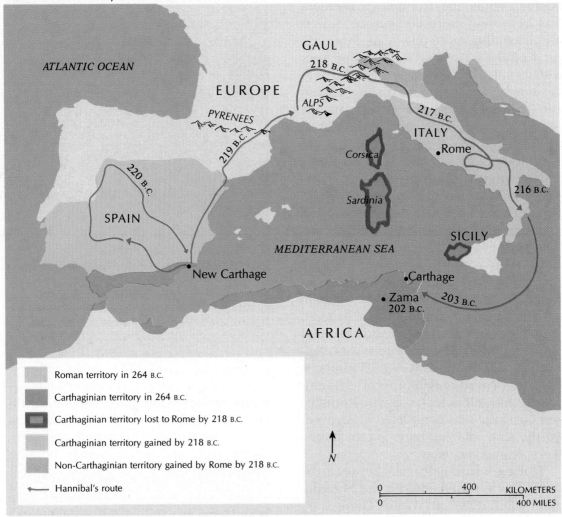

This map shows the rivalry between Rome and Carthage.
- By 218 B.C., Rome had conquered part of Sicily and what other two islands from Carthage?
- Over what two mountain ranges did Hannibal travel to invade Italy?

Poor unemployed laborers became quite discontented.

In an effort to distract the crowds of unemployed and hungry people, Roman politicians offered bread and entertainment. The bread filled their stomachs and the circuses offered violent entertainment. In the circuses there were fights to the death between men and animals or between gladiators.

These measures helped keep control for a while, but the old fight between the patricians and the plebeians broke out again. This time the results were tragic, since neither group was willing to compromise or give in.

Two patricians, the brothers Tiberius [tī bēr′ē əs] and Gaius [gā′əs] Gracchus [grak′əs], tried to pass laws to give land to farmers who did not have any. They

62

tried to encourage employment. They tried to give the plebeians a greater voice in the government. The Senate would not accept the changes that the brothers suggested were needed to calm the common people. By 123 B.C., both Gracchi brothers were dead. One was assassinated and one committed suicide. Civil war broke out as a result of their attempts to get more freedom and economic opportunity for the common people.

During the difficult period after the deaths of the Gracchi, various generals fought one another for political power. No sooner did one become a hero through a great victory than he tried to become consul and even dictator. One general, Marius [mär'ē əs], served as consul six times between 108 B.C. and 100 B.C. Then his power was successfully challenged by Sulla [sul'ə], another general. When Sulla died, a new struggle for power began. It was now Julius Caesar's [sē'zərz] turn to become master of Rome. He would succeed in becoming dictator where others failed. Let us see, briefly, what he did and how he did it.

How Caesar Became Master of Rome

Although born to a noble family, Julius Caesar (100 B.C.–44 B.C.) owed his success to his popularity among the common Romans. Caesar endeared himself to the masses by spending large sums of money in their behalf. He organized spectacular public games and gave bribes and gifts of food. He married Cornelia [kôr nē'lyə], the daughter of the popular leader Cinna [sin'ə]. In doing this, his position as a popular politician was assured among the common people.

Caesar's marriage gained him the hostility of Sulla, the leader of the aristocrats (the ruling and privileged class). The aristocrats and patricians ordered Caesar to divorce his wife. Caesar refused. He seemed marked for death, but he fled Rome to join the Roman army in the Middle East.

When Sulla died in 78 B.C., Caesar returned to Rome. His great ability as a speaker won him renewed fame. In 60 B.C. the *First Triumvirate* [trī um'vər it] took power. (A triumvirate is the rule of three people.) Three men made up this union: Caesar, Crassus [kras'əs], and Pompey [pom'pē]. Caesar's popularity, Crassus' wealth, and Pompey's military strength made the First Triumvirate especially powerful.

Caesar held the positions of consul and general in the First Triumvirate. He proved his ability as military leader by winning victories in Gaul. His conquest of Gaul and his invasion of Britain in 55 B.C. brought large areas under Roman rule. While in Gaul, he wrote his *Commentaries on the Gallic Wars*. He told the story of his military campaigns and victories. These stories spread far and wide and established Caesar as a brilliant mili-

Julius Caesar united the Roman Empire but ruled it for only five years. Why was he assassinated?

63

tary commander. His fame helped prepare the way for his return to Rome where civil war had broken out.

While Caesar was winning victories in Gaul and building an army, Crassus was fighting in Persia. After Crassus was killed in battle in 53 B.C., Pompey ruled Rome with nearly dictatorial powers. Rome was soon torn by civil war. Pompey felt his powers were not secure as long as Caesar was in Gaul with an intensely loyal army supporting him. The Senate ordered Caesar to resign and to disband his army. It feared his popularity with the army and with the Roman people. Caesar refused to give up his position as general. Instead, in 49 B.C., he crossed the Rubicon [rü′bə kon′] River and entered Italy. During four long years of bloody fighting, Caesar pursued and defeated his enemies in Spain and in Egypt, as well as in Italy. Finally, he entered Rome in triumph. He became dictator of Rome. Pompey, defeated, escaped to Egypt where he was murdered. Thus ended the First Triumvirate.

Caesar ruled for only five years. In 44 B.C., he was assassinated by some aristocrats and former friends who feared that Caesar might become king. In the Senate on the Ides of March (March 15), his trusted friend Brutus, and others, stabbed and killed him.

Why Caesar Deserves to Be Remembered

Although he served as leader of Rome for only a few years, Caesar launched many reforms. By increasing the number of people in the Senate, he expected to gain a majority vote for his reforms. A national census was taken. Caesar tried to provide for the poor by redistributing land. He tried to establish a stable government by pardoning aristocrats who had opposed him. He tried to rebuild the republic by giving people in the Roman provinces equal rights with the people of Rome. He tried to improve the government by making the Senate representative of the conquered lands and not of Italy alone. He also was responsible for the adoption of a new calendar, called the *Julian Calendar*.

Despite his achievements, Caesar was a dictator first and a reformer second. He was tribune, consul, and even religious leader. Had he lived, it is likely that he would have been worshipped as a god.

How Augustus Came to Power

As a result of Caesar's assassination, the reforms he began were short-lived. After another period of violent civil war the Roman Empire was established. It began in 27 B.C. and lasted until A.D. 476.

From 27 B.C., *monarchy* was the chief form of government of the Roman Empire. (A monarchy is a government in which a single person, such as a king, queen, or emperor, inherits the power to rule.) When the ruler was capable, government went well and there was peace. When the ruler was weak, ambitious people tried to take power and civil war followed.

The first and perhaps the ablest of the Roman emperors was Caesar's nephew, Octavian [ok tā′ vē ən]. He took the title Augustus [ô gus′təs]. Octavian (63 B.C.–A.D. 14) was a nineteen-year-old student in Greece when Julius Caesar was assassinated. He hurried home to avenge his uncle's death. In a struggle for power Octavian successfully forced his rival, Mark Antony, to share power with him. Together, Mark Antony and Octavian defeated the republican armies of Brutus and Cassius, two of the murderers of Caesar. They then divided the Roman Empire between them. Octavian ruled the western part, and Antony ruled the eastern part.

64

Cleopatra (69 B.C. -30 B.C.)

Cleopatra [klē'ə pat' rə] was the daughter of an Egyptian ruler. He provided that upon his death Cleopatra would share power with her brother Ptolemy XII as joint rulers of Egypt. He further provided that Rome would serve as the guardian of Egyptian welfare. In a civil war in 49 B.C., Cleopatra was forced to flee to Syria and leave her brother on the throne as the sole ruler of Egypt. This ambitious woman, however, was determined to return to Egypt as ruler.

Cleopatra was helped by Julius Caesar who claimed the right to decide who would rule in Egypt. She escaped from Syria in a small boat and made her way to Alexandria. In Alexandria, she had herself rolled up in a carpet and carried into Caesar's presence by one of her guards. The next day Caesar announced his decision to restore Cleopatra to the throne of Egypt as joint ruler with Ptolemy XII.

Despite Caesar's intervention, war followed. During the course of the war, Ptolemy XII was drowned in the Nile. Caesar could have made Egypt a Roman province. Instead, he restored Cleopatra to the Egyptian throne. However, he required her, as was the Egyptian custom, to marry her eleven-year-old brother Ptolemy XIII. Caesar remained in Egypt for a time. When he returned to Rome, Caesar asked the Roman Senate to pass a law permitting him to marry Cleopatra. In 46 B.C., Cleopatra followed Caesar to Rome.

Caesar requested the Senate's permission to divorce his Roman wife and marry Cleopatra. This was, in part, responsible for his assassination in 44 B.C. There was fear in Rome that by marrying Egyptian royalty, Caesar was preparing to rule as king with Cleopatra as queen. When he placed a gold statue of Cleopatra in the temple of Venus, he seemed to be mocking Roman religion. Upon Caesar's death, Cleopatra recognized how unpopular she was in Rome and returned to Alexandria.

In 43 B.C., upon the death of Ptolemy XIII, Cleopatra became sole ruler of Egypt. In the war that followed Caesar's death (see p. 64) Cleopatra supported, with ships and soldiers, the Triumvirate of Mark Antony, Octavius, and Lepidus. The Triumvirate won the Battle of Philippi in 42 B.C. Mark Antony became ruler of Rome's Eastern Empire, of which Egypt was part. Through Cleopatra's cunning, Egypt remained an independent country instead of becoming a Roman province. Antony, like Caesar before him, lingered in Alexandria. Between 40 and 32 B.C. Antony, aided by Cleopatra, conquered such lands as Phoenica, northern Judea, and Syria. In return for

65

her help, Antony declared Cleopatra to be Queen of Queens and appointed her children rulers of the conquered lands.

In the Roman Senate, Octavius denounced Antony for giving away Roman conquests. He declared war on Cleopatra in 32 B.C. In 31 B.C., at the Battle of Actium, Octavius won a decisive victory. Antony committed suicide in the mistaken belief that Cleopatra had already done so. Cleopatra sought mercy from Octavius but her luck or her skill in diplomacy failed her. Octavius sought her death. In a tomb where she had gone to hide, she allowed herself to be bitten by an asp, a poisonous snake. She died on August 29, 30 B.C. and was buried beside Mark Antony. With her death the Ptolemaic Dynasty that Alexander the Great had put in power in 323 B.C. ended, and Egypt became a Roman province.

Antony went to Egypt to enjoy the luxuries of the court of Cleopatra. Upon learning that Antony and Cleopatra were preparing to attack the western part of the Empire, the Roman Senate declared war. Octavian defeated Antony and Cleopatra at the naval battle of Actium in 31 B.C. He then became the sole ruler of the Roman Empire.

Octavian, now called Augustus, ruled an empire at peace with itself. He carried out many of Caesar's reforms. Like his uncle before him, he tried to hide his power by keeping the name but not the features of a republican government. Augustus rebuilt highways, collected taxes fairly, made sure the laws were just and justly carried out. It has been said of him that he "found Rome of brick and left it of marble."

Augustus was Rome's first emperor and one of its most outstanding. During his reign there was a long period of peaceful development. Trade and commerce flourished, building increased, and there was prosperity. The most notable achievement of the reign of Augustus was the establishment of the *Pax Romana* [paks rō mā′nə], the 200 years of peace that began in A.D. 27.

How Rome Was Ruled Under the Empire

Augustus, who liked to be known as "the restorer of the Roman Republic," was really the founder of the Roman Empire. The historian Tacitus [tas′i təs], writing a century after the reign of Augustus, tells us that Augustus "first conciliated [won over] the army by gratuities [money], the populace by cheapened corn [grain], the world by the amenities [attractive features] of peace, then step by step began to make his ascent and to unite in his own person the functions of the senate, the magistracy, and the legislature."*

Those emperors who immediately followed Augustus were called the *Julian Emperors* because they were related in some way to Julius Caesar. None were as able as Augustus. Tiberius (42 B.C.–A.D. 37), the stepson and son-in-law of Augustus, strengthened the powers of the emperor. Ruling an empire as large as Rome, however, was too much for him. He retreated to the Isle of Capri to hide from his enemies. Caligula (A.D. 12–41), grandnephew

*Tacitus, *The Annals.* Trans. J. Jackson (Cambridge: Harvard University Press; Loeb Classical Library, 1968), Book I, ii.

of Tiberius, was insane and was assassinated. Claudius (10 B.C.–A.D. 54) expanded
Roman rule and customs to Britain
which was then being brought under
Roman rule. He was poisoned by his
wife who sought the throne for Nero, her
son from an earlier marriage.

Nero [nēr'ō] (A.D. 37–68) was perhaps
the worst of the Julian Emperors. Nero's
rule was harsh. He murdered his mother

and then his wife. Nero put hundreds of
Christians to death. He enjoyed appearing in Roman plays and musical events.
In doing so he irritated the people who
thought such behavior undignified for an
emperor. Under Nero a great fire swept
Rome. Because of his role in musical
events, the popular belief was that Nero
fiddled while Rome burned. In 68 B.C.,
Nero was overthrown. He took his own

The Roman Empire at its Height

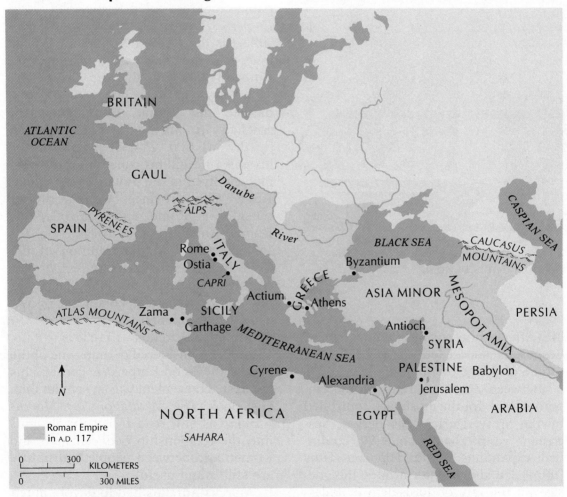

The Roman Empire at its height covered most of the Mediterranean world.
- What mountain range east of the Black Sea served as a northern border of the
  Roman Empire?
- What geographic feature may have blocked the spread of the Roman Empire
  southward in Africa?

A statue of Marcus Aurelius, one of the Good Emperors of Rome.

brother Domitian [də mish′ən] (A.D. 51–96). Domitian was a much hated ruler and was assassinated. Partly because of Domitian's cruelty the Senate decreed that his name be removed from all public places.

Nerva [nər′və] (A.D. 30–98), a citizen of Rome, was supported by those who had plotted against Domitian. He was named emperor. Nerva started the tradition of the emperor adopting as his son the person who would be named the next emperor. Because the emperors were chosen on the basis of ability, many capable emperors ruled Rome. The *Good Emperors*, as they are called, made it possible for the Roman Empire to last as long as it did. The period of the Good Emperors was roughly from A.D. 98–180.

Trajan [trā′jən] (A.D. 53–117) expanded the Roman Empire until it reached its maximum size. Hadrian [hā′drē ən] (A.D. 75–138) is known for his able rule and his concern for the people who lived in the provinces outside of Rome. (The provinces were territories outside of Rome and controlled by Rome.) Antoninus Pius [pī′əs] (A.D. 86–161) continued in the tradition of the Good Emperors by having effective government. However, his long reign was not marked by great conquests or unusual achievements.

Marcus Aurelius [ô rē′lē əs] (A.D. 121–180) is considered perhaps one of the best of the Good Emperors. Perhaps his greatest achievement was in scholarship. His book *The Meditations of Marcus Aurelius* is still read today. Its insights into the relationship between men and women and between people and nature are still found useful.

Marcus Aurelius had to devote much of his time to the tribes who were attacking the borders of his empire along the Danube. The long decline of Rome began at the end of his reign. Under Marcus

life. After a brief struggle among rivals, Vespasian succeeded in winning the throne of Rome for himself.

Between A.D. 68 and A.D. 96 the emperors were, for the most part, controlled by the army. During this period, Vespasian [ves pā′zhən] (A.D. 9–79) continued expanding Rome. His son Titus [tī′təs] led the Roman armies that destroyed the city of Jerusalem in Palestine. During his reign, Vespasian began the building of the Colosseum. When Vespasian died, Titus (A.D. 41–81) became emperor. He was then followed by his

Aurelius the *Pax Romana* ended. A century of civil war followed, until Diocletian [dī'ə klē'shən] (A.D. 284–305) temporarily brought order out of chaos. After his death, however, the decline of Rome continued even more rapidly.

The Good Emperors were wise enough to let the provinces rule themselves for the most part. They tolerated many religions. Nevertheless, from time to time they persecuted Jews and Christians. Several customs helped hold the Roman Empire together. In the provinces, Latin and Greek were common languages. The custom of emperor worship was practiced throughout the Empire. And Roman law governed daily relationships among people and tried to treat people fairly. Under the Good Emperors, Roman citizenship was given to the freemen of the empire. It was a source of great pride, when the empire was at its height, to be a Roman citizen. "No prouder statement could be made from Britain to Egypt, from Mauretania to Armenia, than the simple *'Civis Romanus sum*—I am a Roman Citizen.'"*

Check in Here

1. Why were the Punic Wars important to the growth of Rome?

2. How did Julius Caesar rise to power?

3. Why does Augustus deserve to be remembered?

4. How were the Good Emperors chosen? Was this an effective way of choosing emperors? Why or why not?

*Crane Brinton, John B. Christopher, Robert Lee Wolff, *A History of Civilization* (Englewood Cliffs, New Jersey: Prentice-Hall, Inc., 1956), Volume I, p. 110.

THE LIFE AND LAW OF ROME

What Religion and Family Life Were Like

Romans worshipped many gods. These gods, they thought, guarded their homes or controlled the forces of nature. Romans tried to predict the future by determining whether or not certain signs were favorable. A streak of lightning or an unusually loud thunderclap might be taken as a sign that the gods were angry. These unfavorable omens were sometimes enough to postpone business deals, to stop marching armies, or to delay the outbreak of war. On the other hand, if the signs were favorable, important decisions might safely be made. Roman religion encouraged worship of the emperor and patriotism. Romans were willing to serve in the Roman legions and to die on foreign soil for their country, for their emperor, and for their gods.

"It was Rome," wrote the historian Will Durant, "that raised the family to new heights in the ancient world."* The father was head of the household. He had power of life or death over family members. Healthy sons were hoped for eagerly. If it was the father's wish, a crippled child or a girl was often allowed to die. Women played important roles in rearing and educating children, in directing servants, and in budgeting the family's money.

While women had few legal rights, they were well treated. Parents generally wanted daughters to marry early. Courtship was rare, and most marriages were arranged between families or by marriage brokers. However, being a wife was not the only occupation for women.

*Will Durant, *The Story of Civilization: Caesar and Christ* (New York: Simon and Schuster, 1944), p. 311.

A bas relief showing the interior of a Roman butcher shop.

Large numbers of women worked in shops, and some worked in the cloth trade. Women became doctors; others became lawyers, while some came to serve in politically important posts. To draw on Will Durant again, "legislation [laws] kept women subject, custom made them free."*

Romans at Work and Play

Farming was the basic industry of Rome. However, city life developed in the Roman Empire to a greater degree than in other ancient civilizations. Towns were not unusually large. They were organized for the trade of farm products and supplies. In the early days of the empire, farms were small and individually owned. Later, the small farms were combined into large estates owned by wealthy Romans and worked by slaves. The landlords of the large estates had some industry which, together with farming, was enough to make the estate self-sufficient. That is, the people living

*Durant, p. 370.

on the estate could grow or manufacture what they needed without buying from others.

Much of the wealth of the Empire came from manufacturing and trade. Artisans made handcrafted items which were sold in shops. Wealthy people sometimes tried to mass-produce items. The Roman emperors usually kept a hands-off policy in industry. The government did, however, own the mines and lease them to wealthy people to run.

Trade prospered in the Roman Empire. During the first and second centuries A.D., products from all over the world poured into Rome. Farm crops, weapons, spices, jewelry, and household goods were carried cheaply and, above all, safely on the roads of Rome. A generally stable money supply financed trade with all parts of the world. Bankers served as moneychangers and moneylenders.

When Rome was not at work, it was at play. Roman play was sometimes a bloody affair indeed. In the Colosseum men fought wild animals or with one another for sport. In these contests the loser died, and a chance to die at a later time was the reward of the winner. Sometimes those who took part in such violent games were professional fighters, or gladiators, who fought for a living. More often, however, slaves, war captives, or Christian prisoners were forced to fight for the entertainment of the Romans. Chariot racing was a popular sport. Horsedrawn chariots raced around the track of the Circus Maximus, where death lurked if there was a serious collision.

The Romans used some of their leisure time for schooling as well as for playing. In the Roman schools of that time the chief aim was to turn out boys and girls who knew how to obey. Study was strictly limited to the basic subjects of reading, writing, and arithmetic, the so-called three R's of our present day.

Since many of the teachers were Greek slaves or freemen who had been brought to Rome, Roman education was Greek rather than Roman in nature. But there was little emphasis on bodybuilding, art, or music, as there was in Greek schools. Although "Rome did not invent education . . . she developed it on a scale unknown before."*

*Durant, p. 375.

How Roman Law Was a Model for World Law

Law is the greatest gift of Rome to us. Roman law was based on the Twelve Tables. When these laws became out-of-date, Roman lawyers studied laws passed by the Senate and decisions handed down by Roman judges. They also studied laws that were used in the lands Rome conquered. They tried to build into the law the lasting principles

Trade Routes of the Roman Empire

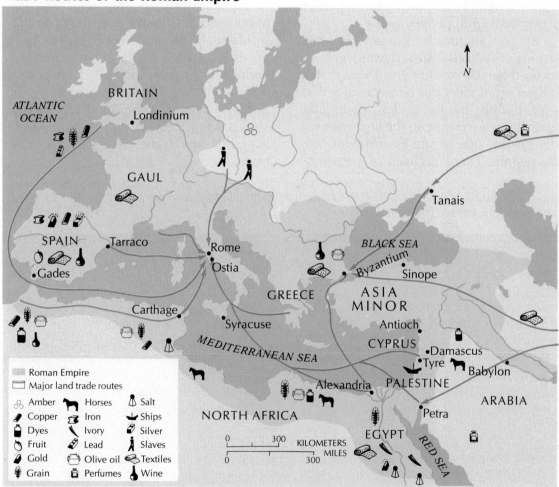

The major trade routes of the Roman Empire centered on Rome and its seaport Ostia on the west coast.
• What products were obtained from Britain?
• From what regions did the Romans get slaves?
• List three seaports on the Mediterranean Sea.

of fairness and justice. In this way Roman law was always changing to meet new conditions.

Roman laws provided for new and better legal methods. Foreign people in the provinces ruled by Rome were allowed to be governed by their own laws. Freemen (Roman citizens) were equally treated regardless of the amount of money they had. Under Roman law, a citizen's life, property, and legal rights were assured. Non-citizens were often more harshly treated. However, one of the greatest contributions of Rome to legal thought is the idea that a person is innocent until proven guilty.

By our standards, Roman law had serious drawbacks. Slavery was legal. An accused person was not given a jury trial. Judges often gave out punishments that were unduly harsh. In any complaint against the government, the law was usually on the side of the government, not the people. Those accused of crimes of theft or murder were harshly treated. Roman law, despite these shortcomings, influenced the law of every European country. It spread throughout the Western world.

Rome's Practical Gifts to the World

There was a major difference between the gifts of Greece to civilization and those of Rome. Those of the Greeks were chiefly artistic, while those of the Romans were chiefly practical. The Greeks enjoyed beauty for its own sake. The Romans tended to make useful things that would make life more comfortable. They produced paved roads, sewers, and aqueducts to provide their cities with fresh water. With a good water supply, public baths become common and Roman streets were cleaned. The Romans built hospitals and some were paid for with taxes.

The Colosseum, as it looks today. In ancient times the Colosseum was used as an entertainment center for Roman citizens.

The *Pantheon* [pan'thē on'] is a fine example of Roman architecture. This is a religious temple completed by Emperor Hadrian. It is a circular building. Its dome is 43 meters (142 feet) across. It still stands in the city of Rome. The arch and dome are distinctive features of the Pantheon and are typical of Roman architecture. They are Rome's unique contribution to the art of building. There were few Roman buildings built solely for religious purposes, however. Rome built many public buildings, including the Colosseum—a stadium bigger than Madison Square Garden or Yankee Stadium. Here, the people were entertained.

In science and engineering too, Romans valued practicality. They invented little that was new, but they made good use of what was already known. Pliny [plin'ē] the Elder proved that the world was round, but he only confirmed a theory that had been known as early as 300 B.C. Surgery was performed in ancient Rome, and operations were often successful. The removal of tonsils was not uncommon. Galen [gā'len] was a Greek (A.D. 131–201) who lived in Rome. He wrote an encyclopedia of medicine which included all the medical knowledge then known.

How Rome Influenced Civilization in Other Ways

The Romans are most noted for the success with which they ruled their empire and for the length of time the empire lasted. The two hundred years of peace which Rome achieved has yet to be achieved in modern times.

In literature, as in education, Romans imitated the Greeks. Rome's greatest writers were Cicero [sis'ə rō'] and Lucretius [lü'krē'shəs], who made their contributions while Rome was still a republic. Virgil [vėr'jəl], Horace [hôr'is], Ovid [ov'id], Seneca [sen'ə kə], and Tacitus [tas'i təs] were writers who became well known during the period of the empire.

Because of its simple style, Caesar's *Commentaries on the Gallic Wars* is still used where Latin is taught. Cicero was a prominent lawyer, politician, and orator. His speeches and other writings are still read by those who wish to study Latin in its purest form. Cicero used his great gifts to defend the Roman republic. Virgil was the official poet of the Emperor Augustus. He wrote the *Aeneid* [i nē'id], which told of the great and good deeds of Rome. Horace urged people to lead simple lives, and Ovid wrote of life's pleasures rather than of its simplicity. Tacitus is regarded as Rome's greatest historian. He warned the Romans of the growing strength of the German tribes.

Roman law became the basic law of Western nations. Latin, the language used by the Romans, became the basis of all the *Romance languages*, which are French, Spanish, Italian, Portuguese, and Romanian. Latin became the language of law, of science, and of the Roman Catholic Church.

The organization of government which made Roman rule successful also made possible the growth of Christianity. As the government in the Empire became weaker, the organization of the Christian church became stronger. In time the Christian faith became the faith of Europe.

Check in Here

1. How does the Roman family resemble or differ from your own?
2. How did the Romans use religion to encourage loyalty to their empire?
3. Why is law regarded as Rome's most lasting contribution to civilization?
4. Give two examples that justify saying that Rome's gifts to civilization were practical ones.

THE RISE OF CHRISTIANITY AND THE FALL OF ROME

How Christianity Rose

As Roman government declined, Christianity rose. It was during the reign of Augustus that Jesus was born in Bethlehem in Judea. At that time, Judea was a part of the Roman Empire. Jesus was a Jew trained in the teachings of the Old Testament. He preached the goodness of people, love of the Lord, and love of the poor, the sick, and the weak. Through his teachings, Jesus appealed to a large number of people. Jesus was called Christ (savior) by those who followed him. A group of his close followers, known as the *apostles* [ə pos′əlz], helped to spread the teachings of Jesus. The teachings of Jesus are found in the New Testament. Paul, who began life as a Jewish teacher, became a leading Christian missionary. He traveled throughout the empire gaining converts to Christianity.

Jesus directed his teachings to all people. As Jesus preached the people listened, and they liked what they heard. The Roman government ordinarily tolerated many religions, but the teachings of Jesus disturbed them greatly.

Although Rome allowed many gods, it expected that everyone would worship the emperor as well. Christians and Jews refused to worship the state (the emperor) because they felt to do so was idol worship. As a result, the Jews and Christians were both persecuted. Despite the persecution, the number of Christians grew steadily. Then in the year 313 the Roman Emperor Constantine issued a command which said that the Christian religion would be tolerated.

How does one explain the success of Christianity? One reason for its success lay in the nature of its teachings. Jesus said that all people were equal in the sight of God. He encouraged all people to believe that a better life would come after death. Another reason for Christianity's success was that it came at a time when Rome was declining. People felt afraid and insecure. Perhaps they felt that their own gods were deserting them. Many thought that Jesus might indeed be the Messiah of whom the Jews had spoken. The Christian belief in God as the protector and in life after death inspired people. It made them feel safe.

The success of Christianity resulted in part from the teachings of Paul. Paul helped make the religion popular with a large number of people in the Roman Empire. He showed them how Christianity could fill their religious needs. Finally, Christianity was successful because it imitated the organization of the Roman Empire. The pope was the head of the Church. The Church was organized into districts of various sizes, which were served by bishops. The smallest district was the parish, whose religious needs were looked after by a priest.

Christianity taught the dignity of work and the brotherhood and sisterhood of humankind. Christianity became a refuge for many troubled people of the world. When political institutions, such as law, government, and the economy, began to crumble, the Church remained stable.

Some of the Reasons for the Fall of Rome

The date for marking the fall of the Roman Empire is generally given as A.D. 476, when invaders defeated the last Roman emperor. It is important to remember that Rome's decline was a process, not an event. Rome was neither built nor destroyed in a day; both took hundreds of years.

The reasons for the fall of Rome can only be summarized here. They reach far

This religious painting decorates the wall of a catacomb near Rome. Why did the Christians bury their dead in catacombs?

back into Roman history. The seeds of destruction may have taken root as early as the first century B.C., when the army was used to fight a civil war. The real decline began in the second century A.D., however, as men of questionable loyalty filled the ranks of the Roman army. These hired soldiers, or mercenaries, could not always be counted upon to stand their ground when the battle seemed lost.

Economics also played a large part in the fall of Rome. The gap between the rich and the poor widened; slaves took the jobs of freemen; there were heavy, unfair taxes and high unemployment; and huge estates were held by a few rich families, while the poor had no land at all. The consuls of Rome, some with unlimited power, fought among themselves and gave little thought to the welfare of the people.

After Rome became an empire in A.D. 27, wise kings ruled well. But unfortunately, Rome did not always have wise rulers. Except during the period of the Good Emperors, succession to the throne followed no orderly pattern. The death of each emperor seemed to be a signal for revolt and civil war. This was

particularly true when generals of the army gained control of the state and sought to become rulers. An important reason that Rome fell was because many of its emperors were weak. Under their rule the nation and the conquered countries were not well-governed.

The moral standards (values) of Rome declined. There was corruption and favoritism in government, luxurious living and idleness among the rich, limited education among the poor, and brutality in the Colosseum and Circus Maximus. The once strong character of the Romans weakened.

Discontent increased due to Rome's failure to extend the privileges of full citizenship to people in the provinces and to give the people a voice in government. When it became evident that the power of Rome was declining, the provinces tried to take advantage of Rome's weaknesses to establish independent nations of their own.

Theodosius [thē′ə dō′shē əs] (A.D. 347–395) was the last Roman emperor to rule over the entire empire. Some Germanic people were allowed to settle within the empire. But most of them were prevented from doing so by the

Roman legions. However, when the West Goths, or Visigoths [viz'ə goths'], were attacked by the fierce Huns from Asia, they sought safety within the Roman Empire. The emperor reluctantly permitted them to enter. The Visigoths became influential in the army, and emperors who followed Theodosius could not control them. When Theodosius died in 395, the empire was divided into the Western Roman Empire and Eastern Roman Empire. Each had a ruler of its own. This division was thought at first to be a temporary one. It proved, however, to be permanent.

The Western part of the Roman Empire was soon dominated by powerful German generals. The Visigoths conquered and destroyed Rome in the year 410. Attila [at'tə lə] the Hun led an attack on Gaul. He was defeated by Aetius [ā ē'shē əs] at the battle of Châlons [shä lôn] in 451. This battle prevented further attacks on Europe by Asiatic invaders. Attila tried to attack Rome but was persuaded not to destroy it by Pope Leo I. Attila died two years later.

By 476 there was nothing left of Rome to "fall." In that year, Odovacar [ō' dō vā' kər], of German birth, overthrew the last Roman emperor. The empire in the west was gone. The eastern part lasted for another thousand years.

We have studied only a few of the reasons for the fall of Rome. Its glory lives on, however, in our language, customs, laws, and ways of thinking.

Check in Here

1. Why did the teachings of Christianity disturb the Roman rulers?

2. How was Paul responsible for the spread of Christianity?

3. Enumerate four reasons for the fall of Rome.

REVIEWING THE BASICS

The rise of the city of Rome, and later of the Roman Empire, was made possible by (1) a favorable geographic location; (2) an ability to adapt ideas and skills from other people, especially the Greeks; (3) a great sense of political organization and the rule of law; (4) a superior army; and (5) a series of emperors who gave the empire strong leadership that was favorable to trade and commerce. The important thing to remember about Rome was that it lasted as long as it did—over 800 years—and that it had a lasting influence on Western civilization. Rome experimented with a variety of governments—republicanism, dictatorship, and rule by emperor—and passed on those experiences to the world.

As Rome declined, Christianity grew and spread. While Roman emperors generally tolerated many religions, they could not tolerate one in which worship of the emperor was forbidden. As a result, early Christians were looked upon as traitors. However, the teachings of the Church and its organization enabled the Church to grow. It became the official religion of the Roman Empire. Much of the organization of the Roman government influenced the organization of the Catholic church.

REVIEWING THE HIGHLIGHTS

**People
to Identify**

Polybius	Domitian	Hannibal	Hadrian
the Gracchi	Caesar	Galen	Marcus Aurelius
Marius	Octavian	Cicero	Theodosius
Sulla	Mark Antony	Virgil	Attila
Pompey	Pliny the	Tacitus	Jesus
Crassus	Elder	Cornelia	Paul
Tiberius	Nero	Diocletian	Visigoths
Caligula	Vespasian	Nerva	Constantine
Claudius	Titus	Trajan	Cleopatra

**Places
to Locate**

City of	Carthage	Gaul	Alps
Rome	Tiber River	Mediterranean Sea	Rubicon River

**Terms
to Understand**

republic	praetors	censor	monarchy
democracy	magistrate	First Triumverate	century
plebeians	consul	Roman Empire	maniples
patricians	Senate	Good Emperors	Christianity
phalanx	tribal	Pax Romana	Visigoths
dictator	assembly	Colosseum	Huns
Etruscans	tribune	Twelve Tables	
Latins	legion		

**Events
to Describe**

Punic Wars	Gallic Wars	Fall of Rome
Macedonian Wars		

**Mastering
the Fundamentals**

1. Explain how Rome was responsible for the spread of Christianity to the Western world?
2. How were the Romans indebted to the Etruscans?
3. What people did the Assembly of Centuries and the Assembly of Tribes represent?
4. Distinguish between the patricians and the plebeians.
5. Why did the plebeians demand changes in the government?
6. Describe the phalanxes of the Roman army.
7. How did the plebeians gain more rights?
8. Why did the Punic Wars mean hardship for many people?
9. Why was Rome able to defeat Carthage?
10. Why did the Gracchi brothers fail in their efforts to help the plebeians?
11. What happened to Rome after the death of Caesar?
12. What are some of the reforms that Caesar tried?
13. Describe the Roman family.
14. How are we indebted to Roman law? How does Roman law differ from our own?

15. What are the Romance languages? Why are they so named?
16. Explain the reasons for the growth of Christianity.
17. Why did Rome persecute the Christians?
18. How did weak emperors play a part in the fall of Rome?
19. Why is it said that the fall of Rome was a gradual rather than a sudden collapse?

THINGS TO DO

1. Prepare a report on the following topic: "Caesar: Hero or Scoundrel."
2. Take a photograph of those buildings in your community that appear to have been influenced by Roman architecture. Bring your pictures to class and explain why you see Roman architectural influence. Add the pictures to your bulletin board.
3. Prepare a "Meet the Press" program in which three or four newspaper reporters interview Marcus Aurelius. What questions would the reporters ask? What answers do you think they might get?

YOU ARE THE HISTORIAN

During the Civil War (44 B.C. to 29 B.C.) following the death of Caesar, the triumvirs, Octavian, Antony, and Lepidus issued an edict requiring 1,400 of the richest women to turn over their property to them. In this way they hoped to pay for the costs of the war. The women, under the leadership of Hortensia, one of the women required to give up her property, protested to the triumvirs. What follows is a report of the historian Appian who lived in Rome during the second century A.D.

HORTENSIA'S SPEECH

The women resolved to beseech* the women-folk of the triumvirs.* With the sister of Octavian and the mother of Antony they did not fail, but they were repulsed* from the doors of Fulvia, the wife of Antony, whose rudeness they could scarce endure.* They then forced their way to the tribunal of the triumvirs in the Forum, the people and the guards dividing to let them pass. There, through the mouth of Hortensia, whom they had selected to speak, they spoke as follows:

"As befitted* women of our rank addressing a petition to you, we had recourse* to the ladies of your households; but having been treated as did not befit us, at the hands of Fulvia, we have been driven by her to the Forum. You have already deprived us of our fathers, our sons, our husbands, and our brothers, whom you accused of having wronged you; if you take away our property also, you reduce us to a condition unbecoming our birth, our manners, our sex. If we have done you wrong, as you say our husbands have, proscribe* us as you do them. But if we women have not voted any of you public enemies, have not torn down your houses, destroyed your army, or led another one against you; if we have not hindered you in obtaining offices and honors, why do we share the penalty when we did not share the guilt?"

"Why should we pay taxes when we have no part in the honors, the commands, the state-craft, for which you contend* against each other with such harmful results? 'Because this is a time of war,' do you say? When have there not been wars, and when have taxes ever been imposed on women, who are exempted* by their sex among all mankind? Our mothers did once rise superior to their sex and made contributions when you were in danger of losing the whole empire and the city itself through the conflict with the Carthaginians. But then they contributed voluntarily, not from their landed property, their fields, their dowries, or their houses, without which life is not possible to free women, but only from their own jewelery, and even these not according to fixed valuation, not under fear of informers or accusers, not by force and violence, but what they themselves were willing to give. What alarm is there now for the empire or the country? Let war with the Gauls or the Parthians come, and we shall not be inferior to our mothers in zeal for the common safety; but for civil wars may we never contribute, nor ever assist you against each other! We did not contribute to Caesar or to Pompey. Neither Marius nor Cinna imposed taxes upon us. Nor did Sulla, who held despotic power in the state, do so, whereas you say that you are reestablishing the commonwealth."

While Hortensia thus spoke the triumvirs were angry that women should dare to hold a public meeting when the men were silent; that they should demand from magistrates the reasons for their acts, and themselves not so much as furnish* money while the men were serving in the army. They ordered the lictors* to drive them away from the tribunal, which they proceeded to do until cries were raised by the multitude outside, when the lictors desisted* and the triumvirs said they would postpone* till the next day the consideration of the matter. On the following day they reduced the number of women, who were to present a valuation of their property, from 1400 to 400, and decreed that all men who possessed more than 100,000 denarii,* both citizens and strangers, freedmen and priests, and men of all nationalities without a single exception, should (under the same dread of penalty and also of informers) lend them at interest a fiftieth part of their property and contribute one year's income to the war expenses.†

Vocabulary

beseech—beg	*contend*—fight against
triumvers—three officials	*exempted*—freed from
repulsed—driven from	*furnish*—provide
endure—stand	*lictors*—minor officials
befitted—suited to	*desisted*—stopped
recourse—right to approach	*postpone*—put off
proscribe—condemn	*denarii*—ancient Roman silver money

†From Appian, *Civil War* Vol. IV, pp. 32–34. As found in Mary R. Lefkowitz and Maureen B. Fant, *Women in Greece and Rome* (Toronto and Sarasota: Samuel-Stevens, 1977), pp. 151–152. Used by permission.

(turn to page 80)

On the basis of your reading of the selection on pages 78 and 79, discuss with your class the answers to the following questions.

1. Before addressing the triumvirs, how did the women try to plead their case?
2. How were they treated by: (a) Fulvia (Antony's wife); (b) Octavian's sister; (c) Antony's mother?
3. Why do the women say that the taxes about to be imposed are unfair?
4. Why do the women object to paying taxes to support this particular war?
5. How had women helped Rome in the past?
6. What was the attitude of the triumvirs toward the women?
7. To what extent were the women successful in their efforts?
8. What do we learn from this selection about the political role of women in ancient Rome?
9. How did the multitude outside the Forum feel about the women's protests?
10. Is this a primary or secondary source? How can you tell?

Vasco da Gama

India and Southeast Asia: Their Ancient Splendors

During the fifteenth century, Europeans were searching for new lands and great riches. They found them in India and in Southeast Asia. In the process of discovering vast wealth, they also discovered America. However, the precious metals, the fine silks, the tasty spices, the precious ivory, and the invaluable jade were at first far more important to them than America was. To the Europeans of the fifteenth century, these riches were worth a search and a struggle.

India and Southeast Asia, like Egypt, Israel, Greece, and Rome, are ancient lands and cradles of civilization. Because India and Southeast Asia are important lands in the world today, an understanding of their interesting past will help you appreciate their present.

THE GEOGRAPHY OF SOUTHEAST ASIA AND ITS INFLUENCE ON ANCIENT INDIA

The Location of India and Southeast Asia

If you take a close look at a map, you will see that Europe is a large peninsula of Asia. To the people of the European peninsula, Asia is the East. That portion of Asia farthest away from Europe is called the Far East. The lands of Egypt and Mesopotamia, which are close to Europe, are called the Middle East.

East Asia, or the Far East, is made up of China, Japan, and Korea. South Asia consists mainly of India, Pakistan, Bang-

The Geography of Asia

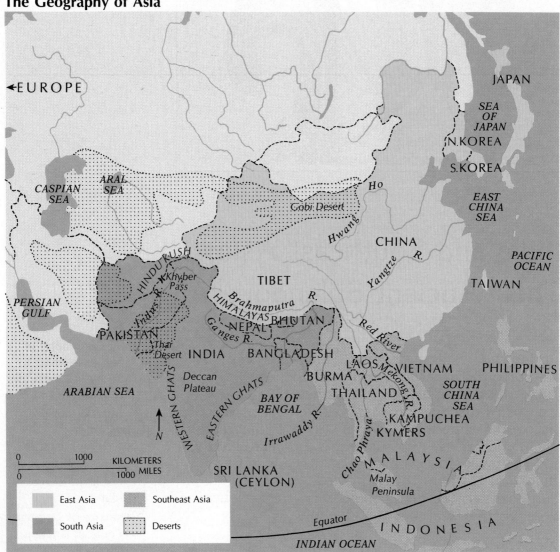

Asia has many important geographic features.
- What is the name of one of the important rivers that flowed through ancient India? Through Southeast Asia?
- In what countries are the mountains known as the Himalayas found?
- Name two Southeast Asian countries not on the Asian mainland.

82

ladesh [bäng glə desh'], Bhutan [bü tän'], Nepal [nə pôl'], and Sri Lanka [srē lang'kə] (Ceylon). Southeast Asia is made up of Thailand [tī'lənd], Burma [bėr'mə], Vietnam [vē et'näm'], Laos [lä'ōs], Kampuchea [kam pü chē'ə], Malaysia [mə lä'zhə], the Philippines [fil'ə pēnz], and Indonesia [in'dō nē'zhə]. All except the last two nations are on the mainland of Asia and form a peninsula jutting out into the South China Sea. The Philippines and Indonesia consist of groups of islands. Indonesia spreads out over 4,830 kilometers (3,000 mi.) of Indian Ocean. This is about the same distance as between New York and California. The Philippines spread out over 2,414 kilometers (1,500 mi.) in the Pacific Ocean.

Because they are situated on or near the equator, the countries of Southeast Asia are hot. Jungles and mountains make transportation and communication within these countries very difficult. On the other hand, even in earliest times it was possible for people in Southeast Asia to sail from one island to another and to the mainland peninsula. It is probably in this way that the islands were settled. Because of their location, the countries of Southeast Asia control the ocean routes of the Indian and Pacific Oceans.

India is a country shaped like a top or inverted triangle. Because it is so large it is often described as a *subcontinent*. A subcontinent is a huge land mass which by itself can almost be considered a continent. India is a land of rugged geography. In the north are the world's highest mountains, the Himalayas, and perhaps the world's most exotic mountains, the Hindu Kush [küsh]. The Khyber [kī'bər] Pass, which cuts through the Hindu Kush, was used many times as an invasion route for armies that tried to conquer India.

The Indus [in'dəs] and the Ganges [gan'jēz] rivers drain the level land of

A section of the Himalayas. Some of the lofty peaks of this Asiatic mountain range soar over 7,500 meters (25,000 ft.).

India. They create a broad fertile valley which became the center for the development of Indian civilization. South of this region is the Deccan [dek'ən] Plateau, an area of relatively high ground between two mountain ranges called the Eastern and Western Ghats [gôts]. The narrow western coast and the wider eastern coast join to form the southern coastline along the Indian triangle. People who lived in these lands in ancient times were seafarers. They bravely sailed across the Arabian Sea to trade with the people of Egypt and Mesopotamia. They crossed the Bay of Bengal to trade with Ceylon and Southeast Asia.

Although the people of Europe and the people of Asia share the same land mass, they had only occasional contact with one another until about the fifteenth century. Chains of mountains, deserts, and rivers kept Asia separate from Europe. These geographic barriers have had an important influence on history. They help explain why the cultures of the

The archaeological site of Mohenjo-Daro was once the industrial heart of an Indus river valley civilization. What clues did archaeologists discover about life and culture in Mohenjo-Daro?

East and the West differ greatly from one another. They also help explain why the people in the two regions found each other's ways of life so strange when they did meet. However, now that modern transportation has "shortened" distances and "leveled" mountains, the East and the West have met, and ways of life are being shared.

What Mohenjo-Daro Tells Us About India's Ancient Past

When Europeans came to India in the late fifteenth century, they found a civilization thousands of years old. Archaeologists made discoveries that shed light on the early civilizations in northern India. They studied a fabulous city, Mohenjo-Daro [mō hen'jō där'ō], located on the banks of the Indus River. From an examination of its ruins, they believed that Indian history is probably as old as those of Sumeria and Babylonia. There was evidence that the Sumerians and Babylonians traded with the people of Mohenjo-Daro as early as 2900 B.C. Sumerian beads and pottery were found in Mohenjo-Daro.

What kind of city was Mohenjo-Daro? What do the ruins tell about the people who lived, worked, played, and died there? As early as 2900 B.C., a rich civilization existed. The straight, wide streets of Mohenjo-Daro ran north to south and east to west, crossing each other at right angles. With such a pattern for their streets, people were able to go easily from place to place in Mohenjo-Daro. The people had homes in brick apartment houses in which several families lived. Bathrooms with toilets were common. A drainage (sewer) system served the city.

Archaeologists found evidence of business skills and manufacturing. Coins they found proved that the people of Mohenjo-Daro had a money system. The people used attractively decorated pottery dishes, jugs, and jars. They knew how to grow cotton and weave it into cloth and how to make gold and silver ornaments, copper weapons, and bronze figures. The potter's wheel was known and used. All this evidence tells us about the high level of civilization at Mohenjo-Daro. Not until thousands of years later would Europeans enjoy such a level of civilization. Yet the civilization of Mohenjo-Daro disappeared about 2000 B.C.

Why the city of Mohenjo-Daro died is not known. It is also not known what happened to its people. Historians do know that about the year 2000 B.C., a people called *Dravidians* [drə vid'ē ənz] were living in northern India. How they came to be there or why they were given this name remains one of the many mysteries of Indian history. They were dark-skinned and had black hair. They were the ancestors of a large portion of the people living in India today. They developed a religion. In wooden temples, they prayed to snakes, their holy symbol. Today the snake remains a symbol in the Hindu religion.

The Dravidians were followed by a people who had light skin and hair. These *Indo-Aryans* [in'dō ar'ē ənz], as they were called, played an important role in the unfolding history of India.

How the Indo-Aryans Lived

Where the Indo-Aryans came from is unknown. They may have come from the

Ancient India

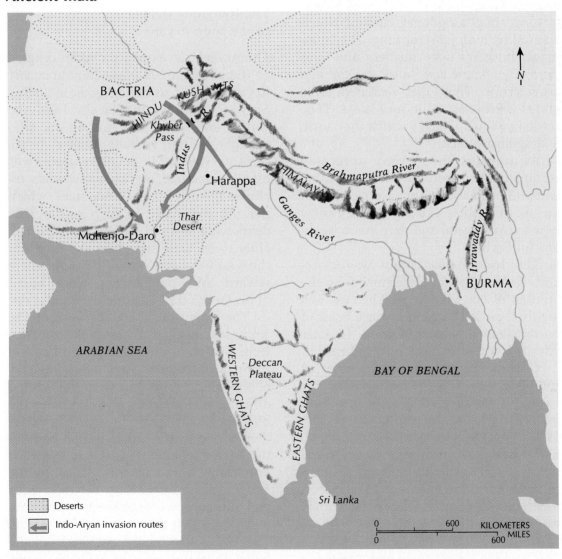

• The ancient Indian city of Mohenjo-Daro was located near what important river?
• What mountain pass did many of the Indo-Aryan invaders use?
• In what general direction did these invaders travel?

Middle East, because they were related to the Persians. Beginning about 2000 B.C., the Indo-Aryans came both as conquerors and immigrants to the Indian subcontinent. They made slaves of the original dark-skinned Dravidians. They established their own government and religion, which were to have great influence upon the people of India.

The Indo-Aryans first lived in tribes that were related to each other. Each tribe was ruled by a chief and a tribal council. Later some of the tribes joined to form small kingdoms, each of which was led by a *raj* [räj], or king. The Indo-Aryan invaders were farmers and warriors. They knew how to till the soil and grow crops. Their diet included milk, grain, vegetables, fruit, and meat. They settled in small villages which they fortified against attack.

As warriors the Aryans were well equipped. They used the horse for riding and pulling chariots. They were skilled in the use of the bow and arrow. They knew how to work metal and they made weapons and armor.

The Indo-Aryan family was close-knit. Its wealth was determined by the number of cows it owned. The cow was highly regarded because it was a beast of burden and a source of food. In later days the cow became a holy animal.

One of the prominent features of Indo-Aryan life was the *caste system*. The caste system divided society into four main groups. The three chief castes were 1) *Brahmans* [brä'mənz], or priests; 2) *Kshatriyas* [ka shat'rē əz], or nobles and fighters; and 3) *Vaisyas* [vis'yəz], or plain people such as merchants and workers. A fourth caste, known as *Shudras* [shü'drəz], was made up of servants. Below these castes there were the "untouchables." This was the lowest caste and was made up of the large numbers who performed tasks believed to be unclean. In the beginning there were only four castes, but over time, the number of castes increased significantly.

The caste system began because the priests wanted to keep their high positions in society. At first the rules and regulations governing the relationships among the castes were not nearly as strict as they later became. Differences in occupations and differences in color hardened dividing lines and relationships among the castes.

The Religious Beliefs of the Indo-Aryans

The Aryans developed the main religion of India, called *Hinduism* [hin'dü iz'əm]. Aryans prayed to nature gods including Surya the sun, Varuna the sky, Indra the storm, and Signi the fire. Indra, who brought the rain so badly needed, in ancient as well as in modern times, was highly esteemed. Aryan ceremonies included the drinking of soma juice, which put the worshiper in high spirits. The dead were burned rather than buried. Holy songs were sung to make sure that the soul went to *Karma* [kar'mə], where reward and punishment were based upon the kind of life one lived on earth.

The holy songs and prayers of the Aryans are called *Vedas* [vā'dəz]. They were written in the Vedic [vā'dik] period from 1500–1000 B.C. They tell the history of the Hindu faith, but were not written down until hundreds of years after the birth of Christ. The *Rig-Veda* [rig vā'də] is regarded as the oldest Indian book of the Hindu religion. It is one of the most important works in the *Vedas*. In the *Vedas*, the relationships between gods and humans are explained, as are the ways by which the gods may be served. The *Vedas* also record change from the belief in many gods to a belief in one God.

The most famous of the religious books, the *Upanishads* [ü pan'i shadz],

Hindus worshipping. The Hindus believe in reincarnation, or rebirth into another form after death. What are some other religious beliefs of Hindus?

were handed down by word of mouth for about 300 years (800 B.C. to 500 B.C.) and later put into written form. Here may be found the beginning of the idea that humans are reborn, often in another form, after death. Each time a person dies he or she is *reincarnated*, or born into another body. This thought has had a great influence on the Hindu faith. The *Upanishads* also express the idea that through knowledge one can achieve a oneness with God.

The *Vedas* and *Upanishads* were written in a language called *Sanskrit* [san'skrit]. Along with Greek, Latin, and Hebrew, Sanskrit is one of the great classical languages of the world.

The Hindu religion has deep roots in the ancient history of India. Today, it is the religion of more than 475 million people and the most important religion in India. The Hindus believe that life is usually evil. It is possible to avoid evil by following the teachings of the Brahmans,

or priestly caste. Among these teachings are those which insist upon strict caste separation. A member of one caste is not permitted to marry, to eat, or to work with one of another caste. A person cannot change the caste into which he or she is born. A person's caste is the reward or punishment for good or bad deeds committed in a previous life.

The Hindu faith was not without competitors. At about the time the *Upanishads* were being handed down, various religious teachers spread ideas of their own. One such teacher, Mahavira [mə hä′vēr′ə], organized a group called *Jains* [jīnz]. They believed that all living things had souls. Therefore, there was a strict rule against killing a person, a beast, or even an insect. True Jains sweep the street before they take a step, lest they kill an innocent life. The Jains were really trying to set up a simpler, less rigid religion than Hinduism. A bigger competitor to Hinduism was Buddhism.

Buddha (about 563 B.C.–483 B.C.)

About the year 563 B.C., a prince was born in a village at the foot of the Himalayas. Gautama [gou'tə mə], as he was called, is said to have been born under a lucky star. There is a story that at his birth a great light shone in the sky and those who were ill were made well. Gautama lived amid luxury; his father was determined that he would never know sorrow. In spite of efforts to keep the knowledge of reality from him, Gautama soon learned about evil, illness, and suffering. Legend has it that Gautama was so moved by what he learned that he left his wealth and position to live in the forest. There he exposed himself to much suffering and torment. He hoped to find the answers to life's problems. After seven years, Gautama felt he had found the answers and returned to civilization. He left the forest for the cities where he began to spread his ideas.

To his followers Gautama was the *Buddha* [büd'ə], or the Enlightened One. He wished to bring the light or the answers to others through talks, stories, and conversation. Buddha did not write his ideas down. They have come to us through the writings of other people. Buddha never believed that he was a god. He cared little about the way people prayed. He said that to be happy one must be unselfish. The desire for material things, he taught, was the cause of pain and evil.

The followers of Buddha taught that such things as gossip, lies, stealing, and killing were bad. They said that people who obeyed the laws would enjoy peace and happiness. Buddha felt that a painless and ideal existence called *nirvana* [nir vä'nə] was possible to reach. Nirvana was a release from reincarnation and worldly suffering. By following the teachings of the *Eightfold Path* one could reach nirvana. These teachings included right thinking, right speech, and right action.

Buddhism began in India and had great influence until about A.D. 200. But it died out in India and spread to countries of the Far East.

Buddha lived until the age of eighty. During his long life he taught people how they might achieve happiness and peace. Today, throughout the Far East, many statues and temples of Buddha may be seen, evidence of the influence of Buddhism. In art, the face of Buddha takes many forms. Each face attempts to express the artist's understanding of what Buddha meant when he urged his followers to seek nirvana.

1. List the countries of the Far East. List the countries of South Asia. Locate them on a map.

2. What do the ruins of Mohenjo-Daro tell us about the life and skills of the people there?

3. What are the religious beliefs of Hinduism?

4. What were the religious beliefs of Buddha?

INDIA IS UNITED AND ENTERS ITS GOLDEN AGE

How the Mauryas United India

During the Vedic period (1500–1000 B.C.), India was made up of many small kingdoms. Many religious beliefs were practiced and there was little unity among the kingdoms. These divisions made India weak. They encouraged other people to try to win the wealth of India for themselves. About 510 B.C., Darius I of Persia was among the first to try. He successfully conquered northern India, where Persian influence can be seen today.

Alexander the Great invaded India in 326 B.C. This is regarded as the first exact date in Indian history. In a fierce battle, in which 200 Indian elephants took part and 12,000 lives were lost, Alexander won a great victory in northern India. This victory was only temporary. In 323 B.C., Alexander died, and his troops left India.

Limited and short though the conquests of Alexander were, they had lasting results. For one thing, early contact helped introduce the West and the Far East. When Greece declined, its culture lived on in parts of India. In northwestern India, Hellenistic culture met Buddhist culture and influenced its art, its painting, and its sculpture. Alexander's conquest taught that without some unity northern India would be subject to frequent invasions.

Chandragupta Maurya [mour′ē ə] (322–298 B.C.) was a young noble who sought to unify northern India. He was largely successful. Chandragupta conquered many small kingdoms from the Indus River to the Ganges River and united them into a strong nation. Its capital, Pataliputra [pä tä li pu′trə], was visited by Greeks who readily agreed that it was every bit as good as their cities. Chandragupta's government was a monarchy in which the king had great power. It was a highly organized and efficient government.

Chandragupta won fame as a soldier. His grandson Asoka [ə sō′kə] (273–232 B.C.) won even more fame, but as a man of peace. As a great monarch Asoka deserves an honored place in Indian history. His kingdom was the greatest one India had seen up to that time. He started his reign as a warrior. He soon became a convert to Buddhism and was

A section of the wall paintings in the Ajanta Caves done during the Gupta period. It shows the Buddha at prayer.

Maurya Empire Under Asoka, 250 B.C.

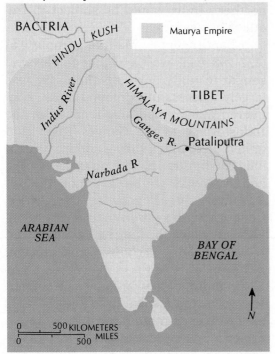

Gupta Empire, A.D. 400

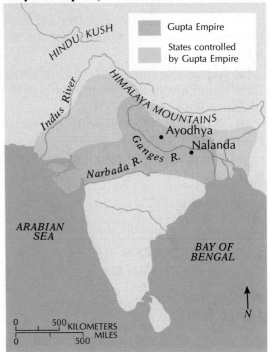

Ancient India had a number of important empires.
- Which of the empires shown on the maps on pages 90 and 91 covered the largest region?
- What was the important city of Asoka's Maurya Empire?
- What river formed the southern border of the Gupta Empire?

responsible for the growth of that faith. He had the teachings of Buddha written on huge stone columns so that all people might see them. Buddhist monks went to many parts of the Eastern world to spread their teachings. Although he built a Buddhist nation, Asoka tolerated all other religions.

The Maurya kings who followed Asoka were not able men. The kingdom, which Chandragupta had united by force of arms and which Asoka had united by force of faith, fell apart. After ruling for 137 years, the Maurya dynasty ended in 184 B.C. Buddhism, too, steadily lost influence. In its place, Hinduism took firm root. It remained, and is today, the religion of India.

How the Guptas Ruled India

For 500 years, India knew little peace. There were invasions of tribes from the north. One of these, the Kushans, [küsh'ənz], established the Kushan empire in northwest India during the first century A.D. It ranks with the Roman Empire as one of the great empires in history. King Kanishka [kə nish'ka] ruled the empire wisely and firmly. Like Asoka, he encouraged Buddhism.

To Chandragupta I, who ruled from A.D. 320–30, goes the honor of establishing another great family of kings, the Guptas [gup'təz]. (He was not related to Chandragupta Maurya, who lived 640

Mogul Empire, A.D. 1700

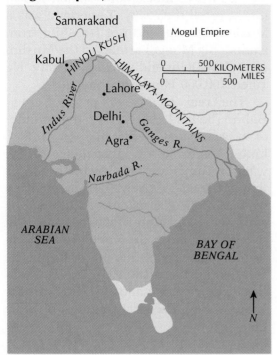

The Mogul Empire was founded by the Mongol invaders of India. (See page 93.)
- On what two large bodies of water did the Mogul Empire have coastlines?

years earlier.) Between A.D. 320–535, the Guptas ruled much of northern India between the banks of the Indus River and the banks of the Ganges River.

This Gupta period has often been looked upon as India's golden age. Under the Guptas, Hinduism became once again the leading religion and Brahmans were appointed to high office. Sanskrit literature was developed. Science and astronomy flourished. Art, architecture, painting, sculpture, poetry, drama, and fables were expertly created.

The Gupta dynasty followed the other dynasties in decay and death in A.D. 535. The death blow was dealt by the Huns, the same Asian tribe that had helped bring about the fall of Rome. These ferocious people successfully brought about the fall of the Gupta Empire. Descend-

ants of the Huns in India were the *Rajputs* [räj'püts], or warriors. As fighters they forced their way into the Hindu caste system and became wealthy princes.

For the next 600 years, the Indian princes and various invaders fought with one another for control of northern India. Invasions and warfare kept northern India divided into several states.

Check in Here

1. Why was Buddha so important a figure in the development of India?

2. What lesson did Alexander's conquest teach India?

3. How did Asoka contribute to the development of ancient India?

4. What were the contributions of the Gupta kings to India's history?

THE RISE AND FALL OF MUSLIM INFLUENCE IN INDIA

How the Muslims Won and Ruled India

In the Battle of Tours, France (A.D. 732), the Muslims were stopped in their march to the West. (The Muslims were followers of the religious leader Mohammed.) In the East, however, the Muslims were more successful. Beginning in the eleventh century, they fought their way to the gates of India. They became masters of India. At first the Muslims were successful only along the coast. By the year A.D. 1000, however, the Muslim invasion, which had started slowly, became an explosion.

In A.D. 1008, Mahmud of Ghazni [guz'nē] began his ruthless invasion of India. He destroyed temples and art that had taken thousands of years to create. Each year for twenty-five years he brought back new wealth and more slaves from northern India to Afghanistan [af gan' i stan].

What was good for Mahmud of Ghazni was good for other Muslim rulers. Soon they too saw an opportunity to fight for wealth and Allah [al′ə], or God. Sultan Kutbuddin Aibak [ā′bak] established his capital at Delhi [del′ē] in northern India. He put hundreds of thousands of Indians to death. By 1206, in a bloodbath, the followers of Mohammed became rulers of most of the land between the Indus and the Ganges rivers. For hundreds of years the Muslims followed a policy of cruelty to Hindus through killing and taxation. The Muslim conquest of India was one of the cruelest stories in history.

By 1398, the Muslim rule in India had spent itself and was ready to fall. Tamerlane [tam′ər lān′] was a Mongol warrior who came from Asiatic Russia. He and his conquering horsemen saw to it that it fell their way. Tamerlane was a Muslim, but this did not stop him from leading his Mongol armies to the Muslim capital of Delhi and sacking the city. He killed 100,000 Hindu prisoners.

The real conqueror of India was Babur [bä′bər] (1483–1530), the founder of a great and noble line of Mongol kings. Babur was a descendant of the warrior Tamerlane. His memoirs tell us that at the age of twelve he became King of Farghana [far ga′nə]; at fifteen, he captured Samarkand [sam′ər kand′]; at twenty-two, he took Kabul [kä′bül] in Afghanistan. From this place, Kabul, he invaded northern India. In 1524, he captured the city of Lahore [lə hōr′] in the Indus Valley. The final conquest of India had begun.

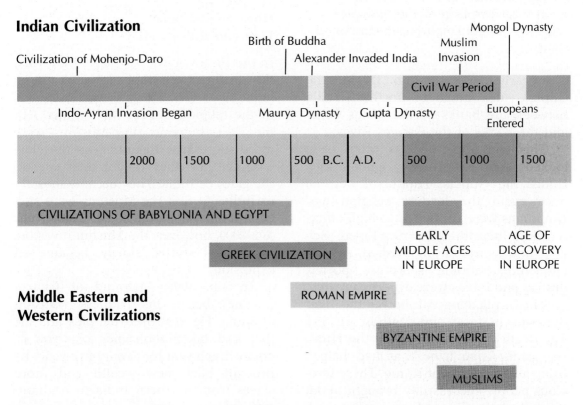

According to the time line, approximately how many years was Buddha born before Jesus?

How the Mogul Dynasty Ruled India

Babur died in 1530. The *Mogul*, or Mongol, dynasty which he established was to have great power and lasting influence. (Mogul refers to the Mongol conquerors of India.) Babur was followed to the throne by his first son, Humayan, who died after a short reign. His second son, became one of the few really great monarchs in all history. He was called Akbar [ak'bär]. His reign occurred at about the same time as the reigns of Philip II (1556–1598) of Spain and Elizabeth I (1558–1603) of England.

Akbar became emperor at thirteen and ruled for over forty years. Early in his reign, he enlarged his empire. He became one of the greatest emperors the world has ever known. Getting an empire is one thing, but ruling it well is another.

Akbar proved equal to the task of ruling, as well as conquering. Akbar was all-powerful. He chose to appoint intelligent advisers and follow their advice. An efficient civil service was formed. Taxes were heavy but fair, and the empire grew rich. Although Akbar had a lavish court, he spent his money carefully. Akbar, who spent much of his time as a judge, listened to the complaints of his people, and tried to come to fair decisions. For this alone he may be considered a great ruler. He was loved by his people.

Akbar was a Muslim who was tolerant of other religions. Unlike Muslim rulers before him, he gave Hindus full freedom. He no longer forced them to pay unfair taxes. When Europeans brought Christianity to India, Akbar was a sympathetic listener. He had the New Testament translated and invited Jesuit missionaries to come to his court at Delhi. "While Catholics were murdering Protestants in France, and Protestants . . . were murdering Catholics in England, and the Inquisition was killing and robbing Jews

The Taj Mahal was built by Shah Jahan as a memorial to his wife.

in Spain, Akbar . . . issued edicts of toleration for every . . . creed."*

Akbar, emperor of India, died in 1605. Thousands of miles away, Elizabeth I, Queen of England, had just ended her reign. In the nineteenth century, 300 years in the future, another queen of England would become Empress of India.

Why the Mogul Dynasty Fell

The emperors who followed Akbar were weak. They thought more of pleasure than of work. Shah Jahan [jə hän'] was a grandson of Akbar. He constructed the beautiful Taj Mahal, which was a tomb for a wife he loved. Under Shah Jahan, the empire that Akbar had put together and ruled so well reached its glorious

*Will Durant, *The Story of Civilization: Our Oriental Heritage* (New York: Simon and Schuster, 1942), p. 469.

height. Its fall, however, came soon after. In 1658, Shah Jahan was forced from the throne by Aurangzeb [ôr'əng zeb'], his son, the last great Mogul emperor. Once emperor, Aurangzeb proved to be intolerant of other faiths. Hindu temples were again destroyed, and the tax on Hindus that Akbar had removed was again imposed. In a few years Aurangzeb destroyed what had taken many centuries to build.

Aurangzeb became emperor of nearly all India. However, after his death, his empire began to fall apart. His intolerance toward Hindus led them to form kingdoms of their own. Aurangzeb was unable to conquer these. He lost the support of the Rajputs (Hindu princes) in northern India. Muslim princes also recognized the weakness of the central government. They took advantage of it to build up their own power. It was not long before India was again made up of many small kingdoms and princely states, most of which were ruled by Muslim princes.

As India grew weak, European influence in India grew. You will read about this in Chapter 21. Now, let us look more closely at the life and culture of India as it was in the days before the Europeans came.

Check in Here

1. What were the achievements and the shortcomings of Muslim rule in India?

2. Why does the text refer to Akbar as one of the greatest monarchs in all of history?

3. Why did Mogul rule of India eventually collapse?

4. What were some of the differences in policy between Akbar and Aurangzeb?

THE LIFE OF ORDINARY PEOPLE IN ANCIENT INDIA

The Nature of Family Life in Ancient India

The family, the caste, and the village formed the circle within which the Hindu lived. The family in India, as in most countries of the East, extended beyond a mother, father, and children. It included grandparents as well as parents, and married as well as unmarried children—brothers, sisters, uncles, aunts, cousins, widows, and grandchildren. The family group also included slaves. In the councils of the family the father was the head of the household and its unquestioned leader.

If the family was to prosper, all members had to do their share of the work. Women prepared the food and ran the household. Men worked in the fields or at their trades. Since most things were made by hand, the family had to weave its own yarn and make its own clothing. Food had to be saved for the days when there would be famine. Property belonged to the father, but upon his death, each son was entitled to a share of it. Each unmarried daughter was entitled to her share of money, probably to be used as a dowry upon marriage.

Children were very important to the ancient Indian family and they remain so to this day. The childless family was looked upon with scorn. Children were expected to help support the family by working in the fields or at a trade. This was especially important when aged parents could no longer support themselves. Moreover, children were desired. They could insure that the souls of the dead parents would rest in peace through proper and frequent prayer. Thus, the family was an important institution in India.

The Role of Women in Ancient India

During the Vedic period (1500–1000 B.C.), women enjoyed more freedom than at later periods of Indian history. Marriage was arranged. Marriage by consent was considered slightly immoral. In those days, Indian women thought it more honorable to be purchased. Polygamy [pə lig'ə mē], the practice which permits a man to have several wives, was common. Polyandry [pol'ē an'drē], the marriage of a woman to several husbands, was not unknown.

It was the husband, however, who had property rights and who could sell wives and children as he wished. Women of Vedic India had some privileges. They often appeared freely at religious ceremonies, at celebrations, and at dances. Women could also study and could engage in philosophic discussion with men. In Vedic India, a woman could remarry if her husband died.

After about 500 B.C., Indian women lost many of their rights. Women were discouraged from intellectual pursuits. Child marriage, arranged by the parents, was the usual rule. There could be no thought about falling in love. It was considered unrespectable to marry simply because you were attracted to someone. It was expected that the bride would live with her husband's family and learn its ways. The future of the woman whose husband died was a sad one. She was expected to die in the funeral fire which burned his dead body. This practice, *suttee* [sut'ē], is now forbidden. Women who chose not to practice suttee, and some did not, remained the lowest member of the family council. Such a woman shaved her head, prepared the food but ate last and then only scraps.

In post-Vedic India, the practice of *purdah* [pur'də], or curtain, grew. Women had to go about veiled and to show themselves only to their husbands and sons. The *Code of Manu* was a kind of guide to the proper behavior in each caste. It said the mother of many children was to be honored. Women could not be beaten, and they were to be dressed attractively so as to adorn the household. The ideal was the humble woman who devoted herself entirely to her husband and who served him faithfully and courageously until she died.

A group of women cadets stands at attention during a military parade. Although change is slow, Indian women today are discarding their traditional roles and taking an active part in the industrial and cultural life of modern India.

How Caste Ruled Everyday Life

Next to the Hindu family, caste was most important in deciding one person's relationship to another. The caste system was made up of strict rules. These rules served to keep people in the caste in which they were born for their entire lives. The members of one caste could not easily take part in the activities of members of another. There was no chance to move up from one cast to a higher one. There were hundreds of castes. Besides the castes already mentioned, there were castes of farmers, carpenters, merchants, herders, metal workers, and barbers, for example. The lowliest tasks, such as tanning leather or cleaning streets, were performed by the untouchables.

An Indian miniature painting from the Jain period.

The Brahmans, the priestly caste, were entitled to many privileges. In return, they prayed for the souls of others. The Brahmans were usually the only ones who could read and write. This learning they did not willingly share with others. It enabled the Brahmans to grow rich and powerful. Invaders came and went throughout the history of India. But the position of the Brahmans remained strong.

Today, the caste system is breaking down in India. Untouchability is illegal. But there are still evidences of caste. In the past it provided a system in which each person knew his or her place. Moreover, the person knew his or her relationship to those in a higher caste, to those of lower caste, and to those who had similar kinds of occupations. These relationships had been the same for centuries and could not be changed easily. They help to explain why in India changes are few and slow in coming. When the government made untouchability illegal in 1947, it was hoped that all Indians would enjoy a greater measure of opportunity and receive fairer treatment in their employment.

Village Life in Ancient India

In ancient India, life in the village seemed indifferent to change. The capital of India was far away, and people were mostly concerned with what went on in their village.

The most prominent person in the village was the *headman*. He was helped by a council with whom he talked over the village problems. The job of the headman was an important one. For one thing, he was appointed by the prince or lord upon whose land the village was located. Secondly, the job was a hereditary one. It was handed down in the same family generation after generation. Thirdly, the job represented the voice of a local but powerful prince. The headman followed the orders of the prince.

The headman tried to get the members of his village to work together for the common good. The sharing of work was necessary since the village would receive little outside help. Villagers had to work together to irrigate the land, to share and save water, and to use it wisely. Failure to cooperate might mean starvation and death in the year ahead.

How People Made a Living in India

Farming was the chief economic activity. Growing vegetables, fruits, and rice was the usual method of making a living. Since Hindus were not allowed to eat meat, farm products were important in the diet of the people. Farming was not easy since the tools were simple. Moreover, it was the custom for a father to divide the land among his sons. In time, the amount of land available for one person to work grew smaller. Therefore, it became more difficult to earn a living. Cotton was one of the early products grown and was an important item of trade in the Deccan Plateau.

Farming was not the only occupation in ancient India. Trade was almost equally important. When Europeans came to India, they found a superior money system; gold, silver, and copper were used as coins. At the bazaar, or market, there were products from all over India and from other countries as well. In ancient times India traded with Sumer, Babylonia, China, Greece, and Rome. The products of India made their way into Europe through the Italian trading cities of Genoa, Venice, and Milan. Spices, such as cloves and ginger, were among the products that the Euro-

peans wanted from the East. Luxuries from the East soon became necessities in the West. Because the luxuries did not come fast enough, the West went after them.

Heavy taxation was a major way in which the central government affected the lives of Indians. Sometimes the taxes amounted to as much as one-half the farmer's crop. Trade between villages and cities was also taxed. The government charged a toll to use the roads. At their height, the capitals of India, at Agra and Delhi, were far wealthier than the capitals in Europe.

Check in Here

1. Explain the importance of the family in India.
2. How was the role of women in ancient India different from that during the post-Vedic period?
3. Describe the role of caste in everyday life in ancient India and India today.
4. Why was the village the center of economic and social life in ancient India?
5. What were some of the ways in which Indians made a living?

INDIA'S CONTRIBUTIONS TO CIVILIZATION

India's Gifts to Science

Science, mathematics, and literature were highly developed during India's golden age (see page 91) and after. Hospitals served people who were sick, and schools taught students. Great progress was made in medical science, mathematics, and astronomy. In the field of literature there was much religious writing, poetry, and fables.

The Arabic numbers which we use today are one of India's greatest gifts to us. These numbers were used as early as the reign of Asoka in 265 B.C. This was

Contemporary Indian women spread dyed cloth to dry in the sun in much the same way their ancestors did.

hundreds and hundreds of years before they appeared in the Muslim world. Though originally from India, they are called *Arabic numbers* because the Europeans learned of them from the Arabs. Similarly, the Pythagorean theorem is said to have been developed by an Indian mathematician. It is called the *Pythagorean theorem* because it is named after a Greek mathematician. It came to us from Greece rather than directly from India.

Aryabhata [är′yə but′ə] lived about the sixth century A.D. He was a great Indian mathematician to whom we owe our knowledge of decimals. He taught about the rotation of the earth on its axis and the value of π (pi). From India, Aryabhata's teaching went to China, Arabia, and the rest of the world.

In chemistry, the Indians were far ahead of the Europeans of the sixteenth and seventeenth centuries. As early as Alexander's invasion (326 B.C.), steel was in use, and a ball of it was given to Alexander as a gift worthy of a conqueror.

The Indians were far ahead of Western Europe in soap making, cloth dyeing, tanning leather, glass blowing, and mixing cement.

In the field of medicine India made progress. The secret of the circulation of the blood was described by Indian doctors a hundred or more years before the English scientist Harvey described it in the seventeenth century. In time, Indian doctors won great fame and the world called for their services.

India's Gifts to Literature and Art

Hindu, Buddhist, and Muslim faiths all played important parts in the history of India. Nowhere can you find more effort to study life and its meaning than you do in India. During the Hindu period there were many schools of philosophy. Students, eager to learn, eager to question, and eager to debate, sat before philosopher-teachers. After the Muslim and Christian invasions, the study of philosophy declined.

In the days of Asoka, it is believed that India had many people who could read and write. Some of the famous universities at Benares, Taxila, and Nalanda were more difficult to enter than are the ivy league schools of today. *Sanskrit* was the language of scholars; *Prakrit* was the language of the people.

Although India developed a great literature, the development of writing was slow. India's earliest literature consisted of songs and poems. The songs and poems were passed down through the ages by word of mouth. The *Mahabharata* [mə hä′bär′ə tə] is an epic poem which was handed down orally for hundreds of years before being written down. Through the years its original 9,000 verses were expanded to 100,000. Some consider it one of the greatest poems ever written. Part of this great epic is known as the

Bhagavad-Gita [bug'ə vəd gē'tä], which means "Song of the Lord." It may be compared with the Old Testament of the Jews and the Christians, or the Koran of the Muslims. It is the holy book of the Hindus.

The *Panchatantra* [pan'chə tun'trə] is one of the earliest Indian fables and was written about A.D. 500. The fable is a form of literature that tries to teach a lesson. Usually, animals in fables talk and act like people.

Songs, dances, and music in India were mostly religious in nature. The ancient instruments would look and sound strange to you. Indian painting would also seem different to you. The most popular forms of Indian painting were miniatures and illustrated manuscripts. When paper came into use, manuscripts became increasingly more illustrated. Architecture and sculpture were closely related in India. Hindu temples were elaborately carved with the images of many gods.

Indian civilization changed greatly over the centuries. Changes began when the West first demanded admission to the empire of India. You will see in later chapters how India's splendor fared during the Age of Discovery and modern times.

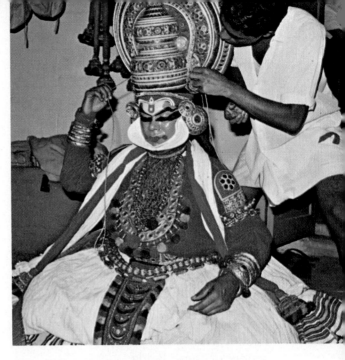

The costume of an ornately dressed dancer is given a final adjustment before a performance.

Check in Here

1. List India's gifts to civilization in each of the following areas: (**a**) science; (**b**) mathematics; (**c**) literature; (**d**) religion.

2. How was India's knowledge of science put to everyday use?

3. How do you explain the great interest in India in philosophy?

4. Explain: (**a**) why our system of numbering is called "Arabic" when it was developed by the Hindus; (**b**) why the Pythagorean theorem is named after a Greek when it was first developed in India?

THE PEOPLE AND HISTORY OF SOUTHEAST ASIA

The People of Southeast Asia

A *crossroads* is an area where two or more paths, coming from different places, meet each other and then move on in different directions. In many ways Southeast Asia is a crossroads. The people of Southeast Asia came from Tibet and China, from India, and from what is now Pakistan. They brought with them the religion of the lands of their birth and often adopted other religious beliefs.

The people of Burma come from Tibet. They came to Burma a thousand years before Jesus was born. They settled along the Irrawaddy [ir'ə wod'ē] River. This river served the Burmese as the Nile served the people of ancient Egypt. Thailand takes its name from the people, Thais, who settled the land. They came from China. The Cambodians came from a people known as Khmers [kmerz], who came mainly from India during the sixth century B.C. They settled in what is now Kampuchea [kam pù chē'ə]. The Khmers established the state of Funan [fü'nan], which grew in power to become one of the great nations in Southeast Asia. The Vietnamese came from the ancient Annamese [an ə mēz'], a people who came to the Red River in Vietnam from China. The Laotians are similar in origin to the Thais. Malaysia, Indonesia, and the Philippines were populated by waves of different peoples who mingled with the primitive Negritos [ni grē'tōz]. The Negritos were probably the earliest people of these lands.

The number of people in Southeast Asia is greater than that of the United States. They are not equally distributed among the countries. In some places, as on Java in Indonesia and on Luzon in the Philippines, there is much overcrowding. In other places, as in Thailand and Kampuchea, the pressure is not as great.

The languages the people of Southeast Asia speak are many and are derived from the languages of India and China. The Buddhist, Hindu, and Muslim faiths dominate the area. In the Philippines, however, most of the people are Catholic. In most countries of Southeast Asia the Chinese make up an influential minority. They are the merchants, bankers, and traders of Southeast Asia. Often their influence is resented, and they are discriminated against.

The people of Southeast Asia are poor. The central fact of Southeast Asian economic life is the overwhelming poverty of the masses. There are a few rich people. However, their existence shows that the main problem is how to distribute wealth evenly and how to raise living standards. There is practically no middle class. The problem of poverty is made even worse by the rapidly increasing population. Any gain in living standards is often lost by the rising number of births. The problems of Southeast Asia today may be traced far back into the history of the area.

What We Know of the History of Southeast Asia

The history of ancient Southeast Asia is a fascinating one. However, all we can do in a small amount of space is touch on its highlights so that you will have some background for understanding the more modern developments.

Burma gained its culture from India. In the eleventh century, Anawrata [ä'nä rä' tə], the first real ruler of Burma, built a powerful nation. Buddhism became the religion of the country. Kublai Khan destroyed the capital city of Pagan [pä'gän], and Burma did not know unity for 400 years. By then it was too late. By the sixteenth century, the Europeans were already on the way. The British became the rulers in Burma as they did in India.

Thailand, once called Siam [sī am'], is the country that became well known to Americans through the play and movie, "The King and I," based on the book *Anna and the King of Siam* by Margaret Landon. The king in the story is King Mongkut [mon'küt] (1851–68), also known as Rama IV. He was well-informed about Western ways and willing to use his knowledge for the benefit of his people. His successors continued his policies.

Hindu and then Buddhist influences came to Siam. Unlike other countries of Southeast Asia, Thailand (Siam) has always kept its independence. Thailand had no products Europeans wanted. This proved to be an advantage.

A section of the Grand Palace in Bangkok, Thailand.

Angkor Wat, a Buddhist temple in Kampuchea (Cambodia), was built in the twelfth century.

Indochina is the name given to the territory of the small countries of Laos, Kampuchea, and Vietnam. The interests of China and India clashed in this area. Annam and Tonking (part of Vietnam) were influenced by India. The rest of the area was influenced by China. The French were driven out of India in the eighteenth century. During the nineteenth century they established themselves in Indochina. There they found the Angkor Wat [ang'kôr wat'], a magnificent ancient Buddhist temple. While business people made profits in Indochina, the French government found Indochina difficult to rule. The native people fought the French and finally defeated them in 1954 at Dien Bien Phu [dyen' byen' fü'].

The Malay Peninsula is about the same size as Florida and occupies a geographically important position. The shortest water route from Europe to the Far East passes the southern end of the Malay Peninsula. In days past, Malaya was influenced by India, China, and the Arab world. The Muslim faith became the faith of most Malaysians.

Indonesia is made up of hundreds of islands in the Indian Ocean. Its culture came from India. As early as the first century B.C., there were settlements of

Indians on the two large islands of Java and Sumatra. The Kingdom of Shrivijaya [shriv i'jä'yə], probably ruled by an Indian prince, included at the height of its power much of Indonesia. In the thirteenth century, the Javanese overthrew the Shrivijaya and built a new kingdom, which was followed in the fourteenth century by the Madjaphit Empire. Islam became the most prominent religion when it was brought in by Arabs in the fifteenth century.

Check in Here

1. Describe the people of Southeast Asia in terms of (**a**) geographic location; (**b**) nationalities; (**c**) languages.

2. In what ways may the area of Southeast Asia be regarded as another cradle of civilization?

3. What evidence of India's influence may be found in Southeast Asia?

4. Why was this area considered important geographically?

REVIEWING THE BASICS

India is an ancient civilization, as old as those of Babylonia and Sumer. The ancient city of Mohenjo-Daro provides evidence that around 3000 B.C. a highly skilled and creative people already lived in India. The original inhabitants of northern India, the Dravidians, were driven out or conquered by the Indo-Aryans. The Indo-Aryans brought with them religious customs and beliefs that form the basis of the Hindu religion. One long lasting effect of Hinduism was the division of Indians into strict castes.

The Hindu religion was challenged by the teachings of Buddha, called the Enlightened One. His views influenced the lives of millions of Indians. Buddhism eventually became more influential in other parts of the world than in India. After the disunity caused by the breakup of Alexander's empire, Chandragupta Maurya united northern India. His warlike reign was followed by the relatively peaceful one of his grandson Asoka. After the golden age under the Gupta kings, a long period of turmoil, nearly 600 years, followed.

The Muslim conquest of India was violent. Muslims tried to convert Hindus to Muslim traditions. Tamerlane, Babur, and Akbar each ruled in turn. Akbar was especially tolerant of all religions. However, after Muslim rule in India declined during the late seventeenth century, India again became weak.

The people of Southeast Asia were enormously influenced by India, as well as by China. Southeast Asia has an ancient past with a highly developed culture and religion. Each country in the area developed different traditions and customs. Southeast Asia became an area attractive to European countries that wanted its wealth.

In the next chapter you will look at another cradle of civilization in the Far East—China. Like India, China had a highly developed Eastern civilization that made many contributions to the Western world.

REVIEWING THE HIGHLIGHTS

**People
to Identify**

Buddha
Alexander
  the Great
Chandragupta
  Maurya

Chandragupta I
Mahmud of Ghazni
Tamerlane
Babur
Rama IV
Asoka

Akbar
Shah Jahan
Aurangzeb
Aryabhata
Anawrata

**Places
to Locate**

Himalaya Mountains
Indus River
Deccan Plateau
Ganges River
Mohenjo-Daro
The Ghats
Agra

Delhi
Angkor Wat
Shrivijaya
Southeast Asia
Burma
Irrawaddy River
Indochina
Khyber Pass

Kampuchea
Vietnam
Thailand
Indonesia
Philippines
Malaysia
Funan

**Terms
to Understand**

Dravidians
Indo-Aryans
subcontinent
untouchables
caste
raj
Buddhism
Brahmans
Kshatriyas
Vaisya
Shudra
Jains

Muslims
Indra
Hinduism
Mogul Dynasty
Mahabharata
Kingdom of
  Shrivijaya
Vedas
Upanishads
Sanskrit
Prakrit
Guptas

Mongols
Hindus
suttee
purdah
Taj Mahal
Bhagavad-Gita
nirvana
Eightfold Path
Panchatantra
crossroads
Khmers

1. How did the geography of India keep that country from uniting?
2. What was the importance of the Indus river valley in India?
3. May India properly be regarded as a cradle of civilization? Why or why not?
4. How did the caste system begin?
5. What ideas are found in the *Vedas* and *Upanishads?*
6. How does the Hindu faith justify the caste system?
7. How do the teachings of Buddhism differ from those of Hinduism?
8. What was the result of Alexander's partial conquest of India?
9. How did the Muslims conquer India?
10. What was the fate of the Hindus under Muslim rule?
11. How did Akbar change some of the Muslim policies?
12. How did Aurangzeb help bring about the fall of the Mogul Empire?
13. Describe family life in ancient India.
14. Describe village life in ancient India.
15. How did caste govern the relationships among people?
16. Describe the economy of ancient India.
17. What is our debt to India in science, mathematics, literature, art, and music?
18. Why is the *Bhagavad-Gita* compared to the Bible?
19. How did India influence the countries of Southeast Asia?

THINGS TO DO

1. Make a map of either or both India and Southeast Asia using papier-mâché or plaster of paris. On your map identify the major mountains, plains, and rivers of these areas.
2. Debate the following topic: Resolved: The caste system of ancient India served the people effectively.
3. Go to your library and review its picture collection. Bring pictures of Angkor Wat to the class. After describing each illustration hang them up on the bulletin board for a short period of time. You may also wish to collect pictures of the Taj Mahal.

A View of India

Between 1960 and 1963 John Kenneth Galbraith was the United States Ambassador to India. He was accompanied by his wife, who had her own views on Indian life and culture. In the preface to his book *Ambassador's Journal,* Mr. Galbraith declared, "My wife's eye for Indian life and culture is better than mine." The excerpt below is from an article Mrs. Galbraith wrote and which is included as Appendix I in the Journal. Read the selection carefully and complete the exercise which follows.

India's history goes back thousands of years. At the time the Pilgrims were building log cabins in Salem,* Shah Jahan was building the Taj Mahal [seventeenth century]. But India became an independent nation [1947]. . . . The contrasts are striking. In Delhi, buses, scooter taxis, and bicycles weave in among the tongas* and oxcarts. New housing developments spring up around old tombs and ancient forts. . . . You go to a village, even on the outskirts of a city, and you see how life has gone on in the same way for centuries. There are the same wooden plows and plodding bullocks, the same cow-dung fires and Persian waterwheels, the same bright saris* bending over the rice fields. . . . You think there has been no change, and then you discover that the village now has a small dispensary,* very simple by our standards; a handful of nurses and a doctor serve thousands of patients . . . [now is] a time of peril for India. Its problems are very great. . . . People are everywhere—in the lonely jungle, clinging to the steep Himalayas, sleeping on the city streets, and clustered all over the plains. Most of these people are poor, customs are diverse, and many tensions have threatened to disunite the nation. . . . There is a sense of urgency and national purpose, and also, initially bewilderment.†

Indicate whether the statements below are *True* and *False* or *Not Stated* in the selection. For each answer, justify your choice by discussing it with your classmates.

1. The selection is an eyewitness account.
2. The selection may be viewed as a primary source for the historian.
3. The history of the United States is much older than that of India.
4. Shah Jahan was a prince in India.
5. Delhi (India's capital) has become a completely modern city.
6. Standards of living are high in India.
7. So much new housing has been built that everyone has a place to sleep.
8. There has been no change in village life in India.
9. Some things have been going on in the same way for many hundreds of years.
10. India and America have close ties.

Vocabulary

Salem—A city in Massachusetts settled by Pilgrims in the early seventeenth century

tongas—Indian two-wheeled vehicles

saris—dresses of silk or cotton worn by Indian women

dispensary—a place where medical help and medication are provided

†John Kenneth Galbraith, *Ambassador's Journal* (Boston: Houghton Mifflin Company, 1969), pp. 609–810. Catherine A. Galbraith, "Mother Doesn't Do Much," *The Atlantic Monthly*, May, 1963. Copyright 1963 by the Atlantic Monthly Company.

Family portrait, Ming Dynasty, 1368–1644

The Far East of Yesterday: The Ancient Past of China, Japan, and Korea

China was once called a sleeping giant because its customs and ways of living—which seemed odd to most Europeans and Americans—had changed little over the centuries. In ancient China ". . . men wore skirts . . . and the women trousers. At banquets . . . dessert came first. Men, in greeting one another, shook their own hands, not the hands of the other. In meeting on the streets gentlemen removed their spectacles, not their hats. White, not black, was the color of mourning. Food was lifted to the mouth with chopsticks and not with forks. . . ."* China is still a giant, but it is now taking its place among the big world powers.

*Kenneth S. Latourette, *A Short History of the Far East*
(New York: The Macmillan Company).

Modern China is different from ancient China, and so our ideas about China must also change.

Japan and Korea are smaller than China, but they are also important countries of the Far East. These countries, although influenced by China, have traditions of their own that help to explain their present role in the modern world.

CHINA'S GEOGRAPHY AND ANCIENT HISTORY

How the Geography of China Influenced Its History

Geography has affected China's history in many ways. China is very large and, therefore, it has been difficult to conquer. At the same time, its very size makes it difficult to unite. Rain causes many of China's rivers to overflow and carry much good soil away. Rivers that overflow their banks may wash away farms. Making a living by farming in the three great river valleys of China has always been risky. The north and west of China are dry and hilly. Because of this, many of the Chinese live in the crowded southern and eastern parts of the country. As a result, although China is vast, its extremely large population of more than a billion people live in a fairly small amount of space. The overcrowding on the eastern coast explains why China has tried to expand its borders at different times.

The Himalayas separate China from its neighbors India and Nepal. The great river valleys of China include the Hwang, [hwäng], Yangtze [yäng'tse'], and Si [sē]. These rivers divide China into north, central, and southern parts. In these river valleys live most of China's people. Much of China is made up of very high mountains. Some of China is made up of sandy deserts, such as the Gobi [gō'bē] Desert in China's northwest.

China is protected from invaders by mountains in the south and west. In the north, no such obstacles to invasion exist. The passes through the Hindu Kush served as invasion routes to India. In a similar way, the plains of northeast China were the invasion routes to China. Huns, Turks, Tartars, Mongols, and Manchus each came in turn. Each left their mark on China's history.

What We Know of China's Early History

A family of rulers is called a *dynasty* [dī'nə stē]. In Chinese history, events are recorded as taking place during the lifetime of a family of rulers, rather than during the lifetime of one ruler. China's first dynasty was the Hsia [shyä] Dynasty (2000–1500 B.C.). Little is known about the Hsia Dynasty. Eventually, it was overthrown by the Shang [shäng] Dynasty. The Shang Dynasty (1500 B.C.) marks the beginning of China's recorded history.

During the Shang Dynasty the Chinese made beautiful art figures and bronze weapons. They used the potter's wheel and made useful and decorative objects of clay. The characters used in Chinese writing were developed during the Shang Dynasty. Many Shang rulers, however, were vicious and amused themselves with cruel games and tortures. Their pagan religion required human and animal sacrifices. After ruling for hundreds of years, these wicked kings were driven out. A new dynasty, the Chou, took the place of the Shang.

Far off in western China was the country of Chou [jō]. From Chou came Duke Fa, a famous fighter. He made war on the dynasty of Shang and overthrew it. This warrior king, known to history as Wu Wang [wü′ wang′], became the first king of the Chou Dynasty (about 1100 B.C.). The Chou Dynasty lasted until around 256 B.C. It ruled for the longest period in Chinese history. Under the Chou, China grew from the sea coast on the east to the Yangtze River valley on the south.

The Chou were strong conquerors, but they proved to be weak rulers. As in Europe over a thousand years later, a *feudal system* developed in China. Under this system the Chou rulers made their friends nobles. They gave them small kingdoms to rule over. The nobles, in return, owed military duty to the king, and the king promised to protect the nobles in time of war. Under the feudal system the nobles, or large landholders, often became more powerful than the king.

The Chou period was marked by frequent wars among the nobles. They carried colorful flags as they rode off to battle. They fought in suits of armor and carried long spears and bows and arrows. They took much pride in how their weapons looked and how they were used. As in feudal Europe, war and sport were closely related. Tournaments were held frequently, and the best fighters emerged as the winners. War, talk of war, and preparation for war ruled the lives of

Bronze objects display the intricate detailing done by the artists of the Shang Dynasty.

Chinese Civilization

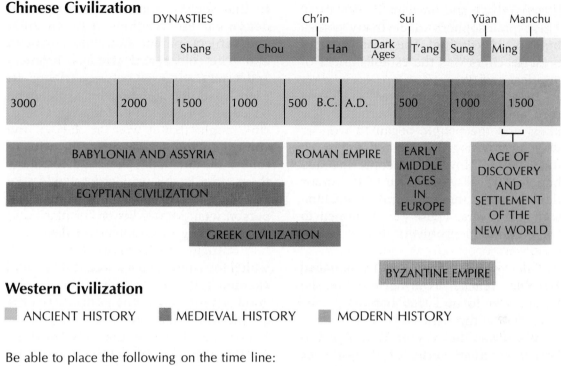

Western Civilization

ANCIENT HISTORY   MEDIEVAL HISTORY   MODERN HISTORY

Be able to place the following on the time line:

	CHINA			EUROPE
551–479 B.C.	Confucius	469–399 B.C.		Socrates
A.D. 600	gunpowder in use	A.D. 1300		gunpowder in use
	1271 Marco Polo visited China			
A.D. 700	block printing	A.D. 1450		printing press
1115 B.C.	compass in use	A.D. 1400		compass in use

many nobles. Fighting many wars made the strong kingdoms stronger. The nobles, or rulers of these kingdoms, had the power to challenge the might of the Chou kings.

In time, after many wars in which the nobles were successful, the Chou rulers were kings in name only. The real power belonged to the rulers of strong kingdoms on the Chou borders. The Ch'in [chin] kingdom in the valley of the Wei [wā] River became very powerful. For more than a quarter of a century, the Ch'in fought to unite the people under them. Finally, Shih Huang Ti succeeded in forcing the smaller kingdoms into one. From this large kingdom, China was born, and a new dynasty began its reign in 221 B.C. (See p. 111.)

The wars during the Chou Dynasty did not lead to a decline in learning, which often happens during times of unrest. Rather, competition among the nobles and contact with other nations encouraged the growth of culture. Under the Chou rulers new ideas thrived among the Chinese. These new ideas brought changes. Let us see what those ideas and changes were and how they came to be.

How Teachers Influenced the People

Ancient Greece gave us the philosophers Socrates, Plato, and Aristotle. From ancient China under the Chou came the thoughts of Lao-tze [lou'tzu'], Confucius

109

[kən fyü′shəs], and Mencius [men′shē əs]. These philosophers made many contributions to learning. The basic goal of these teachers was the establishment of an ideal society.

In a China torn by war, kingdoms rose and fell seemingly overnight. The kings and the people began to wonder what was wrong. How could things be made better? How could people be made happier? These were some of the questions to which the philosophers of China sought answers. These people hoped to solve common problems in a practical way.

Lao-tze (604 B.C.–517 B.C.) was called the Old Teacher. During his life, he taught that to find true happiness one must follow the *right way,* or *Tao.*

What was the way of Tao? The Tao was the natural order of things, over which people had no control. To be happy, people had to allow themselves to be in harmony with the natural order. They had to be humble in spirit. Effort to change the natural way would only upset the Tao and cause unhappiness. Laws, inventions, books, and industries were not the most important accomplishments. An inactive life was the ideal for Lao-tze and his followers.

In this account, the teachings of Lao-tze have been simplified. Lao-tze encouraged the Chinese to accept life as they found it. His teachings made them less willing to improve their lives and less willing to work for human betterment.

Confucius (551 B.C.–479 B.C.) was a far more practical man than Lao-tze. For many years Confucius was an adviser to kings. When his advice was not needed or wanted, however, he frequently found himself looking for work. Periods of unemployment gave Confucius an opportunity to think through his problems and those of his people. Confucius spent his life trying to find an ideal society in which each person knew his or her place.

In that society rules of conduct would determine the relations between ruler and subject, parent and child, husband and wife, older and younger brothers and sisters, and even between friends. In each case the relationship would be based on a leader and a follower. Confucius taught that it was the duty of the subject to follow the ruler, the wife to follow the husband, the child to follow the parent. In this way, order would take the place of disorder in society. Each person would know his or her place and act according to established rules.

Confucius believed in a society in which the ruling classes would set a good example for others to follow. If they set a good example, he thought, the rest of the people would be good. The subject must honor the king, but the king must be worthy of honor. It was the duty of the subject to follow and the duty of the ruler to set a good example. Confucius believed that since people are good, a perfect society is possible.

According to Confucius, a person had to show self-control in order to be good. Self-control was based on the proverb, "Do not do unto others what you would not have others do unto you." With this belief in mind, Confucius encouraged what he believed to be correct behavior for all occasions. Soon this behavior became part of the formal ceremonies which were part of Chinese life.

Confucius' influence led to the worship of ancestors, which became an important part of China's religion. His philosophy also made people slow to change their ways. Because of Confucius, China kept its traditions longer than some other countries.

Confucius, like Socrates, taught by speaking with people. For many years, he wandered from place to place. He looked for a ruler who would find his services useful. Toward the end of his life, he found one. A group of pupils followed wherever he led and listened to what he had to say. His words were later written down in nine books known as the *Confucian Classics*. These classics strengthened the family ties for which China is noted. They contain rules of conduct for the nation and its leaders. Those persons who sought to enter government service were, in time, forced to memorize the sayings of Confucius in order to pass the required tests. Confucian ideas spread to other countries of the Far East where their influence remains.

Mencius (373 B.C.–288 B.C.) followed in the footsteps of Confucius in many ways. Like Confucius, he spent years looking for a ruler wise enough to use his services. However, Mencius tried to answer the question, "What can be done if rulers are not good as Confucius expected them to be?" He decided that in such cases the people have the right to rebel. Although Mencius believed in monarchy, or rule by a king or queen, he insisted that monarchs be effective rulers. He also thought that the people were important. This was an unusual belief at that time. Mencius thought that the people were the real beginning of all political power. He hoped that the future would be better than the period in which he lived.

The philosopher Confucius. His conservative ideas encouraged China to resist changes that would affect the traditional way of life. What were some of his ideas?

CHINA UNITES AND DEVELOPS A GREAT CIVILIZATION

How Shih Huang Ti (221–207 B.C.) Ruled China

Shih Huang Ti [shē'whang'dē'] was determined to forge a nation and to rule as a strong king. To do so would not be easy, for the teachings of Lao-tze and Confucius encouraged passive acceptance of the present and future. Shih Huang Ti wanted to make active changes to prepare for the future. The teachings of Confucius stood in the way of the changes

Check in Here

1. China is an enormously large country, yet there is overcrowding on its eastern coast. Why is this so?

2. How did the Chou Dynasty contribute to the development of ancient China?

3. How was China united?

4. Summarize the main teachings and influence of each of the following: **(a)** Lao-tze; **(b)** Confucius; **(c)** Mencius.

111

Shih Huang Ti had in mind. He ordered the books of Confucius and of the other philosophers burned. By destroying the books, Shih Huang Ti tried to destroy the ideas that stood in his way. Although the emperor burned the philosophy books, he did not burn those on medicine or farming.

Having silenced most of the educated people, Shih Huang Ti then tried to silence the military as well. Kings, dukes, nobles, and the rulers of small kingdoms into which China had been divided were ordered to live at his capital. In this way, the emperor could keep an eye on them. Their presence at his capital also added grace and prestige to his new court. In place of tiny kingdoms, the emperor divided his empire into districts. Each district was ruled by his paid official. The emperor won the loyalty of the peasants by allowing them to own the land on which they worked.

Shih Huang Ti realized that he could not unite China through force of arms

Most of the Great Wall of China was built during the Ming Dynasty as a fortification against invaders from the north.

alone. He built new roads, introduced better standards of weights and measures, and improved irrigation. He ordered wagons to be made of one size and width so that they could travel over the new roads easily. Shih Huang Ti simplified Chinese writing, encouraged science, and built canals.

The emperor knew that he must make his empire safe from foreign enemies. To protect his lands, he began to build the *Great Wall* of China. This wall was built far to the north in order to keep out invaders. The construction of the Great Wall has been compared to the building of the pyramids in Egypt. It was a huge task which called for the forced labor of many people. They had to be housed, clothed, and fed in lands far from their homes. The Great Wall was about 2,415 kilometers (1,500 mi.) long, 6.10 meters (20 ft.) high, and 4.57 meters (15 ft.) wide. In length it would stretch from Kansas City to New York City. Built at great cost in time and labor, it successfully kept out the enemies of China. Later emperors added to and strengthened the wall. To this day, large portions of it still stand.

Shih Huang Ti did much for China. His most important contribution was unifying the nation. During most of its history India lacked unity. The opposite is true of China. Except for short periods, China was a united country most of the time. No other nation in the world can boast of a tradition of unity over a period of 2,000 years.

Unfortunately, the people were not happy under Shih Huang Ti. They paid heavily in lives and taxes to build the Great Wall. Many longed to return to the ways of Confucius. When Shih Huang Ti died, there were few people to cry at his funeral. He was buried in an elegant tomb, but nobles and common people alike were glad that his strict rule had ended.

Shih Huang Ti had hoped that his dynasty would last for hundreds of years. Five years after his death, however, his son was murdered. Their dynasty was brought to a close. In time, it was followed by another dynasty. This new dynasty used different ruling methods. It was destined to leave a greater mark on the history of China.

How the Han Empire Ruled China

When Rome was in its glory in the West, the Empire of the Han [hän] was in its glory in the East. Like the Roman Empire, the Han Empire had lasting influence on the lands and people it touched.

The death of the Ch'in Emperor Shih Huang Ti was a signal that the time had

Ancient China During the Han Empire

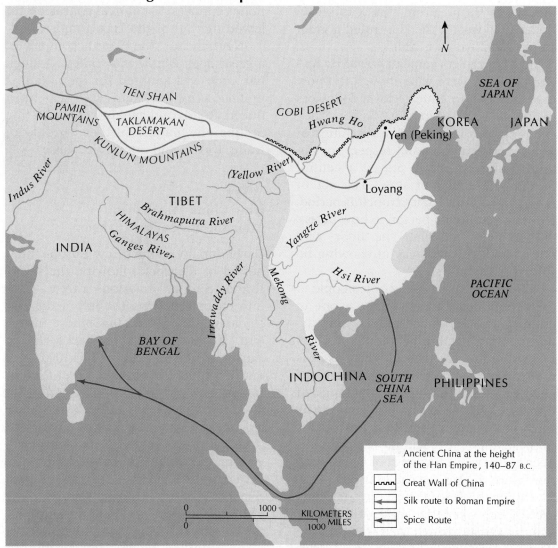

Ancient China at the height of the Han Empire, 140–87 B.C.

〜〜〜 Great Wall of China

← Silk route to Roman Empire

← Spice Route

- What human-made barrier was built along the northern border of the Han Empire?
- What important product did the Han Empire trade with the Roman Empire?

113

come for revolt. In Liu Pang [lyü' bäng'] the people found a leader who drew to him poor people of great ability. Liu Pang grew strong by promising his followers land and power when victory was theirs. He grew strong enough to seize the throne in 202 B.C. Once he accepted the crown, Liu Pang had to fight five more years before the last of the Ch'in nobles gave up. Since Liu Pang lived in the province, or kingdom, of Han, the dynasty which he founded is known by the name Han. From the capital at Loyang [lō yang'], the Han ruled a great empire (202 B.C.–A.D. 220).

The Han rulers came to power by revolution. They were wise enough to know that they had to educate loyal followers if they were to keep their power. They encouraged a return to the teachings of Confucius. Tradition and respect for authority and ceremony played a central part in the affairs of state. The act of *kowtow* [kou'tou'] dates from this period. Kowtow required a person to bow before authority by touching the floor with one's head. It was a way of showing respect for superiors.

The Han rulers needed able people to carry out their orders and to work in important government offices and departments. Selecting people for government jobs was as difficult then as it is today. The rulers of the Han dynasty gave examinations on the teachings of Confucius. These exams provided a way for bright young people to get jobs. Due to these tests, the teachings of Confucius became more firmly a part of China than they were during the Chou Dynasty.

Under the Han, the empire of China grew. None was more successful in contributing to its growth than was the Emperor Wu Ti [wü'tē'] (156–87 B.C.). During a long reign he fought many successful wars against northern tribes. Wu Ti was an efficient ruler as well as a capable general.

Under the Han, the strength of China was probably greater than that of Rome. When Rome fell, the empire fell. When the Han fell, the empire of China lived on. The fall of both Rome and the Han were brought about in part by invasions of barbarian tribes. The Han Empire weakened because it produced a line of young, weak kings and an overemphasis on the ideas of Confucius. New ideas, which were needed to meet the challenge of the invasions, were not encouraged. Four centuries of political confusion followed the fall of the Han Empire.

Nevertheless, the Hans accomplished a great deal. China was united. A single law code was adopted for the nation. A unified writing system was also introduced. Roads and canals were built, thus uniting the nation further by making trade, travel, and commerce easier.

How China Was Ruled After the Barbarian Invasion

Barbarian invasions threw Europe into a period of disorder following the fall of Rome. Similar invasions threw China into chaos following the fall of the Han Dynasty. This period in Chinese history (A.D. 200–600)—like a similar period in European history (A.D. 500–1000)—was one of much confusion. The Chinese fought among themselves on the one hand and against invaders on the other. No one dynasty was strong enough to bring all of China under its control.

This period in China was marked by invasions of Tartars [tär'tərz] who set up dynasties of their own. They adopted Chinese ways and accepted the culture of the country they had invaded. It was also a time marked by the growth of Buddhism. You have read that Buddhism was born in India where, after making some headway, it almost died out. But it grew strong in China.

How China Was Ruled
by the T'ang and the Sung

In A.D. 589, the Sui [sui] Dynasty (589–618) gained control in China. It was followed by the more renowned families of the T'ang [täng] (618–907) and the Sung [süng] (960–1279). Under the T'ang and Sung, China became a strong kingdom with a stable government. Ambassadors from Byzantium, Muslim lands, and India came to China.

One of the greatest rulers of the T'ang family was T'ai Tsung [tī' dzüng'], who ruled from 627–50. He started his rule badly by murdering his brothers and by going to war. He ended his rule in glory by turning to the ways of peace. During the reign of Ming Huang [ming' hwäng'] (712–56), China grew wealthy as never before. Silk was more common in China than in Europe and ". . . fur coats were more frequent in eighth century Ch'angan [the capital] than in twentieth century New York."*

Under the Sung kings, China continued to prosper, although not quite as well as under the T'angs. Wang An-shih (1021–86), an able king, tried to improve conditions for his people. In the process, he made enemies among the rich. In time he was forced from power. Later Sung kings were forced to fight the Mongols who swept down from the north and divided China. These violent people were led by the famous Genghis [geng'gis] Khan. With bloody hands he united his people and led them across the Gobi Desert. His name struck terror in the hearts of people. For many years, he was a warrior no one could match. Upon his death, those who followed him continued to fight. Of these the greatest was Kublai [kü'blä] Khan.

A small sculpture from the T'ang Dynasty shows a man mounted on a horse.

How China Was Ruled
by Its Later Dynasties

The Yüan [yü än'] Dynasty, which Kublai Khan established, lasted from 1279 to 1368. It was the Yüan Dynasty that Marco Polo (a Venetian) visited and wrote about. In his writing Polo vividly described many things about China: the great summer and winter palaces, Kublai's magnificent court, and the efficient systems for collecting taxes and delivering mail. Kublai Khan knew that a civilization could not be built on war and bloodshed. He improved roads and rebuilt canals. In Peking he created a new capital which was far greater than anything in Europe at that time. Its splendors were so great that no one would believe Marco Polo when he wrote about them.

In time, the Yüan Dynasty died as the others had. One reason for its fall was that the Mongol kings were influenced by

(turn to page 117)

*Will Durant, *The Story of Civilization: Our Oriental Heritage* (New York: Simon and Schuster).

115

Genghis Khan (1162–1227)

When Genghis Khan was born, his father—a Mongol warrior and tribal king—had just defeated the Tartars in a great battle. The Tartars were another Asian nomadic tribe. When his father returned home, he found a clot of blood in the palm of the hand of his newborn son. To the superstitious father this was a symbol of his victory over the Tartars, and so he named his son Temuchin [te mü'chin], after a Tartar leader.

When Temuchin was thirteen his father died, and Temuchin became the Mongol king. However, powerful Mongol families were not as willing to be ruled by the son as they had been by the father. Between 1175 and 1206, there was almost ceaseless war among these families. When it was over, Temuchin had become a powerful Mongol king. He was now called Genghis (or Jenghiz) Khan, which means "perfect warrior."

The Mongol armies, led by Genghis and his three sons, overran China to the Yellow River. They swept over western Asia and even reached Europe as far as the Don and Dneiper Rivers. According to legend, city after city was leveled to the ground so that horse and rider could travel in the dark of night without fear of falling. Although he had many victories in China, the superstitious Genghis thought he saw unfavorable omens in the heavens which foretold of defeat. And so he turned back, only to die along the way.

Kublai Khan (1216–1294)

Kublai Khan (1216–94), grandson of Genghis, successfully continued his grandfather's conquest of China. Although the Chinese bravely resisted (100,000 Chinese are said to have killed themselves rather than submit to the Mongol ruler), Kublai Khan founded a new dynasty, the Yüan. He also founded a new capital, Peking.

116

The Khans—Genghis and Kublai—were, first and foremost, warriors of great cruelty. Genghis did not hesitate to boil his prisoners alive or to chop them into little pieces. The death and destruction he wrought are nearly unmatched in history.

His grandson Kublai started his reign in the same brutal manner, but he in time became more civilized. Kublai made friends with the Chinese, accepted their culture, and tolerated many religions. Kublai founded a dynasty, but those who followed him were never able to match his energy, vigor, or ability.

Buddhism. The majority of Chinese did not practice Buddhism and having foreign rulers who did angered them.

The Ming [ming] Dynasty (1365–1644) followed the Yüan Dynasty. The founder of the Ming Dynasty was a Buddhist monk, Hung Wu [hung′ wü′], who led an army that drove the Mongols from China.

In Chinese, Ming means "glorious" or "brilliant." It is a somewhat boastful word to apply to the Ming Dynasty, which was not nearly as great as some of the others. It did not equal the glory of the Chou, Han, T'ang, or Sung. However, it was not without its achievements. In a sense the Ming Dynasty rested on the greatness of the past and made little preparation for the future. Its main ambition was to drive all foreign influence out of China, and in this it was successful. It was so fearful of foreign influence that it withdrew its navies from the seas and tried to build a protective shell around China. All this was to no avail, for it was during the Ming period that Europeans started coming to China.

Nor were the Mings able to keep out the Mongols. From Manchuria came a fresh invasion of Mongols. They drove the Mings from power and set up the Manchu [man chü′] Dynasty (1644–1911). This was China's last dynasty. The story

of its rule and its contacts with the West are found in Chapter 21. We now turn to the daily life of people in ancient China.

Check in Here

1. Identify an important contribution associated with each of the following: **(a)** Shih Huang Ti; **(b)** Liu Pang; **(c)** Wu Ti; **(d)** Hung Wu.

2. Give reasons for the rise and fall of each of the following dynasties: **(a)** Han; **(b)** T'ang; **(c)** Yüan; **(d)** Ming.

3. Describe the conquests of Genghis Khan and Kublai Khan. How did Kublai Khan's policies differ from those of his grandfather Genghis Khan?

4. Were the ancient Chinese eager for contact with people from other countries? In what ways did they show their feelings about foreigners?

THE LIVES OF ORDINARY PEOPLE IN ANCIENT CHINA

How the Common People of China Lived

You have learned about the emperors and conquerors of ancient China. Now you will learn about the ordinary people. They are very important because their lifestyles tell us much about Chinese culture. This section begins with China in

1650. It was about this time that Europeans and then Americans started coming to China in increasingly large numbers. For a period of 2,000 years little had changed in China. The teachings of Confucius taught China to resist change. The changes the Europeans introduced affected the way the Chinese lived and worked. Changes are still taking place in China, even more rapidly than before.

You have seen that in India the family occupied a prominent position in the lives of the people. In China the family was even more important. The family rather than the individual was the center of the Chinese way of life. Confucius had much to say about the family. He taught that the wife had to obey and honor the husband, the children had to obey their parents, and the younger child had to obey and respect the older one.

A porcelain vase made during the Ming Dynasty. The ceramics made during the Ming Dynasty are considered China's finest achievements in the medium.

The family included cousins, uncles, and aunts as well as children and grandchildren. Members of the family who had died were worshipped. Just as the father worshipped his dead parents with appropriate ceremonies, so he expected to be worshipped by his children after his death. The father was absolute master of the household. Although women were treated with indifference, the mother of many sons was often honored. Child marriages were often arranged by parents. After marriage, wives were expected to live with the husband's family, learn its ways, and serve its needs.

As in India, the Chinese family worked together to make a living, usually by farming. Most families lived on small patches of land, which often were too small to provide the family with what it needed. However, if the family was skillful in farming, it could get along. The family farm grew vegetables, cotton (for clothing), rice, and tea, and raised chickens, pigs, ducks, and geese. Although starvation was never far away, the poor farmers did not complain. Instead, they said, "All that a man needs . . . is a hat and a bowl of rice."*

Many Chinese made a living by weaving textiles and by breeding silkworms. Both these occupations became significant industries in ancient China. As early as 300 B.C. there were *guilds* [gildz] of silkweavers, glassblowers, and papermakers. Guilds were made up of workers and owners who decided what wages would be paid, what prices would be charged, and how each item should be made. Guilds came to China hundreds of years before they appeared in Europe.

You may call your dinnerware "china" without realizing the debt you owe the country of China for this beautiful product. In the China of old, the mak-

*Will Durant, *The Story of Civilization: Our Oriental Heritage* (New York: Simon and Schuster).

The Mongol Empires About 1300 A.D.

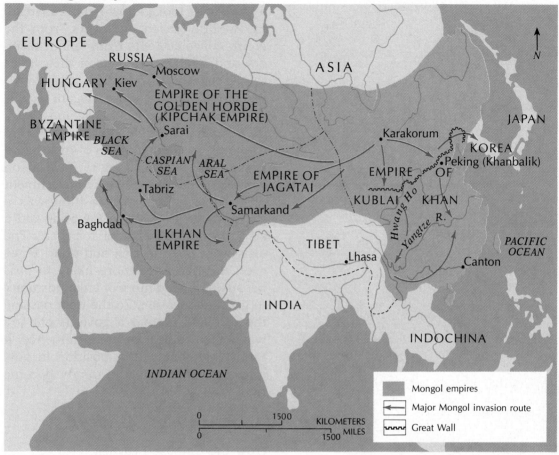

By 1300, the empires of the Mongols stretched from the Pacific Ocean westward into Europe.
• From what city did the Mongol invasions begin?
• What Russian cities were located in the Kipchak Empire?

ing of dinnerware was a big industry and a fine art. The Chinese were so skillful at making dishes that they became world famous in this industry. The Chinese learned to make beautiful clay objects that in color, form, and design have rarely been equaled.

The Chinese were active in buying and selling goods. Chinese goods were shipped to Rome before the empire fell. Merchants did business with the peoples of the Malay Peninsula, India, and Persia. The Chinese sold porcelain, paper, silk, tea, and gunpowder. They bought peanuts, glass, tobacco, and opium. Merchants who needed money could borrow from bankers whose methods of finance, coinage, and paper money made it possible for the Chinese to do business with far-off places. Crops and handicrafts were carried on the backs of unskilled laborers called *coolies*, or they were carried by boat on China's many canals. The Chinese were skilled in business matters, but merchants were not as high on the social ladder as scholars.

A detail from a porcelain plate provides a glimpse of upper-class family life during the Ch'ing Dynasty.

How the Rich People of China Lived and Worked

Among the rich and powerful in China, family ties were the center of life, just as they were for the common people. Ancestor worship played a vital part in the lives of the well-to-do families. They had the wealth to make elaborate altars upon which prayers for dead relatives could be offered. Moreover, since much of the wealth of the upper classes had been inherited, it seemed natural to them to pray for those who had founded the family fortune.

Among the rich, those who worked at a trade were looked down upon. Instead, the wealthy relied on favors from the court, collected rents from tenant farmers, and sold the products of their lands to merchants. To show their distaste for work, the wealthy wore elegant gowns and let their fingernails grow long.

Scholars were highly respected in China. It was the ambition of most families, rich and poor alike, to have a son who could pass the tests for government service. A government position was a great source of pride to the poor and a step up the social ladder for them. The tests were open to rich and poor. However, the rich were more likely to pass because they had more of an opportunity to get an education. To the rich, passing the test and getting a government job was a chance to gain more influence. A family member with a position in government could help the family become rich.

How the Chinese Learned, Worshipped, and Played

To pass the examination for government service one had to memorize the teachings of Confucius. Only the most brilliant scholars could memorize and understand all of his teachings. Because many people studied and tried to pass the examinations, a widespread respect for education developed in China. Those scholars who could pass the tests occupied government posts. Those students who failed sometimes took easier examinations to enter the military service. For those who could not pass either test, the door to advancement in government was closed.

Only a few Chinese students were able to enter government service. Those who could not because they failed the exams had few other opportunities. The emphasis on memorizing Confucius's teachings made it difficult to pass the exams. There was little emphasis on learning new subjects. Scholars who were successful often became snobs and considered working with their hands beneath them. These people formed a new aristocracy, or educated wealthy class. They did not use their education to improve the working and living conditions of their people.

The Chinese followed Buddhism, Taoism, and Confucianism. In addition, they worshipped their ancestors. Because they followed many faiths, the Chinese usually tolerated other religions. Christianity was tolerated, but few Chinese became Christians. The Chinese celebrated many festivals with ceremonies drawn from many faiths and prayers to many gods.

The rich in China could entertain themselves in many ways. A popular form of entertainment was the theater, in which paid actors dressed in elegant costumes and acted out stories before delighted audiences. The audiences had to watch the actors very closely because no stage props were used. Instead, the actors used certain motions to indicate when they were entering a room, closing a door or window, or climbing stairs.

Check in Here

1. How did the teachings of Confucius influence the everyday life of the Chinese?

2. Would you like to be educated the way the ancient Chinese were? Why or why not?

3. Describe some of the ways in which the Chinese made a living.

4. Describe the influence of religion among the people of China.

CHINA'S CONTRIBUTIONS TO CIVILIZATION

How Literature Developed in China

Just as the Egyptians gave us picture writing, so the Chinese gave us a writing system of their own. The Chinese language is difficult to speak or write. As you know, a page of Chinese writing is made up of individual characters written from the top to the bottom of the page, rather than from left to right. The Chinese language does not have an alphabet. Instead, it has thousands of *characters*, each of which is shown by a different symbol, or set of lines.

There are many thousands of these characters, or symbols, used in Chinese writing. The meaning of each character

A scene from a Chinese play in which a comedian is singing a popular song.

varies with its use in a particular sentence. In speaking, the meaning of a character depends upon the tone used in its pronunciation. Each character in written Chinese and each word in the spoken language represents a thing or an idea, not a letter.

There are many spoken Chinese *dialects* [dī′ə lekts′], or different ways of pronouncing Chinese. Some of these are understood by only a few Chinese. However, the written language has changed little through the years and can often be read by other people in the Far East. The Chinese language is probably understood by a greater number of people than any other language.

During the T'ang Dynasty, poetry was the love of China. Poets occupied influential posts and received great admiration and respect. Tu Fu [dü′fü′] and Li Po [lē′pō′] were two well known poets of the period. The following lines tell of Tu Fu's sadness over the war that had taken the lives of many young men:

If I had only known how sad is the
    fate of boys
I would have had my children all girls
    . . .
Boys are only born to be buried
    beneath tall grass.
Still the bones of the war dead of long
    ago are beside
the Blue Sea when you pass.

The interest in writing and books stimulated the growth of block printing. By A.D. 700, block printing was well on its way toward becoming a highly developed art. The demand for textbooks for government examinations and the invention of paper encouraged this development. The world's oldest printed book was found in China and dated A.D. 868.

How Invention Developed in China

The Chinese were an inventive people. As early as A.D. 600, the Chinese knew about and used gunpowder. For centuries it was used for fireworks, not for firearms. It was not until the thirteenth and fourteenth centuries that gunpowder was used to fire weapons.

The compass was known in 1115 B.C., but it was not really used until years later. In China's early history some progress was made in chemistry. However, chemists in China as well as in Europe failed in their attempts to make gold out of less valuable metals. This practice is called *alchemy* [al′kə mē]. The practical results of Chinese chemistry were the development of porcelain-making, the use of lacquers, and the invention of gunpowder.

About the year A.D. 150, the Chinese learned to make paper from rags. The paper was used for painting, writing, and paper money. Since paper was in use at such an early date, China had books early in its history. As a result, the Chinese were especially conscious of the written history of their country.

The Chinese admired beauty as well as knowledge. Under the Sungs, practical objects such as furniture and clothing became objects of beauty. Beautiful pottery was produced. Lovely bronze cups were made for religious purposes. Delicate jade was carved into fantastic figures. Architecture, too, became a fine art. The complex, delicate temples and pagodas which you may associate with China came from this period. Many of the buildings and figures have unfortunately disappeared because the Chinese used wood as a building material.

Under the Sung dynasty, Chinese painting reached its peak. The paintings show insects, fish, birds, or flowers. The landscape of China—hills, waters, des-

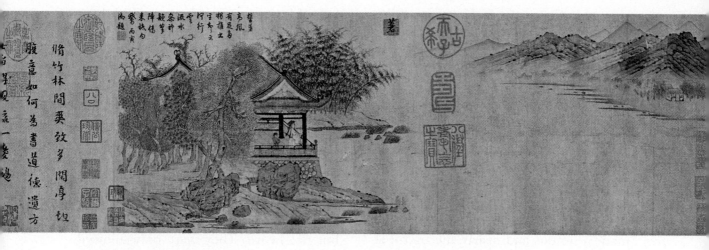

A Chinese scroll painting from the Sung Dynasty. Landscapes were very often the subject matter of the scrolls of this dynasty. Notice the Chinese characters at the left. How do these differ from our alphabet?

erts, and mountains—was painted again and again. Chinese paintings were not made to be hung permanently on walls. They were designed to be rolled or unrolled like a scroll and viewed when the owner wished.

Check in Here

1. Describe the characteristics of the Chinese language.

2. List three practical inventions for which we are indebted to the Chinese.

3. Describe a contribution made to civilization by each of the following: (**a**) T'ang Dynasty; (**b**) Sung Dynasty.

4. When and how did the Chinese learn to make paper? What were the results of the invention?

THE KOREAN LEGACY

What We Know of Korea's History

In 2333 B.C., according to tradition, a dynasty was founded in Korea that ruled for a thousand years. In the twelfth century, a Chinese scholar, Ki Tse [gē′ dzu′], went to Korea with 5,000 followers. They settled among the Koreans they found there and taught them what they knew about Chinese ways of living.

For several hundred years Korea was a divided land until a powerful general, Wang-kon [wang gon′], united it under a single government. It was he who founded the Koryo [kōr′yō] Dynasty (935–1392), which ruled for more than 450 years and gave its name to Korea. In the thirteenth century, Korea fell to the sword of the Mongols. Korea again found itself under foreign rule. In 1392, the Ming Dynasty of China helped Korea rid itself of these unwelcome guests. Who would rule Korea next?

In the Korean revolt against the Mongols, General Yi Tai-jo [yi dī jō′] defeated the Mongols and became a national hero. He also led his troops against the pirates of Japan. Yi declared himself king and won support among the people. Yi was a hard-working ruler for whom the luxuries of court life held little interest. Instead, he was determined to make Korea a strong nation. He began by moving the capital of Korea to Seoul [sä′ōl] and changing the name of Korea to "Chosen," a name by which it is sometimes still called today. Yi improved the government and saw to it that the people were wisely ruled.

During most of the dynasty of Yi, Korea's relations with China were stable. Korea willingly paid tribute to China. In its relations with Japan things were not so peaceful. The Japanese raided the coasts of Korea, and Japanese pirates plundered Korean ships. In 1592, the Japanese under Hideyoshi [hē'de yô'shē] made a serious and nearly successful effort to conquer Korea. The Japanese, for the first time in their history, used firearms in warfare. The Koreans met the challenge with a metal-clad ship called a *tortoise boat*, which was powerful enough to sink a large part of the Japanese navy.

The victory of Korea against Japan exhausted Korea. The war aroused such fear of foreigners that Koreans withdrew from contact with foreign nations. It became a hermit in the family of nations. Even to this day Korea is sometimes called the "Hermit Kingdom."

How Koreans Lived

As in other countries of the Far East, daily life in Korea was built around the family. The father was its head, and his word was law. Women were to be seen but not heard. They were only allowed out at a certain time each day. This was usually early in the evening when men stayed indoors. The separation of men and women was the rule rather than the exception.

The influence of China on Korea was great. From China the Koreans received their spoken and written language and the teachings of Buddha. From China the Koreans learned some of the methods of building and pottery making, and what they produced equaled the best of China. As elsewhere in Asia, most people depended on farming for a living. It was on the farm that the family lived, worked, and died.

Korea made its own contributions to civilization quite independently of the Chinese. Koreans are credited with inventing the spinning wheel, movable metal type, the compass, the observation balloon, a metal clad ship, an instrument to measure rainfall, and developing an alphabet. The modern version of the Yi Palace Orchestra—the original was founded 500 years ago—still performs ancient Korean music. Korean scholars compiled a 112-volume encyclopedia, a copy of which is in the United States Library of Congress. In A.D. 1420, a royal college of literature was established to promote Korean scholarship.

Korea is famous for some of its proverbs. In many of the proverbs may be

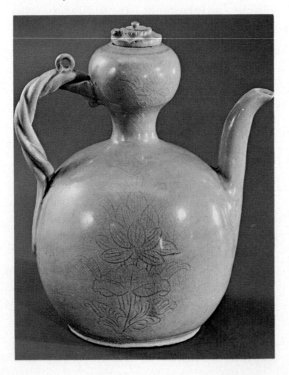

An ancient Korean vessel is adorned with a delicately carved flower.

seen the wisdom of old Korea. Perhaps some of these sound familiar to you.

"Don't draw a sword to kill a mosquito."
"You cannot sit in the valley and see the new moon set."
"It is useless to pour instruction into a sow's ear."
"It is foolish to mourn over a broken vase."

Today, Korea is divided into two countries, North Korea and South Korea. (See p. 682). The division of Korea grew out of World War II. It is a reminder of the difficulty Korea has had through the centuries in keeping both unity and independence.

Check in Here

1. Why has Korea been called the "Hermit Kingdom"?

2. How did China contribute to the development of Korea?

3. How is Korea indebted to Yi Tai-jo?

4. Describe Korean contributions to civilization in (**a**) music; (**b**) inventions; (**c**) literature.

THE LEGACY OF ANCIENT JAPAN

The Early History of Japan

Japan's history may be divided into three parts. The first part, or *ancient age*, began about 660 B.C. and lasted until about A.D. 600. The period from the year 600 to Perry's visit to Japan in 1853 is called the *middle period*. The time since 1853 is called the *modern period*.

There is a legend about the birth of the islands of Japan. The god Izanagi [ē'zä nä'ge] and the god Izanami

Ancient Korea and Japan

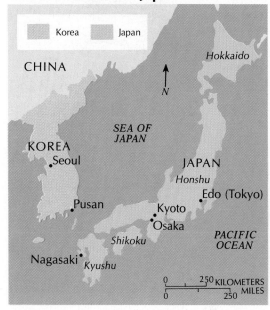

- Korea is a peninsula extending out from the mainland of what continent?
- How many very large islands make up Japan's territory?
- How many kilometers separate Korea from Japan?

[ē'zä nä'mē], who were husband and wife, plunged a spear into the ocean and upon lifting it let the drops fall. These drops, so legend says, became the islands of Japan. On these islands lived the Ainu [ī'nü], an ancient people who came to Japan about the year 1000 B.C. Today, there are only a few remaining Ainu. They live on the northern island of Hokkaido [hôk'kī dô']. They are a quiet people. Their ancestors were not quiet. In ancient days, the Ainu were violent people. By some accounts they were also cannibals.

The Ainu were gradually driven out of most of the islands by newcomers. These people lived in clans made up of family groups who shared common interests. The clans fought one another until one became more powerful than

125

A group of modern Ainu being photographed by tourists.

the rest. The Yamato [yä'mä tō] clan became the most powerful of all and, in time, the people of ancient Japan accepted the leadership of the Yamato chiefs. The first chief was Jimmu Tenno [jē'mō ten'ə] (660 B.C.), which means Child of the Sun. By tradition, he is considered to be the first emperor of Japan. Japanese historical mythology begins with Jimmu.

Under the Yamato, the chief was both a king and a priest to whom other clans listened. When he was strong, they feared his power. When he was weak, they ruled themselves as they pleased. At the dawn of Japanese history life was crude. Civilization was not highly developed, and frequent wars made the soldier an influential figure. The military remained important throughout Japanese history. Religion was based on the worship of nature. It contained little in the way of laws of conduct. This nature-religion became the basis of *Shintoism* [shin'tō izm], still the chief religion of Japan.

While Japanese culture was developing slowly on the islands, Chinese culture was growing rapidly on the mainland. Contact between China and Japan grew. Japan sent ambassadors to the court of the Han Dynasty. These ambassadors brought back valuable learning to the people of Japan. Chinese-style characters used in writing were adopted by Japan. By 500 B.C., Japanese history appears in Chinese records.

The basis of the social organization in Japan was the clan, and the Soga [sō'gə] clan was one of the most important Japanese clans during the early period. The Soga clan learned of Buddhism through its contact with China and Korea. The powerful Sogas determined that Buddhism should become the religion of Japan. As the Soga clan grew in power, the influence of Buddhism grew with it. By 600 B.C., Buddhism was firmly established in Japan, as was the Soga clan. Buddhism lived on in Japan, but the Soga clan lost its power. The Soga's loss of power was due to the coming of another influence from China. This was the idea of centralized government.

How People Lived in Ancient Japan

In Japan, soldiers were more important as a group than in China or Korea. From the *shogun* [shō'gun'], who was the leader, to the *samurai* [sam'ü ri'], who were the warriors, Japan was a nation run by the military. The military dominated the government, the economy, the society, and even the religion of the people. From the seventeenth century, the fighting classes followed a strict code known as *Bushido* [bü'shē dô'], by which the samurai pledged their lives to their lords. Like the knightly code of honor in medieval Europe, Bushido taught the need for loyalty and obedience to a master. Because of the influence of Bushido, the nation and the emperor were given unquestioned obedience by the people. The emperor, however, without loyal samurai had little power of his own. In Japanese society, people knew their place and obeyed those above them.

Family life in Japan was similar to Korea's. The father, as head of the household, was given unquestioned obedience. Obedience was one of the highest virtues. One served one's parents in life and worshipped them after death. And nowhere in Asia was the position of women lower than in Japan. Total and complete obedience to the husband was expected and demanded of a wife. She bowed when she entered a room and when she left it. She served her husband and his children in courtesy and in silence. The loyalty that the father owed his lord was expected in equal measure from his wife and children.

The Japanese were influenced by many religious ideas. Shintoism was the most important religion in Japan. It encouraged obedience, emperor worship, and prayer to gods of nature. Buddhism made much headway in Japan and had many followers among the general population. The teachings of Confucius were popular with the warrior (military) class. The warrior class used Confucianism as a guide for conduct rather than as a religion. Chinese missionaries carried religious ideas to Japan.

Most people in Japan were farmers. Farming was practiced under a feudal system. Most of the farmers did not own the land they worked. The Japanese farmers, like the serfs of medieval Europe, had to give much of what they grew to the lord of the land. Rice, then as today, was a most important food. In addition to farming, fishing was a major industry. Fish and rice made up most of

A Japanese samurai, or warrior. These men pledged their lives to their lords. What was their code of honor called?

the diet of the Japanese. Trade with other countries was limited. The merchant class was therefore small.

Check in Here

1. How did China influence the early development of Japan?

2. When and how did Buddhism become strong in Japan?

3. Explain the importance of each of the following in Japanese society: (**a**) the clan; (**b**) obedience to authority.

When Charlemagne was at his peak in Europe in A.D. 800, the T'angs were ruling China. As great as Charlemagne was, China's power, cultural achievement, and economic wealth were far greater than anything Charlemagne could dream of or even hope to accomplish. Hundreds of years were to pass before Europe could catch up.

Most of China's people live on the coast. The dry, hilly areas in the north and west, where life is hard, force people into the south and east, causing overcrowding. The Chou Dynasty was the first in China's recorded history. It also lasted the longest. Its weak emperors were eventually overthrown by Shih Huang Ti who himself was overturned by the famous Han Dynasty.

After a period of turmoil, the great T'ang Dynasty came to power to be followed by the almost equally important Sung. The Yüan Dynasty, which Kublai Khan established, was of Mongol origins. The Ming and Manchu were the last of China's dynasties, and neither of them could match the greatness at the height of Chinese civilization.

China's contributions to culture are almost unmatched. Printing, gunpowder, silks, writing, to say nothing of great pottery, philosophy, and painting were among China's lavish gifts to humankind. The teachings of Confucius had widespread influence not only in China but around the world as well.

Korea and Japan were enormously influenced by China. Both countries also made important cultural contributions of their own. Korea was known for its music, a 112-volume encyclopedia, and the development of movable metal type. The scholar was important in Chinese society; the warrior, or samurai, was important in Japanese society. The emperor of China was expected to be a powerful figure. In Japan, people were loyal to the emperor, although the shogun and the military dominated Japan. The military leader was called the shogun.

The cultures of East and West went their separate ways. By the seventeenth century, trade, commerce, and exploration increased contacts between Europe and China, Korea, and Japan. At first, the countries of the Far East resisted the coming of the Europeans. They could not, however, keep the Europeans out. These contacts brought far-reaching changes for Asia, Europe, and America.

REVIEWING THE HIGHLIGHTS

People to Identify			
Shih Huang Ti	Kublai Khan	Ki Tse
Liu Pang	Marco Polo	Yi Tai-jo
Confucius	Li Po	Hideyoshi

Mencius	Tu Fu	Jimmu Tenno
Wang An-shih	Wang-kon	Yamato
Genghis Khan	Wu Ti	Lao-tze

**Places
to Locate**

Himalayas	China	Hwang Ho
Peking	Manchuria	Yangzte
Japan	Gobi Desert	Si
Korea	Hokkaido	Great Wall of China

**Terms
to Understand**

ancient age	dynasty	Shang Dynasty
middle period	Bushido	Chou Dynasty
modern period	ancestor worship	Han Empire
feudal	samurai	T'ang Dynasty
kowtow	Shintoism	Sung Dynasty
shogun	Ming Dynasty	Yüan Dynasty
guild	Hsia Dynasty	Soga clan
	Tao	

**Mastering the
Fundamentals**

1. What are some of the advantages and disadvantages of China's geography?
2. Why did the feudal system develop under the Chou Dynasty?
3. How can the building of the Great Wall be compared with the building of the pyramids in Egypt?
4. How did the Han Empire come to power?
5. What improvements did the Han make?
6. What was the purpose of the Chinese examination system?
7. How do the fall of the Han Empire and the fall of Rome resemble each other?
8. Why did disorder follow the fall of the Han Empire?
9. What progress was made in China under the T'ang and Sung dynasties?
10. How did the Mongols become rulers of China?
11. What was the main ambition of the Ming Dynasty?
12. Why was the Ming Dynasty not as great as some of the others?
13. How did the rich entertain themselves in China?
14. How did the guilds regulate China's trade?
15. What is meant by ancestor worship? What part did it play in China?
16. How did Korea defeat Japan?
17. Identify the three major periods of Japanese history.
18. Why was the shogun considered more important than the Japanese emperor?
19. How did Bushido influence family and cultural life in Japan?

THINGS TO DO

1. Using papier-mâché or plaster of paris, make a map showing the mountains, plains, and river valleys of China, Korea, and/or Japan.
2. Debate: *Resolved:* Confucius had a beneficial influence on the civilization of China.
3. Organize a panel program in which a number of reporters interview Genghis and Kublai Khan for their opinions on recent developments in today's China.

YOU ARE THE HISTORIAN

Read the selection below and answer the questions that follow.

Upon the return of the grand khan to his capital he holds a great and splendid court which lasts three days, in the course of which he gives feasts and otherwise entertains those by whom he is surrounded. . . . The multitude of inhabitants and the number of houses in the city, as also in the suburbs without the city . . . is greater than the mind can comprehend. . . .

To this city everything that is most rare and valuable in all parts of the world finds its way; and more especially does this apply to India, which furnishes* precious stones, pearls, and various drugs and spices. From the provinces of Cathay* itself as well as from the other provinces of the empire, whatever there is of value is carried thither, to supply the demands of those multitudes who are induced* to establish their residence in the vicinity of the court. The quantity of merchandise sold there exceeds also the traffic of any other place, for no fewer than a thousand carriages and pack-horses, loaded with raw silk, make their daily entry; and gold tissues and silks of various kinds are manufactured to an immense extent.

Vocabulary
furnishes—provides   *Cathay*—China   *induced*—persuaded

1. Who probably wrote the above? Upon which clues can you base your answer?
2. When was it probably written? Upon which clues can you base your answer?
3. About which country was it probably written? Upon which clues do you base your answer?
4. Why did stories such as these excite the imagination and interest of the Europeans?
5. What do we learn from this selection about the relations between India and China?

Stone Age tools and weapons

Two Continents: South America and Africa Before the Arrival of the Europeans

The ancient roots of the first Americans and the first Africans are steeped in mystery. No one is quite sure how far back they go. Some early American and early African cultures developed a form of written language. Others did not. In addition, several of the written languages have yet to be understood.

Very little is known about how the Native Americans lived before the coming of Christopher Columbus and other European explorers. What we do know is that the Native Americans of North and South America were mainly living in the Stone Age. The European explorers were already living in the Iron Age. Because Europeans had horses, superior weapons, and suits of armor, they were victorious conquerors of the Native Americans. Today, we have become more appreciative of the Native American civilizations of *Pre-Columbian* America. (Pre-Columbian refers to the time before the arrival of Columbus.) The early European conquerors were not sensitive to the high level of civilization that these groups had already developed. They were willing to destroy what the Native Americans had built over many centuries.

Some ancient civilizations of North Africa devised a calendar, a system of numbers, a written alphabet, a plough, and the wheel. In *Sub-Saharan* Africa (south of the Sahara) such developments were unknown. Increasingly, the world has come to admire and understand achievements that developed among the peoples living south of the Sahara. Among the old proverbs of Sub-Saharan Africans are: "Lack of knowledge is darker than night"; "An ignorant person is always a slave." With these proverbs in mind let us see what we can learn of the ancient Sub-Saharan and Pre-Columbian civilizations.

THE UNIQUE CIVILIZATIONS OF THE PRE-COLUMBIANS

The Location of Latin America

Latin America is made up of countries in North, South, and Central America where Spanish, Portuguese, and French are spoken. Latin America gets its name from the people who settled there. They spoke the Romance languages, which are derived from Latin. The term Latin America, however, usually also includes Puerto Rico, Cuba, the British and French West Indies, and Belize [be lēz'], which was formerly British Honduras.

Geographically, Latin America goes from the southern border of Texas to Cape Horn, which is a distance of over 16,093 kilometers (10,000 mi.). Distances between most points in Latin America and those in the United States are very great. It takes longer to fly to most points in Latin America from New York or Chicago than it does to Western Europe. Buenos Aires, the capital of Argentina, is farther from Chicago than is Moscow, the capital of the Soviet Union.

There are twenty countries in Latin America. Brazil is almost as large as the United States. However, most of the countries are quite small. Mexico, the nearest Latin American neighbor of the United States, is a growing world power. Its newly discovered oil wealth makes it a vital neighbor of the United States. Mexico can be expected to play an important part in world events. Tin from Bolivia, oil from Venezuela, iron ore and coffee from Brazil, and cattle from the *pampas* [pam′pəz] or plains, of Argentina, are among the important products Latin America sells to the world.

The climate and geography of Latin America have, on the whole, been obstacles to its development. Most of the countries lie in the tropics. The heat and the humidity make living in these areas difficult. The rain forest region of the Amazon basin is a particularly harsh place in which to live. Yet the country of Brazil, through which much of the Amazon [am′ə zon′] River flows, established a new capital, called Brasília [brä zil′yə], in the heart of this area. Brazil hopes to demonstrate that this region can be made fit for the development of a modern society. While tropical rain forests dominate the climate of Latin America, there are also deserts. The Atacama [at′ə kam′ə] Desert of southern Peru and northern Chile is mostly barren and unable to support life.

The Andes [an′dēz] mountain range runs about 6,440 kilometers (4,000 mi.)

from north to south along the western coast of South America. The Andes are a formidable barrier to transportation and communication. During the nineteenth century, several countries of Latin America fought wars of independence from Spain. Two revolutionary leaders, Simón Bolívar and José de San Martin, crossed the Andes with an effective fighting force. This was a great military accomplishment. The southern tip of Latin America is close to the South Pole and is extremely cold.

The Native American tribes that migrated to the lands of South America probably came from Asia across the Bering [bėr′ing] Strait. They came many thousands of years ago. Some of these people settled in Alaska; others went farther south to what is now Canada and the United States. Others settled in Mexico, Peru, and South America. By 500 B.C., this migration was probably over. Some Native American civilizations never developed beyond the Stone Age.

A section of the Andes mountain range, which spans South America for approximately 6,440 kilometers (4,000 mi.).

Others, in Central and South America, had advanced civilizations. We will study these.

The Mayas

The origins of the Mayas [mä′yəz] are unknown. What we do know we have learned from archaeological remains and from the records made by the conquering Spanish. It is estimated that Mayan civilization began around 2000 B.C. While one can speak of a Mayan civilization, one cannot really speak of a Mayan nation. The Mayan communities were numerous but small. They were united only by a common culture, tradition, trade, and language. There was no capital.

A temple in the central plaza of Palenque is a good example of Mayan architecture. What other ancient culture also built pyramids?

The Mayas in Yucatan [yü′kə tan′] built pyramids similar in design to some of the Egyptian pyramids. The Mayan pyramids were somewhat smaller and were built in steps. The remains of some pyramids can be seen at Tikal [ti kal′] and at Chichen-Itza [chē chen′ēt sä′]. By studying the pyramids archaeologists and historians have learned much about Mayan civilization. The pyramids often occupied the center of the town and were used mainly as places of worship. They were enormous and carefully constructed. This shows that the Mayans had enough knowledge of the principles of physics to move huge blocks of stone into place. The pyramids themselves and the altars at the very top were often placed in such a way that the sun, stars, and moon would shine on them from time to time.

The Mayan people had considerable knowledge of astronomy (the study of the stars and planets). They also had an accurate calendar and a system of arithmetic based on units of 20 (ours is based on units of 10). Their knowledge also included a form of picture writing called *glyph* [glif], which scholars do not yet understand.

Although often thought of as a people tied exclusively to the land, the Mayans sailed the sea for adventure and for trade. They sailed around the Caribbean and along the Gulf coasts. One of the great mysteries in history is the disappearance of the Mayan civilization. The old pyramids are still there in the midst of the jungle, but there is no evidence to explain why the civilization vanished. There is no record of defeat by an enemy.

- What ancient empire was located in the Andes Mountains?
- Name two of the peoples that lived in Central America.

Some Peoples of Pre-Columbian America

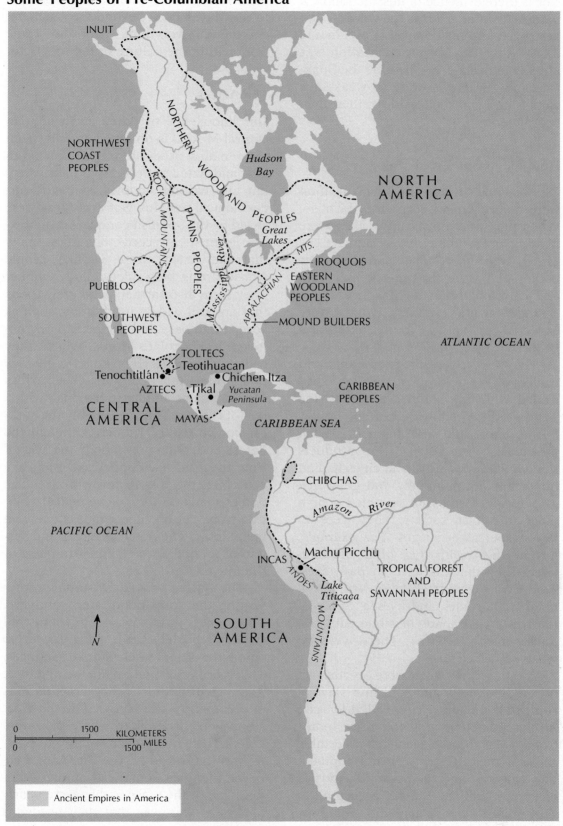

INUIT

NORTHWEST COAST PEOPLES

NORTHERN WOODLAND PEOPLES

ROCKY MOUNTAINS

PLAINS PEOPLES

Hudson Bay

NORTH AMERICA

Great Lakes

Mississippi River

MTS.

IROQUOIS

EASTERN WOODLAND PEOPLES

PUEBLOS

APPALACHIAN

SOUTHWEST PEOPLES

MOUND BUILDERS

ATLANTIC OCEAN

TOLTECS

Teotihuacan

Tenochtitlán

Chichen Itza

AZTECS

Tikal

Yucatan Peninsula

CARIBBEAN PEOPLES

CENTRAL AMERICA

MAYAS

CARIBBEAN SEA

CHIBCHAS

Amazon River

PACIFIC OCEAN

Machu Picchu

INCAS

ANDES

Lake Titicaca

TROPICAL FOREST AND SAVANNAH PEOPLES

N

SOUTH AMERICA

MOUNTAINS

0   1500   KILOMETERS
0   1500   MILES

Ancient Empires in America

Nor is there evidence of destruction by a natural disaster, such as the volcano that destroyed ancient Pompeii (Italy) in A.D. 79. By A.D. 1000 Mayan civilization was already in decline. By the time the Spanish came the Mayas were so weak they were simply pushed aside rather than conquered.

How the Mayas Lived

Most people of the Mayan civilization were maize [māz], or corn, farmers. When they were not farming, they were fighting or building the pyramids. The Mayas were short. They tattooed their bodies and wore their black hair long and carefully braided. Marriages were arranged by matchmakers. Women were expected to marry young and raise children.

The Mayas were the merchants and traders of Pre-Columbian America. They traded with one another and with the Aztecs. Salt, dried fish, cotton, honey, beans, chocolate, and feathers woven into cloaks were some of the products traded. Some of the Mayan cities had an important salt monopoly and grew rich as a result. Merchants occupied a high place in Mayan society. They were allowed special privileges. For example, despite the wealth they often accumulated, they did not have to pay taxes. Trade was conducted over well-developed trade routes and by sea. Some of the roads were made of stone with rest houses along the way. There were no wheeled vehicles.

Although the Mayas were overthrown by the Spaniards and sold into slavery, some of their culture survived. It lives on in the inhabitants of the area today. Some Mayan achievements resemble those of ancient Egypt—the development of a calendar and the pyramid—are two examples. But the Mayas, according to our present knowledge, did not copy them from the Egyptians. Nothing came to the Mayas from beyond the American continent. Everything they did came from within the culture of the Americas.

The Aztecs

Our knowledge of Aztec civilization in central Mexico is obtained, in part, from the remains of stone and stucco buildings and Aztec pottery, from their calendar and writing samples, and other archeological remains. Some of these were saved by the Spanish conquerors of Mexico. From such records, historians know that the Aztecs were warlike people whose strong king ruled a large empire. They were also farmers who grew foods that are still widely used today, such as corn, tomatoes, and peppers. They enjoyed a chocolate drink, which they called *chocollat*, [chō′kō lät]. It was much like hot chocolate. The Aztecs played a game similar to handball with a ball of rubber. This is probably the earliest known use of rubber. Although the Aztecs did not know about the use of iron, they did use copper and tin. They combined the two to form bronze. The Aztecs made pottery, wove delicate fabrics from cotton, and made stone and metal tools. The Aztec calendar and system of numbers were similar to those of the Mayan.

The Aztecs prayed to statues representing the sun, moon, stars, and fire. The chief god was Huitzlopochtli [wē′tsē lō pōch′tlē], the god of war, to whom the Aztecs made human sacrifices. This sacrifice of human life was a part of Aztec civilization. Each year, hundreds of prisoners of war were led up the great stone steps of an altar, where they were killed. Their hearts were removed as offerings to the god of war. The Aztecs believed the gods demanded human sacrifice. One of the reasons they were nearly always at war was that they needed a constant supply of prisoners to be killed for their religious ceremonies.

From 1168 to 1521, the Aztecs dominated the area we now call *Mexico*. In 1521, they were conquered by Cortés, the well-known Spanish explorer. Montezuma [mon'tə zü'mə] was chosen as king of the Aztecs in 1503. The Aztec ruler was selected by a group of distinguished men. They chose a man who displayed outstanding valor or unusual knowledge. This process may seem democratic, but one can hardly say that democracy was practiced as we know it. Nevertheless, the Aztec king was chosen. He was not a hereditary ruler. The king of the Aztecs was a religious leader as well as a political ruler. Eventually, he became a god to be worshipped.

Although a king, Montezuma knew that he was not from the class from which rulers were usually chosen. For this reason he prepared himself to rule. He learned to read glyph, or picture, writing. He studied the religious practices of his people and he learned how to carry out the obligations the Aztec gods imposed upon him. He studied Aztec fighting techniques. Montezuma was the ninth monarch of the Aztec realm, and he was also its last.

How the Aztecs Lived*

For most Aztecs, the day began at 4:00 A.M., when they were awakened by the priests who blew shell trumpets. Farmers went to their fields. Others went about their own activities. Montezuma, at his capital at Tenochititlan [te nôch'tē tlän'], arose early to conduct religious practices. Since water was readily available, Aztecs took steam baths and washed carefully before beginning their working

*This section is based on Victor Von Hagen, *The Aztec: Man and Tribe* (New York: New American Library, 1958), pp. 67–71.

An Aztec mask. Such masks had many uses during Aztec religious ceremonies. How were war and religion related in Aztec culture?

day. Instead of soap, however, they used tree roots to clean themselves.

Supper included tortillas, enriched with turkey, duck, beans, or squash. Eaten during the early evening, about five o'clock, it was the largest meal of the day. The men of the family squatted on mats and helped themselves to food with their fingers. The women served them. Women did not eat with the men. After dark, family members worked by the light of burning pine splinters. Women did sewing, weaving, spinning, or made wine. Men made fish needles, arrowheads, or paddles.

Children were highly regarded, as were the mothers of many children. Because the Aztecs were constantly at war, it was important to have a steady supply of new soldiers. Children were well cared for. The gods were worshipped in hopes that the child would be born under a lucky sign. Children's names were especially important, and advice from religious leaders was anxiously sought before naming.

Aztec society was mobile, that is, people could rise to a higher class. Excellence in anything—farming, hunting, fighting, or even trading—could help a person move up the social ladder. Schooling was available for each group or clan into which the Aztecs were organized. At school, boys learned the arts of war and the myths and legends of their people. Some attempt was made to determine a child's aptitude. Was it for fighting, for making jewelry, or for entering the priesthood? Girls were not as well-educated. For the most part, they were expected to be good homemakers and mothers.

Atahualpa, an Inca leader.

ATHABALIBA
ultimus Rex Peruanorum

The Incas

Atahualpa [ä'tə wäl'pə] was ruler of the Inca Empire at its height in 1532. He ruled all the lands of the Andes from southern Colombia to southern Chile. The center of the empire was located at the magnificent capital of Cuzco [küs'kō].

One very important characteristic of the Inca Empire was its social and political structure. The emperor, known as the *Inca*, was regarded as a descendant of the sun god. He was himself regarded as a god. The empire was governed through high officials who were appointed by the Inca. Often these high officials were related to the Inca. The entire population was closely supervised and was expected to be absolutely loyal to the Inca. Each person was expected to work, at least part of the time, for the state.

Farming was made possible by widespread irrigation and terracing. The irrigation was necessary because much of the land was desert. Terracing was necessary because much of the land was mountainous. The llama [lä'mə] and the alpaca [al pak'ə] were domesticated farm animals. All land was owned by the Inca or the state. The growth and distribution of farm products was determined by the state. The average farmer could expect little more than what could be grown on the farm. During periods of famine, the state stored grain to be made available to the neediest. Those too old, too young, too sick, or physically handicapped were assured of food.

The Incas kept records by means of *quipus* [kē'püz]. These were knotted cords that indicated quantities or amounts of something. The Incas never developed a written language.

The capital, Cuzco, was connected to all parts of the empire by exceptionally good roads. Over these roads, runners provided communication throughout the empire.

How the Incas Lived*

The Incas were farmers. Upon arising at the break of day they went into the fields to work after the scantiest of breakfasts. In the afternoon the family gathered for a meal of corn and chili peppers. A soup made of sun-dried llama meat was often part of the midday meal. The last meal of the day was eaten between four and five o'clock. Men sat in an inner circle eating with their fingers, while women sat outside the circle with their backs to the men. Nights were cold because the Incas lived in the high mountains. Inca fuel, made from llama dung, gave limited warmth. Men described legends of battle

*This section is based on Victor W. Von Hagen, *Realm of the Incas* (New York: New American Library, 1957), pp. 52–57.

while they repaired their tools. Women prepared *aka* [ä′kä], a common beverage of the Incas. It is a mildly intoxicating drink still used today.

As in the Aztec civilization, children were important to the Incas. They were well cared for and were precious to the parents as well as to the state. The education of the child was taken on by the parents, who expected the children to copy them. Upon reaching their early teens, boys of the upper classes made a pilgrimage to Cuzco. A llama was sacrificed. A dab of its blood smeared on the boy's face was a mark that he was making his passage to maturity. A young man of the upper classes was trained to be a soldier or to help administer the state of the Inca emperor.

Usually, men and women of the Incas lived and died in the class into which

The ruins of the Inca fortress city of Macchu Picchu. The design and construction of Macchu Picchu indicate that the Incas had an impressive knowledge of engineering principles.

they were born. Women, however, had a better chance of moving into a higher class. If they were attractive, or especially good at weaving, cooking, or spinning, they might be taken to Cuzco to learn additional skills. Then perhaps they could marry a nobleman.

The Incas were a religious people but they did not perform human sacrifices as did the Aztecs. Prayers to the gods were accompanied by offerings of the first harvests of the fields. Religious practices were kept simple. However, on great occasions of state the official priesthood took part.

The life of the ordinary Inca was hard. The Incas, however, did not expect that it could be any other way.

Check in Here

1. List one major achievement of each of the following: (**a**) the Mayas; (**b**) the Incas; (**c**) the Aztecs.

2. How did the political structures of the Mayas, Incas, and Aztecs differ from one another?

3. How did the religious practices of the Incas, Aztecs, and Mayas resemble each other and differ from one another?

4. Describe the roles of women in the Maya, Aztec, and Inca societies.

AFRICA BEFORE THE COMING OF THE EUROPEANS

What We Know of Africa's Ancient Past*

Africa may well be the birthplace of humans. It is believed that by 10,000 B.C. three types of people were found living in Africa: Bushmen, Pygmies, and a Cau-

*This section is based on Donald L. Wiedner, *A History of Africa South of the Sahara* (New York: Random House, 1962), p. 16.

casian (white) group known as Cushites [küsh'ītz]. About 6,000 B.C., a date that corresponds roughly to the dawn of history in the Middle East, black people began to appear. At first they lived north of the Sahara [sə har'ə] (a desert in northern Africa), but not on the Mediterranean coast. Later, others lived in the Sahara.

At one time the Sahara was not as harsh a place as it is today. A French explorer, Henri Lhôte [lōt], crossed the Sahara in 1956 and found evidence that some farming had been carried on there until approximately 2000 B.C. He also found evidence that there had been enough vegetation to support cattle until about 1000 B.C. Even in the early Roman days, horses were still able to graze there. It was not until about 46 B.C., however, that the Sahara became so barren that it could no longer support farming or grazing. The Romans, at this time, introduced the camel as a means of transportation on the desert. This contrary but useful beast is still seen in Africa.

At some early date, perhaps as early as 5000 B.C. but maybe as late as 1500 B.C., black peoples in Africa developed farming communities. When people learned to plant seeds and produce their own food, there was no need for them to move from place to place in search of food. They were able to settle down and build a stable society. Early Africans made some outstanding contributions to farming. They developed a cotton plant. The fibers of this plant were used to make cloth. Plants which produced vegetable oil were also grown.

Contact Between the Ancient World and Africa

What is known about Africa comes mostly from the writings of the Egyptians, Phoenicians, Greeks, and Romans. According to hieroglyphic inscriptions on the tomb of an Egyptian noble, the

Egyptians had penetrated inner Africa as early as 2340 B.C. Trade led to conquest. An expedition during the reign of Queen Hatshepsut was said to have reached the cape where the Gulf of Aden meets the Arabian Sea.

The Greek historian Herodotus tells us that about 600 B.C., Phoenician sailors sailed around Africa on a journey that took three years. Probably the most extensive ancient exploration of Africa was carried out by the Carthaginian sailor Hanno [han'ō]. About 450 B.C., he sailed first along the Atlantic coast of Africa, where he founded seven towns. He then explored as far south as modern Sierra Leone [sē er'ə lē ōn']. A flourishing trade was established between Phoenicia and parts of Africa.

After Carthage was defeated in the Punic Wars, its outposts in North Africa became part of a Roman province. This province was given the name *Africa* [af'ri kə]. As greater parts of the continent were discovered and explored, the name Africa was applied to an even wider area. In time it came to mean the entire continent. From bases in North Africa, the Romans traded with some countries south of the Sahara. However, they rarely penetrated much of Sub-Saharan Africa. They crossed the Sahara or traded along the coasts for gold and ivory. Slaves were brought from the African interior by North African Berbers [bėr'bərz] to the Roman trading stations.

Foreign contacts with Africa were mostly rather limited. People were ignorant of what the continent of Africa really looked like. Greek geographers guessed at the shape and size of Africa. On a map made by Eratosthenes, most of Sub-Saharan Africa just did not exist. On the other hand, Ptolemy's map showed Africa much larger than it actually was. These early maps were used by the Europeans when, much later, they began their explorations into the interior of Africa.

Early African farmers developed the cotton plant. Craftspeople dyed the fibers and wove cloth such as this piece from Ghana.

How the Kingdom of Ghana Rose and Fell

Ghana [gä'nə] is the name of the West African country located on the Gulf of Guinea [gin'ē]. As a colony of Great Britain it was known for many years as the Gold Coast. When it became an independent nation in 1957, it changed its name to one that was used in its pre-colonial past. *Ghana* was the title of the ruler of the nation that once ruled a large part of West Africa. Ghana also was the name of the land he ruled.

By the eleventh century, Ghana's power was near its peak. It had complete control over the trade routes between the salt mines in the Sahara and the gold mines on its southern boundaries. During the powerful reign of Tenkamenin [ten kə men'in], Ghana became a highly developed state. It had a monarchy similar to the monarchies that ruled in Europe at a later time.

In 1076, ten years after William the Conqueror had crossed the English

African Civilization

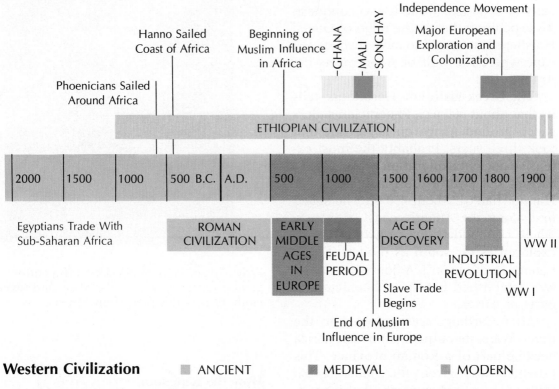

What civilizations existed in Africa before the arrival of the Europeans?

Channel to establish his rule in Britain, Tenkamenin's empire fell. The Almoravids [al′mə rä′vidz], a Muslim group, invaded the kingdom. Although their power was short-lived, Ghana never recovered. Tenkamenin had been a powerful ruler. However, the lands he ruled and the exact borders of his empire were never clearly defined. Rival chiefs were eager to establish themselves as monarchs of a great land. Tribal warfare and petty jealousies interfered with the restoration of the kingdom. Ghana began to decline.

How Rivalry Weakened the Early West African Nations

The history of West Africa from the fall of Ghana in the eleventh century to the coming of Europeans during the fifteenth century may be told in the rivalry of two black Muslim nations. These were Mali [mä′lē], sometimes Melle [mel] or Mandingo [man ding′gō], and Songhay [song′ā]. The modern Republic of Mali takes its name from the black kingdom Mali. This kingdom acquired a firm grip on Ghana in the thirteenth century.

Under its most famous ruler, Mansa Musa [man′sə mü′sə] (1307–32), Muslim scholarship advanced greatly. The city of Timbuktu [tim′buk tü′] became a great center of culture and commerce. Mansa Musa ruled an empire as large as all of Western Europe. Europe, at this time, was still in the feudal era. The European monarchs could make their power felt only over a small area. At a time of chaos and war in Europe, Mansa Musa's realm was orderly and stable.

African States Before European Colonization

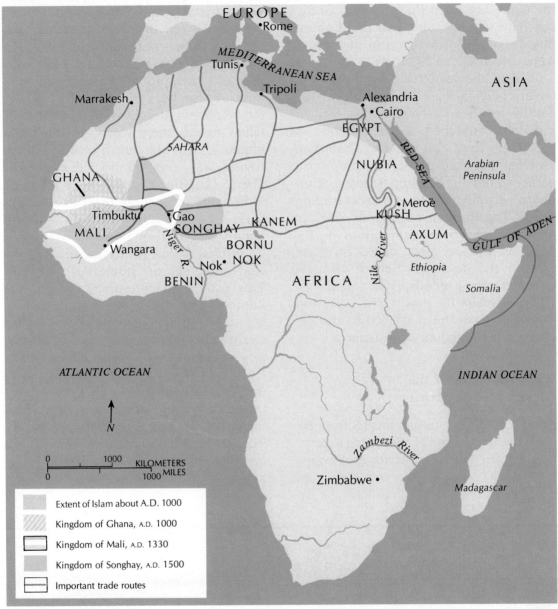

- What ancient states were located along the Nile River?
- Along the Niger River?
- What important ancient African city was located south of the Zambezi River?
- About how many kilometers (miles) did traders have to travel between Marrakesh and Timbuktu?

The kingdoms of Ghana and of Mali depended for wealth and power on the control of the salt and gold trade. Rivalry for the control of trade routes meant that warfare on the borders of the empire was frequent. Other blacks, Arabs, and, later, Europeans tried to take this control away from Mali. The Songhay was a black group displeased at living under the Mali. These people rose up and took over

Timbuktu in 1468. In 1492, Askia [ä′skī ə] the Great ascended the throne of Songhay. This was the same year that Columbus discovered America and the Moors were driven out of Spain.

Under the leadership of Askia the Great (1492–1529), a Muslim black, the empire reached its height. This African kingdom stretched 3,218 kilometers (1,500 mi.) from east to west. Timbuktu, its chief city, had a fine mosque and a great school of Koranic studies. Timbuktu became famous as a great trading center. The tin and leather goods of Songhay were eagerly sought. From as far north as Morocco great camel caravans crossed the desert of Sahara and exchanged various goods, gold, and slaves. In time, rivalry for power, civil war, and invasions from the north led to the decline of the kingdom of Songhay.

What We Know of the History of East Africa

Up to now the discussion has focused on the larger kingdoms of West Africa. Now we turn briefly to East Africa and examine its history. Ethiopia [ē′thē ō′pē ə], whose history can be dated from at least 1000 B.C., is one of the world's oldest nations with a continuous history. The Queen of Sheba, who visited King Solomon of Israel, probably came from Ethiopia. As far back as the sixth century, B.C., Hebrews sought refuge in Ethiopia when their country was overrun by Babylonia. During the fourth century, Christianity was adopted by Ethiopia. The *Coptic* [kop′tik] *Church*, as it is called today, differs in some of its basic ideas from most other Christian groups. Today, one-third of Ethiopia is Muslim.

In East Africa, Arabs traded along the coast and set up numerous outposts. This group of communities, from the Zambezi [zam bē′zē] River north to what is today Somalia [sō mä′lē ə], was collectively called *Zenj* [zenj]. Each community developed as a separate city-state. Each was responsible for its own economy and its own defense. In these cities a mixed Bantu and Arabic language developed. It is known as *Swahili* [swä hē′lē]. This language became and remains the language of much of East Africa.

The ancient African city of Timbuktu. Salt was the most precious trade item of this city. Camel caravans carried huge salt slabs to bartering points in the surrounding area.

Arabs traveled into Africa as far south as Southern Rhodesia [rō dē′zhə]. Here was built Zimbabwe [zim bä′bwā], the famous city of stone. Discovered by explorers in 1871, the stone structures of Zimbabwe are believed to have been built by the Bantu during the fourteenth or fifteenth century. The buildings were elaborately ornamented in gold, which probably came from the rich mines nearby.

How Islam Influenced Africa

Islam sought converts in inner Africa. This religion was more appealing to Africans than was Christianity. The success of Christianity in Ethiopia was the exception rather than the rule.

The coming of Islam brought a religion of a high order to the nations of Sub-Saharan Africa. It gave a measure of religious unity that might otherwise have been lacking. It exposed the people of inner Africa to a culture and a civilization from which they willingly and quickly learned much. They acquired a written language with which they were able to carry on trade and commerce and to write down their own history and oral traditions. They adopted a system of law to govern trade and commerce and to help in building a political organization.

Islam differed markedly from country to country. The religion of Islam permitted adaptations according to the traditions and customs of the people. As a result, the Islamic faith of Sub-Saharan Africa became quite different from what it was in Cairo or Bagdad. Moreover, it never entirely replaced the traditional religion of the Africans, who believed in the worship of natural objects.

Why the Kingdoms of Africa Declined

There were many reasons why the great kingdoms of Africa did not last. One was that they were vast in area and there were few inhabitants. A sparsely inhabited nation has difficulty in defending its territory against attackers.

A second reason for the fall of the great kingdoms of Ghana, Mali, and Songhay is that they had poorly defined borders. Because of this, they were fair game for those who desired their wealth.

A third reason was that each of the great African kingdoms was made up of many different peoples. Some who were unwilling to be ruled by others formed kingdoms of their own. In time, they grew powerful enough to challenge the large kingdoms. Often, people living within the borders of a kingdom were eager to rebel. They were willing to ally themselves with any new conqueror who came along.

Check in Here

1. How was the ancient history of Africa discovered?
2. Why were the ancient maps of Africa inaccurate?
3. Ghana, Mali, and Songhay were among the great kingdoms of Africa. Why did they disappear?
4. What do the ancient ruins at Zimbabwe tell us about the skills of Sub-Saharan Africans?
5. What was the influence of Islam on Sub-Saharan Africa?

AFRICA'S CONTRIBUTIONS TO CIVILIZATION

The Gifts of Africa to Art

African art has a tradition that goes back many thousands of years. While other ancient people of Africa, such as the Egyptians, worked in stone, those who lived in Africa south of the Sahara

A bronze sculpture from Benin, Nigeria.

bronze art. The portrait busts from this area made of ivory or bronze are highly prized today. The Benin method of casting in bronze has not yet been fully understood. African figures often had a lot of religious significance. In Nigeria, art expressed not only religious themes, but the power of the kingdom as well.

In African sculpture the shape of the human body was often distorted, or stylized. The body, eyes, neck, and shape of the head seem out of proportion. The distortion helped the worshipper communicate with his or her gods or ancestors. The freedom to show distortion encouraged originality of expression. African art forms had a great influence on such modern artists as Picasso [pi kä′sō] and Modigliani [mō dēg′lē ä′nē].

When Africans were sold as slaves to the New World, they took their artistic traditions with them. In the history of the United States, for example, there are noted Afro-American artists. Even before the American Revolution, Scipio Morehead was a black artist of some fame. Robert Duncanson (1817–72) became one of the finest landscape painters of America. The greatest Afro-American artist of the nineteenth century was Edward Bannister (1828–1901). Henry O. Tanner (1859–1937) was the first Afro-American artist to be elected to the National Academy of Design. He was also awarded the Legion of Honor by France.

Africa's Gifts to Music

It has been said that there are as many forms of African music as there are African languages. Drums, bells, whistles, rattles, and xylophones were among the major African musical instruments. The one-string bow and the many-stringed harp are also important.

The people of Africa had songs for planting, harvesting, fishing, and fighting. Percussion instruments (drums of

worked mainly in wood. Because stone endures and wood does not, we have far more evidence of artistic achievement in Africa north of the Sahara than south of it.

Africa is a vast continent. As a result, its art forms vary greatly from one area to another. From West Africa and Central Africa come some of the continent's richest and most original works of art. Probably Africa's greatest contribution to art has been in sculpture and in masks made of wood or ivory. Much of the art was made for religious observances. The wooden sculpture was often decorated with shells, feathers, beads, and ivory. Some of it was colorfully painted.

Besides sculpting in wood, many Africans, as in Nigeria, carved in ivory and cast in bronze. The area of Benin [be nēn′], in southwest Nigeria, was the center of

Albert John Luthuli
(1899–1967)

Over the years the Nobel Peace Prize has been awarded to three outstanding blacks: Dr. Ralph Bunche, the Reverend Martin Luther King, Jr., and Albert John Luthuli. Bunche and King were Americans. Luthuli was a Zulu chief living in the Republic of South Africa. Albert John Luthuli was born in 1899 to an upper-class family. His father was an interpreter at the Congregationalist mission, his mother a prominent member of the Zulu tribe, his uncle a Zulu chief.

Albert John Luthuli studied at a local mission school. After school, he tended cattle along with other school children. Luthuli became fluent in English and became a college instructor in 1921. In 1936, he was elected chief of a Zulu tribe. In this capacity Luthuli assumed a leadership role in fighting for the rights of blacks in what is now the Republic of South Africa. His activities on behalf of his country were opposed by the government of the Republic of South Africa. Although he preached nonviolence, he was arrested a number of times. As punishment he was confined to rural areas, where it was thought he would have less influence on his people. While confined, Luthuli spent much of his time cutting sugar cane. He nevertheless retained leadership in the fight for the freedom of blacks to come and go as they wished in the Republic of South Africa. As president of the African National Congress, he became a public figure and continued the struggle for the rights of blacks.

Luthuli was awarded the 1960 Nobel Peace Prize "because in his fight against racial discrimination he had always worked for nonviolent methods." The announcement of the award of the Nobel Peace Prize to Albert John Luthuli was hailed by the world, with the notable exception of South Africa. After great reluctance, the government of the Republic of South Africa agreed to allow Luthuli to go to Oslo, Norway, to receive his much-merited award. When he made his speech accepting the Nobel Peace Prize, he was dressed in rich tribal costume with a blue and black robe, a leopardskin cap fringed with monkey tails, and a necklace made of leopards' teeth. In this way, he expressed in both his words and in his person the deep attachment of blacks the world over for their African cultural heritage. "I think as an African," he once said. "I act as an African, and as an African I worship the God whose children we all are."

Luthuli died in 1967 under somewhat obscure circumstances. It is not clear whether he died from natural causes. His life was an example of how, despite great obstacles, one person can make a difference in the lives of others by leadership and courage. He drew on his rich Zulu heritage to ennoble blacks and give them confidence to continue their struggle for greater freedom.

African instruments. The Africans used everyday materials such as wood and hides to make these instruments.

various kinds) were particularly important. The best of these drums accompanied ceremonies at religious festivals. Messages from one tribe to another were quickly and effectively sent by the beat of the drum.

The dance has always been important in Africa. There were dances of joy and dances of sadness. There were war dances, and there were peace dances. There were dances for religious observances, and ones for the sheer pleasure of dancing. Drums provided the beat for African dances. Participants were professional dancers, warriors off to battle, or

priests leading a religious ritual. Included in African dance were the arts of *mimicry* [mim'ik rē] and *pantomime* [pan'tə mīm']. Both are valued expressions of dramatic art today. In mimicry, the sounds of birds and animals are imitated. In pantomime, the actions of animals or the folk tales of the tribe are dramatized without the use of words.

Much of modern Western music (jazz, blues) and dance, as well as spirituals, have at least some of their roots in African artistic and musical traditions. Under the impact of European civilization, however, African art, music, and dance have been undergoing rapid change. Some art forms are disappearing as tribal elders die. New art forms are emerging under the influence of a reborn nationalism and independence.

Africa's Gifts to Literature

The Africans developed an oral tradition of storytelling and history. Out of the folklore of myths, riddles, proverbs, and tales grew an African literature. Often literature was accompanied by song, dance, and responses in unison by the listeners. Professional storytellers, men and women known as *griots* [grē'ōts], went through a long period of preparation. Griots were supposed to have faultless memories. It was their responsibility to learn the history and tales of their people and to repeat them from memory without error.

1. How does the evidence of artistic achievements among the ancient people of North Africa differ from that of Sub-Saharan Africa?

2. Describe briefly the contributions of Africa to (a) art and sculpture; (b) music; (c) literature.

3. Describe ways in which African art and music have influenced our own American culture.

4. Is it appropriate to call a griot a historian? Why or why not?

REVIEWING THE BASICS

The first Americans were the Native Americans of North and South America. The Mayas, Aztecs, and Incas developed highly sophisticated civilizations. They developed a calendar and built pyramids for religious purposes. They were good astronomers; and some, like the Aztecs and Mayas, developed a written language. The people of Sub-Saharan Africa developed a precious oral tradition that gives us insight into their ancient past.

The roots of the civilizations in South America are mostly unknown. The written glyph language of the Mayas has yet to be understood. We do not know all the details of how the Incas could keep a unified empire together, from southern Colombia to southern Chile, without having a written language. The quipu, or knotted rope, was their only form of record keeping. However, their statistics are outstanding for their accuracy.

In Sub-Saharan Africa, a number of mighty kingdoms rose and fell. These included the West African country of Ghana, which reached the height of its ancient glory during the reign of Tenkamenin. The people of Mali, too, developed strong traditions under their king Mansa Musa. In Sub-Saharan Africa, Muslim practices grew in influence. In East Africa, an old city of stone, Zimbabwe, was discovered and is believed to have been built by the Bantu people. A sparse population spread out over a great area contributed to the fall of great ancient African kingdoms. Wood, ivory, and bronze sculptures are among Sub-Saharan Africa's artistic contributions. In music, percussion instruments (drums of various kinds) were important.

The Indian nations of South America had little contact with the world outside the Americas, although the Mayas were seafarers. The pyramids and their calendars were altogether their own. When the Europeans came to South America, the Aztecs, Incas, and Mayas were already weakened peoples. The Spaniards hastened their fall. In Sub-Saharan Africa, the African nations fell under the European onslaught.

REVIEWING THE HIGHLIGHTS

People to Identify

Mayas	Edward Bannister	Bantu
Aztecs	Incas	Scipio Morehead
Tenkamenin	Montezuma	Atahualpa
Askia the Great	Henri Lhôte	Mansa Musa
Robert Duncanson	Almoravids	Henry O. Tanner

Places to Locate

Ghana	Peru	Zimbabwe
Songhay	Mexico	Timbuktu
Zenj	Central America	Cape Horn
Yucatan	Andes	Sahara
Latin America	Atacama Desert	Somalia
Amazon	Cuzco	Benin
Chile	Caribbean	Nigeria
Brazil	Mali	Venezuela

Terms to Understand

Pre-Columbian America	Coptic Church	Swahili
Sub-Saharan Africa	griot	ghana
glyph	quipu	

Mastering the Fundamentals

1. List the countries that make up Latin America. How did Latin America get its name?
2. Why have the Latin American climate and land been obstacles to its development?
3. How did the Native Americans get to the Americas?
4. Despite the existence of a form of picture writing, we do not know a great deal about the Mayas. Why not?
5. Why are we unable to speak of a Mayan nation?
6. The Incas kept an enormous empire together. Yet they had neither the wheel nor a written language. How did they do it?
7. When Henri Lhôte crossed the Sahara in 1956 what did he learn?
8. Describe the early contacts ancient Egypt, Greece, and Rome had with Sub-Saharan Africa.
9. What were three important features of Aztec civilization?
10. What did Sub-Saharan Africa contribute to agriculture?
11. Explain the rise and fall of Ghana.
12. What practices among the Incas made farming possible?
13. Why did Islam appeal to the people of Sub-Saharan Africa?
14. How did African music influence modern music?
15. Why did African artists distort the human body? How did African art influence modern art?
16. What was the religious significance of African art?

17. What is the griot tradition in Africa?
18. What did Sub-Saharan Africa contribute to dance?
19. Describe the ancient city of Zimbabwe. What is its historical significance?

THINGS TO DO

1. Draw a map of Pre-Columbian America and Sub-Saharan Africa showing the location of the following: (a) Mayas; (b) Aztecs; (c) Incas; (d) Ghana; (e) Mali; (f) Songhay; (g) Zimbabwe.
2. Prepare a report using illustrations to show the influence of Sub-Saharan Africa on: (a) modern art; (b) modern music.
3. Read and report on Thornton Wilder's famous story, *The Bridge of San Luis Rey*. In your report emphasize such subjects as: (a) Incan bridge building; (b) Indian traditions.

YOU ARE THE HISTORIAN

Below is an illustration showing two forms of glyph, or picture writing. Study the illustrations and answer the questions that follow. Discuss your answers with your class.

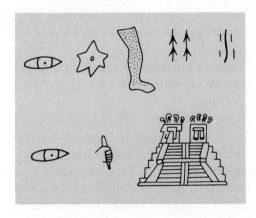
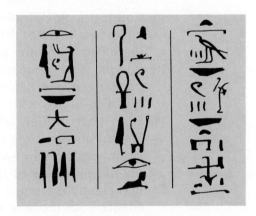

1. Which of the above is Egyptian writing and which is Aztec writing? How can you tell?
2. Form a theory about the story that is being told in each picture. Defend your point of view.
3. Form a theory about the age of each form of writing. Defend your point of view.
4. Would you regard these illustrations as primary or secondary sources? Explain your answer.
5. What questions about the writing above might a historian ask?

UNIT ACTIVITIES

1. Draw a map of the world. On it show the location of those areas that may be called cradles of civilization. Which modern countries are located in those regions?
2. Prepare a time line showing the leading events in the history of ancient Egypt, Greece, Rome, China, and India.
3. Using the materials in this unit plus those in your library, compare and contrast the role of women in each of the following ancient civilizations: Babylonia, Egypt, Greece, Rome, India, and China.
4. Make a collection of newspaper articles showing recent archaeological discoveries in Latin America and Sub-Saharan Africa.
5. Write a composition with the title "Hero or Scoundrel?" In it discuss the life of one person mentioned in this unit about whom some doubt exists. Tamerlane, Socrates, Nero, and Shih Huang Ti are possible subjects.
6. As a radio or television sportscaster, report on a gladiatorial contest held in the Colosseum.
7. Prepare an illustrated talk on: (a) the teachings of Buddha; or (b) religious practices among the Aztecs.
8. Prepare an illustrated talk on any buildings in your community that have Greek or Roman architectural features. You might take pictures of these buildings for your report.
9. Conduct a mock trial of Socrates. The class can serve as jury, while two teams of three students can serve as the lawyers for the defense and the prosecution.
10. Buddha and Confucius were contemporaries. Prepare for dramatization on television a conversation that these two might have had with each other.
11. From travel folders of Korea and Japan cut out pictures of famous ancient sites a tourist would want to visit. In a paragraph, explain why each is important to a better understanding of the history of those countries.
12. In oral reports, compare and contrast the Olympics of ancient Greece with those of today. Among the topics to be considered are: (a) purposes; (b) importance; (c) participants; (d) honors to the winners.
13. Hold a panel discussion with your classmates on the question: "How Does One Explain the Interest in Sub-Saharan Africa?"
14. If you live in or near a large city you will probably find restaurants serving Greek, Indian, Japanese, Chinese, and Mexican food. Get the menus of these restaurants and report to the class what they reveal about food preferences.
15. Prepare a group report on the building of one or more of the following: (a) the Great Pyramid at Gizeh; (b) the Parthenon; (c) the Colosseum; (d) the Taj Mahal; (e) the Stone City of

Zimbabwe. For each, indicate the labor that was used and how it was obtained, the length of time it took to build, the purpose of building, the way the building was paid for. What do these buildings tell us about the society that built them?

BIBLIOGRAPHY

*Best, Allena C. *Honey of the Nile.* Oxford University Press. An entertaining story of a trip down the Nile River in ancient Egypt.

Ceram, C. W. *Gods, Graves and Scholars.* Knopf. This is an account of archaeologists at work among the world's ancient ruins.

Chander, Anna. *Dragons on Guard.* J. D. Lippincott. A book that describes the luxury of the T'ang, Sung, and Yüan dynasties.

Chiera, Edward. *They Wrote in Clay.* University of Chicago Press. A beautifully illustrated account of the ancient culture of Babylonia.

*Coolidge, Olivia F. *Egyptian Adventures.* Houghton Mifflin Co. A book of short stories based on life in ancient Egypt.

Davidson, Basil. *The African Past.* Little, Brown & Company. Legend and myth are skillfully woven into history.

Farb, Peter. *Humankind.* Houghton Mifflin Company. A fascinating account of humankind's origins.

Gaer, Joseph. *The Fables of India.* Little, Brown & Company. Stories from the *Panchatantra* and other great books of India.

*Gere, Frances. *Boy of Babylon.* Longmans Green & Co. A history about a youth in the time of Hammurabi.

Gunther, John. *Alexander the Great.* Random House. A biography of a colorful historical figure.

Harris, Marvin. *The Origins of Cultures.* Random House. A discussion of the interaction of ecology and technology in the development of culture.

Heaton, Marc. *Everyday Life in Old Testament Times.* Scribner. This volume describes daily life among the ancient Hebrews.

Komroff, Manuel. *Julius Caesar.* Julian Messner. A simply-written account of Rome's most famous son.

Kumer, Frederick A. *The First Days of History.* Doubleday & Company. A book that tells about the ancient civilizations in a most simple way.

Lamb, Harold. *Alexander of Macedon.* Doubleday & Company. An exciting biography of an outstanding hero.

Lamb, Harold. *Hannibal: One Man Against Rome.* Bantam. This is an easy-to-read biography of the only man who tried but failed to conquer Rome.

*Lawrence, Isabelle. *Gift of the Golden Cup.* The Bobbs-Merrill Company. A swiftly-moving tale of pirates in the time of Caesar.

Leakey, Richard E. and Roger Lewin. *Origins.* Dutton. Famous anthropologists speculate on the origins of the human species.

Seeger, Elizabeth. *Pageant of Chinese History.* Longmans Green & Company. The sweep of Chinese history from its beginning to nearly modern times, engagingly told.

Von Hagen, Victor. *The Aztec Man and Tribe; World of the Maya; Realm of the Incas.* New American Library. These three books skillfully survey the old civilizations of Mexico, Central, and South America.

*Indicates Fiction.

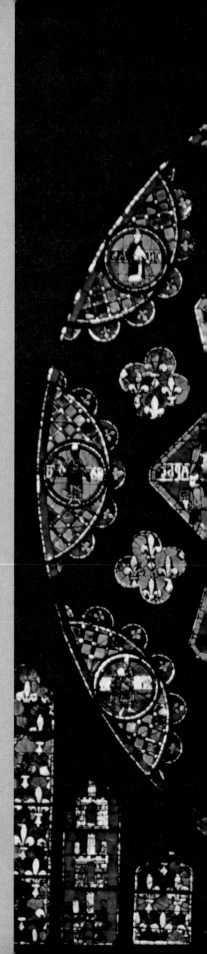

UNIT
II

A Journey from Medieval to Modern Times

North Rose Window, Chartres Cathedral

154

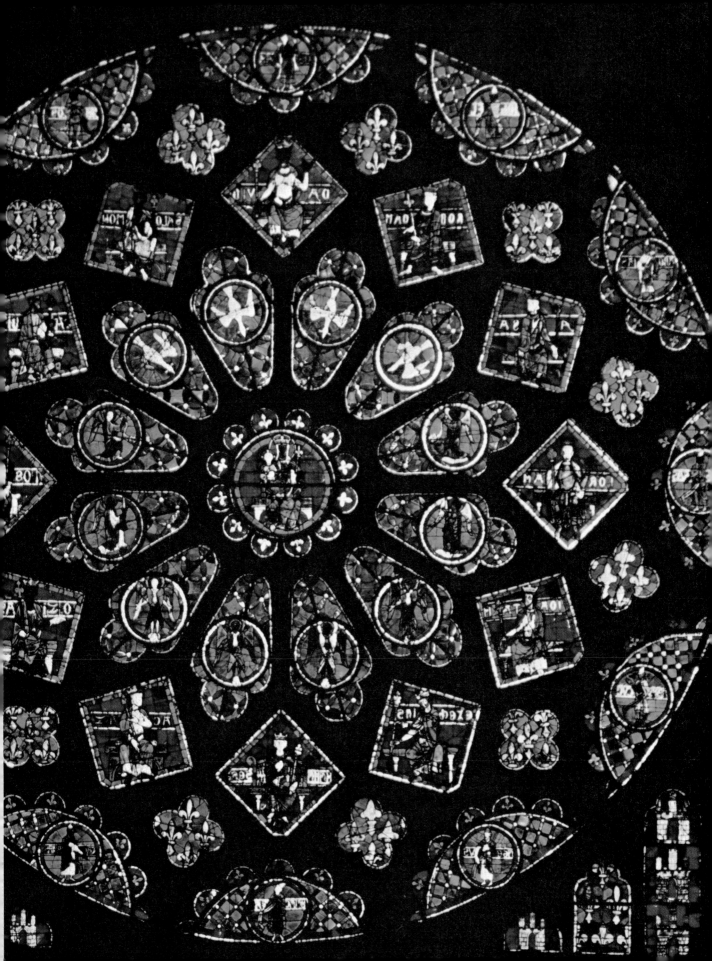

A page from a Byzantine manuscript

The Medieval World: Byzantium and Islam During the Middle Ages

Historically, the *Middle Ages* is that period between the fall of Rome in A.D. 476 and the discovery of America in 1492. It is a period that stands between ancient history and modern history. These dates, however, are more convenient than precise. As you learn about the Middle Ages, also called the *Medieval* [mē′dē′vəl] *Period,* you will discover that the roots of modern times may be found in the Middle Ages.

The Middle Ages was a time of uneven growth in Europe. The culture of ancient Greece and Rome seemed lost. Toward the end of the Middle Ages during the *Feudal* [fyüd′əl] *Period,* land, castles, knights, and serfs were controlled by the nobles. These nobles often fought each other to gain more power.

During the Middle Ages a flourishing civilization developed in the Byzantine [biz′ən tēn] Empire in southeast Europe. The Muslim civilization was flourishing in the Middle East. The modern world has ties to these civilizations.

THE POLITICS OF BYZANTIUM

The Byzantine Empire

The Byzantine culture of southeastern Europe gets its name from the ancient city of Byzantium, which in turn owes its name to its mythical founder, Byzas [bī′zəs]. The city was rebuilt by Emperor Constantine. It was renamed Constantinople [kon′stan tə nō′ pəl] and became the capital of the Eastern Roman Empire, which historians call the *Byzantine Empire*. When Rome fell, the Byzantine Empire lived on. While Western Europe struggled to gain a high level of economic development and political stability, the Byzantine Empire thrived.

The ancient city of Byzantium is today the modern city of Istanbul [is′tan būl′]. It is one of the most strategically located cities in the world. A careful study of a map will tell you why Byzantium's location was important in ancient times. Notice that the city of Byzantium is surrounded on three sides by water. Byzantium is located on both sides of the Bosphorous [bos′fər əs]. It is at the entrance to the Sea of Marmara [mär′mə rə]. To the northeast lies the entrance to the Black Sea. To the southwest lie the Dardanelles [där′də nelz′], through which ships can pass into the Aegean and from there into the Mediterranean. The Dardanelles, the Sea of Marmara, and the Bosphorous form a water passage that divides Europe from Asia. From the fall of Rome in A.D. 476 until 1453, when the Turks captured Constantinople, Byzantium was the nerve center of a great civilization and a great empire.

Geographically, the extent of the Byzantine Empire is difficult to define. This is because it alternately grew with conquest and shrank with defeat. Present-day Greece, Turkey, Bulgaria, Hungary, Yugoslavia, and Romania were areas once part of the Byzantine Empire.

The Byzantine Throne

In the Byzantine Empire, the emperor was all powerful. He was not, however, worshipped as a god. The emperor believed he was a servant of God and that God meant him to be the ruler. The major emperors of the Byzantines were Justinian [jus tin′ē ən] (483–565), Heraclius [her′ə klī′əs] (575–641), Leo III [lē′ō] (717–741), Basil I [baz′əl] (812–886), and Basil II (958–1025). Of these, Justinian was the most important. Justinian tried, but failed, to reunite the Eastern and Western Roman Empires. He was able to encourage trade between the two empires. The Italian cities of Venice and Ravenna became important trade centers. Trade helped spread the great culture of Byzantium to Italy and on to Western Europe.

The Byzantine throne was not necessarily hereditary, although in many cases it was. A future emperor was chosen by the reigning ruler with help from the army, the senate, the people, and the church. In the Byzantine Empire the empress often held and exercised a great deal of power. The portrait of the empress appeared on the coins of the realm. Sometimes empresses ruled alone and exercised full power. The Empress Theodora [thē'ə dôr'ə] (d. 548) was a constant, skillful, and cunning advisor to Emperor Justinian. Irene, the mother of Constantine VI (752–803), later overthrew her son. Between 797 and 802, she ruled Byzantium alone as empress.

Byzantine Emperor Justinian and his court. Did Justinian succeed in his plan to reunite the Roman Empire?

Under Basil II the Byzantine civilization reached its height. Maintaining a large empire required a strong military force and an effective group of administrators. The *Basileu* [bäz'əl yü] (King of Kings), as the emperor of Byzantium came to be called, ruled absolutely. There was much greater wealth, pomp, and ceremony surrounding the emperor of Byzantium than the emperor of Rome—even when the Roman Empire was at its height. The enormous wealth, the many servants, the marble halls, and the gilded columns impressed many visiting rulers from lesser states. They were humbled even before they were presented to the Byzantine rulers.

Constantinople was the center of the Byzantine Empire. It was from there that the emperor ruled. The empire was divided into military districts. Each of these was ruled by a general who was directly responsible to the emperor. Soldiers in the district armies fought for the emperor in return for the land on which they lived. Fighting for their own farms made them brave and loyal fighters.

Byzantine Military Power

The Byzantines were nearly always at war, and warfare became to them almost a fine art. Byzantine armies had intelligent leaders. Soldiers were carefully trained and armed. The music of military bands sent soldiers off to battle in high spirits. Mirrors were used to flash signals for attack or retreat. Later, a medical corps brought the wounded back from battle for the finest medical aid that was then available.

The Byzantine navy was no less renowned than its army. It took exceptional naval skill to launch 1,330 ships in a campaign against an enemy. This was done in warfare with Crete. The Byzantine navy used an ancient Greek device known as *Greek Fire,* which was a combi-

The Byzantine Empire

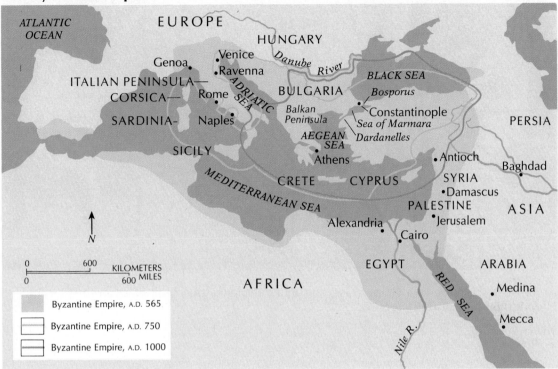

The size of the Byzantine Empire changed throughout its long history. This map shows the Byzantine Empire at three stages.
- What area did the Byzantine Empire control when Justinian ruled?
- During which of three periods shown on the map did the Byzantine Empire control Rome? Jerusalem? North Africa?

nation of naphtha and sulphur. Greek Fire could burn a ship on water. It proved to be a most effective defense against those who tried to defeat Byzantium by sea power.

In the Byzantine Hippodrome

The *Hippodrome* [hip'ə drōm'] of Constantinople was the scene of exciting chariot races. The Hippodrome was also a kind of parliament. Rival *demes* [dēmz], known as Blues and Greens, and their supporters, cheered and booed their favorite charioteers. Demes were political parties. The races were used as an opportunity to express political views. The demes cheered emperors whose policies they liked and jeered those whose policies they disliked. The demes represented opposing points of view on many economic, political, religious, and social questions. In general, the Blues represented the aristocrats and the Greens the working classes. The Blues also stood for orthodoxy (strict observance) in religion. The Greens preferred or sought religious change. Usually, the emperor was supported by one or the other of the demes.

Chariot races at the Hippodrome frequently ended with a political riot. Often, the riots spilled over into the streets and one party would seek to destroy the

159

An ancient sculpture of a chariot race not unlike the ones that took place in the Hippodrome of Constantinople.

homes of the other. It was during a great riot in Constantinople that a church was destroyed. A new church was built in its place. It became the world famous St. Sophia [sō fē′ ə]. By the eighth century the power of the demes was substantially reduced, and the role of the emperor became more secure and powerful.

The strength of Byzantine emperors was reinforced by the support they received from the church. The church was actually an arm of government, and a willing supporter of the emperor. It was a political as well as religious force.

Check in Here

1. List the bodies of water that surrounded Byzantium.

2. How were Byzantine emperors chosen?

3. Why was Byzantium successful in warfare?

THE RELIGION AND ECONOMY OF BYZANTIUM

The Eastern Church

Constantine was the first Christian emperor of the Roman Empire. Those who followed him as emperors of the Byzantine Empire were also Christians. Up to about the fifth century, the Bishop of Rome, the pope, was looked upon as the head of all Christian churches. However, a number of disagreements developed between the *Eastern Church*, and what became known as the *Roman Catholic Church*. These disagreements were political and religious. (The Eastern Church is also known as the Orthodox Church and the Greek Orthodox Church.)

The first religious controversy had to do with the nature of Jesus. Did he have one nature, divine, or two natures, human and divine? The pope believed in the idea that Jesus had two natures. The *Monophysites*, who were important in the churches of the East, believed Jesus had

Empress Theodora
(d. 548)

Procopius [prō kō′pē əs] was a contemporary Byzantine historian. He called Emperor Justinian and Empress Theodora (husband and wife) "fiends in human form." This was probably an extreme view by a biased historian, although Theodora was widely hated and widely envied. It was the custom for Byzantine emperors of those days to choose as empress a woman who pleased them regardless of her social class. Justinian chose Theodora as empress because she was beautiful and had a captivating personality. Justinian met Theodora at the Hippodrome where she had been a dancer and entertainer. These professions were not well-regarded at that time. The nobility neither forgave nor forgot Theodora's lowly origins.

Despite her humble background, Theodora was a woman of iron will. She would let nothing stand in the way of her ambition. She was cruel. She wanted and held power, sharing such power reluctantly but loyally with Justinian. Her political judgment was shrewd. She was devoted to establishing the absolute power of the emperor over the realm. She was known as *Basilissa* [baz′il i′sə] (Queen of Queens). Emperor Justinian consulted her on critical matters of state before reaching a decision. During the serious Nika [ni′kə] riot (532) in Constantinople between the Blues and Greens (see p. 159), the violence grew so great that Justinian was on the verge of abdicating, that is, giving up his throne. It is believed that Theodora strengthened his will and encouraged him to quell the riot with the words, "The imperial purple is a glorious shroud."

Theodora died in 548, but her likeness can be seen in a sixth century mosaic beside one of her husband in the church of San Vitale [san′ vē täl′ē] in Ravenna, Italy. This mosaic in a church, distant from Byzantium, testifies to Theodora's enormous influence during the early days of the Eastern Roman empire.

one nature (mono or single). At the Council of Chalcedon [kal′si′don], in 451, Pope Leo I decreed that Jesus, although one person, had two natures. This doctrine did not satisfy the religious leaders of the Eastern (Orthodox) Church. For one thing, they did not like the fact that the Roman pope had decided for them and thus made them dependent on him. For another, the doctrine itself did not satisfy the powerful Monophysites.

The second religious controversy had

to do with the question of whether or not images were to be allowed in the church. The Eastern Church opposed the use of images. The Western Church believed that images were essential in helping people picture the divine. The controversy raged during the papacy of Leo III (795–816). Like the Monophysite controversy, it was never fully resolved and contributed to the permanent separation of the Eastern and Western Churches in 1054.

This division, or *schism* [siz′əm], was political as well as religious. During the Middle Ages, the Roman Catholic Church of the West was more powerful than the Western monarchs. The Bishop of Rome grew powerful and was recognized as the pope. The patriarchs [pā′trē ärks′], or religious leaders of Constantinople, Alexandria, Antioch, and Jerusalem were unwilling to recognize the power of the pope. They were unwilling to recognize the decision of Pope Leo I in the controversy over the nature of Jesus. They were unwilling to recognize the decision of Leo III on the matter of the use of images in the church. In the East, the emperors of Byzantium dominated the Eastern Church in a way that no emperor of the West could dominate the pope. The Byzantines were angry when the pope took it upon himself to preside over the coronation of Charlemagne as emperor of the Romans. (See p. 178.)

Medieval History

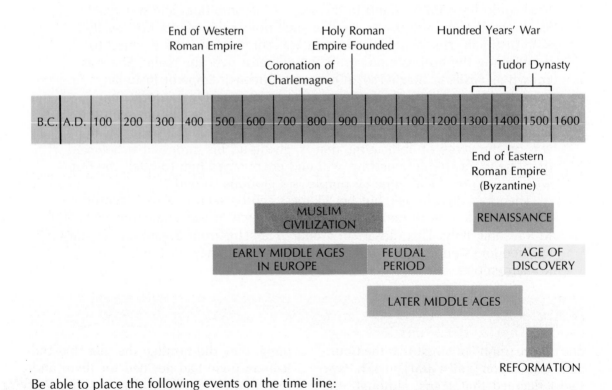

Be able to place the following events on the time line:

395	division of the Roman Empire	732	battle of Tours
476	fall of Western Roman Empire	1066	William invaded England
622	the hegira	1453	fall of Byzantine Empire

The schism (split) between the Eastern Orthodox Church and the (Western) Roman Catholic Church continues today. Throughout history attempts to reconcile the views of these two churches have been unsuccessful.

It is hard to appreciate the influence of religion in the lives of the Byzantines. From birth until death, church leaders were consulted for every important decision that had to be made. In political and intellectual life, as in people's personal lives, the role of the Eastern Church was ever present. For men of high intelligence, the church offered great opportunities for advancement. A career in the church was very desirable.

All Byzantines were caught up in religious questions about the nature of the *Trinity* (union of Father, Son, and Holy Ghost) and the relationship between the human and the divine. The quarrels that took place over issues were not confined to church or intellectual circles. These questions moved the population as a whole and were discussed among soldiers during their off hours and between merchants and customers. Questions of religion dominated daily conversation.

The Eastern Church dominated the political, social, artistic, and personal lives of the people of Byzantium. It affected the economic life as well.

How the Byzantines Earned a Living

Most people in the Byzantine Empire farmed for a living. Trade and commerce, however, were more important. The wealthy merchants of the world and their goods went to Constantinople. Animal skins and furs, salt, wine, slaves, spices, and precious gems were among the common articles of trade.

Later, silk became a major item of Byzantine wealth. It was about A.D. 550 that the Byzantines learned the secret of silk making. For hundreds of years this had been known only to the Chinese. Legend had it that two monks brought silkworm eggs to Constantinople in the hollowed out parts of their walking sticks. From this unusual beginning, a great silk industry, controlled by the emperor, grew and prospered. It added to the wealth of the Byzantine Empire.

In the ancient Roman world trade and commerce were not highly regarded activities. People of noble birth generally shunned engaging in business. In Constantinople the opposite was true. The emperors and nobility of Byzantium were deeply concerned about the economy of the nation and encouraged business activities of all types. It was Justinian who sent monks to China to bring back the knowledge of silk making.

Constantinople was a city of commerce. It was an important manufacturing city. Cloth, jewelry, metal, and enamelware were made using the latest methods. It was in Constantinople that master builders of churches, palaces, and other great buildings learned their trade. So did decorative artists. The city of Constantinople became a commercial center. A rich variety of goods on their way to Asia and Europe passed through it.

Because of its vital role in the economy of the empire, the city of Constantinople was governed separately. It had a police force to catch criminals and courts of law to determine if they were guilty. Workers were organized into trade guilds. Those merchants who tried to cheat buyers were punished by the guilds. The economic vitality of the Byzantine Empire was one reason for its long life. Because it was a dynamic and prosperous empire, it could support a huge government bureaucracy, an extravagant court, and costly wars.

1. How were government and religion related in Byzantium?

2. What reasons explain the separation of the Eastern and Western churches?

3. How did the economy of Byzantium contribute to the strength of the empire?

4. How did Byzantium's attitude toward trade and commerce differ from that of ancient Rome?

THE BYZANTINE CONTRIBUTIONS TO CIVILIZATION

Byzantium's Achievements

For many years Latin was the language of the Byzantine government. It was then replaced by Greek. The great literature of Greece and Rome would have been lost forever if teachers, students, and monks in the Byzantine Empire had not copied them. Libraries and books, schools and teachers, played leading roles in the growth of Byzantine culture. Many of the emperors were themselves learned. Universities supplied educated people for government service. The missionaries Cyril and his brother Methodius knew the Slavic language and invented an alphabet that is still in use today by the Russians, Bulgarians, and Serbs. The brothers are sometimes called the "Apostles to the Slavs." The *Cyrillic* [sir ril'ik] *alphabet,* as it is called, played a significant role in bringing Eastern Orthodox Christianity to those countries.

The Byzantines lived according to Roman law, which dominated peoples' everyday lives. Roman law dominated the affairs of state as well. Emperor Justinian is remembered mostly for having his lawyers organize, simplify, and systematize the laws of ancient Rome.

The *Corpus Juris Civilis* [côr'pəs jü'ris ki vil'is], a Latin title which means the Body of Civil Law, was organized into four parts.

The first part of the collection of laws was the *Code,* which included all the laws since Emperor Hadrian (A.D. 76–138). The second was the *Digest,* which contained the laws of the Roman republic as well as a summary of opinions of famous lawyers. A general textbook on law was also prepared. This, the third part, was called the *Institutes.* Justinian's laws were in the *Novellae* [nō wel'ī]. While the first three volumes were written in Latin, this last was written in Greek. Eventually, Greek came to dominate and to squeeze out Latin as the language of the Byzantine Empire.

The Byzantines contributed a distinctive look to art and architecture. The church of St. Sophia was built in the sixth century and still stands in all its beauty. Its round dome, characteristic of Roman architecture, was fitted to a square building. Interior columns, though Greek in character, were modified so that a totally new Byzantine column resulted. The architectural style of this church has influenced the art and architecture of other churches. With its mosaic inlays and marble veneers on the walls, St. Sophia was originally so colorful that a Byzantine historian had this to say: "One would think we had come upon a meadow full of flowers in bloom. Who would not admire the purple tints of some and the green of others, the glowing red and glittering white, and those too which nature, like a painter, has marked with the strongest contrasts of color."

The Fall of the Byzantine Empire

Byzantium was (1) a continuation of the Roman Empire; (2) a civilization with a

The church of St. Sophia is a fine example of Byzantine architecture. At the left is an exterior view; at the right is an interior view.

St. Sophia was later made into a mosque by the Muslims, which is why Arabic writing can be seen in the interior view.

character of its own; and (3) a cultural bridge between East and West. Yet, despite its important role in world affairs, the Byzantine Empire collapsed. In the paragraphs that follow you will read about some of the reasons that explain the decline and fall of Byzantium.

Through its vast trade and many wars, Byzantine civilization spread to southern Italy, the Balkan countries, and western Russia. Constantinople saved the learning of Greece and Rome and fought one invader after another. In so doing, it gave Europe the time it needed to develop its own ways. Constantinople was a major city when Paris and London were small towns. However, it finally fell as the result of the Turkish invasion.

There is no chief explanation for the fall of the Byzantine Empire. Numerous wars made its enemies stronger and the empire weaker. Its church was more concerned about worldly power than about spiritual power. Its emperors (who enjoyed absolute power) gave the people little voice in the government and few opportunities to improve themselves.

There were people who were jealous of the power and splendor of the Byzantine Empire and were determined to bring about its fall. The Persians and the Arabs took turns fighting the Byzantines. However, they could not defeat them, nor rob the empire of its wealth.

The Byzantine Empire never recovered from two deadly blows that were struck against it. In 1204, the crusaders from Europe went to Palestine to drive out the Seljuk Turks. The latter were believed to have violated Christian holy places in Jerusalem. Envious of the wealth they saw in the Byzantine Empire, they forgot who their enemies were. They destroyed the city of Constantinople. The second blow was when the Ottoman Turks battered down the walls of Constantinople and captured the city in 1453. This date is usually considered by historians as marking the fall of the Byzantine Empire.

A fifteenth century miniature painting shows a group of European knights leaving for a crusade to the Holy Land. How did the crusade in 1204 contribute to the fall of the Byzantine Empire?

Check in Here

1. How was the religion of the Eastern Orthodox Church expanded to other areas of Eastern Europe?

2. What is the significance of the codification of Roman law by Emperor Justinian?

3. Explain each of the following: **(a)** Byzantium as a continuation of the Roman Empire; **(b)** Byzantium as a civilization with its own character; **(c)** Byzantium as a cultural bridge between East and West.

4. Give two major reasons for the decline of Byzantium.

THE TEACHINGS OF MOHAMMED

What We Know About Mohammed

During the Middle Ages the Byzantine civilization shone brilliantly. But it did not shine alone. The civilization of the Muslim world was equally bright.

While Eastern Europe was dominated by the Orthodox Church and Western Europe by the Roman Catholic Church, the Middle East and North Africa were dominated by the faith of *Islam* [is'läm]. The word Islam means surrender—that is, surrender to the will of God. Those who give in to the teachings of Islam are called *Muslims* [muz'lmz].

Mohammed (A.D. 570–632) was the prophet of the new faith. He was born at Mecca [mek'ə] in Arabia. This area had a mixed population made up mostly of nomadic tribes who had to make a livelihood from the desert. Mecca was an old trading city and the center for the worship of tribal gods. Mohammed was a merchant who at the age of twenty-five married Khadija [kə dē'jə], a wealthy widow. As a merchant he crossed the desert with caravans carrying goods to distant parts of the Arabian peninsula. During the course of his journeys he learned a bit about Greek culture, Christian ideas, and the Hebrew religion.

Mohammed was a thoughtful man. He often liked to get away by himself to think about the world around him and his place in it. By the time he was forty he believed that he had been chosen by *Allah* [al'ə] to preach a new faith to the world. (Allah is the Muslim name for God.) He absorbed and accepted many of the ideas of the Jewish and Christian faiths but believed that his revelations, which Allah had given him, were the last true ones.

Mohammed was an attractive looking man with a personality few could resist.

166

He was eloquent in expression and freely shared his revelations with those who would listen. Mohammed taught that there is one God—Allah—and that one person, Mohammed, was his prophet. As do other faiths, Islam teaches kindness, humility, patience, and charity. The holy book of Islam is the *Koran*. Like the Old Testament and the Hebrew Talmud, the Koran is more than a collection of religious ideas. It includes rules of conduct, including those on how to treat children, slaves, and animals.

The rise of the new religion was slow at first. There were many Arabs who would not accept Mohammed as a prophet of Allah. They preferred instead their own tribal gods. Since Arabs looked to Mecca as their holy city, Mohammed thought that Mecca would be a good place in which to spread his ideas. He thought that in this religious center the people would leave their tribal gods and follow him. He was wrong.

In 622, Mohammed was driven out of the holy city of Mecca and fled to the city of Medina [mə dē′nə]. The flight from Mecca to Medina is called the *Hegira* [hi jī′rə]. In Medina, Mohammed was more successful. He began to win converts to his ideas. It was among the Arabs of the desert that the faith of Islam took root. The year 622 is a turning point for the followers of the Muslim faith. It became Year One for the Muslims.

What Muslims Believe

The Muslim faith imposes a number of obligations upon the faithful. These may be listed as follows: (1) Every Muslim must repeat the Muslim Creed in Arabic: "There is no God but Allah and Mohammed is His Prophet"; (2) It is the duty of every Muslim to pray five times daily; (3) Fasting from sunrise to sunset during the holy month of *Ramadan* [ram′ə dän′] is required (Ramadan, the ninth month in the Muslim year, and the one in which Mohammed received his revelations); (4) Every Muslim is required to make a pilgrimage to Mecca at least once during a lifetime; (5) Every devout Muslim is to give charity (alms) to the poor. The *Kaaba* [kä′bə], a holy shrine, is the center of worship in the holy city of Mecca. Any Muslim can lead people at prayer. However, those learned in Muslim teachings and law, called *mullahs* [mul′əz], are treated with great respect and are considered holy.

Devout Muslims make a pilgrimage to Mecca. The Islamic center of worship is shown here. What is it called?

In the Muslim faith, a man was permitted to have only four wives. Outside the Muslim religion, those who could afford to do so could keep a large harem if they wished. While the teachings of Mohammed permitted a man to have more than one wife, it limited the number of wives a man could have at one time. Mohammed sought to improve the role of the family, and at the same time tried to strengthen the position of women.

In his teachings Mohammed sought to protect women. Thus, for example, Mohammed assured women the right to choose a marriage partner. They were also assured the right to inherit property. Generally, a man could easily divorce a woman. However, a contract agreed to in advance of a marriage set forth the conditions under which a divorce would be granted. It listed the rights to property a woman would have when the marriage ended. Mohammed did not require Muslim women to be veiled. This later became a custom as the Muslim religion was influenced by the lands to which it spread. Some of the practices toward women in some modern Muslim countries are different from what Mohammed taught. "One could interpret the history of women in Islam as one long struggle on their part to maintain the rights enunciated [spelled out] by Mohammed. . . ."*

As do Christians, Muslims believe in a Judgment Day. In the Muslim faith, however, whether or not one goes to Paradise, or heaven, is *predetermined* (determined beforehand by Allah). No amount of prayer or good works can change the plan. Muslims believe in *kismet* [kiz'met], that one's time of death and one's fate in another world is predetermined. However, one sure way of getting into Paradise was to die in a *jihad* [ji häd'], or a holy war, against non-Muslims. Because

*Elise Boulding, *The Underside of History* (Westview Press. Boulder, Colorado. 1976), p. 386.

of this belief Muslim fighters knew little fear. The deep faith and courage of the Muslims made the rapid expansion of Islam and the Muslim Empire possible.

Check in Here

1. Identify three basic teachings of the Muslim faith.

2. Identify four major obligations imposed by the faith upon Muslims.

3. Describe the role of women in the Muslim religion.

4. How did the religion of Islam make Muslims brave warriors?

THE WORLD OF ISLAM

How the World of Islam Was Ruled

Mohammed preached a holy war, or jihad, to spread the teachings of Islam. The conquests of Islam began when Mohammed's forces took the city of Medina and the Bedouin [bed'ü in] tribes outside the city. Later, Mohammed conquered Mecca and made it the religious center of Islam. When Mohammed died in 632, he had conquered nearly all of Arabia. He had set an example for future jihads.

In a jihad that swept the Middle East and moved westward, Muslims conquered Arabia, Persia, Egypt, North Africa, and also the Iberian Peninsula (Portugal and Spain). The Muslims then crossed the Pyrenees Mountains and were about to conquer France and Western Europe. They were stopped by Charles Martel, the leader of the Franks, at the Battle of Tours [türz] in 732. In a little over a hundred years from its birth in 622, the Muslim faith had spread and was accepted by a great many people. The Muslim drive westward carried Islam into North Africa and Spain. The

The Spread of Islam

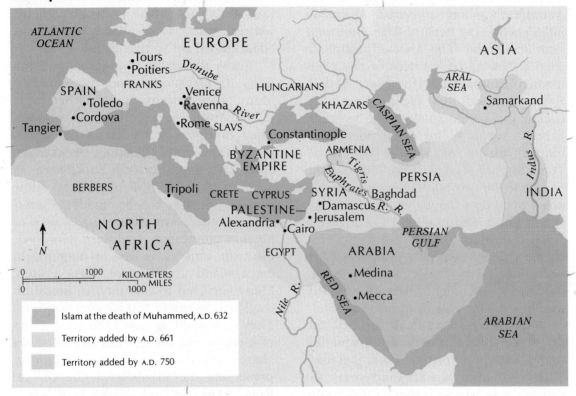

- By what year was much of Spain under Islamic control?
- What empire blocked the spread of Islam into Europe from the east?
- By what year did the Muslims control the entire shoreline of the Persian Gulf?
- By A.D. 750, Rome was how many kilometers (miles) from the closest Islamic-held territory?

Muslims also conquered India, where they stopped at the Indus River. (See p. 92.) Eventually, their influence was felt in the Malay Peninsula, Java, the Philippines, and China. The extent of the Muslim influence was greater than that of the ancient empires of Rome and Persia combined.

The Muslim world was ruled by *caliphs* [kā′lifs]. The first four caliphs were informally chosen by Arab leaders. These were Abu-Bekr [ə bü′bek′ər], Omar [ō′mär], Othman [oth′mən], and Ali [ä′lē]. These four are revered to this day in the Muslim faith. It was under Caliph Omar that the greatest of the jihads were car-

ried out. Upon the death of Ali, however, the traditional way of choosing caliphs ended.

The leader of the Ummayads [ü mī′adz], an Arab family, proclaimed himself caliph and established the *Ummayad Caliphate* with Damascus as its capital. With leadership passing from father to son, the Ummayad Caliphate lasted from 661 to 750. It was overthrown by Abu al-Abbas [a bül′a bas′], the descendant of an uncle of Mohammed.

Under the *Abbasid* [ab′ə sid] *Caliphate*, which Abu al-Abbas established, the Islamic Empire reached its height. A new capital was established at Baghdad

169

[bag′dad]. Especially splendid was the Abbasid Caliphate of Harun Al-Rashid [äl′rä shēd′], the hero of *The Thousand and One Nights*. The Abbasid Caliphate tried to kill all the princes of the overthrown Ummayads. However, Abd-al-Rahman, grandson of the last Ummayad Caliph, escaped to Spain where he established a separate and independent *Ummayad Caliphate of Cordova* [kôr′dō və]. This caliphate lasted from 756 to 1036.

While the two caliphates never recognized or acknowledged each other's authority, both Baghdad and Cordova became centers of power and prosperity. However, even two power centers were not enough for rival claimants to the caliphates, and other centers of authority developed. One was in Cairo (Egypt).

As a result of political disunity, the power of the caliphs declined and fell under the control of the Seljuk [sel jük′] Turks. For over two hundred years the caliphs were largely subject to the rulers of Turkey.

Although the Muslims never achieved political unity, they were united by a strong, common faith and a common language. Arabic was required of all the Muslim faithful in order to read the Koran. The Muslim world was united by the obligation to make a pilgrimage to Mecca at least once in a lifetime. Mecca became a meeting ground for Muslims from many corners of the world. The Muslim world was united by ties of trade and commerce.

What the Muslims Gave to Civilization

The Muslim religion spread rapidly, and a Muslim culture began to develop. The scientific findings of the past were translated into the Arabic language. Muslims studied medicine. Their textbooks on diseases were the best in their fields up until the seventeenth century. Avicenna [av′i sen′ə] (980–1037) is famous for his written summary of all medical knowledge known up to that time.

Arabs also made important contributions to astronomy and mathematics. Many of the caliphs who governed parts of the Arab world were eager to learn. They brought in scholars from many parts of the world. Muslims, Greeks, and Jews gave much to Arab knowledge.

The Muslim faith does not allow human images to be made. Consequently, there was little in the way of Muslim painting or sculpture. However, exquisite objects as well as magnificent carpets and architecture were created. Many survived to this day. In literature the Muslims made notable contributions. They read and translated the great books of Greece and Rome into Arabic. They shared with the Byzantines the credit for preserving the learning of Greece and Rome. The *Arabian Nights* is the best known work of Arab storytellers. Its stories of life and adventure have been translated into many languages and are read throughout the world.

The Muslim world prospered through trade and war. Baghdad (in what is present-day Iraq) and Cairo (in Egypt) became great cities. Trade and travel were carried on in nearly all parts of the known world. Silk fabrics and carpets were skillfully woven, and the Muslims introduced cotton cloth into Europe. At Samarkand [sam′ər kand′] and Baghdad they built factories for the manufacture of paper from rags. These cities also had shops and mosques, synagogues and churches, jails and cemeteries, orphanages, insane asylums, hospitals, schools, and colleges.

Contacts between Europeans and Muslims were few at first. The Christians and Muslims were religious rivals. For a while there was doubt among Europeans about the worth of Muslim scholarship. Yet contacts grew as Muslim learning

An intricately woven Persian carpet displays the highly skilled work of Persian artists.

spread from the great centers of Cordova and Toledo to the rest of Western Europe. The Crusades (see p. 185) also brought Europeans into contact with Muslim culture. An appreciation of Muslim civilization grew. Contacts between Europeans and Muslims were made in Jerusalem, Sicily, and southern Italy. Jewish scholars, some of whom knew Hebrew, Greek, and Latin as well as Arabic, played an important role in making Arab translations of Greek and Latin classics available to scholarly Europeans.

Check in Here

1. List the countries in which the faith of Islam became the dominant one.

2. How does one explain the rapid growth of the Islamic faith?

3. Although political unity was not achieved, the Muslim world was united in other ways. How was this accomplished?

4. What were the strengths and weaknesses of the caliphates?

5. Identify five contributions of the Muslims to Western civilization.

REVIEWING THE BASICS

By the last quarter of the fifth century the glory that was Rome had faded. The eastern portion of the old Roman Empire lived on for a thousand years and contributed much to the civilization of humankind. Byzantium was strategically located and dominated the trade routes of the Aegean. Justinian was a ruler of Byzantium and is best known for having the law codes of ancient Rome rewritten in a systematic way. The law codes were studied and used by later generations.

The prosperity of the Byzantines enabled them to support a magnificent and ceremonial monarchy. The emperor was all-powerful. The chariot races at the Hippodrome became in time more than a sporting event. Political parties known as the Blues and Greens sided with one emperor and then another.

Religion was an important and controversial topic with the people of Byzantium. The patriarchs of the Eastern Church refused to acknowledge the supremacy of the pope. In 1054, Byzantium separated itself from the Roman Church. Political and religious differences were responsible for the schism that remains to this day. The Roman Catholic Church headed by the pope was often more powerful than the rulers of the Western countries. This led in time to quarrels between church and state. In Byzantium, however, the patriarch of Constantinople, head of the Eastern Orthodox Church, was part of the emperor's government.

The Prophet Mohammed was born in Mecca in 570. His ideas became the basis for the third great religion of the world, Islam. Islam spread greatly in a little more than a hundred years after its founding. Its religion imposes obligations upon Muslims. Among the more important are the obligations (1) to visit Mecca at least once during a lifetime, and (2) to fast during specified times during the month of Ramadan.

The Muslim world failed to achieve political unity. Rival caliphates refused to recognize one another and often fought. Nevertheless, Muslims were united by a common religion and a common language, Arabic. Selected works of ancient Greece and Rome were translated into Arabic and thus saved. At Tours in 732, the rapid advance of Islam was stopped. Christianity remained dominant in Western Europe.

REVIEWING THE HIGHLIGHTS

People to Identify			
Justinian	Constantine	Omar	Abbasid
Byzas	Leo III	Methodius	Harun-Al-Rashid
Basil II	Basil I	Othman	Avicenna
Irene	Cyril	Ali	Muslims
Theodora	Mohammed	Abu al-Abbas	Osman
Heraclius	Abu-Beker	Ummayads	

Places to Locate		
Byzantium	Balkan Peninsula	Dardanelles
Middle East	Cordova	Sea of Marmara
Constantinople	Baghdad	Aegean
Mecca	Damascus	Bosphorous
Medina	Tours	Arabian Peninsula

Middle Ages	Hegira	pope
Byzantine Empire	Allah	patriarch
Monophysites	jihad	Islam
schism	kismet	Koran
demes	Roman Catholic Church	Kaaba
Basileu	Eastern Orthodox Church	Corpus Juris Civilis

**Mastering
the Fundamentals**

1. How did Byzantium get its name?
2. Why was Byzantium strategically well-located?
3. Why is it difficult to define the boundaries of the Byzantine Empire?
4. Name the major emperors of the Byzantine empire.
5. Why were the Byzantines excellent fighters?
6. Why can the Hippodrome also be considered a kind of parliament?
7. To what extent is Justinian's reputation as a preserver of Roman law justified?
8. What evidence is there of the importance of religion to the Byzantium civilization?
9. What influence did Queen Theodora have in the early days of the Eastern Roman Empire?
10. How do you account for the prosperity of Byzantium?
11. What were the teachings of Mohammed?
12. How do you explain the rapid expansion of Islam?
13. How did Islam help preserve the classics of ancient Greece and Rome?
14. Why was the Muslim world not politically united?
15. Why is there relatively little painting or sculpture in Islam?
16. How did religion serve to unite the world of Islam?
17. Explain the meaning of the word *Islam*.
18. What are some differences among the Koran, the Old Testament, and the New Testament?
19. How did the idea of kismet help to make the Muslims good warriors?
20. Why were contacts between the Muslim and Christian worlds slow to develop at first?

THINGS TO DO

1. Prepare a speech Empress Theodora might have given urging a greater role for women in the Byzantine Empire.
2. Report to the class on the life of Mohammed. (More is known about Mohammed than is known about Moses or Jesus.)
3. Draw a cartoon illustrating one or more reasons for the fall of Byzantium.

The selection below is taken from the *Secret History* of Procopius, a writer who knew Justinian and Theodora. He observed the way they governed Byzantium. For most of his life he praised their accomplishments in his writing. Later on he wrote what he called a *Secret History* in which he supposedly told the truth about the emperor and empress. Read and study this selection from a *Secret History*. Discuss the questions that follow.

This Emperor was insincere, crafty, hypocritical, dissembling* his anger, double-dealing, clever, a perfect artist in acting out an opinion which he pretended to hold, and even able to produce tears, not from joy or sorrow, but . . . according to the need of the moment, always playing false yet not carelessly, but adding both his signature and the most terrible oaths to bind his agreements. . . . But he departed straightaway from his agreements and his oaths, just like the vilest slaves who, through fear of the tortures hanging over them, are induced to make confession of acts which they had denied on oath. He was a fickle* friend, a truceless enemy, an ardent devotee* of assassination and of robbery. . . .

Such, then, was Justinian. As for Theodora, she had a mind fixed firmly and persistently upon cruelty. For she never did anything at any time as a result of persuasion or compulsion by another person, but she herself, applying a stubborn will, carried out her decision with all her might, no one daring to intercede* for the victim who had given offense. . . . And to state the matter briefly, no one ever saw Theodora reconciled* with the one who had given offense, even after the person had died, but the son of the deceased* received the Empresses' enmity* as an inheritance from him, just as he received anything else that had been his father's, and passed it on to the third generation. . . .

She claimed the right to administer the whole Roman Empire, and if the Emperor should impose* any task upon a man without her consent, that man's affairs would suffer such a turn of fortune that not long thereafter he would be dismissed from his office with the greatest indignities* and would die a most shameful death.†

Vocabulary

dissembling—hiding	*intercede*—plead	*enmity*—anger
fickle—changeable	*reconciled*—made friendly	*impose*—put
devotee—one dedicated	*deceased*—dead	*indignities*—insults

1. Is this a *primary* or *secondary* source? Justify your point of view.
2. How reliable a source would this be if you were attempting to write a new biography of Justinian and Theodora?
3. Why do you think Procopius called his work *Secret History*? Is a secret history likely to be more accurate than other accounts? Why or why not?
4. What actions of Justinian and Theodora might have led to the judgments Procopius made?
5. Prepare a report giving some of the background on the life of Procopius.
6. Compare this judgment of Justinian and Theodora with those of other writers (see bibliography at the end of the unit). Summarize the major differences.

†Procopius, *Secret History*, XIII, XV. Trans. H. B. Dewing (Cambridge: Harvard University Press; Loeb Classical Library, 1950), Vol. VI, pp. 3, 99, 101, 131, 177–181. Used by permission.

The Gothic cathedral of Chartres (France)

The Medieval World:
Western Europe
During the Middle Ages

The culture of Western Europe immediately following the fall of the Roman Empire was poor and backward. The people of Western Europe lacked the money to take part in the rich trade that Byzantium and Islam then enjoyed. Western Europe had to build its own civilization and culture by developing its resources. It had rich farmlands, great forests, fur-bearing animals, and seas. Through the development of these resources, it gradually became one of the richest parts of the world.

In this chapter you will study how Western Europe began to put itself together following the fall of the Roman Empire. You will read how foreigners who lived near the Rhine and Danube Rivers—people the Romans called "barbarians"—helped bring about the fall of Rome. Their invasions plunged Europe into centuries of economic and political upheaval. Nevertheless, during the *Early Middle Ages* (500-1100), as those years are called, Europeans made a new beginning upon which to build a distinctive civilization.

EUROPE DURING THE EARLY MIDDLE AGES

Why German Tribes Entered Rome

For hundreds of years German tribes lived on or near the borders of the Roman Empire. Tacititus, the Roman historian, wrote about these people.

A Frankish warrior. The Franks were one of the fiercest Germanic groups to invade the Roman Empire.

Sometimes the German tribes in the border areas were made part of the Roman Empire through war and conquest. At other times, German families crossed over the borders into Rome peacefully. They tried to secure better farmland for themselves and their followers. On occasion, they were invited into the Roman lands by the Romans. They often joined the Roman army. As Rome declined, the number of Germans who entered the Roman Empire increased. So also did the number of German soldiers in the Roman legions increase.

What the Germanic peoples saw convinced them that they would be able to move into the empire easily. They recognized the advantages of Roman civilization. They were also aware that the government of Rome was beginning to fall. Germans who were in the army could see that the army was badly led. Those who lived in the empire and farmed the land saw that the Roman borders were frequently left unprotected.

What was at first a peaceful and gradual migration and settlement of Germans in the Roman Empire later became a wave and still later a flood. What was its cause? From far-off China, the ferocious Huns stormed across Siberia. They were fierce fighters. All who were in their path fled in fear, as did the Germanic tribes living on the borders of Rome.

The Visigoths, one of the Germanic tribes, crossed the Danube and asked for

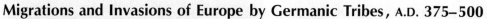

Migrations and Invasions of Europe by Germanic Tribes, A.D. 375–500

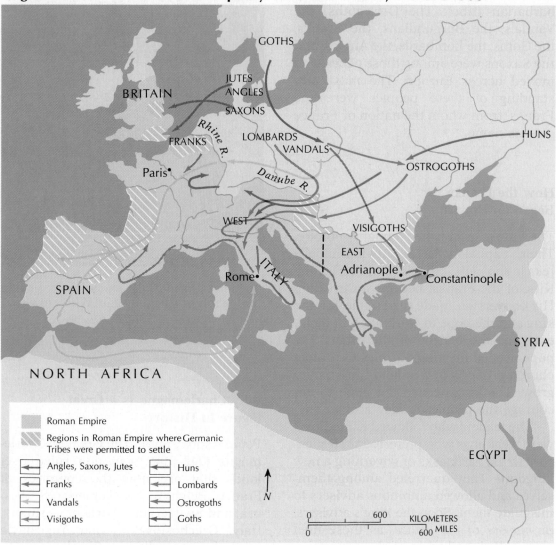

GOTHS

JUTES
ANGLES
BRITAIN
SAXONS

Rhine R.
FRANKS
LOMBARDS
VANDALS
HUNS
OSTROGOTHS

Paris
Danube R.

WEST
VISIGOTHS
EAST
Adrianople
Constantinople

ITALY
Rome

SPAIN

SYRIA

NORTH AFRICA

EGYPT

Roman Empire

Regions in Roman Empire where Germanic
Tribes were permitted to settle

Angles, Saxons, Jutes	Huns
Franks	Lombards
Vandals	Ostrogoths
Visigoths	Goths

N

0   600
KILOMETERS
0   600 MILES

The migrations and invasions of the Roman Empire took place over many years.
• From what continent did the Huns come?
• What Germanic people invaded part of the coast of North Africa?

the protection of Rome. When they discovered that Rome was no longer in a position to help them, the Visigoths attacked the Romans. In the great Battle of Adrianople [ā′drē ə nō′pəl] in 378, they showed that they were a match for the once famous Roman legions. In 410, Alaric [al′ər ik] led the Visigoths [viz′ə goths′] into the city of Rome. They plundered the city for several days. Their victories made them bolder. They pressed their luck and expanded into southern France and then into Spain. There they set up a kingdom. The kingdom collapsed after the Muslims defeated the Visigoths in battle in 711.

The Visigoths were only one of many barbarian tribes. The Ostrogoths, the Vandals, the Burgundians, the Franks, the Goths, the Lombards, the Angles, and the Saxons were among those tribes who moved across Europe. The most outstanding of these peoples were the Franks, from whom the nation of France gets its name.

How the Franks Began an Empire

The Franks established a mighty empire. Their capital was at Aix-la-Chapelle [eks lə shə pel']. Clovis [klō'vis], the King of the Franks, became a Christian. His conversion made it possible for the king and the pope to work hand in hand, each for the benefit of the other. The pope needed the king's armies to protect church property and to help Christianity grow. The king needed the pope to encourage the people to obey him.

The leaders who followed King Clovis were weaklings who preferred their pleasure to the hard tasks of governing a new kingdom. They quarreled among themselves and allowed ambitious advisers to misguide them. Soon the king's advisers, or *mayors of the palace*, as these men were called, had most of the power.

The most influential mayor was Charles Martel [mär tel']. His son, Pepin [pep'in] the Short (747–768), became king with the pope's help. In return, Pepin rushed to the pope's defense when he was threatened by enemies. Pepin gave the pope some land which together with other lands near the city of Rome are called the *Papal States*. This gift, known as the *Donation of Pepin*, gave the pope the status of a prince. The pope already had religious authority. This gift gave him political power as well. Pepin and his son, Charlemagne [shär'lə mān,'] built a great empire.

A medieval manuscript shows the coronation of Charlemagne. Who crowned Charlemagne?

Why Charlemagne Is a Great Figure in History

Pepin's son, Charles the Great or Charlemagne (742–814), won and ruled over lands that are now the countries of France, Belgium, the Netherlands, Austria, and Switzerland. Parts of Germany, Italy, Czechoslovakia, and Yugoslavia were also controlled by Charlemagne.

On Christmas Day in the year 800, Charlemagne was crowned and hailed as emperor by the pope. This event was significant. It meant that Charlemagne accepted the pope as the spiritual ruler of the empire. Later popes could say that they were more powerful than kings. As spiritual leaders, the popes established or claimed the right to overthrow monarchs. This claim led to endless fights between popes and kings.

Charlemagne and the kings who followed him said they had rebuilt the Roman Empire. This, of course, was not true. The establishment of a European empire was a goal that kings would try again and again to achieve.

After Charlemagne died, the rulers were too weak to hold his empire together. The three grandchildren of Charlemagne divided his lands. One grandson took what is now France; another grandson took what is now Germany; and the third grandson took what is now Italy, plus a strip of land along the Rhine River. For nearly two hundred years after Charlemagne's death, there were no strong kings in Europe. The violence and disorder that Charlemagne had stopped began again and grew worse.

How England Began

One of the fiercest groups to attack Europe during the ninth and tenth centuries was the Vikings. They came from Norway, Sweden, and Denmark. They sailed

Charlemagne's Empire, A.D. 814

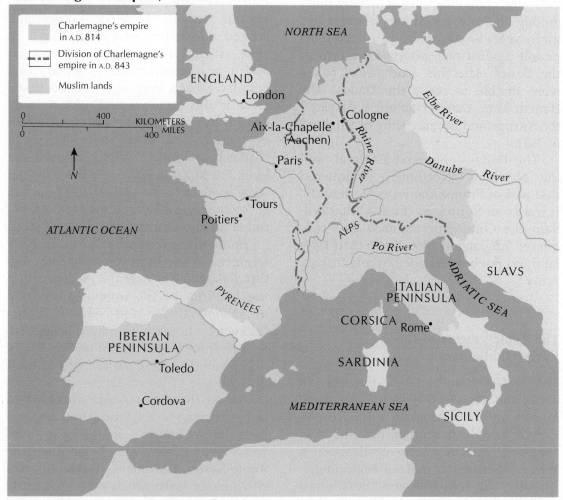

Charlemagne's empire covered much of Western Europe.
- Was Rome a part of his empire?
- Where did Muslim lands border Charlemagne's empire?
- What seas or oceans formed part of the empire's borders?

the seas in small, well-built ships and raided the coasts of France and England. They landed in Iceland and Greenland, and even reached America. Leif Ericson [er'ik sən] was one of the Vikings who probably journeyed to the New World.

The Northmen who attacked the people of the British Isles met resistance from tribes called Angles [ang'gəlz], Saxons [sak'sənz], and Jutes [jüts]. These tribes fought with one another and against the Northmen. Unsuccessful efforts were made to unite Angles, Saxons, and Jutes as a nation. Alfred the Great (849–899) came closest to achieving unity among the peoples of the islands. For many years he successfully protected his people against one group of Northmen, the Danes. After his death weak rulers were unable to resist the Danes. The Danish king, Canute [kə nüt'], defeated the Saxons and became King of England in 1016.

The Danes conquered England, and the Normans (Northmen) conquered that part of France known as Normandy. It was from Normandy (France) that William the Conqueror attacked and conquered England in 1066. Since then England has not been invaded by any foreign army.

The Achievements of the Early Middle Ages

The period from the fall of Rome to about the year 1000 is called the Early Middle Ages. The breakup of the Roman Empire and the barbarian invasions that followed enabled a new civilization in Western Europe to make a beginning.

After the fall of Rome the Church grew in power and prestige. It spread its teachings to France, Scandinavia, and the British Isles. It was responsible for preserving culture during the Early Middle Ages. Its priests and bishops were

almost the only people who could read and write. They helped to save the great books of the ancient world. In a time when life was rough and crude, the Church maintained a high degree of learning.

Faint outlines of today's nations emerged during the Early Middle Ages. Among the characteristics of a nation are established boundaries, a strong central government, and strong feelings of loyalty among the people. These qualities were just beginning to develop at that time. In France and in England this was especially true. In 987, Hugh Capet [kā'pit] became King of France and started a long line of French kings. In 1066, when William the Conqueror invaded and then ruled England, that country took a long step toward unity. Even in this early stage, England developed some of the traditions upon which democracy was later built. The *witan* [wit'ən], or king's council, advised the king. The king could choose to follow the witan's advice or not follow it. The witan is commonly considered the great-grandfather of modern presidential cabinets.

Some rulers of the Early Middle Ages appreciated the importance of learning. Charlemagne, for example, insisted that the children of his nobles work hard in school. Under the scholar Alcuin [al'kwin], whom Charlemagne brought to France from England, the palace school flourished. In fact, Charlemagne himself became one of its students.

Alfred the Great made an effort to bring learning to England. He translated books from Latin to Anglo-Saxon, and was responsible for beginning the *Anglo-Saxon Chronicle*. From Alfred's writings we learn much about the Early Middle Ages. Leaders such as Alfred and Charlemagne contributed much to the Early Middle Ages. However, their contributions to learning and scholarship were small when compared with others.

Check in Here

1. Why were the Germanic tribes able to conquer Rome?
2. List one thing each of the following contributed to the Early Middle Ages: (a) Pepin the Short; (b) Charlemagne; (c) William the Conqueror.
3. On a map (see p. 179), identify those countries that were once ruled in whole or in part by Charlemagne.
4. How did Alfred the Great bring learning to England?

THE FEUDAL PYRAMID CONTROLS MEDIEVAL EUROPE

How Feudalism Was Organized

Following the fall of Rome, there was no strong government or army to protect the lives and the property of the people. Kings and queens were weak and had little power. Landowners were usually wealthy *nobles* who managed to keep their lands, wealth, castles, and possibly, some soldiers and horses. They offered protection to neighboring farmers and peasants who were not able to provide it for themselves. In return, these people served the lord. They were called *vassals* [vas′əlz]. In time, the relationship between the lord and his vassals became the axis around which the political, social, and economic life of the Middle Ages turned. The relationship that existed between them has been given the name *feudalism* [fyüd′ə liz′əm]. The Later Middle Ages in Western Europe are often called the *Feudal Period* (1100–1300).

The political system of feudalism was one in which a powerful noble commanded the obedience of less powerful nobles. They became his vassals. Al-

This illumination, or picture, from an English manuscript portrays the faculty and students of Oxford University.

though nobles held their lands and their authority in the monarch's name, the monarch had little power beyond his or her own land. Many nobles were more powerful than the monarch, and the Church was more powerful than both.

Feudal nobles had their own court. They collected their own taxes. Some even had their own coinage. Feudal nobles expected certain obligations from their vassals. These included ransom money if a feudal noble was captured, a dowry when a noble's daughter married, payment for the ceremony in which a noble's son was knighted, and very possibly armed service in defense of the noble.

The importance of a noble depended upon the size of his estate or property, the strength of his castle, and the number of knights he could command in time of war. Because wars were frequent, feudal nobles spent much of their time in war and in games designed to train them for war. The lord also protected the people who lived near his castle and, generally, tried to rule them justly.

Feudal society can be pictured as a pyramid, with a king or a queen at the top. Some monarchs were quite strong, while others were monarchs in name only. Next in the pyramid came the lords and bishops, some of whom were very powerful, while others were quite poor and powerless. Due to privileges they enjoyed, a poor parish priest and a well-to-do noble's knight both belonged near the top of the pyramid.

At the bottom of the pyramid were the *serfs*. They were not slaves because they could not be bought or sold. Nevertheless, they and their children were bound to the land and owed certain duties to the lord. They worked the land for the lord in exchange for what produce was left after paying their taxes. The serfs paid taxes to the lord in the form of food and work for the privilege of using the lord's road, baking oven, gristmill, or wine press.

There were some *freemen* in the feudal society who were neither lords nor serfs. They were the artisans and merchants who provided specialized services. Although few in number, they increased as the Middle Ages came to an end.

The feudal social system was one in which the nobility was courted and entertained. Courtesy, or court manners, known as *chivalry* [shiv'əl rē], became highly developed. Good manners were valued. The knights were to be brave in war, gallant toward women of noble birth, and faithful to the Christian church. The ideals of bravery, courtesy, loyalty, and honor were not always lived up to. They did, however, provide a base for chivalry and knighthood.

How People Made a Living in Feudal Days

Feudalism was based on agriculture. Serfs lived on a *manor* [man'ər]. It included the lord's land, castle, wine press, flour mill, baking oven, and everything else needed to make the manor independent. The serfs were expected to

Plan of Medieval Manor

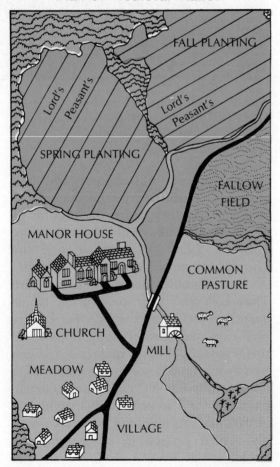

A medieval woman at work. Were women equal to men in feudal society?

A feudal lord receives his vassals. What was the relationship of a powerful noble to his vassals?

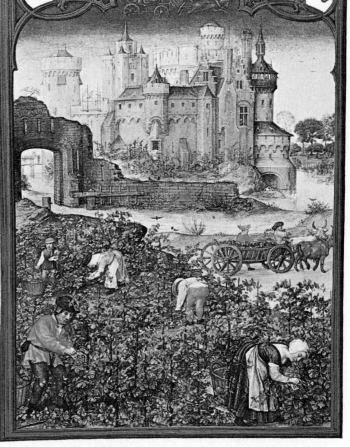

Serfs work the land surrounding the castle of a medieval manor. What were the serfs given in return for their work?

grow enough food to feed those who lived on the manor.

The tools the serfs used were simple, and their farming methods were clumsy. The serfs depended on animals for food, milk, and meat. They worked strips of land scattered throughout the manor. These small strips of land were not easy to farm since it was hard to get from one strip to another. Only two-thirds of the strips were farmed at a time; the other one-third was not used but left *fallow*, or untilled, so that it would be good for

farming later on. The serfs did not know about fertilizers or about rotating crops from year to year in order to get the most from the soil. After paying their obligations to the lord, the serfs had little food, clothing, or time left for themselves.

There was little trading during the Feudal Period because money was scarce and travel was dangerous. Lords bought as little from the other manors as possible. Trade, commerce, and the growth of cities were signs that the Feudal Period was coming to a close.

1. Give three reasons for the development of feudalism.

2. Distinguish between each of the following: (a) serf and slave; (b) lord and vassal; (c) manor and nation.

3. What were the obligations of the lord to the serf? Of the serf to the lord? Of the lord to the monarch? Of the monarch to the lord?

4. Why did serfdom keep most peasants poor?

THE INFLUENCE OF THE CATHOLIC CHURCH IN MEDIEVAL EUROPE

The Role of the Church in Daily Life

During the Middle Ages church and state were not separate as they are in the United States today. Church and government worked hand-in-hand to direct people's lives. Church and government were expected to cooperate with each other. In medieval Europe the Roman Catholic Church had great power and influence.

Medieval people believed that God had the answers to their problems. They believed that God took an active part in their affairs. God cured the sick, brought the rain, caused earthquakes, and made lightning. These were some of the ways in which God's power was made known to people.

The Roman Catholic Church held that those who followed its teachings would go to heaven. Those who did not would lead lives of endless misery in another world. In order to be sure of going to heaven, a person had to observe religous rules and teachings. These included church attendance, prayer, fasting, and confession. Religious rules dominated the lives of noble and serf alike from birth until death.

During the Middle Ages people were looking for meaning in lives that were short and often brutal. The power of the Church was very great. To punish an extremely sinful act, such as *heresy* [her'i sē], the Church *excommunicated* [eks'kə myü'nə kāt'ed], or cut off, people from its protection. (*Heresy* was holding beliefs other than those of the Church.) Excommunicated people could not receive spiritual blessings from priests. They could not marry, and they could not receive the Church's last rites when they died. Through its power of excommunication, the Church controlled the upper as well as the lower classes.

The Role of the Church in Business

Farming was the most important way of making a living in feudal days. The monks were good farmers. Farming church property, they found better ways of growing crops and looking after livestock. They taught these new methods of farming to others.

The Church often regulated the activities of those engaged in business. For example, it forbade the practice of charging interest on money that had been lent to another person. It urged merchants and artisans to charge a just, or fair, price for goods. A *just price* was one that would cover the cost of labor and material and would not include a high profit. Only this fair price could be charged to the customer.

The position of the Church was that people should work because it was good for the soul. Accumulating wealth for its own sake was wrong. Church leaders taught that it was easier for a "camel to get through the eye of a needle than it was for a rich person to get through the gates of heaven." Partly as a result of this viewpoint, business and industry developed slowly.

The Church's Role in Governing

In a real sense the Church was itself a government. It was stronger than any monarch or any noble and was usually able to tell the monarchs and nobles what to do. The Church tried to curb the cruelty of government rulers. To prevent fighting it declared holy days on which fighting was not allowed. As a government it had the power to tax. This tax, known as a *tithe* [tīTH], amounted to a tenth of one's income. Every church member was expected to pay it. Through tithing, the Church got the money to do its work. It also became the world's greatest single landowner. The pope ruled the Papal States in central Italy, where he was head of a government as well as head of the Church. Because of its power, wealth, and lands, the Church was envied by monarchs and nobles.

Today, you expect your government to administer justice, to establish courts of law, to provide for education, to look after the sick, the hungry, and the needy. In medieval days the Church provided these services. The Church had its law, *Canon Law,* and its own courts in which those accused of heresy or other religious crimes were tried. Because education was in the hands of the Church, children of the poor were able to get some schooling. The Church supported hospitals and asylums. It gave to charity and built public buildings, such as churches and monasteries.

Because of its great influence, the Church could make and unmake monarchs. In 800, Charlemagne accepted his crown from the hands of the pope. Later, in 962, another king, Otto I, was crowned Holy Roman Emperor by the pope. In 962, the Holy Roman Empire was made up of loosely joined countries which are present-day Holland, Belgium, Switzerland, northern Italy, Austria, and East and West Germany. The land and titles of a monarch were held only with the consent of the pope. Without land and titles, a monarch could not hope to rule. Conflict as well as cooperation between pope and monarch were part of medieval life.

How Monarchs and Popes Cooperated in the Crusades

A *crusade* may be defined as a vigorous fight for a cause. In 1095, Pope Urban II called upon the monarchs, their nobles, and their people to help the Church by driving the Muslims out of Palestine. People were eager to join the crusade. The pope urged war against the Muslims

Interior of the Gothic Cathedral of Notre Dame in Paris. The Cathedral was built in the Middle Ages.

The Crusades

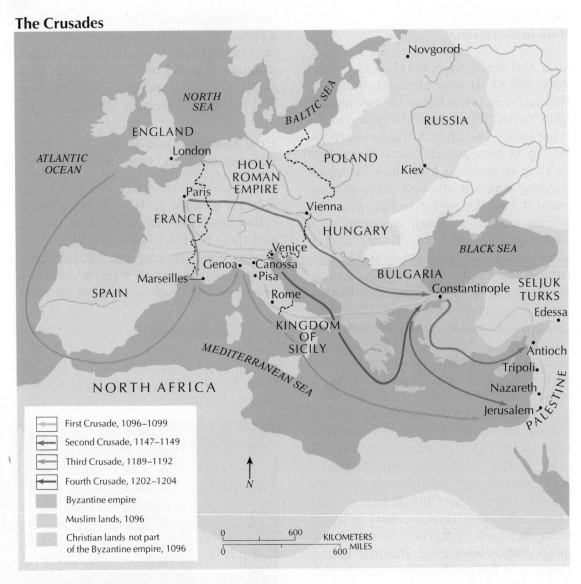

The crusaders left Europe and traveled to Palestine.
• In what general direction did the crusaders travel?
• Some of the crusaders went by ship. What bodies of water did they cross?

who, he said, were interfering with the right of Christians to worship in Jerusalem. These Muslims were Seljuk Turks who had recently adopted Islam as their religion. (See p. 170.) The Turks were making Christian pilgrimages to the Holy City of Jerusalem unsafe. They were also threatening the Eastern Orthodox Church in the Byzantine Empire. Religious enthusiasm and the possibilities of more land in the East brought many recruits. Stories about the great wealth of the East also lured Europeans.

Four major Crusades were undertaken, but they failed to recapture the Holy Land. The First Crusade (1096–99) was the most successful. Jerusalem was temporarily recaptured from the Muslims. The Second Crusade started in answer to calls for help from crusaders who had remained in the Middle East as monarchs of independent states. That crusade ended in 1149 with quarrels among the leaders.

In 1187, the Muslim warrior Saladin [sal′ə din] recaptured Jerusalem. A call for a Third Crusade was sounded. This crusade is famous in history because three great and rival kings took part in it. Despite these royal celebrities, the Third Crusade failed. Emperor Frederick Barbarossa [bär′bə räs′ə] from the Holy Roman Empire drowned on the way to the crusade. Philip Augustus of France got tired of crusading and went home. Richard the Lion-Hearted of England fought bravely and well, but he finally returned to England without having recaptured the Holy Land.

In the Fourth Crusade, the crusaders forgot that their enemies were Muslims. Political and financial reasons caused them to plunder the wealth of their fellow Christians in Constantinople. This was one of the blows that shattered Byzantine civilization. Other Crusades were tried, but they too were unsuccessful. One of them was undertaken by children. It was a dismal failure; many children died, and others were captured and sold into slavery. It showed, however, the tremendous religious faith of the people.

In fighting for Christianity, crusaders attacked Jews. As they made their way east, they spread terror in the sections of the cities in which Jews were forced to live. These sections were called *ghettos* [get′ōz]. Many Jews were killed and saw their homes burned to the ground and their possessions stolen.

The Results of the Crusades

The Crusades increased the prestige of the pope, held back the Turks for two hundred years, and increased contact between Western Europe and the Middle East. The Crusades contributed to the

German emperor Frederick Barbarossa, who took part in the Third Crusade.

growth of trade and commerce. Necessities and luxuries such as sugar, rice, lemons, cotton, muslin, damask, and precious gems were introduced into Western Europe. As trade increased, money, banking, and credit, long frowned upon by the Catholic Church, became necessary to carry on business.

The Crusades contributed to the growth of towns. People were encouraged to leave the land for towns where there were better opportunities.

To some extent the Crusades also brought about an increase in the power of the monarchs over the nobles. The monarchs were able to strengthen their taxing power to raise money for the Crusades. When the Crusades ended, the power to tax remained in the hands of the monarchs. The establishment of town life and the growth in the power of the monarchs were forces which led to the decline of the Feudal Period.

Results of the Crusades

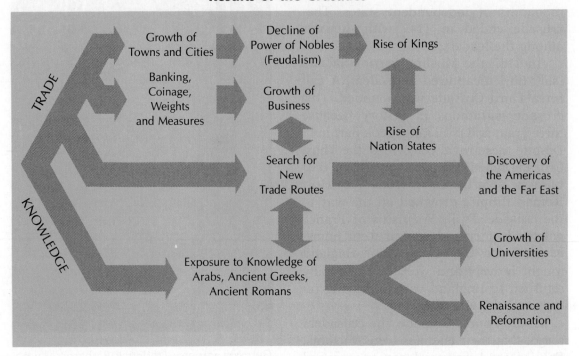

Growth of Towns and Cities

Decline of Power of Nobles (Feudalism)

Rise of Kings

TRADE

Banking, Coinage, Weights and Measures

Growth of Business

Rise of Nation States

KNOWLEDGE

Search for New Trade Routes

Discovery of the Americas and the Far East

Growth of Universities

Exposure to Knowledge of Arabs, Ancient Greeks, Ancient Romans

Renaissance and Reformation

In a later chapter you will read about the Age of Discovery, in which the New World was found. The crusaders were in some ways similar to the explorers and the discoverers of later years. Surely the New World would have been discovered whether or not the Crusades had taken place, but the Crusades speeded up the process of discovery by encouraging an interest in new lands.

How Monarch and Pope Come into Conflict

Because the Church was powerful, it was envied by the monarchs. Because the Church was rich, it was envied by less wealthy monarchs. Because there was no separation of church and state, the powers of the monarch and those of the pope were often in conflict.

In medieval days almost the only people who were well educated were bishops, monks, abbots, and abbesses. Monarchs often appointed bishops to help them run their governments. As payment for their services, bishops were given land by the monarchs. The bishops controlled church affairs over a large area. Parish priests and the administrators of large areas of Church land were under their control. Like the feudal lords, the bishops were vassals of the monarch; and as vassals, they swore to support the monarch. As bishops, they were also subject to the commands of the Church.

Since a bishop was an official of the Church, the pope claimed the power to choose him and to inherit his land when he died. Since a bishop was also a vassal of the monarch, the monarch claimed the right to do so. These issues led to a test of strength between monarch and pope.

Why Henry IV Went to Canossa

Under Pope Gregory VII (1073–85) the conflict between monarch and pope came to a head. Gregory was determined that the pope would be obeyed and that he alone had the right to crown and uncrown kings and queens. He insisted that only the pope, and not the monarch, had the power to appoint bishops.

The argument over who would appoint bishops angered Henry IV (1050–1106), the Holy Roman Emperor. When he refused to obey the pope, a struggle followed. Gregory excommunicated Henry. Because Henry was denied the benefits of the Church, his people were afraid to follow him. They did not wish also to be excommunicated. To make matters worse, Henry's nobles sided with the pope; they feared for their souls.

Henry nearly lost his kingdom. He seemed to be no match for Pope Gregory. Henry decided to make a pilgrimage to Canossa [kə nos'ə] in northern Italy to plead for the pope's forgiveness. In 1077, in the cold of winter and dressed in rags amid a snowstorm, he waited for the pope to appear. For three days he stood thus. Finally, the pope gave in and removed the sentence of excommunication. Henry was again accepted into the Church. Henry's pilgrimage to Canossa served to illustrate the vast powers of the pope.

How Henry's Quarrel with the Pope Ended

In the dispute between Henry and the pope, the pope won the first round. However, the argument was not yet over. Henry returned to his country where he behaved as before. Again, he was excommunicated. This time Henry marched against Rome with military troops and defeated Gregory in 1081. Gregory died in 1085, but other popes continued the struggle.

In 1122, under Henry V (1106–25), a compromise between the pope and the king was worked out. The *Concordat* [kon kôr'dat] *of Worms* [wėrmz] decreed that the pope and the king would share the loyalty of bishops and other church officials. On behalf of the king, the bishops were responsible for affairs of state. On behalf of the pope, the bishops were responsible for the affairs of God. The king gave the bishop lands, and the pope appointed the bishop and gave him religious authority.

The results of this quarrel between monarch and pope showed the comparative power of each. As monarchs grew stronger, they became more sure of their own authority. They were less willing to give the pope a share of it. In Germany and in Italy, the struggle for power among pope, monarch, and noble delayed the growth of these lands into modern countries.

Check in Here

1. How do you explain the authority of the Church in the Middle Ages?

2. List three results of the Crusades.

3. What were the terms of the Concordat of Worms?

4. How did the Church try to do each of the following: (**a**) regulate business; (**b**) encourage better farming; (**c**) maintain peace?

TOWNS GREW AS TRADE AND COMMERCE REVIVED

How Town Life Grew in Europe

Many cities in the Roman Empire declined after the fall of the Roman Empire. As a result, in Western Europe, the manor, and not the town, became the center of community life. In the later Middle Ages, town life began to develop.

The self-sufficient feudal manor was often the beginning of town life. As the manor became more and more crowded, tradespeople and farmers began to live outside the manor walls. Sometimes these settlements grew. For example, if the lord's castle was located near a strategic position, such as a bend in a river, merchants might stop to rest. Sometimes a manor would become the site of fairs where people gathered to exchange goods. Sometimes a monastery became the site of a town. Merchants and tradespeople settled nearby to supply the needs of the pilgrims who journeyed to the monastery.

As trade increased, in the later Feudal Period (around 1300), towns grew in number and in size. As towns increased in population the townspeople gradually came to resent the rule of lord or monas-

tery. They tried to govern and tax themselves. As towns grew in importance, they administered justice, coined money, built streets, and erected town halls. Many towns joined one another in leagues to promote trade and to secure protection from thieves and pirates. The cities of Italy and those of northern Europe formed important and powerful leagues. An example of such a union was the Hanseatic League in northern Europe. (See map, page 193.)

Why Lords Opposed the Growth of Towns

The growth of towns was viewed with alarm by feudal lords. The growth of trade meant that the town had a chance to become wealthier than the manor. Business people who lived in towns

Medieval History

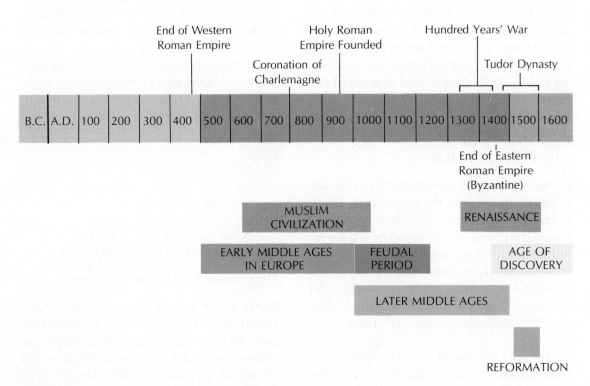

What civilization was declining at the beginning of the Feudal Period in Europe?

could become richer than lords. The wealth of the feudal lords was in land, but the wealth of the townspeople was in money, goods, and services. As townspeople traded and manufactured goods, their wealth increased and living conditions improved. A lord's manor was self-sufficient. This means it was able to supply its own needs. There was little opportunity for the people living on the manor to improve their living conditions.

Monarchs gave the towns certain rights and privileges and in return received money. Sometimes townspeople were relieved of their feudal obligations to the lord. Taxes were paid in money rather than in the form of work or goods. This gave people more freedom and monarchs more power. With the money they got from towns, monarchs were able to hire soldiers of their own and no longer had to depend on the feudal obligations of their vassals.

With money enough to maintain a standing army, monarchs could extend their power and authority. As monarchs got stronger, the idea of a country or nation headed by a central authority became a realistic possibility.

Serfs and their families began to leave the manor for the town, where there were more opportunities than on the manor. In the town it was possible for a serf to climb from a low level in society to a higher one. Wealth, not birth, was what made for class differences in the town. When serfs became rich they were highly regarded. Serfs who ran away to towns often became free and escaped their feudal obligations to the lord. In towns there were many more opportunities for success.

How Trade and Commerce Grew

When Rome declined, trade in Europe declined. Byzantine and Muslim traders did a flourishing business in Eastern Europe and the Middle East. Trade in Western Europe, however, was hurt by the lack of a strong central government to enforce the law and to protect private property. Thieves made the transportation of goods risky and expensive. Roads were poor, and using the best roads was costly since tolls were collected at frequent intervals by feudal nobles. Merchants could not afford to pay the high tolls. Trade and commerce did not move freely.

Another obstacle to trade in feudal times was the lack of a sound money system. Feudal banks were not as numerous nor as able to serve the needs of business people as were the banks of ancient Rome. *Barter,* the exchange of goods for other goods, was frequent. The unwillingness of the Church to allow profit making on moneylending acted as another obstacle in the growth of medieval trade.

The Crusades encouraged the growth of trade and commerce by introducing the crusaders to new products such as sugar, silk, and precious spices. The luxuries of the East in time became necessities to Europeans, and merchants tried to supply Europe with them. The Italian cities of Genoa, Venice, Milan, Florence, and Pisa became leading centers for world commerce. These cities, suitably located for trade near the Mediterranean Sea, specialized in spices, silks, and luxury goods. Trade in northern Europe was based on more ordinary, but probably more important goods such as fish, furs, skins, and leather.

Since overland travel was dangerous, sea travel became highly developed as stronger and larger ships were built. These ships could travel farther and faster than previous ships. The merchants' desire for trade encouraged the explorations and colonization of the New World. Improved methods of coining money, banking, and the weighing and measuring of goods all contributed to a revival of trade.

Population growth also contributed to a growth in trade and commerce. More people had to be fed and clothed. To feed and clothe more people required that farm and nonfarm goods be shipped from one part of Europe to another. As population grew, many serfs fled to the towns where they had to find work. They found jobs in trade, in commerce, and in cloth weaving. They made shoes or baked bread. These products had to be sold in exchange for money with which to buy the food that grew on manorial lands. Younger sons of noblemen could not inherit the manors from their fathers. Since the older son claimed the manor, the younger sons left the manor to establish new lives in the towns, where growing wealth made trade and commerce possible.

A medieval pharmacy. Although medicines were prepared for illnesses in pharmacies like this one, people strongly believed that God, not science, cured the sick.

How Guilds Controlled Business Life

In medieval times *craft* and *merchant guilds* controlled the prices and the quality of products made and sold in the towns. The craft guilds were made up of male and female *artisans* (craftspeople) and merchants in the various trades. Thus, a medieval town might have guilds of stone masons, weavers, clockmakers, butchers, tanners, shoemakers, bakers, and lacemakers. Guilds regulated business dealings. They created minimum standards of quality for the manufactured products. They provided a system through which an *apprentice* (beginner) rose to the rank of *journeyman* (one who has learned the trade). After passing a difficult test, he or she became a *master* artisan. The guilds guarded the trade secrets that were peculiar to their individual crafts. The guild determined the wages of apprentices and the prices of goods.

Guilds tried to charge a just price. That is, they tried to charge a price that they and the Church believed to be fair to the consumer. Since there could be little or no price competition, a shopper looking for a pair of shoes could hardly expect to get a bargain. There was no oversupply of goods since most products were made as they were needed.

The guilds tried to discourage too many people from entering crafts. To limit the number of apprentices, guild masters made entrance examinations difficult. When the guilds became older, it became almost impossible for a newcomer to enter the guild unless his or her father or mother had been a member.

Trade Centers and Trade Routes During the Middle Ages

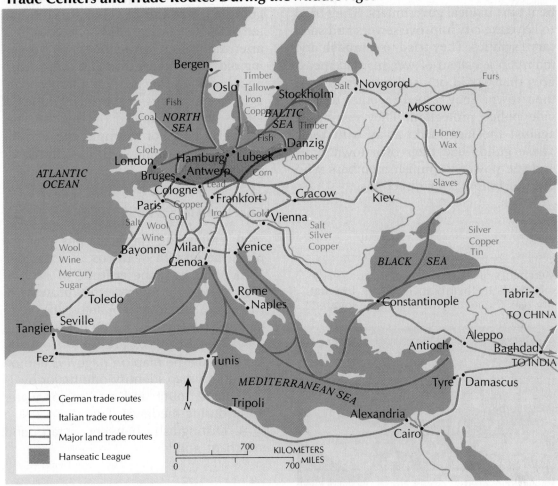

- Across which two bodies of water did the Hanseatic League control most of the trade routes?
- List two of the products that came from the region east of Moscow and Novgorod.

How Merchant Guilds and Craft Guilds Differed

Craft guilds controlled the making of products, but the merchant guilds controlled their sale. Because of their important position between maker and buyer, the merchant guilds became more powerful than the craft guilds. They were particularly important in Italy, where Venice became the center of trade in luxury goods. Venice led other cities in trading along the Mediterranean Sea.

The *Hanseatic* [han′sē at′ik] *League*, with the city of Lübeck [lü′bek] as its center, was the dominant merchant guild in northern Europe. The Hanseatic League dominated the North and Baltic Seas. At its height it was made up of over fifty cities. The ships of the Hanseatic League controlled the profitable wool trade between England and Flanders. Its ships also transported furs, fish, and lumber to London and elsewhere. Refer to the map above.

193

The merchant guilds took a prominent part in local government. They tried to have the city improve sewers and sanitary facilities. They tried to establish and maintain a system of weights and measures that would be used by everyone in their town. They joined together to provide police protection. They combined against the lord to do away with tolls. These guilds had their own town halls and the power to punish members who did not follow their directions.

Merchants of the Hanseatic League ready shipments to their branch offices. In what city was the center of the League located?

Each guild had a patron saint (special guardian), and the town hall was the center of its social life. Guilds tried to look after the welfare of members by providing old-age benefits, fire and theft insurance, and building hospitals and orphanages. Today, many of the social duties of guilds are still carried out by fraternal organizations. For example, the Masons of today are somewhat like the craft guilds of medieval days.

Check in Here

1. Enumerate three reasons that explain the growth of towns.

2. What was the attitude of each of the following toward the growth of towns: (**a**) medieval monarchs; (**b**) medieval lords; (**c**) medieval merchants; (**d**) medieval serfs?

3. Study the map on page 193 and on an outline map identify one major overland trade route and one major water route during medieval days.

4. Distinguish between craft and merchant guilds.

THE CONTRIBUTIONS OF MEN AND WOMEN TO MEDIEVAL CIVILIZATION

The Position of Women in Medieval Europe

Church teachings generally kept women in a second-class position. According to the Church, man, not woman was made in the image of God. To the Church of medieval Europe, women were considered "a necessary evil, a natural temptation, a desirable calamity, a domestic peril, a deadly fascination, a painted ill."* The great theologian Thomas Aquinas [ə kwī′nəs] also thought little of

*Will Durant, *The Age of Faith* (New York: Simon and Schuster, 1950), p. 825.

194

women. He said, "The woman is subject to the man on account of the weakness of her nature, both of mind and of body."*

Men and women were expected to marry. During the Middle Ages they did so when they were very young. Among the nobility, marriage contracts were extremely important. They could be used to seal treaties or to establish alliances. According to Church law, it was the duty of the husband to protect the wife and the duty of the wife to obey her husband. Wife beating was common and was not a crime either under Church or civil law. In a court of law, women could not testify or give evidence. Nor could women take formal part in government, although some noble women participated. No woman could become a licensed physician, although some women practiced medicine despite the law.

Women as well as men were expected to work in the fields. In addition, they were expected to care for the family, cook, bake, mend clothing, make soap and candles, brew beer, and mix medicines. In the towns, women did most of the spinning and weaving in the textile guilds. There were often as many women as men in the guilds because women were encouraged to help their husbands at their crafts. Several guilds, devoted to the manufacture of women's clothing, were made up entirely of women. Women usually received lower wages for the same work; and in guilds made up of both men and women it was rare for a woman to become a master.

Some noble women learned to read, write, and play musical instruments, activities sometimes considered beneath the dignity of warrior knights. With men often away at war, upper-class women had to manage the family estate, which required hard work and skill. Women

*Durant, p. 825

often joined in pilgrimages to holy places, and some shared with men the difficulties and the dangers of the Crusades. Sometimes, dressed in suits of armor, women fought side by side with men.

The lot of medieval women was a mixed one. Church and civil laws kept women in a lesser position than men. In practice, however, some women had great influence over their husbands, their families, and in some cases, over the affairs of state as well.

What School Was Like in Medieval Days

Education in the Middle Ages, although not as highly developed as it is today, was better than is generally realized. Church schools grew up around parish churches and monasteries. Since education was mostly in the hands of the Church, it was free from those who could, or would, spare their children from the farms. However, many parents in those days needed their children as workers or failed to realize the importance of education. Many did not let their children take advantage of the schooling the Church offered.

Many universities were founded by the Church during the Middle Ages. The teachers were often religious leaders. However, subjects other than religion were studied and taught. Medicine and law, as well as theology, were studied by those who were getting ready for these professions. Universities were established at London, Paris, Salerno, Padua, Salamanca, and Bologna. During the Late Middle Ages, universities were founded that had little connection with the Church.

University student life was much different from what it is today. One unique feature of college life in southern Europe

Eleanor of Aquitaine
(1122–1204)

Eleanor of Aquitaine [ak′wi tān′] was a famous medieval woman. She was the daughter of William X, Duke of Aquitaine. To his noble estate in Bordeaux [bôr dō′] in southern France went the best of the intellectual and artistic talent in Europe. Eleanor absorbed both the grace and the intellectual vitality of this glamorous court.

When she was fifteen, she married Louis VII, the king of France. Through marriage to Eleanor, Louis was able to attach the great duchy of Aquitaine to his holdings. The court of Louis VII was too dull for Eleanor's free spirit. To relieve the boredom she accompanied Louis to Palestine on the Second Crusade in 1147. Eleanor wore a suit of armor and boldly set forth.

Neither the bonds of matrimony nor tradition could keep Eleanor married to Louis VII. After fifteen years of marriage she sued him for a divorce on the grounds that they were remotely related to each other. The reason was accepted by the church. Her divorce was granted even though she and Louis had two daughters.

Eleanor returned to Bordeaux where she was immediately courted by many distinguished suitors. She finally chose Henry Plantagenet [plan taj′ə nit], heir to the throne of England. Two years later he became King Henry II. Eleanor of Aquitaine, once the queen of France was now queen of England as well. Eleanor and Henry had three daughters and five sons. This marriage failed also. In protest against Henry's unfaithfulness to her, Eleanor decided to return to her kingdom of Aquitaine. Henry then deposed (removed from the throne) Eleanor. In Aquitaine, Eleanor was captured by Henry's knights and kept imprisoned for fourteen years.

With two of her sons, Eleanor plotted unsuccessfully to overthrow Henry. When Henry died in 1189, their son Richard became king of England. He became known in history as Richard the Lion-Hearted. Richard released his mother and made her regent (acting ruler) of England while he went on the famous Third Crusade. During Richard's absence Eleanor prevented a plot to overthrow him. When Richard was held captive, it was Eleanor who raised the money for the ransom to free him. Richard died in 1199. Eleanor then supported her other son, John, in his claim to the throne.

From her court at Poitiers [pwä tyā′] in France, Eleanor encouraged education, art, and literature. She was a popular woman in her own time and medieval troubadours sang of her charm and talents.

was that the university was run by the students. By forming themselves into student guilds, students could help establish the rules that they needed. Students decided which teachers should be hired and what they should be paid. In the early universities, the teachers received their pay directly from the students. If a teacher's lecture was too long or too boring, students could leave.

One of the main roadblocks to the advancement of learning in the Middle Ages was the scarcity of books. There was no printing and most of the teaching was done by reading orally from the few books that were available. Even the simplest book was expensive. It is estimated that just an ordinary volume cost several hundred dollars. Books, copied on parchment by monks, were often handsomely illustrated. In an ordinary household, books were precious and were handed down from generation to generation. People of Western Europe did not have free libraries.

Medieval Achievements in Science

In the field of science, scholars of the Middle Ages were followers of the ancient scientists Aristotle, Galen, and Ptolemy. Roger Bacon, one of the most famous of the medieval scientists, used observation and experimentation in chemistry. In spite of his emphasis on observation and interpretation, magic and alchemy were often confused with science. Through *alchemy* scientists tried to change metals into gold and to find ways to lengthen human life. To change ordinary metals to gold was a false hope and served only to hold back the science of chemistry.

As science in the Middle Ages became more mature, there was less emphasis on magic and alchemy and more emphasis on observation and experimentation. Although the scientific method had not yet fully developed, there were a number of useful advances. The Arabic numbering system was taken from the Middle East. Mirrors, lenses, and clocks were among the practical medieval inventions.

What Medieval Europeans Read

An *epic* is a long poem telling of a hero's brave deeds. The Middle Ages was, among other things, an age when chivalry was an ideal. Epics of great heroes were an important part of the literature. One of the earliest epic poems, *Beowulf*, tells of the heroic deeds of Beowulf against wicked people and ferocious animals. Other epics of this period that have come down to us are the stories of *King Arthur and the Knights of the Round Table*. The French contributed the *Song of Roland*, and from the Germans came the *Nibelungenlied* [nē′bə lüng′ən lēt′]. These epics tell of heroic deeds of brave men and women. This early literature was used as a source for later poetry and music.

In this age of chivalry, the idea of romantic love played as crucial a role as bravery. Stories of romance were often sung by *troubadours* (poet musicians) who wandered from castle to castle singing songs of love and telling of the charms of fair ladies. Troubadours made the rounds in France, and minstrels performed the same duties in England.

A *fable* is a story that teaches a lesson. In medieval days, *Reynard the Fox* was the best known fable. In this collection of stories, the animals take on human qualities. Those who read the stories cannot help laughing at the foolish ways in which people behave, especially when they are pointed out to them by animals.

Drama was used by the Church as a means of telling people what it expected of them. Plays based on stories from the Bible were called *mystery plays;* those based on religious events not in the Bible were called *miracle plays;* those that tried to show the continuing struggle between good and evil were called *morality plays.* The theme of the plays was that it paid to be good.

The Most Delectable

HISTORY
O F
Reynard the Fox.

Newly Corrected and Purged, from all grofsnefs in Phrase and Matter.

Augmented and Enlarged with fundry Excellent Morals and Expofitions upon every feveral Chapter.

To which may now be added a Second Part of the said History: As alfo the Shifts of *Reynardine* the Son of *Reynard* the F O X, Together with his Life and Death, &c.

LONDON, Printed by *Tho. James,* for *Edward Brewfter,* at the Sign of the *Crane* in St. *Palus* Church-Yard. 1694.

A title page from a seventeenth century edition of *Reynard the Fox.* A favorite fable of medieval children, it still is read today.

What Medieval Philosophers Taught

Scholasticism [skə las'ti siz'əm] was the philosophy that dominated the medieval period. It held that faith could be achieved through logical reasoning. The scholastic method was not unlike the method used in the study of geometry. Geometry tries to prove theorems in a number of logical steps. It is necessary to write down what is given, to state what has to be proven, and to list the steps of the actual proof. In medieval times, formal logic was used to try to prove the most difficult questions of faith.

One great scholastic teacher was Peter Abelard [ab'ə lärd'] (1079–1142). His unhappy love affair with the brilliant and beautiful Heloise [el'ō ēz'] got him into difficulty with the Church. More troubles beset him when he wrote his well-known book, *Sic et Non,* or *Yes and No,* which showed that the Bible could be interpreted in many ways. The idea shocked many Catholic church leaders, who believed that there was only one correct way to interpret the Bible. Abelard became unpopular with Church leaders, but he was so respected by students that they flocked to his lectures. The attendance at his lectures was so large that he is said to be responsible for starting the University of Paris.

Thomas Aquinas [ə kwī'nəs] is noted for his book *Summa Theologica.* It is an encyclopedia of Christian teachings, but not the same kind as today's encyclopedia. Aquinas tried to show that Christian teachings did not disagree with reason. He said that if there was disagreement, then the method of reasoning must be wrong. Aquinas gave logical proof of the existence of God, for life after death, and for the authority of the Church. Thomas Aquinas was probably the greatest of all the scholastic philosophers of medieval days.

What Medieval Church Architecture Was Like

The period of the Middle Ages was also an age of faith. An expression of that faith was the medieval cathedral. The building of a cathedral was a community affair. It was paid for by the people of the community in which it was built, and was often built with their labor and talents. The cathedral was important to them.

Architecture was probably the greatest of the medieval arts. The Gothic style was characteristic of the period. It brings to mind tall spires, pointed arches, flying buttresses, stained glass windows, and carved statues. By using the flying buttress, medieval builders were able to make high roofs and thin walls. They cre-ated tall, impressive buildings. The Cathedral of Notre Dame and the Cathedral of Chartres are the best examples of Gothic architecture.

Check in Here

1. Explain the role of the Church in: (a) providing education in medieval days; (b) determining the role of medieval women.

2. Define each of the following: (a) epic poem; (b) morality play; (c) fable; (d) mystery play.

3. What did each of these people contribute to medieval philosophy: (a) Abelard; (b) Thomas Aquinas?

4. Why does the cathedral show that the Middle Ages was an age of faith?

REVIEWING THE BASICS

When Roman government collapsed it was replaced by a feudal system in Western Europe. In this system, vassals and serfs owed obligations to those who could protect them, usually a lord of some prominence. The great lords of medieval days were often more powerful than kings. Nations as we know them were beginning to develop, but there was no sense of national loyalty or patriotism or allegiance to a monarch. The Roman Catholic Church was all-powerful. It crowned monarchs and influenced every aspect of political, economic, and social life of the medieval people.

The power of the Church was demonstrated in the Crusades, which were undertaken to try to retake the Holy Land from the Muslims. In this effort, the Crusades were unsuccessful. However, they stimulated travel, trade, and commerce which eventually led to the development of towns. The medieval manor was gradually replaced as the center of economic and political life.

For the ordinary person, life in the medieval period was harsh. Disease was ever present and death never far away. There was a general acceptance of life as it was and little notion that the quality of one's life could be improved upon. Nevertheless, schools and colleges developed, courts of justice had their beginnings, merchant and craft guilds tried to look after the material benefits of their members, and the Church looked after souls. Scholasticism was the dominant philosophy.

REVIEWING THE HIGHLIGHTS

People to Identify

Huns
Visigoths
Alaric
Franks
Clovis
Charlemagne
Alfred the Great
Pepin the Short
Philip Augustus
Henry II

Angles, Saxons, Jutes
Danes
Canute
William the Conqueror
Hugh Capet
Vikings
Leif Ericson
Charles Martel
Henry IV

Otto I
Peter Abelard
Thomas Aquinas
Urban II
Gregory VII
Henry V
Eleanor of Aquitaine
Frederick Barbarossa
Saladin
Richard the Lion-Hearted

Places to Locate

Aix-la-Chapelle
Jerusalem
Rome
Canossa

Genoa
Venice
Milan
Florence

Pisa
Papal States
Holy Roman Empire

Terms to Identify

Middle Ages
medieval
Donation of Pepin
vassal
noble
serf
knight
scholasticism
Canon Law

Concordat of Worms
Hanseatic League
just price
chivalry
manor
craft guild
Gothic
Feudal Period
excommunication
bishop

ghetto
witan
apprentice
journeyman
merchant guild
heresy
alchemy
Crusades
freemen

Events to Describe

Battle of Adrianople

Mastering the Fundamentals

1. Describe the relationship between church and state during feudal times.
2. How did the German tribes react to the fall of Rome?
3. What is the significance of the crowning of Charlemagne by the pope?
4. What is meant by feudalism?

5. Why can it be said that feudalism was a political, social, and economic system unto itself?
6. Why did the Church play an important role in the affairs of people during medieval times?
7. Why was excommunication a severe punishment?
8. Why did Pope Urban II call for the first Crusade?
9. What reasons, other than religious ones, explain why many were eager to go on the Crusades? To what extent were the Crusades successful?
10. What were the causes of conflict between popes and kings during the medieval period?
11. Why did Henry IV go to Canossa? How was the dispute between him and Pope Gregory VII settled?
12. What were some of the ways that guilds controlled business in medieval times?
13. Why did feudal lords oppose the growth of towns? Give reasons why the lords were not successful in limiting the growth of the towns.
14. How did the growth of towns strengthen monarchs?
15. What was the role of women in the economic, political, and social life of the medieval period?
16. What reasons explain the growth of trade and commerce in medieval Europe?
17. What was the Hanseatic League?
18. Why were the merchant guilds more powerful than the craft guilds?
19. What were the chief obstacles to the spread of learning in medieval Europe?
20. Give one example of medieval contributions to: (a) science; (b) architecture; (c) literature.

THINGS TO DO

1. Draw a cartoon or diagram illustrating your understanding of the structure of the feudal manor.
2. Research project: Medieval education has been underestimated. Try to find out more about the following: (a) What schooling was available to the masses of people? (b) How did the Church provide schooling? (c) What schooling was available to women?
3. Write a speech for Pope Urban II urging everybody to go on the Crusade.

To historians every scrap of written evidence may be valuable in the efforts to interpret the past accurately. Documents of state or even personal letters are of value to the historian. Below is a letter from a university student written during the medieval period. It was not written with the idea that it would ever appear in any book, yet historians have studied it.

Well-beloved father, I have not a penny nor can I get any save through you, for all things at the University are so dear; nor can I study in my Code or my Digest,* for they are all tattered. Moreover, I owe ten crowns due to the Provost,* and can find no man to lend them to me: I send you word of greetings and of money.

   The Student hath need of many things if he will profit here; his father and his kin* must needs supply him freely, that he be not compelled to pawn his books, but have ready money in his purse, with gowns and furs and decent clothing, or he will be damned for a beggar; wherefore, that men may not take me for a beast; I send you word of greetings and of money.

   Wines are dear, and hostels,* and other good things; I owe in every street, and am hard bested to free myself from such snares. Dear father, deign* to help me! I fear to be excommunicated. . . . If I find not the money before this feast of Easter, the church door will be shut in my face; wherefore, grant my supplication,* for I send you word of greetings and of money.†

Vocabulary
Code and Digest—textbooks
provost—university official
kin—relatives
hostels—inns
deign—stoop
supplication—plea

1. Why is the selection above of interest to the historian?
2. What does it reveal to you about university life during the medieval period?
3. As a historian, what precautions would you have to take in order to interpret this document correctly?
4. Is this a *primary* or *secondary* source? Justify your position.
5. What does the document appear to reveal about the relationships between the university and the Church?
6. *Optional:* What kinds of things would a university student of today ask for?

†G. G. Coulton, *Life in the Middle Ages* (Cambridge, England: Cambridge University Press, 1929), Vol. III, p. 113.

A panel from the Sistine Chapel painted by Michelangelo

The Renaissance and the Reformation: New Views in Learning and Religion

You might be proud of the fact that you live in the modern world. To most people, modern means skyscrapers, telephones, suburban communities, airplanes, automobiles, computers, space satellites, and television. Being modern, however, means more than believing in material improvements and comforts. Modern thinking suggests that the quality of life can be improved through our own effort and education.

During the fourteenth through the sixteenth centuries, a period known as the *Renaissance* [ren'i säns'], modern times began to develop in Europe. The word "renaissance" means rebirth. During the Middle Ages, interest in learning

203

declined. Then during the fourteenth through the sixteenth centuries there was a reawakened interest in the learning of the past. Ancient works were read with new interest. Experiments were tried in writing, painting, science, and technology. People became optimistic and bold. They became "modern," in the sense that they believed that people could make things better if they worked to do so.

THE RENAISSANCE: DEFINED AND EXPLAINED

The Nature of the Renaissance

Educated people in the early medieval period spoke and wrote mostly in Latin. Ordinary people could neither write nor read Latin. During the Renaissance, books were written in everyday language. However, most people were not educated. In different areas different languages developed and grew. These special forms of Latin became known as the *Romance languages*. They varied from place to place and formed the basis of the French, Spanish, Italian, Portuguese, and Romanian languages.

Everyday language is known as *vernacular* [vər nak'yə lər]. This is the native language of a region, such as Italian. During the Renaissance, books were written in the vernacular rather than in pure Latin. Dante [dan'tē] (1265–1321) led the movement toward the vernacular with *The Divine Comedy*. Written in Italian, this is a story poem that tells of an imaginary trip to the hereafter. The *Song Book* by Petrarch [pē'trärk] (1304–1374), also written in Italian, encouraged the development of the Italian language. *The Canterbury Tales* by Chaucer [chô'sər] (1340–1400) was written in English. This is a collection of stories in verse told by pilgrims on their way to and from the Thomas à Becket shrine at Canterbury.

During the Middle Ages, religion was the most important influence in the lives and thoughts of the people. They worried about what would happen to their bodies and souls after death. They depended on the Church for answers to many of their questions. In the Renaissance, some people began to question some of the beliefs held during the Middle Ages. Life on earth concerned them more than life after death. Some said people could lead full, rich lives here on earth. Those who taught this were called *humanists*. The humanists turned to the thinking of ancient Greeks and Romans, such as Plato, Socrates, and Aristotle. They were no longer willing to accept knowledge and beliefs without question.

Erasmus [i raz'məs] was one of the great humanists. In his book, *The Praise of Folly*, he poked fun at the privileged position of the nobles. Although a critic of the Church, he did not believe in breaking away from it. Erasmus encouraged people to try to improve their lives by following Christian principles. Another humanist and close friend of Erasmus was the Englishman, Thomas More. In his book *Utopia* [yü tō'pē ə], More drew a picture of a perfect society that people might try to attain. More regarded property as the root of all evil.

People of the Renaissance began to raise questions. Was everything in the Bible true? Was Aristotle right or wrong?

Renaissance men and women wanted to test old beliefs. They wanted proof before they were satisfied that certain things were true. Some superstitious beliefs that they once held closely were given up one by one.

Where the Renaissance Began

Italy was made up of a number of city-states including Florence, Genoa, Pisa, Venice, and others. Because of Italy's location in the Mediterranean, these city-states traded with the Middle East and became prosperous. The existence of trade and cultural contact with other civilizations is one of the reasons why the Renaissance began in Italy in the fourteenth century.

The Italian city-states competed for wealth, power, and glory. Competition encouraged the city-states to try out new forms of government, new ways of doing business, and new forms of art. Through competition each city-state tried to gain an advantage over the other. Enough freedom existed in the Italian city-states to encourage a desire for learning. At that time, wars hindered the growth of other nations of northern Europe. The small Italian city-states survived because they were not strong enough to destroy one another in war. These developments further explain why the Renaissance began in Italy.

Italy was the home of ancient Rome. Scholars from all over Europe went to Italy to study the famous writings of the past and the remains of many ancient buildings. Italy was also the center of the Church, which used its wealth to promote painting, learning, and writing. Thus, the Church helped the rebirth of learning.

We have seen that the Renaissance began in Italy for four reasons. First, the Italian city-states were rich; second, Italy

Sir Thomas More, a humanist, wrote a book in which he suggested ways that society might be reformed. What was its title?

was the birthplace of Roman civilization; third, Italy was the host to many scholars; and fourth, the Church encouraged learning and culture. From Italy, the Renaissance crossed the Alps and spread to northern Europe.

Check in Here

1. Define the term *Renaissance*.
2. List the leading Italian city-states in which the Renaissance began.
3. Identify three reasons why the Renaissance began in Italy.
4. Identify four characteristics of the Renaissance.

Renaissance Europe

Why was Italy's location favorable to the development of trade in Renaissance Europe?

- Why was Italy's location favorable to the development of trade in Renaissance Europe?
- Locate and name four Italian city-states.

GREAT PEOPLE
AND GREAT CITIES:
SYMBOLS OF
THE RENAISSANCE

Why Leonardo da Vinci Is a Symbol of the Renaissance

The Renaissance had many geniuses in art, literature, and science. A list of them would not tell about the restless spirit, the inquiring mind, and the ability to do many things well that marked the individuality of the age. It is important to remember, nevertheless, that the Renaissance was mostly an upper-class movement. Only gradually did it help improve conditions for the people in the lower classes. The spirit of the times was one that encouraged asking questions and doing many things well.

No one is more typical of the spirit of the Renaissance than Leonardo da Vinci [də vin'chē] (1452–1519). Leonardo is best known as a great painter. The "Last Supper" and "Mona Lisa" are two of his well-known masterpieces. Leonardo was also a sculptor, a scientist, an engineer, and an inventor. All these things he did almost equally well. His drawings of the human form were used by medical students in their studies. Leonardo was active in every science. He wanted to test everything by experience rather than accept authority. He made significant studies in astronomy, and understood physics, sound, sight, and light.

As an inventor, Leonardo was a genius. He is credited with having made a thread-cutting machine and an improved water wheel. He designed a machine gun, military fortifications, and weapons. He was fascinated with the idea of flight. Doing many things well was characteristic of many people in the Renaissance. However, even for the Renaissance Leonardo was outstanding for his versatility.

Other Giants of the Renaissance

Leonardo da Vinci was a giant among giants. There were other geniuses who contributed to the Renaissance. They, like Leonardo, could do many things well. Artists learned to use line, light, and shadow to show realism in their canvases and *frescoes* (paintings on plaster). They experimented with color and used oil paints. Renaissance artists painted mostly religious subjects, although non-religious themes were sometimes introduced. Painting is perhaps one of the greatest contributions of the geniuses of the Renaissance.

Giotto [jōt'ō] (1276–1337) is known for his effective use of light and shade to add depth to his paintings. In this way he influenced many Renaissance artists and changed their ideas about what art should look like.

Raphael [raf'ē əl] (1483–1520) was a gentle soul. His paintings were not vigorous or dynamic; they reflected his quiet ways. Many of his paintings glorify the teachings of Greece. In his painting "School of Athens," Plato and Aristotle, among others, debate the finer points of philosophy.

During the Renaissance art flowered in Italy. Artists from northern Europe learned techniques from Italian artists and made contributions of their own. Painters from Holland, Spain, and what is now Belgium and Germany traveled to Italy to study under the great Italian masters. As a result, northern Europe too experienced a rebirth of art.

Some of the Leading Women of the Renaissance*

Many women contributed to the development of the Renaissance, particularly in Italy. Italian women of the upper classes knew Latin, wrote sonnets, and became patrons of the arts. They often supported some of the great male Renaissance artists. Writers such as Petrarch respected the great women at the court of Naples. Lucrezia Borgia [bôr'jə] (1480–1519) is falsely known in history as a depraved and violent woman. She was in fact kind and brilliant. Many artists and poets flourished under her protection at her sparkling court at Ferrara, Italy.

*This section is based on Elise Boulding, *The Underside of History* (Boulder, Colorado: Westview Press, 1976), pp. 541–546.

Michelangelo Buonarroti (1475–1564)

As were so many of the other great leaders of the Renaissance, Michelangelo [mĭ'kəl an' jə lō'] was a product of the City of Florence. In the household of Lorenzo de Medici, Michelangelo came under the influence of the humanists. They encouraged him to create such varied works as a sculpture of "Bacchus" [bak'əs] and the "Pietà" [pē'ä tä']. "Bacchus" shows the young god nibbling on grapes. The "Pietà" shows Mary holding her dead son Jesus. Among Michelangelo's other great sculptures are the giant marble figures of "David" and "Moses."

Michelangelo is also famous for his paintings on the ceiling of the Sistine [sis'tēn] Chapel in the Vatican. The ceiling was done for Pope Julius II, who constantly prodded Michelangelo to get the task done so that it could be proudly shown. Michelangelo, however, would not be hurried. Originally, he had some artists to help him, but later he sent them all away. Alone, lying on his back on the scaffold, he worked. His progress was slow and painful, but he produced a work of art that remains one of the glories of the Western world.

Michelangelo was the chief architect of St. Peter's Cathedral in Rome, an assignment he took in 1546 at the age of seventy. He died long before the cathedral was completed, but it was his plan that was followed. He designed the main feature of St. Peter's, the great dome that rises 130 meters (435 ft.) above the floor. Although large in size, it looks smaller than it really is.

In an age when rich people dressed with elegance and flair, Michelangelo chose to go about in rags. Although he had enough money to live comfortably, he chose to live among the poor. He slept in his clothes and often shared his bed with his workers. He gave most of his earnings to less successful relatives and preferred being alone. Thoughtful and brooding, Michelangelo died knowing few moments of contentment or peace of mind.

Italian Renaissance women who were well known as great composers were Vittoria Alcotte [äl côt'ā], Francesca Baglonclea [bäg lôn klē'ə], and Orsina Vizzani [vi zan'ē]. Caterina de Virgri [vir'grē] was a painter in the city of Fer-rara and a patroness of the arts as well. She was made a saint and became the protector of academies and art institutions of the Catholic world. Properzia de'Rossi [ros'ē] of Bologna, was a popular sculptor who aroused much jealousy among her male competitors. So sharp did this competition become that men campaigned against her so that her work was not displayed on the building for which it had been carved. She died at the age of forty.

Anna Maria Ardoin [är dō in'] was a poet and an artist as well as a musician. Sophonisba [sō fō nis' bə] of Cremona (1535–1625) was in demand all over Europe as a portrait painter; Lavinia Fontana [fôn tän'ə] of Bologna (1552–1614) was an active and popular artist, as was Catharina van Hemessen [he'me sən] (1528–1587). Artemisia Gentileschi [jen tēl es'kī] (1593–1652) was considered to be the greatest of the Italian women artists. She worked in Rome, Florence, Genoa, Naples, and London and was an important influence on the development of the Neapolitan School of Painting.

An outstanding Renaissance woman was Tarquinia Molza [môl'tsə]. She "had a rare knowledge of astronomy, and mathematics, Latin, Greek, and Hebrew. So great was the esteem in which she was held that the Senate of Rome conferred upon her the singular honor of Roman citizenship. . . ."*

In other European countries there were also many important Renaissance women. In Spain, Queen Isabella was a very learned woman who encouraged scholarship among the women of her court. Beatriz Galindo [gə lēn'dō] founded schools, hospitals, and convents all over Spain. Olivia Sabuco [sa bü'kō] de Nantes, at the age of twenty-five, wrote a seventy-volume series of books. The subjects were biology, psychology, anthropology, medicine, and agriculture.

In France, a notable Renaissance woman was Marie de Jars de Gournay [də gür nā'] (1565–1655). She was a fine scholar and a writer whose books on

Lucrezia Borgia, whose court at Ferrara attracted many artists and writers.

education and public affairs were dedicated to Henry IV and to Marie de'Medici, her patrons. Her books were widely read, including her translations of Virgil, Ovid, and Tacitus. She was one of the few Renaissance women who actually made a living from her writings. Marie de Jars de Gournay was an early feminist. She vigorously attacked a society in which it was difficult for women to achieve recognition for their intellects. She commented in one of her works: "Lucky are you, reader, if you happen not to be of that sex to whom it is forbidden all good things, to whom liberty is denied; to whom almost all virtues are denied; lucky are you if you are one of those who can be wise without its being a crime."**

Accomplishments by women during the Renaissance were made against great odds. Schooling for them was possible only if men permitted it and encouraged them. In most countries such permission and encouragement were grudgingly

*Boulding, p. 541.

**Boulding, p. 545.

A Renaissance painting portrays Lorenzo de Medici on horseback. How did he encourage the arts in Florence?

given, and then usually only to the upper-class women. In Italy and Spain women of the upper classes could attend universities. However, this was not the case elsewhere. Most women did not rebel against their status. With the exception of Marie de Gournay and a few others, most women were content to remain in the shadows and expected little more.

Why Florence Is a Symbol of Renaissance Culture

In the northern part of the Italian peninsula were a number of rich city-states, each of which competed with the others for leadership. One of the most impor-tant of the Italian Renaissance cities was Florence. Except for Venice, Florence was the richest city in Italy. In its early years, it had been somewhat democratic. It had an alert and public-minded citizenry. Later, it became the scene of political plotting as various people sought to win control of the city for their families. Out of this struggle the Medici [med'ə chē'] family became powerful in Florence.

Lorenzo [lō ren'zō] the Magnificent (1449–92) was the most famous member of the Medici family. He was probably the richest man in Florence and, perhaps, in all of Italy. He was everything a Renaissance ruler was expected to be. He was ruthless and cunning, but also generous as a patron of art and learning.

He was a scholar in his own right, and he encouraged scholarship in the schools. Through his generosity, he supported the development of the Italian language and made Florence a renowned center for artists. Under his rule, Florence became a brilliant city filled with beautiful buildings and statues.

One of the victims of the political scheming in Florence was Niccolo Machiavelli [mak′ē ə vel′ē] (1469–1527). In an effort to get back his position, wealth, and glory, Machiavelli wrote a book called *The Prince*. He stated that a king need not be bound by any considerations of right and wrong when governing his kingdom. Rather, the ends justified the means. Violence and trickery were to be excused if they kept the king in power and made the nation strong. Dictators since then have often taken instruction from the writings of Machiavelli.

Numerous geniuses in art and architecture fill the history of the city of Florence. The architecture of Filippo Brunelleschi [brün′ə les′kē] moved the Gothic style into more delicate forms. The bronze doors of Lorenzo Ghiberti [gē ber′tē], done in fine relief, illustrated the New and Old Testaments. Donatello [dôn′ə tel′ō] studied and surpassed his master, Ghiberti. He went on to sculpt the bronze figure of "David," which rivaled the "David" of Michelangelo. There were many geniuses of the Florentine Renaissance. They were the outstanding leaders of an artistic industry that included glass blowing, metal engraving, making weapons, and furniture making. Artists created products that were both decorative and useful.

In literature, Pico della Mirandola [mir an dō′lə] demonstrated the qualities of humanism. His mind was open to and tolerant of every philosophy and every faith. He understood but did not agree with scholasticism. He admired Arabic and Jewish thought. Pico tried to blend the great religions of Judaism, Christianity, and Islam, not only with one another, but with the teachings of Plato and Aristotle. Although he was unsuccessful in his effort, his attempt helps us understand the nature of the Renaissance.

Why Venice Is a Symbol of Renaissance Commerce

Venice was a republic headed by a *Doge* [dōj], or Duke. The Doge was chosen by a Council of Ten made up of wealthy and important families. Venice sent ambassadors to the great cities of Europe and the Middle East. The government used some of its wealth to build the Grand Canal, the Palace of the Doges, and the Church of St. Mark. In Venice, the great schools of painting of Titian [tish′ən] and Tintoretto [tēn′tô ret′ō] flourished. The government and the culture of Venice were made possible by the city's importance as a trading center. If Florence

Lorenzo Ghiberti sculpted the bronze doors of the baptistry at Florence. This panel tells the story of Esau and Jacob.

represented Italian Renaissance culture, then Venice represented Renaissance commerce. Both cities, however, were centers of business and culture.

Venice was one of the many Italian cities whose economies flourished during the Crusades. Genoa, Pisa, Milan, and Florence also profited. Venice, however, prospered more than the others. It was known as the "Queen of the Adriatic" and the "Mistress of the Mediterranean." Venetian trade was carried on far and wide. Venetian *galleys* (ships) were the envy of the world. These sleek vessels had room for 225 tonnes (250 short tons) of cargo, which was a lot for those days. Venetians made such good use of sails that oarsmen were used only for getting in and out of port. Fleets of these vessels carried wines and spices and other products to Flanders, Beirut, and London. These vessels made regular all-water trade possible between Italy and Europe. All-water routes were cheaper and safer than overland routes.

Because of its industry, Venice was central to the economic life of southern Europe. Venice was known for the finest cloth and glass and leather products, which were eagerly bought in the markets of Europe and Asia. All the products were made by hand, without the help of power-driven machinery.

One of the major characteristics of the Renaissance was a growth in finance and banking. During the Middle Ages money-lending and charging interest on borrowed money were forbidden by the Church. During the Renaissance these were still regarded with suspicion, but increasingly recognized as necessary to trade, commerce, and manufacturing. Kings, popes, and merchants needed money to finance their activities. Banks grew in number and wealth and performed many functions. They loaned money and enabled merchants to change money from one currency to another.

Without such services commerce could not be carried out.

The Italians were the bankers of the Renaissance. Venice played an important role in banking, but not as great as that played by Florence under the two great banking houses of Bardi [bär′dē] and Peruzzi [pə rü′tsē].

The importance of Venice as a trading community began to decline in the fifteenth century. The discovery of the New World made the Atlantic more important than the Mediterranean as a commercial waterway. Gradually, the importance of Venice as a commercial center faded away.

What the Renaissance Achieved in Science and Technology

Along with the artistic growth of the Renaissance there were also advances in technology and science. In technology, the development of printing was the most important. The Chinese invented printing, but they printed books from blocks, each of which represented a full page. Each block was carved so that the raised letters showed up. The ink was then spread on the block and the paper pressed down upon it.

In Germany, printer Johann Gutenberg [güt′ən bėrg] developed a new printing method in 1450. He used wood and cut out each letter separately. Individual letters could then be bound together in words on a slotted board. When the printing process was finished, the letters could be separated and another group of words arranged for printing another page. In this way, printing by means of *movable type* was born. Later, Gutenberg learned how to make letters from metal and how to press the paper evenly onto the type. The printing press, together with a method for making cheap paper, made possible the spread of learning throughout the world.

Modern science was also born during the Renaissance. The anatomical drawings of the human body by Leonardo da Vinci provided a better understanding of how the body worked and how blood circulated. In medicine, Vesalius [vi sā'lē əs] (1514–64) wrote *The Structure of the Human Body*. It contained the most accurate illustrations of the human body available up to that time.

The astronomer Nicolaus Copernicus [kō per'nə kəs] (1473–1543) made an important scientific discovery. Copernicus discovered and said that the sun, and not the earth, was the center of the universe. This upset the theory of Ptolemy, which scientists had believed for centuries. Ptolemy believed that the earth was at the center of the universe. Copernicus said that the earth made a circular path about the sun. We now know that the path is an oval. The findings of Copernicus helped prepare the way for greater advances in astronomy in the seventeenth century.

Renaissance science laid the foundation for the great scientific progress that was to take place during the seventeenth and eighteenth centuries. However, one of the limitations of Renaissance science was a great dependence on the learning of Greece and Rome. The humanists believed that little of scientific value could be discovered beyond what Galen in medicine or Ptolemy in astronomy had already described. Leonardo da Vinci himself kept notes on subjects that interested him. Leonardo, however, kept his

Venice was a wealthy seafaring city during the Middle Ages and early Renaissance. Its beautiful buildings on the Grand Canal have been painted by artists over the centuries. This painting of Venice was done in the eighteenth century by Canaletto.

(*top*) The Gutenberg printing press, which introduced movable type. How did this invention affect the Renaissance world?

(*bottom*) Part of a page from Leonardo da Vinci's notebook showing sketches for flying machines. Note the mirror-image handwriting.

notebooks secret. He did not, as do modern scientists, anxiously seek to publish new discoveries. He also lacked the modern scientist's technique of systematic observation. He often questioned authority, yet on occasion he was awed by it.

Check in Here

1. Compare and contrast Venice and Florence as Renaissance cities in the areas of: (**a**) culture; (**b**) business and industry.

2. In your view, is Leonardo da Vinci an appropriate symbol of the Renaissance? Why or why not?

3. What were some of the achievements of the Renaissance in science and technology?

4. Identify a contribution of each of the following to Renaissance science or technology: (**a**) Johann Gutenberg; (**b**) Vesalius; (**c**) Nicolaus Copernicus; (**d**) Leonardo da Vinci.

5. What were some of the shortcomings of Renaissance science?

CHURCH ABUSES THAT LED TO THE PROTESTANT REFORMATION

The Protestant Reformation

During the Middle Ages, all Christians in Western Europe were Roman Catholics. They were members of the Church and followed the directions of the pope as handed down through bishops and local parish priests. The Church, up to 1500

A.D., had been many things. It was a government that taxed and a court that administered justice. It controlled the life of the lowliest individual and that of the haughtiest monarch. But this situation did not continue unaltered. It changed in a way that influenced the daily lives of people.

Some historians called this change the *Protestant Reformation*. It was called "protestant" because it was led by people who protested against or opposed some of the practices of the Church. It was called a "reformation" because in the beginning there were many people who simply wanted to make the Church better, or to reform it. The religious changes are also sometimes referred to as the *Protestant Revolt*. Some saw the changes as a revolt against the established Church. Whether a reformation or revolt, the religious changes of the sixteenth century had far-reaching results.

The Causes of the Protestant Reformation

By the sixteenth century, the Christian Church was over fifteen hundred years old. It was the oldest and most established institution in the Western world. It was older than any government. With its growth had come such wealth and power that it was feared by monarchs and commoners alike.

With riches, age, and power came certain abuses. The Church had allowed its priests to become more concerned with worldly affairs than with affairs of the spirit. Church jobs were sometimes bought and sold. The Church had taught that proper prayer and repentance would open the gate of heaven to sinners. However, by 1500, the power of the Church to grant *indulgences* [in dul'jən səs] (partial forgiveness for sins) had become subject to much abuse. Indulgences were sold,

making forgiveness a matter of money rather than conscience. The large sums of money raised by selling indulgences went to the pope in Rome.

In 1514, Pope Leo X sought funds to rebuild St. Peter's Church in Rome. He hoped to raise the money through the sale of many indulgences. An ambitious Dominican monk named Johann Tetzel [tet'səl] traveled around northern Germany urging people to buy an indulgence and thus be forgiven for their sins. "So soon as the coin in coffer [treasury] rings," declared Tetzel, "the soul from purgatory [hell] springs." In his great enthusiasm Tetzel declared that if one gave generously enough, sins committed in the future could be forgiven. By saying this, Tetzel strayed very far from traditional Church teachings.

In the past, religious thinkers spoke against Church practices. John Wycliffe [wī'klif] (1320–84) in England and John Huss [hus] (1369–1415) in Bohemia voiced their concern about the authority of the Church in the fourteenth century. Wycliffe produced the first complete English translation of the Bible. People could then read the Bible for themselves. Both Huss and Wycliffe were punished for their views. While Wycliffe escaped with his life, John Huss, who followed the teachings of Wycliffe, was burned at the stake. Erasmus [i raz'məs], a Dutch humanist, remained within the Roman Catholic Church, but he, too, pointed out that certain practices in the Church needed to be changed.

The influence of the Church began to decline as a result of the so-called "Babylonian Captivity" (1309–77). Between 1378 and 1417, French and Italian popes fought each other for sole authority over the Church. French cardinals in Avignon [a vē nyôn'] supported a French pope. Italian cardinals in Rome supported an Italian one. The rivalry between the two popes did not end easily. Most European nations sided with one or the other of the popes. Between 1414 and 1418, a Church Council met in Constance, Germany. For four years the council argued over who should be pope and how the abuses of the Church should be overcome. The council finally elected a new pope who would lead the Church from Rome. Although the council members knew what reforms were needed, they were unable to bring them about.

Ambitious monarchs did not like to share power with the pope. They sometimes encouraged people who tried to break away from the established Church. In addition, trade and commerce were thriving as people settled new lands and financed new businesses. The Roman Catholic Church opposed the making of profits by charging interest for loans. Its teachings were not always followed, and in this way its power weakened.

The Renaissance encouraged learning. Books became more easily available. People read more and were less likely to accept ideas without questioning. The ideas of the Church, like those of science or literature, were closely examined. A combination of these trends led to the Protestant Reformation.

How Luther Contributed to the Protestant Reformation

Two outstanding leaders of the Reformation were Martin Luther [lü′thər] (1483–1546) and John Calvin [kal′vin] (1509–64). Luther in Germany and Calvin in France and Switzerland protested against some medieval practices of the Church. Their views differed so from those of the Catholic Church that in time new religious groups were formed.

Martin Luther began his career in the Church as a monk, but later he left the monastery to start an individual crusade against Church practices. He fasted, prayed, and taught the Bible, as was usual among brothers of his monastery. However, his mind and soul were not at rest. From his reading of the Bible, Luther came to believe that faith in God was all a person needed in order to be saved. He reasoned that if faith alone were needed for salvation, then the services of the Church and pope were not necessary. He felt that those who were faithful could interpret the Bible for themselves without the aid of priests.

Luther wrote about his ideas and about Church abuses while he was still in the Church. He attacked the sale of indulgences, or pardons for sin. In 1517, he nailed a list of statements about indulgences to the doors of the Wittenberg [wit′ən bėrg] Cathedral. These were known as the *Ninety-Five Theses*. In days when there were no newspapers, posting a public notice on the church door was the usual way of getting one's ideas before the people. This way, Luther publicly invited scholars to debate his views.

Johann Eck [ek], one of the most distinguished scholars and speakers in the Church, took up the challenge to debate Martin Luther. While the immediate issue was the question of the sale of indulgences, the debate quickly spread to other teachings of the Church. From his responses to Eck's challenges, it became evident that Luther could not stay within the Church. When questioned about whether or not he would obey the authority of the Church in matter of indulgences and other practices, Luther responded that he would refer to the Bible alone. This was a position not unlike that taken by John Huss, who was burned at the stake for his views.

With the aid of the new printing presses, Luther's ideas spread quickly throughout Europe. Luther wrote to the kings and princes of Germany's many states clarifying his position but not backing away from it. Luther attacked the Church and urged the German princes to join him in ridding the German states of Church influence in political affairs. At first, the Church took little notice of Luther. As Luther moved further away from official Church teachings, a break, however, in their relations seemed to be the only possible course. Luther's ideas spread quickly. In 1520, Pope Leo X (1513–1521) excommunicated Luther from the Church. Emperor Charles V declared him an outlaw who was to be killed on sight. Luther was neither captured nor killed, due, in large measure, to the German princes, who liked his ideas and helped him escape.

Although Luther was excommunicated by the pope, he continued to write and speak against the Church. He wrote in German, the language of the people, and what he wrote was widely read. He translated the New Testament into German. By doing so, he helped to develop German as a common language for the German people. Luther also translated the Old Testament into German. In his pamphlets he urged that the papacy be resisted as any other foreign power. Luther declared that taxes going to support the pope could better be used to help the poor at home.

Luther's beliefs were based on the idea that salvation could be achieved through faith in the Bible. The traditional sacraments, except for baptism, communion, and penance, were eliminated. Luther also eliminated the structure of the Roman Catholic Church from his new faith. For reasons of their own, German princes were quick to adopt Luther's ideas. Some responded favorably because they genuinely believed in what he said. Others used Luther's beliefs as a chance to rid their lands of the influence of the Roman Catholic Church. They wanted to take over Church lands and wealth.

Martin Luther, one of the leaders of the Protestant Reformation. What were some of his criticisms of the Catholic Church?

Luther did not understand what he had done. He believed that individuals could interpret the Bible for themselves and that salvation would come through faith alone. He thereby encouraged different interpretations of the Bible. When some rejected Luther's ideas as well as Catholicism, Luther was upset.

Encouraged to interpret the Bible for themselves, some people took independent political and economic views as well. If one could think independently in religion, why not in other areas too? In 1523–1524 a *Peasants' War* broke out. Peasants sought to improve their lots in life. They rose up, murdered nobles, and destroyed castles. Martin Luther then encouraged the princes to suppress the rebellion harshly.

Luther, violently hostile to Jews, was also intolerant of Christians who did not interpret the Bible as he did. This, however, did not prevent the growth of other Protestant faiths. *Lutheranism* was the Protestant faith founded by Luther. Many German lands adopted Luther's religious ideas. Others, such as the Scandinavians, adopted them too.

In 1546, shortly after Luther's death, a war broke out between the rulers who had chosen Luther's ideas and Charles V and his Roman Catholic supporters. The war ended in 1555 with the *Peace of Augsburg* [ôgz′bėrg]. It was agreed that the religion of the prince would be the religion of the state. The peace treaty did not take into account the will of the people. It was important, however, because it contained the idea that different religious beliefs were possible.

Check in Here

1. Summarize three basic reasons for the Protestant Reformation.

2. How did the sale of indulgences differ from the traditional teachings of the Church?

3. Why was Luther saved from death while Huss was not?

THE PROTESTANT REFORMATION SPREADS TO OTHER COUNTRIES

What Calvin Contributed to the Protestant Reformation

Just as Germany became the birthplace of Lutheranism, so did the Swiss cities become the birthplace of *Calvinism*. The cities of Switzerland, like the states of Germany, were seething with dissatisfaction over abusive practices in the Church. Ulrich Zwingli [zwing′lē] (1484–1531) of Zurich was the first organizer who fought for reform. He knew the teachings of Luther thoroughly, but did not accept them fully. Zwingli was eager to free Zurich and other Swiss cities from the domination of the Church. When war broke out between the Catholic Swiss cities and Protestant Zurich, Zwingli led his people in battle. He was defeated and killed. Reform would come with John Calvin [kal′vin] (1509–1564), a more powerful leader.

The city of Geneva was the center of the Protestant Revolution led by Calvin. Under John Calvin's leadership, Geneva became the model of Calvinistic teachings and practices. Calvin made his views known in his famous work *Institutes of the Christian Religion* (1536). It is one of the great books of the Protestant faith. Calvin and his followers believed that only the people whom God had chosen would be saved. Neither good works nor faith could change God's plans. Calvinists were taught that they must lead God-fearing lives since they did not know whether or not they were saved or doomed.

Calvin's ideas had wide appeal. He departed even further from traditional Catholic doctrine than did Luther. Calvin rejected the ceremonies and the rites of the Catholic Church. The church building itself was shorn of any decorations. Instead, it became a place for direct communication between the worshippers and the Lord. For twenty-three years, Calvin ruled Geneva. In time it became a *theocracy* [thē ok′rə sē], a place where government and religion were one.

Under Calvin, Geneva became a city in which merriment was absent. Calvin and his followers frowned on luxury, idleness, games, and dancing. These things were viewed as sinful. No one really knew who was assured of salvation. Therefore, it was only wise to behave as if one was of the elect of God. Everyone in Geneva was expected to work hard because the "devil waits for idle hands."

Protestant and Catholic Europe About 1600

By 1600, most of Europe was divided between the Protestant and Catholic religions.
- Of what religion were the majority of the people in the northern part of the Holy Roman Empire?
- Were there Protestants in Poland?
- What was the main religion in Hungary?

Despite its stern ideas, Calvin's teachings spread to other lands. Calvinism had wide appeal for the growing class of business people. It encouraged such practices as industry and thrift and did not discourage either profit making or money lending. The *Institutes* of Calvin were widely read and became influential.

Calvinism also offered a strong system of church government that required strict discipline. Since Calvinism looked neither to the papacy nor to the government of the state for support, it had to survive through its own efforts and discipline. In France, the followers of Calvin were called *Huguenots* [hyü′gə nots′], and in

King Henry VIII. What action of his led to England's break with the Catholic Church?

England they were *Puritans*. Presbyterian and Congregational faiths originally based their teachings on the ideas of Calvin.

Why England Broke with Rome

In England, too, a movement against the Church was underway. There, politics was more important than religious belief in separating England from its Catholicism. Ill feeling had developed between the people of England and the pope. The government no longer wanted the pope's interference in national affairs. The government had to pay heavy taxes to the Church, and the people did not like foreigners occupying church offices in England. In the fourteenth century, John Wycliffe daringly attacked the wealth and earthly power of the Church's priests and bishops. The humanists Sir Thomas More and Erasmus, who was Dutch, had discussed Church reform. Lutheranism had found its way to England through merchants and wandering scholars. The printing press helped spread Protestant literature.

When Henry VIII began to rebel against Roman Catholic authortiy, he received much popular support. No male heir to the throne had been born during his marriage to Catherine of Aragon. Henry wanted a divorce from her to marry the younger Anne Boleyn [bủl'in]. The pope refused to give Henry his divorce because Henry's wife, Catherine, was related to the powerful Catholic king, Charles V of Spain. Moreover, the pope had given Henry special permission for his marriage to Catherine in the first place.

Despite the pope's opposition, Henry was determined to marry Anne Boleyn. The English Parliament was willing to break with the Church. Then the vast Church lands would come under government control and the influence of the pope would be lessened in England. After the necessary laws had been passed, the Church of England was established with Henry, and not the pope, as its head. The Church of England, referred to as the *Anglican* [ang'glə kən] Church, differed little from the Catholic Church in doctrine. It did not, however, serve the pope in Rome. Opposition to the Church of England from those who preferred the Catholic Church continued throughout Henry's reign. It was not until the end of the reign of his daughter, Elizabeth I, that the Anglican Church was firmly established.

The Counter Reformation

Wise Church leaders began to feel that the time had come for the Catholic Church to take the reform movement into its own hands. They started what is known as the *Counter Reformation.* Many efforts were made in Spain, Italy, and Rome to reform the Church. At the *Council of Trent,* which began to meet in 1545, an attempt was made to reform the Catholic Church. The debate continued over a period of eighteen years. The Council restated the main teachings of the Church. In addition, it issued a new edition of the Bible and made a number of important reforms that enabled the Church to stop further losses to Protestantism. As a result of its reforms, the Church was strengthened. Through a powerful missionary order, the Society of Jesus, or *Jesuits* [jezh'ü its], the Catholic Church won new recruits in far-off places of the world. It was led by Ignatius Loyola [loi ō'lə].

During the Counter Reformation, the Catholic Church changed some of its practices. Priests devoted themselves to spiritual rather than to wordly matters. The worst church abuses, such as the sale of indulgences, were abolished. But the *Inquisition* [in'kwi zish'ən], a special court which tried heretics, was strengthened. It became an instrument to hold back the growth of Protestantism.

The Results of the Reformation

An immediate result of the Protestant Reformation was the start of a long series of religious wars. These lasted until the middle of the seventeenth century. There were political as well as religious reasons for the wars. They began, however, mostly because Protestants and

Modern History

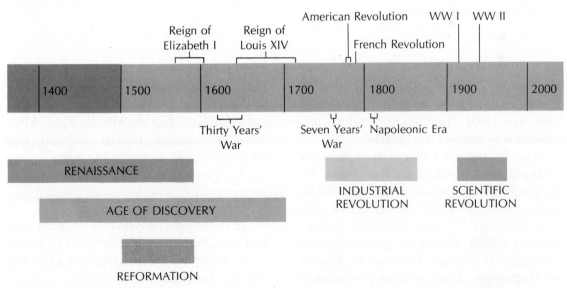

Be able to place the following on the time line:

1450	Gutenberg invented printing press
1517	Martin Luther at Wittenberg
1452–1519	Leonardo da Vinci

1534	Henry VIII broke with Rome
1545	Council of Trent
1598	Edict of Nantes

The grand council of the Inquisition condemned to death those accused of heresy. Why was the Inquisition established?

Catholics each believed that they had the only true faith. The idea of religious tolerance was not yet accepted.

The Protestant Reformation brought changes that reached further than the religious wars. Many Christian faiths began, and they had to learn to live with one another. In the *Edict of Nantes* [nants] (1598), Henry IV gave religious tolerance to French Protestants known as Huguenots. However, religious tolerance faced a long, hard fight.

One result of the Reformation was that the all-embracing influence of religion in people's lives was reduced. Religion occupied a less important position in the lives of people or in the affairs of state than it did in the Middle Ages. After the Reformation, people thought less about the hereafter and miracles.

Check in Here

1. How do the views of Calvin and Luther differ on the subject of salvation?

2. What was the significance of the Edict of Nantes?

3. How did the reasons for Henry VIII's break with the Church differ from those of Calvin and Luther?

4. Summarize three major results of the Protestant Reformation.

REVIEWING THE BASICS

The Renaissance and the Reformation led to new ideas in learning and in religion. Italy was the home of the Renaissance. The Italian city-states had prospered through trade with Byzantium, the Muslim world, and by helping the Crusaders reach the Holy Land.

Leading artists of the Renaissance were Leonardo da Vinci, Michelangelo, and Raphael. The Renaissance was often torn by a renewed interest in ancient writings and a desire to remain within the teachings of the Catholic Church. The humanists, chief of whom was Erasmus, emphasized humankind and life on earth over life in a hereafter.

During the Renaissance, there was a rebirth of interest in science and technology as well as in art. This activity was made possible by growth in industry, commerce, trade, and banking. However, neither science nor commerce fully emerged from the shackles of tradition. The printing press was invented by Gutenberg; Copernicus showed that the sun and not the earth was at the center of the universe. Despite some scientific advances, the scientific method was not fully developed. Venice and Florence were leading artistic and commercial centers. The Church's traditional position against profit-making and the charging of interest slowly diminished as commerce and manufacturing grew.

The Protestant Reformation was an outgrowth of the ideas of the Renaissance and of the widespread abuses of power within the Roman Catholic Church. John Huss, John Wycliffe, Martin Luther, and John Calvin were among the leading Protestant reformers. In England, Henry VIII established the Anglican faith, mostly to achieve political ambitions. The Protestant Reformation eliminated the complete control of the Catholic Church in the religion of Western Europe. In the Counter Reformation, the Church sought to reform itself.

REVIEWING THE HIGHLIGHTS

People to Identify

Dante	Donatello	Ignatius Loyola
Petrarch	Pico della Mirandola	Henry VIII
Chaucer	Lorenzo de Medici	John Eck
Erasmus	Johann Gutenberg	Michelangelo
Thomas More	Vesalius	Raphael
Leonardo da Vinci	Nicolaus Copernicus	Brunelleschi
Giotto	John Wycliffe	Machiavelli
Lucretia Borgia	Martin Luther	Charles V
Maria de Jars de Gournay	Ulrich Zwingli	John Huss
Ghiberti	John Calvin	Tetzel

223

Places to Locate	Geneva	Alps	Bohemia	Florence
	Avignon	Holland	Scandinavia	Genoa
	Wittenberg	Spain	Holland	Pisa
	Nantes	Belgium	Venice	Milan

Terms to Understand	Renaissance	Protestant	Inquisition
	Reformation	indulgences	Babylonian Captivity
	humanists	Ninety-Five Theses	*The Prince*
	Utopia	Edict of Nantes	Huguenot
	Anglican Church	Counter Reformation	Doge
	vernacular	Jesuits	Peace of Augsburg
		Romance languages	

Events to Describe Council of Trent   Peasants' War

Mastering the Fundamentals

1. What are the Romance languages? How did they develop?
2. What did the humanists teach?
3. How did Gutenberg's printing press improve upon the Chinese method of block printing?
4. How did trade with the East help in some ways to bring about the Renaissance?
5. Why did the Renaissance develop more fully in southern Europe than it did in northern Europe?
6. What were some of the main characteristics of Renaissance painting?
7. What were the teachings of Machiavelli?
8. What contributions did Michelangelo make to the Renaissance?
9. Why was it difficult for some prominent Renaissance women to be recognized for their accomplishments?
10. Why was the Catholic Church criticized by some religious leaders?
11. What was the Protestant Reformation?
12. What were the significant results of the Protestant Reformation?
13. Why did Martin Luther nail his comments to the doors of the Wittenberg Cathedral?
14. How did Luther's teachings differ from those of the Catholic Church?
15. How did the teachings of John Calvin differ from those of the Church?
16. How did the teachings of Calvin differ from those of Luther?
17. Why did England break away from the Church?
18. What practices did the Catholic Church change as a result of the Counter Reformation?
19. What were the significant results of the Protestant Reformation?

1. Write a letter that you as a Venetian merchant might have written to a merchant in another city. Explain the advantage of Venice as a commercial center.

2. Prepare a *Meet the Press* program in which you and a group of student reporters interview either Martin Luther or John Calvin, or both.

3. Write a report on the subject: "The Most Distinguished Woman of the Renaissance."

YOU ARE THE HISTORIAN

Study the data below and on the basis of it, indicate whether the statements that follow are either true, false, or not stated. Discuss the reasons for your answers with your class.

Printing Presses Established in the Various Countries to the End of 1480 and 1500

	To 1480	To 1500
Italy	236	532
Germany	78	214
France	20	147
Holland	14	40
Spain	6	71
Elsewhere in Europe	28	46
Total	382	1,050

1. There were more than twice the number of printing presses in Europe in 1500 as there were twenty years earlier.

2. The greatest growth in the number of printing presses was in Spain.

3. In 1480, Germany had nearly four times the number of printing presses as did France.

4. By 1500, France had caught up with Germany in the number of printing presses.

5. Italy was the country that held the lead in the number of printing presses between 1480 and 1500.

6. The printing press contributed to the growth in the ability of people to read.

7. There were no printing presses in England in either 1480 or 1500.

8. In 1480, as well as in 1500, Italy had more printing presses than all the other countries combined.

9. After 1500, the number of printing presses grew so rapidly that it was not possible to keep records.

10. Germany and Italy combined had more than twice the number of printing presses as the other countries.

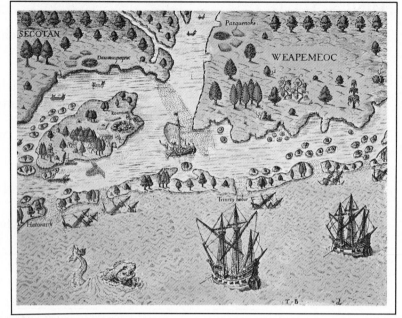

Jamestown, Virginia

New Nations and Empires: The Monarchies of Europe and Their Expansion Overseas

During the Middle Ages, *patriotism,* or love of country, was limited to a particular city such as Florence in Italy, or to a province such as Burgundy in France. The idea of a nation had not yet developed. *Nationalism,* or the desire to form a nation, has been a powerful force in history. This process of nation-building began as early as the eleventh century when England became a nation. Nation-building is still going on in the twentieth century as new nations are formed, such as Indonesia, Ghana, Tanzania, and Zimbabwe.

From the eleventh to the fifteenth century, the growth of nations was in the hands of strong monarchs. The people had little direct influence upon their nation's growth. Later, patriotism on the part of the common people became important to the growth of nations. In this chapter you will learn how countries developed, how they earned the loyalty of their people, and how the new nations expanded their power.

ENGLAND AND FRANCE BECOME MODERN NATIONS

Some Characteristics of a Nation

Nations share a number of characteristics, namely, land, boundaries, resources, and government. Without any one of these characteristics a nation probably could not exist. Land refers to the geographic area in which a people who have something in common—language, religion, or special interests—live. Boundaries set off the land of one nation from another. They may be natural ones such as rivers, oceans, or mountains, or they may be agreed-upon borders. England and France developed into nations early. They had specific territories with defensible borders.

If a nation is to prosper, it must have natural resources to develop a sound economy. Good land for farming is most important, and the existence of stores of energy such as coal or oil are others. It is not necessary for every nation to have all the resources that it needs. No nation has all the resources it would like to have. Yet, to survive, a nation should have a reasonable share of natural resources upon which to build its economy, its trade with other people, and a decent standard of living at home. An industrious, hard-working people is a human resource that may overcome a lack of some natural resources.

For people to build a nation there must be agreement about the kind of government to have. The government of a nation, whether a monarchy or a democracy, must have the power and authority to do as it wishes within its borders. This characteristic of a nation is called *sovereignty* [sov'rin tē]. It means that a nation, through its government, has the power to make its own decisions freely and independently.

Thomas Hobbes [hobz] (1588–1679) was a famous political theorist. According to his views, the growth of a system of government based on absolute monarchs who ruled nation-states was the most important development in the history of humankind. Hobbes believed that without the development of strong nations the lives of most people would be "solitary, poor, nasty, brutish, and short." The system of nation-states that Hobbes praised so much began to develop in Western Europe about the middle of the fourteenth century.

However, the growth of nation-states had some undesirable aspects. War had always been a fact of life. With the rise of nations it was conducted on a much larger scale than before and with more determination. As nations grew they sought power, wealth, and security. To achieve these they made war on other nations. Powerful monarchs, with the support of a loyal people, could raise money and large armies. In some ways

227

war became a national obsession. It is small wonder that Thomas Hobbes chose the term *Leviathan* [li vī'ə thən] as the title for his book about nation-states. The word describes a powerful sea monster.

The Rise of Nations in Europe

During the Early Middle Ages monarchs were often weaker than the lords who served them as vassals. As towns and commerce grew, a *middle class* developed. Monarchs gave the middle class special privileges and rights in exchange for money. This money and taxes made the monarchs rich and helped them pay for an army of their own. Monarchs no longer had to ask the feudal lords for help in fighting wars. Soon, with the help of the towns and the middle class, the monarchs became powerful leaders. The growth of nations began when monarchs became strong enough to unify and control large numbers of vassals.

There were other reasons for the rise of nations. As national languages developed, nation-states grew with them. English, French, Spanish, Portugese, and other languages encouraged those who spoke the same tongue to unify. A common language provided a bond for people. Geography was another factor that played a part in the growth of nations. Rivers, oceans, or mountains often brought people together or separated them from those who were different. In addition to these factors, monarchs were able to take advantage of the Protestant Reformation. They could reduce the influence of the Roman Catholic Church and substitute their own power.

England and France became nations in the Middle Ages. Other countries such as Germany and Italy were not unified until the nineteenth century. From the eleventh to the fifteenth century, the growth of nations was in the hands of strong monarchs.

How England Became a Nation

The English were one of the first groups of people to form a nation of their own. They were separated by the English Channel from the continent of Europe and so were relatively free from its wars and problems. The English were a people easy to unite because they lived in a small area, spoke the same language, and shared the same history.

Despite having so much in common, the English under the Anglo-Saxons (see p. 180) could not agree among themselves. There was much disagreement, for example, about who would follow the Anglo-Saxon king known as Edward the Confessor. When Edward died, the Anglo-Saxons chose Edward's son Earl Harold to become king. However, William, Duke of Normandy, also claimed the throne as the cousin of Edward's mother. William challenged Harold's claim to the throne. In the summer of 1066, William the Conquerer, with an army of 5,000, crossed the English Channel from Normandy (in present-day France) and invaded England. At the Battle of Hastings, he defeated the Anglo-Saxon King Harold and made himself king of England. William proceeded to build a nation. The Anglo-Saxon's had tried but failed to do so.

William and his successors were able rulers. Henry II (1133–89) was a strong king who improved the legal system and established king's courts throughout the country. A *grand jury* reported to the king's judges those who were believed to have committed crimes. A *petit jury*, made up of twelve men, listened to a case to decide whether or not a crime had indeed been committed. The judges made the law, based on the customs of the people. The body of law that developed is

The Battle of Hastings as shown on the Bayeux Tapestry. During this battle, William the Conqueror defeated the English. He then crowned himself King of England.

called *common law.* For common law and for the jury system, we are indebted to the rule of Henry II.

The death of Richard the Lion-Hearted (1157–99) brought King John (1167–1216) to the throne of England. King John is remembered for his troubles with the pope and the English nobles. He had to pay tribute to the pope and was forced to give up some powers to the nobles. The *Magna Carta,* which John signed at Runnymede [run'ē mēd'] in 1215, stated that no taxes could be levied without the consent of the *Great Council.* The Great Council was made up of prominent nobles and church officials who advised the monarchs. The Magna Carta also stated that no free person could be put into prison without a trial by jury or be punished except in accordance with law.

The Magna Carta outlined several fundamental rights that we take for granted in modern times. In the thirteenth century most people were serfs,

and serfs were not free. The principles of the Magna Carta did not apply to them. Nevertheless, the Magna Carta was a political milestone; it showed that a monarch's power could be limited by law. Gradually, the principles of the Magna Carta were applied to a greater number of people and became the basic rights of the English.

Early in the reign of William the Conquerer, the beginnings of representative government were made. The Great Council was at first an advisory body. As its influence slowly grew, the king had to get the council's approval before reaching a decision. Later, the Great Council came to be known as *Parliament* [pär'lə mənt].

On the principle "Let that which toucheth all be approved by all," King Edward I (1239–1307) called for a meeting. This has been named the *Model Parliament* (1295). It was made up of clergy, nobles, and commoners, or *burgesses.* The Model Parliament soon became divided into a *House of Lords* and a

The Magna Carta. What fundamental rights did it give the English people? How did it check the power of the monarch?

How France Became a Nation

France did not become a nation as quickly as England. Since France was on the continent of Europe, it was involved in Europe's wars and could be easily invaded. Charlemagne (742–814) thought in terms of an empire, not in terms of a nation. (See p. 178.) At his death, Charlemagne divided his empire into three parts. This division was a setback for France because it encouraged a social disorder that took it hundreds of years from which to emerge.

When Hugh Capet [kā'pit] became king in 987, he began a line of kings that spanned 350 years. While Capet was recognized as a king, many feudal lords were far more powerful than he was. The Duke of Normandy was one of these strong lords in northern France, and in 1066 he was strong enough to conquer England.

When Philip Augustus (1165–1223) began his reign, he governed only a small portion of land around Paris. Many of his vassals, including King John of England, were more powerful than he was. Philip decided to do something about this difference in power. He boldly took John's French lands away from him and the lands of other nobles as well. He granted favors to the middle class to enlist their support in reducing the power of the lords. By extending his authority over a greater territory, by weakening the power of the lords, and by enlisting the help of the middle classes, Philip Augustus helped France become a nation.

Philip the Fair (1268–1314) organized a French parliament called the *Estates-General*. This body did not become as powerful as did the English parliament since it met only when the king called upon it. It was, however, a start toward representative government and contributed to the decline of feudalism. The

House of Commons. In the Model Parliament, the representatives to the House of Lords and the representatives to the House of Commons met in one room. Later, the House of Lords and the House of Commons met separately.

The year 1066 is the date usually given for the beginning of England as a nation. By the end of the Middle Ages, England had a strong monarch, a united country and a kind of representative government. It was on the road toward establishing a democratic government.

decline of feudalism and the development of an Estates-General encouraged greater loyalty to the government and helped make the French nation.

Check in Here

1. Define the term *nation*.
2. What factors explain why France became a nation relatively early in European history?
3. What factors explain why England became a nation relatively early in European history?

THE HUNDRED YEARS' WAR

The Causes of the Hundred Years' War

The long series of wars between England and France from 1338–1453 are known as the *Hundred Years' War*. This struggle had important results for both countries.

For many years the ruler of England, who held land in France, was a vassal of the French ruler. As the feeling of nationalism grew stronger, the English came to resent their relationship with France. Hostility between France and England also grew over rivalry in Flanders, where both nations sought to control the wool trade. When France aided Scotland in its troubles with England, the English were irritated still more.

When the French king Charles IV (1322–28) died, there was no direct heir to the French throne. Edward III (1327–77), the king of England, thought the time had come to settle accounts with France and make England supreme. He felt that he should be king of France. Because his mother was the daughter of Philip the Fair, a French king, Edward thought he had the best claim to the French throne. However, just as the English did not want a French king, so the French did not want an English king.

The Hundred Years' War was, in a sense, the first modern war. National pride and honor, as well as arguments about land and trade rights, were among the important causes of the war.

The Hundred Years' War, 1338–1453

This map shows the areas held by England and France during the Hundred Years' War.

- Was Paris ever under English control?
- What body of water separates England from Normandy?
- What city in France did England still control in 1453?
- How does the map indicate the growth of French nationalism?

231

How the Hundred Years' War Was Fought

The equipment of the English and French armies was quite different. The English army was made up of foot soldiers, each of whom was equipped with a long bow and a supply of arrows. The French army was made up of knights dressed in armor and mounted on horses that were also protected by coats of metal.

At the great battles of Crécy [kres′ē] (1346), Poitiers [pwä tyā′] (1356), and Agincourt [aj′in kôrt′] (1415), the English showed that the days of armored knights and hand-to-hand fighting were over. Arrows shot from long bows could cover great distances and accurately reach their victims. The arrows could pierce the armor of a horse or of a rider. Showers of arrows, as thick as rain, were enough to strike terror in the hearts of the bravest knights. These new English weapons meant the beginning of the end for armored knights and hand-to-hand fighting.

The long bow was a cheap weapon that could be given to many soldiers. A king who could command an army so equipped had a winning force. Such a king did not have to depend on expensively clad knights. In these battles, gunpowder was also used for the first time to load small cannon. The use of gunpowder brought about great changes in how warfare was conducted.

The Hundred Years' War caused much hardship among the French people. Though their lords fought the war, the peasants were forced to pay for it. The French peasants found their payments more and more difficult to make because the fighting was taking place in France, and French farms were being destroyed. Disease and famine killed many people, and hatred grew between lord and peasant. In 1358, an unsuccessful peasant uprising known as the *Jacquerie* [zhäk ə rē′] took place. The desperate peasants revolted. They killed their lords and burned their castles. There was much bloodshed before the uprising was finally put down. The Jacquerie, by challenging the power of feudal nobles, showed that feudalism was on its way out.

How Joan of Arc Helped the French

Henry V (1413–22) of England wanted to win the war with France. He landed an army in France and was near his goal when he died. France was nearly defeated, but Joan of Arc rallied the nation.

Joan of Arc (1412–31) was born in the village of Domremy [dôn rə mē′] to a poor peasant family. As a child, she was eager to help her country—most of which was occupied by the English. In 1428, the English were laying siege to the French city of Orleans [ôr′lā änz] and it appeared as if France would lose the Hundred Years' War. Joan came to the rescue. She claimed that she had received messages from God in the form of dreams or visions in which she was told that only she could save France.

Many believed that Joan was insane and that it was foolish for a nation to follow a seventeen-year-old peasant girl. Joan successfully convinced the French leader, Charles VII, to let her try to save Orleans and unite France. Mounted on a fine horse and dressed in a suit of shining armor, she led a French army in the direction of Orleans. Holding aloft a sword that glistened in the sun and a French banner that fluttered in the wind, she inspired the tired French soldiers. They defeated the English. By 1429, the English were finally driven from the city of Orleans, and Charles VII was crowned king in the cathedral at Reims [rēmz].

Joan led the French in other battles, but she failed to bring further victories to

Joan of Arc led the French to victory in the Battle of Orleans. On this tapestry she is shown entering the castle of Chignon.

France. A year after the Battle of Orleans, she was captured by the Burgundians and sold to the English. In May 1431, after a church trial, Joan was convicted of witchcraft and burned at the stake in the city of Rouen [rü än']. In her short lifetime, she had united the French. At her death, the French people swore they would not rest until the English had been driven from France. In 1453, this was finally done.

Joan of Arc, sometimes known as the Maid of Orleans, is famous in French history. A few years after her death, the charges against her were withdrawn. In 1919, she was declared a saint by the Roman Catholic Church.

The Results of the War for England

After the English lost the war and most of their land in France, they began to concentrate on uniting their nation. There were rival claims to the English throne. The attempt to gain control of the monarchy resulted in a series of civil wars that lasted thirty years. These were known as the *Wars of the Roses* (1455–85). The House of Lancaster (whose symbol was a red rose) fought the House of York (whose symbol was a white rose) for the throne of England. The outcome was significant in England's history.

The Tudors were the victors in the Wars of the Roses. Henry Tudor was a descendent of the House of Lancaster. On Bosworth Field, in 1485, he defeated Richard III of the House of York. He took the throne as King Henry VII of England (1457–1509). As a result of these wars, feudalism in England was also destroyed, for the nobles had destroyed one another.

Henry's marriage to a Yorkist united the nation as it had never been united.

233

Beginning with his reign, the Tudor family ruled over England for many years. It gave England a number of great rulers, including Henry VIII (1509–47) and Elizabeth I (1558–1603). These rulers broke with the Catholic Church, encouraged trade, and participated in the Age of Discovery, about which you will learn.

The Results of War for France

By winning the Hundred Years' War, France rid itself of a foreign enemy that had been on its soil for many years. Charles VII (1422–61) began to exert greater authority. In 1438, in the *Pragmatic Sanction of Bourges* [bùrzh], he took power away from the Church and reduced the influence of the pope. In 1440, he won the agreement of the Estates-General to a land tax called the *taille* [tä′yə]. In this way, he helped solve the financial problems of France. These measures enabled him to establish a small but efficient standing army. His son, Louis XI (1423–83), further strengthened the monarchy by bringing about the defeat of Charles the Bold.

The Wars of the Roses ended feudalism in England. A war also ended feudalism in France. Charles the Bold, the Duke of Burgundy, was a powerful ruler who governed much of France and portions of the Netherlands. He was the greatest threat to the power of the French king, Louis XI. He wanted more power for himself. During the Hundred Years' War, the Duke of Burgundy sided with the English. When the war was over, he was ambitious enough to want the royal title. Louis XI was more crafty than courageous. (He was called "The Spider" because of his diplomatic skills.) He convinced both the Swiss and the Holy Roman Emperor that Charles the Bold was a threat to them. In the end, in a battle against the Swiss, Charles the

Bold, Duke of Burgundy, was killed. Louis XI claimed most of the Duchy of Burgundy. He thereby further strengthened the power of the French king, and helped unite the French nation even more.

Check in Here

1. On a map of France and England, locate the following: Crécy, Agincourt, Poitiers, Rouen, Hastings, Reims, Runnymede, and Orleans. Which ones are important in French history? In English history?

2. List three causes of the Hundred Years' War.

3. List three results of the Hundred Years' War.

4. How did Charles VII and Louis XI contribute to the growth of the French nation?

MORE NEW NATIONS—SOME SUCCEED, OTHERS FAIL

How Spain and Portugal Became Nations

During the Hundred Years' War, feudalism declined and France and England took giant steps forward and became strong nations. But France and England were only two of many countries developing in Europe. How did other European nations grow?

On the *Iberian* [ī bēr′ē ən] *Peninsula* are the two countries of Spain and Portugal. In the eighth century, much of the Iberian Peninsula was conquered by the Muslims. (See p. 168.) Their civilization was superior to that of most European countries at that time.

Slowly, small Christian kingdoms grew up in the northern part of the Iberian Peninsula. These Christian kingdoms began a successful fight against the

234

Muslims. In 1147, Alfonso I, Count of Portugal, took the city of Lisbon from the Muslims. He extended his lands to the River Tagus [tā′gəs]. By the time Alfonso died in 1185, the Kingdom of Portugal was born.

The Iberian Peninsula, 1037–1492

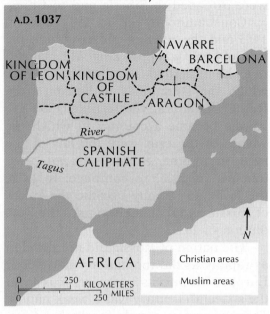

A.D. 1037

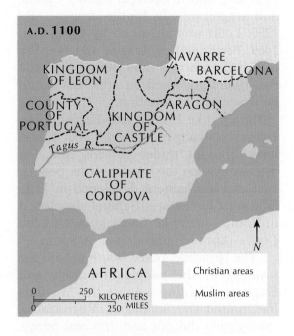

A.D. 1100

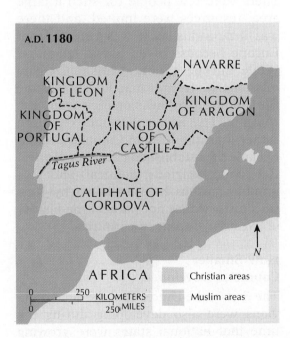

A.D. 1180

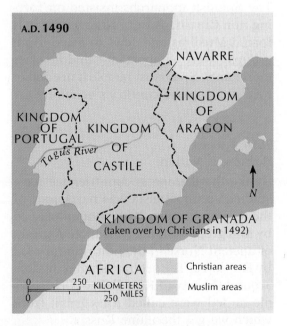

A.D. 1490

These maps show the spread of Christian control over the Iberian Peninsula.
- In 1037, what was the largest Christian kingdom on the peninsula?
- By about the year 1100 was Portugal under Muslim or Christian control?
- What was the last region on the peninsula that the Muslims controlled?
- In what year was that region taken over by the Christians?

The establishment of Spain as a nation-state took somewhat longer. In 1200, there were four Spanish kingdoms: Navarre [nə vär′], León [le ôn′], Castile [kas tēl′], and Aragon [ar′ə gän′]. Castile and Aragon were by far the strongest. By 1230, León was absorbed by Castile. In 1469, Ferdinand of Aragon and Isabella of Castile married, and before long the two rulers governed an area that could be described as a nation.

Spain, like France and England, developed a strong monarchy. Local nobles were brought under control, and the monarchy won the loyalty of the people. Just as a parliament developed in England and an Estates-General developed in France, a similar body, known as the *Cortes* [kôr tez′], developed in Spain.

The Hundred Years' War had won the loyalties of the people in France and England. Fighting against the Muslims had united the Spaniards. Regrettably, the fighting did not end in a real peace. The Spanish monarchs insisted on forcing non-Christians out of the country. It forced Muslims and Jews to leave. Both groups were important middle-class merchants. Spain lost people it needed to help develop the country's economy.

How Russia Became a Nation

Unlike the European countries we have studied so far, Russia was never part of the Roman Empire. It was not influenced by that great Roman civilization. A group of ancient Norse in the ninth century led by Rurik [rūr′ik], set up a small kingdom around the city of Kiev [kē ev′]. The people he led were called *Russ* [rüs], from which we get the name Russia.

In 1237, Kiev was destroyed by the Mongols, who ruled for 300 years. They left Russia as much an Asiatic country as a European one. During the fourteenth century the principality of Moscow grew in strength. The princes of Moscow at first served the Mongols and paid tribute to them. Under Ivan the Great (1440–1505) Mongol rule ended. Russian expansion took place, and Russian borders were extended to Siberia and to China.

Constantinople fell to the Turks in 1453 and the ruler of Moscow took the title of *czar* [zär], or king. He claimed that he inherited the imperial power which the Byzantines had taken from Rome. Under Ivan the Terrible (1530–84), Russia became a country in which the wishes of the czar were the law of the land. In no other country was *autocracy* (one-person rule) so complete. In 1613, the Romanov family became the rulers of Russia and remained so until the Revolution of 1917.

The nation of Russia did not develop as rapidly as did the nations of Western Europe. Despite its vast size, Russia in the sixteenth century was a weak nation. There were few people for such a large area, resources were limited, and there was little industry. It was cut off from Europe because of its Slavic language. While Europe became Christianized by missionaries from Rome, Russia became Christianized by missionaries from Byzantium. The Eastern Orthodox Church rather than the Roman Catholic Church became the established church in Russia. Economic, religious, political, and geographic reasons help explain why Russia's history does not parallel the history of Western European countries.

How Smaller Countries Developed

The Swiss, the Dutch, and the Scandinavians were also developing during the time that national states were growing elsewhere. Although their periods of greatness did not last long, their influence on history has been great.

Early in their history, the Swiss realized the value of uniting. By 1386, an in-

Modern History

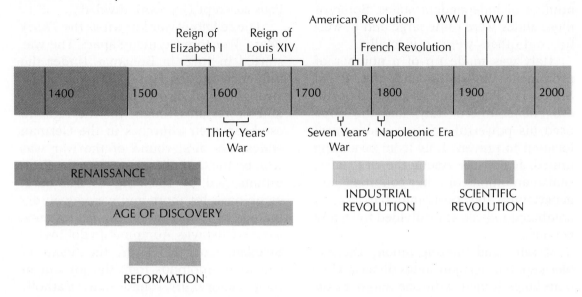

Be able to place the following events on the time line:

987	Hugh Capet became king of France
1215	Magna Carta
1237	Kiev destroyed by Mongols
1295	Model Parliament
1386	Switzerland became a nation
1431	Joan of Arc burned at stake
1453	English driven from France
1455–85	Wars of the Roses

1469	Moors driven from Spain
1492	Columbus reached West Indies
1498	da Gama reached India
1565	St. Augustine established
1581	Holland became independent
1607	English settled Jamestown
1613	Romanovs began reign
1618–48	Thirty Years' War

dependent Swiss nation was born. Switzerland was protected by the Alps. Switzerland's geographic location made it possible for this small nation to establish unity and to keep its independence.

Bordering on the North Sea were a group of provinces that had been part of Charlemagne's empire. After Charlemagne's death, they came under the rule of more powerful neighbors. The northern group of provinces we know as Holland; the southern group later became Belgium. In the sixteenth century, the provinces were controlled by Catholic Spain. The Dutch, who lived in Holland, adopted the Protestant faith. In Belgium, the people remained Catholic. The Dutch revolted against Spain and, in 1581, Holland became independent.

The Scandinavian countries—Norway, Sweden, and Denmark—have much in common, but they have not often been united as a group. They played a prominent role in the settlement of much of Europe. They lost the chance to become more powerful because they fought among themselves.

Why Germany and Italy Remained Divided

Many great European nations developed from small beginnings. In the cases of Germany and Italy, unification into nations did not happen until the nineteenth century. While the names Germany and Italy were used during the Middle Ages, they were really only geographic terms.

237

Germany and Italy were made up of a number of independent states. Some of these states were quite large and powerful, and others were very small.

Italy was made up of a number of prominent city-states and the Papal States. The Papal States separated northern and southern Italy, and the pope used his powerful position and central location to prevent Italy from becoming united. Jealousies among the city-states, selfish ambitions of other countries, and geographic and economic barriers all combined to keep Italy divided for many centuries.

Rivalry and fighting among the nobles kept the German states divided. German kings fought with one another and with foreign nations. In time, the Hapsburg family in Austria came to hold the title of Holy Roman Emperor. It was truthfully said of them that they were neither "holy" nor "Roman" nor "emperors." However, the Hapsburg rulers owned much land outside of Austria, especially in northern Italy where they had a great deal of influence. Competition between the Hapsburgs of Austria and the Hohenzollerns, of what later was Prussia, kept Germany divided.

The religious war known as the *Thirty Years' War* tore Germany apart. The war started in 1618, in Bohemia. Under the influence of John Huss, Germany was a stronghold of Protestantism. Catholics and Protestants fought for the right to establish their churches in the German states. The first round of the war was won by the Catholics. However, the Protestants, led by the king of Denmark, came back for more and were again defeated. In round three, the Protestants, led by Gustavus Adolphus [ə dol'fəs] of Sweden, won. However, the death of Gustavus Adolphus took the joy out of their victory. In round four, Catholic France, under the leadership of Richelieu, joined the Protestants in hopes of becoming the strongest country in Europe. With French help, the Protestants were successful.

In 1648, the *Peace of Westphalia* ended the Thirty Years' War. According to the terms of the peace treaty, German princes could decide whether or not the people in their states would be Catholic,

In 1648, the Peace of Westphalia was signed. What war did it end?

Lutheran, or Calvinist. Switzerland and the Netherlands were assured of their independence. It took Germany almost two hundred years to recover from the war. Not until 1969, when fighting broke out between Catholics and Protestants in Ulster, was religion again a cause of armed conflict in Europe.

Europe, 1648

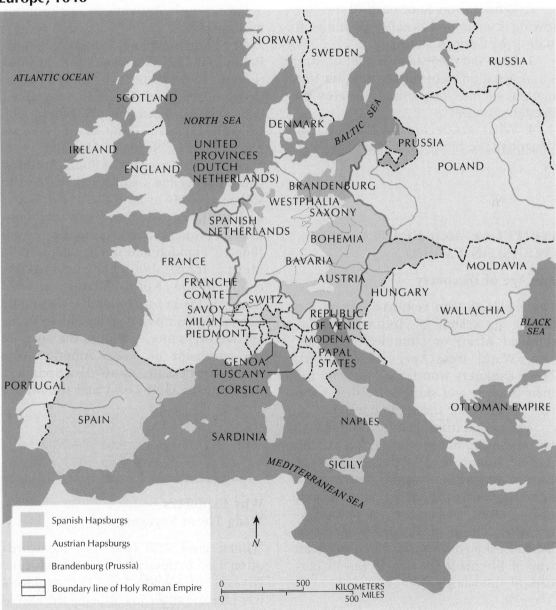

One result of the Treaty of Westphalia in 1648 was that the Catholic and Protestant states were to be on complete equality in all affairs of the Holy Roman Empire. Another result was that Brandenburg received the region called Prussia.
• Was Prussia part of the Holy Roman Empire?
• Name some of the states within the Holy Roman Empire.

1. Use the map on page 239 to locate the following: **(a)** Iberian Peninsula; **(b)** Scandinavian countries; **(c)** Papal States; **(d)** Prussia; **(e)** the area controlled by the Spanish Hapsburgs.

2. What factors kept each of the following from uniting as nations: **(a)** Italian states; **(b)** German states?

3. How did the establishment of Russia as a nation-state differ from the formation of the other nation-states of Western Europe?

4. What was decided by the Peace of Westphalia in terms of religion?

PORTUGAL AND SPAIN GAIN OVERSEAS EMPIRES

The Age of Discovery

The explorers who ventured out on the oceans in search of India and who rounded Africa or stumbled upon the New World were very great indeed. These explorers won fame, not only for their bravery and skill, but also for the vast wealth their travels uncovered.

The period from the fifteenth through the seventeenth centuries is called the *Age of Discovery*. The new nations of Europe, having built strong governments at home, were ready to set out in search of new lands. During the Age of Discovery, the culture of Europe was established in the New World. The European way of life made its way to far-off corners of the world.

The Heroes of the Age of Discovery

Columbus was just one of several explorers who opened new areas of the world to trade and commerce. Bartholomeu Diaz [dē'əs] (1450–1500), a Portuguese navigator, sailed around the Cape of Good Hope. Another Portuguese, Vasco da Gama [də gäm'ə], completed the ocean trip around the southern tip of Africa to reach India in 1498. Further Spanish and Portuguese discoveries opened South America to explorations by Europeans.

A Spanish explorer, Vasco Núñez de Balboa [bal bō'ə], crossed the Isthmus [is'məs] of Panama and saw the Pacific Ocean. Ferdinand Magellan [mə jel'ən] was a brave Portuguese explorer who sailed through the strait that now bears his name. The Strait of Magellan is located near the very tip of South America. One of Magellan's ships was the first to sail completely around the world. Ponce de León [pôn'se de le ôn'] explored Florida for Spain, and Hernando Cortés [kôr tez'] landed and made conquests in Mexico. John Cabot, sailing for England, explored the North Atlantic, as did Henry Hudson for Holland. Giovanni da Verrazano [ver'ə zä'nō], an Italian in the service of France, explored the coast of the continent of North America. And Hernando de Soto [də sō'tō], a Spaniard, explored the Gulf Coast and the Mississippi River area.

Why Explorers Made These Voyages

"Glory, gold, and God" are the words often used to describe the reasons for the voyages of exploration. The explorers went for the sheer joy of being the first to find and conquer new worlds. Gold proved to be a powerful magnet, drawing people from all nations. Religious zeal, the desire to make Christians of other people, was another powerful force behind the explorations.

Christopher Columbus
(1451–1506)

As a youth, Christopher Columbus served sailors food and wine in his father's tavern in the Italian port of Genoa. He listened to the tall tales sailors told. The sailors claimed that they had reached the Green Islands of Barbary and had sailed past the Pillars of Hercules to the fantastic but mythical island of Atlantis. These stories stirred the imagination of young Christopher. He was convinced the time would soon come when he would leave his father's tavern and see the world for himself.

When Columbus was twenty, his father was forced to close the tavern. For eight years Columbus shifted for himself. He then fell in love with the beautiful and rich Donna Filepa Perestrello [per ə strā′lō] and they married. The elder Perestrello, Donna Filepa's father, had been a sailor. It was his belief that the world was round and not flat. In his library were many books that encouraged belief in this theory. These books exposed Columbus to new ideas. From them, and from talks with map makers and adventurous sailors, Columbus began to believe that one could reach the rich lands of the East by sailing west.

Columbus needed sailors, money, and ships to prove that he was right. He journeyed to the courts of Portugal, Spain, England, and France seeking help. But everywhere he was refused. His disappointment mounted when his beloved Donna Filepa died and he was left to carry on alone. His search for someone to help him left him penniless. When things looked darkest, Columbus was called to the court of Ferdinand and Isabella of Spain. They agreed to pay for three ships and a journey to the East. Columbus landed on islands off the coasts of North and South America. He believed the islands were the East Indies. Today, the islands are known as the *West Indies.* They are located in the Caribbean Sea.

Columbus made four more voyages. He died thinking he had reached the East. Columbus never found either the short route to the East or the gold he sought. His failure to find gold infuriated King Ferdinand, who had Columbus brought home in chains and imprisoned. Broken in mind and spirit, feeling cheated and wronged, Columbus died a poor and little-known man.

European Explorations, 1488–1610

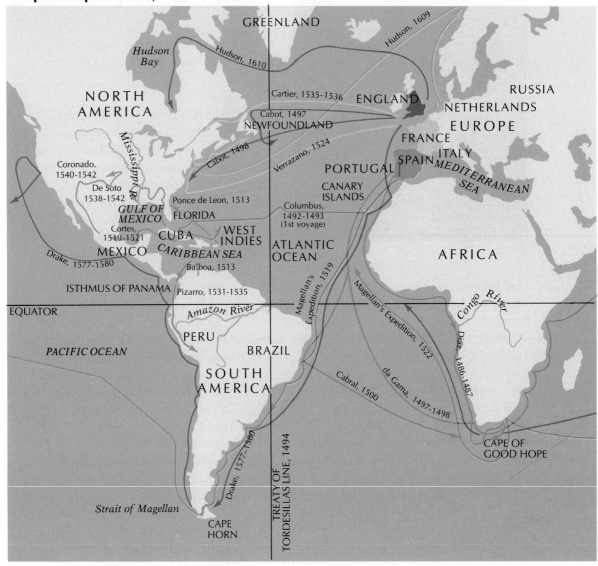

During the Age of Discovery, European explorers traveled to many regions of the world.

- According to the map, which country sent the most explorers to the New World?
- What explorer for Portugal sailed to Brazil?
- What explorer sailed for both England and the Netherlands?

In addition to gold, glory, and God, there were other reasons for the explorations. By the fifteenth century, it was possible to make trips that went far out of sight of land. The magnetic compass had been in use for some time as a navigation aid on the open sea. Ships were made better and were therefore able to withstand heavy seas and high winds. Among the navigators there was greater confidence that the world was round and that there was little danger of falling off the edge of a plate-shaped world. The Age of Discovery was really a part of the

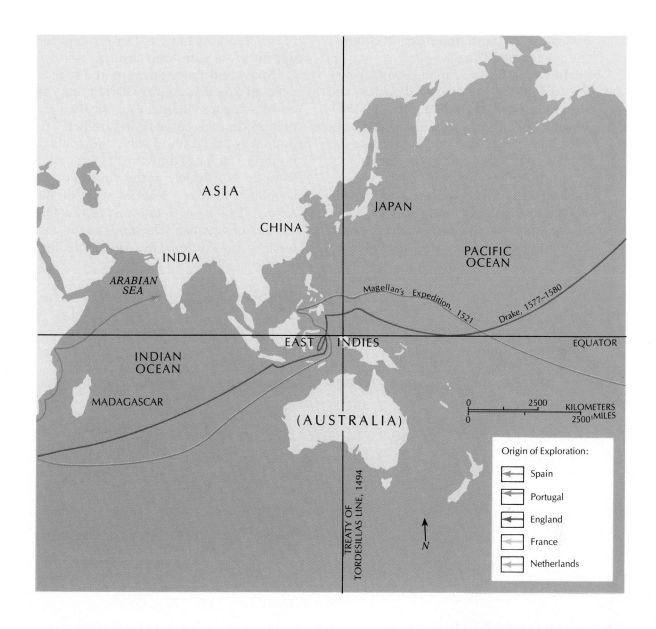

Renaissance. People were greatly interested in what lay on the other side of the known world.

How the Portuguese Gained an Empire

The Portuguese were among the first to brave the unknown seas. Under the leadership of Prince Henry the Navigator (1394–1460), Portuguese sailors sailed along the west coast of Africa. Portuguese sea captains take credit for finding the first and much desired all-water route to the East. Portuguese sailors boldly sailed westward across the Atlantic Ocean. They eventually landed on the east coast of South America and claimed the area called Brazil.

In India, China, Japan, South America, and along the coasts of Africa, the Portuguese set up trading posts. In 1500, Pinzón [pēn thôn′] reached Brazil. In each place they settled the Portuguese traded such things as guns, cheap fabrics, and knives for gold, silver, spices, silks, and luxuries. For the most part, the Portuguese did not settle in the places where they established trading posts. They did not interfere with the rulers at those places as long as those rulers did not interfere with their profits.

Spain and Portugal were in a race to develop overseas empires. Often Spanish and Portuguese claims to what their explorers discovered were in conflict. The pope was called on to solve the conflict. Pope Alexander VI drew an imaginary line from the North Pole to the South Pole at a point a hundred leagues west of the Azores. The lands to the west of this line were to be Spanish. The lands to the east were to be Portuguese. This settlement

A sixteenth-century world map.

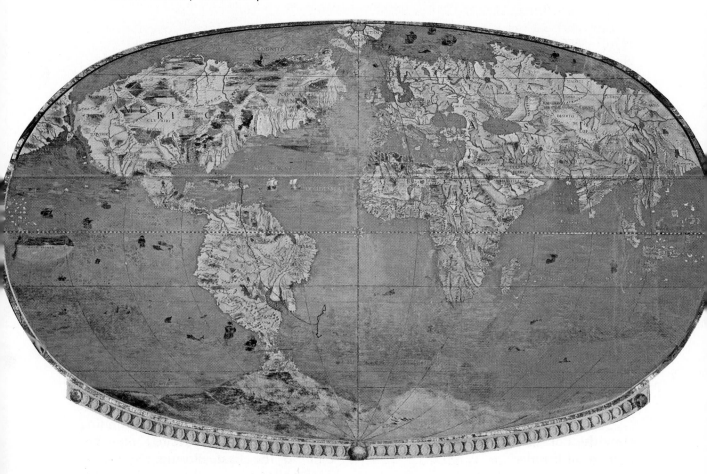

did not satisfy the Portuguese, and in a separate agreement called the *Treaty of Tordesillas* [tôr′the sē′lyäs] (1494), Spain and Portugal moved the imaginary line drawn by the pope. The line they agreed upon was 46′ 30″ West Longitude. It cuts Brazil off from the rest of South America. This agreement assured the dominance of Portugal in Brazil, where the language and customs remain Portuguese to this day.

How the Spaniards Gained an Empire

The New World Empire of Spain was won by the brutal military conquests of the *conquistadors* [kän kēs′tə dôrz′], the Spanish conquerors. Mounted on horses and armed with guns, these Spanish conquerors were feared as gods by the Indian tribes of Central and South America. In 1511, Cuba was settled. Under the able management of Diego Velasquez [və las′kez], the colony prospered and became a jumping-off point for further discovery and exploration in the New World. In 1513, Balboa [bal bō′ə] crossed the Isthmus of Panama and reached the Pacific. In 1512, Ponce de Leon unsuccessfully tried to build a colony in Florida. In 1517, Francisco de Cordova [kôr′də və] discovered the Mayan civilization. A year later, Hernando Cortés [kôr tez′] made his way to the palace of Montezuma [mon′ti zü′ mə], where he found some of the wealth that he was seeking. In 1565, the Spanish established the city of St. Augustine (Florida). It is the oldest city in the United States.

Cortés was a conquistador who took Mexico by military force. His soldiers willingly followed him to Mexico, where some met fame and fortune and some met death. With 11 ships and 600 soldiers armed with guns and gunpowder, cannons, and horses, Cortés set out from Cuba for Mexico. He landed at what is

The meeting of Cortés and Montezuma. What did Montezuma do to try to avoid this meeting?

now Vera Cruz [ver′ə krüz′]. He headed in the direction of the Aztec capital, Tenochtitlán [te nôch′tē tlän′], now Mexico City.

Cortés met large numbers of Indians who regarded Montezuma, the Aztec leader, as their chief. Some of the Indians had suffered at the hands of Montezuma and were willing to see him defeated by newcomers. Montezuma knew that the coming of these strange people meant the days of his empire were few. He first ordered, then bribed, and finally begged Cortés not to come to Tenochtitlán. But Cortés went to the capital. In time, he conquered the king, the people, and the capital. Tenochtitlán was burned, and Mexico City was built in its place.

Success made the Spanish bold. They wanted to find a short route to riches of the East. Hernando de Soto [də sō′tō] left Cuba with a great number of men,

245

The Spanish Empire in the Americas, 1620

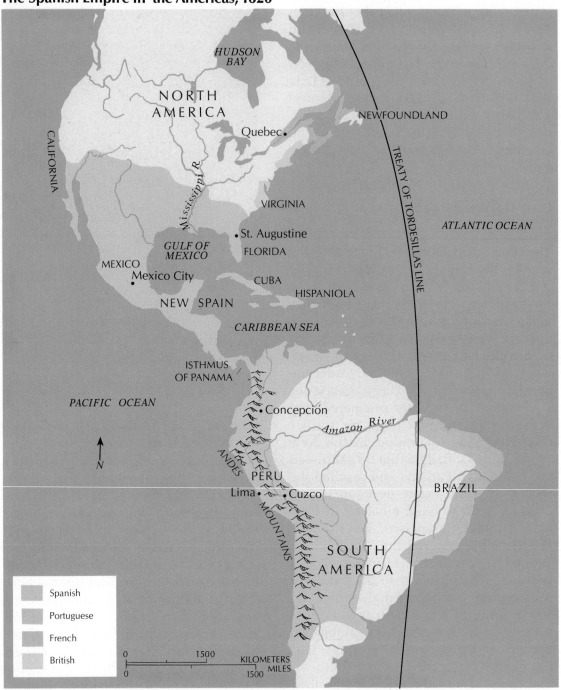

By 1620, the Spanish Empire in the New World stretched for thousands of miles through North and South America.

- What city in New Spain was built on the site of Tenochtilán?
- Name two important islands in the Caribbean Sea that the Spanish controlled.
- Which European country had land in South America east of the Treaty of Tordesillas line?

horses, and food. He explored the lands between what are now the American states of Georgia and Oklahoma. He died a disappointed man, for he found no gold. In 1540, Francisco Coronado [kôr′ə nä′dō] tried his luck in what is now the American southwest. With a group larger than that of de Soto, he sought the great riches of El Dorado [el də rä′dō], about which the Indians had hinted. No matter how far he traveled, however, he never found El Dorado. Although he discovered more than he realized at the time, Coronado died heartbroken.

Francisco Pizarro [pi zär′ō] discovered the Inca Indians in Peru in 1531. Although he did not find the short cut to the Far East, he found lands that proved to be, for a time, the richest in South America. Pizarro could neither read nor write, but he was both determined and brutal. Upon hearing news of a great people and a great wealth, Pizarro tried unsuccessfully to get men and ships together to make the conquest. He went all the way back to Spain and got permission and money from Charles V, King of Spain, for the conquest of Peru. Success smiled on Pizarro.

Atahualpa [ä′tä wäl′pä] was the trusting king of the Incas in the land of Peru. The Inca king seemed eager to please Pizarro, but Pizarro cruelly slaughtered Atahualpa's people and captured the king. To ransom their ruler, the Incas filled a room measuring 5.18 meters (17 ft.) by 7.32 meters (22 ft.) and high as a person could reach, with treasure valued at more than five million dollars. All this wealth was not enough to prevent the treacherous murder of the Inca king.

The Spanish empire in South America was ruled from Spain by agents of the monarch who lived in the New World. In all things and in every way, the colonial empire of Spain existed for the single purpose of making Spain, the parent

Quetzalcoatl [ket säl′ kō ät′l], the principal god of the Aztecs. He was also called the feathered serpent.

country, rich. The once proud and highly developed Aztec and Inca civilizations were slaughtered by the Spanish. These people were given a place on the lowest rung of the social ladder and were often enslaved by the Spaniards.

Missionaries tried to teach Christianity to the native peoples. A Catholic priest, Las Casas [läs kä′səs], fought for their rights and laws were passed in Spain protecting these rights. However, more often than not, these laws were not obeyed by the Spanish conquistadors. Encouraged by its conquest of South America, Spain moved vigorously to establish colonies in the New World. Some of the Spanish, as well as Portuguese, colonies would be hundreds of years old before the first English colonies were established in North America at Jamestown and Plymouth.

1. Why did the explorers of the sixteenth century make their dangerous voyages? What made these voyages so dangerous?

2. Explain how Brazil became Portuguese rather than Spanish.

3. How did the Spanish conquistadores conquer much of South America?

4. How did the Spanish treat the native peoples?

5. What skills and qualities did explorers require to be successful?

FRANCE, ENGLAND, AND OTHER COUNTRIES GAIN OVERSEAS EMPIRES

How the Dutch and French Gained Empires

The Dutch founded trading colonies in the New World. The Dutch empire in the New World included the Hudson River in New York, Hudson's Bay in Canada, and the settlement of New York, which was called *New Amsterdam.* However, by 1664, the Dutch were slowly pushed out of the New World. The Dutch East India Company, established in 1602, built up a rich trade with the Far East. It occupied what came to be called the *Dutch East Indies.* These islands, which include Java and Sumatra, remained in Dutch control until World War II. In South Africa, too, the Dutch began a settlement. Today, descendants of the Dutch control the government of the Republic of South Africa.

Montreal in the province of Quebec is a French-speaking city and Canada's largest urban center. The French came to the New World during the Age of Discovery. In what is now Canada and the Mississippi River valley of America, they built a large number of trading posts. Furs were the chief source of wealth and one of the chief items of trade. The French empire spread to West Africa and to the island of Madagascar. While France lost most of its empire in the New World, its empire in Africa and the Far East grew. France held part of this empire until the last half of the twentieth century.

How the English Gained an Empire

The English were latecomers to the Age of Discovery. At first, they did not lead voyages of exploration. Rather, they preferred to attack the Spanish ships and to take the wealth that was being taken from the colonies back to Spain. Two English sailors, John Hawkins and Francis Drake, became famous for plundering Spanish ships. In 1607, the first English settlement was made at Jamestown. It was followed by settlement of what became the thirteen American colonies. The English settlers who came to live in the New World wanted religious freedom and a chance to make a good living. They brought with them the beginnings of democratic ways, which developed into an important part of American life.

The French and English settlers clashed in the New World. English settlers in the New World came with the desire to establish permanent homes. They thus came for different reasons than either the French or Spanish settlers. The French and Spanish, for the most part, came to get rich quickly and hoped to enjoy their wealth back home. The English dissenters wanted to settle in the New World. The French and Spanish settlers were under direct control of both the government and the Roman Catholic Church. The English settlers enjoyed more freedom from government restrictions than the settlers of Spain and France.

New York in 1673. The Dutch settled New York in the early seventeenth century. What was it called by the Dutch?

The British East India Company gradually pushed the Portuguese, Dutch, and French out of most of India. In time, India came almost completely under British rule and remained so until after World War II. By the seventeenth century, the English were well on their way toward the establishment of the largest colonial empire in the world.

The Benefits of the Age of Discovery

One result of the Age of Discovery was that the Atlantic Ocean, and not the Mediterranean Sea, became the main highway of commerce. This new trade route meant that England, France, and Holland became powerful commercial countries. Italy, Spain, and Portugal became less important in foreign trade. The naval defeat of the Spanish *Armada* (fleet of warships) in 1588 by the English marked the beginning of the decline of Spain's power and prestige and the beginning of the naval supremacy of England.

The Age of Discovery brought with it an increase in the amount of gold and silver that came into use. With the increase in money came an increase in banking and in moneylending. Overseas adventures required a great deal of money, usually more than one person had. The savings of many were needed to pay for overseas travels. The selling of shares of stock in such adventures became common. The joint stock company and, later, the corporation became the chief ways in which business ventures were organized and financed.

One of the results of the Age of Discovery was the growth of *capitalism*. Capitalism is an economic system based on competition, private property, the investment of money for profit, and freedom from government interference. It is based upon the pooling of vast sums of money from many people who invest in commercial activities in order to try to make a profit. A middle class is made possible from among those of moderate wealth. Their power is based on profits made from business rather than from the land. Capitalism became the main economic institution of modern times. So great were the changes in methods of doing business that the Age of Discovery has sometimes been called a "commercial revolution."

Major European Empires, 1700

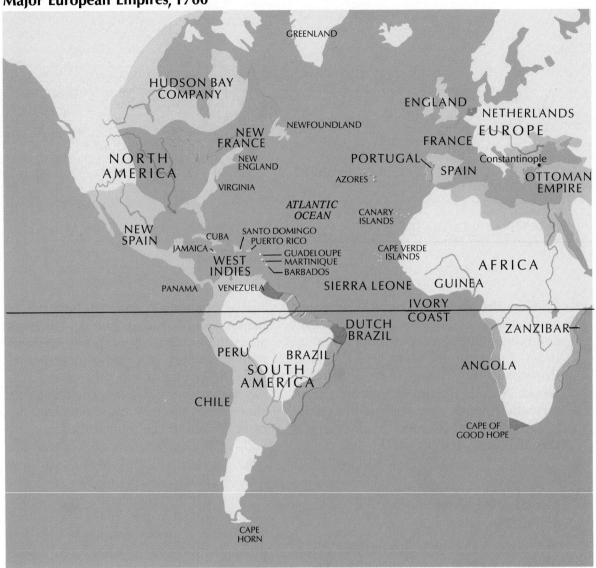

By 1700, several European countries had vast overseas empires.
• What European countries had territory in both America and the Far East?
• The Phillipine Islands were part of what empire?

Problems Created by the Voyages of Discovery

Not all the results of the Age of Discovery were beneficial. As national governments took more interest in colonies, there were new causes for war among nations. Each nation tried to own the richest colony or to take riches away from the other nations. Because of the competition for wealth, power, and glory, the native peoples who lived in the newly found lands were often harshly treated. Wealth came first; life and liberty, second.

The new wealth of the Age of Discovery created high prices for goods and

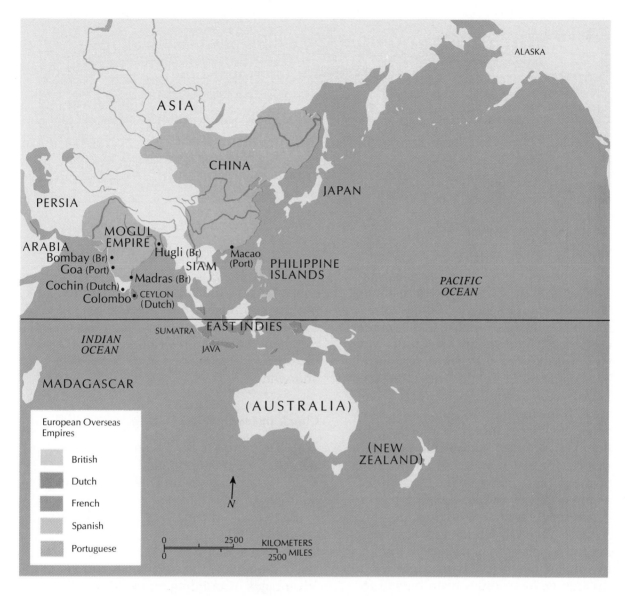

- What city on the China coast did Portugal control?
- List three overseas areas that were part of the Dutch empire.
- To which European empire did Bombay and Virginia both belong?

products. Ordinary people found that the things they needed cost a great deal of money. The increase in prices, or inflation, caused considerable hardship for many people. They did not understand the reasons for the high cost of living and were upset.

Greedy explorers enslaved people and stole much of their wealth, espe-

cially in the New World. African slavery was introduced in the New World to provide cheap labor for the silver mines. The slave trade became very profitable for sea captains, merchants, financiers, and investors. Many problems that we face today may be traced to the slave trade, including the racial problems of the United States in the twentieth century.

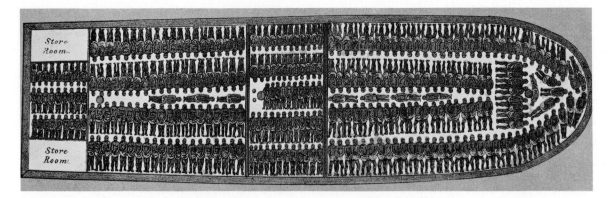

The lower deck of a slave ship headed for the Americas. Why were slaves arranged this way?

The view developed generally among European countries that colonies existed for the exclusive benefit of the parent countries. The colonies had to do what they were told by the parent, or controlling, country. From this view, the idea known as *mercantilism* [mėr'kən til izm] grew. It meant that the people in the colonies would produce raw materials for the parent country and would provide a market for the manufactured products of the parent country. Since wealth was as important as power, a nation tried to get as much gold and silver as possible. In order to grow rich the parent country needed to sell its manufactured products to foreign countries. It also needed to discourage its colonies from buying foreign goods. The parent country did this by taxing goods coming from other countries into the colonies. How best to put mercantilism into practice was a source of endless argument. The colonies resented the trade restrictions and the taxes. This discontent led to revolution and war.

Check in Here

1. How did the French and the Dutch start their colonial empires?

2. What progress did England make in building an empire?

3. How did the motives of the English in establishing an empire differ from those of the Spanish?

4. What were the advantages and disadvantages of building empires?

5. How did the theory of mercantilism develop?

REVIEWING THE BASICS

One of the most important developments of modern world history was the rise of nation-states and the empires they built. A national government provides protection for its people, raises money, and improves the way people live. Nations develop loyalty among their peoples. Clashes between nations occur when their goals conflict, or when their people observe a different religion, or speak another language.

England and France developed early as nations. Spain and Portugal followed somewhat later. Although England and France were each governed by a monarch, political institutions emerged that were later used to control the unlimited rule of the monarch. The Hundred Years' War between England and France marked the end of feudalism. It ended the claims that each nation made upon the other. Russia developed as a nation more slowly, but eventually occupied a large landmass. Holland, Switzerland, and the Scandinavian nations also developed gradually. Germany and Italy remained divided, however, and did not become nations until the nineteenth century. Many countries of Africa and Asia did not become nations until the twentieth century. Nationalism continues to influence world affairs today.

The search for empires was a powerful force. Portugal and Spain led the world in discovering new lands overseas in Africa, Asia, and South America. Spain in particular built up an empire in the New World. Portugal dominated Brazil and established colonies in Asia, India, and the islands of the Pacific. England established colonies in what is now Canada and the United States. It competed with France, which also had colonies in the New World. Mercantilism was a system whereby colonies existed for the betterment of the controlling country. Conquered peoples were often cruelly treated. Their wealth and resources were drained by their conquerors.

REVIEWING THE HIGHLIGHTS

People to Identify

Thomas Hobbes	Alfonso I	Magellan
William the Conqueror	Charles the Bold	Balboa
	Richard III	Cortés
Henry II	Montezuma	Atahualpa
King John	Rurik	De Soto
Hugh Capet	Romanovs	Ponce de León
Philip Augustus	Philip the Fair	Henry Hudson
Joan of Arc	Gustavus Adolphus	Verrazano
Henry VII	Prince Henry	Las Casas
Queen Isabella	Vasco da Gama	Coronado
King Ferdinand	Columbus	Pinzón
Ivan the Great	Diaz	Pizarro

Places to Locate

Iberian Peninsula	Canada	Kiev
English Channel	New Amsterdam	Orleans
Holland	Cape of Good Hope	Strait of Magellan
Flanders		Scandinavia
New World	Brazil	Crécy
Isthmus of Panama	Dutch East Indies	Poitiers
Mexico	West Indies	Agincourt
Tenonchtitlán	Runnymede	Jamestown

nationalism	nation-state	grand jury
Great Council	capitalism	Cortes
Magna Carta	Age of Discovery	petit jury
Parliament	mercantilism	burgesses
Model Parliament	conquistador	Peace of Westphalia
common law	Pragmatic Sanction	Treaty of Tordesillas
Estates-General	of Bourges	czar
middle class	sovereignty	

**Events
to Describe**

Wars of the Roses	Jacquerie	Thirty Years' War
	Hundred Years' War	

**Mastering
the Fundamentals**

1. List the factors that encouraged or discouraged the rise of nation-states.
2. How did monarchs free themselves from the necessity of asking their vassals for help?
3. What did Henry II of England contribute to our system of law?
4. How did Philip Augustus strengthen the French monarchy?
5. How did Philip the Fair strengthen the French monarchy?
6. How did the weapons the English used in the Hundred Years' War change the way warfare was conducted?
7. Why did the English win the important battles in the Hundred Years' War?
8. What factors may have influenced Queen Isabella and King Ferdinand to support the proposed voyage of Columbus?
9. Explain how Joan of Arc helped the French.
10. What is the significance of the Wars of the Roses?
11. How did Louis XI strengthen the French monarchy?
12. How did the development of Russia differ from that of other countries?
13. What reason explains why Russia became an Asiatic as well as a European nation?
14. Explain why Germany failed to become a nation until later in history.
15. What is the significance of the Thirty Years' War?
16. What reasons explain why explorers searched for new lands?
17. Describe the empires of the Spanish, Portuguese, Dutch, French, and English.
18. List the significant results of the Age of Discovery.
19. List some problems brought about by the Age of Discovery.
20. Explain why the Age of Discovery is also called a "commercial revolution"?

THINGS TO DO

1. Use an outline map to trace the journeys of discovery of the major explorers mentioned in this chapter.
2. Prepare a report on the subject "Shipboard Life During the Age of Discovery."
3. Write a letter home that an ordinary soldier might have written describing his feelings about the Battle of Poitiers.

YOU ARE THE HISTORIAN

Queen Elizabeth and Her Master Mariners

. . . Twenty years on the throne had taught her [Queen Elizabeth] statecraft* in the school of experience. She was excommunicated by the pope in 1570, and in *de facto** war even before the declared war with Spain, whose ambassador financed an unsuccessful plot to assassinate her, Elizabeth found security only in the hearts of her subjects. They rendered* to their queen a love and loyalty that no English monarch had yet received or would receive for centuries to come. "Gloriana," as the poets named her, called the wisest men in the kingdom to her council, but she was wiser than some and shrewder than any. More than any European prince she encouraged with her patronage* and supported from her privy purse* the overseas voyages of her subjects. . . . She had a 'good liking' to all, . . . and showed her approval both of Drake's circumnavigation* and of his despoiling* a Spanish treasure ship by knighting him on the deck of the *Golden Hind* when he returned in November 1590. In this queen England found her destiny.†

Vocabulary

mariners—sailors
statecraft—skill in managing
de facto—actual, in fact
rendered—gave

patronage—support
privy purse—personal fund
circumnavigation—sail around the world
despoiling—robbing

On the basis of the selection above answer the questions that follow.

1. What was Elizabeth's attitude toward overseas discoveries?
2. What was her attitude toward Drake's attacks on Spanish ships?
3. Why does the passage say that "Elizabeth found security only in the hearts of her subjects"?
4. How was Elizabeth referred to in literature? Why do you think she was given this name?
5. Where did she learn how to be a monarch?
6. How did the Spanish ambassador threaten her?
7. How did the pope threaten her?
8. What does the writer of this selection think of Elizabeth's intelligence? How can you tell?
9. How did she support the voyages of discovery?

†Samuel Eliot Morison, *The European Discovery of America: Northern Voyages* (New York: Oxford University Press, 1971), p. 496.

UNIT ACTIVITIES

1. Prepare a "Town Meeting of the World" to be presented through Telstar. You, as moderator, interview Erasmus, Luther, and Calvin.
2. Make a graph showing the early growth of democracy in England to 1300.
3. Write a composition comparing the Age of Discovery with the Space Age.
4. Debate. *Resolved:* Modern astronauts are more courageous than were the explorers of the sixteenth century.
5. Draw a plan of a feudal manor. Draw a comparable plan of a present-day farm. Discuss the differences in the role played by each in the life of the people.
6. Dramatize each of the following: (a) The trial of Joan of Arc; (b) The coronation of Charlemagne.
7. In a "Meet the Press" type of program, prepare to interview Eleanor of Acquitaine on the subject of women during the Medieval Period.
8. Prepare an oral report on each of the following technological advances in the medieval period: (a) mining; (b) transportation; (c) textile weaving.
9. Prepare an illustrated talk on the teachings of Mohammed.
10. Prepare a debate that a candidate of the Blues might have had with the Greens. It is important to identify appropriate issues in politics and religion in Byzantium.
11. Prepare a time line showing the major events in this unit.
12. Draw a cartoon illustrating one or more of the following: (a) Henry IV going to Canossa; (b) The Children's Crusade; (c) The Battle of Poitiers.
13. Conduct a round table discussion in which a person representing each of the following discusses ways and means of raising living standards: (a) a member of a craft guild; (b) a member of a merchant guild; (c) a member of a modern trade union; (d) a member of a modern chamber of commerce.
14. On a map trace the routes taken by each of the following: (a) Vasco da Gama; (b) Columbus; (c) Magellan.
15. On a map show the extent of each of the following: (a) the Empire of Byzantium at its height; (b) the Muslim Empire at its height.

BIBLIOGRAPHY

*Andrews, Frank. *For Charlemagne!* Harper & Row. The story of a youth who went to Charlemagne's court to study.

Churchill, Winston S. *A History of the English-Speaking Peoples: The Birth of*

*Indicates fiction.

Britain. Dodd Mead & Co. The history of England from its earliest days under Roman rule to the end of the feudal period.

*Clemens, Samuel. *A Connecticut Yankee in King Arthur's Court*. Globe Book Co. The humorous story of an American who dreams of visiting England in medieval times. He has numerous experiences.

Cooke, Donald E. *The Romance of Capitalism*. Winston. This is an account of how great fortunes were built and what capitalism meant in the development of Western civilization.

*Costain, Thomas B. *The Black Rose*. Doubleday & Co. A novel of England and China during the Middle Ages.

*Costain, Thomas B. *The Moneyman*. Doubleday & Co. The adventures of the first capitalist of the world, Jacques Coeur.

Durant, Will. *The Story of Civilization: The Age of Faith; The Story of Civilization: The Reformation; The Story of Civilization: The Renaissance*. Simon and Schuster. The famous *Story of Civilization* which traces, in a readable style, the Middle Ages, the Renaissance, and the Reformation.

Hahn, Emily. *Leonardo da Vinci*. Random House. Another easy-to-read biography in the Landmark Series of that most Renaissance of men.

*Holt, Victoria. *My Enemy the Queen*. Doubleday. An historical novel based on the life of Elizabeth I.

Howarth, David. *1066: The Year of the Conquest*. Viking. A new interpretation of the conquest of England by William of Normandy.

*Kent, Louise. *He Went With Magellan*. Houghton Mifflin Co. An exciting story based on the first circumnavigation of the globe.

*Kent, Louise. *He Went With Vasco Da Gama*. Houghton Mifflin Co. An exciting story of the trip around the Cape of Good Hope to India.

Komroff, Manuel (ed.). *The Travels of Marco Polo*. Liveright Publishing Corp. A firsthand account of far-off Cathay in the days of the Great Khan.

Ladurie, LeRoy Emmanuel. *Carnival in Romans*. Braziller. A dramatic account of a tax revolt in a province of southern France during the late sixteenth century.

Lamb, Harold. *Earth Shakers*. Doubleday & Co. Exploits of Genghis Khan and Tamerlane.

Mattingly, Garrett. *The Armada*. Houghton Mifflin Co. A scholarly account of the defeat of the Spanish fleet by the English, excitingly told.

Maude La Claviere, R. de. *The Women of the Renaissance*. Deals with notable women of the Renaissance.

Meade, Marion. *Eleanor of Acquitaine*. Hawthorne Books. The turbulent life of a prominent woman of the Middle Ages.

Morison, Samuel Eliot. *Admiral of the Ocean Sea*. Little, Brown & Co., Inc. An enjoyable account of Columbus' voyages told by a famous naval historian.

Picktall, Marmaduke. *The Meaning of the Glorious Koran*. New American Library. A good introduction to the Islamic holy book.

Tuchman, Barbara W. *A Distant Mirror: The Calamitous Fourteenth Century*. Knopf. This modern best-seller describes vividly a period of time which, the author says, is a distant mirror of our own.

Wilson, Kerek. *Francis Drake and His Great Voyage*. Harper & Row. A short and exciting account of the voyages of this great seafarer.

Democracy Triumphs over Absolutism in Europe

The execution of Louis XVI of France, 1793

Louis XIV of France

The Age of Absolutism:
The Might
of Mighty Rulers

If you have read *Alice in Wonderland,* you may remember that at Alice's first meeting with the Queen of Hearts, the queen shouted, "Off with her head!" The king and queen in Alice's adventures were part of a dream, but the power of rulers was real to the people of seventeenth-and eighteenth-century Europe.

The complete power of a monarch over his or her people is called *absolutism* [ab'sə lü'tiz em]. During the Age of Absolutism, roughly between the sixteenth and eighteenth centuries (1500–1700), mighty monarchs ruled from expensive palaces where they lived in splendor. Absolutism reached its peak sooner in some countries of Europe than in others, but it was a feature of all countries. Because monarchs held all the political power, they were flattered and admired by those who wished royal favor or had desires for more power. Monarchs set the fashion in clothes, the taste in music and books, and the nation's moral and social patterns. How well they ruled depended upon their ability and on the ability of their advisers.

Today, Americans accept the idea that government should be based upon the will of the people. During the Age of Absolutism, the monarchs of Europe claimed they ruled by the will of God. The *divine right theory,* as this is called, was generally used by the monarchs in ruling their people. Machiavelli (1469–1527) said that a prince did not have to ask the people for permission to do the things he wanted done. Later, Thomas Hobbes (1588–1679) said that an absolute monarchy was the best of all forms of government. In this chapter you will examine absolutism as it worked in various countries of Europe. You will also read about the Age of Absolutism, which played a prominent role in the beginning of modern European history.

THE RISE AND DECLINE OF ABSOLUTISM IN SPAIN

How Charles V Ruled an Empire

Charles I of Spain (1516–56) was one of the best examples of an absolute monarch in Europe. He controlled more lands than any other ruler since Charlemagne and had many titles. As a member of the Hapsburg family, Charles I of Spain was Charles V of the Holy Roman Empire, king of the Netherlands, king of part of Italy, and ruler of Spain's lands overseas. A combination of luck and skill was responsible for his success. Charles V inherited much of his land and power from his grandparents Ferdinand and Isabella, and from the powerful Hapsburg family which ruled Austria. He played an important role in the affairs of Europe. How well did he play that role?

Keeping the center of the European stage was not an easy thing for Charles V. Two other powerful kings, Henry VIII of England (1491–1547) and Francis I of France (1494–1547), wanted to share the stage with him. Shakespeare said, "Uneasy lies the head that wears a crown." Certainly Charles and many other monarchs had uneasy times. War between Charles V and Francis I could not be avoided since each wanted to be supreme in Europe. Francis I in particular did not like to see his country surrounded by lands ruled by Charles V. War between the two kings was almost constant. Even when Francis I died, the fighting continued. It did not end until a tired Charles V gave up and retired to a monastery.

Charles V left his German lands to his brother Ferdinand and his Spanish lands to his son, Philip II. The wars between France and Spain ended in a tie. A tie was a good thing for Henry VIII of England, who would have been in a bad position if one or the other had become supreme on the continent of Europe. It was England's plan to stop any one power from becoming too strong in Europe. Such a plan is known as keeping the *balance of power*.

Why Spain Lost Its Power

The reign of Charles V was a glorious one for the king and the country, but not long after his death, Spain began to decline and never recovered. Why? Charles V was Holy Roman Emperor as well as King of Spain and King of the Netherlands. He was the most powerful monarch in Europe, but one ruler could not successfully govern all these countries. What was good for Spain was bad for the Netherlands. What was right for him to do as Holy Roman Emperor was wrong for him to do as king of Spain. Charles V was a faithful Roman Catholic who became involved in Martin Luther's attack on the Church. (See p. 216.)

In 1521, to meet the problems of uniting the empire and to stop Luther, Charles V called the *Diet of Worms* [wėrmz]. (Diet means assembly, and Worms is a city in Germany.) Charles demanded that Luther give up his ideas, but Martin Luther remained firm in his stand against certain practices in the Roman Catholic Church. Through his efforts at the Diet, Charles tried to halt the spread of Luther's ideas in Europe.

Martin Luther speaking before the Diet of Worms. Why did Charles V order this meeting of the Diet?

However, he neither unified his empire nor stopped Luther's influence. Charles's rule as Holy Roman Emperor was generally unsuccessful, and he ended his reign a very disappointed man.

From its lands in the New World, Spain received much gold and silver. Spanish conquistadors stole gold and silver from the Aztecs and the Incas and sent the wealth back to Spain. So much wealth made it seem as if Spain did not have to manufacture or grow things to be prosperous. The gold and silver forced prices up so high that the people of Spain found that no one would buy their goods. When the flow of gold and silver from the New World stopped, Spain became poor.

The Spanish *Armada,* which was defeated by the British navy in 1588. How did the loss affect Spain's power?

How Philip II Futhered the Decline of Spain

Charles V divided his empire in 1556 and left the rule of Spain and the Netherlands to his son, Philip II (1556–98). Philip had less to rule than his father. However, he was also less able, and he ruled Spain in an absolute but misdirected way. Philip believed that God expected him to save the Church from Protestantism and to make Spain the strongest country in Europe. He tried to make Spain powerful by driving out or destroying those who were not Catholics. He achieved this part of his plan. He proposed to stamp out *heresy* (rejection of Church beliefs) by bringing back the *Inquisition.* The Inquisition tried and punished those who were not Catholics or those who worked against the Catholic Church. It stopped heresy in Spain.

Philip's plan to make Spain a stronger nation, however, was not very successful. He saw that Spain was getting poorer, not richer. He established more absolute control over the nation by filling government offices with people who were responsible to and depended upon him alone. Because of this he did not benefit from the wise ideas of other leaders. The flow of gold and silver from the New World was slowing down. He saw, too, that trade was making the Netherlands prosperous.

Philip grew jealous of the Netherlands and treated the people so harshly that they rebelled. The Dutch were led by William the Silent. Under a Spanish army led by the Duke of Alva, the people of the Netherlands were treated with great cruelty, but even this could not put down the revolution. Philip II lost the best part of his Netherlands possessions, which became the Dutch Republic in 1581.

Philip II tried to make up for his loss of part of the Netherlands by conquering Portugal. Sixty years later, Portugal too broke away from the Spanish rule. In 1588, Philip II sent his *Armada* (a fleet of warships) against England, only to suffer a stunning defeat by the British navy.

263

Why Absolutism
Was Harmful to Spain

Charles V and Philip II both tried to do what they thought was right, but neither king was able to meet the problems he faced. For its success, absolute government depends on the leadership of one person. When the monarch was able, absolutism sometimes succeeded for short periods of time. When the monarch made too many mistakes, government failed and the people suffered. Spanish glory dimmed in spite of all the wealth of the New World. Under Charles V parts of the empire began to break away. This process continued during much of Spanish history.

Under Spanish kings there was religious intolerance and persecution. People such as the Moors and the Jews, who might have helped Spain become rich, were persecuted and driven out. Soon Spain, once a leading country of Europe, fell to second place in the commercial and political affairs of Europe.

Check in Here

1. Using the map on p. 269, identify the major countries that were ruled by Charles V at the height of his powers.

2. What is meant by the term "balance of power"? Why was maintaining a balance of power a useful goal for Henry VIII of England?

3. List three mistakes made by the Spanish king, Philip II.

4. How did absolutism in Spain demonstrate the strengths and weaknesses of this type of system?

ABSOLUTISM UNDER ENGLAND'S TUDORS

How the Tudors Ruled England

As a result of the War of the Roses, the Tudor family took the leadership in England. (See p. 233). In 1485, Henry Tudor, known as Henry VII, became king of England. He was followed by Henry VIII (1509–47). After the brief reigns of Edward VI and Mary, Elizabeth I (1558–1603) ruled as the last Tudor.

The Tudor monarchs had much in common. Let us look at them as a group. Under Henry VII, England began to expand overseas and to grow in wealth and strength. Under Henry VIII, England broke with the Catholic Church. (See p. 220.) England also tried to keep the balance of power in Europe. (See p. 262.) When Henry VIII died, there was some confusion about who would follow him. His son Edward VI, who became king, died after a short reign. He was followed by Mary Tudor (1516–1558), who was a devout Catholic.

For a time during Mary's rule, the Catholic Church was again the leading church in England. Mary then married Philip II of Spain. Under his influence Mary earned the title of "Bloody Mary" for her persecution of heretics and non-Catholics. Upon Mary's death, Elizabeth became queen. She was the strongest Tudor.

Elizabeth I restored the Protestant (Anglican) church in England. She tried to steer a course somewhere between Catholicism and Protestantism and dissatisfied many people. The Puritans left England because the Church of England was "too Catholic" to suit them. Elizabeth wanted a national church which was free of Rome, but subject to the Crown.

Scotland was ruled by Mary Stuart, a great-granddaughter of Henry VII. Since Mary Stuart was married to the heir to the French throne, the influence of France was great. France, a Catholic country, sought to prevent the growth of Protestantism in Scotland. Elizabeth allied herself with the Calvinist (Protestant) Party in Scotland. Mary, Queen of Scots, tried to resist the power of the

Protestant movement but was unsuccessful. She was forced to give up the throne in 1567. She fled Scotland and sought refuge in England.

Mary Stuart, however, was a threat to Elizabeth I. As a great-granddaughter of Henry VII, she had a claim to the English throne. As a strong Catholic she opposed Elizabeth's attempt to keep Anglicanism strong. Elizabeth I had Mary Stuart executed on the grounds that she had conspired with Philip II of Spain against England.

To avenge Mary's death and to restore Catholicism to England, Philip II launched an enormous fleet of ships, the *Armada*, to invade England. Bad weather and poor planning helped doom the attack. The *Armada* was soundly defeated by the English. After this, Spain declined further, and under Elizabeth, England became stronger among the nations of Europe.

Elizabeth I was one of England's most popular and powerful queens. Yet her power was never as absolute as that of the kings of Spain. Elizabeth I, like her father and grandfather, knew how to get her way with the Parliament. She did not do away with Parliament but used it to serve her own purposes. Although this practice did not encourage democracy, the people nevertheless loved and respected Elizabeth.

During Elizabeth I's reign, England became a great seagoing nation. Improvements in the kinds of vessels available and their handling gave England a superior navy. Under the leadership of the sea adventurers Drake and Hawkins, England began to build an empire.

It was under Queen Elizabeth that the great works of English literature of the Tudor period (1485–1603) were written. William Shakespeare (1564–1616) was the leading poet and dramatist of this early modern period. His dramas—comedies, tragedies, and historical plays—are still performed and widely enjoyed. The Elizabethan theater became world famous, but to a modern theatergoer it might seem strange. There was no curtain and little scenery, and men and boys did all of the acting.

England After Tudor Rule

Among England's gifts to the world are the great dramas of Shakespeare, models of great lawmaking bodies such as Parliament, and democratic traditions such as jury trial. Under the Tudors, these expressions of democracy did not die, but served the monarch. The Tudors were able rulers. Although they did not follow the theory of divine right, they ruled as absolute monarchs. They twisted the meaning of democracy to suit their own

The Globe Theater was a large outdoor theater built in 1599. Shakespeare's plays were performed there.

Elizabeth I (1533–1603)

On September 7, 1533, a daughter was born to Henry VIII and Anne Boleyn [bül'in]. Had the baby been a boy, there would have been great rejoicing because the king would have had a male heir. The king's disappointment was very great. The birth of a girl resulted in the fall of Anne Boleyn from royal favor. In 1536, she was sent to the Tower of London, an infamous prison. On May 19, she was beheaded.

Elizabeth I, the daughter whose birth so disappointed her parents, grew up to become one of England's greatest monarchs. Although as a child she had no mother, Elizabeth's early years were relatively happy ones. She was cared for by Lady Bryan, who often complained about the late hours Elizabeth kept and the improper food she was encouraged to eat. Lady Bryan also complained that Elizabeth did not have all the petticoats, skirts, gowns, and stockings one would expect a young princess of the House of Tudor to have. Yet Elizabeth received her share of attention, and her tempermental father loved her despite his displeasure with Anne Boleyn.

Elizabeth was born during the Renaissance when learning for women began to be encouraged. The court of Henry VIII was filled with scholars of note and reputation. Elizabeth was quick to take advantage of the opportunity for learning their presence offered. By the age of ten she was studying Latin and Italian as well as French. Later, she studied Greek and the New Testament. At sixteen she had won the praise of her learned teachers who admired her genuine love of knowledge.

Upon the death of Mary Tudor in 1558, Elizabeth was crowned monarch amid pomp and ceremony. As the ruler of a potentially rich nation, Elizabeth was the best match in Europe. Every eligible bachelor of noble birth hoped that Elizabeth would choose him to share the throne. There was to be no royal wedding, however. Elizabeth preferred to rule alone. Her strategy was to win favors from powerful men and nations by dangling bait. The bait? The promise of marriage to her. Elizabeth used this to bring about favorable alliances between her suitor's country and England.

Under Elizabeth I, England grew and prospered. Its ships, commanded by Sir Francis Drake, sailed around the world and later defeated the Spanish *Armada* (navy), crushing forever the power of Spain. When Elizabeth died in 1603, she left England richer in spirit and wealthier.

needs. Yet, such great lawmaking bodies as Parliament grew in power. Democratic traditions such as jury trial also expanded. The Tudors were followed by the Stuarts, who did not know how to follow the Tudor example.

The son of Mary Stuart (Queen of Scots) was James Stuart. He had been brought up in the Protestant faith. On the death of Queen Elizabeth I, he became King James I of England and began the Stuart line. Under the Stuart kings a more strict form of absolute monarchy was tried. As a result, rebellious groups arose. How the English felt about the Stuart style of absolutism and what the English did about it will be told in Chapter 13.

Check in Here

1. Explain how Elizabeth became queen of England.

2. Why was Elizabeth regarded as a less absolute ruler than Philip II?

3. What was Elizabeth's religious policy? Was it successful?

4. Why was the defeat of the Spanish *Armada* a significant event in England's history?

ABSOLUTISM IN FRANCE UNDER LOUIS XIV

France Was Made Ready for Absolutism

The best example of absolutism and of the divine right of kings was the reign of Louis XIV (1638–1715) of France. The magnificence of Louis's reign would not have been possible without the work of many people who came before him.

Henry IV (1553–1610) came to the throne of France as a result of a series of religious wars. Henry was Protestant, and many French people did not wish to see a Protestant on the throne of France.

To make peace, to get on with the business of governing, and to rebuild a nation that had been torn by war, Henry became a Catholic.

Henry IV ruled wisely and well. With the aid of his brilliant adviser Sully [sul′ē] (1560–1641), he cut government expenses, carefully collected taxes, and rebuilt bridges, roads, and canals. Henry wanted France and its people to develop commercially and industrially. Under Henry the silk textile industry, for which France became world famous, was born. Henry was responsible for a milestone in religious tolerance, the *Edict of Nantes* [nants] (1598). By this law, Protestants were given the right to worship and to hold public office.

Henry IV was truly interested in the good of the people. Despite the fact that Henry was well liked and a good king, he did have at least one enemy. As he was about to go to war against the Hapsburgs (rulers of Austria), he was killed by a fanatic. Thus France lost a fine king.

On the death of Henry IV, his young son, Louis XIII, became king. Since Louis was too young to rule, his mother, Marie de' Medici [də med′i chē], ruled for him. She ruled badly, and France was weakened through her mistakes. It was not until Cardinal Richelieu [rish′ə lü′] (1585–1642) was given permission to govern by Louis XIII that France regained its old importance.

Louis XIII let Richelieu rule France between 1624 and 1642. Richelieu, popular with no one, not even the king, ruled forcefully and was feared by all. He wanted absolute control by the Crown, and he wanted France to be the strongest nation in Europe. Unfortunately, his way was not always the best way for the French people. Henry IV had been interested in his people, but Richelieu referred to them as mules that had to be driven.

To drive the "mules" Richelieu placed his trust in new government officers, called the *intendants* [in ten′dənts]. These served as local government officers. They were loyal middle-class men, who served as Richelieu's eyes and ears as well as his tax collectors. It was their job to report disloyal people who would undermine the king's power.

The death of Richelieu was followed shortly by the death of King Louis. The four-year-old boy who became the new king of France was destined to have a long and glorious reign. His actions produced a page in history which is still remembered. His title was Louis XIV. A four-year-old child can hardly be expected to rule, but Louis and France were fortunate in finding a new minister, Mazarin [maz′ə rin].

Though not quite the equal of Richelieu in cunning, Mazarin was able to rule France along the lines established by Richelieu. Mazarin led France successfully through the remaining years of the Thirty Years' War. (See p. 238.) At the time of his death, Mazarin had the satisfaction of knowing that his efforts had made France the foremost country in Europe. It was indeed a nation fit for a king, and Louis XIV, the Grand Monarch, and Sun King, was ready to take over the leadership of this nation.

France Under Louis XIV

From 1643 to 1715, King Louis XIV was the absolute ruler of France and the most influential king on the European continent. Other kings copied him. By studying his reign, one can learn much about absolutism in France and elsewhere.

Louis XIV was ambitious and wanted to expand the lands he ruled. To satisfy his ambition, he waged war during much of his reign—in America as well as in Europe, on land as well as on sea. Beginning in 1667 and continuing for the next forty years, Louis made war on his neighbors. He hoped to push the borders of France to the Pyrenees, the Mediterranean Sea, the Atlantic Ocean, the English Channel, the Alps, and the Rhine River. He looked upon these physical features as the natural and rightful borders of France. But Louis was not successful in expanding France to these borders.

The *War of the Spanish Succession* (1701–14) was fought over the title of King of Spain. Charles II of Spain had made a will in which he gave his lands to Louis's grandson. This gift, of course, was good for Louis, but bad for the other European kings. They did not like to see the crown of Spain and the crown of France in the same family. England especially did not like to see the balance of power upset this way, and so France and England went to war.

The results of the war were disappointing for France, since little was gained and much was lost. The *Treaty of Utrecht* [yü′trekt] (1713) ended the War of the Spanish Succession. According to its terms France lost land in the New World to Great Britain. Nova Scotia, Newfoundland, land in the Hudson's Bay region, and islands in the Caribbean Sea came under English control. Besides getting these lands, England gained Gibraltar—the gateway to the Mediterranean Sea. France gained something, too. Louis's grandson was allowed to keep the title to the throne of Spain, but the crowns of the two countries were never united.

How Louis XIV Lived at Versailles

Louis XIV was clever and shrewd and worked hard at the job of being king. He wanted to have powerful nobles near him, where he could keep his eye on them. In order to keep the nobles occupied, he established a dazzling court at Versailles [ver sī′], where he entertained

Europe About 1721

Under Louis XIV and his successors France fought many wars.
- What physical features did Louis XIV consider to be the natural borders of France?
- In what city was the treaty that ended the War of the Spanish Succession signed?
- What did England gain in the Mediterranean as a result of the Treaty of Utrecht?
  Clue: Spain in the twentieth century wants England to return this site.

lavishly. Decorative furniture, sparkling chandeliers, mirrors, and water fountains filled the glittering and fascinating court of Versailles.

Here, for the king's favorite people, life was a continuous ball. Elegant fash-ions for men and women were created and worn. To be among Louis's favorites was a sign of high rank and prestige. Members of the nobility helped Louis dress. Even handling his towel was a high honor. From morning to night, life

269

was a constant series of grand ceremonies, lavish parties, and court love affairs, all of which followed strict rules of court etiquette.

Monarchs and nobles throughout Europe envied Louis and copied his court and fashions. Yet many people today enjoy comforts and luxuries which even royalty could not have in those days. Plumbing, electricity, and central heating were unknown at the court of Louis XIV. The royal palace at Versailles was hot in summer, cold in winter, and lighted by candles and torches. Because proper sanitation and washing facilities did not exist, strong and unpleasant odors were common, and perfumes were used to hide them.

How Louis XIV Paid His Expenses

King Louis XIV had wise advisers. Perhaps he should have followed their advice more than he did. Among the most influential of Louis's advisers was Colbert [kôl ber′], his brilliant minister of finance. Colbert introduced a budget system and made other financial changes that encouraged French industry. He tried to improve manufacturing and farming. He supervised a number of public works and thereby increased employment throughout France.

Colbert was responsible for bringing the system of economics widely known as *mercantilism* [mėr′kən ti liz′əm] into

The Palace of Versailles was built by Louis XIV. There are hundreds of rooms in the palace, including the Hall of Mirrors shown here.

Modern History
1500-Present

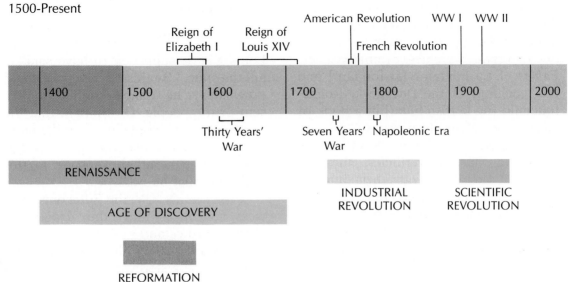

Be able to place the following events on the time line:

1500–1700	Age of Absolutism	1618–48	Thirty Years' War
1509	Henry VIII—King of England	1689	Peter—Czar of Russia
1521	Diet of Worms	1713	Treaty of Utrecht
1534	Henry VIII—broke with Rome	1740	Frederick II—King of Prussia
1588	Spanish Armada defeated	1762	Catherine—Czarina of Russia
1598	Edict of Nantes	1780	Joseph II—Emperor of Austria

France. According to its teachings, each country measured its riches by the amount of gold and silver that poured into it. Since gold and silver were used as money, a country increased its amount of gold and silver by buying fewer goods than it sold. Another way was to have colonies that supplied the things the parent country needed for manufacturing. Mercantilism taught that high *tariffs* (taxes on goods coming into a country) helped a nation get rich. These high tariffs made prices on foreign goods higher than the prices of goods produced in the home country. The high prices on foreign goods encouraged the people to buy the homemade, less expensive goods.

Colbert did not start this system, but it is most closely associated with his name. He tried to make France a strong nation in industry and in agriculture.

Cultural Growth Under Louis XIV

Just as Henry IV, Richelieu, and Mazarin set the political stage for absolutism, so, too, certain French writers set the stage for French cultural growth. In his influential books, *Gargantua* [gär gan'chü ə] and *Pantagruel* [pan tag'rü el'], the author Rabelais [rab'ə lā'] (1494–1553) wrote that life was meant to be enjoyed. Montaigne (1533–92) wrote a series of brilliant essays in which he expressed his deepest thoughts on life. In 1635, Richelieu established the French Academy to encourage French writing. Some years later, Colbert established the French Academy of Science to encourage the growth of science.

It was under Louis XIV that a great age in French writing was born. Great tragedies were written by Corneille [kôr nā′yə] (1606–84) and great comedies by Molière [mōl yer′] (1622–73). Racine [rä sēn′] (1639–99) is considered one of France's greatest dramatists. The *Fables* of La Fontaine [lə fon tān′] and the teachings of the Duc de la Rochefoucauld [də lə rōsh′fü kō] in a book of *Maxims* are prized to this day.

Louis XIV and his lords and ladies had many faults. Nevertheless, they encouraged literature with their interest and wealth. You have read that the countries of Europe copied the royal court of France. They copied and borrowed French literature as well. French poems, plays, and stories reached many parts of the world.

During Louis's reign the city of Paris became a model for other cities. Some of the old slums were destroyed, and new parts of the city were built. Some of the streets were paved and widened, and a few were even lighted by torches. Paris

Although Molière wrote in the seventeenth century, audiences still find much to laugh at in his comedies.

became a capital worthy of a mighty king and a mighty nation.

Louis XIV Evaluated

Louis XIV is supposed to have said, "I am the state." By this he meant he could do whatever he wished without the consent of the people. He thought that the nation and the people lived for the monarch. Did Louis use this great power wisely? In general, the answer to this question must be no.

Under Louis XIV, the Edict of Nantes was canceled, and the *Huguenots* (French Protestants) were driven out of the country. Driving the Huguenots out proved to be a step which was nearly as harmful to France as the expulsion of the Moors and Jews from Spain proved to be in that country. The Huguenots were hard-working people and helped make the country prosperous.

Because he was a spendthrift, Louis XIV left a heavy financial burden for others to pay after he died. He had devoted more time to the cause of war than to the paths of peace, and the results of his military adventures did little to improve France.

A wise monarch was needed to undo the evils begun by Louix XIV. Unfortunately, those who followed him were not wise. Under Louis XV, France lost control of Canada. During the reign of Louis XVI, the French Revolution took place.

Check in Here

1. List one achievement of each of the following people: Richelieu, Mazarin, Sully, Colbert.

2. Why is the reign of Louis XIV regarded as a good example of absolutism?

3. Why was Louis XIV frequently at war with other countries?

4. Identify four cultural accomplishments made in France during the reign of Louis XIV.

ABSOLUTISM IN RUSSIA UNDER PETER AND CATHERINE

Why Absolutism Developed in Russia

In Russian history there are some outstanding examples of very powerful rulers. The foundations of modern Russia were laid by Peter the Great (1672–1725). While Louis XIV was declaring, "I am the state," Peter was calling himself the Czar of all Russia. Like many other monarchs of Europe, Peter wished to copy certain things from France. He was determined that Russia would catch up with the countries of Western Europe, but he had to find out more about them.

Peter became a European tourist. In disguise he visited the famous capitals, where he saw and learned much about Western European civilization. He was interested in many fields, but European ships interested him most. In England and the Netherlands he actually worked in shipyards and learned how to build ships. He would have stayed in Europe longer, but a revolution in Russia made it necessary for him to come home. He put down the revolution forcefully by killing its leaders.

The Growth of Russia to 1796

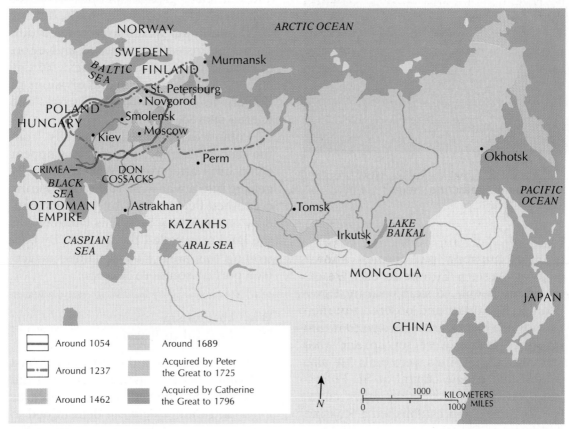

This map shows the increase in the area of Russia over many centuries.
- When did Russia experience its greatest growth?
- Which was larger, the Russia of 1054 or the Russia of 1462?
- Under what ruler did Russia acquire most of its territory on the Baltic Sea?
- Locate one area acquired by Catherine the Great.

273

Catherine the Great of Russia. How would you describe Catherine's reign?

Peter hurriedly put his new knowledge of Western Europe to use. He ordered his people to start wearing European-style clothes and ordered the men to shorten their beards. He saw to it that printing presses were set up and that schools and hospitals were built. He also established a new capital at St. Petersburg. He sent Russians to other countries to study, and established a Russian Academy of Science.

Peter helped to make Russia a powerful country. One of Russia's problems was the fact that it had few ports or, as Peter called them, "windows to the west." Peter thought that Russia needed ports so that trade could move between Russia and Western Europe. With the object of getting an outlet to the West, Peter the Great of Russia declared war on Charles XII of Sweden. The gallant and intelligent Charles was defeated. Peter won his window on the Baltic Sea, and Sweden never again became a major power.

Absolutism Grew Under Catherine

Peter's death brought to the throne several weak rulers. These were followed by Catherine II, known as Catherine the Great (1729–96). Catherine meant well and wanted to give her people privileges that they had not before enjoyed, but her good intentions were never carried out. Catherine instead spent time and effort in expanding Russia in the West. To this end, she took part in several divisions of Poland, in which Austria, Prussia, and Russia shared.

Poland disappeared eventually from the map of Europe, and did not appear again until after World War I (1918). By getting into a war with Turkey, Catherine continued Peter's work by gaining a window on the Black Sea. This window was the land area called the Crimea. By controlling this area, Russia gained an ice-free port in southern Europe.

Why Absolutism Was Harmful to Russia

Nowhere in Europe did absolutism last as long or become as complete as it did in Russia. Strong willed rulers such as Peter and Catherine were determined to have their way. A Parliament and an Estates-General had been formed in England and France respectively, and the American Revolution brought independence to America. But Russian rulers allowed no check on their royal powers,

274

and the Russian people became used to absolutism under a monarch.

To the monarchs of Europe, Russia seemed more Asiatic than European. But Peter and Catherine were determined that Russia would become a European power. As a result, Russia became deeply involved in European affairs. Yet, because Russia straddled the continents of Europe and Asia, it looked East as well as West. Because Russia wanted to find new ice-free ports, to defend its territory, and to expand its influence in the Middle East, it often clashed with the countries of Europe.

Check in Here

1. What did Peter the Great hope to learn from the West?

2. Why did Peter seek ice-free ports? Using a map, explain where Peter might have looked for such ports.

3. How did Peter find new ports to the West for Russia?

4. How did Catherine continue Peter's policies?

5. Was absolutism harmful or beneficial for Russia? Give reasons for your point of view.

HOW ABSOLUTISM FARED IN PRUSSIA AND AUSTRIA

How Absolutism Began in Prussia

Today, Germany is a divided country, just as it was during the eighteenth century. Then it was divided into many parts—over three hundred—some so small that you could hardly call them countries. They were part of a loose assortment of states called the Holy Roman Empire.

The Hohenzollern [hō'ən zol'ərn] family was important to the development of Germany. In 1415, the Hohenzollern family became rulers of the small German district of Brandenburg. Some members of the family were *electors* (princes entitled to take part in choosing the Holy Roman Emperor). Through them the Hohenzollerns were gradually able to extend their power and gain control of Prussia which, like Brandenburg, was only a small state.

The little state of Brandenburg in northern Germany grew and became the important state of Prussia during the seventeenth century. The Great Elector, Frederick William of Hohenzollern (1620–88), started Prussia on the road it followed for many years. He built a strong army, stable government, and sound economy. His grandson, Frederick William I (1688–1740), continued in his footsteps by building the army and the treasury and by expanding the size of Prussia.

Prussia Under Frederick the Great

Credit must go to Frederick the Great (1712–1786) for making Prussia a really strong nation. As a youth, Frederick liked philosophy, music, poetry, and books. From his father, he learned about armies, war, and power. Under his father's rough hand, Frederick served in almost every department of the kingdom. He learned from experience about the inner workings of government and the job of being a king.

In a series of wars, Frederick added to Prussia's power and to his own prestige. Allied with Spain and France, Prussia made war on Austria, Britain, and the Netherlands. The war was known as the *War of the Austrian Succession* (1740–1748). Austria's new empress, Maria Theresa, lost Silesia [sī lē' zhə] to Prussia. Peace was not achieved by this war. The *Seven Years' War* (1756–1763) soon followed.

Europe, 1763

- Locate the German state ruled by the Hohenzollern family.
- Locate the countries that opposed each other in the War of the Austrian Succession. In the Seven Years' War.
- By 1763, what country controlled Silesia?

The Seven Years' War seemed like another inning in the game the monarchs of Europe were playing. Although the game was the same, the sides were different. Britain and Prussia had been on opposite sides before; now they were on the same side. Fear of growing Prussian strength drew France and Austria together. The desire to maintain the balance of power and the outbreak of war between France and Britain in the New World drove Prussia and Britain together. This change in sides has been called a *diplomatic revolution*. It referred to a great change in the way nations bargained or dealt with one another. The search for power, glory, and land in the New World as well as in the Old World was one reason for the diplomatic revolution. As a result of the Seven Years' War, Prussia increased in size and still kept Silesia. Since Prussia also took part in the division of Poland, that too added to Frederick's fame.

Frederick's Peaceful Achievements

Frederick's ability in war was very great indeed; in peace, he was no less great. He looked upon himself as "the first servant of the state," and as such, he was up early and worked late. The pleasures which could be found at the French palace at Versailles were not for him. He built schools and hospitals, gave land and seed to the poor, and tried to repair the damage caused by the war. He was interested in the welfare of the people.

Frederick tolerated nearly all religions and expected each to give something to the glory of the country. Frederick, too, found much to copy from France. He himself preferred to speak and write in French, not in German. The French philosopher Voltaire was at home in Frederick's palace, which had a French name *Sans Souci* (without worry). Frederick saw to it that the law was fair to rich and poor alike. He tried to encourage study in science, and he founded the Berlin Academy of Science. Frederick died peacefully in a chair by the fire; he had given much of himself to the development of Prussia.

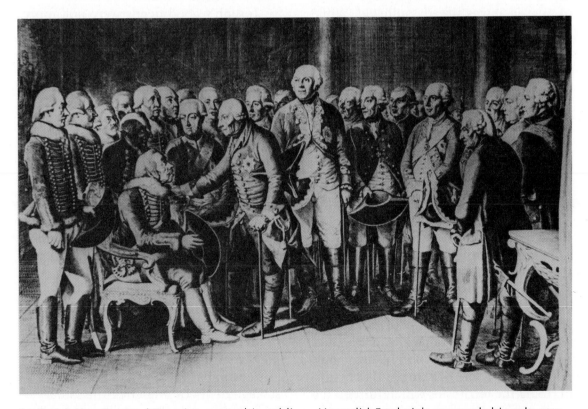

Frederick the Great of Prussia among his soldiers. How did Frederick approach his role as a peacetime leader?

Why Absolutism Was Harmful to Prussia

As great as the Hohenzollerns were, their influence was, in the long run, harmful to their country. Under the Hohenzollerns, the Germans learned to obey commands, to respect the army, and to accept authority. They rarely questioned authority and rarely asked to take part in the government. Although Prussia's early kings were able, they never gave the German people the opportunity to govern themselves. When it became necessary for the Germans to do so, they had difficulty because they had been accustomed to following the orders of strong leaders. Some historians have traced the rise of Hitler in 1933 to German willingness to accept authority.

How Absolutism Grew in Austria

To the Hohenzollerns of Prussia, absolute power was a fairly new development; but to the Hapsburgs [haps'burgz] of Austria, it was already quite old. While the absolute power of the Hohenzollerns was growing, that of the Hapsburgs was declining.

In 1273, Rudolf of Hapsburg was elected Holy Roman Emperor. This election added to the fame and fortune of the Hapsburg family. Gradually, from control over a small area in Switzerland, the Hapsburgs came to rule all of Austria. Through marriage, the influence of the family spread to other lands including Spain, the Netherlands, Hungary, and Bohemia.

When Charles VI (1685–1740) died, his Hapsburg lands (including Austria, Hungary, and northern Italy) went to his young daughter, Maria Theresa (1717–80). She was wise and tried to be a good ruler. Under her father, Austria had fallen upon difficult days. The army had not been paid, and the king had difficulty in ruling the territories which formed his empire. The rise of the Hohenzollerns in Germany had challenged his power.

Maria Theresa wanted to strengthen Austria. To do this, she decided to copy Prussia, a country she disliked, but whose government she admired. Maria Theresa increased taxes and pressed the nobles to pay their fair share. In 1722, she took part in the division of Poland and added to her lands.

Her son, Joseph II (1741–90), tried hard to make conditions better for his people. While other absolute monarchs tried to make themselves more powerful, Joseph tried to give the people the freedom he thought they wanted. He tolerated all religions and freed the Jews from many restrictions. He built schools and encouraged learning. Unlike schools in other countries, these schools were not for the rich alone. The poor went to the schools that Joseph built. Joseph abolished the death penalty for certain crimes, freed the serfs, and canceled many of their feudal obligations.

Joseph's good deeds were not appreciated. The nobles did not like to see their ancient feudal rights taken away. The peasants were discontented because Joseph seemed to interfere with their age-old habits. Joseph was also unsuccessful in war and lost out in dealings with other countries.

In Austria, absolutism was being worn down. The rulers of Austria controlled many lands made up of different groups of people. Their laws were not followed much. By the early 1800s, the proud but empty title, Holy Roman Emperor, vanished.

Check in Here

1. How did Frederick the Great strengthen Prussia?

2. Summarize the major peaceful achievements of Frederick the Great.

3. How did the policies of Maria Theresa of Austria differ from those of her son Joseph II? Which of these was the more powerful ruler? Why?

4. Why was absolutism harmful for both Prussia and Austria?

ABSOLUTISM EVALUATED

Absolutism: A Help and a Hindrance to Civilization

Under absolutism, there were many good things done for the people and nations of Europe. For one thing, absolutism was a better form of government than feudalism. It brought people together to form nations, to create national law, and to build national armies. A strong central government could collect taxes from many people and build the nation's trade and industry. It united large groups of people under an organized central government. People learned that there is strength in numbers, especially when groups of people are led by a strong person.

Nevertheless, absolutism probably should be more condemned than praised. Waging costly wars that took many lives was absolutism's greatest evil. Wars were fought over religion, power, prestige, and land in the New World as well as in the Old World. In order to support the wars, the monarchs taxed the peasants heavily. In the present day, taxes are supposed to be based on one's ability to pay, but ability to pay was not considered in the days of absolutism. The poorest people often paid the heaviest taxes and carried the burdens of foolish and unnecessary wars. These people also had to pay for the court life of an idle and privileged nobility. The people who were least able to pay had to pay the most to support the costly system of absolutism.

Absolutism did not serve civilization well because it did not provide stable

Empress Maria Theresa of Austria

and lasting government. Absolutism depends upon the ability of one person, the ruler. When such a person dies, the government often falls into weaker hands, and whatever progress has been made is then lost. This happened when the government of Spain fell from the hands of Charles V to Philip II.

One reason absolutism caught and held the minds of the people was the general feeling that things could not be better. The Renaissance helped pave the way for weakening the acceptance of absolutism. The idea grew that people could improve themselves through effort, and that they could make a more peaceful and comfortable world. Writers and philosophers taught that government had a responsibility for taking care of the people.

Even rulers such as Catherine, Frederick, and Joseph II came to believe that they had responsibilities toward the people. These rulers are sometimes called *enlightened despots,* meaning rulers with good intentions. They were enlightened because they believed that they had an obligation to serve. Frederick the Great, for example, called himself the first servant of the state. But the rulers were despots because they would not give up their power and authority. Also, they would not give up the idea that they ruled by the will of God. The enlightened despots showed, however, that change was on the way; there would be more concern for the welfare of ordinary people. Exciting discoveries in science, changes in philosophy, and new ideas about how a country should be governed, prepared the way for change. You will read about these discoveries and ideas in the next chapter.

Check in Here

1. Define *absolutism.*

2. List and explain three advantages of absolutism.

3. List and explain three disadvantages of absolutism.

4. How did so-called enlightened despots pave the way for change?

REVIEWING THE BASICS

Absolutism may be defined as a form of government by a hereditary ruler who claims to have absolute power received from God. This is called the divine right theory of government.

During the Age of Absolutism (1500–1700), absolute rulers held nations together, raised powerful armies, and encouraged the growth of literature and science. They made wars as they sought to increase their powers or to protect their nations. In Spain, Charles V ruled the most extensive empire. When his son, Philip II, was defeated by England in the battle that destroyed his *Armada,* the Spanish empire began a marked decline. In England, Henry VII and Henry VIII were followed by Elizabeth I, probably England's most popular ruler. She was an absolute monarch. Elizabeth did not so much rule without Parliament as she ignored it.

The height of absolutism and its classic example was the reign of Louis XIV of France. Louis built the palace of Versailles, which was envied by all the absolute monarchs in Europe. Louis XIV said, "I am the state," thus indicating his absolute authority. Peter the Great called himself the Czar of all the Russians, thus demonstrating how he sought to unite his far-flung nation. Catherine the Great consolidated much of Peter's power. In Prussia one of the greatest of monarchs was Frederick the Great. Maria Theresa of Austria and her son, Joseph II, never quite achieved the power the other monarchs did. This was because their empire was made up of many people who spoke different languages and who were difficult to unite.

REVIEWING THE HIGHLIGHTS

People to Identify

Thomas Hobbes
Charles V
Philip II
Francis I
Henry VIII
Elizabeth I
William Shakespeare
Henry IV of France
Sully
Anne Boleyn

Louis XIII
Marie de'Medici
Richelieu
La Fontaine
Rabelais
Corneille
Molière
Racine
Peter the Great
Catherine the Great

Mary Tudor
Mary Stuart
James I
Louis XIV
Mazarin
Colbert
Frederick the Great
Maria Theresa
Joseph II

Places to Locate

Versailles
Dutch Republic
Gibraltar
Pyrenees
Rhine River

St. Petersburg
Baltic Sea
Poland
Black Sea
Brandenburg

Prussia
Austria
Silesia
Crimea

Terms to Understand

Holy Roman Empire
absolutism
divine right
balance of power
Inquisition
heresy
Treaty of Utrecht
Tudor

Hapsburg
intendants
mercantilism
tariffs
Age of Absolutism
Edict of Nantes
Diet of Worms

balance of power
diplomatic revolution
enlightened despots
Huguenots
Hohenzollern
Armada
Stuart

Events to Describe

Defeat of the Spanish Armada
War of the Spanish Succession
War of the Austrian Succession
Seven Years' War

Mastering the Fundamentals

1. Why did France and Spain go to war during the respective reigns of Francis I and Charles V?
2. Why was it good for England that neither France nor Spain won the wars between them?
3. What evils of absolutism are illustrated by the reigns of Charles V and Philip II?

4. How did the absolutism of Elizabeth I differ from that of Philip II?
5. Why was Mary Stuart executed by Queen Elizabeth?
6. How did Henry IV prepare the way for French greatness?
7. Louis XIV was a child when made king. How was this a danger of absolutism?
8. How did Richelieu and Mazarin set the stage for France's greatness?
9. Why was the War of the Spanish Succession costly for France?
10. How did Colbert try to make France a prosperous nation?
11. Why were the Huguenots driven from France?
12. What evils of the system of absolutism are illustrated by the reign of Louis XIV?
13. What did Louis XIV mean when he said, "I am the state"?
14. How did Peter the Great try to westernize Russia?
15. What evils of absolutism are illustrated by the reigns of Peter the Great and Catherine the Great?
16. Why is it said that Frederick the Great was great in peace as well as war?
17. How did former enemies become friends in the Seven Years' War? What was this shift in alliances called?
18. What did Frederick the Great gain by the War of the Austrian Succession?
19. Why did Poland disappear from the map of Europe?
20. How did Joseph II of Austria differ from other absolute monarchs in Europe at the time?

THINGS TO DO

1. Hold an *Issues and Answers* program in which a group from your class interviews Frederick the Great. See if you can identify, through your questions, the great issues of the day.
2. Hold a *Meeting of Minds.* Suggest a conversation of thirty minutes in which students portraying Peter the Great, Catherine the Great, Elizabeth I, and Charles V exchange views on the nature of absolutism as they saw it.
3. Draw a cartoon illustrating one of the following quotations: Louis XIV: "I am the state"; Frederick the Great: "I am the first servant of the state"; Peter the Great: "Czar of all the Russians."

Read the following letter written to a diplomat by an absolute monarch referred to in this chapter. On the basis of internal evidence, that is, interpreting what the letter says, try to answer the questions that follow it and discuss them with your class.

The unfortunate partition* of Poland is costing me ten years of my life. . . . How many times have I refused to agree to it! But disaster after disaster heaped upon us by the Turks, misery, famine, and pestilence* at home, no hope of assistance from either France or England, and the prospect of being left isolated and threatened with war both by Prussia and Russia—it was all these considerations that finally forced me to accept that unhappy proposal which will remain a blot on my reign. God grant that I be not held responsible for it in the other world! I confess that I cannot keep from talking about this affair. I have taken it so to heart that it poisons and embitters all my days.†

Vocabulary
partition—division
pestilence—disease

1. Who wrote the letter? How can you tell?
2. To what event does the letter refer? How can you tell?
3. Is the writer sincere? Give reasons for your point of view.
4. How does the writer justify the part she or he played in the event?
5. What are the writer's fears?

†Joseph R. Strayer and Hans W. Gatzke, *The Mainstream of Civilization* (New York: Harcourt Brace Jovanovich, Inc., 1979), p. 514. Abbreviated version, *Readings in Western Civilization.* Paul L. Hughes and Robert F. Fried (Eds.) (Paterson, New Jersey: Lifflefield Adams, 1960), p. 134.

The Attributes of the Sciences by J.B. Chardin

The Age of Reason:
The Might of Mind and Pen

The crowd that came to see the scientific wonder of the age was noisy and curious. The date was June 5, 1783. The place was outside the city of Lyons, France, where the Montgolfier [mon′gul fē′er] brothers sent the first balloon into the sky. A 32-meter (105-foot) linen globe was filled with smoke and then released. It rose to a great height and returned to earth about one and a half miles away from where it was launched.

The crowd cheered at the success of the experimental balloon, and the Montgolfier brothers were looked upon as scientific heroes. Chickens, pigs, dogs, and cats were later sent aloft, and finally a human being went up in a balloon. The seventeenth and eighteenth centuries were filled with scientific wonders and with scientific and intellectual heroes of many kinds.

The Age of Reason is sometimes called the *Enlightenment.* It is a period of time that dates roughly from the publication in 1687 of *Principia,* [prin'chip'ē ə] by Sir Isaac Newton to the outbreak of the French Revolution in 1789. It is called the Enlightenment because during these hundred years there was concern about improving the way people lived and were governed. To enlighten is to free from ignorance. Scientists, writers, philosophers, and artists sought to free people by teaching them how the laws of nature and the laws by which they were governed could be used to better the human condition.

REASON GIVES BIRTH TO THE SCIENTIFIC METHOD

The Age of Reason

You have already studied other great periods in history, such as the Age of Discovery and the Age of Absolutism. When used in this way, the word "age" means a time period which is dominated by a single important idea. During the Age of Discovery, explorers found new lands and during the Age of Absolutism, monarchs said they ruled by the will of God, or divine right.

The Age of Reason was a time when people used their reasoning abilities to find answers to disturbing questions. They explored the mysteries of nature. They put their faith in reason and in their ability to make scientific observations and interpretations. They believed that by experimenting they could find the answers to their questions.

The Age of Reason was in many respects a continuation of the Renaissance. Many of the creative activities of the Renaissance took place in Italy. Much of the great work of the Enlightenment was done in northern Europe and later in America. The Renaissance may be seen as a preparation for the accomplishments of the Age of Reason. The Age of Reason is considered a glorious chapter in history. It was a period of great human accomplishment. It also prepared the way for future achievements in science, literature, and government.

How the Scientific Method Was Born

In high school science laboratories today students perform experiments in chemistry and physics. They watch their experiments carefully and write down exactly what they see. After noting the facts and their observations, students make interpretations. From their interpretations, they form conclusions. This, in brief, is an example of the *scientific method.* For this method, science is indebted to Francis Bacon (1561–1626). He believed that scientific progress would be based on the scientific method.

Scientific thinking was not widespread in the seventeenth century. Many people were too willing to accept the words and ideas of others instead of finding out for themselves. However, in the seventeenth century scientific observation of nature was made somewhat easier by the invention of the telescope (1608) and the microscope (1610). With these inventions the use of the scientific method became more widespread.

Two of Galileo's telescopes. What were some other scientific breakthroughs of the seventeenth century?

How the Scientific Method Worked

In the sixteenth century, Nicolaus Copernicus [kō pėr′nə kəs] said that the sun was the center of the universe and that the earth and other planets moved around the sun. In Copernicus's time this fact had not yet been proven. Few people believed him. The accepted theory was that the earth was the center of the universe. An Italian scientist, Galileo [gal′ə lē′ō] Galilei (1564–1642), put his faith in experimentation and observation. It is said that he climbed the Leaning Tower of Pisa and dropped some weights to the ground. In this way he proved that falling objects of different weights fall at the same rate of speed. This story illustrates how Galileo made use of the scientific method. Galileo also used the scientific method in studying the movement of the solar system through a telescope. He became convinced that the Copernican theory of the universe was right.

Galileo described what he saw to the world. At first the people would not accept his ideas. He was called before the Inquisition for heresy. It was the position of the Church that the earth was at the center of the universe. Galileo was forced to say that his observations were untrue. It is said that when the trial was over and no one was looking, Galileo shook his fist in the direction of his tormentors and whispered, "It (the earth) moves just the same!" But how did it move and why? These questions needed to be answered.

A German astronomer, Johannes Kepler [kep′lər] (1571–1630), knew about the theories of Copernicus. Kepler believed Copernicus was right about the earth revolving around the sun, but that he was wrong about the shape of the earth's orbit around the sun. Using data from his teacher Tycho Brahe [brä′hē] (1546–1601), Kepler arrived at another conclusion: the path of the earth around the sun was elliptical and not circular. Using evidence from mathematics Kepler improved on the work of Copernicus. Kepler showed that mathematics could be used to solve the mysteries of nature.

The importance of mathematics in the scientific method was demonstrated by René Descartes [dā kärt'] (1596–1650), a philosopher and mathematician. All things in nature, he said, could be proved on a mathematical basis. The world is a machine whose movements can be measured and predicted.

Another great thinker, the Englishman Sir Isaac Newton (1642–1727), opened the door to our understanding of the world and the universe. From the shoulders of giants (the scientists who came before him), Newton saw farther than many had ever seen before.

There is a well-known story about Newton. An apple fell from a tree, hitting Newton on the head. Newton is said to have wondered why the apple fell down instead of up. Newton's *laws of gravity* explain not only why apples and everything else fall down, but also partially explain the universe as a whole. Why do the planets move as they do? What keeps them from hitting one another? Why can people walk on a spinning earth? What keeps the planets from falling down? These are among the questions Newton answered many years ago. When travel through space becomes common, Newton will still stand among the heroes of science who made it possible.

Modern History
1500-Present

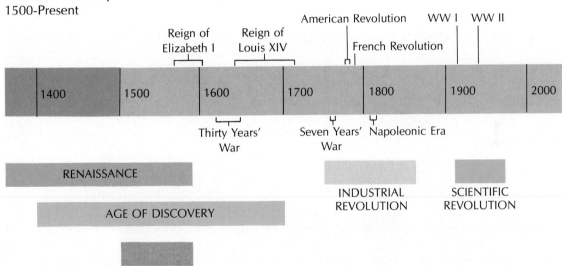

Be able to place the following on the time line:

1650–1775	Age of Reason	1665	Newton—theory of gravitation	1726	Swift—*Gulliver's Travels*
1543	Copernicus—earth revolves around sun	1690	Locke—*Two Treatises on Government*	1762	Rousseau—*Social Contract*
1596–1650	Descartes	1750	Montesquieu—*Spirit of the Laws*	1776	Smith—*The Wealth of Nations*
1609	Galileo—telescope				
1620	Bacon—scientific method	1719	Defoe—*Robinson Crusoe*	1665	Wren—St. Paul's
				1606–69	Rembrandt
1628	Harvey—circulation of the blood	1759	Voltaire—*Candide*	1756–91	Mozart

How the Scientific Method Served the Advance of Chemistry and Physics

During the medieval period, magic and chemistry were closely related. Chemists tried to make gold from other metals.

Using the scientific method, Robert Boyle (1627–1691) described a difference between compounds and mixtures. Boyle devoted his life to studying such problems as why metals rust and what makes fire.

Henry Cavendish [kav′ən dish] (1731–1810) discovered what he called inflammable air (hydrogen), and Joseph Priestley [prēst′lē] (1733–1804) discovered oxygen. Antoine Lavoisier [lə vwä zyā′] (1743–94), called the father of modern chemistry, correctly explained what happens when things burn. Lavoisier also determined the role that oxygen serves in the respiratory systems of both plants and animals.

Galileo, Descartes, and Newton laid the foundation for physics. Evangelista Torricelli [tôr′i chel′ē] (1608–47) developed the barometer and improved upon the telescope. Blaise Pascal [pas kal′] (1623–62) determined the weight of air. The properties of heat, light, and sound were among the other subjects that the scientific observers of the age studied.

The science of electricity was founded by the English physicist William Gilbert (1540–1603). The American Benjamin Franklin (1706–90) proved that lightning was electricity. Franklin found that lightning could be carried, or conducted, through wire. He also invented the lightning rod, which could be used to protect buildings from lightning.

Antoine Lavoisier, the father of modern chemistry. Marie Anne Paulze, his wife, worked with him. Here, she records the results of his experiment.

An Italian, Alexander Volta [vōl′tə] (1745–1827), found a way to make electricity run in continuous currents. Because of the work of these people, electricity became the servant of humankind.

How the Scientific Method Helped Medicine

Medicine made progress during the seventeenth and eighteenth centuries as doctors became willing to use the scientific method. By performing experiments on the bodies of animals and humans, William Harvey (1578–1657) discovered that blood flows, or circulates, through the human body. Doctors became more expert in diagnosing different types of sickness. They measured blood pressure and used stethoscopes to listen to sounds within the human body.

The Dutch naturalist Anton van Leeuwenhoek [lā′vən hük′] (1632–1723) improved the microscope. He was then able to see bacteria. Other scientists later saw a connection between some of these living things and sickness. In the fields of biology and zoology, Carl Linnaeus [li nē′əs] (1707–78) developed a method for classifying plants, and Comte de Buffon [də bü fôn′] (1707–88) created a system for the classification of animals.

Check in Here

1. Define the term *reason* as used in this chapter.

2. Identify and explain three aspects of the scientific method.

3. Why did the Inquisition fear Galileo's ideas?

4. How was the scientific method applied to physics and chemistry?

5. How did mathematics contribute to the scientific method?

REASON ENCOURAGES LITERARY AND ARTISTIC EXPRESSION

Many Different Kinds of Books

The Age of Reason encouraged creative expression in literature. Writers described what they saw or how they felt in new forms of writing. The novel, or long story, was one such form. In novels writers not only told a story but often were critical of the way people behaved. Stories written in the seventeenth and eighteenth centuries became part of the world's great literature. The stories in *Gulliver's Travels* by Jonathan Swift (1667–1745) amuse readers, but they were written to point out the silly behavior of people and the foolish causes of war. In the land of Lilliput, people are tiny because of the petty and mean things they do to one another.

Robinson Crusoe by Daniel Defoe [di fō′] (1659–1731) is regarded by some as the first novel in the English language. There had been stories before, but the idea of expressing reality through stories was new. The novel, with its realism, was an outstanding gift to literature. Henry Fielding's (1707–54) *Tom Jones* is a novel that shows a great understanding of eighteenth-century English life. Oliver Goldsmith's (1728–74) *The Vicar of Wakefield* is still read and enjoyed.

No discussion of English literature could leave out Samuel Johnson (1709–84), a great literary personality. He compiled one of the first complete English dictionaries entitled *Dictionary of the English Language.* Johnson's brilliance and wit made him the center of attraction in many social gatherings.

In poetry the work of Alexander Pope (1688–1744) expresses well the spirit of

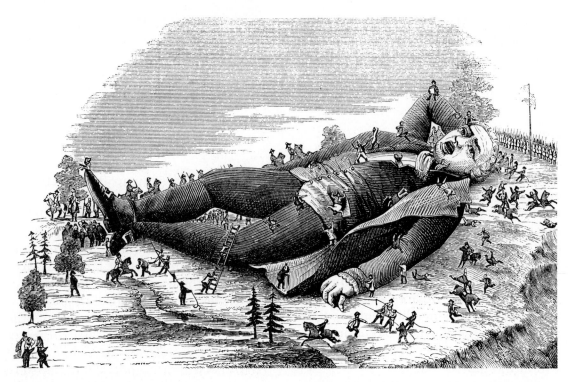

The hero of Jonathan Swift's *Gulliver's Travels* is tied down by tiny folk, called Lilliputians, whom he meets during his journey.

the Age of Reason. The following lines are from his *Essay on Man:*

Self-love, the spring of motion, acts the soul;
Reason's comparing balance rules the whole.
Man, but for that, no action could attend,
And, but for this, were active to no end.

In German writing, the works of Johann Friedrich von Schiller [shil'ər] (1759–1805) and Johann Wolfgang von Goethe [ger'tə] (1749–1832) stand out. In Schiller's *Wilhelm Tell*, the author describes Tell's eager search for liberty. Goethe's *Faust* tells the story of a man who sold his soul to the devil in exchange for knowledge and pleasure. This plot has formed the basis of many stories.

In Spain, in the seventeenth century, the novel *Don Quixote* [dän kē ō'tē] appeared, written by Miguel de Cervantes [sėr van'tēz] (1547–1616). In this celebrated book, the author laughs at the habits of the people around him.

The Artistic and Musical Contributions of the Period

During the Middle Ages, outstanding buildings were almost always churches. In the seventeenth and eighteenth centuries, private homes and public buildings as well as churches became works of art. Christopher Wren (1632–1723) was the greatest architect of the period. After a great fire destroyed much of London in 1666, Christopher Wren was a major contributor to its rebuilding. The Cathedral of St. Paul and many smaller churches are his most lasting gifts. The steeples on New England churches reflect the influence of Wren.

The simplicity of Greek and Roman buildings also influenced the architecture of this period. The homes of George Washington and Thomas Jefferson are examples of this classic style.

In painting, as in other artistic fields, Renaissance influences continued. The paintings of the Dutch artists Peter Paul Rubens [rü'bənz] (1577–1640) and Rembrandt [rem'brant] (1606–69) are characteristic of the painting of the period. The subjects vary from landscapes to sacred subjects. Rubens showed a mastering of the use of color, while Rembrandt was noted for his use of light and shadow. In France, Jean Watteau [wä tō'] (1684–1721) and in England, Thomas Gainsborough [gānz'bėr'ō] (1727–88) were artists for their kings. Spain, too, had its golden age in art. Among its outstanding painters were El Greco [el grek'ō] (1547–1614), Murillo [mü rē'lyō] (1617–82), and Velásquez [və las'kes] (1599–1660).

The opera, which combined the talents of singers, musicians, and actors, was a new form of musical expression. Claudio Monteverdi [môn'te ver'dē] (1567–1643) was the first great figure in the development of opera. His operas were offered in the first public opera house, which was opened in 1637 in Venice. Among the great composers of the age were George Frederick Handel [han'dəl] (1685–1759), Johann Sebastian Bach [bäkh] (1685–1750), and Wolfgang Amadeus Mozart [mōt'särt] (1756–1791).

Check in Here

1. Why was the development of the novel an important literary milestone?

2. How did Samuel Johnson contribute to the English language?

3. Explain the influence of Sir Christopher Wren on American architecture.

The Cathedral of St. Paul in London, which was designed by Christopher Wren.

4. Summarize two important achievements of the period in art and music.

5. To what extent do the lines of Alexander Pope (see p. 290) accurately describe the spirit of the Age of Reason?

REASON ENCOURAGES CRITICISM OF GOVERNMENT AND SOCIETY

How Absolutism Was Opposed

Had there been newspapers as we know them in the seventeenth and eighteenth centuries, some of the headlines might have read:

GALILEO PROVES THE EARTH MOVES AROUND THE SUN

SIR ISAAC NEWTON EXPLAINS THE LAW
OF GRAVITY

DISCOVERY OF THE CIRCULATION OF
BLOOD IN THE HUMAN BODY

LIVING THINGS UNSEEN BEFORE ARE
SEEN THROUGH MICROSCOPE

The Age of Reason was an exciting time. New ideas offered possibilities for a better life. Old-fashioned ways of thinking and doing things were changing.

Changes and new ideas make people think and ask questions. If these new ideas in mathematics and science were true, was it nevertheless still true that monarchs ruled by the will of God? Was it reasonable for the poor to pay higher taxes than the rich? If there were permanent laws controlling nature, were not laws to control government also possible? Did some have to be very rich and others very poor? These were the kinds of questions intelligent people started asking themselves. Thought led to talk, and talk led to action.

A group of philosophers was largely responsible for the thought, the talk, and the writing of the Age of Reason. Today the word "intellectual" would be used to describe the philosophers. Many philosophers of the eighteenth century were French, and the term *philosophes* [fē lô zōfs'] has been widely used to identify them. The philosophers of the eighteenth century frequently described themselves as *deists* [dē'ists]. Deism was a religious point of view. A deist believes in the existence of God as proven by the normal events which take place in history and nature. As deists, the philosophers did not believe in formal religion or in supernatural happenings, such as revelation. These philosophers were free-thinkers who tried to solve problems through the use of reason.

In the days when newspapers were few and radio and television did not exist, books and pamphlets written by the philosophers were vital in spreading new ideas. Their views were to shake the power of absolute monarchs and to change the thinking of the enlightened despots. The flames of revolution were beginning to burn brightly. In England, they devoured the absolutist Stuarts. The days of absolute rulers in France and elsewhere were also numbered.

What the Philosophers Thought and Wrote

Voltaire [vōl ter'] (1694–1778) was a writer who made fun of prominent people and of accepted beliefs. He wanted freedom of thought and freedom of religion. He especially criticized the Church because he felt that it discouraged freedom of thought. He wrote a book called *Letters on the English*, in which he made fun of the French. He used the term "English" to make the title seem harmless to government leaders. In France, freedom of speech and of the press did not exist. Voltaire taught tolerance in religion and politics. Surprisingly, he was popular at the courts of the absolute rulers Frederick of Prussia and Catherine of Russia.

Another French writer, Baron de Montesquieu [män'təs kyü'] (1689–1755), wrote a book which had a great influence on government. His book *The Spirit of the Laws* praised the government of England because it was democratic. He urged that the three branches of the government—the law-enforcing, the law-making, and the law-interpreting—be separated so that one might check upon the other. Montesquieu's book influenced the writers of the American Constitution. The Americans provided for a government in which there is a president to enforce the laws, a congress to make the laws, and a supreme court to tell what the laws mean. Each branch has a specific job to do.

John Locke [lok] (1632–1704) believed that a government should exist only with the consent of the governed (the people). This idea grew out of his experiences with the English Revolution of 1688. (See Chapter 13.) It was further developed by the Frenchman Jean Jacques Rousseau [rü sō'] (1712–78), an emotional and influential person.

Jean Jacques Rousseau thought that people were happier in the past because they were closer to nature. There were neither wars nor taxes to disturb them. When people found they needed laws to live by, they established governments. Rousseau expressed his ideas in a book called *The Social Contract*. He believed that the people give government the right to rule. When the government rules unwisely, people can take power away from it. These thoughts were expanded upon by Thomas Jefferson in the Declaration of Independence.

Voltaire, Montesquieu, and Rousseau were the greatest of the *philosophes*. They disagreed in many ways, but they did agree on one thing—society could be better than it was.

In the field of economics, too, there were writers who demanded more freedom. Perhaps no one had more influence than Adam Smith (1722–90), who wrote a book in 1776 entitled *The Wealth of Nations*. In this work, Smith said that it would be better if business were not closely controlled by the government. He criticized the old mercantile theory. He wanted the government to provide an army to protect property and to provide for a sound currency. He felt that competition and the laws of supply and demand would be enough to control wages, prices, and profits. The term *laissez faire* [les'ā fer'] comes from the French language. It means that government should keep hands off business. Both *The Wealth of Nations* and the Declaration of Independence were written in 1776. The first asked for economic independence; the second asked for political independence.

The *Encyclopedists* were a group of *philosophes* that included Rousseau, Montesquieu, and Voltaire. Under the direction of Denis Diderot [dē'də rō'], (1713–84), they wrote articles for a new encyclopedia. This was not merely a reference book. It contained many of the new ideas which were to pave the way for a change from absolutism to democracy. In the encyclopedia could be found the latest in scientific information. There were also articles in opposition to slavery, cruel punishments, unfair taxation, and religious intolerance. Because of their advanced thinking the contributors to the encyclopedia were often in danger of their lives.

A temple built in honor of Rousseau in the eighteenth century.

Jean Jacques Rousseau (1712–78)

Jean Jacques Rousseau was born in Geneva to a French family. When he grew up, he yearned for the life of the artist and writer. He longed to be different, and he was. He is remembered for his courage to be different.

Rousseau wrote many books which have greatly influenced poetry, education, and literature. His *Confessions* is widely read. Rousseau wrote frankly about the most intimate details of his early life. He described his early life as a vagabond, tramping from place to place, working as a valet, waiter, and secretary, but never finding himself and never getting along with his employers. Rousseau seemed to arouse the pity of older women, who sent him to school from time to time. This enabled him to acquire some formal schooling.

In his *Confessions* Rousseau said, "I am not like anyone else I have been acquainted with, perhaps like no one in existence." Rousseau has been described as a mad genius who lived a mad life. He eventually married an ignorant and simple serving girl who never learned to count money, tell time, or name the months of the year. Yet perhaps because of her ignorance he was relatively happy in her company.

In *Émile* [ā mēl'], Rousseau insisted that children were basically good. For this reason, children should be allowed freedom to develop their natural talents. Rousseau said that adolescence was a special time of life. Older people, parents and teachers, should not try to teach adolescents through formal instruction. Despite his concern for young people, Rousseau was unable or unwilling to bring up five children of his own. Each of his children was placed in an orphanage at birth.

Rousseau dared to be different. His genius lay in his revolt against the unimaginative deeds and thoughts of his day.

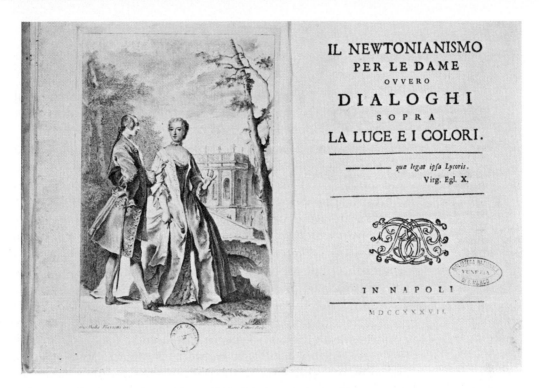

The introductory pages of an Italian book, *Newtonianism for Women.*

What Women Contributed to the Age of Reason

Not all of the *philosophes* were men. Several women opened their *salons* (homes) to writers, artists, poets, and essayists of both sexes. These people came together to talk freely about their ideas and contributed importantly to the Age of Reason. In the salons, geniuses sharpened their wits by trying out new ideas in politics and science.

Among the great salons of the day were those of Marie-Thérèse Geoffrin [zhô fran'] (1699–1777), Marie du Deffand [dü de fän'] (1697–1780), and Julie de Lespinasse [də les pē näs'] (1732–76). "It was not beauty that distinguished these . . . salons; . . . it was that complex of intelligence, grace, influence, and unobtrusive money that enabled a hostess . . . to make a gathering sparkle with wit or wisdom. . . ."*

*Will and Ariel Durant, *The Story of Civilization: Rousseau and Revolution* (New York: Simon and Schuster, 1967), p. 118.

The salons helped keep alive the ideas of the Age of Reason. What *philosophes* wrote could be burned and often was. What they said in the salons of France, Prussia, Austria, England, and elsewhere could not be destroyed. Their ideas were passed on by others in a revolutionary fire which swept America and Europe before long.

Check in Here

1. Is it appropriate to call the philosophers described in these pages intellectuals? Why or why not?

2. Identify three changes in government that the philosophers collectively sought to bring about.

3. How did the ideas of Montesquieu differ from the divine right theory?

4. What freedoms did the economist Adam Smith seek?

REVIEWING THE BASICS

Another name for the Age of Reason is the Enlightenment. During this period three forces came together to prepare the way for changes in government and society. (1) The development of scientific knowledge, which questioned the traditional ways of looking at nature. Scientists suggested that what was unknown in nature could, in time, be understood by people who used a scientific approach to solve problems. (2) The growth of new forms of literature, especially the novel, which became a convenient way in which writers could comment on reality and morality. (3) The work of intellectuals called philosophes. The books and articles the philosophes wrote encouraged a rethinking of political ideas as well as scientific ideas.

Among the things the philosophes as a group wanted was greater freedom of speech and freedom of the press. These were nonexistent on the European continent and existed in part only in England. Philosophers also wanted to replace absolutism with government responsible to the people. In economics, Adam Smith maintained that the laws of the marketplace were enough to guide a nation's and a person's economic decisions. Interference by government in the workings of the economy was unnecessary. The ideas of the Age of Reason prepared the way for revolution in England, America, and France.

REVIEWING THE HIGHLIGHTS

People to Identify			
Francis Bacon	Rousseau	Marie du Deffand
Galileo	John Locke	Jonathan Swift
Descartes	Adam Smith	Samuel Johnson
Isaac Newton	Johann Sebastian Bach	Alexander Pope
Rembrandt	Benjamin Franklin	Christopher Wren
Voltaire	Montesquieu	

Terms to Understand		
Age of Reason	Encylopedists	laissez faire
Enlightenment	scientific method	deism
salons	philosophes	

Mastering the Fundamentals

1. Describe the chief characteristics of the Age of Reason.
2. How is the Age of Reason related to the Renaissance?
3. How did Copernicus's views of the universe differ from those which had been held up to that time?

4. How did Descartes's ideas make the workings of the universe less mysterious?
5. Why may Newton be regarded as a scientific genius?
6. What progress was made in the science of chemistry during the seventeenth and eighteenth centuries?
7. Describe the progress made in medicine.
8. What evidence is given in this chapter that the Age of Reason led to a growth of interest in books and literature?
9. How were the art and music of the Age of Reason different from the art and music of medieval times?
10. How did the Age of Reason prepare the way for rebellion against absolutism?
11. What were the religious views of the philosophes?
12. How did the ideas of Rousseau and Locke differ from the divine right theory?
13. How is the government of the United States indebted to Montesquieu?
14. Why were the lives of the Encyclopedists often in danger during the eighteenth century?
15. Why might Thomas Jefferson be called a *philosophe?*
16. How did women help spread the revolutionary ideas of the Age of Reason?
17. To what extent does this chapter prove or disprove the statement that the pen is mightier than the sword?
18. What beliefs of the philosophes are still held today?
19. How are we indebted to the Age of Reason?
20. May the age we live in also be called an Age of Reason? Why or why not?

THINGS TO DO

1. Research and report using Diderot's *Encyclopedia* on some of the new advances in science and technology that the Encyclopedists were making available to the general reader. Diderot's *Encyclopedia,* in recent editions, is still available in major libraries.
2. Prepare a newspaper for June 5, 1783, the date the Montgolfier brothers launched a balloon into the sky. Write a headline and an article for the event. Also, what other events might be included? What cartoons would be appropriate? Assign someone in the class to do an editorial and someone else to write a letter to the editor.
3. Write a book review on one of the following: (a) Defoe's *Robinson Crusoe;* (b) Rousseau's *Émile.*

Mary Wollstonecraft (1759–97) was the leading feminist of her day, and her ideas were far in advance of those of the eighteenth century. She wrote *A Vindication of the Rights of Women*. The selection below compares the ideas of Wollstonecraft and Rousseau on the education and character of women. Read the selection below and discuss with other members of your class the questions that follow.

Rousseau: "The education of women should be always relative to men. To please, to be useful to us, to make us love them, to render * our lives easy and agreeable; these are the duties of women at all times, and what they should be taught in infancy."

Wollstonecraft: "Woman was not created merely to be the solace * of man. . . . On this sexual error has all the false system been erected, which robs our whole sex of its dignity. . . . Whilst man remains . . . the slave of his appetites . . . our sex is degraded* by a necessity."

Rousseau: "Girls must be subject all their lives to the most constant and severe restraint*, . . . that they may the more readily learn to submit to the will of others. . . But is it not just that this sex should partake* of the sufferings which arise from those evils it hath caused *us?*"

Wollstonecraft: "How can a woman believe that she was made to submit to man—a being like herself, her equal?"

Rousseau: "Boys love sports and noise and activity: to whip the top, to beat the drum, to drag about their little carts; girls on the other hand are fond of things of show and ornament—trinkets, mirrors, dolls."

Wollstonecraft: "Little girls are forced to sit still and play with trinkets. Who can say whether they are fond of them or not?"†

Vocabulary

render—to make
solace—comfort
degraded—lowered in rank
restraint—reserve
partake—took part

1. How do the ideas of Rousseau on the education of women differ from those of Mary Wollstonecraft? How do you account for the difference in their views?
2. How do the ideas of Rousseau and Mary Wollstonecraft differ on the character of women?
3. Why does Mary Wollstonecraft continue to be regarded as a forerunner of the women's liberation movement?
4. What reasons might possibly explain Rousseau's views on the education of women? Why may it be considered strange that Rousseau should have such views?

†Elizabeth Gould Davis, *The First Sex* (New York: Penguin Books, 1971), pp. 297–8.

A scene from the American Revolution by Alonzo Chappel

Revolution in England and America: Shots That Were Heard Around the World

Democracy must be learned through experience as well as through books. That is why many schools encourage student government. Through your participation in student government you learn to support the best candidates or, perhaps, become a candidate for office yourself. You listen to many viewpoints, and you learn to respect the wishes of the majority as well as the rights of the minority. In short, you learn the habits of fair play that democracy demands. Democracy requires and expects more of its people than do other forms of government.

In this chapter and in those that follow, you will study the further growth of political freedom and democracy. You will find out how men and women gained political freedom. By understanding how the world's great democracies were born, you will be in a better position to understand democracy in the United States and throughout the world. By knowing what freedom and democracy mean, you will be better able to extend their practice in the world. You will also be able to defend them against those who say that freedom and democracy do not have the answers to the problems people face.

SWITZERLAND AND HOLLAND BECOME DEMOCRACIES

Democracy Defined

Democracy means more than the voting, candidates, campaigns, speeches, and political parties. H.G. Wells, an English historian, once said, "Votes in themselves are useless things!" What he meant was that the right to vote is useless if the people do not know why or for what they are voting. The process of voting is useless if people are not able to make free choices or if they are forced to vote against their wishes.

Democracy depends upon an informed people. Therefore, people must have the opportunity for education and the freedom to discuss problems. To become informed, people must have freedom of speech. They also need freedom of the press, religious liberty, and freedom of assembly. These freedoms give people the opportunity to read about, listen to, and discuss many different points of view.

In a democracy people must be assured of having fair and quick trials. Those accused of crime are assured freedom from cruel or unusual punishments. In a democracy people are not forced to give information about themselves if by

doing so they could damage their reputations or incriminate (appear guilty) themselves. Without this safeguard, persons could be forced—by torture or threats—to admit to crimes they did not do.

Democracy is based on government by the people. The majority decides who will govern them and how they will be governed. In a democracy people have more rights than under other forms of government. Yet with each right goes the responsibility not to abuse it.

Democracy can take many forms. For example, today the United States, France, the United Kingdom, the Netherlands, Belgium, and the Scandinavian countries have different forms of democracies. Some of these countries have governments headed by a king or queen. Others are republics. But these countries are in many ways similar. In each of these countries people have equal rights. In each, there is respect for the rights of the individual and for the wishes of the majority. In each, the law allows for peaceful change.

These countries became democratic only after long and difficult struggles. In all democratic countries, the struggle for further democracy is still going on. Freedom requires constant attention if democratic gains are to last.

How Switzerland and The Dutch Republic Gained Democracy

In 1291, several Swiss *cantons* (districts) broke away from the Holy Roman Empire and set up governments of their own. In the middle of the fourteenth century, they were joined by other cantons, and the country of Switzerland was born. There was no one person to act as a monarch or central ruler. Instead, each of the small political divisions made up laws of their own. These cantons elected a common body of officials to act as a central government. Each canton still kept much of its independence. This group of small divisions with a central government was called the *Swiss Confederation.* Switzerland was the first country in Europe to take an important step toward democracy.

In 1648, the independence of Switzerland was recognized by the European countries in the Peace of Westphalia. It has remained free and independent ever since.

The hero and liberator of Holland was William the Silent (1533–1584). He is looked upon as the father of his country. Just as Washington led the thirteen colonies in North America in fighting the English, so William led the Dutch in fighting the Spanish. In 1581, the Dutch Republic (at that time officially called the *United Provinces*) was formed. It was made up of the Protestant northern provinces of the Netherlands. Holland was its most important province. William became the republic's *stadtholder* [stad′hōl′dər], or ruler. Although William was killed by an assassin in 1584, the republic to which he had devoted his life lived on. The Peace of Westphalia in 1648 recognized the independence of the Dutch Republic as well as that of Switzerland. The Dutch southern provinces, however, remained under Spanish control.

William the Silent. Why do the Dutch regard him as the father of the Netherlands?

Check in Here

1. List three of the freedoms necessary for democracy to work.

2. Why is the story of the development of democracy an unfinished one?

3. Describe the major steps leading toward independence and democracy in Switzerland and in the Dutch Republic.

THE STUARTS IRRITATE THE ENGLISH

How the Tudor Monarchs Ruled England

In 1485, Henry VII of the House of Tudor became king of England after a long period of civil war. Henry hoped that he could bring peace to England. He favored the middle classes and worked closely with Parliament. Henry VII brought the powerful nobility under his control and put an end to the nobles' private armies. A strong central government was set up by advisers appointed by the king. Since Henry VII was both strong and tactful, he usually got what he wanted. Henry VIII and his daughter Elizabeth I followed in the footsteps of Henry VII. They dominated Parliament as he had done. They brought religious life under royal control. The rights of the subjects and of Parliament were ignored from time to time. Yet, for the most part, the English people did not seem to mind.

By and large, the English were fond of the Tudors. The Tudors maintained peace and order in England and were successful in fighting foreign wars. The Tudors never claimed to rule by divine right. They respected Parliament. Nor did they try to rule as absolute monarchs. They found they could get what they wanted by bending the people and Parliament to their will. Under the rule of the Tudors, the central government gained greater power than previous English rulers had possessed. However, although the Tudors did little to encourage Parliament, jury trial, or common law, they did not seem to discourage them.

Why James I Irritated Parliament

The arrival of the Stuarts brought much change. After the Tudor rulers King James VI of Scotland established the Stuarts on the throne of England. King James VI was Elizabeth's cousin and upon her death had the strongest right to the English Crown. He became James I,

Modern History
1500-Present

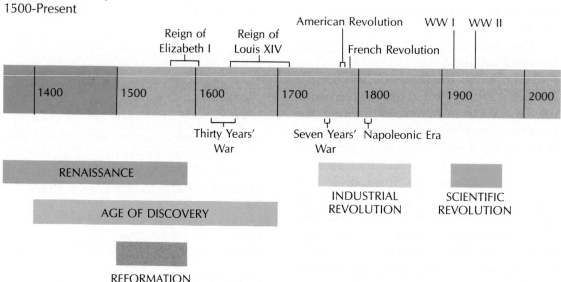

Be able to place the following events on the time line:

1581	Dutch Republic formed	1660–85	Restoration
1628	Right of Petition	1688	Glorious Revolution and the Bill of Rights
1630	Puritans settled Massachusetts		
1640–60	Long Parliament	1707	Act of Union
1649	Charles I beheaded	1776	Declaration of Independence

king of England in 1603. James, a Scot, was looked upon as a foreigner. He was disliked by the English. To make matters worse, James was arrogant, although intelligent. He was "wise in booklearning, but a poor judge of men,"* undignified in appearance, and a person with whom it was difficult to get along.

The Tudors knew how to get along with Parliament. James, however, was ignorant of English laws and traditions, and did not get along with Parliament. James insisted that he ruled by divine right, because he liked the power he thought it gave him. To the English, divine right of kings and queens was repulsive. James's lack of common sense and lack of tact made his reign a failure.

Many mistakes on his part made James I unpopular with the English people. His first mistake had to do with a religious issue. Henry VIII had established the *Anglican* [ang'li kən] *Church*. Its services were similar to those of the Catholic Church, but it did not follow the pope at Rome. The *Puritans* were dissatisfied with the Anglican Church and wanted to purify it by following the teachings of John Calvin. They wanted to simplify church services and to organize their church on a democratic basis. James was determined that the Puritans should follow the Anglican Church, of which he was head.

On religious matters James I ran into conflict with several religious groups. Although he was sympathetic to the views of Roman Catholics, he did not appear to support the Catholics strongly enough. When he upheld the Anglican Church, Catholics were irritated. *Presbyterians* [prez'bə tir'ē əns] wanted to set up their own national church. It would be similar to the one that John Knox had set up as early as 1560. The Presbyterians would set up their own congregation

*George M. Trevelyan, *History of England* (London: Longmans Green and Company, 1937), p. 381.

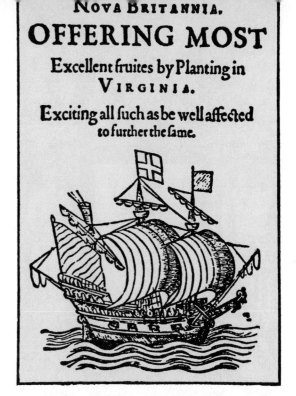

NOVA BRITANNIA.
OFFERING MOST
Excellent fruites by Planting in VIRGINIA.
Exciting all such as be well affected to further the same.

An advertisement to attract colonists to America. Why would some English people want to emigrate?

under an elected body of elders, called presbyters. There were others, including the *Pilgrims* [pil'grəmz], who wanted no established church at all. The Pilgrims were among the earliest to leave England to set up churches of their own in America.

The support James I gave to the Anglican Church was a mistake because it did not satisfy the many Puritans in England. Religious arguments between James and the Puritans continued during most of the king's reign. When Puritans sought religious reform, James resisted. His support of Roman Catholic Spain and his failure to help the Protestants of Germany in the Thirty Years' War (see p. 238) irritated the Puritans still more. Because there were many Puritans in Parliament, that body was unwilling to do what James I wanted. Thus, religious arguments limited the king's ability to govern.

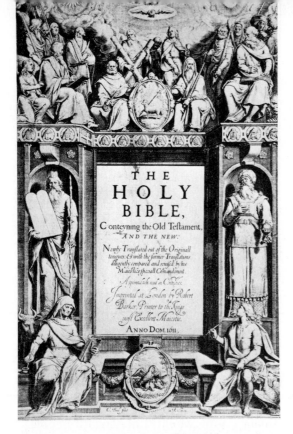

The frontispiece of the original King James version of the Bible. It reads: "Newly translated out of the original tongues and with the former translations diligently compared and revised by His Majesty's special commandment. Appointed to be read in churches."

Some good, however, did come from these religious disputes. James I, upon the urging of the Puritans, appointed a group of scholars who wrote what came to be called the King James version of the Bible. It included some, but far from all, of the changes for which the Puritans had hoped. The *King James Bible*, or a revised version of it, is used by most English-speaking Protestant churches in the world today.

Financial problems proved to be as troublesome as religious ones. Parliament controlled the *purse strings* (money). It was often unwilling to let James have the money he needed because he had irritated the people and

Parliament. When he said he ruled by divine right, Parliament would not listen. When he said that all must join the Anglican Church, he made matters worse. When Parliament did not give James the money he needed, he became exasperated and dismissed the stubborn body.

James was forced to call Parliament back into session as economic conditions in England were unsound. The growth of the woolen industry caused many landowners to switch from farming to the more profitable sheep raising. These landowners often seized land that had been held in common by farmers. They fenced it off so that sheep could graze within the confines of the fences. The *enclosure movement,* as this was called, forced many farmers off their farms.

Unemployment grew. A great increase of gold and silver in England caused a sudden rise in prices. England's new wealth came from the sale of woolens and other goods to foreign countries and from the treasure captured from Spanish ships. The sale of woolens and other goods to Spain and other countries led to a great increase in gold and silver in England. To this treasure was added the gold and silver England obtained from the capture of Spanish ships. Because of the increase in gold and silver a sudden price rise took place. *Inflation,* as this economic situation is called, meant that James I needed more money to govern the nation. He also needed more money if he was to live as well as he liked. Relations between James I and Parliament grew worse each year. James's son Charles paid for his father's mistakes.

How Charles I Irritated Parliament

In 1625, James I died and was followed to the throne by his son, Charles I (1625–49). It is said that Charles never forgot anything and that he never learned anything. Charles did not forget how badly Parliament had treated his father, nor did he ever learn how to get along with— or without—Parliament.

Money problems, religious problems, and foreign problems brought about a clash between monarch and Parliament. These problems were closely related to one another. When Charles I wanted money to carry on the work of the government and fight foreign wars, Parliament refused to levy the necessary taxes. Charles then tried to rule without Parliament and used unlawful means of raising the money he needed. As his father had done, Charles sold titles of nobility, gave special monopoly rights to those who could pay the price, and taxed cities that had not been taxed before. He forced rich people to make loans to the government that were never repaid. His efforts to raise money in these ways further angered the people and Parliament.

Charles I was unable to raise enough money by illegal methods and finally had to go to Parliament to ask for more money. Parliament was not fast in giving Charles the money he wanted. First, Parliament made Charles sign an agreement that he would not force people to pay a tax or to make a loan without first asking Parliament. Charles was forced to do away with special courts such as the *Court of Star Chamber*, which had imprisoned people unjustly. He had to agree not to make further arrests without giving reasons for the arrests. Charles had to promise that soldiers would no longer be housed in people's homes if the homeowners did not want them. These new rules were included in the *Petition of Right* (1628), which Parliament forced the reluctant Charles I to sign. The changes listed in the Petition of Right were only slowly carried out, but they show several of the rights for which some English people were fighting.

Like his father, Charles I had religious troubles. He tried to make the Anglican Church even more Catholic than it was. He wanted everyone to worship the way he did. This caused the Puritans to begin to leave England for America in large numbers. These thrifty, hard-working people helped America grow, and England was the poorer for losing them.

How Parliament Got the Better of Charles I

After signing the Petition of Right, Charles I decided to break the agreement and rule without Parliament. He was more determined than ever to rule by absolute methods. From 1629 to 1640 he did so until his religious policies led to trouble with Scotland. Scotland was a Protestant country. The Scots did not follow the Anglican religious service and disliked any attempt to force them to worship in a way they did not believe was right. When Charles tried to compel them to do so, they raised an army to fight him. Charles needed an army to fight back, but strong armies cost more money than Charles had. He was forced to call another meeting of Parliament. Parliament once again refused to give him the money he wanted, whereupon Charles dismissed Parliament in anger. The spirit of rebellion was alive, but the signal for rebellion came from Scotland.

The Scots invaded England and forced Charles I to pay them to get out of the country. The king was forced to call another Parliament in order to get the necessary funds. Charles was caught between a hostile Scotland and a hostile Parliament. The awkward position in which the king found himself brought about his downfall.

The new Parliament was made up of mostly Charles's enemies. It is known to history as the *Long Parliament* because it met from 1640 to 1660. First, it ordered the execution of two of Charles's chief advisers. Then, it passed laws to limit the monarch's powers. Among these laws were those which said that Parliament could not be sent home without its own consent and that Parliament must agree to all taxes imposed on the people.

While these laws were being passed inside the Parliament building, there was mob violence outside. Charles I began to fear for his life. Then he took a step that he was to regret. He went in person to try to arrest five of the members of the House of Commons. However, when he got there, the leaders of Parliament had vanished. The members of Parliament were out to break the absolute powers of the monarch. Charles's attempt to use force was met with force. Civil war began.

Charles I in his attempt to arrest five members of the House of Commons. Why was Parliament against Charles?

The Cavaliers and the Roundheads

Civil war, which lasted from 1642 to 1646, was fought between the *Cavaliers* (those who supported the king) and the *Roundheads* (those who supported Parliament). The Cavaliers were made up of aristocrats, Catholics, Anglicans, and landholders. The Roundheads were made up of merchants and Puritans. The Roundheads won, and Charles I was captured and imprisoned.

Religious questions soon started the Roundheads fighting among themselves. A powerful minority (less than half of the group) gained control of the Long Parliament. They set up a special court and tried and sentenced the king to death. Charles I, after a reign of turmoil, was beheaded on January 30, 1649.

Oliver Cromwell, the leader of the Roundheads, became military dictator. Under Cromwell, Puritanism was the dominant religious faith, and Puritans tried to impose their ways on everyone. Since the Puritans frowned on dancing, games, and the theater, these forms of entertainment were made illegal. England became a stern and somber place in which to live. Cromwell's dictatorship was not popular with the people. When he died, the Long Parliament realized that the people had become tired of Cromwell's military dictatorship and Puritan ways. It restored the Stuarts to the throne by inviting Charles II to return to England from exile.

Check in Here

1. Describe three ways in which the Stuarts angered Parliament.

2. How were each of the following responsible for the difficulties James I had with Parliament: **(a)** money problems; **(b)** religious problems; **(c)** political problems? (turn to p. 308)

Aphra Behn (1640–1689)

Had she been a man, Aphra Behn [af'rə bān'] might have been better known in history and literature than she is. She wrote at a time when writing for money and for fame was considered an activity appropriate only for men. Therefore, her works have frequently been overlooked. Even Aphra Behn considered her talent to be unfeminine in nature. For example, she said, "All I ask, is the privilege for my masculine part, the poet in me."

Aphra Behn was born in Kent, England. Historians do not know who her parents were or what their name was. Behn was Aphra's married name. When she was in her twenties she went to Surinam (in northeast South America). Although that area had originally been settled by the Dutch, it became English during a series of wars between England and the Netherlands. It was there that she learned to speak Dutch. In Surinam she supported the cause of rebellious black slaves and sympathized with the poverty of the Indian population. When Surinam was returned to the Netherlands in exchange for New Netherlands (New York), Aphra Behn went back to England. She married a Dutch merchant named Behn, who died shortly afterwards, probably of the plague that swept England at that time.

Because of her knowledge of Dutch Behn was enlisted as a spy in the service of Charles II. She was a devoted Royalist but her services as a spy were little appreciated. Her warning that the Dutch were planning to sail up the River Thames to destroy the British ships was correct but was disregarded. Despite her loyal service to the government, Behn was dismissed without reward. Deprived of income, she was sent to debtors' prison for a brief time. Her poverty may have forced her to turn to writing as a means of making a living.

Behn's writing career began in the 1670s with the publication of her first play, *The Forc'd Marriage*. That play and others were unusually successful and were widely performed. She wrote poetry under the pen name of Astrea. However, her most important contributions were her novels. Her first novel was published in 1680. Her most famous novel was *Oroonoko* which was published a year before she died. It was based on a romance that took place in Surinam during the period she was there. Her writing demonstrates qualities that matched the best of the male writers who were to become far better known. It shows a wide range of interests. *The City Heiress* and *The Roundheads* were attacks on the Puritans. They show her involvement in the politics of her day. The play *The Widow Ranter* was based on the story of a rebellion in the colony of Virginia.

Aphra Behn was the first woman in England to earn her living by writing. Today, with growing interest in the history of women, the life of Aphra Behn is being increasingly studied for the light it sheds on the role of women and on the development of literature in Western civilization.

3. How did the Tudors and the Stuarts differ on the subject of absolutism?

4. How did Charles I try to get along without Parliament?

5. How did Charles I have to give in to Parliament?

THE RESTORATION FAILS, BUT THE REVOLUTION SUCCEEDS

How Charles II Ruled England

The return of the Stuart family in the person of Charles II (1660–85) to the English throne is called the *Restoration.* The English were happy to have a king once more, but their rejoicing did not last long because Charles II intended to rule as much as possible without Parliament. In this, he was nearly successful.

Charles II was able to get along without Parliament because his friend, Louis XIV of France, gave him some of the money he needed to govern. In addition, Charles found in Parliament a group of friends, known as *Tories,* who favored the monarchy. Those who opposed him became known as *Whigs.* The division between Whigs and Tories marks the beginning of the two-party system in England.

Under Charles II, the *Test Act* was passed. According to it only Anglicans could take part in government. With this act of religious intolerance, democracy took a step backward. However, democracy was advanced when the people were assured of fair and speedy trials by the *Habeas Corpus Act* of 1679.

During the reign of Charles II, John Milton (1608–1674) wrote the great classic *Paradise Lost,* and John Bunyan (1628–1688) wrote *Pilgrim's Progress.* Ironically, these two celebrated books were written by Puritans at a time when Puritans found it difficult to worship as they pleased.

In contrast to its somber mood under Cromwell, England was a festive country under Charles II. But these happy times did not last. Charles II died suddenly in 1685, and was succeeded by his brother James II. The reign of James II was brief and turbulent.

Why the Glorious Revolution Succeeded

James II (1633–1701), a Catholic, continued his brother's plans; however, he was unsuccessful. He tactlessly seemed to favor the Catholics. When the queen gave birth to a son and the people realized that another Catholic would follow James to the throne, they felt that something had to be done. Leaders in Parliament invited William III of Orange (Holland) and his wife, Mary Stuart (a daughter of James II), to become king and queen of England. William welcomed this opportunity. He disliked James II because James had been a friend of Louis XIV, who was trying to destroy Holland. William

John Milton and his daughters. Although Milton was blind, he produced one of the great classics of English literature, *Paradise Lost.*

wanted to become king of England to save Holland from France.

William III landed in England on November 5, 1688, fully expecting to fight another civil war. But James II, having found few friends, fled to France. William and Mary became king and queen of England without a fight. A bloodless revolution had taken place. It is known as the *Glorious Revolution.*

The result of the Glorious Revolution was a *limited monarchy* in England. Before William and Mary could become king and queen, they had to agree that they would not do certain things. They agreed to a *Bill of Rights,* which made the laws of Parliament supreme in England. Parliament was to be called each year and was given the sole power to levy taxes. The people were given the right of *petition;* that is, they could ask the monarch to correct abuses. People were guar-anteed fair and speedy trials. A standing army in peacetime was declared illegal. A *Toleration Act,* passed in 1689, gave Puritans the right to have their own churches. The *Act of Settlement,* passed in 1701, gave only those of the Protestant faith the right to rule England.

Mary's sister Anne followed William and Mary to the throne. During Queen Anne's reign (1702–14) the *Act of Union* was passed (1707) whereby England and Wales were united with Scotland to form one nation, Great Britain. From this time the history of England became the history of Great Britain, and the British Parliament ruled these countries.

The Results of the Glorious Revolution

As a result of its struggles England had made a number of worthwhile advances

XXVIII. WILLIAM the THIRD and MARY the SECOND, from 1688 to 1702.

BILL OF RIGHTS

William and Mary. Why were they not as powerful as previous English monarchs?

Why Undemocratic Features Remained in England

Democracy is not achieved all at once and for all times. Its gains are won slowly and must be preserved by constant vigilance. Many undemocratic features of English government remained even after the Glorious Revolution. For example, only owners of large amounts of land could vote, and only Anglicans could hold office.

At this time, Paliament was not a truly democratic body because the wealthy people, or artistocrats, were in control. In the House of Lords, membership was by birth rather than by ballot. The House of Lords held the power to veto laws passed by the House of Commons. Freedom of speech and freedom of the press were not well established. There was much political corruption, partly because the secret ballot had not yet been developed. Intolerance to Catholics and Jews continued, and punishments for crimes remained cruel.

Nevertheless, by 1688 England had taken a big step toward having a democratic government. Government by the consent of the governed became the rallying cry for other revolutions, notably in America and in France.

along the road to democracy. The monarch's power was limited. Kings and queens could not make or veto laws, or levy taxes, or keep an army without Parliament's consent. The law courts of England were free of royal influence since no one could be put into prison without being given a fair and speedy trial by a jury of one's *peers* (equals).

Many new political developments helped the growth of democracy in England. One major one was the two-party system. The custom of choosing the cabinet from the majority party of the House of Commons was another. The prime minister was the leader of the most numerous party in the House of Commons. He was not merely the king's favorite at court. The House of Commons itself became more powerful at the same time more responsible to the people.

Check in Here

1. Distinguish between Cavaliers and Roundheads.

2. Why is the arrival to the throne of William and Mary described as a "Glorious Revolution"?

3. Identify three accomplishments of the Glorious Revolution.

4. Identify three ways in which further progress toward democracy was needed in England.

5. Why did James II flee England?

THE AMERICAN REVOLUTION BRINGS FREEDOM AND DEMOCRACY TO THE COLONISTS

Some Causes of the American Revolution

The people in the thirteen American colonies believed that some of the democratic advances of the Glorious Revolution in Britain would be spread to the colonies. Britain was the most democratic country in Europe and its thirteen American colonies came to expect democratic treatment. The people living in the colonies thought of themselves as loyal British subjects who had the same rights as British subjects living in the parent country. When the colonists thought they were being treated less democratically than the people at home, they rebelled. The American Revolution soon followed.

The causes of the American Revolution are many. One cause was that George III wanted to be king in fact as well as in name. He wanted to rule as an absolute monarch. The English in Britain as well as the English in America opposed him in this.

Another important cause of the revolution was the *mercantile* [mėr'kən tīl] *system*. This said that colonies should support the parent country economically. Under the mercantile system, Britain could limit manufacturing in the colonies. It could tax the products that Americans made as well as any products that were shipped into the colonies. The American colonists were opposed to the mercantile system. No taxation without representation meant that the colonists had no elected representatives in the House of Commons. They therefore had no part in choosing what taxes they would pay. They felt they were not being treated democratically. Some colonists were willing to try revolution.

Because the colonies were many miles away from Britain, they had been allowed to govern themselves. In early colonial lawmaking bodies they developed independent ways which they wanted to keep. There were colonists who wanted to make colonial America entirely independent of British control. When the revolution took place, most of the colonists had lost their ties to England. Many children of English colonial parents had never been in England. Many others were from Germany, Sweden, the Netherlands, and France. These people were not likely to be loyal to Britain.

How the Colonists Prepared for Revolution

John Adams said of the American Revolution: "Even before the outbreak of the revolution many Americans were prepared emotionally to separate from England. To wage a successful revolution people must have—in addition to guns and armies—the determination to fight." John Adams also said, "The Revolution was effected [accomplished] before the war began. It was in the minds and hearts of the people."

Many Americans had ideas similar to those of the European philosophers who were helping prepare the way for change in Europe. Thomas Paine and Thomas Jefferson were as much a part of the Age of Reason as were Locke and Rousseau. In a pamphlet, *Common Sense*, Thomas Paine helped prepare the minds of the colonists for separation from Britain. He showed that independence was a reasonable thing for which to ask. After the battles of Lexington and Concord, Paine said that it was not right to work for a settlement with Britain. Instead, it was time to part.

North America, 1763

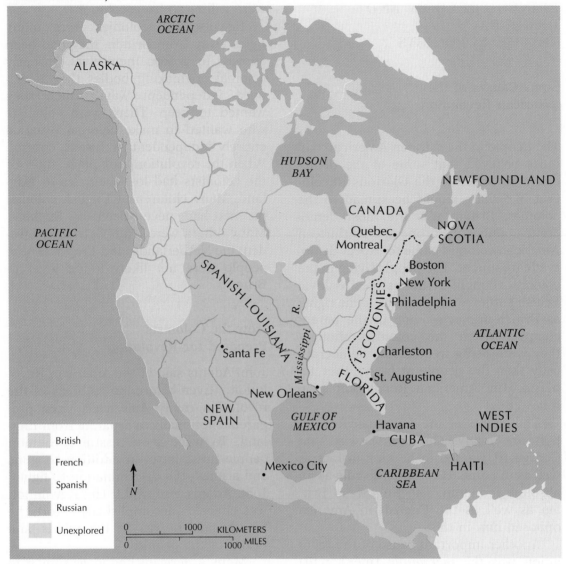

- Refer to the map on page 250. What additional territory had Spain acquired in America since 1700?
- How do the two maps (pages 312 and 313) show one result of the American Revolution?
- In 1783, the United States extended as far as what river?
- Locate two areas where there were land disputes in 1783.

In the *Declaration of Independence* of 1776 the colonies declared their independence of Britain and described the revolutionary ideals of the day. The Declaration of Independence said that people are created equal and have the right to life, liberty, and the pursuit of happiness. These are rights which no one can take away, and governments are made to protect them. The powers of the government, the Declaration went on to say, are derived from the people. When a government no longer protects the people's rights, people should abolish it.

North America, 1783

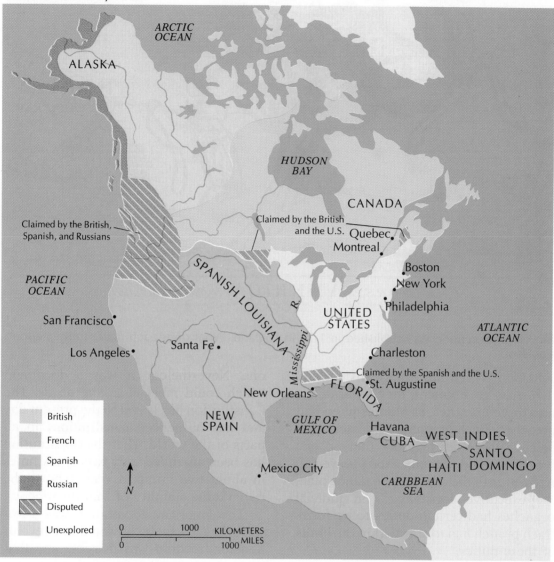

In the second part of the Declaration, King George III was charged with numerous crimes. George III was probably not as bad as the Declaration made him out to be, but it was easier and simpler to blame the king rather than Parliament. The Declaration of Independence was a revolutionary document, written to stir the minds of people and to help bring about great changes. The last part of the Declaration announced the separation from Britain: "These United Colonies are . . . Independent States. . . ."

The Results of the American Revolution

The American Revolution has been called the shot heard around the world because it influenced and inspired other nations to fight for freedom. The American colonies were influenced by the writings of Locke, Montesquieu, Paine, and

THE HORSE AMERICA, throwing his Master.
Pub.d as the Act directs. Aug.t 1.st 1779. by W.m White, Angel Court, Westminster.

This editorial cartoon was published in 1779 in England. What does each figure in the cartoon represent?

Jefferson. When the Americans formed their new government, they separated it into three branches, as Montesquieu had preached. Each branch would check and balance the other in order that no one branch would become too powerful. According to the check and balance plan, the executive, legislative, and judicial branches had certain duties to perform. Each branch had to stay within the limits of these duties.

The *Bill of Rights*—the first ten amendments to the Constitution—guaranteed to the people the individual rights of which Locke, Jefferson, and others spoke. Included in these rights were freedom of speech, freedom of the press, freedom of religion, freedom of assembly, jury trial, freedom from unusual or cruel punishments, freedom from excessive bail, and the right not to be forced to give evidence that might hurt one's reputation or that might be used to convict oneself.

The United States *Constitution*, which was written in 1789, did not please everyone. Nevertheless, it was a document which could meet changing needs. The Constitution has lasted to the present day and has influenced constitutions in all parts of the world. That the Constitution has been amended only twenty-six times in about two hundred years, shows the remarkable stability of that document.

The American Revolution was a lesson to the world. It showed that a revolution for freedom was possible and that there are times when revolution is necessary. It showed that a government could be established without a monarch. These lessons were not lost on the people and the nations of Europe. The shots that were fired at Lexington and Concord were heard in Paris, where a more terrible revolution was about to break out. The French Revolution was next in the series of shots which marked the beginning of Europe's march toward political freedom. The ideas of the American and French Revolutions continued to inspire worldwide political change in the nineteenth and twentieth centuries.

314

1. List three causes of the American Revolution.

2. How did each of the following contribute to the Revolution: **(a)** Paine; **(b)** Jefferson?

3. Why was the American Revolution a lesson to the world? How is it still a lesson to countries today?

4. How was the American Constitution influenced by the ideas of Locke and Montesquieu?

REVIEWING THE BASICS

During the seventeenth and eighteenth centuries, democracy grew in England, in various northern European countries, and in America. Significant advances were made in the rights and freedoms we associate with democracy today.

James I, Charles I, James II, and Charles II are collectively referred to as "the Stuarts." James I angered Parliament because he claimed to rule by divine right. James was torn by money as well as religious problems. He was dependent upon a Parliament he disliked. To the English he appeared a foreigner because he was a Scot. Charles I was even less successful than James. He violated the laws and traditions of England by taxing unfairly and by unjustly imprisoning his opponents.

Charles was unable to raise enough money through illegal methods and was forced to call Parliament into session. Parliament forced Charles to sign the Petition of Right in 1628. The Court of Star Chamber was abolished, and Charles was forced to agree to getting Parliament's approval before imposing taxes. Charles tried to rule without Parliament once again. For eleven years he did so. However, war broke out as a result of his attempt to impose the Anglican church on Scotland. Charles I was forced to call Parliament into session once again.

The new Parliament is known to history as the Long Parliament. Charles tried to dissolve the Parliament by force, and in the process was captured and later tried and beheaded. Under Oliver Cromwell, leader of the victorious Roundheads, the Cavaliers were defeated and a dictatorship was established. When Cromwell died, the Parliament reluctantly turned to Charles II, and so the Stuarts returned to the English throne.

Charles II was unsuccessful in reestablishing the authority of the Stuarts. Although he was willing to compromise, his tolerance of Catholics was not well received after a long period of Protestant domination. Under his reign a two-party system developed in England, and the Habeas Corpus Act was passed in 1679.

When James II came to the throne, the idea of a Catholic succession was enough to anger Parliament and unite its leaders against him. These leaders invited William and Mary of Holland to the throne of England. The peaceful arrival of William and Mary to the throne has been called the Glorious Revolution.

In America the events of the Glorious Revolution had great influence. The colonists sought self-government on the one hand and freedom from monarchy on the other. They were influenced by the writings of philosophers, especially Thomas Paine, Thomas Jefferson, and others. These writings helped prepare the colonists mentally for separation from England. Upon victory over England, the new government framed a Constitution based on the principles of Locke and Montesquieu. It provided for separation of the three branches of government and a system of checks and balances so that one branch could not become stronger than the others. A Bill of Rights was attached to the Constitution so that every individual could be guaranteed the personal rights of which Locke, Jefferson, and others had written.

REVIEWING THE HIGHLIGHTS

People to Identify			
William the Silent	Oliver Cromwell	Charles I	
Queen Anne	Charles II	John Bunyan	
Thomas Paine	James I	James II	
Thomas Jefferson	William and Mary	John Milton	
	Aphra Behn		

Places to Locate		
England	Holland	Belgium
Scotland	Wales	Switzerland
	Great Britain	

Terms to Understand		
Anglican Church	Tudor	peers
Petition of Right	King James Bible	Star Chamber
Puritans	Tories	Test Act
cantons	Act of Settlement	Habeas Corpus Act
democracy	(1701)	Toleration Act
Cavaliers	United States	Whigs
Roundheads	Constitution	Act of Union (1707)
Long Parliament	Bill of Rights	Declaration of
Swiss Confederation	Parliament	Independence
stadtholder	limited monarchy	Pilgrims
Stuart	Petition of Right	

Events to Describe		
the Restoration	Glorious Revolution	American Revolution

316

1. What are the chief characteristics of democracy?
2. Describe the growth of democracy in Switzerland and the Netherlands.
3. Why was absolutism not as strong in England as elsewhere?
4. How did James I irritate the people and Parliament?
5. Why were the Puritans dissatisfied with the Anglican Church?
6. Why is the Petition of Right an important step toward the development of democracy?
7. How did the Scottish invasion of England make matters worse for Charles I?
8. Why was Charles I beheaded?
9. Why was Oliver Cromwell unpopular?
10. Why were the Stuarts restored to the throne?
11. What democratic steps forward were taken during the reign of Charles II?
12. Why did Charles II find it unnecessary to go to Parliament for money?
13. Why was James II forced to leave England?
14. Explain the political positions of the Tories and the Whigs.
15. Why is the Revolution of 1688 called the Glorious Revolution?
16. To what extent was democracy advanced in England as a result of the Glorious Revolution?
17. What remained undemocratic in England after the Glorious Revolution had taken place?
18. How did the colonists prepare for the American Revolution?
19. What revolutionary ideas could be found in the Declaration of Independence?
20. Why was this chapter called "Shots That Were Heard Around the World"?

THINGS TO DO

1. Hold a mock trial of Charles I. Have a "jury" decide whether he was guilty or not guilty of the crimes of which he was accused. Base your trial on the account by the first Earl of Clarendon entitled *The History of the Rebellion*. (See p. 318 in the text for an excerpt.)
2. Draw a cartoon illustrating an aspect of Oliver Cromwell's dictatorship.

Below is a selection by an observer of the trial of Charles I. Read it carefully and answer the questions that follow.

Trial of King Charles I

When he was first brought to Westminster Hall, which was upon the twentieth of January, 1649, before the high court of justice, he looked upon them and sat down without any manifestation* of trouble, never doffing* his hat. . . . He was impeached* for . . . treasons and crimes . . . as a tyrant, traitor, and murderer, and a public enemy to the commonwealth of England. . . . President Bradshaw, after he had insolently* reprimanded* the king for not having doffed his hat or showing more respect . . . asked the king what answer he made to that impeachment.

The king . . . told them he would first know of them by what authority they presumed by force to bring him before them, and who gave them power to judge his actions, for which he was accountable to none but to God. . . . He told them that he was their king and they his subjects, who owed him duty and obedience; that no parliament had authority to call him before them. . . . As there were many persons present at that woeful spectacle who felt a real compassion* for the king, so there were others of so barbarous and brutal a behavior toward him that they called him . . . murderer; and one spat in his face which His Majesty without expressing any resentment wiped off with his handkerchief. . . .

Of the execution of the sentence . . . no more shall be said here of that lamentable* tragedy, so much to the dishonor of the nation. . . .†

Vocabulary

manifestation—sign	impeached—charged	compassion—sympathy
doffing—removing	insolently—rudely	lamentable—sad
	reprimanded—scolded	

1. Does the author show greater sympathy for the king or for Parliament? How can you tell?
2. How does the author describe the conduct of Charles I?
3. Which lines prove that Charles I believed in divine right?
4. What "sentence" does the author refer to in the last paragraph?
5. May this be regarded as a *primary* or *secondary* source? Justify your answer.

†*The History of the Rebellion,* by Edward Hyde, first Earl of Clarendon (1609–1674), found in *Readings in Medieval and Modern History,* by Hutton Webster. D.C. Heath and Company, Boston. 1917.

The palace and gardens of Versailles

The French Revolution and Napoleon: A Close Look at a Revolution

"It was the best of times, it was the worst of times. . . ." So begins Charles Dickens's *A Tale of Two Cities,* a novel based on the French Revolution. The two cities, London and Paris, were the hearts of two great nations and the seats of two strong governments. And both cities were the centers of revolution.

It was the year 1775. Important events were taking place in various countries. In North America, the thirteen colonies were almost ready to declare their independence from England. In France, the great revolution was only a few years away. In

319

their glittering palace at Versailles, Louis XVI and Marie Antoinette went about their round of pleasures, unmindful that France would be the next stage for the drama of revolution. Out of the French Revolution the First Republic of France was formed.

Other republican governments followed. Some came as a result of further violence. Others, as in the case of the Fifth French Republic, formed in 1958, were born without bloodshed.

THE OLD REGIME ABUSES THE FRENCH PEOPLE

The Old Regime

If a French family of the Middle Ages had been transported to the France of 1789, it would have found conditions unchanged in many ways. It would have been quite familiar with the division of society into privileged and unprivileged classes. It would have known about unfair taxation, under which the poor paid more than the rich. And it would also have known about the highway tolls, which interfered with transportation.

The form of government and the way society was organized before the French Revolution is described as the *Old Regime* [rə zhēm']. Government and society under the Old Regime had many features that had not changed since feudal days. The needs of the French nation, or people, of 1789 were not served by the Old Regime. Perhaps the most outstanding feature of the Old Regime was that the monarch still had absolute power.

In 1789, the power of governing was in the hands of a well meaning but feeble king, Louis XVI. He had inherited many problems from Louis XV, who boasted that after his reign there would be a del-

uge. He meant that after his reign there would be a flood of troubles. He was right. The wife of Louis XVI was Marie Antoinette [an'twə net'], Austrian by birth. Her thoughtlessness and extravagance hurt her reputation and her position. The king and queen, together with the lords and ladies at court, spent their time thinking about comforts and luxuries rather than about the problems of the nation. Both king and queen wanted to do the right things but did not know how. They were often misled by selfish friends and did not recognize or take good advice.

How Society Was Divided Under the Old Regime

The French people were divided into three groups, or *estates*. The First Estate, made up of religious leaders and clergy, represented less than one percent of the 25 million French people. This small minority, however, owned or controlled one-fifth of the land. Members of the First Estate enjoyed special rights. They were free from carrying the burden of taxes.

The Second Estate, made up of the nobles, included less than two percent of the population, but it, too, had many privileges and owned much land. Today, taxes are paid by those best able to pay them, but this was not so during the Old Regime in France. The nobles were best able to pay, but they paid few or no taxes and retained many feudal privileges. The nobles held the best political jobs and had a great deal of influence with the monarch. They spent most of their time leading lives of ease at the royal palace at Versailles.

Among members of the First and Second Estates there were also many poor and well-meaning people. The parish priests served the religious needs of their people and received few rewards. Furthermore, there were many nobles who knew that the privileges they had were unfair. Some of the thoughtful people among the nobles and the clergy were to help remove these privileges.

To the Third Estate belonged 95 percent of the people, more than 24 million of them. This group included serfs who were still bound to the soil, members of the middle class (some were very rich), and peasants. The average person of the Third Estate was a poor peasant. Servants, skilled and unskilled workers, doctors, lawyers, teachers, storekeepers, and laborers were in the Third Estate.

The people of the Third Estate were the backbone of the country, but they had few privileges. They paid most of the taxes, but they had little influence on the monarch. The Third Estate had no voice in the government.

The *Estates-General* was a kind of lawmaking group without much democratic influence. It had been in existence since 1302, but did not meet regularly. In the Estates-General voting was done separately by Estate. The Third Estate was always doomed to lose by a vote of two to one. The First and Second Estates always overruled any laws that would help the people of the Third Estate. Thus, most people were unhappy with conditions in France.

Marie Antoinette with her children. Why did the people of France turn against her?

Why Revolution Came to France

The government and society of France under the Old Regime were little different from other countries of Europe. Except for Great Britain, other European countries were ruled by undemocratic governments. Why then did revolution on the continent come first to France?

France was the home of Voltaire, Rousseau, and others who taught that freedom of thought and action is important. Revolution came first to France because the peasants were not as oppressed as peasants in other countries. The French peasants were better treated and had more privileges than other peasants in Europe. Revolution often occurs

321

A French working-class family in the eighteenth century. This painting by Louis Le Nain is entitled *The Dairywoman's Family.*

not when conditions are the worst, but when they are beginning to improve. People begin to expect even better conditions when they see that there is the possibility of change. The underprivileged in France believed that things could be better. Revolution came first to France because a growing middle class was getting rich and was demanding a voice in the government. The inability of the king to solve France's problems was another reason for the revolution.

Many fundamental and immediate causes brought about revolution in France. A *fundamental cause* is one that has deep roots in the past. Under the Old Regime, there were many feudal laws and customs that were not in step with modern thinking. The thinking and attitudes of the people were changing. These were among the fundamental causes of the revolution.

An *immediate cause* is one that directly leads to action. The switch that set the French Revolution in motion was the need for money to pay the costs of running the government and supporting a costly court. The debt was so great that the interest on it was the nation's greatest single expense. French income did not equal French expenses, a dangerous situation. Many people were dissatisfied with Louis XVI and his inefficient ways.

On his deathbed, Louis XIV (see p. 272) had warned those who followed him not to spend too much money and not to fight costly wars. The monarchs who followed him did not take his advice. Instead, they followed his bad example. Since they were less skilled in governing than he, the results were serious for France. Although France gave aid to America during its revolution, it could not financially afford to give this aid. Its loans to the American Revolution contributed to its bankruptcy.

Louis XVI and Marie Antoinette might have held off bankruptcy and

322

saved the monarchy if they had listened to their wise finance ministers, Jacques Necker [nek'ər] and Robert Turgot [tür gō']. However, the foolish king and queen and the selfish nobility would not do what was needed to save France or themselves. They refused to lower expenses, and they would not allow themselves to be taxed. The able finance ministers, Turgot and Necker, who suggested these necessary measures were dismissed by the king.

Check in Here

1. What is the Old Regime?

2. Identify three ways in which the Old Regime abused the French people.

3. What were the differences among the First, Second, and Third Estates?

4. Why was the method of voting in the Estates-General unfair?

5. Distinguish between a fundamental and an immediate cause. Give an example of each as they apply to the French Revolution.

THE FRENCH BRING AN END TO ABSOLUTISM

Why the Estates-General Was Called to Meet

French bankruptcy made Louis XVI desperate. He decided to call a meeting of the Estates-General; perhaps this group would have an idea. Louis was playing with fire, and he got burned. The meeting of the Estates-General gave the people a voice in the government. They were eager to make the most of this meeting, which they saw as a golden opportunity. Their king needed money. The Estates-General could help him get it.

But first, the Third Estate (middle class, peasants, and serfs) would make the king give in a little. Wasn't this the way the English Parliament became strong under Charles I? Didn't the philosophers tell them that governments are to be run by the people? Didn't the American Declaration of Independence state that when government destroys the people's rights, it should be changed? With these thoughts to guide them, various groups met in large and small cities. They drew up lists of dislikes and criticisms of the monarchy and put them in books called *cahiers* [kä yäs'].

The cahiers told of some of the new democratic ideas of the day. However, for the most part they did not demand extreme changes in the government. They did not say that the monarch must be killed or leave the throne. Instead, they asked only that special privileges for the nobles be abolished, that taxes be fair for all the people, and that the Estates-General should meet more often to discuss government affairs. In the cahiers, the people demanded that the government allow freedom of speech and press and that the government leave business alone. The people wanted freedom from an irresponsible government guaranteed by a written constitution for France.

How the Estates-General Became the National Assembly

The Estates-General met in 1789. The First and Second Estates had three hundred members each. The Third Estate had about six hundred. The members of the Third Estate were angry, however, to find that they were being outvoted by two to one. How could this be? The Third Estate should have had at least six hundred votes. According to custom, voting was not done by individuals, but by an entire Estate. Thus, although the Third Estate had six hundred members, it had only one vote. Because the First and Second Estates usually voted against the wishes of the Third Estate, the Third Estate was usually outvoted two to one.

This method of voting struck hard at the high hopes with which the members of the Third Estate came to Paris. However, they were determined not to go away empty handed. They declared themselves to be the *National Assembly* for all of France. They invited members (priests and nobles) of the other estates to join them. Because the meeting hall was closed to them, they met on an indoor tennis court and swore that they would not disband until they had given France a constitution. Only when they had gained a constitution would they give their attention to the king's

money problems. The *Tennis Court Oath* of June 20, 1789, was a significant step in the French Revolution. It showed that the three estates could unite, at least for a time, against the crown. But Louis XVI would not listen to the demand of the Third Estate for a constitution. He told them that they were wasting time, and he threatened to send them home.

By the time Louis XVI had decided to listen to the Third Estate, the French Revolution had begun. The demand of the Third Estate for a constitution was cheered by the people of Paris. Angry mobs showed their approval by attacking the *Bastille* [bas tėl'], an old fortress used as a prison. It was a symbol of the Old Regime. This action, taken on July

Members of the Third Estate meet on a tennis court to formulate a constitution for France. How did Louis XVI react to their assembly?

14, 1789, is remembered by the French today. Bastille Day is celebrated as a national holiday. July 14 has the same meaning for the French that July 4 has for Americans.

What the Revolutionaries Wanted

The Bastille in Paris was taken, and there were riots outside the city. Economic depression, as well as revolution, gripped the country. Unemployment was widespread; troops seemed to be everywhere. The people were afraid and uneasy. A rumor that the queen had told the people to eat cake if they had no bread aroused French women to action. In the rain, they marched from Paris to the palace at Versailles. They wanted to force "The baker, the baker's wife, and the baker's little boy"—that is, the king and queen and their son—to come back to Paris with them and to provide them with more grain. Enthusiasm for the revolution was high.

At the National Assembly, which met from 1789–91, important work was being done. On the night of August 4, 1789, a noble stood up to make the shocking suggestion that the nobles and clergy give up their special privileges. The members of the Third Estate cheered with delight. This suggestion was the beginning of reforms. This was the opportunity for which they had been waiting. Other suggestions were made to make the nobles pay more taxes and to do away with the nobility's ancient feudal privileges.

The Third Estate introduced the *Declaration of the Rights of Man* in August 1789. It repeated some of the new ideas of the time, such as "Men are born and remain free and equal in rights." The rights of liberty, ownership of property, and resistance to oppression were de-

This representation of the capture of the Bastille was painted by an eyewitness.

fended. All citizens were to have a voice in the government, to be equal before the law, and to be free from unfair arrest. These were great days for the people, who seemed to be getting what they wanted.

But the honeymoon period was soon over. The Third Estate controlled the National Assembly and was made up of the *bourgeoisie* [bür′zhwä zē′], or middle class, who wanted to control the government. It was made up of peasants who wanted to own land and city workers who wanted liberty, better wages and working conditions, and more extreme reforms. A three-way conflict developed among these groups. You will see how the demands of each of these groups were at least partially, if not fully, met as a result of the French Revolution.

325

How the Assembly Met Money Problems

The resolutions of August 4 and the Declaration of the Rights of Man did not solve the money problems of France. The king needed money, and good ideas did not give him the money he needed. It was one thing to say that all should be taxed according to their ability, but it took time to collect the money, even from the nobles. In the meantime, how were the financial problems to be solved?

The National Assembly found that one answer was to take away the Church lands, which were worth a great deal. Against the high value of these lands, the National Assembly printed *assignats* [as'ig nats'], or paper money. The money was to be used to pay the nation's debts. The land taken from the Catholic Church was to be sold at low prices to the French peasants. In this way, two problems would be solved at one time. The national government would have money to pay its debts, and the peasants would be strengthened by becoming landowners.

However, this financial idea backfired because soon more paper money was printed than the lands were worth. This forced prices of food, clothing, and shelter to rise so high that the people could not pay for the things they needed. Church officials were angry that their lands had been taken away. People were angry that they could not buy the necessities of life. Printing paper money had been a good idea. However, it created more problems than it solved.

The peasants of France were the only ones who were content because the lands taken from the Church had been sold to them. In the years before the revolution, French peasants were slowly becoming independent farmers. Now they wanted more land, and for this reason they supported the revolution. To own even a small amount of land was important to a French peasant family. A family was especially eager to gain land if it had not owned any before. When a peasant family got the land it wanted, it was satisfied. For that peasant family the revolution was over. Partly as a result of the sale of land to peasants, the agricultural areas of France today are dominated by small privately owned farms.

The Plans of the National Assembly

In the famous Tennis Court Oath, the members of the National Assembly had sworn to give France a constitution. After two years of discussions, the Constitution of 1791 was adopted. It allowed the monarch to keep the throne provided that the rules of limited monarchy were observed. These rules denied the monarch many powers. French rulers would be limited to those activities approved by the people's representatives.

The National Assembly granted freedom to all religious groups. It wanted to weaken the power of the Roman Catholic Church. It had done so, in part, by taking Church lands. By the *Civil Constitution of the Clergy*, the priests and other officials of the Church were placed under state control. In the opinion of many religious French people, this act of the National Assembly went too far. They remembered the good work of the parish priests, and they had no wish to see them become salaried servants of the government. Many people who had supported the idea of the revolution, including many poor and sincere parish priests, turned against it.

The National Assembly divided France into 83 departments, or local districts, and created a one-house lawmaking body to be elected by the people. The right to vote was limited to people who could pay taxes. This voting restriction did not agree with the spirit or the letter of the Declaration of the Rights of Man, which said that all citizens had a right to take part in government. At this time the revolution was in the hands of the middle class, which was responsible for the unfair voting restriction in the new French Constitution. The middle class controlled the government, and the peasants had bought farmland. The city workers and the laboring classes had so far gained little from the new government. They had a right to be disappointed. The revolution had not gone far enough; they meant to push it further.

Why the Limited Monarchy Failed

The limited monarchy failed because it lacked sufficient support. The Legislative Assembly which was provided for in the Constitution met for a little less than a year. During this time there were bitter arguments between those who felt the revolution had not gone far enough (workers) and those who felt the revolution had gone too far (nobles and bourgeoisie). The bourgeoisie and the workers were quite far apart in their ideas of what changes were necessary for France. The majority of the old Third Estate did not know exactly what they wanted. They were usually unable to make up their minds, whether to support the limited monarchy or to encourage further revolution.

It often happens that the few people who know what they want can sway the many who do not. The workers, relatively few in number, were supported by *Jacobin* [jak'ə bin] *Clubs*. These were made up mostly of Parisian laborers who felt that the revolution had been sold out

Workers forge musket barrels to aid the French Revolutionary Army.

A woman cooks and sells cabbage and other vegetables to the workers of Paris. In the early days of the First Republic food was scarce and prices were high.

by the French nobles now living in other countries. They felt they had been betrayed by the king who, unhappy at being only a limited monarch, had been caught trying to leave the country. They felt that France was surrounded by enemies who were trying to return the king to power. The Jacobins, who were in the minority, forced the majority to declare war on the enemies of France—Austria and Prussia. The war that came provided an excuse to remove the king. The National Assembly was abolished. It was replaced by the *National Convention,* which would form the *First Republic.* The undecided majority of the Third Estate accepted what the minority wanted.

How the First Republic Governed France

The National Convention, which represented the working people, governed the First Republic (1792–1795). Although France was fighting a war, Georges Jacques Danton [dan'tən], one of the revolutionary leaders, demanded that France be bold. The Parisian mob took his advice and began a wave of killings in the city that spread to the countryside. The people who were not in favor of carrying on with the revolution were looked upon as enemies and were not safe from the revolutionary mob.

France was having a difficult time. The nation was undergoing revolution at home and fighting a war abroad. The National Convention was trying to keep order in France and defend it from invasions. The French went out to fight against the foreign enemy and to fight for Liberty, Equality, and Fraternity. They marched to the tune of a new song that became the French national anthem, *La Marseillaise* [lä mär'sə yez'].

In the National Convention, those who favored extreme measures were in control. On January 15, 1793, Citizen Louis Capet (King Louis XVI) was declared guilty of treason and condemned to the guillotine. He was killed within a week.

Most members of the National Convention did not like what had been done, but there was little that they could do to change it. Armed Parisians forced their way into the National Convention, where they arrested and put to death many of those who were against extreme measures. The *Reign of Terror* had begun.

Check in Here

1. What is the significance of the Tennis Court Oath?

2. Why did the clergy and nobility give up their special privileges?

3. To what extent was issuing paper money backed by Church lands a good idea?

4. Why were the workers of Paris dissatisfied with the progress of the French Revolution?

5. Why was Louis XVI killed?

TERROR AND WARFARE LEAD TO NAPOLEON

The Nature of the Reign of Terror

Killing without reason is usually a sign of weakness, not of strength. This was true of France during the Reign of Terror. Rioting and war, disagreement over the kind of government to have, little leadership, hard times, unemployment, high prices, and food shortages had weakened France. The nation stood alone fighting the countries of Europe and hoping to save the gains of the revolution. America was asked for help, but America was not in a position to give help because it was trying to establish itself after winning its own revolution.

The National Convention voted a new democratic constitution that gave all men the right to vote and all lawmaking power to a single legislative body. However, it did not put these provisions into practice. Rather than following the constitution, the National Convention appointed a twelve-man committee, known as the *Committee of Public Safety*.

The Committee of Public Safety, which had unlimited power to rule the nation, was headed by Maximilien de Robespierre [rōbz′pyer]. The committee paid no attention to the democratic constitution. It arrested and put to death those who were even suspected of not being in complete agreement with the revolutionary ideas of the National Convention. Danton, an early leader, lost his life; later the queen, Marie Antoinette, was also beheaded. Thousands of people were executed in the name of the republic. Some were real enemies, many others were not.

Before the Reign of Terror had worn itself out, Robespierre himself was killed. Upon the death of Robespierre, those who favored less extreme measures won control of France.

A patriotic women's club meets during the French Revolution. How did women help the cause?

The Role of Women During the French Revolution*

Many women took part in the French Revolution. Among the women were shopkeepers, fish vendors, launderers, tailors, journalists, and actors. Between 1725 and 1783 there were frequent bread riots in the streets of Paris and elsewhere. During these riots, women gained experience in revolutionary tactics.

The women who marched on Versailles in 1789 were street fighters. They marched twenty miles to Versailles to bring the king back to Paris so that he could see at first hand what starvation was really like. During the long march they were led by Madelaine Chabray [shü brā′], a seventeen-year-old, unemployed sculptor who sold flowers for a living. She was successful in getting the king to distribute grain, which she hoped would relieve starvation in France.

Women were disappointed with the results of the National Assembly. While a Declaration of the Rights of Man was

*This section is based on Elise Boulding. *The Underside of History.* (Boulder, Colorado: Westview Press) pp. 588–593.

329

being written and adopted, a Declaration on the Rights of Women prepared by Claire Lacombe [la kōm'] and Olympe de Gouges [də güj] was turned down. The National Assembly went so far as to prevent women from holding any kind of meeting in the future. Women tried to resist this act of the National Assembly. They were unsuccessful. Many women, as well as men, felt it was improper for women to take an active or violent role in the political life of the nation.

Madame de Condorcet [də kôn dôr sā'] and her husband championed the cause of equality of women. Condorcet himself spoke out strongly for the political rights of women in the National Assembly. He hid from the guillotine with the aid of his wife, but was later found and was killed during the Terror.

Madame Manon Roland was another woman who was actively involved during the revolution's early days. As a member of the upper-middle class she sought to establish a limited monarchy, not a republic in France. Those who favored a limited monarchy felt that she was not doing enough to make such a government possible. Those who favored a republic thought that she was doing too much to encourage a limited monarchy. She was despised by both groups. In the end, she too died in the Terror.

Marie Antoinette, who has not been well treated by historians, was very upset because she could not help her husband. In a letter to a friend in 1792 she wrote:

I could do anything, and appear on horseback were it needed; but that would be furnishing [supplying] weapons to the king's enemies: throughout all of France a cry against the Austrian and the rule of a woman would be raised instantly. By coming forward I should, moreover, reduce the king to a humiliating and inferior position. A queen who, like me, is nothing in her own right—who is not even a regent, has but one part to act—to wait the event silently, and prepare to die.*

Marie Antoinette died in dignity on the guillotine, as did many other women during the Reign of Terror.

While women took part in the French Revolution, their role was limited. Public opinion did not support them. Most women were not ready to take bold political action. Women had much to learn about politics and economics and there were few to teach them. The process of thinking through the role of women in government, in society, and in the economic life of the community was a long and slow one. That process may be said to have begun during the time of the French Revolution.

How the National Convention Changed France

The National Convention should be remembered for more than violence. It attempted to change all aspects of French life. Nothing of the Old Regime was to remain. The National Convention adopted a new calendar. September 22, 1792, the first day of the new government, became the Year 1 of the new calendar. The Convention even changed the names of the months. For example, the month of September became Vendémiaire [vän dā myer'] and October became Brumaire [brü mer'].

The National Convention made other changes in the old way of doing things. It ordered men to wear long pants, rather than knee breeches, and women to wear simple dresses. The words "Monsieur" and "Madame" were replaced by French words meaning "Citizen."

*Boulding, p. 588.

330

The Invalides was a hospital for officers and soldiers. Like the Bastille it was a symbol of the Old Regime and was attacked by Parisians during the revolution. In this period of French history, violence occurred often in the streets of France. It continued until the leadership of Napoleon provided stability.

More lasting reforms were also made. The metric system of weights and measures was adopted. It was considered by some people to be a better system than the English and American system of pounds and ounces. Imprisonment for debt was abolished, as was slavery in the French colonies. Plans for a national system of education were made.

Events After the Reign of Terror

Following the Reign of Terror, the people were tired of disorder and wanted peace. The National Convention dismissed the Committee of Public Safety and adopted the Constitution of 1795. This was less democratic than the one produced by the National Assembly. The new government included a two-house lawmaking body and a five-person law enforcing body known as the *Directory*. This government was a far cry from the high ideals the National Assembly had formed in 1791.

It is said that two heads are better than one. If two heads are better than one, then perhaps five heads are better than two. Such must have been the thinking of the people of the National Convention. However, in the case of the Directory (1795–1799), the five heads did not have the answers to the problems that bothered France. These problems included finding money to run the government, ending the foreign war with victory, and providing law and order for France.

The Directory was not equal to the difficult job it had. The dissatisfied people were looking for a strong leader who could bring them peace, glory, and lasting victory. Such a leader soon came. His name was Napoleon Bonaparte [bō'nə pärt'].

331

1. How did the National Convention make France more democratic?

2. List three lasting additional reforms of the National Convention.

3. Why did the Committee of Public Safety launch a Reign of Terror?

4. Why were women disappointed with the results of the French Revolution? What had they expected?

5. What were the problems of the Directory?

THE RISE AND FALL OF NAPOLEON BONAPARTE

How Napoleon Rose to Power

As a young man, Napoleon supported the French Revolution by fighting against the foreign enemies of France as an officer in the army. He was noticed by the Directory when he saved the National Convention from an attack made by a Parisian mob. By the timely use of what was called a "whiff of grapeshot" (artillery fire), Napoleon held back the mob. As a reward, he was made a general and given command of the French armies in northern Italy, where he defeated the Austrians, whose armies controlled this region. Later, he went to Egypt and unsuccessfully attempted to destroy the British trade route to the Middle East and India. Upon hearing that there was unrest at home, Napoleon felt that the time had come for him to become master of France.

He returned to France and soon took control. With the help of his brother and two members of the Directory, he successfully forced that body from power. A revolution of this kind, in which the existing government is suddenly changed, is known as a *coup d'etat* [kü′ dā tä′]. Napoleon quickly issued a new constitution in which power was given to the *First Consul* [kon súl] of a three-person *Consulate* [kon súl et]. The new constitution was acceptable to the people. Napoleon was popular, and he became First Consul and ruler of France.

What Napoleon Did for France

By 1802, Napoleon had brought victory to France and peace to Europe. He took advantage of this interval of peace to make a number of lasting changes in France.

After gaining peace, Napoleon turned his skill to the problem of making a strong central government. So effectively did he place all power in the hands of the national government that even today France is largely ruled from Paris as Napoleon had planned. The *Napoleonic Law Code* helped to centralize power. It is important because it included many democratic principles, such as religious tolerance, jury trial, abolition of serfdom, and fair legal methods.

To strengthen the government further, Napoleon established the University of France. This was not a college, but a supervisory bureau charged with the responsibility of looking after the schools of France. Napoleon made sure that the schools taught what Napoleon wanted them to teach. In so doing, he set the pattern for the dictators of modern times.

The age-old problems of money also called for an answer. Napoleon organized the Bank of France, which provided a basis for an economic system that could help make France a prosperous nation. He efficiently collected taxes and enforced economy in government. Business was encouraged.

The French Revolution had left Church officials unhappy. Their lands had been taken away, and they had been forced to accept the Civil Constitution of

Napoleon Bonaparte
(1769–1821)

Napoleon Bonaparte was born in Corsica [kôr sə kä], an island off the coast of Italy. Only three months before he was born the island became a French possession. It is interesting to imagine how things might have been different for Napoleon, France, and Europe if Corsica had not become French territory.

Napoleon, who rose from humble origins to become Emperor of France, was sent as a child of five to a school for girls. His mother hoped that Napoleon would become less stubborn and easier to handle. This, however, was not to be the case. Napoleon, who was the second of the eight Bonaparte children, was strong-willed, obstinate, and often disagreeable.

Napoleon's parents then sent him to a Jesuit school where his older brother was a student. The Jesuit school apparently made a good impression on Napoleon because as emperor he rewarded his reading teacher with the sum of twenty thousand francs as a token of his gratitude for what he had learned. As a student, Napoleon devoured books of all kinds. When he was finally admitted on a scholarship to a French military academy and later to the Military College of France, his reading enabled him to stay near the top of his class.

Napoleon's career was one meteoric rise from poverty to power, and then an almost equally swift decline. When he was defeated by the English at Waterloo in 1815, Napoleon was made prisoner and taken to St. Helena, an isolated island in the south Atlantic. With him were his jailers from Great Britain, Austria, Russia, and France, four companions to keep him company, a doctor to keep him well, and twelve servants.

At first, Napoleon tried to make the best of things, but in time he became bored and irritated. When he was called general, not emperor, he became furious. When his letters to his son in Austria were unanswered, he grew sick at heart. Napoleon tried to work and to dictate his memoirs, but ill health dogged his footsteps. His legs swelled. His energy flagged. He knew death was not far away. He wrote a will in which his last request was that his ashes might rest on the banks of the Seine, "in the midst of the people I so greatly loved." Napoleon died at the age of fifty-two, but twenty years were to pass before his body was returned to France as he had wished.

the Clergy. To regain the confidence and support of Church leaders Napoleon made an agreement with the pope. The *Concordat* [kon kôr′dat] (the agreement) made Catholicism once again the official religion of France. In exchange for the Concordat, the pope gave up all claims to the lands taken from the Church by the National Assembly.

Napoleon gave his attention to making France more beautiful. He undertook many public works, improved the roads, dug canals, and deepened harbors. He

Napoleon crowns his wife Josephine empress. At his own coronation Napoleon took the crown from the pope and placed it on his head. He wanted to prove that he alone had earned the right to wear it.

tried to enlist the support of prominent people for these jobs. To get their support, he established the now famous Legion of Honor, which honors people who have made outstanding contributions to France.

Because of his successes at home and abroad, the people were ready to give Napoleon whatever he wanted. He wanted to be First Consul for life, and this amounted to a dictatorship. France agreed. He wanted to become emperor. Again, the people agreed. By 1804, Napoleon, Emperor of France, was looking for new worlds to conquer.

What Napoleon Did In Europe

An emperor frequently needs new victories to remind himself and the people of his greatness. Napoleon started war with Great Britain (1803) and, later, most of the nations of the world became involved. On land, Napoleon was usually successful against the British, but on the sea the British admiral, Horatio Nelson, defeated Napoleon. Admiral Nelson's naval victory over the French at Cape Trafalgar [trä fal gur] was one of history's outstanding sea battles. It proved that Great Britain controlled the seas.

On land, the battles at Austerlitz, Jena, Friedland, and Wagram ended as significant victories for Napoleon. Napoleon became the most feared person in Europe, and France became the continent's most powerful nation.

Napoleon tried to reorganize Europe so that France could keep its powerful position. He united the German states into the *Confederation of the Rhine* and placed his relatives on many of the European thrones. With Alexander I of Russia, Napoleon made a strong alliance for mutual protection. By 1807, Europe was in Napoleon's palm. But Great Britain remained a threat to him.

Napoleon's Empire

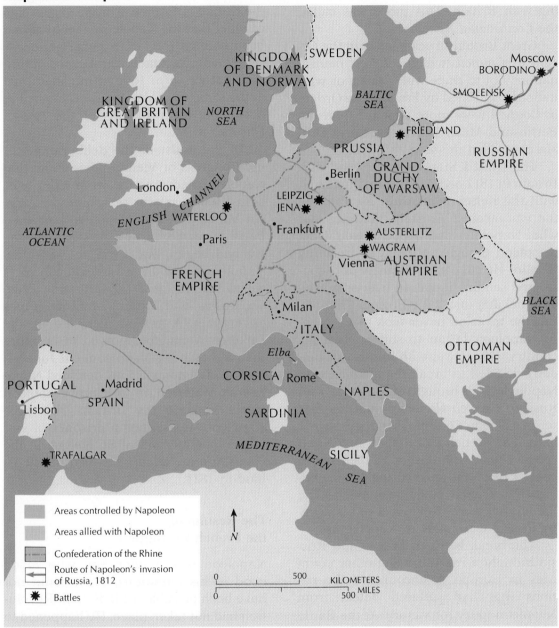

Napoleon's Empire extended over much of Europe.

- Napoleon united the German states. What was the union called and where was it located?
- About how many kilometers (miles) is the distance between Paris and Moscow?
- The Battle of Trafalgar was fought off the coast of what country?

The Final Defeat of Napoleon

When he failed to defeat Great Britain by military means, Napoleon decided he would crush what he called the "nation of shopkeepers." He would prevent Great Britain from trading on the continent of Europe. In his *Berlin Decree* and *Milan Decree,* Napoleon ordered all the countries under his control to stop trading with Britain. This move was called the *Continental System.*

Great Britain struck back with the *Orders in Council,* which ordered neutral nations not to trade with France or with nations controlled by France. The Orders in Council were more effective than the Berlin and Milan Decrees because Britain controlled the seas.

The United States went to war with Britain in 1812 because Britain interfered with the rights of neutrals. By entering the war against England, America did what Napoleon had hoped it would do. Napoleon thought seriously of invading Britain. He prepared his army and considered sending it over in balloons or by a tunnel dug under the English Channel. But the invasion never took place.

Napoleon began to suffer when his country went to war with Russia. Alexander I decided to break the alliance with Napoleon. This brought about a war with Russia in which Napoleon met his first serious defeat. Conditions in Russia were hard. The French had to fight in ice and snow. The Russians shot at them from behind trees and burned their cities before the French could take them. The French fell back. The defeat of his army by Russia was costly to Napoleon.

The break between France and Russia brought a reaction from other countries in Europe. It encouraged the nations that had suffered defeat from Napoleon to try for victory. At the Battle of Leipzig in 1813, these nations combined to inflict another serious defeat on Napoleon. He was forced to give up the emperorship and was sent to live on the tiny island of Elba in the Mediterranean Sea.

After the defeat of Napoleon, the monarchs in Europe were restored to power, and peace was reestablished. Louis XVIII, one of the older brothers of Louis XVI, became king of France. At the restoration of the Bourbon kings to the throne of France, Europe gave a sigh of relief that the Napoleonic menace had been banned forever. A generous peace settlement was made with France. A brilliant gathering of foreign ministers met at the *Congress of Vienna* for the purpose of solving the problems of the rest of Europe.

In the midst of the deliberations of the Congress of Vienna news came that Napoleon had escaped from Elba and, with 1,500 men, was marching on Paris. On March 20, 1815, Napoleon reentered Paris. It seemed as if a new Napoleonic era had begun, but it did not last long. Napoleon's new drive to regain control is called the *Hundred Days.* Austria, Prussia, Russia, and Britain combined forces once again. A million men, led by the Duke of Wellington, proved to be more than a match for Napoleon. On June 18, 1815, Wellington's troops defeated Napoleon at Waterloo, in Belgium. Napoleon surrendered to the British. This time Napoleon was sent as a prisoner of war to the lonely island of St. Helena in the south Atlantic Ocean. He died on the island in 1821.

The Results of the French Revolution

Napoleon was a poor boy who made good in his ambitions. This would not have been possible if the French Revolution had not taken place. He happened to be in the right place at the right time. Although Napoleon destroyed political freedom as we understand it, he was responsible for saving and spreading some of the democratic ideas behind the French Revolution.

Under Napoleon there was general religious tolerance and equality before the law. Under the rallying cry of "Liberty, Equality, Fraternity," France experienced a growth of nationalism and patriotism. This feeling of national pride enabled soldiers and travelers to spread French revolutionary ideals to other lands.

But France failed to gain one of the most important features of democracy—political freedom. The French Revolution destroyed absolutism in government; Napoleon brought it back, not as monarch but as emperor. The French Revolution separated church and state; Napoleon joined them again. The French Revolution established free speech and freedom of the press; Napoleon took them away.

The democratic values of the French Revolution were only temporarily destroyed by Napoleon. These gains and ideas lived on to gather new strength after Napoleon himself was destroyed. Probably without knowing it or even without caring, Napoleon planted the seeds of revolution in other countries. In the soil of Europe and Latin America, these seeds took root—some grew strong, and some were crushed. The struggle for democracy went on after Napoleon's death.

Check in Here

1. Give three reasons for Napoleon's rapid rise to power.

2. What were Napoleon's major contributions to France?

3. How did Napoleon hope to defeat England? Why did he fail?

4. Why was Napoleon's invasion of Russia a mistake?

5. List three important results of the French Revolution that Napoleon's rule temporarily overturned.

REVIEWING THE BASICS

One reason the French Revolution came to France was that the French peasants were somewhat better off than peasants in the rest of Europe. Bankruptcy was the immediate cause of the French Revolution. Because the king grew desperate for money he was forced to call the Estates-General into session. On a tennis court, the Third Estate declared that it was the National Assembly of France and invited the First and Second Estates to join it. They did so, and agreed that voting would be done by individuals rather than by Estate. When, on the night of August 4, 1789, nobles agreed to give up some of their privileges it seemed as if a bloodless revolution had taken place. This was not the case, however. The Declaration of the Rights of Man essentially gave privileges to middle-class men. Peasants and workers had not been helped as yet.

Workers were disappointed in the failure of the revolution to provide them with any real benefits. They demanded that more be done. War provided an excuse to remove the king and to form a republic. In time the king was put to death. The queen, Marie Antoinette, was put to death not long after, during what has been called the Reign of Terror. Danton and later Robespierre led the Terror in which people who opposed the violence of the revolution were killed at the guillotine. Danton and Robespierre were later themselves killed. The Terror gradually ended and a five-person Directory was set up.

The Directory failed to solve the immediate problems of France. There was still prosperity at home to achieve and enemies abroad to defeat. Napoleon was successful in staging a palace revolution, or *coup d'état,* in which he wrested power from the Directory. He established a national bank, made peace with the Church, and centralized the educational and administrative systems of France.

In Europe, Napoleon was a superb general in defeating Austria, Prussia, and Spain. Napoleon was unsuccessful in defeating Britain at sea. Napoleon made a fatal mistake by invading Russia. The Russian winter and a long campaign combined to defeat him. The nations of Europe united against him, and he was finally defeated. He was exiled to St. Helena, where he died.

REVIEWING THE HIGHLIGHTS

People to Identify		
Louis XV	Marie Antoinette	Napoleon Bonaparte
Louis XVI	Georges Jacques Danton	Horatio Nelson
Madame Manon Roland	Maximilien de Robespierre	Alexander I
		Duke of Wellington

Places to Locate		
Trafalgar	Friedland	Elba
Austerlitz	Leipzig	St. Helena
Jena	Waterloo	Versailles
	Austria	

Terms to Understand		
Old Regime	Declaration of the Rights of Man	Committee of Public Safety
Estates-General	Declaration of the Rights of Women	Directory
National Assembly		Civil Constitution of the Clergy
cahiers	*assignats*	
National Convention	Concordat	Continental System
coup d'état	Napoleonic Law Code	Orders in Council
French Revolution	Republic of France	Congress of Vienna
bourgeoisie		
estates		

Events to Describe		
Tennis Court Oath	Battle of Trafalgar	Hundred Days
taking of the Bastille	Reign of Terror	Battle of Waterloo
march on Versailles	night of August 4, 1789	

1. Describe the main features of the Old Regime in France.
2. Why did revolution come first to the country of France on the continent of Europe?
3. What similarities could be found in the France of the Middle Ages and the France of 1789?
4. What was the main purpose in calling the Estates-General?
5. What complaints were made by the *cahiers?*
6. How did the Estates-General become the National Assembly?
7. How did the voting method in the National Assembly differ from that in the Estates-General?
8. How did the National Assembly try to solve the financial problems of the French?
9. How did the National Assembly weaken the Church?
10. How did the National Assembly please the peasants?
11. What was undemocratic about the Constitution of 1791?
12. Why was there dissatisfaction with what had been accomplished in the revolution up to 1792?
13. Why was the Reign of Terror begun?
14. What were some of the peaceful accomplishments of the National Convention?
15. Evaluate the role of women during the French Revolution.
16. Describe Napoleon's peaceful accomplishments.
17. Why was Napoleon unable to defeat Britain?
18. Why were the Orders in Council more successful than Napoleon's Berlin and Milan Decrees?
19. To what extent did Napoleon carry out or fail to carry out the ideals of the French Revolution?
20. How did the French Revolution prepare the way for other revolutions in Europe and Latin America?

THINGS TO DO

1. Research the biographies of leading women during the era of the French Revolution: Charlotte Corday, Madame Roland, Madame Condorcet, Olympe de Gouges, Madelaine Chabray. (A useful starting place: Sokolnikova, Galina Osipovna, *Nine Women: Drawn from the Epoch of the French Revolution.* Translated by H. C. Stevens. Freeport, New York: Books for Libraries Press. Reprint of 1932 edition.)
2. Write a letter to your cousin in the country in which you describe what you saw the day the Bastille fell.
3. Draw a cartoon of your own describing conditions before and after the French Revolution. Use the cartoons on page 340 as your guide. Try a cartoon showing the rise and/or the fall of Napoleon.

CARTOON A

CARTOON B

1. Which one of these cartoons may be looked upon as a cause of the French Revolution? Which of these may be looked upon as a result of the French Revolution?
2. What do the three figures in **Cartoon A** represent? How can you tell? What does this cartoon tell us about the relationship among the Three Estates?
3. How has the situation changed in **Cartoon B?**
4. Both cartoons were published in the year 1789. What event or events might have given the cartoonist ideas for drawing these cartoons in the eighteenth century?
5. What significance do you attach to the fact that the peasant is carrying a sword in **Cartoon B?**
6. Among the privileges the peasants wanted was the right to kill the animals that ate their crops. They were not allowed to kill animals because under the Old Regime, hunting was a privilege of the First and Second Estates. How is this wrong illustrated in **Cartoon A?** According to **Cartoon B** has this problem been solved?
7. What other groups in the Third Estate might feel in the same position as the peasant in **Cartoon A?** Why?
8. Make up titles for these cartoons.

View of the Belvedere, Vienna (detail) by Belotto

The Congress of Vienna and Its Aftermath: The Uphill Fight for Freedom in Europe and Latin America

Had you received an invitation to attend the Congress of Vienna, you would have been honored. It would have meant that you were at or near the top of the social and political ladder. At the Congress of Vienna you would have rubbed shoulders with kings and queens, dukes and duchesses, lords and ladies, princes, counts, and all kinds of diplomats. The Congress of Vienna was an important social and diplomatic event. It was, above all, the settlement that ended the Napoleonic Wars and brought peace to Europe.

When you reached Vienna, you would have found a holiday mood in the air. The members of the Congress of Vienna, as well as people throughout

Europe, felt that now they could relax. Europe had been freed from the grip of the French Revolution and Napoleon. The world which had been turned upside down could now be set rightside up.

The Old Regime that had been destroyed could now be partially rebuilt. The privileges that had been taken away could now be partially restored. Some of the land that Napoleon had won could now be returned to its rightful owners. Some of the monarchs Napoleon had removed from power could now be returned to their rightful thrones. In short, the members of the Congress of Vienna were determined to turn back the clock of history. Let us see how they went about their work.

THE CONGRESS OF VIENNA REDRAWS THE MAP OF EUROPE

The Work of the Congress of Vienna

Fox hunting by day, dancing by night, and parties in between took up the time of many delegates to the Congress of Vienna. Delegates who took time out for serious work were determined to redraw the map of Europe more to their liking. Among them was Prince Metternich [met′ər nik], the Austrian minister of foreign affairs, the host at the Congress, and its leading figure. Czar Alexander I of Russia (1777–1825), the ruler of the largest country at the Congress, had an influential voice in the discussions. Great Britain sent its war hero, the Duke of Wellington, who had defeated Napoleon, and Lord Castlereagh [kas′əl rā′], Britain's foreign minister. The king of Prussia was there, and so was Charles de Talleyrand [tal′ē rand′], the leading French policymaker and diplomat.

Talleyrand had the most difficult job. It was in his country that the French

Revolution had taken place, and it was his country that had been at war with Europe for nearly twenty-five years. France was the villain at the Congress of Vienna, and Talleyrand had to see that his nation was not punished severely. Talleyrand did his work very well.

The Big Four—Castlereagh, Metternich, Alexander I, and Talleyrand—wanted to turn back the clock. They returned to power the rulers whose families had been removed from the throne by Napoleon. The Bourbons, in the person of Louis XVIII (1755–1824), had already been restored to the French throne. The French king was not, however, an absolute monarch. In a charter he gave France, a two-house, lawmaking body was set up. It was made up of a *Chamber of Peers* and a *Chamber of Deputies.* The Deputies were elected by the very wealthy of France. Louis XVIII's was the most liberal monarchy in all of Europe.

Absolute kings in Prussia, Austria, Spain, and some of the smaller states of the Italian peninsula, were returned to the thrones from which they had fallen.

A meeting of the Congress of Vienna. These men determined the course of Europe after the Napoleonic Wars. Metternich stands at the left.

The Big Four at the Congress of Vienna wanted to stabilize the European governments and the political boundaries as they had been before 1789. They were not, however, always able to turn back the course of history. For example, rulers of many of the smaller German states never regained the thrones they had lost.

Besides trying to reestablish former monarchs in Europe, the Congress of Vienna wanted to repay each country for lands lost to Napoleon. Greed, however, rather than justice guided the thinking of the members of the Congress. Foreign delegates tried to get as much land as possible for their own countries, while Talleyrand of France tried to lose as little as possible. Due to his great diplomatic skills, Talleyrand was largely successful. In the end, France was merely reduced to the size it had been in 1790. This was little punishment indeed for the nation that had plunged much of the world into war.

In remaking the map of Europe, the leading foreign diplomats paid little attention to the wishes of the people. Russia was given Finland and part of Poland, and Norway was taken from Denmark and handed to Sweden. Holland acquired Belgium, and Austria obtained lands in northern Italy. Great Britain got the islands of Malta and Ceylon and the land at the southern point of Africa called the Cape of Good Hope. A *German Confederation* of thirty-nine states was formed, thus ending forever the Holy Roman Empire.

The Congress of Vienna thought it had reached its goal by making Europe similar to what it had been before 1789. The Congress wanted to be sure that its work would not be undone. The *Metternich System*, as the work of the Congress of Vienna was called, was designed to keep France from starting other wars. The Metternich system was only partially successful in rolling back the map of Europe to what it had been before the Napoleonic Wars.

To protect the settlement at Vienna, the leaders of Great Britain, Prussia, Russia, and Austria signed the *Quadruple Alliance*. The four nations agreed to act as the "fire department" of Europe. This

343

Europe After the Congress of Vienna, 1815

The Congress of Vienna redrew the map of Europe. Compare this map with the one on page 335.

- What areas did France lose in 1815?
- What territory did the Austrian Empire acquire in 1815?
- The Congress of Vienna united thirty-nine German states under what name?

means that they agreed to use their armies to put out the flames of revolution wherever they burned. The signers agreed to meet from time to time to see what needed to be done to hold back the tide of change.

The Congress of Vienna Evaluated

In some ways, the Congress of Vienna did its work very well. The chief delegates had come to redraw the political boundaries on the European map. They did. They had come to build a peaceful and stable Europe. They did. Except for revolutions which began to overthrow old governments, there were no big wars in Europe until the Crimean War of 1853. And there was no world war for a hundred years, until 1914. All this is to the credit of the Congress of Vienna.

Alexander I of Russia was an important member of the Congress of Vienna. He tried to do even more to control the course of history in Europe. Alexander was the author of the *Holy Alliance* and wanted the nations present to accept it. According to the Holy Alliance, nations would let God guide their relations. They agreed to help one another so that a peaceful world for all would be possible. Although most of the countries at the Congress of Vienna joined the Holy Alliance, they did so with tongue in cheek. They did not believe that the noble ideas of the Holy Alliance could be carried out.

More work of lasting merit may be credited to the Congress of Vienna. Switzerland was made bigger. Its neutrality was assured when the larger nations agreed not to send troops across its borders. The diplomats at the Congress of Vienna said that the Rhine River should be open to travel to all countries. They condemned the slave trade in which African blacks were captured and sold in North and South America. The diplomats at the Congress of Vienna were cautious people who had seen the violence of the French Revolution and hoped to avoid revolutions in the future.

The Congress of Vienna tried to kill the spirit of the French Revolution and nearly succeeded in doing so. But that spirit died hard. Liberty, Equality, and Fraternity were the goals of the leaders of the French Revolution. By liberty they hoped to write constitutions that would provide freedom of speech, freedom of the press, and freedom from the heavy hand of absolute monarchs. By equality they hoped that special privileges would be abolished. By fraternity they meant the unity of the people in wanting a better life and a free government.

Check in Here

1. List the leading figures at the Congress of Vienna.

2. What did the diplomats at Vienna try to accomplish?

3. To what extent were they successful in achieving their objectives?

4. Using the maps found on pages 335 and 344 identify the major territorial changes brought about by the Congress of Vienna.

5. What was the purpose of each of the following: **(a)** Quadruple Alliance; **(b)** Holy Alliance?

Alexander I of Russia. His troops defeated Napoleon's army.

REVOLUTION SPREADS TO EUROPE AND LATIN AMERICA

Why the Fight for Freedom Continued

It has been said that when France has a cold, all Europe sneezes. In other words, what happens in France influences most of the rest of the countries in Europe. To the Congress of Vienna, the French Revolution was a dangerous sickness. Despite the efforts of the Congress of Vienna to stop its symptoms, the fever of revolution spread to many other parts of Europe.

In Spain, Portugal, Naples, and Russia, revolutions broke out. In the first three, the forces of revolution made temporary democratic gains. But the Quadruple Alliance (with France as a replacement for Great Britain) sent troops to put out the revolutionary fires. The organized military troops of the Quadruple Alliance easily defeated the disorganized rioting mobs of revolution. So the gains that were made were soon lost.

After the death of Alexander I in 1825, revolution broke out in Russia. His successor, Nicholas I (1825–1855), was determined to be more of an absolute ruler than Alexander, and he ruthlessly put down the revolution. Not for him were the high ideals of freedom which the French Revolution had let loose. For the Russian people the fight for freedom was never won.

In 1821, the Greeks began their fight for independence from the Turks. The fierce eight-year struggle between Muslim Turkey and Christian Greece aroused the interest of the world. The poet Lord Byron gave up his life in the Greek cause. The victory of Greece over Turkey was due to help from Great Britain, France, and Russia. The Greek victory was not a complete one for democratic rule, since a king was put on the throne. However, it proved that the Metternich System was built on shaky foundations. The Metternich System was showing signs of not being able to hold back revolutions in Europe. The cracks in the Metternich System were particularly obvious because members of the Quadruple Alliance had come to the aid of the Greek revolution.

How Spain and Portugal Ruled Their Empires

The success of the United States in separating from England gave the Spanish colonies something to think about. They were dissatisfied with the heavy hand of Spanish rule. Wealth flowed from the Latin American colonies to Spain, but little wealth came back to the colonies. The colonists had no voice in government, and Liberty, Equality, and Fraternity remained dreams for them.

The kings of Spain and Portugal were absolute rulers in the New World, as they were in Europe. For Spain, the *Royal and Supreme Council of the Indies* was given the job of ruling the Spanish colonies in America. It was this group, made up of nobles and responsible to the king alone, that did the thinking for the colonies. The council made all the laws it thought were needed to control the colonies.

Establishing full control was no easy matter. It was especially difficult to control the islands of the Caribbean known in history as the *Spanish Main*. Until the eighteenth century this area was subject to frequent raids by Dutch, French, and British pirates. They plundered the Spanish Main and stole the gold and precious jewels the Spanish were stealing from the original inhabitants of Latin America.

After finally suppressing piracy, the Supreme Council expanded its control over Latin America. It established strong *Viceroyalties* each headed by a *viceroy* who was the king's representative. The viceroy had absolute power which was exercised from an elaborately maintained court. From here he ran the colonial activities, chose colonial officials, and controlled colonial justice. The area over which a viceroy governed was very great. For example, the Viceroyalty of Peru, one of the earliest established, controlled the former Inca Empire. From time to time, governmental visitors from Spain were sent to check the activities of the viceroy. But Spain was very far away and the viceroy was generally able to do as he wished.

To help the viceroy carry out his duties, and to limit his power, the Spanish government established the *audiencia* [ô′dē en′sē ə]. This advised the viceroy and served as a colonial supreme court. It was a kind of lawmaking body for the colony. It was to the viceroy what the Council of the Indies was to the king.

The Viceroyalty of New Granada had its capital at Bogotá and included the present-day countries of Colombia, Ecuador, Panama, and Venezuela. The Viceroyalty of the United Provinces of the Rio de la Plata, established in 1776, included Argentina, Paraguay, and the southern third of Bolivia. The Viceroyalty of New Spain consisted of Mexico, which at that time extended far into what is now the United States west of the Mississippi to the Pacific and into much of what is now Central America.

The Portuguese system of ruling its empire was similar to that of Spain. Portugal tried to regulate the trade and economy of Brazil very closely. It set up the Viceroyalty of Brazil which had a structure similar to that of the Spanish viceroyalties. The administration of Brazil from Portugal was far more flexible than that exercised by Spain over its colonies. Many local matters were left in the hands of the colonists.

Under Portuguese rule, Brazil never developed quite as prosperously as the

Workers on the estate of a Spanish viceroy in South America. In general, how were Indian workers treated by their Spanish conquerors?

Spanish colonies. Sugar, tobacco, cotton, and coffee became important crops. These crops were cultivated by Indians and by slaves who were brought to Brazil from Africa. Mining of gold and diamonds became important industries, but mining was not as important to Portugal as it was to Spain.

The Catholic Church was the major religious, cultural, and educational force in the colony of Brazil. Cultural life in Brazil, however, never became as rich and varied as it was in the Spanish colonies. Schools were not as numerous, and those who sought a college education had to get it in Portugal. In Brazil, Indians were fewer and Africans more numerous than in the Spanish colonies. Portuguese, African, and Indian populations mingled freely in the colony of Brazil. Because Portugal was more flexible than Spain in governing its colony, Brazilian dissatisfaction was therefore never as great as in the Spanish colonies.

How well did this strict system of colonial government work? Although Spain and Portugal eventually lost their colonies in the New World, their colonial empires lasted for more than 300 years. The Spanish and Portuguese system of governing a colonial empire had many strikes against it. For one thing, the New World was so far from home. Good laws written in Spain and Portugal were not always carried out in America. Able and willing viceroys and officials were difficult to find and were hard to keep in the colonies. They were generally eager to get rich quickly in the colonies and return to a life of luxury and ease in Spain or Portugal. Neither the Indians nor the colonial-born Spaniards nor Portuguese were given a chance to rule themselves. This closely supervised control by the parent countries became a source of friction between the colonies and the parent country.

How People Lived in the New World Empires

At first, the Spanish made slaves of the Indians in the New World. That slavery did not become worse was due to the good work of Bartolemé de Las Casas [də läs kä′säs]. He was a Spanish missionary who converted many people to Christianity and taught about the evils of slavery. The Indians became serfs who were as bound to the land as were the serfs of medieval Europe. They worked the *encomienda* [en kō′mē en′də] (estate) of a Spanish noble, on whom they depended for a minimum of food, clothing, and shelter. In time, this serfdom was made illegal. A system of forced labor was a feature of colonial life in the New World empires of Spain and Portugal.

The African blacks were treated even worse than the Indians. The Spaniards brought blacks from Africa to the colonies, where they were sold as slaves. Blacks remained slaves for hundreds of years. Las Casas, who was kind to the Indians, encouraged black slavery in the hopes that blacks would replace the Indian slave labor on farms and in mines. Blacks proved to be able farm workers, but Indians continued to be used for work in the mines.

A profitable form of trade came from the *asiento* [ä sē en′tō], which was a special trading privilege. The king granted this privilege to a person or a group of persons. It gave them the right to sell a certain number of slaves in the New World. Taking blacks from Africa against their will and selling them in the New World became a profitable business for Europeans.

The Spanish government allowed their colonies to do little manufacturing. Despite this restriction, the colonists developed a textile industry and wove beautiful cloth of cotton and wool. These textiles were valued for their design, quality, and color. Cloth, cigars, and wines were among the industries to be found in many of the Spanish and Portuguese colonies. In Peru and Mexico, large quantities of silver were mined. Precious stones such as emeralds were eagerly sought in the mines as were pearls in the Caribbean Sea.

The search for gold and silver lured adventurers to the New World. These people were impatient and not willing to earn wealth through farming, which took time. In time, farming increased and sugar cane, grapes, oranges, rice, and native products such as corn and potatoes were grown on plantations. A plantation system of agriculture developed, typical of Spanish and Portuguese America. A few Spanish landlords owned vast holdings and grew wealthy. However, they denied the peasants the right to own land.

Few rich people and many poor people were found in the colonial empires of Spain and Portugal. The officials who came from Spain to rule were at the top

Latin America, 1800

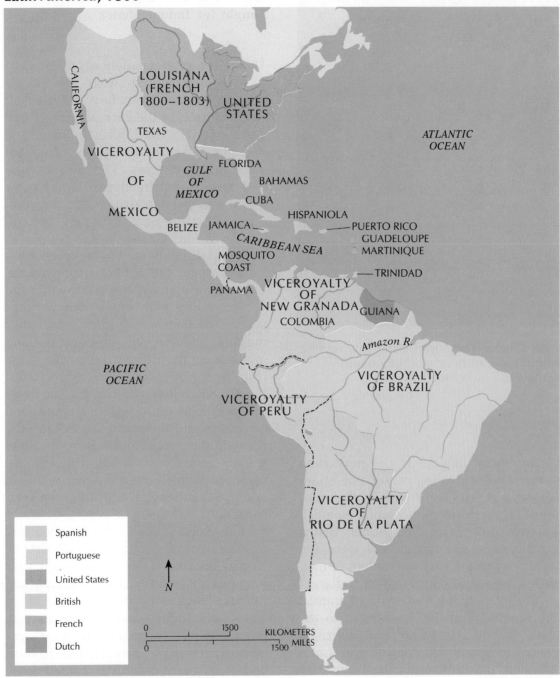

Latin America, 1800

CALIFORNIA

LOUISIANA
(FRENCH
1800–1803)

UNITED
STATES

TEXAS

VICEROYALTY

OF

MEXICO

GULF
OF
MEXICO

FLORIDA

BAHAMAS

CUBA

BELIZE   JAMAICA

HISPANIOLA

PUERTO RICO
GUADELOUPE
MARTINIQUE

CARIBBEAN SEA

MOSQUITO
COAST

PANAMA

VICEROYALTY
OF
NEW GRANADA

TRINIDAD

GUIANA

COLOMBIA

Amazon R.

ATLANTIC
OCEAN

PACIFIC
OCEAN

VICEROYALTY
OF PERU

VICEROYALTY
OF BRAZIL

VICEROYALTY
OF
RIO DE LA PLATA

Spanish

Portuguese

United States

British

French

Dutch

N

0   1500
                    KILOMETERS
0   MILES
              1500

- By 1800, Spain had lost what territory in North America? To help you answer this refer to the maps on pages 312 and 313.
- According to the map, Latin America was divided between what two countries? Refer to the map on pages 242–243 and explain why Latin America was divided this way.

A small silver llama from Peru. The promise of gold and silver attracted European settlers to South America.

of the social ladder. At the next rung were *creoles* [krē′ōlz], persons of Spanish descent who were born in the colonies. To these people, colonial Spanish America, not Spain, was home. Below the Spanish and the creoles were the *mestizos* [mes tē′zōs], or children of marriages between Spaniards and Indians.

Catholic missionaries accompanied the Spanish and the Portuguese to the New World. As Spain and Portugal gained firm political control over Latin America, they converted the Indians to Catholicism. Catholic missions became religious centers in many communities. They played an important part in trying to replace Indian values with Christian ones. Many of the missionaries were devoted people who were helpful in making the treatment of these people less harsh than it might otherwise have been.

Why Latin America Fought for Independence

The fight for independence is never easy. This is especially so when the people seeking independence have been under strict control. In the case of Latin America it was very hard because Spain and Portugal had ruled with an iron hand for three hundred years. The people, who had never tasted freedom, did not know that it was worth a struggle. In a revolution against the parent country, the colony needs the support of the people.

It was often difficult for revolutionary leaders to get full support from people. There were many racial groups that did not get along with one another. Some people felt they would merely exchange masters, and they saw no point in fighting. Among the whites, those who came from Spain opposed independence. But the Creoles clamored for it. Relatively few people in Latin America could read or understand the reasoning behind the revolutionary movement. Revolutionary leaders found it difficult to arouse the common people's interest and to tell them how independence would improve their condition.

The colonists of Latin America had as many complaints as the colonists of North America. They could point to a long history of unfair treatment and unfair taxes such as the *alcabala* [äl kä bä′lə] (sales tax). Rich people did not have to pay many of these taxes. The poor were often forced to pay heavily. The Spanish and Portuguese colonists wanted more freedom to trade, and they wanted laws that encouraged settlers to come and live in the colonies. Moved by the new ideas of the English, American, and French revolutions, the Latin American colonies finally revolted. The colonists wanted to get rid of the heavy yoke of Spanish and Portuguese rule.

The Fight
for Independence

The colonies of Latin America were ready to revolt. In Mexico the fight for independence was led by the Catholic priests Miguel Hidalgo [ē däl'gō] and José Morelos [mô rā'lôs]. In the course of the struggle, both men were captured and killed, but not before Morelos declared Mexican independence.

Agustín de Iturbide [dā ē'tür bē'dā] was a soldier of fortune who deserted the Spaniards when he saw a chance for fame and fortune. He joined the revolutionary forces. His fight against Spain succeeded, and he became emperor of Mexico in February, 1821. The empire that Iturbide hoped to rule included Central America as well as Mexico. This scheme satisfied no one and Mexico and Central America went their separate ways. After a brief attempt at a Federation of Central American States, the countries of Central America became completely separate and self-governing.

The fight for independence went on in Spanish America. Francisco Miranda [mē rän'də] (1756–1816), was a Venezuelan creole who had taken part in the French Revolution. He had learned the meaning of freedom and hoped to bring it to Spanish America. Miranda got his ideas from some of the most prominent people of the day. These included leaders such as Alexander Hamilton, John Adams, James Madison, and Thomas Jefferson in the United States, and Catherine the Great, the Czarina of Russia. Miranda was in touch with the revolutionary leaders in other parts of Spanish America, including Simón Bolívar and Bernardo O'Higgins. In the second of two attempts to free Venezuela, Miranda was captured and died in prison in 1816.

Miranda's ideas were adopted by Simón Bolívar [bô lē'vär] (1783–1830).

Bolívar had helped Miranda in a second try at revolution. This attempt failed, and Bolívar allowed Miranda to fall into the hands of the Spanish. Miranda was put in a Spanish prison for the rest of his life. Later, Bolívar became the hero of a great part of Latin America's fight for independence. Bolívar was a tireless worker. With the cry, "War to the Death!" he led his armies to victory. He succeeded in achieving freedom for the Viceroyalty of New Granada. He made the present-day countries of Colombia, Venezuela, Ecuador, and Panama independent of Spain.

In 1822, José de Sucre [dā sü'krā] was a follower of Bolívar. He freed Ecuador. Another revolutionary leader, José de San Martín [dā sän mär tēn'] (1778–1850), freed parts of Peru and Argentina. Bernardo O'Higgins (1778–1842) is the patriotic hero of Chile's struggle for independence. As a result of his work, the Spanish were finally defeated in 1818. O'Higgins was eventually ousted from power because of disputes over the reforms he wished to make.

How Brazil
Won Independence

The independence movement in Brazil took a different and somewhat more peaceful course. The coming of Napoleon's army to Portugal forced King John VI to flee to his colony of Brazil. King John declared the colony free of Portugal and an independent nation. While in Brazil John did much to improve conditions in his new country. The Brazilians, however, were displeased with him. He favored members of the royal family, and put Portuguese nobles, not Brazilians, into high offices. After Napoleon was defeated in Europe, the people of Brazil demanded that John VI go back to Portugal. A revolutionary army forced him to leave Brazil on April 26, 1821.

Simón Bolívar

(1783–1830)

Simón Bolívar was born to a wealthy family in Venezuela, where he lived and grew up. By the time he was nine, his parents had died. Bolívar grew up to become a rebellious and bold young man. His close friends taught him the need for revolution and urged him to prepare himself for the time when he would lead the fight for South American independence. (Much of South America was controlled by Spain.) Bolívar went to Europe several times, where he met some of the most important people of the day. He was especially impressed with Napoleon Bonaparte, whose crowning he witnessed in 1804.

The time for revolution was ripe in South America. Bolívar's call for volunteers was answered by soldiers of Venezuela and Colombia (then New Granada). With two hundred men on rafts, Bolívar pushed up the Magdalena River to a Spanish fort at Tenerife. Here, in the dead of night, Bolívar hid with his soldiers. He ordered them to make a lot of noise, and then demanded that the Spanish general surrender or be blown up by cannon. Thinking he was surrounded by a large army with cannon, the Spanish officer quickly gave up. Actually, Bolívar had no cannon and only a few soldiers, yet he won a brilliant victory.

This was only the beginning of Bolívar's gallant fight for the liberation of South America from Spain. Despite his successful efforts against Spain, Bolívar was regarded by some as a dictator. Others were jealous of the glory he had achieved. Revolts against his rule flared up all around him. One time Bolívar had at least five hundred men executed in order to put down a revolt. The cruelty which he used and the cruelty to which he had been subjected contributed to his becoming fatally ill. Bolívar died in poverty and loneliness.

Often called the George Washington of South America, Simón Bolívar was the father of more than one nation. Today, he is a national hero in Venezuela, Colombia, Panama, Ecuador, Bolivia (which is named after him), and Peru. For his military accomplishments Simón Bolívar is known as "The Liberator."

John VI left his son Dom Pedro I in charge of his colony of Brazil. The Brazilian Parliament demanded complete separation from Portugal, and some were eager to drive Pedro from Brazil. Determined to stay, Pedro declared, "I remain." That day, January 9, 1822, has been known to Brazilians ever since as "I Remain Day." In September, he proclaimed Brazil independent of Portugal. In October, 1822, Dom Pedro became constitutional emperor of an independent nation. A revolution for independence had been won, and scarcely a shot had been fired.

The Results of the Latin American Fight for Independence

The wars for independence were over in 1825. Some of the countries that emerged were larger than they are today. For example, Mexico and Central America were united, and Colombia included Venezuela, Ecuador, and Colombia. These nations were divided into a number of smaller ones. In time, the Latin American countries of today were formed.

The Quadruple Alliance (Russia, Austria, France, and Great Britain) threatened to punish the countries of Latin America that had broken away from their parent countries. A number of things prevented the Alliance from carrying out its plans. For one thing, the colonies were far away from the reach of the Alliance. For another, Great Britain, no longer a member of the Quadruple Alliance, was enjoying a rich trade with the new independent nations of Latin America. It did not wish to see them go back under Spanish control.

The United States thought it would be to its advantage to support the new nations of Latin America. In 1823, President James Monroe made a speech in which he warned Europe to stay out of the Western Hemisphere. This warning to the European nations came to be called the *Monroe Doctrine*. (See p. 535) The Doctrine supposedly had the support of Great Britain. No European nation immediately challenged the authority of the Monroe Doctrine.

In Mexico, the imperial government of Iturbide fell in 1824. The kind of government that would replace it was in question. After a period of violence and disorder, the revolutionary general Santa Anna [san'tə an'ə] gained control of the government as president. As a dictator, Santa Anna was without ability; as a man, without mercy; and as a patriot, without loyalty. Nevertheless, Santa Anna controlled Mexico until 1855.

Santa Anna lost the territory of Texas. In 1836, Texas declared itself independent from Mexico. It later became one of the American states. Santa Anna was defeated by the United States Army in the Mexican War in 1847. As a result of that war, Mexico gave up most of what is now California, Arizona, New Mexico, and Texas to the United States.

Argentina's history has been marked by military dictatorships and revolutions. For several years, 1829–52, Argentina was ruled by a dictator, Juan de Rosas [dä rô'sus]. Discontented groups drove him out and wrote a constitution like that of the United States. Unhappily, it did not work well in Argentina. The government remained largely in the hands of big landowners and cattle ranchers who controlled the politics of the nation.

When Pedro I of Brazil tried to get more power than the constitution gave him, he was forced from the throne in 1831. The government was left in the hands of his five-year-old son who became Emperor Pedro II in 1840. Under Pedro II's long and happy reign, Brazil made great progress. Slaves were freed, railways built, and coffee production

Latin America, 1825

By 1825, most of Central and Latin America were independent of European powers. (See also the map on page 349.)

- List two regions that were still European colonies.
- California and Texas were part of what empire?
- What was the name of the country on Mexico's northeastern border?
- What empire ruled most of eastern Latin America?

Emperor Dom Pedro II of Brazil.

Check in Here

1. List three complaints that Spanish Americans had against Spain.

2. Why did the revolutions described in this chapter take place in stages rather than all at once?

3. What was the importance of the Monroe Doctrine?

4. List three problems common to the countries that had freed themselves from the parent country, Spain.

5. How did Brazil become a republic?

THE REVOLUTIONS OF 1830 AND 1848 HAVE UNCERTAIN RESULTS

How the Revolutions Continued in the 1830s

The revolutions of the 1820s were not entirely successful in Europe. In the 1830s, another round of revolutions occurred. In France, the fever of revolution was again running high. Louis XVIII, who had been returned to the throne by the Congress of Vienna, knew that many people disliked him and the way he had become king. His reign could boast of few accomplishments.

When Louis XVIII died, his place was taken by Charles X (1757–1836), who tried to rule as an absolute monarch. Although he had the support of the nobility, his attempt to return to the days and ways of the Old Regime was a mistake. The French remembered their revolution, and so they knew how to deal with a king whose policies they opposed.

In 1830, the French revolted against Charles X when he tried to dissolve the Chamber of Deputies. They put up barricades, behind which they prepared to fight the army and the police if these forces came to the defense of the monarch. These preparations were unnecessary. Neither the army nor the police

was increased. Despite these gains, there was a large influential group that wanted no emperor at all. So, in 1889, Pedro II was driven from the throne and sent to live permanently in Portugal. In 1891, Brazil became a republic.

Earlier than most countries of Latin America, Chile developed a stable (if not always democratic) government. O'Higgins, the liberator of Chile, ruled from 1818 to 1823 as a dictator. He made so many enemies that a revolt forced him to resign. One weak government after another tried to maintain law and order, but each was unable to do so. Finally, in 1833, a group of business leaders, religious leaders, and landowners, led by Diego Portales [pôr tal'es], wrote a new constitution. With minor changes, it was the constitution of Chile until 1925.

would have fired on the people with whom they sympathized. Without bloodshed, the rioters captured the City Hall of Paris and prepared to take over the government of France.

Charles X began to worry. He pictured the beheading of Louis XVI. The guillotine was not what he wanted. Charles X fled to England for safety and left the throne to Louis Philippe (1773–1850). Because those who fought in the revolution of 1830 could not agree on whether or not to have a republic or a monarchy, the Chamber of Deputies decided upon a limited monarchy. But who would be king? The Chamber chose Louis Philippe, Duke of Orléans. The duke had been living in Paris as a member of the upper-middle class. He looked like a man who would not seek absolute power. Lafayette, a hero in Europe and America, supported Louis Philippe and played an important part in getting the people to accept another monarch.

The fever of revolution spread in Europe. Protestant Holland and Catholic Belgium had been joined by the Congress of Vienna in a union that was doomed to fail. In August and September of 1830, the Belgians rebelled and successfully drove out the Dutch. A limited monarchy was set up in Belgium, the neutrality and independence of which were guaranteed by the big powers. The success of the Belgian revolution widened the crack in the Metternich System. The Metternich System did not last long after this time.

In the United States, a revolution of another kind took place. In 1828, Andrew Jackson, a man of humble origins, was elected president. His election showed that the people had enough voice in government to elect one of their own to the highest office in the land. By 1828, nearly all white men could vote. Neither lack of property nor religious beliefs could keep a person from taking part in the government. The Jacksonian Era brought more freedom and a new democratic spirit.

The 1830 revolutions, like those of 1820, were not completely successful. France had a new king; Belgium won independence; America had a "people's" president. But elsewhere, in Poland, Italy, and Germany, the revolutions had failed. In those countries the Old Regime was still firmly entrenched. Privilege, absolutism, and autocracy remained.

How Revolution Continued in France

The revolutions of 1848 were far more serious than any since the French Revolution. In France, revolutionary fever was again high, as people were disappointed with Louis Philippe. He had started out being a man of the people, but as the years went by he became more interested in the affairs of the nobility. He became more and more a servant of the rich and a master of the poor. When depression and hunger came to France, as they did in 1848, people blamed Louis Philippe.

The French, particularly the Parisians, were used to revolution. Up went the barricades in 1848. This time the fighting was more than the rioting of 1830. Many people were killed and injured. Louis Philippe, having no wish to lose his head by the guillotine, soon packed and left for the safety of England.

The *Terrible June Days*, when the people were undecided about the kind of government to have, were at hand. For three days in June of 1848, France was torn by class war as the middle class and the working class fought one another for control of the government. The middle class won and its leaders fiercely put down the revolt.

A new National Assembly was formed. It gave France a constitution which gave all men the vote. France was

During the early nineteenth century, there were revolutions throughout Europe. In the United States, Andrew Jackson (shown campaigning) was elected president. Why may his election be considered revolutionary?

to have a one-house lawmaking body and an elected president. But who was the new president to be? When the votes were counted, the president was Louis Napoleon Bonaparte, a nephew of the great Napoleon. Louis Napoleon won because the people hoped for some kind of magic from this Bonaparte. Not long before, the body of Napoleon I had been brought home from St. Helena and placed with loving care in a huge and expensive tomb. It had been built to remind the French people of the glory Napoleon had brought to their nation. The election offered further proof that the name of Napoleon was still revered by the French.

For three years, Louis Napoleon governed as the first and only president of the Second French Republic. When he yearned to become emperor as his uncle had done, he arrested his enemies, dissolved the legislature, and asked the people to approve his acts. His name, however, continued to have magic. The French agreed to Louis Napoleon's request that the Second French Republic be replaced with the Second French Empire, with Louis Napoleon as emperor. Louis Napoleon married the beautiful and talented Eugenie of Spain. As emperor and empress they governed the Second French Empire until its downfall in 1871.

How Revolutions Continued in Europe

In Germany, the fight for freedom failed. In the city of Berlin, the barricades were put up as they had been in Paris, and many people were killed in the rioting. The rioters fought their way into the king's palace. They forced a frightened King Frederick to call a meeting for the purpose of writing a democratic constitution for Germany.

A meeting was held in Frankfurt to draft a constitution. King Frederick changed his mind before the Frankfurt Assembly could complete its work. Months of talk, differences of opinion, and unwillingness to compromise gave the king time to think over his situation. A fair constitution was finally written. It united Germany and made the king a limited monarch. But King Frederick turned it down. He believed he was king by divine right and would not take a crown offered by the people. Since there was no united revolutionary group to come to its rescue, the constitution born at Frankfurt died in infancy. The failure of the *Frankfurt Assembly* to establish the constitutional monarchy was a setback for the unification and democracy of Germany. It would be many years before Germany achieved these.

In Vienna, Austria, the barricades were up, and blood was spilled in the rioting. Metternich was forced to resign and had to leave the country. He hid in a laundry wagon and escaped to England.

Under Louis Kossuth [kos'süth], the Hungarians fought for independence from the Austrian Empire, but it was only partly successful. A constitution granting freedom of speech, freedom of press, and freedom of religion was written as a result of the revolution. The Hungarians were guaranteed a lawmaking body of their own. Russian troops finally came to the aid of the Austrian Empire, and the Austrians put down the Hungarian revolt.

The Results of the Revolutions of 1848

The year 1848 was a year of revolution on the continent of Europe. Everywhere the forces of democracy made a slow, uphill fight with little immediate progress. Nevertheless, the revolutions showed that democratic ideas had great strength and would not quickly die. The revolutions of 1848 taught that careful planning was necessary before a revolution could succeed. Too often the people who fought for freedom also fought among themselves about their goals.

Europe, nevertheless, was free from the Old Regime. Metternich was overthrown, and his system of absolutism fell with him. The Old Regime had been defeated. Political action, the speaker's platform, and the ballot box became the means to achieve greater democratic reforms in Europe.

Check in Here

1. Why did the French become dissatisfied with Louis Philippe?

2. Why did the French choose Louis Napoleon?

3. Why was the revolution of 1848 in Germany unsuccessful?

4. What were the results of the revolution of 1848 in these two countries: (a) Hungary; (b) Austria?

5. Summarize the results of the revolutions of 1848.

REVIEWING THE BASICS

The Congress of Vienna tried to redraw the map of Europe. It restored monarchs who had lost their thrones to Napoleon. The Congress also tried to compensate those countries that had been defeated by Napoleon by giving them new lands elsewhere. In the main, the Congress of Vienna did its work well. Because of it there was no world war for a hundred years. Its real intention, however, was to return to the days of absolutism and the Old Regime. A revolutionary period from 1820–1850 upset the peace.

During the 1820s, Greece won its independence from Turkey, and Latin American colonies won their independence from Spain. In America, Andrew Jackson was elected president, reflecting the popular democracy in the United States. During the 1830s, Belgium and Holland were separated from each other; and in France, Louis Philippe became a monarch with limited powers.

In the revolutions of 1848, Louis Napoleon replaced Louis Philippe, only to become, in due course, an emperor as Napoleon Bonaparte had been. In Germany, there was so much debate about the kind of government to have that the German emperor was able to play off one side against the other and retain his crown and his absolute power. German unification and democratization would have to wait many years.

In Russia, autocracy continued until 1916. Hungary made an unsuccessful attempt at independence. In Austria, Metternich was finally forced from power, and with him fell what he had built, the Metternich System.

REVIEWING THE HIGHLIGHTS

People to Identify

Prince Metternich	King John VI	José San Martín
Alexander I	Charles X	Andrew Jackson
Lord Castlereagh	Louis Philippe	Louis Napoleon
Duke of Wellington	Nicholas I	King Frederick
Charles de Talleyrand	Francisco de Miranda	Louis Kossuth
Louis XVIII	Bernardo O'Higgins	Pedro I
Miguel Hidalgo	José Morelos	Pedro II
Agustín de Iturbide	Símon Bolívar	Santa Anna
		Bartolemé de Las Casas

Places to Locate

Vienna	Malta	Brazil
Frankfurt	Turkey	Mexico
Finland	Berlin	Bolivia
Norway	Hungary	Venezuela
Denmark	Peru	Chile
	Spanish Main	

Terms to Understand

Quadruple Alliance	German Confederation	viceroy
Holy Alliance	Second French Empire	Metternich System
audiencia	creole	alcabala
encomienda	mestizo	Second French Republic
Frankfurt Assembly	asiento	Monroe Doctrine
Royal and Supreme Council of the Indies	Congress of Vienna	

Events
to Describe

"I Remain Day"

Terrible June Days

revolutions
of 1848

Mastering
the Fundamentals

1. What was the purpose of the Metternich System?
2. Why was Talleyrand's job at the Congress of Vienna a difficult one?
3. How did the Congress of Vienna turn back the clock?
4. Explain how greed influenced the members of the Congress of Vienna in repaying the countries that had lost land to Napoleon.
5. To what extent did the Congress of Vienna succeed in achieving its purposes?
6. In what ways was the Holy Alliance different from the Quadruple Alliance?
7. What was meant by "Liberty, Equality, and Fraternity"?
8. To what extent were the revolutions of the 1820s successful?
9. Describe the Latin American fight for independence as it took place in two countries.
10. When did the Greeks win their fight for independence?
11. Why did Britain and the United States support Latin American independence?
12. How did the monarchy of Louis Philippe differ from that of Charles X?
13. How did Belgium gain independence?
14. Why did the French people become disappointed with King Louis Philippe?
15. How did Louis Napoleon become president of the Second French Republic?
16. Why was the Frankfurt Assembly a failure?
17. Why was the Quadruple Alliance called the fire department of Europe?
18. Why might the Congress of Vienna be described as a summit meeting?
19. Why were Charles X, Louis Philippe, and Metternich forced to flee to England?

THINGS TO DO

1. Using the map on page 344 draw a map of your own showing the major changes of the Congress of Vienna.
2. Using the Almanac and other references indicate the size of the population of the leading countries of Europe in 1848.
3. Hold a "Meet the Press" conference in which a group of student reporters questions Metternich immediately after his arrival in England after having been driven from power in Austria.

Below are two opinions about Prince Metternich, whose influence on Europe between 1815 and 1848 was probably greater than that of any other individual. As you read each passage, keep the questions that follow in mind for class and group discussions.

Prince Metternich

He was a statesman of unusual proportions: the greatest foreign minister that Austria ever had, and one of the greatest masters of international politics in the history of the modern European states. . . . He lifted Austria from its deepest downfall to a proud height. . . . He had the greatest part in bringing it about that for thirty years Europe enjoyed comparative international peace, and that during that time, in the center of the continent, learning and art could have a period of the most salutory*, quiet cultivation*; capital and the spirit of enterprise* could undergo a strong increase, and . . . religious communities could experience intensification and consolidation*.†

The question has often been raised whether he was not rather a good diplomat than a statesman. The question appears to be thoroughly justified: he lacked virtually all the characteristics necessary to a real and great statesman—courage, resolution, strength, seriousness, the gifts of breadth of vision, the correct evaluation of the fruitful forces of the future, in brief, everything creative. . . . All revolutions, he held, came not from economic misery or dissatisfaction with bad political conditions, but arose from the secret societies, visionaries*, and doctrinaires*. The new, world-moving forces, the idea of national self-determination, counted for nothing with him. Peoples, in his eyes, were "children or nervous women," "simpletons." Liberalism* to him was a "spectre"* which must be banished by forceful action, a mere fog, which would disappear of its own accord.‡

Vocabulary

salutory—helpful	visionaries—people	liberalism—belief
cultivation—improvement	who see visions	in reform of political
enterprise—business	doctrinaires—people	and social institutions
consolidation—unity	who hold rigid ideas	spectre—ghost

1. How is it possible for two writers to describe the same person in such different terms?
2. Which of the two views comes closest to reflecting your own view? Why?
3. Which of the two seems to present the stronger case? Why?
4. How would you try to find out which of these views was closer to the truth?

†Quoted in Joseph R. Strayer and Hans W. Gatzke, *The Mainstream of Civilization* (New York: Harcourt Brace Jovanovich, Inc., 1979), p. 548.
‡Quoted by Henry F. Schwarz, (Ed.) *Metternich: The "Coachman of Europe,"* (Boston: Heath, 1962), pp. 15–16, 22–23.

1. Prepare a "You Are There" program based on one of the following topics: (**a**) the execution of Charles I; (**b**) the Battle of Trafalgar; (**c**) the Battle of Austerlitz; (**d**) the Retreat from Moscow; (**e**) the Battle of Waterloo; (**f**) the opening of the Congress of Vienna; (**g**) the trial of Galileo; (**h**) the building of St. Petersburg or Versailles.

2. Write an illustrated biography on one of the following scientists: (**a**) Copernicus; (**b**) Galileo; (**c**) Newton; (**d**) Descartes; (**e**)Boyle; (**f**) Lavoisier; (**g**) Priestley; (**h**) Cavendish; (**i**) Harvey.

3. Discuss Newton's contributions to science with your science teacher and then prepare a report for your history class explaining Newton's Laws.

4. Report on one of the following: *The Three Musketeers; Gulliver's Travels; Robinson Crusoe.*

5. Prepare a "Meeting of Minds" program in which you talk with the following absolute monarchs: (**a**) Louis XIV; (**b**) Peter the Great; (**c**) Catherine the Great; (**d**) Maria Theresa; (**e**) Frederick the Great.

6. As a war correspondent, write an article describing some of the battles fought by Prussia under Frederick the Great.

7. Prepare a "Meet the Press" program in which reporters interview one of the following: (**a**) Sully; (**b**) Richelieu; (**c**) Voltaire; (**d**) Locke; (**e**) Rousseau. Indicate the questions that might be asked and the answers that might be expected.

8. Prepare oral reports on warfare during the period 1750–1850 on one or more of the following topics: (**a**) Strategy and Tactics in Naval Warfare; (**b**) Supplying an Army in Battle; (**c**) The Organization of Armies and Navies.

9. Imagine that you have been sent as a reporter to visit Napoleon in his final exile at St. Helena. Report to the class on what you found.

10. Draw cartoons which sum up your impressions of one of the following: (**a**) the chief reasons for the fall of Napoleon; (**b**) the chief results of the Glorious Revolution; (**c**) the chief aims of the Vienna Congress.

11. The Congress of Vienna was a social as well as a political event. For the fashion column of a newspaper, prepare an article on the latest men's and women's clothing at that time.

12. History is full of ifs. Describe how history might have been different if one of the following had occurred: (**a**) if Cromwell had become king; (**b**) if George Washington had become king; (**c**) if the Bastille had not been taken; (**d**) if Louis XVI had made a successful escape; (**e**) if Bolívar had been defeated.

13. Draw a cartoon illustrating the purpose and strength of the Monroe Doctrine.

BIBLIOGRAPHY

Baker, Nina. *He Wouldn't Be King*. Vanguard Press. A simple biography of Simón Bolívar.

Baker, Nina. *Peter the Great*. Vanguard Press. A well written and easy-to-read story of the life of a brilliant but ruthless ruler.

Baker, Nina. *William the Silent*. Vanguard Press. The story of William the Silent in Holland's fight for freedom.

Camelot, Andre. *Queen of France*. Harper & Row. A sympathetic account of the life of Marie Antoinette.

*Costain, Thomas. *Ride with Me*. Doubleday & Co. A fascinating tale of adventure based on the fortunes of Napoleon's armies in England, France, Russia, and Spain.

Churchill, Winston. *A History of the English-Speaking Peoples: The Age of Revolution*. Dodd, Mead & Co. The story of English, French, and American revolutions as seen through the eyes of the English.

*Dickens, Charles. *A Tale of Two Cities*. The Macmillan Co. A famous English novel based on heroism and sacrifice during the French Revolution.

*Dumas, Alexander. *The Three Musketeers*. Dodd, Mead & Co. A thrilling book of adventures in the days of Louis XIII.

Durant, Will and Ariel. *The Story of Civilization: The Age of Rousseau; The Story of Civilization: The Age of Voltaire*. Simon & Schuster. These books are in the famous series by the Durants. They can be selectively read by students.

*Forester, Cecil. *Lord Hornblower*. Little, Brown & Co. A tale of naval warfare during the Napoleonic Wars.

Foster, Genevieve. *George Washington's World*. Charles Scribner's Sons. A simple account of how the events in Europe affected the colonies in the eighteenth century.

Fraser, Antonia. *Royal Charles*. Knopf. A friendly look at the reign of Charles II.

Guedalla, Philip. *The Hundred Days*. Grosset & Dunlap. A magnificently told story of the hundred exciting days when Napoleon tried to regain the rule of France.

Hackett, Francis. *Francis the First*. Doubleday & Co. A lively biography of Francis I of France.

Komroff, Manuel. *Napoleon*. Julian Messner. An easy-to-read biography of Napoleon.

Lamb, Harold. *The March of Muscovy*. Doubleday & Co. An account of the Mongols' and the Tartars' attempts to gain control of the Muscovite Empire from the Russians.

Lofts, Norah. *Queens of England*. Doubleday & Co. Exciting biographies of 45 queens of England.

Manceron, Claude. *Twilight of the Old Order*. Knopf. A readable anecdotal history of the French Revolution.

Peck, Anne M. *The Pageant of South American History*. McKay. A survey of the sweep of events in South America.

*Shellabarger, Samuel. *King's Cavalier*. Little, Brown & Co. An exciting story told against the background of Francis I of France.

Snyder, Louis L. *The Age of Reason*. D. Van Nostrand Co. A short but valuable book with extracts from important documents from the Age of Reason.

van Loon, Heinrich. *Life and Times of Simón Bolívar*. Dodd, Mead & Co. An account of the George Washington of South America.

*Weyman, S.J. *Under the Red Robe*. Grosset and Dunlap. A story told against the exciting background of France in the days of Richelieu.

*Indicates Fiction.

UNIT
IV

The Dominance
of Europe

The Triumph of Steam and Electricity, an English lithograph, 1897

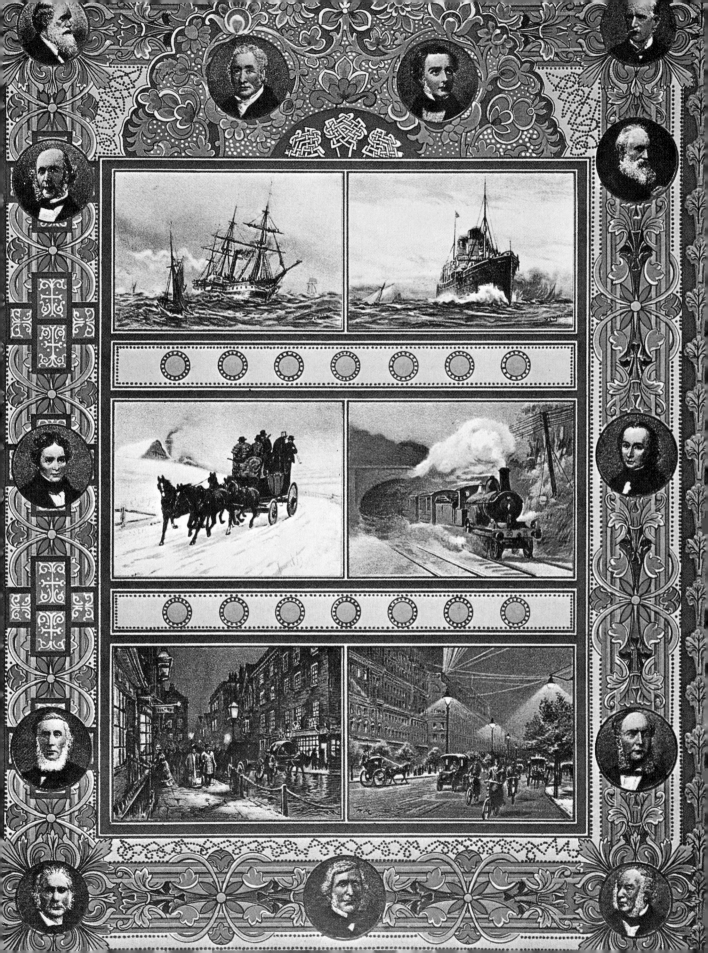

A village holiday in Europe

Nationalism: New European Nations Are Born

When you salute the flag or when you sing the national anthem, you express love for your country, or *patriotism*. After the French Revolution patriotism helped unite the French people and preserve the accomplishments of the revolution. Sometimes, however, patriotism is harmful. Hitler played upon the patriotism of the Germans to build up a strong military dictatorship.

The desire of a people to be a nation is called *nationalism*. The desire comes from common interests among people. Common language, common customs and beliefs, common literature, and common economic interests serve as ingredients in the cement which holds people together in a nation.

During the nineteenth and twentieth centuries, nationalism was a powerful force. Sometimes, nationalism made one nation out of many, as happened in Germany and Italy. Other times, nationalism broke up one nation into many, as it did in Austria-Hungary and Turkey. Nationalism has been a cause of war, as in World War I and World War II. Often it has encouraged colonies to seek independence from their parent countries, as in the cases of India, Indonesia, and the new nations of Africa. Nationalism takes many forms and may be used for good or evil purposes, but certain factors must be present before it can grow. Let us see what some of these factors are.

THE ITALIAN STATES UNITE

Barriers to Italian Nationalism

When Prince Metternich of Austria said that Italy was a "geographic expression," he meant that it was not a nation. Italy was divided into several states of different sizes. It could, therefore, be easily ignored. Italy was divided and offered no threat to the balance of power that existed in Europe.

After the Congress of Vienna in 1815, Italy was made up of nine states. The largest of these was Piedmont-Sardinia [pēd'mont sär din'yə]. The northern provinces of Venetia and Lombardy belonged to Austria; the pope ruled the Papal States in central Italy; and the rest of Italy was ruled by a number of foreign princes under the control of Austria.

There were many things that stood in the way of Italian unification, among them the geography of Italy itself. The Apennine [a'pen nīn] Mountains are like a backbone running down through the center of the country. They separate Italy, east and west. The Po [pō] River divides Italy, north and south. These physical features divided the country

and the people into sections and discouraged the growth of nationalism.

Nationalism was slow in coming to Italy for several reasons. Many people in Italy could neither read nor write. Because of this handicap, it was difficult to lead them and arouse their enthusiasm by written messages. The pope felt that a united Italy would interfere with his rights in the Papal States. The other states of Italy could not agree on who should lead in making Italy a nation. Nor could they agree on the kind of government to have after Italy had become a nation. Many European countries were afraid that a strong Italy would interfere with their plans. They, too, often stood in the way of Italy's becoming a nation.

How Italy Was United

Machiavelli, the Italian statesman, dreamed of an Italian nation. That was early in the fifteenth century. Not until the nineteenth century did this dream come true. Nationalism in Italy was encouraged by Italy's geography. Italy was separated from the rest of Europe by the Alps Mountains in the north, and it was

This is a nineteenth-century artist's view of the Po, Italy's longest river.

surrounded on three sides by water. This enabled the people of the boot-shaped peninsula to develop their own ways. Nationalism in Italy was encouraged also by Italy's history. Italy had been the home of the Renaissance, and Italians were proud of the contributions their people had made. They were also conscious of the shame brought on Italy by Napoleon's conquest. To be sure that Italy would not again be conquered, Italians sought strength through unity as a nation.

The joining of the numerous Italian city-states is called the *unification of Italy*. Italian unification centered around the following three men: Giuseppe Mazzini [mät tsē′nē] (1805–72), Giuseppe Garibaldi [gar′ə bôl′dē] (1807–82), and Count Cavour [kä vür′] (1810–61).

Mazzini, the prophet of Italian unification, was a young man violently in favor of a united Italy. During the revolutionary period of the 1820s and 1830s, he was a member of the *Carbonari* [kär′bə när′ē], a secret group which used

violence to obtain what it wanted. The Carbonari tried to unite Italy, but failed. Mazzini decided to try other ways to build a united Italy.

Mazzini formed a group, *Young Italy*, made up of young people whose job it was to arouse enthusiasm for a united nation. Its members made speeches and told the people what a great and good thing a united Italy would be. In 1848, Young Italy tried revolution, but this failed. Although Mazzini had to leave the country, his work was not a loss. He prepared the way for Cavour, who took more realistic steps to create a united Italy.

Camillo di Cavour, sometimes called the architect of Italian unification, wanted to do good things for his people. By making Piedmont-Sardinia strong and democratic, he set an example for a united Italy. Italy's greatest obstacle to unification was Austria. Sardinia could not unite Italy without outside help to defeat Austria. This help came from Napoleon III of France.

The Unification of Italy, 1859–1870

- How many years did it take for Italy to become united?
- When did the Kingdom of the Two Sicilies unite with other parts of Italy?
- What was the empire north of Venetia?
- What three territories did France possess in the region during the period of Italian unification?

First, Cavour had Sardinia join Britain and France against Russia in the Crimean War (1853–56). Britain and France won the war. Cavour then made an agreement with France that in case of war between Austria and Sardinia, France would help Sardinia. The Austro-Sardinian War followed the agreement. Napoleon III (the French ruler) suddenly changed his mind and withdrew his help, but not before Lombardy

(an Italian city-state) was united with Sardinia. Sardinia's success encouraged a number of smaller Italian states to revolt against Austria and join Sardinia in a growing united Italy. The tempo of Italian unification was increasing.

The Kingdom of the Two Sicilies (southern Italy and the island of Sicily) was a large area which had not yet joined Sardinia. A fiery leader named Giuseppe Garibaldi invaded the Kingdom of the

Two Sicilies. With his "Thousand Red Shirts" (soldiers), Garibaldi won Sicily for Italy. As victor, he could have kept Sicily for himself and become its emperor. In the interests of unification, Garibaldi urged the Sicilian people to join Piedmont-Sardinia under the leadership of Victor Emmanuel [i man'yü el], King of Sardinia. This move earned for Garibaldi the title "sword of Italian unification." On this page there is a cartoon interpretation of this event. Garibaldi hands over the conquered areas to Victor Emmanuel.

The next step in unification was the addition of the Papal States. This Garibaldi was eager to do. Cavour was opposed lest Garibaldi's attack bring about a conflict with France and the pope. Instead, Victor Emmanuel marched through the Papal States, conquered them, and stopped Garibaldi's further advance. Garibaldi, disappointed at not being allowed to conquer the rest of Italy, retired to his farm. Unification, however, was nearly complete.

In 1860, elections were held in all of Italy, with the exception of Venetia and Rome. In those elections, the Italians strongly supported a united nation. In 1861, in the city of Turin, representatives of a united nation formed a parliament and proclaimed the establishment of the Kingdom of Italy under Victor Emmanuel II. While the unification of Italy had been proclaimed, Italy was not fully united. Venetia still belonged to Austria. The pope still ruled Rome. Cavour died before these additions to a united Italy were made. Before his death, however, he realized that nothing could stand in the way of a united Italy.

In 1866, Italy fought with Prussia in a war against Austria. As a reward for helping Prussia defeat Austria, Venetia was made part of Italy. In 1870, with French troops away from Rome to fight in the Franco-Prussian War (see p. 375) Italian soldiers entered the city of Rome. Citizens of Rome greeted the Italian troops warmly. In an election the people of Rome voted strongly to join the Italian nation. In 1870, Rome also became the capital of a now fully united Italy.

The papacy, fearing the strength of a united Italy, had been against Italian unification, and later popes refused to work with the new government. They made themselves "prisoners" of the Vatican (center of the Roman Catholic Church in Rome). It was not until 1929 that an agreement with the Italian government was reached. In the agreement, the pope became ruler of a tiny area known as *Vatican* [vat'ə kən] *City*. The Church was paid for the loss of the Papal States.

RIGHT LEG IN THE BOOT AT LAST.

A nineteenth-century English cartoon comments on the unification of Italy. Who are the two figures in the cartoon? How can you tell?

Problems Faced by a United Italy

In February, 1861, Victor Emmanuel II became king of Italy as a constitutional monarch. Although Italy copied its form of government from that of Great Britain, its new government did not work well. Since the right to vote was limited to educated property holders of the upper-and middle-classes, most people could not take part in the government. Furthermore, because the pope was against Italian unification, many Catholics refused either to help or to take an interest in the government.

The lower classes, poor and uneducated, did not understand how people should behave in a democracy. Bribery and corruption were frequent, and many political parties made it more difficult for the nation to be well governed.

In addition to misunderstandings about the new government, Italy had many other problems. There were still Italian-speaking areas that were not united to the central government. There were some who felt that Italy should become a world power and fight for colonies. The country was poor in industrial development, agriculture, and natural resources. Prices were high, and people could not afford manufactured goods. All these conditions meant that Italy had a long, rough road before it.

Check in Here

1. Summarize the factors encouraging and discouraging the unification of Italy.
2. What did each of the following contribute to Italian unification: (a) Mazzini; (b) Garibaldi; (c) Cavour?
3. Why did the pope prefer a divided rather than a united Italy?
4. What problems remained in Italy after unification?

A GERMAN NATION IS FORGED

Factors that Stood in the Way of German Unification

Before the French Revolution, there were more than 300 German states; Prussia and Austria were the two biggest. At the Congress of Vienna the number of states was reduced to thirty-nine. The decrease in the number of states helped move the Germans toward unity. It encouraged a growing spirit of national patriotism.

There were many factors that stood in the way of German unification. Among them was Germany's neighbors. France, Germany's western neighbor, preferred thirty-nine weak states to one large nation. Austria, a German-speaking state to the south, also opposed unification. It knew that a united Germany would mean that Prussia, not Austria, would be the more powerful German state. Many of the rulers of the smaller German states felt that their power would decline if Germany were united. Hostility among the German states was increased by the still unhealed scars of the Thirty Years' War (1618–48), which set Protestants and Catholics against one another. Economic differences between the industrial states of the west and the agricultural states of the east also stood in the way of German unification.

Factors that Encouraged German Unification

Despite numerous obstacles, there were signs that pointed in the direction of a united Germany. Many German teachers, writers, and philosophers taught that Germany should become a great nation. Heinrich von Treitschke [trīch'kə] declared that in the future a German fatherland would be created. Other poets and writers, such as Goethe [gėrt'ə] and Schiller [shil'ər], taught the idea of a

A haymarket at Cologne, Germany. Cologne was part of the Zollverein.

common nationality to be shared by all Germans. This nationality included a common language, literature, and customs. German language and culture served to make the Germans look upon themselves as a nation.

A number of steps had already been taken which furthered the possibility of German unification. Napoleon had conquered much of Germany and had aroused the national hopes of many Germans. He had reduced the number of German states. He had combined them in a loose union, called the *Confederation of the Rhine*, with himself as protector. The Napoleonic Code had been adopted by the Confederation of the Rhine. It helped destroy what was left of feudalism, by encouraging uniform laws, jury trial, and religious tolerance. The Congress of Vienna had encouraged unity by forming a new *German Confederation* made up of about thirty-nine states.

A *confederation* is a loose association of states in which each state is practically independent. Thus, in the German Confederation each state had its own govern-ment, coinage, postal system, and taxes. Differences in laws made it difficult for one state to do business with another.

To do away with some of these problems and to increase trade, a tariff union called the *Zollverein* [tsôl′fer īn′] was set up among the German states in the middle of the nineteenth century. Those German states that were in the Zollverein agreed not to place taxes on goods coming from other member states. This trade agreement proved to be a good thing for all members. It showed what financial benefits a united Germany might bring.

How Bismarck United Germany

German unification was led by Prussia, and Prussia was led by Otto von Bismarck [biz′märk] (1815–98). The history of the unification of Germany centered around the actions and the personality of this man. Bismarck was a wealthy landowner who trusted neither the people nor democracy. William I, king of Prussia, called Bismarck to be his chief minis-

The Unification of Germany, 1866–1871

By 1871, Germany was one of the most powerful nations in Europe.
- What state led the drive for German unification?
- What region did Germany take from France in 1871?
- What lands included in the German Confederation were not part of the German Empire?

ter. He knew that Bismarck stood for absolutism, divine right monarchy, and the Protestant Lutheran Church. He felt that Bismarck could manage the Prussian Parliament that had been created in 1848. Bismarck soon made his policy clear. He said, "Not by speeches and resolutions of majorities are the great ques-tions of the time decided upon—but by blood and iron." Bismarck was ready to put his policy of blood and iron into effect at once.

First, Bismarck proved the strength of Prussia by winning a series of wars. The *Danish War* (1864), the *Austro-Prussian War* (1866), and the *Franco-Prussian*

War (1870–71) helped unify Germany. In the first war, Prussia joined with Austria and easily defeated Denmark. Then, when Prussia and Austria quarreled over the division of the spoils, they went to war with each other, as Bismarck had planned. Prussia was ready for this war, but Austria was not. Prussia won the Austro-Prussian War in seven weeks, and

Austria was removed as an obstacle to German unification. Following the defeat of Austria, the *North German Confederation* was created, with Prussia as its leading state.

Bismarck knew that a war with France would not only help unification but would prove popular, especially if he could get France to declare war on Prussia. If Prussia won such a war, the prestige of Prussia would be great, and those states that had not yet joined the North German Confederation would do so. Bismarck waited for a chance to fight France.

A revolution in Spain gave him the opportunity he wanted. When the leaders of the Spanish revolution drove their ruler from the throne, they offered the crown to a relative of the king of Prussia. For the crown of Spain and the crown of Prussia to be in the same family was dangerous to France.

Louis Napoleon, emperor of France, was successful in getting the German prince to refuse the Spanish crown. He remained dissatisfied, however. He sent an *envoy*, or special messenger, to William I of Prussia, telling him that the Hohenzollerns (William's family) must never accept such a crown. King William became impatient and sent the messenger away.

From the city of Ems, William I sent a telegram to Bismarck telling him of the demand made by the French envoy. The telegram gave Bismarck the opportunity to provoke France into declaring war on Prussia. Bismarck read the telegram, changed its wording, and had it printed in the newspapers. When the Prussians read it, they were angry that the French had made unfair demands upon their king. When the French read the same telegram, they felt that Prussia had insulted France.

The *Ems* [emz] *Dispatch*, as this message is called in history, brought about

An American cartoon done in 1887. Why is Otto von Bismarck shown as a juggler?

war between France and Prussia. This is known as the Franco-Prussian War. France declared war and, in so doing, made a very big mistake. Prussia was ready for war, but France was not. Prussia's victory over France brought Prussia the French provinces of Alsace and Lorraine and a huge sum of money, which France was forced to pay to cover the costs of the war.

The Franco-Prussian War completed the unification of Germany. The south German states had joined the North German Confederation to fight their old common enemy, France. In the palace of Versailles, in 1871, the German Empire was proclaimed, with William I of Prussia as emperor.

Problems Faced by a United Germany

The government of the German Empire was a federal union of states with the king of Prussia as the nation's ruler. A two-house legislature made the laws; but the upper house, made up of 61 members appointed by the states, was very powerful. The lower house, made up of 400 members, was chosen by *universal male suffrage* (the right of all men to vote). It had little power.

Germany was far from being a very democratic nation. It had a strong king who commanded the army and made government appointments. It had a powerful upper house that could override the wishes of the lower house. Bismarck, the Iron Chancellor, did little to encourage democratic growth. Soldiers were prominent in society, and army officers became influential in political affairs. Germany, now a united military nation, was eager to catch up with the big powers of the world in every way. Because of its success in doing so Germany was to prove a formidable opponent.

Bismarck tried to stamp out those who opposed him, especially the socialists, whom he hated most of all. First, he tried measures which made the socialist parties illegal. When these measures failed to wipe them out, he tried to win the support of the working classes by passing laws which made the lot of the workers somewhat better. Social security gave money to workers when they were too old to work. Health and accident insurance gave workers an income when they were sick or hurt. These workers' benefits were available in undemocratic Germany before they were available in most democratic nations. National and religious minorities, however, were persecuted. This was especially true of the Catholics, for whom Bismarck made life very difficult.

In the field of foreign affairs, Bismarck tried to isolate France by forming friendships with Austria and Russia. France would then be unable to seek revenge on Germany for its defeat in the Franco-Prussian War. Bismarck, however, was not able to carry out his plans. In 1888, William II became king and decided to be his own prime minister. The strong personalities of William II and Bismarck clashed. William II dismissed Bismarck in 1890 and began to carry out his own domestic and foreign plans. These were not always successful, and during his reign World War I began.

Check in Here

1. What factors encouraged and discouraged German unification?

2. How did Napoleon and Bismarck contribute to German unification?

3. What was the role of each of the following in contributing to the unification of Germany: (**a**) Zollverein; (**b**) Ems Dispatch; (**c**) Franco-Prussian War?

4. What were some of the problems that faced a united Germany?

THE AUSTRIAN AND OTTOMAN EMPIRES ARE SHATTERED

How Nationalism Broke the Austro-Hungarian Empire

You have seen that in Italy and in Germany, nationalism served as a cement to bind the people into nations. In Austria and in Turkey, nationalism acted as a hammer and broke those empires apart. Let us see what happened in the Austrian Empire and in the Ottoman, or Turkish, Empire.

Bismarck did not want Austria in a united Germany because Austria was a country made up of many nationalities. A *nationality* is a people who share common history, customs, beliefs, and language. They do not always have a country of their own. In the Austrian Empire, there were Germans, Hungarians, Italians, Russians, Poles, Czechs, Croats, and Slovenes. At one time or another these peoples had common histories handed down through legends. They were proud of their different backgrounds and each group wanted a country of its own. They were humiliated by German rule.

Austria was defeated first at the hands of Sardinia and later at the hands of Prussia. This encouraged the various nationalities in the Empire to ask for a greater voice in government and for independence. The Hungarians were the most numerous and influential people in the Empire. They demanded and were given a large measure of independence. Austria and Hungary made an agreement that established the *Dual Monarchy* of Austria-Hungary. Emperor Franz Joseph of Austria was to be the ruler of the Dual Monarchy. The agreement was called the *Ausgleich* [ous'glīkh].

The term Ausgleich is a German one which means compromise. This agreement of 1867 was a compromise between the wishes of Austria and the aims of Hungary. According to this agreement, each country was to have its own language and its own government. Emperor Franz Joseph of Austria was to be king of Hungary as well. Foreign affairs, war, and money matters were to be the same for both countries. In domestic matters, the separate peoples of Austria and Hungary were to govern themselves.

Austria and Hungary each had its own parliament which made up the laws. Each treated its subject peoples as it wished. Strangely enough, the Hungarians, who fought for their own rights when ruled by others, were not willing to give the same rights to the peoples they ruled. Hungarian children were favored in the schools. The Hungarian language was used in all newspapers and magazines to the exclusion of other language groups. Both Austria and Hungary were made up of different peoples with different languages and customs. The discontent of the peoples ruled by Austria and Hungary was to be one cause of World War I.

How Nationalism Broke Up the Ottoman Empire

Turkish rule in Europe extended to the city of Vienna, which the Turks nearly captured in 1683. The Turks ruled many peoples, including Arabs, Egyptians, Albanians, Slavs, Romanians, Bulgarians, and Greeks. The rulers of Turkey were Muslim. The countries of the Balkan Peninsula were, for the most part, Christian and belonged to the Greek Orthodox Church.

During the nineteenth century, Turkey had many domestic and foreign problems. Russian Czar Nicholas I called Turkey the "sick man" of Europe. Russia was especially eager to hasten the death of the sick man. In particular, Russia was eager to get control of Constantinople.

The Dual Monarchy and Ottoman Empire, 1867

- What two major countries made up the Dual Monarchy in 1867?
- Name two countries that shared borders with the Dual Monarchy.

Great Britain, however, sought to keep the sick man alive. Its business people felt that their trade with the countries of the Mediterranean region would suffer if Constantinople fell under Russian rule. Britons were also very fearful that Russian control of Constantinople would threaten British control of India. Most importantly, since the failure of Napoleon's invasion of Russia in 1812, Great Britain and France were afraid of Russia. They saw it as unconquerable and feared its size and its might.

The first to take advantage of Turkey's weakness were the Greeks. They succeeded in gaining their independence of Turkey in 1829. As Turkey weakened still further, Russia and France tried to annex (add on) Turkish provinces.

In 1853, Great Britain tried to prevent the breakup of Turkey at the hands of Russia. It sent troops to the Crimea [crī mē′ə], a Russian peninsula extending into the Black Sea. The *Crimean War* (1853–1856) was between Russia on the one hand and Turkey, Great Britain, France, and Sardinia on the other. Sardinia entered the war for its own purposes. (See p. 369.) England and France preferred to keep the sick man alive rather than let Russia gain control of Constantinople and the Dardanelles. The Dardanelles are the straits that connect the Black Sea with the Mediterranean.

There were heavy losses on both sides. Russia and Great Britain and France eagerly agreed to end the war. Diplomats met at Paris in 1856 and tried to work out a settlement. The lasting results of the *Treaty of Paris*, however, were not territorial. What is remembered is the attempt to limit the violence of war and to protect the rights of neutrals. These principles have often been viola-

Decline of the Ottoman Empire, 1867–1912

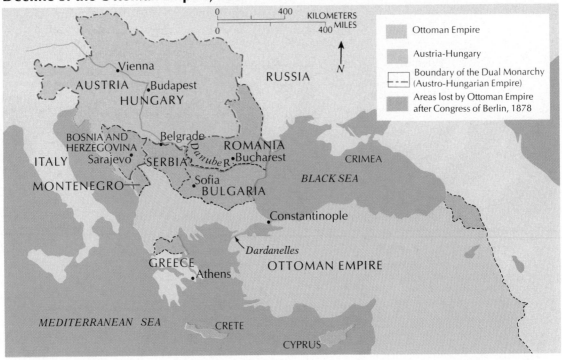

• Name two areas lost by the Ottoman Empire as a result of the Congress of Berlin.

ted. The Treaty of Paris, however, marks the first time an attempt was made to limit the cruelty that war encourages.

Russia tried again to get control of Constantinople in the *Russo-Turkish War* (1877-78). It easily defeated Turkey. At the *Congress of Berlin*, which ended the war, Bismarck presided as the so-called "honest broker." Bismarck claimed he wanted to see that Turkey was fairly treated. His plan was actually to prevent Russia from enjoying the fruits of her victory—taking over the Balkan countries. Instead, Montenegro, Romania, and Serbia gained complete independence; Bulgaria remained partly under the Ottoman Empire, but the northern part was allowed to govern itself. The island of Cyprus, which had belonged to Turkey, was given to Great Britian. Russia gained a province on the Black Sea. The former territory of Turkey was protected by the major European powers.

After World War I, some long-needed reforms were begun in Turkey. The reform movement was undertaken by Turkey's president, Mustapha Kemal Atatürk [at′ə tėrk′]. In seeking to build a strong, modern nation, Turkey borrowed Western ideas. In October of 1923, Kemal Atatürk declared Turkey a republic. In 1961, a new constitution made reforms and a Second Republic was established.

Check in Here

1. What factors encouraged the breakup of Austria and Turkey.

2. Was the Ausgleich a compromise that worked? Why or why not?

3. Why was Turkey called the "sick man" of Europe?

4. Why did Bismarck strive to play the part of the honest broker?

Mustapha Kemal Atatürk (1881–1938)

Latife Hanum and Kemal Atatürk

As a boy, the father of modern Turkey was known only as Mustapha. Against his family's wishes young Mustapha sought a military education. At military school he was popular among his classmates and looked upon as a leader. Because of his excellence in mathematics, his teacher gave him the name Kemal [ke mal], which means perfection. When he became the first president and virtual dictator of Turkey, the Turkish National Assembly voted him the name Atatürk. That means chief of the Turks. Mustapha was handsome and had great personal magnetism.

Mustapha married Latife Hanum [ha num], the daughter of a wealthy merchant. She had lived in Paris, spoke many languages well, and believed that women should not be forced to occupy positions inferior to men. Latife and Mustapha were married in a brief ceremony. It was said to be the first Turkish marriage in which both the bride and groom were present. Custom and tradition required that the wedding take place with the bride alone. The groom was present in name only. With Latife, Mustapha Kemal shared his thoughts and his plans for a modernized and Westernized Turkey.

Kemal Atatürk founded the Republic of Turkey. He was its president from 1923 to 1938. As president he sought to modernize his country. He freed Turkey from foreign influence and tried to establish friendly relations with Turkey's neighbors. Religious tolerance was encouraged. In 1928, the Latin alphabet was adopted in place of the Arabic script. Turkish citizens under the age of forty were expected to attend school to learn the new alphabet. In 1930, the name Constantinople, no longer the capital, was changed to Istanbul. In 1934, women were given the right to vote.

These changes were achieved over much opposition from those who wanted the old traditions. Wealthier classes were quicker to adopt Atatürk's modernization than were the poorer classes. Although modernization continues, Turkey became a different nation because of Atatürk's determination. Along with Sun Yat-sen (China) and Mahatma Gandhi (India), Kemal Ataturk ranks high. He was one of a group of Asian leaders who broke with tradition and led their countries to adopt new ways.

Modern History

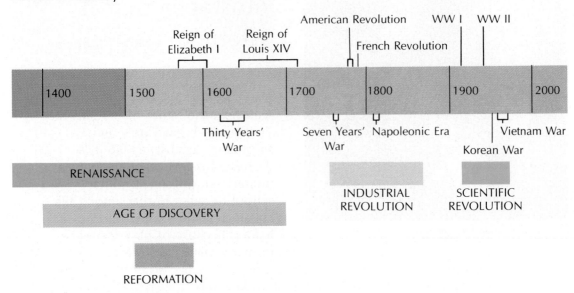

Be able to place the following events on the time line:

1861–65	American Civil War	1870–71	Franco-Prussian War
1867	Dual Monarchy established	1871	unification of Germany
1870	unification of Italy	1878	Congress of Berlin

THE CIVIL WAR PROVES THE UNITED STATES IS ONE NATION

How Nationalism Affected the United States

The Declaration of Independence was written in 1776, and a new government was established in 1789. At that time, it was by no means certain that the United States would succeed as a nation. Some people expected that after winning independence from England, the states would become separate and independent countries. Under the government of the Articles of Confederation, each state did go its own way. The national government could not force the states to follow the Articles of Confederation.

The *Constitution*, which was drawn up in 1789 to form a more perfect union, became the supreme law of the land. All the states agreed to follow the Constitution. A federal union was formed. The central government was given the right to tax, to raise an army, and to enforce the country's laws.

As time went on, the powers of the national government were questioned. The federal union was tested when the farmers of Pennsylvania rose in a rebellion against the right of the government to tax them. Later, Virginia and Kentucky questioned the right of the government to pass certain laws. In 1814, during the War of 1812, the New England states threatened to leave the nation. In 1828, South Carolina questioned the right of the government to enforce tariffs of which it did not approve.

In 1861, the South questioned the right of the government to limit slavery. The *Civil War* (1861–1865) between the North and South was a war over slavery. It was also a war over the question of the powers of the central government over the wishes of individual states. On November 19, 1863, following the Union army's victory at Gettysburg, Lincoln delivered his famous Gettysburg Address. These lines from that speech show that Lincoln believed that the war was a test of whether a united nation would endure.

Four score and seven years ago our fathers brought forth on this continent a new nation conceived in liberty and dedicated to the proposition that all men are created equal. Now we are engaged in a great civil war, testing whether that nation or any nation so conceived and so dedicated can long endure.

President Abraham Lincoln delivering the Gettysburg Address.

The disastrous Civil War ended in 1865. The nation, born in liberty in 1776, had been preserved. The federal union of states was not dissolved and would remain as a nation. The Civil War proved that the United States was indeed a solid union.

In the nineteenth century, nationalism helped to unite the United States just as it had Germany and Italy. Nationalism remains a vital force in world politics. Recent events in Africa and Asia cannot be understood without understanding nationalism. In later chapters, you will learn about the force of nationalism in the twentieth century.

While Europe and America were struggling to establish democracy and nationalism, they were also making revolutionary progress in industry and agriculture. It is to developments in these fields that we turn in the next chapter.

Check in Here

1. How was the authority of the new government of the United States established by the Constitution of 1789?

2. What were Lincoln's aims in the Civil War?

3. How was the Civil War a test of nationalism?

381

Nationalism refers to the desire of people with common interests, background, and history to become a nation. Sometimes nationalism shatters nations which have been joined together for many centuries, as in the case of Austria and Turkey. At other times, it joins countries together which had been separate for many centuries, as in the cases of Italy and Germany. In the United States, nationalism was tested in the great Civil War. The war was fought as much to save the union as to free the slaves.

In Italy, geographic factors contributed to keeping the independent states apart. The pope and Italy's neighbors (Austria and France) all sought to keep Italy a geographic expression. Under the leadership of Mazzini, Garibaldi, and Cavour, Italy was united in 1861 under Victor Emmanuel II.

In Germany, the move toward unification was led by Otto von Bismarck. Writers began to express the need for a German fatherland. A tariff union known as a Zollverein showed its members the economic advantages of working together. The customs union provided for trade among twenty-three German states including Prussia. For the states in the Zollverein there was no tax (customs) charged on products crossing borders. Under Bismarck, three wars for unification were fought: the Danish War, the Austro-Prussian War, and finally the Franco-Prussian War. These wars demonstrated Bismarck's approach to the problems of unification: namely, the approach of blood and iron.

Despite the existence of universal male suffrage in Germany, little was done to encourage democracy. Instead, a strong military state was established. When William II became king in 1888, he decided to be his own prime minister. Bismarck was dismissed.

Austria was a country made up of many peoples speaking different languages and having different traditions. There, nationalism served to make many nations out of one. The Ausgleich brought only a temporary compromise between Austria and Hungary. It held two countries together that would later separate. Under a common monarch, Emperor Franz Joseph, each country governed itself internally. Both left foreign affairs and related matters to the emperor. However, this compromise satisfied few people. Discontent among these people weakened Austria-Hungary and was one of the causes of World War I.

Turkey, the so-called "sick man" of Europe, was also made up of people whose customs, languages, and traditions were very different from one another. The Greeks, in 1829, were among the first to challenge Turkey and to successfully establish a nation of their own. During the Crimean War, England saved Turkey from defeat at Russia's hands. In the Russo-Turkish War of 1877–1878,

Turkey was easily defeated. Bismarck did not allow Russia to get as much control over Turkey as Russia would have wished. Montenegro, Romania, and Serbia gained independence, while Bulgaria remained mainly under Turkish rule. These arrangements barely kept Turkey alive. Under Kemal Atatürk, a new era in Turkish modernization began.

REVIEWING THE HIGHLIGHTS

People to Identify		
Giuseppe Mazzini	Mustapha Kemal Atatürk	Otto von Bismarck
Giuseppe Garibaldi		
Camilio di Cavour	Heinrich von Treitschke	William I
Victor Emmanuel II		William II

Places to Locate		
Apennines	Prussia	Montenegro
Po River	Alsace-Lorraine	Romania
Piedmont-Sardinia	Turkey	Serbia
Rome	Balkan Peninsula	Bulgaria
Papal States	Dardanelles	Cyprus
Kingdom of the Two Sicilies	Black Sea	Turkey
	Austria	
	Crimea	

Terms to Understand		
nationalism	United States Constitution	geographic expression
Confederation of the Rhine	universal male suffrage	Ems Dispatch
Zollverein		Treaty of Paris
blood and iron	Carbonari	Young Italy
Ausgleich	sick man of Europe	unification

Events to Describe		
Franco-Prussian War	Crimean War	American Civil War
	Congress of Berlin	

Mastering the Fundamentals

1. List the factors that usually encourage the growth of nationalism among a people.
2. What did Metternich mean when he called Italy a "geographic expression"?

3. Explain how patriotism can be both helpful and harmful.
4. How did the work of the Carbonari differ from that of Young Italy?
5. How did Italy's past history influence its desire for unification?
6. How did the Napoleonic Code help encourage German unification?
7. What is a confederation? Give an example from this chapter.
8. What kind of government did Germany establish after 1871?
9. Why was Bismarck known as the Iron Chancellor?
10. Why did Bismarck have laws to help the working classes?
11. Why was the arrangement between Austria and Hungary known as the Dual Monarchy?
12. What is especially memorable about the Treaty of Paris?
13. Although universal male suffrage existed in Germany, that nation was not democratic. Why?
14. What similarities exist between the effects of nationalism on Austria and Turkey?
15. Why did Britain want to keep the "sick man" of Europe alive?
16. Describe two ways the federal union of the United States was tested before the Civil War.
17. The union of the United States was tested by the Civil War. What were the results?
18. Was Bismarck's policy of unification by blood and iron wise? Why or why not?
19. Why has Austria sometimes been referred to as a "ramshackle empire"?
20. Why was the Ausgleich only a temporary agreement between Austria and Hungary?

THINGS TO DO

1. Debate: *Resolved:* Germany had a right to demand a huge payment from France because of German victory in the Franco-Prussian War.
2. Draw a map of Europe in 1875. Identify the major territorial changes that had taken place since 1815.
3. Draw your own cartoons, commenting on such events as: (a) the defeat of Napoleon III; (b) the practical results of the Ausgleich; (c) Atatürk's attempt to modernize Turkey; (d) Turkey as the sick man of Europe.

Study the cartoon below. It was taken from a nineteenth-century newspaper. As part of an individual or group activity answer the questions that follow it, either orally or in writing.

"Dropping the Pilot" by Sir John Tenniel

1. To which event does the cartoon refer? How can you tell?
2. In which country did the event referred to in the cartoon take place?
3. Who are the two figures in the cartoon? Justify your choice with evidence.
4. When did the event referred to in the cartoon take place?
5. What reasons might explain why it took place?
6. Does the cartoonist appear to be expressing an opinion? How can you tell?

Watt steam pumping engine, English coal mine, 1790s

People, Money, and Machines: The Agricultural and Industrial Revolutions

By the turn of a switch, a home can be lighted. With the flick of the thumb, a skyscraper can be automatically heated. With the turn of a key, an automobile can be started.

Modern forms of energy and power may not seem unusual to you. You see them all around you every day. Yet, not many years ago, heating or lighting a home was a difficult task. Railroads, airplanes, and automobiles were unknown. It was not long ago that human and animal muscles were the main sources of power.

The great changes that took place in farming and manufacturing have been described as revolutions. Today, science and technology are being applied to new fields of activity. It may be said that we continue to live through revolutions in transportation, communications, and manufacturing. We travel and transport goods via jets that fly faster than the speed of sound; we communicate via satellites; and we manufacture products with the help of computers.

Today, fossil fuels such as oil are more difficult and more expensive to obtain. Nuclear and solar power are possible answers. How we shall provide for the long term energy needs of planet earth is a major problem for our time. Today, the advances of technology are so enormous that we must pick the areas we wish to develop. Will people make wise choices? Let us examine the choices those who came before us made.

THE INDUSTRIAL AND AGRICULTURAL REVOLUTIONS IN ENGLAND

The Industrial Revolution

During the later Middle Ages, physical work was done in small shops under the direction of craft guilds. On feudal manors it was done under the supervision of an overlord. With the discovery of the New World, wealth grew and commerce increased. There was a greater demand for the world's goods. With this increased demand for goods, merchants began to seek new ways to produce more manufactured products. People who had large amounts of money bought raw materials, which they gave to workers whom they hired to make the finished products at home. In the *domestic system,* as this arrangement was called, workers owned simple machines such as spinning wheels or hand-operated looms. They manufactured cloth and yarn. In time, the domestic system could

no longer meet the demand for manufactured goods, and it became necessary to invent faster methods of production.

The necessity of producing manufactured goods on a large scale prompted the invention of many new machines which were driven by new sources of power. The domestic system could not make use of these new inventions. The machines were too expensive to be owned by any one worker and too big to be kept in a home. Because the operation of these power-driven machines did not call for much skill, large numbers of unskilled workers could be hired. The new steam-powered machines and large numbers of unskilled workers were housed in large buildings called *factories.* This change from the domestic system to the factory system and all the effects that followed has been called the *Industrial Revolution.*

Revolution—a word that you have seen before—may be defined as a big or complete change. In previous chapters, you read about the English, American, and French revolutions, in which big changes in government were made. In England, an absolute monarchy became a limited constitutional monarchy; in America, a group of colonies became an independent nation; and in France, a kingdom became a republic.

The Industrial Revolution was a different kind of change. First of all, the Industrial Revolution was an economic rather than a political change. That is, it brought about changes in how goods were produced and in how people earned a living. Second, it was a gradual and not a sudden change. People knew when the American Revolution and the French Revolution took place. They were probably not aware that an industrial revolution was going on at the same time.

Between 1750 and 1850, Great Britain was the home of the Industrial Revolution. While the Industrial Revolution is most often associated with England, it was not confined to that nation. Instead, it took place in many countries of Europe and in the United States. It spread to other parts of the world as well.

How the Way Was Prepared for the Industrial Revolution

The Industrial Revolution was a gradual rather than a sudden development. Because it was gradual, some historians think that the term revolution is inaccurate. Those who hold this view maintain that the technology for the industrial revolution began developing long before 1750 and in countries besides England.

Between 1550 and 1750, an industrial age began to emerge in many European countries. New improvements in mining methods made mining one of the oldest and earliest of the large-scale enterprises. Iron ore and coal were particularly important minerals. Coal provided the energy to make iron into new forms of machinery. Other minerals mined included tin, lead, and copper. Coal mines were large-scale enterprises that required hundreds of workers. By the mid-seventeenth century coal mines were dug deeper, and provision had to be made for draining water from them and allowing air into them.

The mining of coal required that this heavy but cheap source of energy be carried cheaply over great distances. The locomotive was still in the future, but the technique of putting down parallel railroad tracks was known. Along these tracks, or wagon-ways as they were called, horse-drawn wagons were pulled. By the mid-eighteenth century, a network of tracks was widespread in England and Western Europe.

These wagon-ways were forerunners of the modern railroad age. The burning of coal led to the making of iron and steel products. Efforts to remove water from the mines led to the widespread use of steam. In these ways, England, other European countries, and America were made ready for the coming of an industrial revolution.

Why the Industrial Revolution Began in England

England was the birthplace of the Industrial Revolution. It was the only country with the conditions necessary for a change from the domestic system to the factory system. There was a plentiful supply of labor for new factories. A wealthy class of merchants used its money to invest in new businesses and inventions. England was blessed with good harbors, natural resources, and a favorable climate. The moist climate was an advantage for the textile industry. Without moisture in the air, cotton threads broke easily. England's abundant supply of natural resources included coal and iron. Coal was used as a

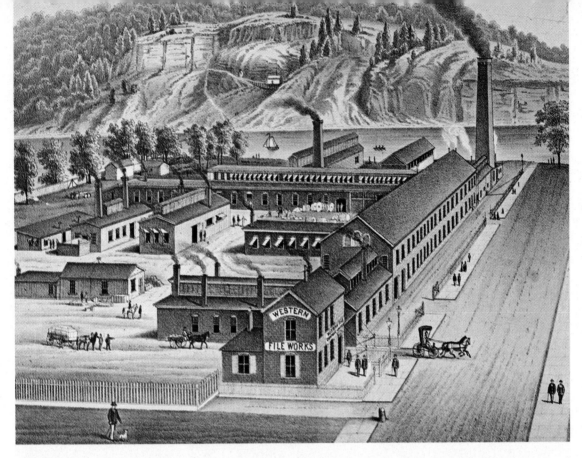

Western file works, Beaver Falls, Pennsylvania. The Industrial Revolution spread from England to other Western European countries and to the United States. By the late nineteenth century, the United States was a leading industrial nation.

power source to drive the new machines of the Industrial Revolution. Iron was used to build machines and tools. The goods produced by England's factories had markets at home and in the far-flung colonial empire.

England had skilled workers who learned how to operate and repair the new machines. England also had large numbers of unskilled workers who wanted to work in factories rather than on farms. A number of changes in agriculture forced many farm laborers into the cities. Improved methods of agriculture made large-scale farming possible. Small farmers, unable to compete, joined the labor force needed by the Industrial Revolution.

Manufactured goods sell best in areas where many people have the money to buy them. England's large population provided a good market for textiles, furniture, household utensils, saddles, coaches, and farm implements. In addition to the home market, England had many colonies where people were willing to buy these manufactured goods. Good markets at home and abroad did much to aid the growth of the Industrial Revolution.

The Industrial Revolution was based on the use of water and steam power applied to new machines. In the early stages of the Industrial Revolution, the machines were run by water wheels, which were turned by running water from creeks and rivers. In the first part of the nineteenth century, steam engines were used to supply the energy for machines. Coal, which was needed to

Interior of an early cotton mill in Manchester, England. Why did the mechanization of the textile industry result in increased production and profits?

produce steam, was so plentiful in England and so important to England's wealth that it was called black gold. Iron ore was another important natural resource that supported the Industrial Revolution. England had a supply of iron ore, too. Iron ore provided the raw material for iron and steel tools and machines.

England was a united country with a democratic government. The interests of the middle class were important to Parliament and to political leaders. The middle classes were important to the growth of factories and industry. They were not as important in other countries. Because England enjoyed longer periods of peace than most countries in Europe, it was able to make use of the industrial changes that were taking place.

Inventions that Changed Life During the Industrial Revolution

Historians could probably not agree on which inventions have had the greatest influence on our lives. There are many important inventions which made great changes in the way we live. As you read, decide whether or not you agree with the choices made.

Among the inventions that contributed to the growth of the textile industry are the following. John Kay's *flying shuttle* (1733) increased the speed of weaving, and James Hargreaves's [här grēvz'] *spinning jenny* (1764) increased the speed of spinning yarn. The spinning jenny made many threads at one time. It was an improvement over the spinning wheel that spun only a single thread. Richard Arkwright [ark′rīt] invented the *water frame* (1769). For the first time, water power was used to drive the spinning machine. This machine spun thread more quickly than ever before. In 1779, Samuel Crompton's invention of the *spinning mule* was an improvement over both the spinning jenny and the water frame. The *power loom* (1785) invented by Edmund Cartwright to weave yarns into cloth made use of water power to drive it. The demand for cotton textiles grew rapidly. In 1793, Eli Whitney (an American) invented the *cotton gin*, a machine which quickly separated raw cotton from seeds. In 1769, James Watt improved on the earlier steam engines. By the beginning of the nineteenth century, this remarkable source of power, the steam engine, was running looms for the manufacture of cloth. This meant that more cloth could be produced.

Just as important as the inventions in the textile industry were those in the coal mining industry. The mining of coal was a dangerous job. Coal gas inside the mine exploded when exposed to open flame. Sir Humphrey Davy's *safety lamp*, invented in 1816, enabled miners to see where they were going. At the same time, it kept them safe from explosions because the flame of the lamp was enclosed. Engineers provided for air in mine tunnels and strengthened the tunnels. They increased mining safety and the amount of coal mined. While coal mining remained a dangerous job, coal was the base upon which the Industrial Revolution rested.

Inventions also furthered the growth of the iron industry and manufacturing. When iron comes from the ground, it has many impurities which must be removed by a blast furnace. As blast furnaces became increasingly larger they produced iron in bigger quantities. Iron was used in bridges, buildings, and machinery.

Nevertheless, a stronger material was needed in construction. Steel soon came into widespread use.

By 1800, the manufacture of steel was possible. Its production was so expensive, however, that for the first half of the nineteenth century steel was scarce. In 1856, Henry Bessemer [bes′sə mur] invented a process which changed iron into steel by removing still more of the impurities. Steel took the place of iron as the most important product of the Industrial Revolution. A later improvement in the making of steel was the *open-hearth* process. It was cheaper and could handle larger amounts of iron than the Bessemer process.

Industrial growth cannot take place unless people and materials can be moved quickly and cheaply over long distances. The need to move things from place to place resulted in many changes in transportation and communication. Great steps were made in land transportation. John McAdam, a Scot, improved roads by using crushed stone which, when spread on the road surfaces, made them passable in rainy weather.

Also important were the inventions of steam-powered trains and boats. Horse-drawn rail cars were rather common in England by 1820. In 1829, George Stephenson invented a steam locomotive. Steam power was also successfully used by Robert Fulton on a steamboat. His steamboat, the *Clermont,* made a successful trip up the Hudson River in 1807. In 1840, the first transoceanic crossing under steam power took place. By 1860, it became clear that the days of the sailing vessel and horse-drawn vehicles were numbered. Steam-powered vehicles had taken the lead.

Cheap but quick postal service was provided by the government of Great Britain in 1840. Other nations followed in improving and in speeding up the delivery of mail. The development of cheap

Robert Fulton's steamboat, the *Clermont,* made a trip up the Hudson River in 1807.

newspapers made possible the spread of information needed in daily business activities. "What hath God wrought?" was the first telegraph message sent by Samuel F.B. Morse in 1844. In 1876, Alexander Graham Bell spoke through his new invention—the telephone.

How a Revolution in Agriculture Began

The *Agricultural Revolution* contributed to and accompanied the Industrial Revolution. Before the eighteenth century, English farmers farmed separate strips of land in a number of fields. In addition, they shared common lands to feed their livestock and woodlands for timber to heat their homes. The *open field system,* as this was called, was good for small farmers who grew food for their own use. It was not good if food was to be grown inexpensively and sold to people living in cities or even in other countries. If farming was to be made more efficient,

the open field system would have to be eliminated.

The *enclosure movement* took place between the sixteenth and eighteenth centuries in England. Lands that had been scattered in several fields were enclosed or combined into a single farm under a single ownership. Lands that were held in common, such as pasture land and wood land, were also consolidated, or enclosed. Between 1702 and 1797, literally thousands of laws were passed by Parliament encouraging the enclosure of millions of acres of English farmland.

The enclosure movement encouraged the development of new inventions, since a single owner was now free to experiment with land on a single farm. Land so consolidated could be used more efficiently and productively. However, with every enclosure act of Parliament, some poor farmers were driven from the land. They did not benefit from the consolidated farms, and what was left to them was too small for providing for their own needs. These poor farmers often left the land, headed for the city, and became skilled or unskilled workers. They worked in the factories developed during the Industrial Revolution. The farmers still on the land sought better and more efficient ways of farming.

The search for improved and easier farming techniques led to an Agricultural Revolution in England. Later, the changes in farming methods adopted in England would spread to many other countries. During the seventeenth century, the usual way of planting was simply to scatter the seeds by hand. Many of the seeds, unevenly scattered on top of the soil, did not grow into plants. In 1701, Jethro Tull invented a drill for planting seeds in straight rows.

About the mid-eighteenth century, Viscount Townshend [toun'shend] told farmers that they should periodically change the kind of crops grown in the same soil. *Crop rotation*, as this method is called, makes it possible for the soil to retain valuable minerals and stay fertile longer. Robert Bakewell taught farmers how to breed and produce the kinds of cattle that gave better beef and dairy products.

Many improvements were made in farm machinery. Steel plows took the place of wooden ones. The *reaper*, invented in 1834 by Cyrus McCormick, made it possible to cut grain more rapidly than a farmer could cut it with a hand scythe. The reaper was designed to cut and tie the grain into bundles. The *thresher* was a stationary machine designed to strip the grain from the stems. In the twentieth century, a mobile machine called the *combine* performs several of these jobs. It cuts the grain and separates the seed from the stems in one operation. The new inventions, plus the use of natural and chemical fertilizers, were outstanding developments of the Agricultural Revolution.

"OUR FIELD IS THE WORLD."

LIGHT DRAFT. SUPERIOR DESIGN.

CLEAN AND RAPID CUTTER.

McCormick Harvesting Machine Co., Chicago.
ESTABLISHED 1831.

An early advertisement for a McCormick reaper. How did this invention help the business of farming?

Check in Here

1. What is meant by the term *revolution,* as in the term Industrial Revolution?

2. Give three reasons why the Industrial Revolution took place first in England instead of somewhere else?

3. Identify three inventions that greatly contributed to revolutionary changes in industry.

4. Identify three inventions that greatly contributed to revolutionary changes in agriculture.

5. Describe the direct relationship between the Industrial and Agricultural Revolutions.

INDUSTRIAL AND AGRICULTURAL REVOLUTIONS BRING GOOD AND EVIL

Benefits of the Agricultural and Industrial Revolutions

The comforts we take for granted were not even imagined during the early part of the eighteenth century. More and better food, shelter, and clothing are the significant beneficial results of the Industrial Revolution and the Agricultural Revolution. Because of machines, we have comforts and even luxuries which Louis XIV did not have in his fabulous palace at Versailles. Not only is better clothing available, but more is available and at prices many people can afford. This is true of hundreds of items in use in our daily lives. For the most part, living conditions for the average person have improved greatly in those countries where the Industrial Revolution and Agricultural Revolution took place.

As living conditions in the industrialized countries improved, population increased and cities grew in number and size. The increase in population was due in large part to the fact that the death rate was lowered as health conditions improved. People's lives were bettered in cities by public sanitation and police protection. City life was made more pleasant by the benefits of public libraries and the inspiration that came from the mingling of different peoples.

Another favorable result of the Industrial Revolution was the creation of new forms of business. The most important new form of business organization was the *corporation*. A corporation is a business organization. It is formed by people who are given permission by the government to sell shares of *stock* (certificates of ownership) in the corporation to the public. The sale of stock gives the purchaser part ownership in a corporation. In this way, the corporation can raise more money than a single individual is likely to have.

Why are people willing to buy the shares of corporation stock? People invest their money in the hope that the corporation will make a profit. If the corporation does make a profit, it pays *dividends* (shares of the profits) to each of the stockholders. The stock shares may also increase in value. People who have small amounts of money can own a share in business and get some of the rewards. The stockholder also shares the risk of a loss. If the company does not make a profit, the stockholder may receive no dividend and the value of his or her stock may also decline. The corporation is a widely used form of business organization.

Before the Industrial Revolution the English population was divided into fixed classes. There was a small upper class (the very rich), a small middle class (the moderately wealthy), and a large lower class (the poor). The Industrial Revolution made possible the rise of a powerful middle class which owed its position in society not to birth but to its ability to gain wealth. If ability rather than birth was the key to financial success, then it was possible for poor but ambitious people to grow rich.

Scientific farming methods and the use of machines helped increase food supplies and thereby reduced the threat of hunger. Railroad and steamship facilities brought fresh foods to the dinner tables of Europe, America, and to some people in other parts of the world.

The Industrial Revolution made possible better care of the sick and the aged. Better hospital facilities were provided by cities and towns. New medical equipment became available for the sick and for those wounded on battlefields.

The use of machines meant that many people had more time for education. The hours of labor for factory workers usually allowed them some time off for holidays and vacations. Public schools, paid for by taxes, became common. The public schools made it possible for workers' children to learn to read and write and perhaps get better jobs. When compulsory education was adopted, sending children to school was a way of keeping them out of the factory. Workers realized that education was a means of self-improvement. The industrial and agricultural revolutions performed a service by placing at our fingertips the means to improve and enjoy the world.

Problems Caused By the Agricultural and Industrial Revolutions

There was another side to the Industrial Revolution that was not so pleasant. Although the middle class was in the saddle, that saddle was worn by the workers of the lower class. The middle class had economic power and high hopes that they could gain political power. The workers, on the other hand, often considered their position hopeless.

Workers were mainly concerned with wages, hours, and conditions of work. During the early period of the Industrial Revolution, wages were so low that a factory worker could not support a family. Women and children had to do factory work alongside men. Working hours were long—fourteen to sixteen hours a day. Factories were unhealthy and dirty places with little light or circulating air. Since machines were expensive and labor was cheap, the machines were often more carefully protected than the people who ran them. Many factory owners provided no safety devices. Often the work was dangerous, and accidents were frequent when unskilled workers came in contact with the machines. This was particularly true when workers got tired and careless after the long hours. The factory owners could punish, through fines or beatings, those workers who failed to keep up with the work.

To make matters worse, employment was uncertain since it depended on the demand for whatever the factories made. Because sickness was frequent, workers could not always count on a full week's pay. Not only did they lose wages, but in some cases workers paid fines for being absent. A worker might escape paying a fine for an absence if he or she could find a substitute.

There was much unemployment as new machines took the place of people. Workers who lost their jobs because a new machine could do it better found it difficult to learn a new trade. Frequently, laborers started riots against the introduction of machines which could reduce the need for labor.

While factory conditions were bad, with low pay, long hours, and poor working conditions, conditions were not much better in the homes. Cities were growing rapidly; often buildings were built faster than streets or water and sewerage systems. In every large industrial city, workers lived in wretched

In the nineteenth century, there were artists and writers who portrayed the evils brought about by the Industrial Revolution. Gustave Doré made many engravings that showed how the different classes lived in London. His scenes of crowded slums convey human misery.

slums. Whole families often occupied one room which was too hot in summer and too cold in winter. Stuffy and unsanitary, these living quarters were breeding places of crime and disease. During the eighteenth century, when industrialism began in earnest, government did nothing about improving the living conditions of the working classes.

Many farmers who owned small farms could not afford to use the new farm machines. Nor could they compete with those farmers who did use machines. In the past there had been a *common,* an area farmers could use to pasture cows and sheep or to cut trees for firewood. With the coming of farm machines, the common land was absorbed into large farms, adding to the suffering of small farmers. To survive the competition, owners of small farms did one of three things: (1) they kept their farms and worked harder to produce a small income; or (2) they gave up their farms and became poorly paid farm workers; or (3) they went to the city in search of factory jobs.

Farm machinery made it possible to grow food in great quantities at low prices. Because English landlords wanted to get high prices for their grains (rye, barley, oats), they tried to keep cheaper foreign grain from coming into England. The landowners had a great deal of influence in Parliament and were able to get the *Corn Laws* passed. These provided for taxes on grain that came from other countries. (All small grains— wheat, barley, oats—in England are called corn. Very little corn is raised in England.)

The Corn Laws made the prices of bread and cereals unnecessarily high. The Corn Laws were good for the landlords but bad for the workers and for the factory owners. Factory owners would have liked cheap grains so that they would not have to pay high salaries to their workers. When the factory owners became more powerful than the landowners, the Corn laws were finally dropped in 1846.

Check in Here

1. List three beneficial results of the Agricultural and Industrial Revolutions.

2. List three harmful results of these revolutions.

3. Why are some people often willing to invest their money by buying stock in a corporation?

4. How did the Industrial Revolution lead to the creation of slums?

5. Why were the Corn Laws good for landowners but bad for factory workers and factory owners?

PROPOSALS ARE MADE FOR THE PROBLEMS OF INDUSTRIALISM

How Laissez Faire Helped the Factory Owners

Factory workers and small farmers faced poor living and working conditions, unemployment, and starvation. Some people believed that the Industrial Revolution had to be brought under control or its evils would ruin the lives of people who could not escape.

Many people saw the evils that industrial change had brought. However, there were those who said that these evils would not last long. Long hours, poor living conditions, and unemployment would be corrected. They thought that if industry and farming were left to themselves, everything would work out in the long run. It was felt that interference by government would only make the situation worse.

Those who believed in these ideas were followers of *laissez faire* [les′ā fer′].

Modern History

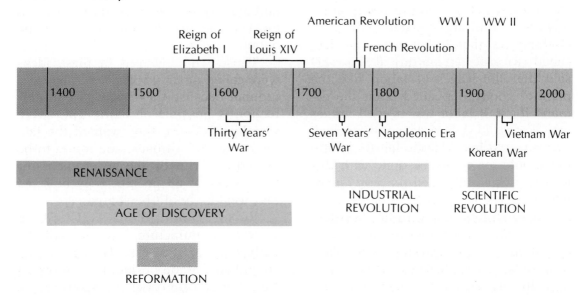

Be able to place the following events on the time line:

1769	Watt—steam engine
1807	Fulton—steam boat
1829	Stephenson—steam locomotive
1750c	Townshend—crop rotation
1793	Whitney—cotton gin
1834	McCormick—reaper
1844	Morse—telegraph
1856	Bessemer—steel
1876	Bell—telephone

1776	Smith—*The Wealth of Nations*
1800	Owen—New Lanark
1803	Malthus—population theory
1817	Ricardo—"iron law of wages"
1846	Corn Laws repealed
1847	ten-hour work week for women and children
1848	Marx—*Communist Manifesto*
1867	Marx—*Das Capital*

The term was used to describe the belief that the government should keep "hands off" business. In his book, *The Wealth of Nations,* Adam Smith (1723–90) said that a government should only ". . . protect society from violence . . . protect society from injustice, and maintain certain public works." According to Adam Smith, a free market was guided by an "invisible hand." That is, if each person pursued his or her own self interest, the common interest of all would also advance. Many factory owners, landowners, and merchants felt that Adam Smith was right.

The theory that government should not interfere with business was good for growing commerce and industry. This theory was interpreted to mean that business people did not have to clean up the wastes their factories created in the environment. They did not have to provide safe and healthful working conditions. They did not have to provide shorter hours or better wages for their workers. The theory of laissez faire suggested that if industry were left to itself, competition among business people would lead to improvements for workers and consumers as well as for owners.

The writings of other thinkers held out little hope for wage earners. Thomas Malthus [mal'ᴛʜəs] (1766–1834) was a writer who said that the population would grow faster than the ability of industry and farming to provide the food, clothing, and shelter that people needed. David Ricardo [ri kär′dō] (1772–1823) said that the wages of labor, like the price of goods, depended upon the demand for it. If labor was needed, wages would rise. If labor was not needed, wages would fall. Ricardo felt that nothing should, or could, be done with this process, which he called the *iron law of wages*.

These writers took a rather hopeless view of the possibilities of improving conditions for the working class. They were satisfied that, because of the Industrial Revolution, total wealth was increasing. They were not concerned that this wealth was not evenly distributed among people. Competition in industry would, they felt, lead to better products, lower prices, higher wages, and a general improvement in the quality of life for all people. Many writers and economic thinkers were interested only in the growth of national wealth.

People came to believe that the inventions of the Industrial Revolution assured humankind of a world of plenty. Today many people are no longer sure of this. Many feel that Malthus may yet prove to be right. They point to shortages of food, energy resources, and fertilizers. There is widespread worldwide hunger. Unless the well-to-do are satisfied to live less lavishly, there may not be enough of the world's resources for all to share.

Help for the Working Classes

If there were some writers who thought that improvement for most people was hopeless, there were others who thought that things could become perfect. *Utopia* [yü tō′pe ə] was an imaginary place with perfect government, perfect law, and perfect economy. Extremes of wealth and poverty did not exist. Under such an ideal system, people were supposed to be happy.

Those who believed in these ideas were called *utopian socialists*. They were utopian because they believed that perfection is possible on earth. They were socialists because they wanted the factories, farms, railroads, and mines to be owned and run by the government for the benefit of all people. They believed that wealth should be shared.

Robert Owen [ō′in] (1771-1858), a wealthy manufacturer, was one of the early utopian socialists. He was a successful, self-made business executive. At New Lanark [lan′ərk], in Scotland, he built an industrial community that paid high profits to the owners and high wages to the workers. He reduced work hours, raised wages, and improved working conditions. He made it possible for workers to get a better education and would not hire any children under ten. These reforms were socially advanced for those days.

When the New Lanark community grew rich, Owen tried to build another utopian society at New Harmony, Indiana. Although this one failed, Owen spent the rest of his life trying to convince others that his social experiments were worthwhile.

In France, others had utopian ideals, too. Count Saint-Simon [san sē môn] (1760–1825) and Charles Fourier [fü ryā′] (1772–1837) favored communities in which people would work together for the common good. Fourier wanted to organize groups of people into cooperative bodies of about 1,800 called *phalanstères* [fal′ən ster′ēz]. In these, individuals would do the kind of work he or she could do best. Fourier hoped that some rich person would come along and pay for an experiment to prove his idea. No one ever came.

New Lanark, Scotland, the industrial community founded by utopian socialist Robert Owen.

In 1841, an unsuccessful attempt was made to establish a cooperative community in America. In Massachusetts, the community of Brook Farm tried to carry out some of the ideas of a utopian community.

In 1848, another French socialist, Louis Blanc [blän] (1811–1882), urged the formation of National Workshops. These would be owned and operated by the workers who would share in the profits. For a brief time Blanc's National Workshops were tried in France. They did help to relieve unemployment. In the long run they were not successful because National Workshops required a new form of industrial organization for which France was not yet ready.

What Marx Said
About the Working Classes

There were other socialists who were not utopians, or perfectionists. They, too, saw evils in the industrial society and wanted to do something about them at once. They did not believe a perfect society could exist and laughed at the utopians as dreamers. They felt that the workers could take steps to get better working conditions and a share of industrial profits.

The most prominent person who felt this way was Karl Marx [märks] (1818–83). In his pamphlet, *Communist Manifesto*, and in his three-volume study, *Das Kapital* [dä kap'ē tal], Marx outlined his beliefs. There are two basic ideas found in the writings of Karl Marx. The first is that history is determined by how people make a living, that is, by economics. In addition to his economic interpretation of history, Marx believed in *class struggle*.

Marx thought of all history as a struggle between the rich and the poor. In the industrial age that struggle was between owners and workers. From his reading

Karl Marx (1818–1883)

Karl Marx was born in Germany to a comfortable upper-middle-class family. His theories of history, economics, and the nature of the working class guided the communist movement. Marx went to the local high school or gymnasium, as it is known in Germany. When he was seventeen, he took the examination for college. He did poorly on the exam in math but was outstanding in composition. After being admitted to college, he wrote a required essay entitled, "A Young Man's Choice of His Career." In it, Marx advised young people to listen to an inner voice and not to be misled by the lure of ambition or money.

After receiving his degree, Marx decided to make journalism his career. He joined a small newspaper and soon made his extreme views on politics and economics known. In Paris, where he went for further study, he met Friedrich Engels [eng'əls] (1820–1895) who became his lifelong friend. Marx's views became even more radical.

Marx married and his family began to grow. But supporting a family seemed trivial for a great thinker and writer. Despite the mounting bills and debts Marx went on with his work, first in Cologne, and then in Paris. Forced to move to London because of his views, he lived on handouts from friends and admirers. Marx was generally a kind husband, and his wife, Jenny, a devoted wife. Although she came from a prominent family, she shared the poverty of her husband and did what she could to care for the family.

Marx spent many years in London's British Museum working on his great work *Das Kapital*. In this work he predicted the downfall of capitalism and the victory of communism. Marx failed to complete his work before he died. On March 14, 1883, Engels found his friend in an armchair—dead.

and understanding of history, Marx insisted that the workers were bound to win this fight. In the *Communist Manifesto*, Marx called capitalism a Frankenstein monster which would destroy society. Marx and his followers were successful in organizing political groups in many countries.

Both communists and socialists were influenced by the ideas of Marx. Communists teach the use of revolution to gain their goals. Socialists maintain that their goals can be reached through orderly democratic processes. Communists want the government to own all industries. Under the socialists, government would own just the large industries.

Others Who Tried
To Help the Workers

Anarchists [an'ər kists] and Christian Socialists were other groups who in their different ways sought to make conditions better for the workers. Marx had insisted that in the struggle between workers and owners (capitalists) the workers were bound to win. That struggle, Marx felt, would be a long one. Anarchists believed that capitalism had to be overthrown more quickly and more violently. *Anarchism* was an attempt to overthrow capitalism and to do away with government altogether. The two most famous anarchists were Pierre Joseph Proudhon [prü dôn'] (1808–1865) and the Russian Mikhail Bakunin [bä kü'nin] (1814–1876). While anarchism and communism both were hostile to private property, the anarchists were opposed to any kind of government at all. Government, anarchists felt, was guilty of preventing workers from having a better life. Bakunin went to jail many times for taking part in violent attempts to overthrow the government of Russia.

In England, some Christian churches took part in a movement called *Christian Socialism*. The leaders of the movement were Charles Kingsley, a clergyman and writer, and the Anglican leader Frederick Denison Maurice. These men and the Christian Socialists urged churches to unite so that workers and their families could be more fairly treated by industry. Christian Socialists sought to accomplish their aims through peaceful means. They urged the formation of workers' cooperatives so that workers could get the benefits of their labor. They formed schools for women and for workers. The Christian Socialists felt that the teachings of Jesus could help workers overcome the evils of the industrial revolution. Christian Socialism encouraged the movement toward reform.

In England, workers themselves tried to improve their position by forming *labor unions*. At first these organizations were not allowed to exist. By 1824, despite strong business opposition, labor unions were legal in England. However, they had yet to win the right to strike or to engage in other activities that would interrupt their work.

As English workers organized and gained the right to vote, they chose people who would help improve labor conditions. As early as 1819, the labor of children under ten was made illegal. In 1842, the labor of women and children was reduced to ten hours per day. Later laws regulated health and safety conditions for English workers.

Workers were not entirely satisfied with the improvements that were made. To improve their situation still more, they needed political power. They sought to extend and enjoy the benefits of democracy.

Check in Here

1. Summarize the laissez faire economic system. What are the advantages of such a system? Disadvantages?

2. What is meant by *utopia*? Is a utopia possible? Why or why not?

3. How did the views of Marx differ from those of the utopian socialists?

4. How did workers hope to improve their position by forming labor unions?

5. What were the views of the anarchists? Of the Christian Socialists?

The startling developments in industry and agriculture that took place roughly during the hundred years between 1750 and 1850 have been described as a revolution. Unlike other revolutions, this was a gradual change that transformed the lives of people all over the world.

England was the home of the Industrial and Agricultural Revolutions. That country had skilled and unskilled labor, a democratic government, and the natural resources, especially iron and coal, needed to make industrial progress possible. As the enclosure movement drove more and more people from their farms, workers were increasingly taking jobs in the industries of the nation. The revolution in agriculture and industry which began first in England spread rapidly to other nations.

Revolutions in agriculture and industry brought mainly good results. There was general abundance and in the main less poverty. A new and increasingly powerful middle class grew and a hereditary aristocracy declined in importance. In 1846, the Corn Laws were repealed. This showed the greater political strength of the industrial middle class. The revolutions in agriculture and industry contributed to a growth in population and cities grew in size. The corporation became the most important form of business organization as a growing number of people sought to invest in new industries.

The benefits of the Industrial and Agricultural Revolutions were not uniformly distributed. The greatest evils were in the factory system. Women and children as well as men worked fourteen or sixteen hours a day under conditions that threatened health and life. Accidents were frequent, and wages were barely enough to keep a family fed and sheltered. In agriculture, those who were forced from their homes on the farms often found it difficult to get work in factories. Slums developed, as did related ills such as crime and delinquency.

The laissez-faire economic point of view held that the invisible hand of the marketplace would regulate the economy so that poverty could never be very long lasting or very deep. Government interference in the economy was regarded as unwise, as such interference would limit the ability of the marketplace to correct abuses.

The economy, however, did not always regulate itself in the interests of the majority. Some people felt that government intervention was necessary. Utopian socialists hoped to establish perfect societies in which poverty would not exist. Communists, led by Karl Marx, believed that a class struggle between workers and owners was inevitable and that in such a struggle the workers would win. Anarchists sought the overthrow of government, while Christian Socialists encouraged a spirit of reform through the churches.

REVIEWING THE HIGHLIGHTS

People to Identify

James Hargreaves	Sir Humphrey Davy	Thomas Malthus
Richard Arkwright	Samuel F.B. Morse	David Ricardo
Samuel Crompton	Robert Fulton	Adam Smith
Edmund Cartwright	John McAdam	Robert Owen
Eli Whitney	Alexander Bell	Charles Fourier
Joseph Proudhon	Mikhail Bakunin	Count Saint-Simon
James Watt	Jethro Tull	Frederick Maurice
Henry Bessemer	Robert Bakewell	Karl Marx
George Stephenson	Cyrus McCormick	Louis Blanc

Terms to Understand

domestic system	safety lamp	corporation
Industrial Revolution	Bessemer process	anarchism
spinning jenny	open-hearth	enclosure
cotton gin	process	movement
Agricultural	crop rotation	iron law of wages
Revolution	Christian Socialists	utopian socialists
Das Kapital	Corn Laws	class struggle
blast furnace	laissez faire	factories

Mastering the Fundamentals

1. How did the Industrial Revolution differ from the English, American, and French Revolutions?
2. Explain the domestic system, and tell why this system was unable to meet the growing demand for manufactured goods.
3. How did the early Industrial Revolution depend on water power, coal, and iron?
4. How did the Industrial Revolution better living conditions?
5. How did the Industrial Revolution create a middle class?

6. How did the Agricultural Revolution lessen the constant threat of hunger?
7. How did the Agricultural Revolution and the Industrial Revolution lengthen life?
8. How did the Agricultural Revolution and the Industrial Revolution promote health?
9. How did the Industrial Revolution encourage the labor of women and children?
10. What dangers faced factory workers?
11. Why did workers riot against labor-saving machinery?
12. Why did the Industrial Revolution lead to slums?
13. How did the Agricultural Revolution force many farmers off the land?
14. Explain the Corn Laws. Why were the landlords unsuccessful in keeping them?
15. How does the philosophy of laissez faire differ from the philosophy of mercantilism?
16. Describe a utopian plan of the eighteenth or nineteenth century. Explain why it was successful or unsuccessful?
17. What were the main ideas of Karl Marx?
18. Explain the utopian ideals of Count Saint-Simon and Charles Fourier. Were their ideas ever realized?
19. Explain how the ideas of socialists differ from the ideas of communists.

THINGS TO DO

1. Build a model of the spinning jenny—if you are handy with tools. When it is finished, bring it to class and demonstrate it.
2. Construct a diorama showing the interior of a factory during the early days of the Industrial Revolution in England; or, build a diorama showing the application of farm machinery to agriculture. Display and explain your concept to the class.
3. Make a speech on one of the following topics: The Invisible Hand Is the Only Control the Economy Needs; Intervention by Government in the Economy Is Necessary if Justice for All Is To Be Achieved.

In 1832, a Parliamentary committee looked into the conditions of child labor in the factories in England. The testimony below was obtained from the parent of several working children. Read it, and answer the questions that follow.

Question: At what time in the morning, in the brisk time [busy season] did your girls go to the mills?
Answer: In the brisk time, for about six weeks, they have gone at three o'clock in the morning and ended at ten or nearly half-past, at night.

Question: What intervals were allowed for rest or refreshment?
Answer: Breakfast a quarter of an hour, and dinner half an hour, and drinking a quarter of an hour.

Question: Had you not great difficulty in awakening your children to this excessive labor?
Answer: Yes, in the early time we had to take them up asleep and shake them when we got them on the floor to dress them, before we could get them off to work; but not so in the common hours.

Question: The common [regular] hours of labor were from six in the morning till half-past eight at night?
Answer: Yes.

Question: Did this excessive term of labor occasion much cruelty also?
Answer: Yes, with being so very fatigued, the strap was frequently used.

Question: Have any of your children been strapped?
Answer: Yes, every one.

1. If you had been on the committee, what questions would you have asked?
2. As a historian, what conclusions, if any, would you come to as a result of the evidence presented?
3. What general ideas about the nature of the Industrial Revolution could reasonably be drawn? Why?
4. Would you regard the above as primary or secondary material? Why?
5. What other evidence would you look for during the course of your study?

The World Republic, illustrating the revolutions of 1848

The Further Trials of Democracy: Democratic Reform in England and France

Here are some significant dates in history: 1688, 1776, and 1789. Do you know what great event is associated with each? You would be right if you said the Glorious Revolution in England, the American Revolution, and the French Revolution. While each event marked an important advance in democracy, the institutions of democracy continue to evolve into new and better forms.

During the revolutions of 1820, 1830, and 1848, people in many European countries tried to make their governments more democratic. They sought the freedom to vote as they wished, the right to read books and newspapers without censorship, the right to attend public meetings, and the right to be represented by elected officials. These advances were slow in coming.

In this chapter we will review the democratic gains made by England and France. We will see how their governments developed and the steps they took to achieve democracy. They did not achieve democracy all at once, but over a period of time. In the nineteenth century, England and France made important reforms that prevented those countries from losing democracy altogether.

GREAT BRITAIN UNDERTAKES REFORMS

Why Great Britain Was in Need of Reform

If a time machine were to carry you back in time and place to Great Britain of 150 years ago, you would come upon a number of shocking, undemocratic practices. Parliament was made up of two Houses, the House of Commons and the House of Lords. Membership in the House of Commons was decided by election, but membership in the House of Lords was determined by birth. Neither House was democratic because only a handful of rich and powerful men ran the government as they saw fit.

In order to vote, it was necessary to own a certain amount of property. Most people did not own any property. They could not vote. In order to serve in Parliament one had to be rich since members of Parliament were not paid. Only members of the Anglican Church could serve in Parliament. Therefore, government service was closed to Catholics and Jews. Because there was no secret ballot, many people were afraid to express their choices, especially if they depended upon a factory owner or a landowner for their living. So elections did not show actual representation of the people's wants.

In addition, representation in the House of Commons had not changed in years. Representation was based on voting districts, called *boroughs* [bèr'ōz]. The number of representatives from each borough stayed the same whether population had either increased or decreased. With the coming of the Industrial Revolution (see p. 387), there was a growth of new cities, such as Leeds and Manchester. These cities were not represented by members in the House of Commons. On the other hand, as some communities grew smaller or disappeared altogether, they kept their representation in Parliament. There were boroughs with few or no people living in them. In some boroughs, the wealthy people bribed the majority of electors to vote for a representative of the wealthy class. These were known as *rotten boroughs.*

Sometimes, a representative was hand-picked by a rich landlord rather than by the people. The name *pocket borough* has been used to describe this kind of situation because the landowner was said to have the district in his pocket. Many a rich—and sometimes able—young man got his start in Parliament in this way. Pocket and rotten boroughs made it possible for rich people to control Parliament to their advantage.

407

The Death of the "Rotten Borough"

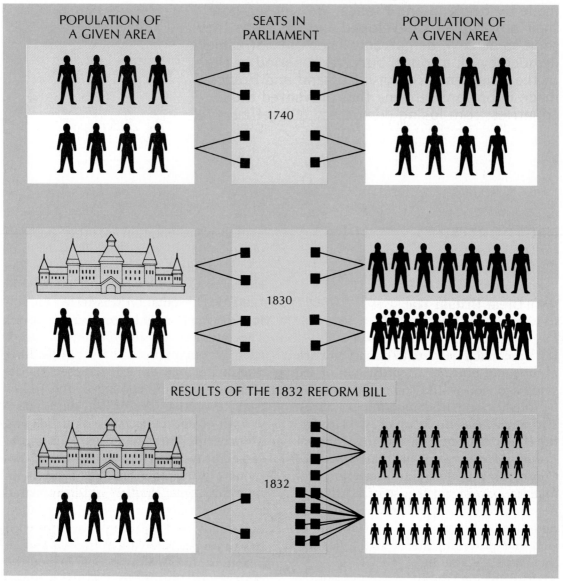

What happened to representation from the "rotten borough"?

How the Reform Bill of 1832 Became a Law

The need for reform had been expressed for more than a hundred years. The middle class, which was stronger as a result of the Industrial Revolution, wanted more power in the British Parliament.

Factory workers, farm workers, and women wanted the right to vote. But those whose wealth was based on land controlled Parliament and wanted to remain in control. They opposed granting the right to vote to other people. Because the *Reform Bill of 1832* met some of these demands of the middle class and others, it marked a giant step in the growth of democracy in Britain.

After much debate in and out of Parliament, a Reform Bill was passed by the House of Commons. It was turned down twice by the House of Lords. The people wanted the Reform Bill, and they were angry when the House of Lords would not accept the plan for reform. The problem was how to get the House of Lords to accept change.

The king was also opposed to change. Prime Minister Earl Grey, who wanted the bill passed, was forced to resign. The king then appointed the popular war hero, the Duke of Wellington, to be the new prime minister. The Iron Duke was a better soldier than a statesman. He unsuccessfully tried to kill the Reform Bill.

The Reform Bill was gaining in popular support. Wellington soon realized that it was impossible to stop the passage of the bill, so he quit as prime minister. Earl Grey was recalled. This time he said he would not become prime minister unless the king agreed to appoint more members of the House of Lords who would vote for the Reform Bill. This the king agreed to do. The mere threat of creating more lords was enough for the members of the House of Lords. They did not want any upstarts sitting in the old and dignified House. When the Reform Bill of 1832 came up for a third time, it passed in the House of Commons and the House of Lords as well and became a law of the land. It was a milestone in British political history.

William Hogarth was an eighteenth-century painter. Through his paintings he made observations, often critical, about English society. This painting, *The Polling*, shows Englishmen arriving at the polls. What do you think Hogarth was trying to say about the kind of people who were entitled to vote? Remember, this was before the Reform Bill of 1832.

John Constable's *Dedham Mill*. As a result of the Reform Bill of 1832, owners of small businesses like this mill were able to vote.

The Importance of the Reform Bill of 1832

The Reform Bill of 1832 is important for the way it was passed and became a law. The bill brought a great change—almost a revolution. Yet there was no serious violence. The people waited for Parliament to make the democratic changes that they wanted. They were patient, and they accepted delays and compromise. They saw that democracy was the way through which wrongs could be made right without resort to rebellion and violence. When the wealthy saw that they could not stop reform or change from taking place, they gave in. The threat of creating more lords was used again, at a later time, when the members of the House of Lords refused to make changes.

Because of the nonviolent way in which the Reform Bill of 1832 was passed, some historians say that England became more democratic by evolution than by revolution. By *evolution* they mean a gradual change to a better way of doing things. By *revolution* they mean a quick violent change, such as the French Revolution. Evolution, not revolution, was the course England took.

The importance of the Reform Bill of 1832 was that it took the power to run the government away from the nobles. It lowered the property qualifications for voting, and so extended the right to vote to the middle class (merchants, traders, bankers, factory owners, and mill owners). It did away with many of the rotten boroughs and gave representatives in Parliament to the new industrial cities. With the passage of the Reform Bill the leaders of industry became more important than the large landowners and nobles. This in itself was a great change. People in the cities became as influential as people in the country.

Dissatisfaction with the Reform Bill

In a democracy, it is difficult to satisfy everyone all the time. People accept the idea that the majority rules. The results of the Reform Bill of 1832 did not satisfy everyone because many people still did not get the right to vote. They had good reason to be disappointed. Industrial leaders of the middle class now controlled Parliament. Factory workers feared that laws would be passed that would favor factory owners rather than factory workers. The result was that workers started demanding further changes.

The demands of the workers were outlined in a petition, known as a *charter* (guarantee of rights). The *Chartists*, as those who signed the charter were called, demanded that all men be given the right to vote and that voting be done by secret ballot. They wanted annual meetings of Parliament, payment of salaries to members of Parliament, and the abolition of property qualifications for membership in Parliament. Many of these demands were looked upon as unreasonable; yet, slowly, nearly all of the demands of the Chartists were met in England and other democratic countries.

Why More People Gained the Right to Vote

Both of Great Britain's major political parties wanted to get the credit for extending the right to vote. The Liberals had been responsible for the Reform Bill of 1832. In 1867, the Tories, under the leadership of Benjamin Disraeli, had secured the passage of a bill to reduce voting restrictions which would allow city workers to vote.

If the Tories could do it, the Liberals thought they had better do the same thing if they were to gain power. In 1884, William Gladstone, a liberal, was responsible for further extension of the right to vote. By 1918, all men had gained the right to vote and so had women over thirty years of age. Ten years later, all women over twenty-one had won the privilege of voting.

Why Parliament Became More Democratic

The British government was made still more democratic. Catholics, in 1829, and Jews, in 1858, could be elected to Parliament. In 1872, the secret ballot was adopted, which made it possible to vote as one wished without the fear or threat of losing one's job.

Parliament itself needed to change more if England were to be a truly democratic country. The House of Commons, to which the people elected representatives, had to become more powerful than the House of Lords, whose members inherited office.

The House of Commons finally became more powerful in the early part of the twentieth century. Members of the House of Commons decided that the power of the House of Lords would be reduced if money bills were controlled by Commons. The *Parliament Act of 1911* was designed to overpower the House of Lords. According to this law, all money bills passed by the House of Commons were to become law with or without the approval of the House of Lords. The problem was how to get the House of Lords to pass a bill which would mean signing its own death warrant. You may remember that, in 1832, when the House of Lords refused to do something, the king then threatened to appoint more members to the House of Lords in order to gain a majority for the Reform Bill. (See p. 409.) This same threat was enough to make the House of Lords accept the Parliament Act of 1911.

In 1947, another bill reduced the power of the House of Lords still further and, today, the House of Lords plays a rather unimportant part in English politics. Its members may debate, but they cannot stop a law that the House of Commons wants passed. The House of Commons is now the representative and law-making body of Great Britain.

Check in Here

1. List three undemocratic features of the government of Great Britain in 1830.

2. Trace the steps by which the Reform Bill of 1832 was passed.

3. What were the demands of the Chartists?

4. How did the House of Commons become more powerful than the House of Lords?

HOW THE GOVERNMENT OF GREAT BRITAIN WORKS

How Great Britain Is Governed

In Great Britain the queen reigns but does not rule. The monarch is a figurehead who has no real power. Governing power is in the House of Commons which makes parliamentary laws. The prime minister is chosen by the monarch from the House of Commons. He or she must be the leader of the party that has a majority of the members of that body. Since there are usually only two main parties, the monarch does not have to make a difficult decision.

The prime minister chooses others from her or his party to fill the cabinet posts. The prime minister traditionally selects the cabinet from members of the House of Commons and the House of Lords. The cabinet and prime minister remain in office only as long as they have the support of the majority of the House of Commons. If the House of Commons refuses to pass a bill that the prime minister and the cabinet want, the prime minister has lost the support of the majority. The prime minister then asks the monarch to dissolve the Parliament and hold a general election.

In a general election the parties wage a political battle for control of Parliament. This step is called *going to the people* or *to the country*. In a general election the voters elect members to Parliament who will vote on bills as the voters wish.

There are two main parties in Parliament, and each party tries to stay in control as long as it can. Party members are expected to vote the way the party leaders vote, since voting against the party could result in a defeat for the party leadership and would force a new general election or the appointment of a new cabinet. To guard against one party staying in power too long, however, elections must be held at least every five years. The party in power can ask for elections sooner and may say when it wants such an election held.

Today, the two main parties in the British Parliament are the *Tory* (Conservative) *Party* and *Labour Party*. The Tory Party represents the thought of those who prefer private ownership of property rather than government control. They are willing to enter anticommunist alliances. The Labour Party is a relatively new party. Its members believe in government ownership of industry, favor socialized medicine, and do not want to become involved in anticommunist alliances. The Labour Party grew in strength

412

William Gladstone   Benjamin Disraeli

Benjamin Disraeli
(1804–81)
William Gladstone
(1809–98)

Disraeli and Gladstone were rival leaders of the Tory and Liberal parties respectively. They alternately governed England between 1868 and 1885. Disraeli privately wrote that Gladstone was an "unprincipled maniac," while Gladstone said of Disraeli that ". . . the man was more false than his doctrine."* Despite such conflict, England's prestige and power grew, making it a world leader in the nineteenth century.

Young Disraeli, or Dizzy as he was nicknamed, was by his own admission, a miserable child in school. As a young man he failed at nearly everything he tried. He found that he was not suited for the law, and an unsuccessful investment in South America plunged him into debt. He tried to publish a newspaper, but this venture failed also.

Disraeli's first great success was in literature, not politics. His novel *Vivian Grey* became very popular, and Disraeli seemed embarked on a literary career. But his enormous ambition tempted him to run for Parliament. After a number of defeats, he finally won a seat in the House of Commons as a Tory. His first speech was met with laughter and jeers, and another failure seemed on the horizon. His elaborate and colorful dress and his exaggerated style of speaking were noted by his opponents. They stood ready to make a mockery of his first public speaking efforts. Disraeli, however, had the last laugh. In time, he became the most popular speaker in Parliament, and people waited for hours for a chance to listen to him.

Several aspects of Gladstone's life stand in contrast to those of Disraeli. While Disraeli began his career as a successful author, Gladstone first considered entering the church. Upon his father's advice Gladstone entered politics instead, and from the start made a thorough success of it. If Disraeli cut an awkward and ungainly figure in Parliament, Gladstone at thirty-six was handsome, erect, and dignified. He had enormous energy, and it was said of him that he could do in four hours what it would take others some sixteen to do. He was the master of any subject to which he put his mind. Gladstone put his great talents to work in liberal and humanitarian causes. Where Disraeli concentrated on expanding England's

*Winston S. Churchill, *A History of the English-Speaking Peoples: The Great Democracies* (New York: Dodd, Mead and Company, 1958), p. 283.

413

colonial rule, Gladstone concentrated on making that rule just wherever it existed.

Disraeli and Gladstone both served the queen and the nation they loved, yet of the two, it was Disraeli who found greater favor with Queen Victoria. Gladstone, the queen complained, spoke to her as if she were at a public meeting. Disraeli, on the other hand, charmed his monarch, made her Empress of India, for which she made him Earl of Beaconsfield. Gladstone, although less loved by the queen, was at his death deeply mourned by people the world over. A great and good man had passed away.

when the old Liberal Party (which still elects a few members to Parliament) was too slow in bringing about social and economic changes.

How the Democracies of Britain and the United States Are Alike

The governments of Great Britain and the United States are similar in that both are democracies in which the voice of the majority of the people rules. In both, there are freedom of the press, freedom of speech, and freedom of worship. In Great Britain and in the United States there are powerful lawmaking bodies chosen by the people. The lawmakers come from the two powerful political parties that share a belief in democracy. The party out of power tries to develop plans which will appeal to voters in future elections. The two parties each work for popular support. In this way no one party can get too strong or stay in power for too long.

In each country the government is one of laws, not of people. The law is the same for all people. Both countries have fair laws and fair trials which apply to all the people. In both countries, democracy grew slowly, and generally speaking, without revolution and violence. Elections are decided by ballots rather than bullets, and the political decisions of the majority are respected.

How the Two Great Democracies Are Different

Despite the significant similarities in the governments of Great Britain and the United States, there are some differences to be noted. Great Britain is a *limited monarchy* in which the monarch reigns but does not rule. Elizabeth II, queen of England, works hard but has no real power. She serves as a symbol of the past glories and the future promise of Great Britain. She serves to unify the nation and helps to unite the members of the Commonwealth. The queen of England receives loyalty from the people of Canada and Australia, which are members of the Commonwealth of Nations. She inspires loyalty and patriotism among British subjects.

The United States is a *federal republic*. That is, governmental power is shared between the national government in Washington, D.C. and the fifty state governments.

Unlike England's monarch, the president of the United States is elected to be the national leader and chief executive. The president may be reelected for a second term. The president has great power. The president is commander-in-chief of

414

Washington, D.C. is the seat of the United States government. This is a view of the Jefferson Memorial in Washington.

the armed forces, is responsible for making plans in foreign affairs, and is the leader of the political party in office. The power of the veto also enables the president to influence legislation. As ceremonial leader, the president represents the nation by greeting important visitors and by taking part in national ceremonies.

It is said that the British have an *unwritten constitution*. That means there is no single written document that spells out the exact form of the British government. Their constitution is a group of documents such as the Magna Carta and the Bill of Rights. Also included in the British constitution are the laws of Parliament and the customs developed through the years.

The United States has a *written constitution*, a brief document which outlines the organization of the government and the duties of chief officials. The English have no similar document to which they can refer. However, in the organization of American government, there are many parts not described in the Constitution. So the United States, too, has an unwritten constitution including our two-party system.

The prime minister of Great Britain plays a similar political role as the president of the United States. However, the prime minister gets his or her job in a different way. The prime minister is chosen because he or she is the head of the party with a majority in the House of Commons. The prime minister holds the job as long as his or her party controls Parliament.

In the United States, the Congress passes the laws, and the president sees that the laws are carried out. The president may be of one party, and a majority of the members of Congress may be of another. The president of the United States serves for four years. To get elected, the president must campaign all over the country asking for votes.

In Great Britain, no one campaigns to become prime minister. If a British voter wants a conservative for prime minister, all the person can do is vote for the Tory candidate who is running in his or her district for the House of Commons. If a majority of Tories is elected to the House of Commons, the leader of that party will become the prime minister. The House of Commons must pass laws which support the prime minister's views and the plans of the prime minister's party. Congress does not have to pass laws which the president and the president's party want.

The differences between the government of Great Britain and that of the United States may be summed up in this way. Britain is a democracy in which Parliament is supreme. The United States is a democracy in which there is a *separation of powers* among the three branches of its government—the legislative (Congress), the executive (president), and the judicial (Supreme Court). The Supreme Court (the highest court in the nation) has the power to say that a law of Congress or an act of the president is *unconstitutional*. That is, it is illegal because it goes against the Constitution. The president can veto an act of Congress. In Great Britain, there is no such system of check and balances.

A woman has never served as president of the United States. In 1979, Margaret Thatcher became the first woman prime minister. She served in that capacity as the leader of the Tory Party because that party won the election that year.

Check in Here

1. What is meant by the statement: "The queen of England reigns but does not rule"?

2. How is the prime minister of Great Britain chosen?

3. What are the two chief parties in Britain and what are the main principles they follow?

4. Show two ways in which democracy in the United States and Britain are similar.

5. Show two ways in which democracy in the United States and Britain are dissimilar.

THE GOVERNMENT OF FRANCE STRUGGLES TO BECOME STRONGER

The Second French Republic and the Second Empire

Louis Napoleon was nephew of the great Napoleon. He was elected president of the Second French Republic after Louis Philippe was driven from office. (See p. 356.) The main aim of Louis Napoleon's presidency was to destroy the Second Republic and set himself up as Napoleon III, Emperor of France. It was Louis Napoleon's dream to become as great as his uncle had been. Skillfully, Louis Napoleon sought help from both the aristocracy and the middle class. He won the support of ordinary men when he introduced universal male suffrage (voting rights for all men).

As his uncle had done before him, Louis Napoleon asked the people to vote to extend his term of office and give him more power. This the people did. But Louis Napoleon was not yet emperor, and so was still not satisfied. In 1852, in yet another vote, Louis Napoleon was made emperor. He was given the title Napoleon III, thereby suggesting falsely that his father had been the son of Napoleon I.

As emperor, Napoleon III did not have an easy time. He faced too much opposition. *Monarchists* (those who favor a monarchy) viewed him as an upstart and sought to seize power from him. The middle class felt that his policies should favor business and independent farmers since these groups had supported his desire to be emperor. Catholics wanted him to work with the Church. Napoleon tried to satisfy everyone and wound up satisfying no one. He made Paris beautiful, thereby giving employment to many workers while making his capital more attractive. He built railroads and imposed tariffs (taxes on products coming into France) so as to encourage French industry by making imported goods more expensive.

As emperor, Napoleon III destroyed democracy. His word was law, as there was no effective legislature to check his powers. There was no free press and criticism of the emperor was forbidden. Those believed to be hostile to the emperor could be imprisoned or even forced to leave the country. Under such pressures, the people grew restless and some began to regret the decision to make Napoleon emperor.

Napoleon tried to win people over by restoring France to its former glory. Napoleon III took part in the Crimean War in which France and England fought Russia. The war was a useless one, known best for its military inefficiency and wasteful loss of life. (See p. 377.)

In 1863, Napoleon III forced Benito Juárez [wär'ez] (1806–1872) from office as president of Mexico. Juárez had won this post after he led the overthrow of the dictatorship of Santa Anna. (See p. 353.) As president, Juárez refused to repay the debts that Mexico owed England, France, and Spain. Spain and England reached an agreement with Juárez. Napoleon III thought he saw an opportunity to establish a foothold in the New World. Supported by the guns of French troops, he then placed Maximilian [mak'sə mil'yən] of Austria and his Spanish-born wife, Carlotta [kär lô'tä] on the throne of Mexico. The United States was deeply involved in the Civil War, and Napoleon III felt that a puppet emperor on the Mexican throne would add glory to his reign.

When the Civil War ended, the United States at once applied the principles of the Monroe Doctrine. The United States sent its troops to the Mexican border. Juárez was encouraged to overthrow Maximilian, and the United States threatened to invade that country. Maximilian, thoroughly despised by Mexicans, was captured and killed. Juárez was reelected the president of Mexico (1867–1872). Under pressure, Napoleon III had flinched and had not dared to send troops to support his ill-advised adventure.

In a French cartoon Victor Hugo, a writer, and Emile Girardin, a journalist, attempt to upset Louis Napoleon. Why are they doing this?

Modern History

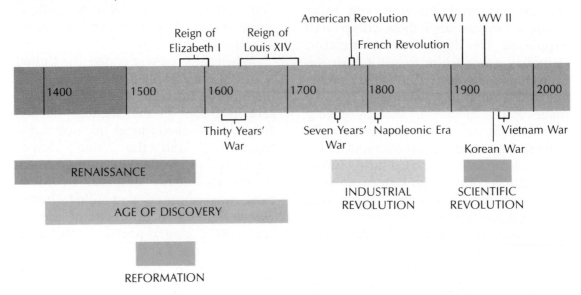

Be able to place the following events on the time line:

1832	Reform Bill	1928	women won vote in Britain
1867	city workers won vote	1852–71	Second French Empire
1911	Parliament Act	1958	de Gaulle became President

Other foreign adventures of Napoleon III included strengthening French rule in Algeria and establishing French influence in Cambodia and Indo-China. In 1859, Napoleon III began the building of the Suez Canal. Despite these adventures, Napoleon III made his greatest mistake when he let himself be lured into the Franco-Prussian War with Bismarck. (See p. 375.) This led to the end of the Second French Empire and the beginning of the *Third French Republic.*

The Problems Faced by the Third French Republic

The Third French Republic was born under unfavorable conditions. For one thing, the defeat of France in the Franco-Prussian War was a great disappointment to the French. The harsh terms of the peace treaty France signed with Germany added insult to injury. In the assembly, which was elected to establish the Third Republic, there were many royalists who wanted a king. Only because these royalists could not agree among themselves was it possible for France to establish the Third French Republic.

From time to time, there were incidents that threatened the Third Republic with replacement by a monarchy. In the *Boulanger* [bü län zhā′] *Affair* a heroic French general tried unsuccessfully to seize control of the government for the royalists. Another incident arose when someone was caught sneaking secrets from the French war office and selling them to the Germans. Captain Alfred Dreyfus [drā′fəs], a Jew, was falsely blamed. He was imprisoned in the French prison on Devil's Island, off the

418

coast of South America. The *Dreyfus Affair* hurt the Republic and gave the monarchists, or royalists, another excuse to urge a king on France. However, they were unsuccessful.

The Third Republic was faced with many serious crises. One was the question of the separation of church and state. This question was important. At issue was whether tax money should be used to support the Catholic Church and whether the Church would control education and laws governing marriage and divorce. In 1905, the Church and government separated. The struggle between church and state caused the rise and fall of more than one premier.

Other crises were two world wars. In both wars, France was near defeat because French premiers were unable to prepare the nation properly for war with Germany. The Third French Republic lasted until 1940, when the Nazis conquered France. After World War II ended, the *Fourth French Republic* was established. It lasted until 1958, when the *Fifth French Republic* was born under the leadership of Charles de Gaulle. Under the Fifth French Republic, which exists today, France is a strong, democratic, and prosperous country.

The Growth of Democracy

Great Britain, America, and France were not the only countries in which democracy grew. They were among the largest countries, and they therefore set examples for others to follow. Among those that accepted democratic ways were the Netherlands, Belgium, Switzerland, and the Scandinavian countries. Switzerland became a republic, while the others became limited monarchies. Norway declared its independence from Sweden and peacefully separated in 1905. All these countries have strong democratic governments.

In a democracy, people can take part in the decisions that are being made by government. In the chapter that follows, you will see how democracy improved the lives of the people.

Check in Here

1. Why were the French dissatisfied with the government of Louis Napoleon?

2. What incidents threatened the stability of the Third French Republic?

3. Why was instability characteristic of France under the Third Republic?

4. List three criteria necessary for a democracy.

REVIEWING THE BASICS

This chapter was devoted to a review of the further trials of democracy in England and in France. In England, it has been said, democracy developed by evolution, in France by revolution. These are convenient ways to remember how democracy was achieved in those countries.

Following the Glorious Revolution of 1688 more progress had to be made before England could be considered a democratic nation. As late as 1832, few men could vote. The House of Lords was far more powerful than the House of Commons and so could stop reform. Moreover, as a result of the Industrial Revolution many people moved closer to the factories in which they worked.

In this way, new cities were formed. The people living in these cities were, however, often unrepresented in Parliament.

Between 1832 and 1928, Britain became more democratic. Parliament was forced to pass a number of reform measures which gave more men and, later, women the right to vote. It was not until 1925 that universal suffrage (all adult men and women having the right to vote) was achieved. Legislation also, in time, made the House of Commons far more powerful than the House of Lords.

Great Britain's constitution is essentially an unwritten one in that it is made up of a series of great documents rather than a single one. The United States has a written constitution, but it also has a great number of practices, such as the two-party system, which are not provided for in the Constitution at all. The prime minister of Great Britain gets power by being head of the party that has a majority in the House of Commons. The prime minister serves as long as he or she retains such a majority or for a maximum of five years. In the United States, the president is elected independently of Congress. The president is part of the executive, or law enforcing branch, rather than the lawmaking branch of government. In England, the prime minister is both a law enforcer and a lawmaker because separation of powers does not exist.

When Napoleon III was overthrown, the Third French Republic was set up. The Dreyfus Affair and the Boulanger Affair were two scandals that made it difficult for that government to function as well as it could. French premiers get their position in a manner similar to that of the prime minister in England. Because there were many parties, the French experienced the rise and fall of many governments. This had a weakening effect on France.

REVIEWING THE HIGHLIGHTS

People to Identify		
Earl Grey	Benjamin Disraeli	Charles de Gaulle
Queen Victoria	William Gladstone	Elizabeth II
Napoleon III	Margaret Thatcher	Maximilian and
Duke of Wellington	Benito Juárez	Carlotta
	Alfred Dreyfus	

Terms to Understand		
Reform Bill of 1832	Parliament Act	Third French Republic
House of Commons	of 1911	Fifth French Republic
House of Lords	Chartists	limited monarchy
secret ballot	cabinet	federal republic
rotten borough	Tory Party	written constitution
pocket borough	Liberal Party	unwritten constitution
Boulanger Affair	Labour Party	separation of powers
Dreyfus Affair	Congress	

Mastering the Fundamentals

Mastering the Fundamentals

1. List the undemocratic features of nineteenth-century Great Britain.
2. How does membership in the House of Lords differ from membership in the House of Commons?
3. Only a small percentage of English males could vote or hold office in the nineteenth century. Why?
4. What do the terms *rotten boroughs* and *pocket boroughs* mean?
5. Why is the Reform Bill of 1832 called a "revolution"?
6. How did the Reform Bill of 1832 make Great Britain more democratic?
7. What people were dissatisfied with the Reform Bill of 1832?
8. Explain the importance of the Parliament Act of 1911.
9. Show how Great Britain gradually achieved the goal of universal suffrage.
10. How was the House of Lords forced to reduce its own power?
11. How does the power of the House of Commons differ from that of the House of Lords?
12. Why is the secret ballot considered a milestone in the march of democracy?
13. How did the personality and political beliefs of Benjamin Disraeli contrast with those of William Gladstone?
14. How does one win or lose the job of prime minister of Great Britain?
15. Distinguish between the membership and ideas of the Tory Party and the Labour Party.
16. What are the three branches of the United States government?
17. How does the American government differ from that of Great Britain?
18. Why was Louis Napoleon called ambitious?
19. Explain the term *male suffrage:* Who introduced it to France and why?
20. How did the Boulanger Affair and the Dreyfus Affair threaten the Third Republic?

THINGS TO DO

1. Prepare a speech you might make as a member of Parliament urging the House of Lords to vote *for* the Reform Bill of 1832.
2. Draw a cartoon illustrating one or more of the demands of the Chartists.
3. Research and report on the following: Dreyfus and the Miscarriage of Justice; or, Boulanger: Adventurer on Horseback.

Using the chart below where it is applicable, discuss the questions that follow.

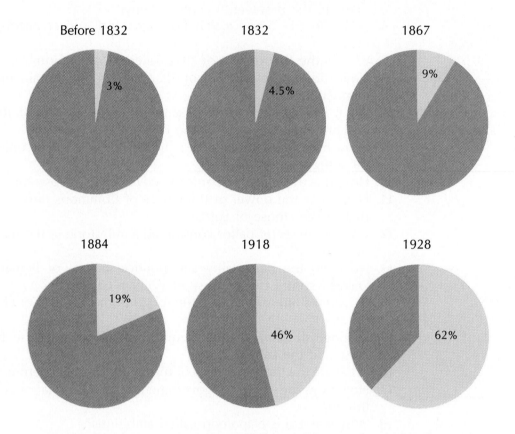

Before 1832 — 3%
1832 — 4.5%
1867 — 9%
1884 — 19%
1918 — 46%
1928 — 62%

1. The right to vote increased by only 1.5 percent in 1832. Why is the 1832 Reform Bill considered a great milestone on the march to democracy in Great Britain?

2. How do you account for the fact that the percentage of voters before 1925 never equals 100 percent? If this chart were brought up to date, would it equal 100 percent? Why or why not?

3. During which year was the suffrage increased the most? What circumstances help to explain that increase?

4. In evaluating the democracy of any nation is it enough to know the extent of suffrage? What else should be known? Why?

5. To what extent did the extension of suffrage in France and in the United States follow a pattern similar to that in England?

The Crystal Palace, 1851

The Victorian Era: Europeans During the Nineteenth Century

If you had lived in the middle of the nineteenth century in England, one of the exciting things in your life might have been a trip to the Crystal Palace in London. There you would have seen an exhibit of the great inventions of the day from all over the world. You would have been amazed at all the mechanical wonders gathered in one place. The Crystal Palace was an engineering marvel of iron and glass. It was opened to the public in May, 1851, by Queen Victoria. Thousands of visitors came to see the "Works of Industry of All Nations." As an English person, you would have been proud of the exposition. It was held in London, and at its opening, Queen Victoria of England delivered a speech. The exhibits would have delighted you because many of the inventions were English. The *Victorian Era* (1837–1901) was England's golden age, and the English people had a right to be proud of their industrial and democratic progress.

The exhibit at the Crystal Palace was really a World's Fair. It showed that many nations were seeking a better world in the industrial age. The Industrial Revolution and the growth of democracy, which were going on in several countries, brought in a new period of comfortable living for many people.

POPULATION GROWS AS LIVING CONDITIONS IMPROVE

Why Population Increased in the Nineteenth Century

After 1650 the world's population began to rise rapidly. There were many causes for this increase. For one thing, medical advances made over the centuries helped people live longer. For another, in Europe and in much of Asia, the growth of law and order made death from violence and civil war less frequent. This was especially so in Europe. In Africa, tribal wars, encouraged by the demands of the slave trade, held back the population growth of that continent.

In addition, the Agricultural Revolution made growing more and better food possible. As a result, the English were able to reduce much of the famine in India. The Dutch were able to do the same in Java. In Europe, too, many people got more to eat. A better food supply caused an increase in life expectancy. As the death rate fell population grew.

A rapid population growth was especially characteristic of Europe. Partially because of it, European civilization began to dominate the world during the nineteenth and early twentieth centuries. Europe's population was not greater than that of any other continent. But its rapid growth enabled it to keep pace, at least in numbers, with the other conti-

nents. A larger population made workers available for growing industry. More people provided more consumers for Europe's goods.

The population of Europe grew because the death rate declined. It did not grow because of an increase in the birth rate. In fact, around 1800, the birth rate in Europe began to fall. This was especially true in France. Families, which at one time had as many as ten children, now had only two. Many factors help explain why families decreased in size. Probably one of the most important factors was that in rich countries, families preferred to have fewer but more well-cared for children. To keep their living standards high, families tended to limit the number of children they had. The availability of compulsory public education meant that children would be in school for a long time. Children in school had to be clothed and fed. These were costs parents had to pay. With fewer children the costs of raising them were more easily met.

Why People Moved to the Cities

Along with the growth in population occurred the growth of cities. The growth of cities was made possible by the expansion of industry and by railroads which served the cities's needs. Up to 1800, most people lived on farms or in rural areas.

During the nineteenth century, this began to change rapidly. By 1851, a little more than half the people of Great Britain (50.8 percent) were living in urban, or city, areas. The growth of cities took place faster in Great Britain than in France or in Germany. Today, in most countries of Europe and in the United States, more people live in cities than in the rural areas.

Urbanization, as this movement to the city is called, had many effects. People went to cities because they were forced off the land as farm machines rapidly replaced farm labor. They went to cities in search of jobs or wealth. Most people never found wealth. Urban poverty—bad as it was—was rarely as bad as rural poverty. People went to the city in search of opportunities—to get an education, to enjoy the cultural advantages of museums and libraries, and to have better medical care. People were followed to the cities by friends and relatives, who were also eager to improve their lives.

City life is different from country life in many ways. In the country, families tend to be large. In the cities, families tend to be small. Country life is often very traditional. In the city, traditions may be more difficult to keep. In the country, people are sometimes slow to change. In the city, people may change quickly. In the country, one person's misfortunes are felt by neighbors, who offer to help. But in the city, it may sometimes seem that no one cares.

Partly because no one seemed to care, cities had to develop services to look after people. Thus, a police force was developed to curb crime and regulate growing traffic. A fire department was created to prevent and to fight fire. Sanitation facilities were set up to keep the city clean. Hospitals were supported at public expense.

It was in the city that the tempo of life grew faster. The goods of the world were brought to the city by railroads and were available to all who could pay. Newspapers sparked an interest in public affairs and stimulated public participation in politics. When people lived so close together, they had to learn to work together. They worked together to form giant businesses. They worked together to form giant unions to protect workers. These unions bargained with businesses for higher wages and shorter hours. It was in the city that a better world was born during the mid-nineteenth century.

How the Workers Lived in the Nineteenth Century

Nevertheless, by present-day standards, early nineteenth-century life remained hard for most people, especially for the laboring classes. Factory workers lived in small, crowded apartments located close

A mounted police officer. Why do you think increased urbanization during the nineteenth century created a need for effective police and firefighting forces?

to their workplaces. It was not unusual for four or five people to share a two-room apartment in which gas was used for heating and lighting. Early in the twentieth century electric lights came into use. Indoor toilets and running water were common, but most workers did not have the luxury of private bathrooms. To most factory workers central heating was unknown in their drafty apartment buildings.

The working day was long. Laws reducing work hours were passed gradually, allowing some time for leisure. Family events, such as births, marriages, and deaths, were among the more important and exciting episodes in the workers' lives. In these activities, religion played a smaller part than it once did.

As the daily hours of work decreased, the workers' interests in affairs outside the factory rose. They had fun watching and taking part in sports, in riding or

A bookstore in Boston, Massachusetts. Reading became an increasingly popular pastime in the nineteenth century.

walking in the parks, or in going out to the country. The price of books was slowly coming within their reach. Some workers enjoyed the novels of the great Victorian writers Charles Dickens and William Thackeray. They bought these books almost as readily as they did the penny newspapers which they could also now afford. Workers enjoyed reading the news of the day, the cartoons, the sports pages, book-length features, and the advertisements. During the nineteenth century, there were no movies to which city workers could go. As the nineteenth century drew to a close, movies began to be shown in Paris and in London.

Factory working conditions were poor. They began to improve in the latter part of the nineteenth century. In general, wages for factory work were higher than farm wages. Living conditions were generally better in the city than in the country. Nevertheless, slums, crooked streets, foul and unpleasant odors, and crowded conditions were all a part of city life. Eventually, public housing, city sewerage, public schools, and publicly cleaned streets improved living conditions. Modern transportation—refrigerated freight cars and ships—brought fresh fruit and vegetables to city markets. Modern communication such as the telegraph and telephone increased the pace of life by shortening distances and by keeping people in touch with others.

During the nineteenth century, workers won the right to join together in labor unions. The *Trades Union Act of 1871* assured labor unions that union members would not be punished for striking. Union workers bargained with employers for shorter hours, better working conditions, and higher wages. Labor unions sought political as well as economic power. They helped workers fight for the right to vote. (See p. 411.) In this way, the political power of workers grew. With greater political and economic power they were in a better position to fight for a greater share of the good things of the world.

How the Middle Class Lived

The middle class was made up of many people. Some members of the middle class lived little better than factory workers. Other members of the middle class were rich. Generally speaking, the term middle class means those who own small amounts of property. In this group were small farmers, storekeepers, and some of the more skilled workers. Also included were professional people such as doctors, lawyers, engineers, and teachers.

The so-called upper middle class was often very prosperous. In this class were the factory owners, merchants, and bankers. The upper middle class had been the real winners of the French Revolution. This class had controlled the English Parliament and had gained most from the reform bills in nineteenth-century England.

For the most part, the members of the middle class lived better than the lower class, or laboring class. Their homes were well furnished, with private baths and modern plumbing. Furniture was decorative and ornate, as well as formal and uncomfortable. On the dinner tables of the middle class was a rather wide variety of food. Members of the middle class often had more leisure hours than the lower class. They read and went to concerts, operas, and the theater. They saw to it that their children received good educations. The middle class had won a voice in government and were enjoying the fruits of the Industrial Revolution and the growth of democracy.

How the Upper Class Lived

In the late nineteenth century, the members of the upper class were the owners

An omnibus, as carriages were called, carries its crowded travelers. Today's traveler often fares no better.

of large amounts of land and the owners of large factories. The landowners who often rented their lands to others and lived off the rents (*absentee landlords*) were becoming fewer in number. The tenant farmer, however, often became deeply indebted to the landlord. In this case, a lord and master relationship remained between landlord and tenant.

The factory owners were capitalists. They owned the machines of industry and the banks. It was from their money as well as from their work that the factory owners grew rich. In the town houses and country estates, they enjoyed the best of city and country life. They entertained lavishly. No expense was spared to bring the products of the farms and factories to their homes or tables. They owned the means of production, and they managed them forcefully.

Music, painting, theater, and opera were supported by the upper class. Golf, tennis, hunting, and horse racing were

Fox hunting was enjoyed by the British upper class. It was a sport for people with leisure time and money.

the sports they enjoyed. They had much leisure time. They also had the time and money to pursue higher education. Since they did not work for a living, some sons of the upper class tried to make a mark in military or political affairs. Many members of the upper class—Sir Winston Churchill, for example—took life seriously and made important contributions to society.

Health Conditions in the Nineteenth Century

The Industrial Revolution opened the way to a cleaner and healthier life. Transportation improvements in railroads, roads, and steamships made it possible for many people to eat fresh meat and fruit for the first time. Improved farm machinery increased the amount of food that could be grown. Public sewerage and sanitary facilities made homes and cities cleaner places in which to live. The result was that people were healthier and lived longer. Fewer children died at birth or during infancy, and there were fewer epidemics of disease. Population grew

due to the decrease in both disease and the death rate.

Edward Jenner [jen′ər] (1749–1823), an English medical doctor, discovered vaccination as a means to prevent smallpox. Until then smallpox had been the cause of many deaths and much human misery. Before 1800, almost no family escaped smallpox. Jenner's vaccination method showed that the disease could be prevented. When a patient is vaccinated, a small dose of the virus of cowpox is given. By building up resistance, the body can fight off smallpox. The process of building up resistance to a disease is called *immunization*.

Today, adults and children are made immune to many diseases by vaccination. In Jenner's day most people were afraid of being vaccinated. Not until the king and queen of England urged vaccination did it become common. From England, smallpox vaccine and the knowledge of vaccination spread to other parts of the world. The smallpox vaccine was as great a blessing then as the polio vaccine was in the 1950s.

Louis Pasteur [pa stür′] (1822–95), French chemist and pioneer in medicine, found that bacteria caused many diseases. Bacteria are tiny living creatures that cannot be seen with the naked eye. Pasteur said that bacteria turned milk sour and made humans and animals ill. *Pasteurization* is a method of treating foods (especially milk) to make them safe for human consumption. It kills bacteria through heat. Our debt to Pasteur is great. It was he who also showed how to save farm animals from certain diseases and how to prevent and treat rabies.

Joseph Lister [lis′tur] (1827–1912), an English surgeon, used Pasteur's discovery of bacteria. Lister's patients did not get infections after being operated on. This was because Lister used carbolic acid to keep his medical instruments and the wounds of his patients clean and free of bacteria. Dr. Lister became known as the founder of antiseptic surgery.

Others took advantage of the pioneering work done by Pasteur. In 1876, Robert Koch [käch] (1843–1910), a German doctor, found that specific bacteria caused specific diseases. The problem was how to identify which bacteria caused the disease and which were harmless or even beneficial. He found which bacteria caused anthrax, tuberculosis, cholera, and other diseases. In 1905, he was awarded the Nobel Prize for his work in developing a test which determines if a patient has tuberculosis.

Florence Nightingale (1820–1910), English nurse and hospital reformer, devoted her life to the care of the unfortunate. She established a barrack hospital and gave medical aid to wounded soldiers of the Crimean War. (See p. 377). To the soldiers of this war she was known as the "Angel of the Crimea."

Marie Curie [cür ē'] (1867–1934), French chemist and physicist, made outstanding contributions to the field of medicine. She is best known for her work with radioactivity, including the discovery of radium. She was awarded two Nobel Prizes for her work.

Check in Here

1. Give three reasons for the growth of world population.

2. Give three reasons which explain why people moved to the cities.

3. How did the life of factory workers gradually improve?

4. Compare and contrast the life styles of the working classes with those of the middle and upper classes.

5. How do improvements in sanitation and in transportation help bring about improvements in the health conditions of the people?

Victorian society did not approve of women becoming involved in war. When Florence Nightingale went to the Crimea she was resented at first. After saving many soldiers' lives and working under terrible conditions, she won the respect and gratitude of the English. Later, she made important reforms in the field of nursing.

EDUCATION AND DEMOCRACY MAKE LIFE BETTER

How Free Education Grew in Democracy

Up to the nineteenth century there was little attempt on the part of governments to educate people. As the right to vote was slowly given to more people, it became obvious to thoughtful people that the vote by itself was useless. Thomas Jefferson once stated that if we expect to be ignorant and free in a state of civilization, we expect what has never been and never will be. For democracy to work well the people need education.

In the United States the idea of free public education was adopted early in some parts of America. This education was mostly training in the three R's and religion. Nevertheless, the education was open to all and free. In 1821, the first public high school in the United States was opened in Boston, Massachusetts. In 1837, Massachusetts organized the first state Board of Education, with Horace Mann as its secretary. Henry Barnard, another American pioneer in education, served as America's first United States Commissioner of Education (1867–70). By 1860, a majority of northern and western states had free public schooling.

In Europe, education was readily available for the rich. Europeans were slow, however, to accept the idea that all people should be sent to school. In England, the first gift of public money for free schooling was made in 1832. It was not until 1870 that a national system of free public schools was born. Soon all children from five to fourteen were forced by law to attend school. In France, the *Ferry Laws* of the 1880s provided free and compulsory education. In England, France, Germany, Belgium, the Netherlands, and the Scandinavian countries, free education gained a firm foothold in the late nineteenth century.

Pioneers in education, like pioneers in science, politics, and exploration, deserve an important place in history. One of the more outstanding figures in education was Swiss educational reformer Johann Pestalozzi [pes'tə lot'sē] (1746–1827). He taught that the ills of society could be improved through education. He improved methods of teaching reading, writing, and arithmetic.

Pestalozzi tried to put new ideas about education into practice. Pestalozzi thought that the teacher-pupil relationship should be one of love. This suggestion was shocking because, in those days, teachers were harsh and often brutal. They did not spare the rod.

Johann Herbart [her'bärt] (1776–1841), German thinker and educator, learned from Pestalozzi and improved upon his methods. Herbart believed that a teacher should try to hold the attention of students through interesting subjects rather than through beatings. He felt that schools should develop good character traits among students.

Friedrich Froebel was a German educator. What was his contribution to education?

In the United States and Western Europe women worked hard to achieve one of the basic democratic rights: the right to vote. These women in New York City were among those commited to the cause. In 1919, the United States passed the Nineteenth Amendment giving women the right to vote.

Friedrich Froebel [frō'bəl] (1782–1852), a German educator, may be looked upon as the founder of the kindergarten system. In the kindergarten children were taught through play. They were prepared to learn the skills of reading and writing in higher grades.

Maria Montessori [mon'ti sôr'ē] (1870–1952) was the first Italian woman to become a doctor. She earned fame, however, as a teacher who developed new ways of teaching the very young. Her methods are still widely used in Europe and in the United States.

John Dewey [dü'ē] (1859–1952), American educator and thinker, was one of the greatest of the educational pioneers. He was responsible for developing the belief that students learn best by doing. His main idea was that there should be close ties among the home, the school, and the neighborhood. He believed that schools should teach students how to solve life's problems. Education is life, not merely getting ready for it, and therefore education goes on throughout life. Dewey's ideas have influenced education in nearly every country in the world.

How Women Gained Rights in Democracy

Women's struggle for equal rights with men has been a long and difficult one and is not yet over. One of the early fighters for women's rights was Mary Wollstonecraft (1759–97), an English author. (See p. 298.) Because of her efforts to achieve equality, she was called a "hyena in petticoats." She fought for the right of women to vote, to enjoy educational opportunities, and to hold property. She faced a long, hard, uphill battle.

Among the first victories of women was their admission to colleges and universities. For many years, men were hostile to the idea of women receiving an advanced education. Yet, some progress was made. In the United States, Oberlin College admitted women as well as men in 1833. In 1836, Mount Holyoke College in Massachusetts became the first college for women in America. In 1847, Elizabeth Blackwell was admitted to the study of medicine in the United States. In Geneva, New York, the first women's medical college was opened in 1865.

In Europe, the admission of women to higher education was somewhat slower. The University of Zurich (Switzerland) was a forerunner in the admission of women. In 1866, the University of Paris admitted women and men students on an equal basis as did Italian universities. In 1869, however, there were riots in Edinburgh, Scotland, when a small group of women was admitted to the study of medicine. Sweden and later England admitted women to colleges and universities. By 1880, however, it was still difficult for women to be admitted to many colleges and universities. It was not until 1919, for example, that England allowed women to become lawyers. Once in the university, women had to have strong personalities to withstand criticism from male students, from their parents, and from other women.

As difficult as the struggle for women to get an education in colleges and universities was, the struggle to gain the right to vote was even more difficult for them. In America, Elizabeth Cady Stanton [stan′tən] (1815–1902) took the lead in fighting for the rights of women. She organized the first women's rights meeting. At the Seneca Falls Convention which met in New York in 1848, women took a strong stand against the tyranny of men. The convention marked the beginning of the American *suffragist* [səf′rə gist] *movement*. This was a militant movement that sought to win voting rights for women.

As time went on, women became louder and sometimes more violent in demanding their rights. In the early 1900s, the suffragist movement in England became more militant. The suffragists were led by Emmeline Pankhurst [pangk′hurst] (1858–1928). They sought the right to vote for women. Suffragists spoke on street corners, held parades and demonstrations (breaking windows and setting off bombs to gain attention), and rallied members of their sex to action. For ten years, violence in one form or another broke out. Meetings of Parliament were interrupted and parliamentary leaders were shouted down when they tried to speak in public. Men and women began to take notice.

Women's fight for the right to vote was first won in 1895 in Australia. In 1902, the right was granted in New Zealand; in 1907, in Norway; in 1919, in the United States. In England, women won the right to vote on a piecemeal basis. Older women were given this right in 1918, and in 1928, women over twenty-one were allowed to vote. In France, women had to wait until 1945 before they could vote, and in Switzerland, women's right to vote was granted as late as 1971.

The rights of women to higher education and to the vote have been largely won. Another struggle women had to win was the right to buy, sell, own, or inherit property on an equal basis with men. During most of the nineteenth century, a woman's wealth became the property of her husband. Only he could buy, sell, or give it away. Gradually, in the United States and in Europe women gained greater rights over their own property. Today, women seek to achieve equal job opportunity and equal pay with men.

How Democracy Helped the Unfortunate

During the nineteenth century, some private individuals and organizations did what they could to help those who were helpless, particularly orphans. As governments became more democratic and responsible for people's welfare, they

(turn to page 434)

Harriet Martineau

(1802–1876)

Harriet Martineau [mär'ti nō'] was the first important woman social scientist of the nineteenth century. She ranks with Adam Smith, Thomas Malthus, and David Ricardo (see pp. 397–398) in helping to make the economy of an industrial society understandable. More than the male writers, however, she took special pains in helping working men and women, as well as members of Parliament, understand how the growth of commerce and industry was changing the world about them.

She was born in England of a family with a French Protestant background. As a child, Martineau was generally in frail health. She was shy, timid, fearful, and had no sense of smell or taste. Before long she became partially deaf. At fifteen, Martineau was sent to a boarding school kept by her aunt. There her life brightened considerably. In 1821, she began to write. Upon her father's death she began to write for a living. The very modest inheritance she received was not enough for her to live on without a source of income.

Her most famous work, and the one that brought her national fame, was first published in 1832. It was entitled *Illustrations of Political Economy*. This nine-volume work did not add any new economic theories. Rather, it illustrated in understandable ways the economic and political problems of the day. Martineau dealt with the subjects of population growth and the impact of the factory system on workers. Her books were read by cotton mill hands, domestic servants, and inmates of workhouses.

In 1834, Harriet Martineau paid a long visit to America. She wrote *Society in America*, which was based on her visit. This work is one of the better known foreign writings on the American people. Because she took a strong abolitionist stand against slavery, Harriet Martineau was never very popular in the United States. During her visit, she was threatened several times. Just as she was concerned about the plight of the slave, so too was she concerned about the plight of women. She became an important leader among women activists in England and in America.

Harriet Martineau wrote novels and was especially successful in writing stories for children. In 1846, despite difficulty with a heart ailment, she went with some friends to Egypt, Palestine, and Syria. Upon her return she published *Eastern Life, Present and Past*. Basically, this was a study of religions over the years. It was part of the new interest in the role of religion in a more scientific era.

Harriet Martineau's life was rich but controversial. Her books spoke to the needs of her time. They were eagerly read by people who had begun to earn the money with which to buy books. These people had the education to read and to understand what Martineau's books contained.

took over a large share of caring for unfortunate people.

During the eighteenth and nineteenth centuries, the slave trade proved profitable. Many failed to see that it was wrong. With the growth of democracy came the demand that the slave trade, if not slavery itself, be stopped. Denmark was the first country to stop the slave trade. Later, the United States and Great Britain abolished slave trading. Although the slave trade was slowly being abolished, slavery continued for some years. In 1833, William Wilberforce [wil'bər force] persuaded Parliament to end slavery in the British colonies.

It took a great Civil War and the *Emancipation Proclamation* of 1863 to end slavery in the United States. Before this, slaves were sold at auction and families were disrupted. The slave had no rights and was denied the opportunity for an education. Even after emancipation the struggle of blacks for equal rights was long and hard. The barriers of segregation and discrimination fell slowly. The black revolution of modern times is is a continuation of the struggle for equal opportunities.

During the nineteenth century, government made little effort to relieve the burdens of the poor. Private organizations provided some relief. Among private groups, the *Salvation Army* is probably the best known. It was begun by William Booth [büth] (1829–1912), an English preacher. He tried to form a group that would give religious and material help to the needy. The Salvation

Army was organized on military lines—with ministers as officers and members as soldiers. Booth took the idea of the Salvation Army to several continents.

In America, Jane Addams [ad'əmz] (1860–1935) pioneered in social work by helping Chicago's poor. Helen Keller [kel'ər] (1880–1968) set an example to the handicapped by overcoming blindness and deafness.

To Henri Dunant [dü nän'] (1828–1910), a Swiss philanthropist, goes the honor of establishing the *International Red Cross*. It was his work that led to a meeting in Geneva in 1864. There it was agreed to establish an organization for giving aid to wounded soldiers. At first, only a few nations agreed to do so. Later, an International Red Cross was established. Its job became one of helping those hurt by disasters: floods, earthquakes, and war. In America, the work of the Red Cross (established 1881) was carried forward by Clara Barton [bär'tun]. Today, although most nations are members of the International Red Cross, it is often hard to make all nations obey its rules.

In most countries of the nineteenth century punishments for crime were more severe than was necessary. In both Europe and the United States death was the punishment for serious crimes. Imprisonment for debt was the rule. This was particularly harsh because in debtor's prison a person could not earn money to pay what was owed. If the prisoner was the only or chief wage earner, the family was often left in hunger and cold. The prisons themselves were filthy, and no attempt was made to make better persons of the prisoners.

Gradually, change did come. An Italian professor of law, Cesare Beccaria [bek är'ē ə] (1738–94), was the first to call attention to the harsh penalties and the inhuman treatment of prisoners. His book, *Crimes and Punishments,* was written in 1764. It advocated doing away with torture and the death penalty. The influence of the book spread rapidly.

John Howard and Elizabeth Fry were both reformers who brought about changes for the better in English prisons. In 1829, Robert Peel [pēl] (1788–1850), as England's Home Secretary, organized England's first police force. The police of England are still called *bobbies* after Peel's first name.

Check in Here

1. If democracy is to succeed, the masses of people need to be educated. Why?

2. List three gains of women during the nineteenth and twentieth centuries.

3. What changes took place during the nineteenth century in the way society treated the poor and helpless?

4. Why do some people say that the right to vote by itself is a useless thing? Do you agree or disagree?

SCIENCE AND TECHNOLOGY CLASH WITH RELIGION

The New Scientific Theories of the Nineteenth Century

As books and newspapers increased in circulation during the nineteenth century, people were stimulated to think about new ideas. They began to wonder about how the earth was formed and when life first appeared on it. In the middle of the nineteenth century, these topics were on every lip.

Elizabeth Fry sought English prison reform in the nineteenth century. What other social reforms were being made at this time?

John Dalton [dôl'tən] (1766–1844), an English chemist, discovered that elements are made up of tiny parts. He said that elements are the basic building blocks of matter. Elements are composed of extremely small particles called *atoms.* Dalton's work led to further developments in physics and chemistry. Only since 1900 have scientists learned to split the atom and put its energy to work.

Throughout history people have been interested in Earth's relation to the

435

Sun and to the other bodies (planets) of the solar system. They have wondered about the age of the earth. Sir Charles Lyell [lī′əl] (1797–1875), a British geologist, gave us one of the early theories about the question of the Earth's age. In 1830, he wrote a book in which he said that the face of the Earth is changing all the time. Rivers wear down mountains. Earthquakes, water, wind, and rain—each in its own way—constantly change the face of the earth. These forces of nature bring changes which help explain why the earth looks the way it does. These changes take place over thousands of years. Lyell thought that the Earth is many millions of years old.

If the Earth is millions of years old, when did living things first appear? When did men and women first appear? Some scientists are not sure of the answers to these questions. However, the ideas of Charles Darwin [där′win] (1809–82), an English naturalist, are accepted by many scientists today. Darwin's book, *On the Origin of Species*, which was published in 1859, described his theory of evolution. It is one of the most important books ever written. Darwin said that all forms of life, including human life, began from simple forms millions of years ago. The slow process of change from simple forms to complex forms is called *evolution*. In the process of evolution some forms of life die. Those that are best fitted to their environment live. This part of the process of evolution is called the *survival of the fittest*. Darwin pointed out that life is a constant struggle between the strong and the weak. This struggle, he said, will always continue.

Darwin's views had great impact on the nineteenth century, as they still do today. That impact was felt in science and in attitudes toward the relations among human beings as well. If nature was a biological struggle for the survival of the fittest, was there not also a social struggle in which the able survive and the less able fall by the way?

Herbert Spencer [spen′sər] (1820–1903) was a British philosopher. He took Darwin's theory and applied it to groups of people and even to whole nations. History, he said, was but a struggle among individuals, and only the most fit survive. This view is sometimes referred to as *Social Darwinism*. In the nineteenth century it allowed the rich to justify the wealth they accumulated. At the same time, it encouraged a disregard for the needs of the poor and the weak. Among

After studying plant and animal life all over the world, Darwin returned to England. There he wrote books and continued his observations.

nations, Social Darwinism invited warfare. War was believed to be the ultimate test of who was fit to survive and who was not.

Social Darwinism also influenced people's thinking about race. If carried far enough, the theory suggested that some races were more fit to survive than were others. Arthur de Gobineau [də gō'bin ō] (1816–1882) was among the first to declare the superiority of the white race. Within the white race, according to Gobineau's false beliefs, the Germans were those most fit to survive. The Anglo-Saxons were slightly less fit, while the Jews and Slavs were considered unfit by him. Gobineau's racist views were later used by Nazi Germany to persecute Jews. Yet, during much of the nineteenth century the idea of the superiority of the white Anglo-Saxon race was accepted. It was used to justify conquest of the so-called lesser races of the world.

How Science and Religion Clashed

The new scientific ideas of the nineteenth century conflicted with traditional religious views. *Creationists*, people who follow traditional religion, believe the Bible is true as written. In the Bible it says that the world was created in six days. According to the Bible, from the very beginning all the heavenly bodies were in place, as were the plants and animals, except for some that might have died in the flood. According to traditionalists, the world is about 6,000 years old. Some people believe that the Bible holds the only true explanation of the world. Science, they believe, can explain only the period after the world's creation.

Science and religion can sometimes be harmonized. The scientist Isaac Newton, for example, was a deeply religious man. He was satisfied, however, that the laws of gravity and thermodynamics that he developed were in keeping with the divine creation of the universe. He supposed, for example, that in the beginning the planets had been hurled into orbit by the hand of God. What happened after that he attributed to the laws of gravity.

Darwin's ideas, rather than Newton's, however, clashed with the prevailing religious ideas of the time. They caused turmoil in religion. Nevertheless, people were fascinated by the notion that humans were a part of nature as much as plants and other forms of life. Darwin was accepted by those who believed that progress was inevitable.

The theory of evolution challenged the biblical view of creation. It did so by making humans part of evolution. Humans too had evolved from a simple form of life to a more complex one. This idea raised questions. If Darwin was right, did humans really have an immortal soul? And if they did, why were they alone in having one? In 1864, Pope Pius IX wrote a document entitled, "A Syllabus of the Principal Errors of Our Times." It condemned, among other things, the new theory of evolution and the scientific ways of thinking upon which it was based.

Six years later a Church council proclaimed the dogma of *papal infallibility*. This meant that on matters of morals and faith the pope could not be wrong. The reason for taking this stand was to make the pope stronger. He could then attack Darwinism, especially as it applied to human beings. Under Pope Leo XIII a more moderate position was taken by the Church in its attitude toward scientific developments. Nevertheless, it continued to oppose strongly the doctrine of evolution.

Protestants, and to some extent Jews, were also upset by the theory of evolution. Some Protestants made their own individual peace with evolution. Protestant *Fundamentalists*, especially in the

United States, insist upon the story of creation as given in the Book of Genesis. Fundamentalists believe the Bible is a factual record of history. This group has never accepted the theory of evolution.

Despite its conflict with religion, Darwin's theory of evolution gained rapid acceptance during the nineteenth and twentieth centuries. One reason was that people had a great deal of faith in science and its ability to find answers. Today, not all scientists agree on the origins of the creation of the earth. Some have suggested that perhaps the universe was created in a major geological happening. Science has not yet solved the mysteries of the universe. The theory of evolution remains an important but uncertain one in a world that seeks answers to questions in many ways.

Religion in the Nineteenth Century

The clash of science and religion was one aspect of the changing role of religion in society. During much of history, church and state were very close. The state often required people of all faiths to pay taxes to support the churches. Sometimes, the state enforced attendance at church services. At other times, the state expected members of the government to be of the religion supported by the state.

During the eighteenth century, the United States led the way in separating church and state. The United States Constitution makes it unlawful to establish a state religion. No religious requirement for holding office can be established. In separating church and state other countries followed the United States.

In France, church and state parted company in 1905. (See p. 419.) In Italy, the relations of church and state were complicated because of the hostility of the papacy toward a unified Italy. This problem was partially solved in 1929, when Mussolini signed an agreement with the pope. (See p. 554.) In England, church and state were never completely separated. However, religious liberty was gradually established. The separation of church and state helped expand religious tolerance. This encouraged the practice of all faiths. Religious differences are an accepted feature of modern times.

In the nineteenth century the scientific way of thinking was applied to religion itself. The Bible was subjected to what some have called a "higher criticism." Attempts were made to find out who wrote the Bible and when it was written. Some scholars found that parts of the Bible may have been written long after the events they describe were supposed to have taken place. Some compared Christianity with other religions. They found more similarities than differences in what different religions taught. Still other scholars took the daring view that perhaps Jesus was only a superior human being who had neither performed any miracles nor risen from the dead. This view was expressed by Ernest Renan [ri nan'] (1823–1892) in his book *Life of Jesus.*

A new attitude was growing: all areas of life were worthy of further study and review. The result was that new mysteries were marked for exploration.

Check in Here

1. How did some of the scientific work of the nineteenth century lead to the development of modern atomic energy?

2. How did Darwin benefit from the work of Lyell?

3. How did Darwin's theory of survival of the fittest also encourage the theory that might makes right?

4. How did Darwin's theory of evolution clash with people's traditional religious beliefs?

5. How was the scientific way of thinking applied to religion itself?

LITERATURE, MUSIC, AND ART REFLECT THE SPIRIT OF THE TIMES

How Literature Grew in the Nineteenth Century

In the nineteenth century, there was a large audience for books. More people were learning to read and had more time to read as well. Short stories and poetry were popular with many readers. The poems of Wordsworth, Byron, Keats, and Shelley were well known. These English poets were moved by the great events that touched their lives, including the French Revolution and the fight for Greek independence. Their feelings for these events found expression in their works. *Prometheus Unbound* by Percy Bysshe Shelley [shel'ē] (1792–1822) is a good example of this. William Wordsworth [wurdz'wurth'] (1770–1850) was an English poet of distinction. He wrote of the natural beauty he found around him.

Samuel Taylor Coleridge [kōl'rij] in *Rime of the Ancient Mariner* moves the imagination of countless readers as he tells a story of a strange ship:

Alone, alone, all, all alone;
Alone on a wide, wide sea.

Later poets were influenced by the Industrial Revolution, science, democracy, and nationalism. Among the more eminent of these were Alfred Lord Tennyson [ten'i sən] (1809–1892) and Elizabeth Barret Browning [brou'ning] (1806–1861) and Robert Browning (1812–1889). In Tennyson's "The Charge of the Light Brigade," the heroism of soldiers in the Crimean War is vividly recalled.

Everyone likes to read a good story, and nineteenth century England had many fine novelists, or storytellers. Charles Dickens [dik'əns] (1812–70) is probably the best known. In *A Tale of Two Cities* he wrote about the French

Captain Alfred Dreyfus was falsely accused of selling military secrets to the Germans. He was sent to Devil's Island. When Zola defended him, he too was sent to prison.

Revolution. In *David Copperfield, Oliver Twist,* and *Great Expectations,* he told about the lives, loves, adventures, triumphs, and disappointments of poor boys in industrial England.

In France there were several literary giants. Victor Hugo [hü'gō] (1802–85) wrote a novel, *Les Misérables,* which was a best seller. His great name in nineteenth century literature was matched by Alexandre Dumas [dü mä'], Guy de Maupassant [mō'pə sänt'], and Honoré de Balzac [bal' zak]. Émile Zola [zō'lə] (1840–1902) was a giant among giants. He was a storyteller as well as a newspaperman. It was his celebrated newspaper article, *J'Accuse,* which helped reopen the Dreyfus Case and free an innocent man from prison.

Russia was the home of many writers. *Crime and Punishment* by Fyodor Dostoevski [dos'tə yef'skē] (1821–81) and *War and Peace* by Leo Tolstoy [tol'stoi] (1828–1910) were among Russia's gifts to the world of good books.

439

How Music Developed in the Nineteenth Century

Music has universal appeal. In the nineteenth century, certain qualities of music were more richly expressed by the development of new instruments and techniques. People had more time to listen to good music, and the number of orchestras and outstanding musicians greatly increased.

There were many great composers in Europe in the nineteenth century. Ludwig van Beethoven [bā'tō vən] (1770–1827), a German composer, wrote nine symphonies after developing a hearing defect which led to complete deafness. Other German composers were Felix Mendelssohn [men'dəl sən] (1809–47), Johannes Brahms [brämz] (1833–97), and Richard Wagner [väg'nər] (1813–83). They must be included among the great composers. Their music is still played, and happy couples still get married to the accompaniment of Mendelssohn's *Wedding March*.

From Hungary came Franz Liszt [list] (1811–86), noted for his Hungarian rhapsodies. From Poland came Frederic Chopin [shō'pan] (1810–49), famous for his piano music. The story of the defeat of Napoleon at the hands of Russia was told by Peter Tchaikovsky [chī kôf'skē] (1840–93) in his *1812 Overture*. America did not produce such great composers during the nineteenth century. Nevertheless, Americans can be proud of the folk songs of Stephen Foster (1826–64) and the hymns of Lowell Mason (1792–1872).

Modern History

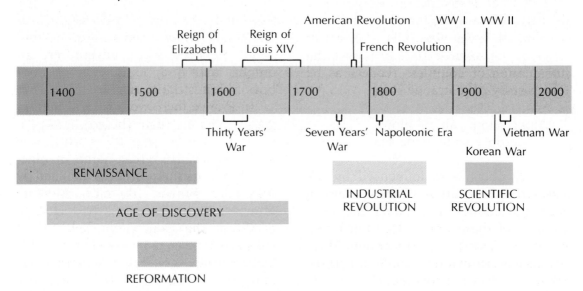

Be able to place the following events on the time line:

1837–1901	Victorian Era	1862	Pasteur—disease caused by bacteria
1821	first U.S. public high school	1865	Lister—antiseptics in surgery
1870	free public schools in Britain	1898	Curies—radium
1833	slavery ended in British colonies	1859	Darwin—*Origin of Species*
1863	slavery ended in U.S.	1919	women won vote in U.S.
1829	police force founded in Britain	1928	women won vote in Britain
1881	Red Cross founded	1945	women won vote in France
1796	Jenner—small pox vaccine		

Claude Monet's *Terrace at Sainte-Adresse.* Monet was fascinated by the effects of sunlight at different times of the day. Notice the long shadows and the colors in this painting. What is the name of the school of painting to which Monet belonged?

How Art Developed
in the Nineteenth Century

Art, in the form of painting, sculpture, and architecture, made advances during the nineteenth century. The French painter Eugene Delacroix [də la krwä'] (1799–1863) painted canvases and murals in rich and lively colors. Many are on display in Paris and in the library of Luxembourg. Honoré Daumier [dō myā'] (1808–79), a cartoonist by profession, ridiculed middle-class life in his cartoons. The French are known for the *Impressionist* [im pre'sion ist] school of painting, in which artists painted their impressions of what they saw around them. Édouard Manet [ma nā'] (1832–83), Pierre Renoir [ren'wär] (1841–1919), Claude Monet [mō nā'] (1840–1926), and Paul Cézanne [si zan'] (1839–1906) were among these painters. Rosa Bonheur [bo nur'] (1822–99) was a French painter whose pictures of horses and animal life gave her widespread fame.

It was in architecture that the marriage of art and industry can best be seen. Industry developed new materials and used old materials in new ways. Iron and steel made it possible to build taller buildings. The styles of Greek and

441

Roman buildings were copied for structures such as libraries, railroad stations and other public buildings.

Steel, iron, brick, glass, and stone were used as construction materials in homes, schools, hospitals, libraries, and hotels. Louis Sullivan [sul'ə vən] (1856–1924) and Frank Lloyd Wright [rīt] (1869–1959) were pioneers in modern American architecture. They said that good design in building did not depend on decoration. Rather, a building's location and purpose should determine its shape and the materials used to build it. If these were properly balanced, a beautiful building would be the result. The skyscrapers with which you are familiar are the result of this thinking in design.

Check in Here

1. Why was there an unusually large audience for literature during the nineteenth century?

2. List two contributions of the nineteenth century to each of the following: music, literature, and art.

3. What evidence of a marriage between industry and art can be seen during the nineteenth century?

REVIEWING THE BASICS

In this chapter, the story of monarchs and wars was left behind. The nineteenth century has been described in terms of the democratic and industrial growth which made everyday life more comfortable and enjoyable. During the nineteenth century, population grew. The death rate declined as a result of better health care and improved sanitation. People moved from farm to city. Many agricultural laborers became factory laborers. While factory conditions left much to be desired, they were often an improvement over the backbreaking labor the landless farmer performed.

Among the working class of the city, life was hard. The city was crowded. At least four or five people shared a two-room apartment in which there was little heat and little privacy. Working hours were long, but they were gradually reduced. Men and women took advantage of the shorter hours to enjoy sports, to participate in games, to get some schooling, to read books, and, most importantly, to buy and read the newspaper. The middle and upper class led easier lives than the poor, but the style of life varied considerably as some were very rich and others were moderately well off.

There was a great intellectual awakening in the nineteenth century. The most important development was Darwin's theory of evolution and the survival of the fittest. This view clashed with the traditional religious view which followed the biblical story of the creation of the world.

The nineteenth century was marked by a number of important developments. There was the clash between the views of evolutionism and those of creationism. The nonreligious nature of society clashed with traditional religious views. There was an attempt to apply higher criticism to the Bible. There was a change from rural to urban ways of living. The scientific way of thinking was applied to many areas of thought.

These developments were reflected in the art, music, and architecture of the period. Education was gradually extended to the masses. Women began pressing for their rights in education, work, politics, and the ownership of property. Eventually, women won the right to vote. People convicted of crime were more humanely treated. The times were filled with hope. The improvements of the nineteenth century, however, were not well distributed among Europeans, to say nothing about the people in other parts of the world.

REVIEWING THE HIGHLIGHTS

People to Identify

Jane Addams	Robert Peel	Pope Pius IX
Horace Mann	Maria Montessori	Helen Keller
Henry Barnard	Clara Barton	Charles Dickens
Johann Pestalozzi	Cesare Beccaria	Victor Hugo
Johann Herbart	Louis Pasteur	Émile Zola
Friedrich Froebel	Joseph Lister	Leo Tolstoy
John Dewey	Robert Koch	Ludwig van
Elizabeth Cady Stanton	Florence Nightingale	Beethoven
Emmeline Pankhurst	Marie Curie	Peter Tchaikovsky
Harriet Martineau	John Dalton	Frank Lloyd Wright
Mary Wollstonecraft	Charles Lyell	Honoré Daumier
William Booth	Charles Darwin	Rosa Bonheur
Arthur de Gobineau	Samuel Coleridge	Pope Leo XIII
Herbert Spencer	Ernest Renan	Queen Victoria

Terms to Understand

Ferry Laws	urban	Impressionists
Salvation Army	urbanization	immunization
survival of the fittest	rural	pasteurization
class	evolution	Trades Union Act
creationist	Social Darwinism	Seneca Falls Convention
	suffragist movement	

1. What two forces were largely responsible for the birth of a better world in the nineteenth century?
2. Despite some improvements why was life in the nineteenth century still hard for the working class?
3. What effect did the Trades Union Act of 1871 have on the working class?
4. Why did the upper classes live better than the working classes during the nineteenth century?
5. What were the main ideas of Johann Pestalozzi and Johann Herbart with respect to education?
6. Where was the first breakthrough in the fight for women's rights made?
7. How did the Salvation Army try to relieve the burdens of the poor?
8. Why was the Red Cross formed?
9. Why was imprisonment for debt a harsh punishment?
10. What reforms were advocated in *Crimes and Punishments* by Cesare Beccaria?
11. What is the principle upon which vaccination is based?
12. How did Joseph Lister use the findings of Louis Pasteur to advance his own research?
13. What is meant by *urbanization?* Why did cities grow rapidly during the nineteenth century?
14. Why was there an increased interest in reading during the nineteenth century?
15. What is the main idea of *On the Origin of Species?*
16. What were the new developments in music and painting during the nineteenth century?
17. Why did the theory of evolution clash with the Bible's story of creation?
18. To what extent does the idea of survival of the fittest apply to groups of people and to nations? Give reasons for your point of view.

THINGS TO DO

1. Draw a cartoon in support of Darwin's theory of evolution and survival of the fittest. Draw a cartoon opposing this point of view.
2. Write a letter describing what impressed you as an American tourist about the World's Fair at the Crystal Palace held in 1851.
3. Conduct an interview that you as a reporter might have had with men and women of Victorian England that may be of special interest to readers of your newspaper.

The Victorian Woman

The selection below describes the changing nature of women's employment during two decades (1840s and 1850s) of the Victorian Era. Read the selection with care and discuss in class the questions that follow it.

Young ladies did not work; women did. The convention* which kept a middle-class miss idle in the drawing-room did not apply to the lower classes; economic necessity was too strong. In 1841, when the first census of the new reign* was taken, the percentage of women and girls in employment in Great Britain was 22.9—just over two million out of a total female population of nine-and-a-half million (9,514,800). They were employed in more than 300 trades. But almost all of these accounted for only about one quarter of the women employed. The three categories of domestic service*, textiles and dress manufacture, and agriculture together employed 1,604,000 women and girls—almost three-quarters of the total female working population of 2,176,500. The chief occupation for an employed woman in Britain was to be a domestic servant, an extension, in fact, of the daily life that most of the 7,338,300 non-employed women in the country led. One in every ten of the total female population was a domestic servant. . . .

In 1851, when the second census of the reign was taken, the number of women and girls in employment in Great Britain had increased to almost three million (2,988,600) out of a total female population of 10,659,600. The percentage of females employed had also increased substantially to 28.9. Domestic service, textile and dress manufacture, and agriculture were still the main occupations. They now employed 2,460,000—over four-fifths (82.3 percent) of the total female working population as against 58.8 percent in 1841. However, there had been changes in their order of importance. Manufacturing as a whole came first, its numbers having more than doubled in ten years; indeed the number employed in textiles and dyeing alone was larger than 'all manufacturing' in 1841. A significant increase was in the number of female metalworkers. This reflected the increase in the metal-working trades as a whole, which showed the growing sophistication of British industry. Another sign of a more complex economy was that new employments began to make their appearance. For example, in 1854 women clerks, suitably chaperoned, were employed by the Electric Telegraph Company in Manchester.†

Vocabulary

convention—custom
reign—rule, in this case, of Queen Victoria
domestic service—work in the home

1. Explain the meaning of, "Young ladies did not work; women did."
2. What reasons explain the shift in the nature of the employment of women between 1841 and 1851?
3. What significance may be attached to the employment of women as clerks by the Electric Telegraph Company?
4. What were the major occupations in which women found employment? Why these?
5. What work did non-employed women in Britain do?

†Duncan Crow, *The Victorian Woman* (London: George Allen & Unwin, Ltd., 1971), pp. 72–73. Used by permission.

1. Prepare a television program based on the life of one of the following: (**a**) James Watt; (**b**) Eli Whitney; (**c**) Clara Barton; (**d**) Florence Nightingale; (**e**) Louis Pasteur; (**f**) Emmeline Pankhurst; (**g**) Benjamin Disraeli.

2. Prepare a "Meeting of Minds" in which students take the views of Bismarck, Cavour, and Louis Napoleon and discuss nationalism.

3. Draw a cartoon illustrating one of the following: (**a**) The advance of science, (**b**) The emerging role of women.

4. Make sketches or models of the following: (**a**) Men's and women's dress during the 1850s; (**b**) Selected inventions of the early Industrial Revolution.

5. Prepare a map of Europe showing the trend toward urbanization between 1850 and 1900.

6. Select an area of artistic interest (painting, sculpture, or music) and prepare a report for the class showing how world events shaped developments in one of these areas.

7. Identify pioneers in education other than those mentioned in this unit and prepare a report for the class.

8. Debate. *Resolved:* The theory of evolution best explains today's natural world.

9. Make a scrapbook of pictures, newspaper articles, and cartoons illustrating the changing role of women during the nineteenth century.

10. Prepare a newspaper for the date May 1, 1851—Crystal Palace Exhibit—in which you include articles about the exhibit, advertising, cartoons, a comic, and other real events that took place in England on the same day. If space permits, include *real* events that took place elsewhere in the world.

11. Conduct a forum with your class in which you discuss the following: The Industrial Revolution Is Still Going On.

12. Debate. *Resolved:* Nationalism remains a vital force in world affairs.

13. Hold a "Meet the Press" conference in which a group of reporters tries to get a story from each of the following: (**a**) Dreyfus; (**b**) Boulanger.

14. Read Émile Zola's *J'Accuse* and report on your reading to the class.

15. Make a time line for the Victorian Era showing significant developments in the advance of democracy in England, France, and the United States.

16. Report to the class on the developments in health care during the nineteenth century.

BIBLIOGRAPHY

Ausbel, Herman. *The Late Victorians*. D. Van Nostrand Co. A brief account of the life, times, and problems in Victorian England.

Churchill, Winston. *A History of the English-Speaking Peoples: The Great Democracies*. Dodd, Mead & Co. The growth of democracy in England and America during the nineteenth century as related in this fourth volume of the former prime minister's history.

Doorly, Eleanor. *The Radium Woman: A Life of Marie Curie*. Roy Publishing. A well-written account of a great lady of science.

Foner, Philip S. (ed.) *The Factory Girls*. University of Illinois Press. Letters, essays, songs, and poems of the early women's rights movement.

Heilbroner, Robert. *The Worldly Philosophers*. Simon & Schuster. Well-written accounts of the ideas of the great economists of the nineteenth century.

Langford, Elizabeth. *Queen Victoria: Born to Succeed*. Pyramid Books. A superb account of the life of England's great queen.

*Llewellyn, Richard. *How Green Was My Valley*. The Macmillan Company. A story of the effects of the Industrial Revolution on a Welsh mining town.

Lyons, F. S. *Charles Stewart Parnell*. Oxford University Press. A judicious biography of the life and times of an extraordinary leader of the Fenians.

Stern, Fritz. *Gold and Iron*. Knopf. This is an account of the role of money in helping Bismarck unify Germany.

Williams, Roger L. *The World of Napoleon III*. Free Press. This is a good brief account of diplomatic affairs under Louis Napoleon.

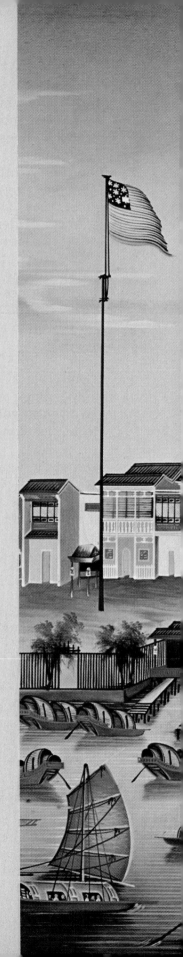

UNIT
V

The Beginning of
a Global Society

A European map of Africa, 1630

Europe in Search of Empire: Imperialism in Africa

If you were interested in buying a new house, you would probably have questions about the neighborhood that the house is in, the amount of land on which the house is built, and tax costs. You would want the house to be in a good location, that is, near schools, shopping centers, and transportation. These are important considerations if you want to be happy in the house you choose.

Leaders of nations often have similar considerations on a much larger scale. They too are concerned about their neighbors and their locations. They want to be near great ocean-water routes. They want to own islands that can be used as naval bases or refueling stations. They want land that has rich natural resources, such as coal, oil, and iron ore. And they want enough land to support their people in comfort.

Throughout history nations have acquired overseas colonies. This process of building empires is called *imperialism*. It strengthens a nation's economy and provides political security. In this chapter you will see how imperialism affected Africa. It changed the ways Africans traditionally lived and thought. Imperialism also changed the ways Europeans lived and thought. You will have to decide for yourself whether imperialism has been a force for good or for evil.

IMPERIALISM OLD AND NEW

The "Old" Imperialism

This is the first chapter in this book on the subject of imperialism. It is not, however, the first time you have read about it at work in history. Imperialism was at work when Egypt conquered its neighbors, when Alexander the Great conquered northern India, when Rome overpowered Carthage, and when Genghis Khan overran China. You have read about the revolution in commerce and about the Age of Discovery. Then imperialism was somewhat different. From the fifteenth through the seventeenth centuries, imperialism took the form of finding new lands and seeking converts to Christianity. During the age of *"old" imperialism*, people searched for "gold, glory, and God."

"The search for gold" meant that nations desired to increase their wealth. This could be done by discovering gold and silver in far-off places. It could also be done by establishing colonies in those places. Colonies provided valuable raw materials that could be used by the imperialists or parent country. The parent country made products from the raw materials. When it sold the products, the profits—gold and silver—poured into its treasury.

"The search for glory" meant the desire of adventurers and explorers for fame. Men such as Captain Cook and Sir Francis Drake found fame and fortune by sailing the uncharted oceans of the world. "The search for God" meant the desire of Christian missionaries to find converts.

The "New" Imperialism

The *"new" imperialism* is closely tied to the Industrial Revolution. During the Industrial Revolution, the factories of Western Europe needed raw materials. They needed cotton, coal, and iron ore. Later, they needed oil, copper, rubber, tin, and uranium. They found these in the Far East, the Middle East, and Africa.

The countries of Western Europe also needed foreign markets where they could sell the goods that their factories were making. The people at home could not buy as much as the factories could turn out. The "new" imperialists thought that big populations of Asia and Africa would buy these goods if they could be taught to use them.

The Industrial Revolution made it possible for some people to get very rich. The owners of some business firms thought that they could make big profits if they used their money to build factories where there were none. However, before taking chances on investing their money in far-off places, they encouraged their own countries to seize control of those places. Under the protection of their own governments, business owners could be sure that their money would be

Elephant ivory and hides for sale in a market in South Africa. Why did many Europeans support their governments' search for colonies?

safe. Sometimes business owners built factories and railroads in foreign countries even before they were sure that their own governments would protect them. When their overseas investments grew large enough, some business owners asked their governments to protect them. In this way, they convinced their own governments to get control of a foreign land.

Of course, most Europeans were not rich. They were farm and factory workers. They were not in business, they did not need raw materials, they did not have any goods to sell, nor did they have extra money to invest in foreign business. Strangely enough, these people also wanted their nation to have colonies.

Patriotism was strong. Most Europeans felt that their own nation should have colonies if their own country was to be counted among the powerful of the world. Europeans were *nationalistic*, or proud of their own country.

Some also felt that people in less well developed countries should have schools and be taught about good health and sanitation. Others wanted to make Christians out of people who had other religions. In addition, military men found glory and prestige in taking over new lands. They wanted to create large armies in which there would be opportunity for promotion and advancement. For these people nationalism—not the Industrial Revolution—encouraged their interest in colonies.

Imperialism takes many forms. In a *colonial system*, colonies are owned outright and ruled by the parent country. Under a *protectorate*, a weaker nation and its ruler are under the control of a stronger nation. A *sphere of influence* is an area in a country in which a foreign nation holds special trading privileges.

Check in Here

1. How does imperialism differ from nationalism? How is imperialism related to nationalism?

2. What were the major motives of people who supported the "old" imperialism? Give two examples.

3. What were the major motives of people who supported the "new" imperialism? Give two examples.

4. What was the role of nationalism in the desire for colonies?

5. Define: (a) colonial system; (b) protectorate; (c) sphere of influence.

HOW EUROPEANS CAME TO AFRICA

How Europe "Discovered" Africa

During the Age of Discovery (see p. 240), Europeans found a new all-water route to India and the East. In this same period they also reached the New World. Europeans had long known that Africa existed, but its shape and size remained a mystery to them. So deep was European ignorance about Africa that all kinds of myths grew up about the land and the people of that continent.

Among the more famous myths was that of Prester John. Europeans believed that he ruled a vast kingdom in Asia or Africa. In his kingdom there were no poor people. Everyone was treated justly. Prester John was a model of what a good Christian king should be.

The search for the legendary kingdom of Prester John was only one of the reasons Europeans were interested in Africa. "Gold, glory, and God" were the motives of Europeans in their dealings with Africa.

The Portuguese were the first of the modern Europeans to come to Africa in significant numbers. They were searching for a short water route to the East. In their travels, they sailed up some of the larger African rivers. In this way, they discovered inner Africa.

Vasco da Gama, sailing for Portugal, was the most successful of the early explorers. He found the long-sought water route to India. After this success, Portugal protected the route. It established bases along both the east and west coasts of Africa.

The desire to bring Christianity to Africans was often as intense as the desire to possess their wealth. In the regions near the mouth of the Congo River, missionaries converted some of the people to Christianity. However, the conversions were often short-lived.

In 1580, Portugal and Spain were united. As Spanish interests leaned more to the New World, Portugal's grip on Africa weakened. Finally, Portugal lost its hold on African trade to the Dutch and others. However, the Portuguese ruled Angola, Mozambique, and some tiny coastal lands in Africa until 1975.

The Dutch, the English, the French, the Danes, and the Swedes all made their way to Africa. They established trading posts. Gold, ivory, spices, vegetable oils, and slaves were the products they traded.

Why the African Slave Trade Was Evil

Slavery—the ownership of people as property—is as old as civilization. It is mentioned in the Bible. The pharaohs of Egypt used slaves to build the pyramids. Slaves fought in the Colosseum for the amusement of the Romans. Slaves were often captives taken in battle. Sometimes people badly in debt became the property of those to whom they owed money. In most societies, slaves made up the labor force.

Both slavery and slave trading were common in Africa. Among the Africans, slaves had certain rights. These rights were protected in the laws and customs of African society. The amount of labor that slaves did was limited by law. They could work a portion of the time for themselves. It was also possible for them to buy their freedom. European and American traders justified the slave trade because slavery and slave trading were legal in Africa. Africans legally enslaved in Africa, they said, could be made to serve anywhere their labor was needed.

But when African slaves were traded into another society—Europe or the Americas—they were treated badly. The

A slave market in Zanzibar. Arabs, Africans, and Europeans bought and sold slaves.

laws and customs were different. Slaves had few, if any, personal rights. The amount of labor expected of them was not limited by law. In most cases, they could not work for themselves or earn the money with which to buy their freedom. As a result, cruelty was the rule and kindness the exception.

The slave trade involved the capture, purchase, transportation, and sale of slaves. In Africa it was customary to make slaves of war captives. Because the demand for slaves was high in the New World, white traders encouraged African tribes to make war on one another. The war prisoners were bought as slaves. They were prepared for shipment to the New World at *slave factories*, which were trading stations located in Sub-Saharan Africa. The Congo, Angola, the Gold Coast, and the coast along the Gulf of Guinea became slave-trading centers.

At first, the Portuguese had a monopoly on the slave trade. Soon England, France, Holland, and the United States, among other countries, also entered into this profitable business. Slaves were packed tightly, like cattle, aboard special vessels. Every slave was branded, shackled, and herded aboard. For every slave

who was successfully delivered, at least one died along the way. For those who survived, the trip in the slave ship was just the beginning of the slave's physical and mental suffering. In this way, millions of Africans died from cruel treatment even before they reached their destination in the Americas.

How Africa Was Systematically Explored

The Europeans who were involved in the slave trade knew the coastal areas of Africa. Not until the eighteenth century, however, was the interior of Africa explored. Among the early explorers of Africa was a Scot named James Bruce (1730–94). He was among many who sought the source of the longer White Nile River. Notes of his journey became a guide for other African adventurers.

Mungo Park (1771–1806) was the first European to explore the course of the Niger River. He went to Africa in 1805 to trace the Niger to its source. Unfortunately, his boat was upset by rapids. His party was attacked and Park drowned.

Alexandrine Tinne [tin] (1839–69), a Dutch explorer, chose to devote her wealth and energy to geographic discovery. She explored Sub-Saharan Africa. She wanted to expose the hated slave trade. With a large company of equipment, bearers, and guides, she explored Central Africa (including the Nubian desert) and moved on to Khartoum. Later, she penetrated the unknown regions of the Nile. She was murdered by tribes that thought she had gold.

René Caillié [kī′yā] (1799–1838) of France was the first European to reach Timbuktu [tim′buk tü′]. His exploration efforts were primarily in the Sahara.

Two Britishmen Richard Burton [bur′tən] (1821–1890) and John Speke [spēk] (1827–1864), carried on their work under the sponsorship of the Royal Geographical Association. Speke reached

David Livingstone explored the continent of Africa from 1853–1856. Traveling down the Zambezi River, he discovered the Victoria Falls, which he named after Queen Victoria. The falls are formed as the waters of the Zambezi fall into a fracture in the earth's crust.

Lake Victoria and identified it as the source of the White Nile. Burton worked his way into East Africa and reached Lake Tanganyika [tan′gən yē′kə].

Heinrich Barth [bärt] (1821–65), a German geographer and explorer, crossed the Sahara. He explored the country that lies between Lake Chad and Timbuktu.

Through the work of these explorers, the world learned much about the northern half of Africa. We learned about southern Africa largely through the work of two men: David Livingstone (1813–73) and Henry M. Stanley (1841–1904). Livingstone was a Scottish missionary who went to Africa in 1840 to convert the Africans to Christianity. He remained there for the rest of his life as an explorer as well as a preacher.

The Western world was interested in what Livingstone was doing. For a number of years, however, very little was heard from or about him. Some people thought he had died. The *New York Herald* decided it would make a good story if it could find out what happened to Dr. Livingstone. In 1871, it sent Henry M. Stanley on that assignment. Stanley found Livingstone, but in doing so, he became an explorer himself. He traveled in the Nile River area and saw opportunities for developing business interests.

The explorations of Livingstone and Stanley encouraged the big nations of Europe to make a reckless scramble for colonies in Africa. Germany and Italy, along with Belgium, England, and France, rushed to claim colonies. A study of the map on page 460 will show the parts of Africa that were claimed by European nations by 1914. At that time, 90 percent of Africa was controlled by foreign countries.

Check in Here

1. How did the myth of Prester John help Europeans learn more about Africa?

2. List three reasons for the interest of Europeans in Sub-Saharan Africa.

3. Describe the evils of the slave trade.

4. List the accomplishments of each of the following: (a) Mungo Park; (b) Alexandrine Tinne; (c) David Livingstone and Henry M. Stanley.

The meeting of Henry Stanley and David Livingstone in 1871.

David Livingstone
(1813–73)
Henry M. Stanley
(1841–1904)

David Livingstone was born in Scotland to poor parents. He became a doctor and a missionary and went to Africa to convert Africans to Christianity. There he remained to bring not only the word of God to the people but the benefits of medical science. Livingston was one of the first Europeans to reach and explore much of Africa's interior. He went on to fight the slave trade. As an explorer Livingstone learned the ways of the people among whom he lived. He got along well with them. He often preferred them to the other white explorers, who frequently fell below his high moral standards. Because of his missionary and medical work in Africa, David Livingstone has often been compared to Dr. Albert Schweitzer [shwīt'sər] (1875-1965), who labored for many years for the good of the African people.

Illness and fever took their toll on Livingstone's health. He also suffered a serious injury when he was attacked by a lion. Here is a description of that attack in the words of Livingstone:

I heard a shout. Starting, and looking half round, I saw the lion just in the act of springing upon me. I was upon a little height, he caught my shoulder as he sprang, and we both came to the ground together. Growling horribly close to my ear, he shook me as a terrior does a rat. . . .*

The lion nearly took Livingstone's life. He managed to escape, however, and in time he returned to England. In 1865, he made his last trip to Africa, where he remained until his death. It was during his last journey that the *New York Herald* sent Henry M. Stanley in search of him.

Stanley's early life in Wales was marked by poverty. As a child he was sent to a workhouse that was run by a mad and tyrannical schoolmaster. For nine long, dreary, and painful years, young Henry lived in the workhouse. He finally scraped together enough money to come to the United States. During the Civil War (1861–65), he fought for both the North and the South, once as a soldier and once as a sailor. Later, he became a newspaper reporter and wrote stories about the "wild West."

As a journalist Stanley was sent to Turkey, Persia, Syria, India, and Egypt. He was traveling in Europe and North Africa when he was ordered

---

*Alan Moorehead. *The White Nile* (New York: Harper and Brothers, 1960), p. 102.

to Paris to meet James Gordon Bennett, Jr., of the *New York Herald.* Bennett ordered Stanley to find Livingstone at any cost. After much delay and hardship, Stanley succeeded in locating Livingstone on November 10, 1871. This meeting is described in Stanley's journal:

As I advanced slowly toward him, I noticed that he was pale, looked wearied and wan, that he had grey whiskers and mustache, that he wore a bluish cloth cap with a faded gold band on a red ground around it, and that he had on a red-sleeved waistcoat, and a pair of grey tweed trousers. I . . . would have embraced him, only he, being an Englishman, I did not know how he would receive me; so I did what moral cowardice and false pride suggested was the best thing—walked deliberately to him, took off my hat and said: "Dr. Livingstone, I presume?"
"Yes," says he, with a kind smile, lifting his cap slightly. I replace my hat on my head, and he puts on his cap and we both grasp hands, and I then say aloud: "I thank God, Doctor, I have been permitted to see you!" He answered, "I feel thankful that I am here to welcome you!"*

Stanley gave Livingstone a bundle of letters that he thought he would be glad to have. But instead of turning immediately to the letters from home, Livingstone inquired, "How is the world getting along?" Stanley told him of the events that had made newspaper headlines during Livingstone's absence in Africa: "the Suez Canal was now open, General Grant was President of the United States, the Pacific Railroad had been completed; Prussia had humbled Denmark, France had cowered before Bismarck and the transatlantic cable had been laid."**
Livingstone died two years after he was "found" by Stanley. Stanley went on to become a prominent explorer and to earn fame and fortune. But his rather stuffy greeting to Dr. Livingstone haunted him for the rest of his life and since then has been the subject of much humor.

*Byron Farwell, *The Man Who Presumed* (New York: Henry Holt and Company, 1957), p. 71.
**Farwell, p. 72.

Dr. Livingstone's medical station on the Zambezi River.

The Boers on the Great Trek to the Transvaal and Orange Free State. The journey was hard and dangerous. Why did the Boers leave Cape Colony? What happened after gold and diamonds were discovered in their new home?

EUROPEAN IMPERIALISM IN NORTH AFRICA AND SUB-SAHARAN AFRICA

The Growth of British Influence in Africa

In both East Africa and South Africa, British imperialism succeeded. In South Africa a great deal of work was done by Cecil Rhodes. His dream of empire helped British imperialism develop in South Africa. Rhodes also tried to move British occupation north toward Egypt. One of his goals was to have Britain build a railroad from the southern tip of Africa to Egypt in the north, a Cape-to-Cairo-railroad.

In South Africa the British had competition from the Dutch. The Dutch had settled at Cape Colony as early as 1652. In 1815, the British were given Cape Colony by the Vienna Congress. The Dutch farmers in South Africa opposed British rule. They left Cape Colony in 1836. In the wilderness the *Boers* [bōərz], as the Dutch farmers in South Africa were called, traveled northward in oxdrawn wagons much like those used by the pioneers in the United States. This long journey was called the *Great Trek*. The Boers resettled in lands known as the Transvaal and the Orange Free State. Here they lived peacefully until gold and diamonds were discovered. Cecil Rhodes [rōdz], then prime minister of Cape Colony, decided that some of this wealth must go to England. Because of that decision a conflict between the British and the Boers arose.

The Boer War, which began in 1899, was won by the British. Winston Churchill, who later became prime minister of England, made an early reputation as a war reporter there. The British formed a government that gave the Dutch many rights. In 1910, the two countries of Transvaal and Orange Free State were joined with two other English colonies to form the Union of South Africa. Later, the Union of South Africa became part of the British Commonwealth of Nations.

During the nineteenth century, much

of North Africa was owned by the *sultan,* or, the ruler, of Turkey whose power was declining. Foreign powers took advantage of this decline. They extended their influence to this area. In 1869, the Suez Canal was opened. It connects the Mediterranean Sea with the Red Sea and the Indian Ocean. The powers of Europe wanted to get control of this important water route between Europe and Asia.

At that time, the rulers of Egypt thought more of their pleasures than of their people. They wasted money and allowed Egypt to get into debt. In 1875, an Egyptian ruler gave British Prime Minister Benjamin Disraeli a chance to buy a large interest in the control of the Suez Canal from Egypt. Egyptian money problems continued to mount. In 1882, a British fleet entered Alexandria in answer to cries for help that came from British owners of the Suez Canal. Soon after, Egypt became a British protectorate. The British did not leave until 1956. In that year, Egypt then forced them out and began to operate the canal by itself.

The road to empire was a rocky one for Great Britain. The British made an agreement with Egypt by which the two nations would share in the rule of Egypt's neighbor, the Sudan. The people of the Sudan, however, did not like this idea. The British General, Charles Gordon, tried to fight but he was unsuccessful. In an attempt to put down a Sudanese uprising, Gordon's army—made up of English and Egyptian troops—was trapped in the city of Khartoum. Relief troops arrived only to find Gordon and his army massacred.

The French and British were jealous of each other's influence in North Africa. However, as the clouds of World War I were approaching, the two nations were encouraged to settle their differences in order to face a common enemy: Germany. You will read this story later when you study the causes of World War I.

How Other Powers Gained Control in Parts of Africa

French influence in Africa was mostly in the northern and western areas. France occupied Algeria as early as 1850. Later, French influence spread to Tunisia, Morocco, French West Africa, and French Equatorial Africa.

The Belgians gained control of the huge part of the interior of Africa called the Congo. King Leopold II of Belgium took part in the division of Africa as a private citizen, not as a king. In 1878, he and Henry Stanley formed a company. This company took advantage of the natural resources of the Congo to make huge profits. They treated the Congolese so cruelly that when news of the atrocities reached the outside world the company was deprived of its rights. The Congo then became a Belgian colony. It was called the *Belgian Congo.* The Congo's extensive uranium deposits make it an important area in world affairs today.

Germany and Italy were among the last of the European nations to join the race for colonies in Africa. In 1912, Italy declared war on Turkey and took Tripoli. During the years before 1914, Germany also made efforts to get African colonies. After Germany's defeat in World Wars I and II, its African colonies were taken away. After World War II, all of the other European countries also had to give up their African colonies.

How Europe Treated Africa

The Africans were treated very harshly by the Europeans. African rulers who could neither read nor write were cheated out of their lands. They put their "marks" on treaties that gave away their wealth in minerals, farm land, and rubber to the Europeans. In return, they received gifts of cloth, beads, and sometimes guns.

Imperialism in Africa, 1914

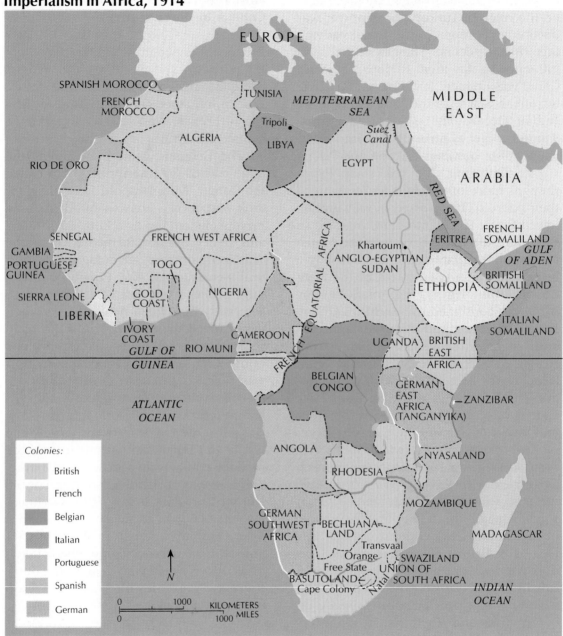

By 1914, Africa had been carved up by the European powers.
- What two countries of Africa were independent as of 1914?
- What German colony separated the British colonies in east Africa?
- What European power controlled most of the northwestern part of the African continent?

African chiefs also forced their people to work under inhuman conditions. They did so either to enrich themselves or under the threat of the guns of European managers. Forced labor continued to exist in much of Africa before World War I. In the Congo, especially, the workers were very badly treated.

After World War II, the cry to improve the worker's lives grew so loud that it could not be ignored. But European efforts to provide better government, schools, hospitals, roads, and a more healthful diet all came too late. One by one the colonies overthrew the foreign governments. They adopted ancient names by which they had been previously known. They became independent members of the family of nations. The twentieth century has been a turning point in the history of African nations.

Check in Here

1. How did each of these countries gain an important role in Africa: (**a**) England; (**b**) France; (**c**) Germany?

2. Was European treatment of Africans generally fair? Justify your point of view.

3. What were the reasons for the conflicts between the English and the Boers?

4. Why was the Suez Canal important to European countries?

5. Study the map of Africa from about 1914. (See p. 460.) What European countries were most important in Africa?

Be able to place the following events on the time line:

1652	Cape Colony settled		1899	Boer War
1836	Great Trek		1910	Union of South Africa formed
1869	Suez Canal		1956	Nasser seized Suez Canal

Modern History

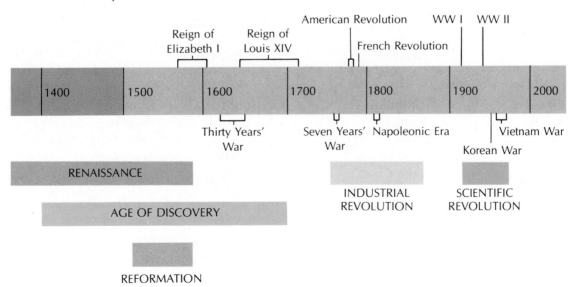

REVIEWING THE BASICS

Imperialism is an old idea in history. In the early days those who sought colonies did so in search of gold (wealth), glory (adventure), and God (to find converts to Christianity). The "new" imperialism involved the search for colonies. The colonies were viewed as places from which to get raw materials cheaply. They were also thought of as the places to sell products the Industrial Revolution was making possible. Imperialism brought many benefits to the developing colonies. It also brought many evils. The major powers drained away the natural wealth of the colonies. They also encouraged the growing evil of slavery and slave trading.

Among the more important explorations of Africa were those of Henry M. Stanley and David Livingstone. Later, Cecil Rhodes sought to develop South Africa as well as Egypt and to bring these huge areas under British control. France, Belgium, Italy, and Germany each scrambled for colonies. By World War I, nearly all of Africa was occupied by European powers.

In South Africa, Britain defeated the Dutch (Boers) who had settled in the Transvaal and the Orange Free State. In North Africa, Britain gained control of the Suez Canal. Belgium gained control of the Congo, where the worst evils of European imperialism occurred. Germany and Italy were among the last to achieve a foothold in Africa.

REVIEWING THE HIGHLIGHTS

People to Identify

Alexandrine Tinne	Prester John	Richard Burton
David Livingstone	James Bruce	John Speke
Henry M. Stanley	Mungo Park	Heinrich Barth
Leopold II	René Caillié	Benjamin Disraeli
Cecil Rhodes	Charles Gordon	

Places to Locate

Timbuktu	Khartoum	Orange Free State
Congo	Lake Victoria	Angola
Zambezi River	Sudan	Lake Tanganyika
Niger River	White Nile	Transvaal
Lake Chad	Cape Colony	Union of South Africa
Gold Coast	Suez Canal	

Terms to Understand

colonial system	"old" imperialism	slave factories
protectorate	"new" imperialism	Boers
sphere of influence		nationalism

462

Great Trek   Boer War

1. Distinguish between the "old" and "new" imperialism.
2. How did the search for the kingdom of Prester John help Europeans to discover Africa?
3. Explain Portugal's entry into Africa.
4. How did early explorers help to open Africa to colonization?
5. Distinguish between slavery and the slave trade.
6. How did slavery as it was practiced in Africa differ from the way it was practiced in America?
7. Why did explorers become interested in Sub-Saharan Africa?
8. How did Europeans justify slave trading?
9. How did the coming of Europeans help Africa? How did it hurt Africa?
10. What were the main causes of the Boer War? What were the results?
11. How did England gain control of the Suez Canal?
12. Where were the French colonies located in Africa?
13. Were the Belgians influential in Africa? In what part?
14. How did the Congo become a colony of Belgium?
15. Why did Rhodes want to build a Cape-to-Cairo railroad?
16. What happened to European control of Africa in the twentieth century?
17. How was the search for colonies in Africa a source of conflict among the major powers?
18. Distinguish between nationalism and imperialism.
19. What is the relationship between the Industrial Revolution and imperialism?

THINGS TO DO

1. Prepare a biographical sketch of Alexandrine Tinne.
2. Prepare a "Meet the Press" program in which you and two or three of your classmates interview for television a fellow student playing the part of Benjamin Disraeli. What questions about Great Britain's role as an imperialistic country would you ask? What answers would you expect?
3. Draw a cartoon (see, for example, "You Are the Historian" for this chapter) in which you express your opinion about an aspect of imperialism in Africa.

Study the cartoon below, and answer the questions that follow it.

The Rhodes Colossus striding from Cape Town to Cairo.†

1. Who or what is the "Rhodes Colossus" meant to be? How can you tell?
2. What is the "colossus" trying to do? How can you tell?
3. Does the cartoonist seem critical or supportive of the "colossus"? Justify your point of view.
4. Why do you think such a cartoon might have been published?
5. In an encyclopedia or other reference book look up information about the ancient Colossus of Rhodes. Then report to the class on where the cartoonist got his idea.

†Cartoon by Sambourne in *Punch*, 1892.

Sepoys, Indian soldiers who served in the British army.

Europe in Search of Empire: Imperialism in Asia

Rudyard Kipling was a British poet. He is known as the "Poet of Imperialism." His most famous poem on the subject is called "The White Man's Burden." One stanza from that poem is worth reading in order to understand imperialism better.

> Take up the White Man's burden—
>   Send forth the best ye breed—
> Go bind your sons to exile
>   To serve your captives' need;
> To wait in heavy harness,
>   On fluttered folk and wild—
> Your new-caught, sullen peoples,
>   Half-devil and half-child.*

* From "The White Man's Burden," by Rudyard Kipling, from *The Five Nations*. By permission of The National Trust, London, England.

The poem expresses one of the most basic reasons for the development of imperialism. Some imperialist nations seemed to want to do good. They thought they could better the lot of the people they considered to be "half-devil, half-child."

Others knew that the desire for colonies was motivated more by the desire to get rich rather than by the desire to do good. Most people, however, were persuaded—or persuaded themselves—that it would be sinful not to take up the "white man's burden." They considered it their duty to bring knowledge of medicine, science, technology, and sanitation to those they believed to be uncivilized. These people pushed their governments to search for colonies in far-off places. In this chapter, you will see how this search for colonies reached Asia. You will again have to decide for yourselves whether imperialism did any good or brought any harm.

HOW THE PORTUGUESE, DUTCH, AND FRENCH CAME TO INDIA

Why the Portuguese Won and Lost India

For hundreds of years India had been invaded by strangers. Most of these invaders came from the northeast through the Khyber Pass and other passes. In the fifteenth century, a new invasion route was opened. In 1498, Vasco da Gama and his Portuguese ships rounded Africa and dropped anchor near the city of Calicut [kal′ə kut′], on the west coast of India. To sailors at sea for eleven months, any land would have been welcome. How much more so were the sights and sounds of India! Da Gama and his sailors spent six months there.

On his return voyage to Portugal, Da Gama carried with him a letter from the Rajah of Malabar who wanted to trade with the Europeans. The Portuguese answered the request for trade by sending 1,200 soldiers under the leadership of Pedro Cabral [kə brôl′]. They were sent to make India a Portuguese colony.

Portugal's main goal in India was to make money. Portugal opened trading posts and factories. Francisco de Almeida [äl mē′də], the first Portuguese *viceroy*, or ruler, in India, increased the profits and the power of the Portuguese traders. Once they established themselves firmly in western India the Portuguese were content. They were happy with the wealth they acquired. They did not try to conquer or settle the land permanently.

In 1510, Alfonso de Albuquerque [al′bə kur′kē], another Portuguese viceroy, captured "Golden Goa," a port city on the west coast of India. At that time, Goa [gō′ə] was one of the world's wealthiest cities. Today, it has declined to a shadow of its former self. Following long

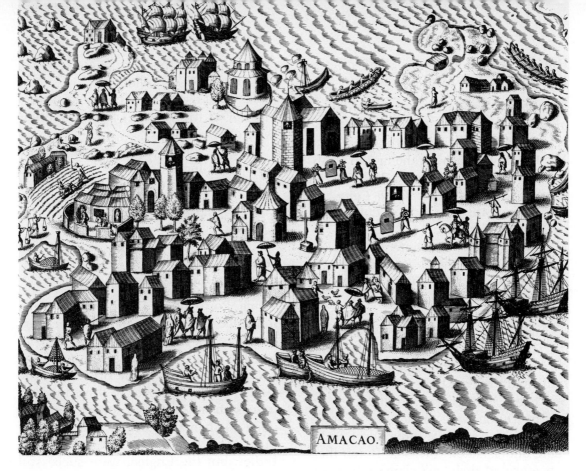

The colony of Macao in the seventeenth century. What European country founded it, and where was it located?

years of struggle with the Portuguese, Goa was forcibly retaken by India in 1961. After more than 450 years, Portugal had to give up the longest held of its overseas colonies.

The Portuguese were the first of the modern Europeans to come to India. Their influence did not last, however. Catholic missionaries followed the Portuguese flag to India. Despite great effort, Christianity never made much headway in India. One reason that the Portuguese did not really leave their mark on India is that they had come too soon. Instead of a weak nation, they found a strong one. Instead of weak kings, they found the mighty Babur and, later, the even mightier Akbar. As a result, there was a

limit to the power and influence Portugal could gain in India. Under Akbar, relations with Portugal were friendly. The Indian ruler tolerated many religions and welcomed the introduction of Christianity. Followers of Akbar were not tolerant of the Christian missionaries. A strong hatred for the newcomers grew when the Portuguese tried to force India to accept the Christian faith. To make matters worse, the climate of India discouraged the Portuguese settlers. They found the heat so distasteful that they were unable to work. At home, Spain and Portugal were growing weaker as a result of wars with France and England. These are some of the reasons why Portugal soon lost out in India.

How the Dutch and French Fared in Asia

Portuguese profits in India did not go unnoticed in Europe. Soon other nations began to dip into the wealth of the East. The Dutch were among the first to establish a foothold there. In 1602, the Dutch formed the *Dutch East India Company*. It was given the sole right of doing business in the Far East.

Many people were interested in becoming wealthy. They found an opportunity to do so by becoming part owners in the Dutch East India Company. Ordinary men and women invested some of their savings in the hope of making great profits. The Dutch East India Company and its owners grew rich as the trade with India and the East Indies, the islands off Southeast Asia, proved profitable.

The Dutch were driven out of India by the British in 1758. India never really came under Dutch rule. The Dutch then concentrated their colonizing efforts on the East Indies, where they were successful. They ruled in the East Indies for over 300 years. It was not until the twentieth century that they were forced to release their grip on these islands.

The Portuguese and the Dutch seemed to be getting a head start in Asia. Other nations did not wish to fall far behind in the race to establish colonies in the Far East. The French, under Louis XIV, made successful efforts to establish French power in India. In 1674, the city of Pondicherry [pon'də cher'ē], on the east coast of India, fell into French hands, where it remained until 1954. As French influence in India grew, it came into conflict with English power.

Check in Here

1. On a map, trace the major routes by which the Portuguese, Dutch, and French came to India.

2. Why did the Portuguese, French, and Dutch fail in India?

3. What did the Europeans want from India? Did they get what they wanted? Why or why not?

4. Why did people invest in the Dutch East India Company?

THE BRITISH INFLUENCE IN INDIA

How the British Built a Lasting Indian Empire

While Portuguese, Dutch, and French influence was growing in India, the English were not idle. They entered the contest for control of this rich land in the seventeenth century. The British and the Dutch worked together to drive the Portuguese from India. No sooner had they done so than they began fighting each other. The Dutch won out in the East Indies, but the English were successful in India. During the seventeenth century, the British built forts at Madras [mə dras'], Calcutta [kal kut' ə], and Bombay [bom bā']. They rented them to the British East India Company. From these forts British trade and control of India grew.

The *British East India Company* was run by London merchants. The company had trading rights in India and hoped to make a profit. This was not easy to do. For one thing, India was a long way from home. For another, since India was broken up into small but independent states, it was necessary for the company to do business with many Indian princes. Sometimes these princes would not give the company what it wanted. As a result, the British East India Company took it upon itself to do what it thought best. If the company wanted to increase its land holdings, it took over new land. If it decided to increase taxes or make war, it did these things too. By taking these actions, the British East India Company became, in fact, the government of India. As the power of the British East India Company grew, it came into conflict with the growing power of the French. A fight for control of India between these two big nations soon took place.

Why the French Were Driven from India

The British and the French were rivals all over the world. In a series of wars sometimes known as the *Second Hundred Years' War*, the British and French fought one another for power in Europe, in the New World, and in India. In these contests the English were victorious, especially in India.

To champion their cause the British put their trust in Robert Clive [klīv] (1725–74). The French found a hero in Joseph Dupleix [dü pleks'] (1697–1763). Dupleix was the governor of the French city of Pondicherry. He dreamed of and worked for a French empire in India. In 1746, he successfully drove the British from Madras. He hoped that he might continue to win more victories, but in 1754 he returned to France and his career in India ended.

Robert Clive went to India at the age of eighteen to seek his fortune. He started as a clerk for the East India Company, but he longed for service in the army, where he soon proved his worth. He made a name for himself in a battle against the French at Arcot [är kot']. Thus began a glorious career in India.

About the middle of the eighteenth century the British began to take complete control of India. In 1756, the prince of Bengal died. He left his throne to a youth who had not yet learned to rule. The young Indian prince attacked the British at Calcutta. In the fighting that followed, the young Indian prince captured many English and threw them into

a military prison. Due to the tropical heat, insufficient air, and lack of water most of the 146 prisoners died. The *Black Hole of Calcutta*, as this imprisonment is known to history, was long remembered. It made the British determined to "get even."

In 1757, the British retook Calcutta. In the same year, at Plassey [plä'sē], the British under Robert Clive defeated the French and Indian troops. As a result of this victory, British rule was firmly established in eastern India. Further fighting with the French followed from time to time. However, the British were in a strong position to govern India and drive out competition.

The Rule of the British East India Company

Robert Clive returned to England. He was given the title Baron Clive of Plassey

Sir Robert Clive drove the Dutch and French out of India and helped to establish the British foothold there. How did his career end?

469

in reward for his good work in India. However, his work in India had just begun. Clive returned to India to improve the profits of the East India Company. He also wanted to improve British relations with the Indian princes. He tried to stop private trading by employees of the company that took profits away from the company. With these reforms Clive "stepped on many important toes." He was called home and accused by his enemies of having taken bribes from Indian princes. The trial proved there was little doubt that Clive had taken gifts from Indian princes. However, since accepting gifts was the custom of the day and of the country, Clive was found innocent of wrongdoing. But the disgrace of this accusation was too much for him. In 1774, he killed himself.

Fortunately for Great Britain, its empire in India did not depend on the work of one person alone. Other English people, as brilliant as Clive, were willing to take his place in handling British affairs in India. One of these men was Warren Hastings (1732–1818), who went to India to join the East India Company.

By 1774, Hastings became governor of India. He tried to reform the government under the East India Company, hoping to make it more efficient. He also wanted the Indian people under him treated more fairly. Hastings was responsible for a law that stopped the directors of the company from receiving gifts from princes and from carrying on private trade. Through these reforms, Hastings annoyed many prominent people. He too was called home, tried, and found innocent of the charges against him. Unlike Robert Clive, however, he lived for a long time after his trial.

When Great Britain lost its grip on thirteen of its colonies in America, it tightened the grip on its colonies in India. Lord Cornwallis, who had been defeated by George Washington at the Battle of Yorktown, served as governor of India from 1786–1793 and again in 1805. He was the first governor to serve under the provisions of a new law called the *India Act*. This law gave the British government a greater voice in the affairs of India and established an awkward "double government" system in India that lasted until 1858. Before the India Act, the East India Company was the final authority in India. That authority had often been harsh and unfair to the people of India.

Under Cornwallis and the India Act, the people were more fairly treated. There was some consideration given to their welfare and interest. Despite Cornwallis's efforts to live at peace with the people of India there were many wars with them. Since the British were always victorious, their influence in India was greatly increased. Gradually, Great Britain gained control of the entire country.

Napoleon thought he could regain India for France. In 1799, he landed an army in Egypt in an unsuccessful effort to cut Great Britain off from India. This was to be the last French attempt to take control of India from the British.

How Britain Gained Complete Control in India

By the middle of the nineteenth century the British government controlled nearly all of India. The influence of the East India Company had declined, however. A large number of states in India remained independent in name only. Their princes had to be content with wealth without power. That power was held by the British government.

By 1857, there was little question that the British had won India. They had done so because they had sent capable governors to India. They also used Indian soldiers, known as *sepoys* [sə pois],

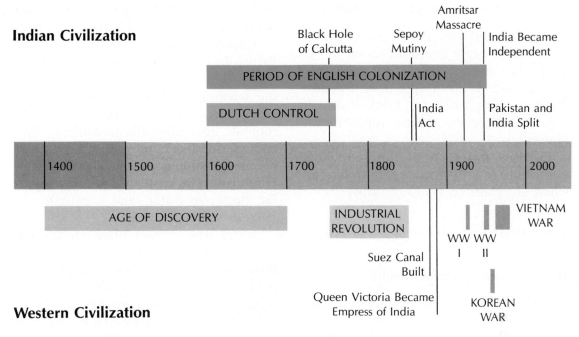

Indian Civilization

Black Hole of Calcutta

Sepoy Mutiny

Amritsar Massacre

India Became Independent

PERIOD OF ENGLISH COLONIZATION

DUTCH CONTROL

India Act

Pakistan and India Split

1400 1500 1600 1700 1800 1900 2000

AGE OF DISCOVERY

INDUSTRIAL REVOLUTION

Suez Canal Built

WW I WW II VIETNAM WAR

Queen Victoria Became Empress of India

KOREAN WAR

Western Civilization

What event made it easier for the British to reach India?

in their armies. The sepoys were loyal to Great Britain. They proved their worth by skill in battle.

However, in 1857, the great *Sepoy Mutiny* took place. It was to be a turning point in Britain's relations with India. As British influence in India spread, the Hindus and the Muslims grew uneasy. Their way of life was changing. Suttee, the practice of burning a widow in her dead husband's funeral pyre, had been made illegal. The development of modern commerce and industry conflicted with the caste system. (See p. 94.) New opportunities for work were opened to those who had previously been denied such opportunities because of caste. There were new kinds of jobs and new ways of doing things. The new jobs were in factories, offices, and on ships. Many changes did not please the Indian people at all. They were some of the causes for revolt.

The immediate cause of the Sepoy

Mutiny can be found in religious beliefs. The British had given the sepoys a new type of bullet. A soldier had to bite the bullet before it could be used. A rumor spread that the grease on the bullet came from a pig or cow. If the grease came from a pig, the religious beliefs of the Muslims were violated. Practicing Muslims are not permitted to eat pig meat. If it came from a cow, the religious beliefs of the Hindus were violated. Mutiny broke out among the sepoys, and fighting followed. It spread to many parts of India and took many months to put down. The ill feelings among Muslims, Hindus, and the English increased.

The Sepoy Mutiny awoke Parliament to its responsibility. No longer could it leave the rule of an empire to a trading company. Parliament ended the powers of the East India Company in India. Ended, too, was the Mogul Empire. In 1877, Queen Victoria became Empress of India.

471

1. Why did the British succeed in India where other countries failed?

2. How did each of the following events mark a turning point in Britain's relations with India: (**a**) Black Hole of Calcutta; (**b**) Sepoy Mutiny; (**c**) Battle of Plassey?

3. How did each of the following contribute to British success in India: (**a**) Clive; (**b**) Hastings (**c**) Cornwallis?

THE BRITISH ROLE IN INDIA EVALUATED

How the British Helped India

In 1858, India was transferred from the rule of the East India Company to the rule of the English Crown. The British promised to treat the people of India fairly. The soldiers in the army of the East India Company became part of the British Army. A viceroy was sent to India to represent the interest of the Crown. However, since India had to pay for the care of the British army, Indian taxes increased.

The British continued to send able and dedicated men to India. They often tried to improve the conditions under which the people of India lived. English and Indian laws were used side by side in courts that provided jury trials. In these courts, educated Indians often served as judges. They made names for themselves by the high quality of their work.

India was divided into a number of provinces. Each province was headed by a governor who was responsible to the viceroy. Those officials were helped by an able group of workers in civil service.

The British brought many good things to India. Elementary schools and colleges, for example, were provided in which history, English, and other foreign languages were taught. The people who graduated from these schools worked for and with the British in ruling India. They made a small but very influential class.

Christian missionaries followed the British to India. They opened schools in which they taught reading, writing, and the teachings of Christianity. The religious ideas did not become deeply rooted, but Christian teachings had enough influence to make the Indian people question some of the practices of Hinduism. The caste system, in particular, began to totter, and eventually, in 1948, it was made illegal.

India was a land often stalked by famine. The British introduced improved farming methods. They helped make poor farmland fertile by drawing water from places where there was plenty to places where there was little or none. In the laboratory and in the field, the British demonstrated how to grow more and better crops. They introduced new farm machines and showed the farmers how to use them.

The British also constructed hospitals and sewerage facilities. Because of this, epidemics from which hundreds of thousands of people died each year were stamped out.

The British built a system of transportation. India is a huge country. During much of its history it lacked unity. This was partly because it was difficult to travel from one part of the country to another. It was also difficult to send goods where they were needed. The British built railroads on which the Indian people could travel to where they wished and send food to places where it was needed. They improved the postal system so that mail could be sent rapidly from place to place. This improvement in transportation and communication served to unite India. Later, the building of telephone and telegraph lines helped even more. India could communicate directly with Europe after the British laid a cable to London.

The traveling distance between India and Europe was shortened when the Suez Canal was opened. The canal made possible the shorter all-water route to the East that Europeans had been seeking for more than 300 years. This route became known as the *British lifeline.* Britain depended on it for the defense of its empire as well as its prosperity at home. Along this lifeline Britain owned strategic lands. It owned the Straits of Gibraltar, from which it could attack vessels that threatened Britain's imperial grip on its empire. Over this route came the raw materials upon which Britain's factories depended. Over this route, too, went Britain's manufactured goods. These were sold at good profit in India and other countries of the East.

How the British Hurt India

The benefits that the British brought to India were not without a price. As it turned out, this price was high enough to make the Indian people question the values of European civilization.

Under the British East India Company the people of India did not fare well. The company charged very high taxes. The taxes were so heavy that people tried to flee to those parts of India that were not under control of the East India Company. Soon, however, there was no place to hide. Some people sold their children into slavery in order to meet the payments demanded by the East India Company. An American historian has this to say about the rule of the East India Company over the people of India, "They had been accustomed to live under tyranny, but never under tyranny like this."*

Under the English crown the people of India fared better. Their problems continued to mount, however. The British brought schools, but soon there were too many educated Indians for whom there was no work. Unemployment brought discontent to the educated class. This discontent eventually led to an open revolt.

The new schools in India were modeled after those in England. The subjects

*Will Durant, *The Story of Civilization: Our Oriental Heritage.* (New York: Simon and Schuster), p. 614.

The British enjoyed many privileges during their colonial rule in India. A British doctor's wife rides in a camel-drawn carriage.

taught were of value to England and the English, but they were not meaningful to most Indians. Subjects included English history and language, science, and arithmetic. The schools taught the culture of England, not the culture of India. There were many Indians who saw that their own culture might disappear under the British system of education. They began to resent the British schools.

English was the language of the schools. It also became the language used almost exclusively by the Indian government officials and educated classes. Their use of English set them apart from their people and aroused resentment against them.

The British who came to India tried to do what they thought was right in managing Indian affairs. However, in their daily lives they sought the company of other English people. Because the English associated mostly with one another, they caused much ill feeling. They made the Indians feel that they were inferior to the British. The British lived well, while most of the Indians lived in poverty. The British were Christians; the Indians were Muslims or Hindus. The British were the rulers; the Indians were the ruled. The British were the owners; the Indians were the servants. The Indians could not help resenting the differences between themselves and the British.

Check in Here

1. List three ways in which the British helped India.

2. List three ways in which the British hurt India.

3. What was the Indian attitude toward the fact that the British modeled the Indian schools after the English schools?

4. How did the British make the Indians feel that they were inferior to the British?

HOW CHINA FELL UNDER EUROPEAN DOMINATION

How China Met Europe

Marco Polo's visit to China in 1255 was the beginning of other foreign visits to China. The Portuguese, the Dutch, the French, and the English were later joined by the Russians, the Germans, the Americans, and the Japanese. The Portuguese were the first to come to China. The Portuguese entered China as pirates rather than as friends. Therfore, they were not allowed to set up a trading post within China itself. They set up a post at Malacca [mə lak'ə] on the Malay Peninsula in Southeast Asia. From there the Portuguese carried on a small amount of trade in the Far East. In 1557, a more permanent Portuguese settlement at Macao [mə kou'] became an active trading post. Macao is a peninsula on the southeast coast of China.

The Spanish followed the Portuguese to China. They too could only establish a trading post near China. Magellan, whose ships were the first to sail around the world, opened a trading settlement in the Philippine Islands. Chinese merchants found their way there, and a trade relationship grew between Spain and China.

The English and French were more interested in India than in China. Because the English were so successful in India, they did not try to trade with China until the nineteenth century. The French, unsuccessful in India, were successful in Southeast Asia. They were not immediately interested in the riches of China either.

By 1644, the Europeans were knocking at the doors of China, but they were not permitted to enter. The Ming Dynasty had successfully fought European advances. Under the Manchus the Chinese were less successful in holding back the foreigners. The European invasion

An illustration from a fourteenth-century map shows Marco Polo's caravan setting out on its journey to the Far East.

that started as a trickle soon became a flood.

Why Europe Wanted to Trade with China

K'ang Hsi [käng'shē'] (1662–1722), of the Manchu dynasty, ruled China. His fame, fortune, and power were as great as any other world ruler. His *banner armies* won and held a mighty empire. The Manchu had eight armies. Each had its own distinctively styled flag. Each banner, or army, was a completely equipped military unit. Each banner was given land, rice, and money in addition to the equipment it needed to fight. The soldiers in each banner were very loyal to their flag. A banner was more than an army. It was like a family in which each man was expected to do his share of the work and of the fighting. It encouraged a high spirit of devotion and sacrifice, which in turn

made it a powerful fighting force. Unfortunately, except for one successor, those who followed K'ang Hsi were not great kings. The Manchu Dynasty remained in power until 1912, but it was the last dynasty to rule in China.

For 200 years after Da Gama found an all-water route to the East, Europe demanded that Asia allow Europe's ships, merchants, and cargoes to enter Asian ports. One by one, India, the East Indies, and Indochina gave in to European demands. China was among the last to give in. Europe wanted a great deal from China, such as silks, porcelain, tea, and spices. There was nothing, however, that China wanted from Europe. The goods of Europe, including coal, road rails, pig lead, firewood, ironware, and tin trays, were not attractive to the Chinese. Nevertheless, Europe kept trying to develop trade relations. In time, formal treaties were signed with China.

Europeans arrive in Canton in the nineteenth century. How can you tell that the artist was Chinese? Why did European merchants think that they were unfairly treated by the Chinese in trading?

Why European Merchants Were Dissatisfied

Carrying on business and trade in China was not easy for the Europeans. They had to learn the ways of the Chinese. The Chinese had grown accustomed to gift-bearing ministers from the countries of Annam, Korea, Manchuria, Tibet, and Turkestan. Through the ministers these countries paid their respect to China. In elaborate ceremonies before the Chinese emperor, foreign ministers would *kowtow* [kou'tou], or bow low. They touched their foreheads to the floor, made their offering, and paid tribute to the "Heavenly Court" of China. In return for this expession of respect, the emperor gave them personal gifts that were often more valuable than the ones they brought. There was also another gift for the people who brought China tribute—the right to trade with its rich cities.

To the people of the Far East this exchange of tribute for trading privileges seemed fair. After all, China was indeed the cultural, business, and imperial center of the Far East. It was also thought to be the biggest and most powerful empire in the world. The leaders of the smaller Asian countries felt that it was only fair and right to honor the emperor of China in this way.

Even in days when weak kings sat upon the "Heavenly Throne," tribute continued to come. In old China and in much of Asia there was much concern with *saving face,* or preserving self-respect. This long-established custom demanded that one not be ridiculed for a blunder or mistake. A person who suffered from humiliation or defeat could save face only by giving up their life to regain prestige.

The Chinese expected that the Europeans who came to China would bring tribute and kowtow to the emperor. The Europeans felt that they came as soldiers or as merchants, not as beggars. They would neither humble themselves nor kowtow. The Chinese saw this attitude as an insult. They called the Europeans "barbarians." These differences in customs caused trouble.

Doing business in China was hard. European merchants were forced to do business with the *Co-hong* [kō'hong], or merchants' guild of Canton. Merchants who were admitted to the Co-hong agreed not to compete with one another. As a result, foreign merchants had to take the prices the Co-hong merchants offered for the goods of Europe. They also paid the prices the Co-hong merchants asked for Chinese goods. The foreign merchants who came to China had to remain in one part of Canton. They also had to depend on the Co-hong for everything they needed. To European merchants, doing business on such unequal terms seemed unfair.

How Europe Gained a Foothold in China

Although Europeans were making profits in China, they were not satisfied. They knew they could make more profits were it not for what they considered unreasonable rules.

The British took the lead in bringing about changes in these rules. The privileges they won were granted to all other European nations as well. More seaports were to be opened to trade with the Chinese. A British representative was to live in Peking where he could talk over trading matters with the emperor. The British wanted to be treated as equals by the Chinese and by all other people doing business there.

Chinese law had to be followed by foreigners seeking to do business in China. Foreigners who committed crimes in China were tried in Chinese courts just as foreigners who committed crimes in England were tried in British courts. The British wanted the English people who were accused of crimes *in China* to be tried under English law in English courts. This principle, known as *extraterritoriality,* was to cause much hard feeling between China and the countries of the West.

What the British were determined to get, all the other countries also wanted. To them, these demands seemed reasonable. To the Chinese, they could not be granted without "loss of face." Because of their success in India, the British were determined to have their way in China. The *First Opium War* (1830–42) was a struggle to decide whether the British would indeed have their way.

How the Opium Wars Forced China to Trade

Opium is a habit-forming drug that has harmful effects on the health of those who use it. It was grown in India and was in great demand by the Chinese. The Manchu emperor had ordered the opium trade stopped. Foreign and Chinese merchants alike winked at the emperor's ruling, and the merchants continued to sell the narcotic opium in China.

Lin Tse-hsu [tsē'shü'], the Chinese governor-general at Canton, was determined to carry out the emperor's wishes. Like the colonists of America who destroyed shiploads of foreign tea in Boston Harbor, Lin Tse-hsu destroyed the foreign opium. Thousands of chests of the narcotic were taken and burned at Canton in 1839.

Unfortunately, Lin was not speaking for the Chinese who wanted opium and for the British who were determined to sell it to them. The British government became involved in the problem. British warships came to Canton and Nanking. War between China and Britain began. The emperor ordered his people to fight back, and they did with crude weapons. The emperor, it was reported, would swim under water and make holes in the bottoms of the British vessels. Firecrackers attached to monkeys would be thrown on board British ships. The monkeys were supposed to jump into the gunpowder rooms and cause the British ships to explode. Needless to say, in the Chinese hour of need, these weapons failed.

The British won the First Opium War in 1842. As a result, the island of Hong Kong became British owned and additional Chinese ports were forced open to trade. The Chinese granted extraterritoriality, which was the right for the British to be tried under British law, not Chinese law. The First Opium War was followed by a *Second Opium War* (1856–60) with similar results. Still more ports were opened to European trade. The importation of the narcotic opium into China was made legal.

The Opium Wars proved that China was no match for the modern power of Europe. These wars were a turning point in Chinese history. The foreigners, having won many privileges, would try to win even more. The days of the Manchu Dynasty were numbered.

Why the Manchu Dynasty Resisted Change

China's defeats meant that its emperor and its people had "lost face." Some Chinese were determined to do something about it. China's problems, however, began to take a turn for the worse. Its population was growing rapidly. Farmers were finding it difficult to grow enough food to eat. Taxes were high; stomachs were empty; peasants were restless. China needed a leader to show them how to solve their problems.

Hung Hsiu-ch'üan [hung′shü′chwan′] proved to be such a leader. Hung had tried and failed in the examinations for government service. He, too, like those he led, knew disappointment. Unlike them, however, he thought he knew what to do for China. Hung had been influenced by Christian missionaries in China. He believed that he was related to Jesus and he urged the peasants to follow him.

For fourteen years, from 1850 to 1864, Hung gathered an army of followers around him. For a time, they made successful rebellions. At Nanking, Hung set up a capital. Plans were made to overthrow the Manchu government at Peking and to set up a new dynasty to be known as *T'ai P'ing* [tī′ ping′], or Great Peace. Hung and his followers were defeated by the armies of the Manchu. Hung killed himself, and the great T'ai P'ing Rebellion died with him.

The T'ai P'ing Rebellion started a debate in China. Some demanded that China adopt Western ways. Others demanded that China resist change. The emperors did not know which side to support. When the side favoring Western ways gained power, some improvements were made. The Chinese were sent to English schools. When the side that wanted to resist change gained power, the foreigners were ordered to go home.

At that time, China was governed by Empress Tzu Hsi [tsu′ shē′] (1861–1908). When her husband died, the throne went to their son, a boy of five. Because a boy of five cannot be expected to rule, his mother ruled instead. When her son was nearly old enough to rule China, he too died. Another minor—a nephew of the empress—was placed on the throne. Again, power remained in the hands of the empress. In the debate that tore China in the years after the T'ai P'ing Rebellion, Tzu Hsi usually sided with the people who sought to resist change. Because of Tzu Hsi's unwillingness to accept change, China had to wait many years before reforms were made.

Foreign Powers Mistreated China

China wanted to improve relations with the United States. For this purpose, Anson Burlingame [bür′lin gām′], an American minister in China until 1867, became the Chinese ambassador to the United States. His appointment gives

Chinese Civilization

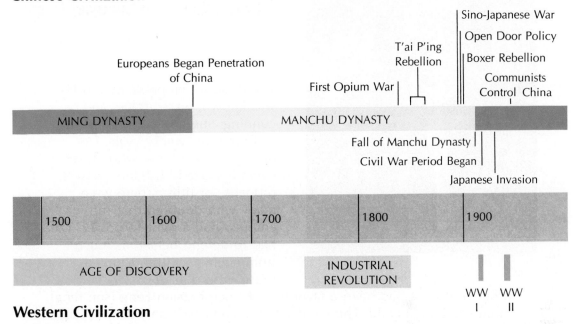

Western Civilization

What events in the nineteenth and twentieth centuries involved contact between China and the West?

you some idea of the respect the Chinese had for him. It also indicates that China wanted to take its place in the family of nations.

In spite of some modernization, China remained a sleeping giant that was easy to attack. In 1895, the Chinese were defeated by Japan in the *Sino-Japanese War*. As a result of this war, Japan obtained Formosa. Japan also gained control of the Pescadores [pes kä dôrs], a group of islands between Formosa and China. It also won trading privileges at four ports. Because China was easily defeated by Japan, other nations felt that they too could defeat China.

Russia, Germany, Great Britain, France, and Portugal expected repayment from China for their help in arranging the peace with Japan. These countries persuaded the Chinese to grant long-term leases on various ports in which they alone had the right to do business. Getting these exclusive leases was a first step toward the actual division

of China by some of the great powers. These nations also gained the rights to build railroads in China. The division of China among the big powers then appeared certain. The big powers had planned the division of China without consulting the United States. The United States opposed the planned division and the plan failed.

The United States took over the Philippines from Spain as a result of its victory in the Spanish-American War. It had become a Far Eastern power as well as a world power as a result. The United States did not wish to see China divided among the big European powers. Therefore, in 1899, American Secretary of State John Hay proposed what came to be known as the *Open Door policy*. This policy sought to get the European powers to agree to leave China open to the trade of all nations. One of the purposes of this policy was to assure the United States its fair share of the trade in China. The Open Door policy was encouraged by

Tzu Hsi   (1834–1908)

The dowager empress, as Tzu Hsi was known, was ruthless and cunning. She guided the destiny of China for twenty years. (A *dowager* is a widow who "takes over" her dead husband's power, property, or title.) There were many who doubted that the empress had a right to power. Tzu had to defend herself as much from enemies within China as those from outside.

In her youth she had been a favorite of Emperor Hsien Feng [sen feng], to whom she bore a child. The child was the emperor's only son. Because of this she was accorded great honors. She also had many privileges at the court. Upon the death of the emperor in 1860, their son became the new emperor of China. It was then that Tzu Hsi became the real authority in China. Her son died just as he was beginning to exercise independent power. She then arranged for another child ruler to take his place so that she could continue to be the real power in China.

Under her rule the imperial court of China had more than its share of conspiracy. She ruled through palace favorites who often did not remain among the favored for very long. Her court was one of sumptuous luxury. Even for those days, it showed arrogance and indifference to the people of China, many of whom were constantly hungry.

When her nephew Kuang Hsü [gwäng shü] (1875–1908) took full authority, he declared that he was in favor of modernization and reform in China. The dowager empress was furious when she heard about this. Her nephew had announced his position without consulting the "Old Buddha," as she was sometimes called. With little hesitation, the dowager empress imprisoned her nephew and withdrew his decrees. She made herself the real authority in China once again. By this act she took the lead in encouraging forces that were against modernization or reform in China. She encouraged the Boxers' violence against the Christian missionaries who were then living in China.

The dowager empress died in 1908. At the end of her life, she did finally encourage some modernization, including the building of a railroad. She was succeeded by Pu-yi [pu yē], who was the last emperor of China.

Great Britain but only mildly supported by other nations. In 1941, America was forced to fight with Japan over the ideas in the Open Door policy.

How the Boxer Rebellion Weakened China

Under the Manchus, China continued to debate the need for reform. A Chinese author wrote a book called *Learn*, in which he suggested that China could learn something from Western ideas. The Manchu Emperor Kuang Hsü seemed to favor reform. He issued orders that ended some outworn Chinese customs. He thought that the Confucian examinations for civil service should be stopped. He also urged that schools and railroads be built. He began to strengthen the army and navy. Although Emperor Kuang Hsü tried to make reforms, Empress Tzu Hsi, as we already know, did not want China to change.

The people who favored the empress's position were called the *Boxers*. They blamed China's difficulties on the presence of foreigners. In a violent uprising that promised "death to the foreigners," the Boxers tried to rid China of its "foreign devils." Over 240 foreigners were slaughtered. Many of the casualties were women, children, and missionaries.

The *Boxer Rebellion* (1900–1903) angered the British, French, Germans, and Americans. These countries sent troops to put down the rebellion. Many Chinese died. The Boxers were defeated, but China was forced to pay for the ill-planned rebellion. The emperor and empress were both forced to flee. China had to agree to Western terms for peace. The terms included payment for the costs of the war, an end to the tribute system, lowering of tariffs, and protection of Western diplomats.

China's punishment for the Boxer Rebellion was severe. The fact that China was not further divided at this time was due to America's insistence upon the Open Door policy. The United States used the money it received for war damages to pay for the education of Chinese youths in the United States.

A Chinese print shows a Boxer trial of foreign captives. The Boxer Rebellion was unable to prevent foreign influence from spreading in China.

1. Why were the Chinese unwilling to allow Europeans to trade with them?

2. Why did the Chinese consider Europeans to be "barbarians"?

3. Why were the Opium Wars a turning point in the relationships between China and Europe? Why was the Boxer Rebellion another important turning point?

4. What is meant by the *open door* in China?

HOW OTHER COUNTRIES OF THE FAR EAST FELL UNDER EUROPEAN CONTROL

Why the Isolation of Japan and Korea Ended

Commodore Perry's arrival in Japan in 1853 marks the beginning of the end of old Japan and Korea. Japan had been a country in which changes had been discouraged, but it soon became a nation most eager to adopt Western ways. In the eyes of the Japanese, the steamships of Perry were objects of wonder. Perry presented a letter from the American president. He asked that American sailors be protected when lost at sea or shipwrecked. He also requested that one or two ports be opened for trade. In 1857, Townsend Harris became United States consul general in Japan. He persuaded the Japanese to open a number of ports to American trade. Foreigners were given the privilege of extraterritoriality.

The coming of foreigners to Japan touched off a disagreement between those who favored learning Western ways and those who wanted to follow traditional ways. After a struggle, the side that felt that Japan should be agreeable to Western diplomats and their ideas was successful. Soon the government under a military leader, called the

Commodore Matthew Perry of the United States navy challenged Japan's isolation. He brought ships into a Japanese harbor and refused to leave. He then demanded to see government officials. Eventually, Japan gave in and signed treaties giving certain privileges to the United States, such as the right to get fuel in Japan.

Imperialism in Asia, 1914

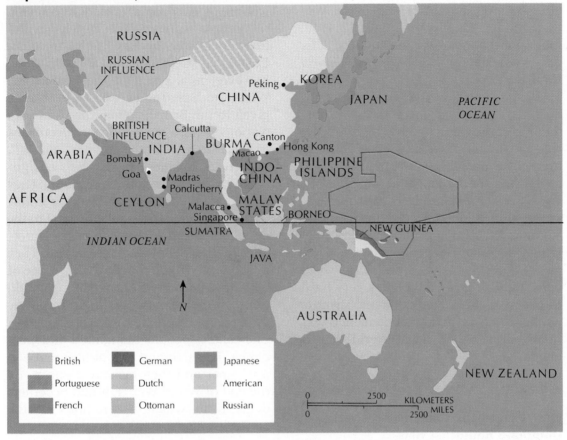

- What European power ruled most of India?
- Locate two regions that were controlled by each of the following: the Dutch, the Americans, the Germans, and the Russians.

shogunate [shō'gun'āt], ended. Emperor Mutsuhito [mü'tsü hē'tō] became the ruler of Japan in fact as well as in name. After 700 years, the old feudal military government had come to an end. China was still debating whether to keep Westerners out. Japan chose the West as its model to copy.

On the farms and in the cities some changes were beginning to take place. The Japanese were quick to buy and use the machines the West had to sell. New factories went up, seemingly overnight. Telephone and telegraph lines crossed the islands and connected cities. Ships flying Japanese flags crossed the seas. The needs of the economy and the needs of the army were uppermost in the minds of Japanese leaders as they rebuilt their nation. It would not be long before a strong Japan would challenge China, Russia, and the United States.

The West had little to do with Korea until the nineteenth century, when it tried to open Korea to trade. British, French, Russian, and American efforts failed, but those of Japan were successful. Three times Japan tried to bring Korea under its rule. The Sino-Japanese War was one attempt, and the Russo-Japanese War was another. Finally, on August 22, 1910, the Japanese took over the country. This day was called *"National Humiliation Day"* by Korea.

Despite the fact that Japan built industry, railroads, highways, and farms, the Koreans were unhappy under the rule of Japan. They had little voice in their government and little freedom. Japanese was the language of the schools. The Koreans were made to serve the Japanese, who were harsh taskmasters. The Koreans kept hoping that one day they would become independent again. During the years between the two world wars, the Koreans had to work very hard in order to make their dreams of independence come true. Independence was finally won in 1945 when World War II ended.

How Europeans Came to Dominate Southeast Asia

The Malay Peninsula is about the same size as Florida. It occupies a very important position geographically. The shortest water route from Europe to the Far East passes the southern end of the Malay Peninsula.

In 1819, Britain gained from the sultan of Jehore [jə hôr'] the port of Singapore at the southern end of the Malay Peninsula. Because of this small island city, the British were able to hold on to the Malay Peninsula until well into the twentieth century.

In the struggle to gain empires, it was the Dutch whose grip proved strongest in the East Indies. You have already read the story of the Dutch East India Company. Like the British East India Company in India, it was for a time the government of the East Indies. The Dutch East India Company became more interested in making profits than in looking after the welfare of the people it ruled. As a result, the people suffered. The Dutch government took over the East Indies from the East India Company in 1798. In 1811, however, as a result of the Napoleonic Wars, the East Indies were temporarily given to the British. When the wars with Napoleon were over, they were returned to the Dutch.

Private business firms were encouraged by the Dutch government. They developed the tea, tin, and rubber industries. These industries became vital to the people of the East Indies, to the Dutch, and to the people of the world. They brought the Dutch much wealth, some of which was used to improve living conditions on the islands. But these improvements came too late and were too few. The island people demanded independence. This demand was at first made in a whisper and then became a shout. By the end of World War II, it had become a demand to which the nations of the world listened.

Check in Here

1. The emergence of modern Japan may be said to date from the end of the shogunate. Why?

2. How did the attitude toward modernization in Japan differ from that of China?

3. Why did Korea fall under Japanese domination rather than under European domination?

4. If the Dutch improved living conditions in the East Indies, why were the people of the islands dissatisfied?

In India, the Portuguese, the French, and the Dutch each came in turn and each left an important influence. It was the British influence, however, which was to be the greatest by far. While the British sent many able and devoted soldiers and statesmen to India, the people of India were not content under British rule. As a result of the Sepoy Mutiny, the British Parliament decided to rule India directly rather than through the British East India Company. In 1877, Queen Victoria became Empress of India.

In China, the Manchu Dynasty resisted the invasion of the "barbarians" from Europe. As a result of the Opium Wars with Britain, China was forced to open more ports to European trade. The principle of *extraterritoriality* weakened the relationships between the Chinese and the Europeans. This was so because it enabled Europeans to violate Chinese law and then to be tried in their own more sympathetic courts. Efforts to remove the Europeans were unsuccessful. China was forced to lease ports and to give special privileges to the countries of Europe. The United States opposed this move and sought to fight for the "open door" in China. That is, the United States sought to end the special privileges of the European nations.

It was the American fleet under Admiral Perry that opened Japan to American and European trade. The Japanese responded by copying the West in its government, armed forces, industry, and economy. The shogunate system, in which a powerful feudal noble ruled and an emperor who was only a figurehead, was overthrown. The emperor became the real ruler of Japan. It was under the emperor that Japan began to modernize.

Korea fell under Japan's rule. The Europeans were unable to win special privileges there. In the East Indies and on the Malay Peninsula, the Dutch and the British ruled until the end of World War II. At that time, independence could no longer be denied to the people of these islands.

REVIEWING THE HIGHLIGHTS

People to Identify			
K'ang Hsi	John Hay	Pedro Cabral
Lin Tse-hsu	Commodore Perry	Alfonso de Albuquerque
Hung Hsiu-ch'üan	Townsend Harris	Robert Clive
Tzu Hsi	Mutsuhito	Joseph Dupleix
Kuang Hsu	Rudyard Kipling	Warren Hastings
Anson Burlingame	Francisco de Almeida	Lord Cornwallis

Places to Locate	Goa	Japan	Manchuria
	Java	China	Mongolia
	Pondicherry	India	Hong Kong
	Southeast Asia	Macao	Bombay
	Madras	Canton	Malay Peninsula
	Calcutta	Peking	Formosa
	Korea	Nanking	Pescadores

Terms to Understand

Dutch East India Company
British East India Company
caste system
tribute
Heavenly Court
kowtow
Manchu Dynasty

extraterritoriality
Co-hong
Open Door policy
"National Humiliation Day"
India Act
British lifeline
banner armies

Events to Describe

Opium Wars
Boxer Rebellion
Sino-Japanese War

Sepoy Mutiny
Black Hole of Calcutta
T'ai P'ing Rebellion

Mastering the Fundamentals

1. Why was Portuguese power in India short-lived?

2. Where in Asia did the Dutch have the most influence? How long did they control that area?

3. What powers, other than strictly commercial ones, did the British East India Company have?

4. What were the underlying causes of the Sepoy Mutiny? What was the immediate cause?

5. Why is the Battle of Plassey a turning point in British history in India?

6. How did the British government improve conditions in India?

7. What was the attitude of China toward the coming of the Europeans?

8. Why was doing business in China difficult for the Europeans?

9. What were the causes and results of the Opium Wars?

10. What were the causes and results of the T'ai P'ing Rebellion?

11. What was the attitude of Empress Tzu Hsi toward reform?

12. Why did the United States insist upon the policy of the Open Door in China?

13. Why was Korea proud to be a tribute state of China?

14. Why is Korea sometimes called the "Hermit Kingdom"?

15. How did the attitude of Japan differ from that of China toward Europeans?

16. How did Perry alter the traditional life and government of Japan?

17. How did Japan seek to modernize?

18. Why was the Malay Peninsula important in Southeast Asia?

19. What did the Dutch accomplish in Indonesia?

20. Why did European influence in East Asia and Southeast Asia last so long?

THINGS TO DO

1. Prepare a Steve Allen "Meeting of Minds" Program in which you develop a conversation Almeida, Robert Clive, and Commodore Perry might have had, had they been able to meet and talk to one another face to face. Be sure your dialogue brings out the similarities as well as the differences of their experiences. Dramatize the conversation you prepare by reading portions of it to your class.

2. Using papier-mâché, prepare a map of any one of the following: India, China, Japan, Indonesia, Korea, Malaya. By using papier-mâché, you can show the terrain and the topography of each country. By using different colors, you can show also the influence of each of the European countries on the country of East Asia or Southeast Asia you choose.

3. The spelling and pronunciation of many of the words in this chapter may be unfamiliar to you. With your class, try a "spelling bee" in which a chairperson reads the word or name and another tries to spell it. By dividing into two teams, one can see which of the teams is more successful in mastering the spelling of difficult names and terms.

Study the charts below. On the basis of the information provided, are the statements below RIGHT or WRONG or is there NOT SUFFICIENT information on which to decide?

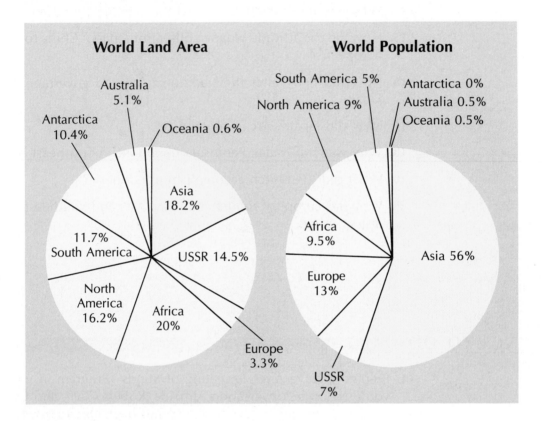

1. Asia has the largest percentage of the world's land area as well as the largest percentage of the world's population.
2. Africa, which has 20% of the world's land area, has only 8% of the world's population.
3. Asia has too many people.
4. There are more people in the USSR than there are in North and South America.
5. North America is a region whose total land area is 2% less than that of Asia.
6. The population of Asia is more than twice that of the combined populations of Europe and Africa.
7. Less than 1% of the world's population live in Antarctica, Australia, Oceania (Pacific Islands).
8. Most of the land area of the world is north of the equator.
9. Asia and Europe occupy 36% of the world's land area and have 77.8% of the world's people.
10. The USSR has about the same number of people as Africa.

American World War I poster promoting war savings stamps

World War I and Its Results: The War to End All Wars

Many of you know the story of the shepherd who cried wolf once too often. When he got tired of watching the sheep he would cry, "Wolf!" He enjoyed watching the other shepherds rush to his defense. He always laughed with delight when he told them that he had fooled them, but he tried this trick once too often. A wolf finally did come. The boy called loudly for help, but the other shepherds, not wishing to be fooled again, did not come.

In some ways, the events that led to World War I may be compared to this story. Between 1895 and 1914, the nations of Europe were near war or at war many times. They disagreed with each other over North Africa, the Balkan Countries, and China. War, or the threat of a major war, was almost a common event. World tension increased, but a big war did not start.

While there was much talk of war, no one believed that it would come when it did. When it might have been avoided, there seemed to be no one to stop it.

THE CAUSES THAT LED TO WORLD WAR I

How Alliances and Armies Led to War

World War I started for many reasons. The causes of World War I can be found in a number of conditions and problems that created great tension in 1914.

The preparation for war started when the countries of the world decided that their safety depended on big armies and big navies. They tried to become stronger than their neighbors. They drafted young men to serve in their armies even though there was no war. Britain insisted on being the "mistress of the seas"; Germany became a "nation at arms." In Germany the army enjoyed much power and glory.

The countries of Europe wanted to become stronger and to protect themselves from attack. They tried making *alliances,* or agreements, with nations that agreed with them on common goals. Bismarck tried to make Germany strong by making alliances with Russia for military protection, but this did not work. In 1882, he formed an alliance with Austria and Italy, which was called the *Triple Alliance.* The three nations in the Triple Alliance

agreed to come to one another's aid in case of war. The Triple Alliance had a central role in the unfolding developments leading to World War I.

France also decided to look for friends. First, that nation made a military agreement with Russia in 1893. In 1907, Great Britain joined Russia and France to form an alliance called the *Triple Entente.* These nations said they would help one another if one of them was attacked by Germany.

When World War I broke out in 1914, the Triple Entente fought against the Triple Alliance. However, Italy, a member of the Triple Alliance, did not live up to its agreement with Germany and Austria. Instead, Italy joined with Great Britain and France to defeat Germany. The Triple Entente bargained with Italy. It made a secret agreement to get Italy's support.

Many of the smaller countries of Europe were also tangled in secret agreements. The countries of Europe did not trust one another. They did not know whether their neighbors were friends or enemies. They did not really know which countries might help them or which might harm them. The climate was ready for the "god of war."

Europe in 1914 Before World War I

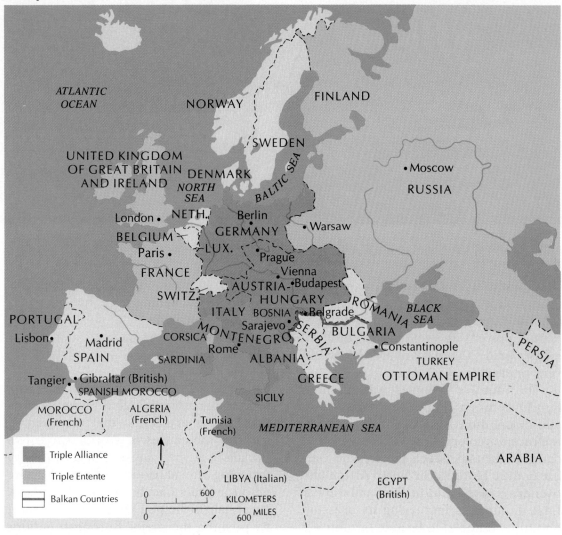

Before World War I, Europe was divided into two military alliances.
• To which alliance did Russia, Austria-Hungary, and Italy belong?
• Locate the members of the Triple Alliance.

How Nationalism and Imperialism Caused War

There were still other factors that helped bring on World War I. Because Germany, Italy, and Japan were late in becoming industrialized, they were trying to make up for lost time. Japan was trying to become a dominant power in the Far East. Germany and Italy wanted to become dominant powers in European and colonial affairs.

The growth of Germany, in particular, upset the balance of power among the European nations. Germany was not content to be just another country. It wanted to be as powerful as Great Britain had been. It began building fine manufacturing plants where quality products

Factories along the Rhine were an indication of Germany's economic power before World War I.

were made. Its manufacturers and merchants were taking business away from other countries. Germany's growing economic power, as well as its military might, made the nations of the world very uneasy.

The race for colonies was, at first, largely between France and Great Britain. Soon, however, Germany entered the race for colonies too. This race led to disagreements between France and Germany over Morocco in North Africa and over areas of the Middle East and the Far East. Japan was increasing its pressure on China. It hoped to be able to control a large part of the wealth of that country. These disagreements brought the world to the edge of war a number of times.

Nationalism, like imperialism, was a factor that helped to bring on World War I. While Germany and France crossed swords over control of Morocco, Austria and Russia argued over the Balkans. Russia tried to act like a big brother to the Slavic peoples who lived there. Russia felt that it should protect those peoples whose language and customs were similar to its own. Serbia, one of Russia's Slavic "little brothers," had no seaport and wanted one badly. Russia decided to help it get one. Austria, fearing growing

Serbian strength, opposed Serbian expansion. Bad feeling grew between Serbia and Austria.

**The Main Causes
of World War I**

Nationalism, imperialism, militarism, secret agreements, and international lawlessness are terms that are used to sum up the causes of World War I. Nationalism helped cause World War I by arousing the patriotic feelings of those who for years had been ruled by others. Imperialism helped cause World War I by pushing the major European nations into the race for colonies. Militarism led to World War I by encouraging arms building and by preparing people and machines for war. Secret agreements among nations led to World War I by causing nations to become distrustful of one another.

International lawlessness means the absence of machinery for the peaceful settlement of disputes among nations. Conflict and war could not be stopped. There was no organization to which the nations of the world could bring their differences. The nations felt they had no place to go for a just and fair hearing and settlement of their complaints.

1. Distinguish between the Triple Alliance and the Triple Entente.

2. Using a map, identify the location of the major members of each of the above alliances.

3. Explain how each of the following was a fundamental cause of World War I: (**a**) nationalism; (**b**) imperialism; (**c**) militarism; (**d**) secret alliances.

4. What is meant by *international lawlessness?* How did it contribute to the outbreak of World War I?

A NUMBER OF INTERNATIONAL CRISES IGNITE THE POWDER KEG OF EUROPE

How Crises in Morocco Brought War Near

In the race for colonies the big powers had overlooked Morocco in North Africa. Now, both France and Germany wanted it. France had soldiers in its nearby colony of Algeria, and it wanted to join Morocco to its Algerian lands. Germany, fearing this move, waited for the chance to stop it.

Germany's chance came in 1905. Since Russia was at war against Japan, it would not be able to help France if a war broke out between France and Germany. The German kaiser said that the sultan of Morocco must remain an independent ruler. France did not like this threat. Luckily for everyone concerned, it was decided to talk about the first Moroccan crisis at an international meeting.

The powerful nations of the world met in 1906 at Algeciras, Spain. They agreed that Morocco was to be independent but that France could have police power in that country. This conference showed which country the nations of the world agreed with in the conflict. Austria supported Germany. Great Britain, Russia, and Italy sided with France.

The agreement at Algeciras had given France police power in Morocco. However, in 1911, France decided to make its grip on Morocco even stronger by sending a French army to Fez, the chief city of Morocco. The Germans answered the challenge by sending a warship to Agadir [ä'gä dēr'] as a warning to France. Preparations for war began. Great Britain and Italy again came to the support of France. Germany backed down. This second Moroccan crisis is known as the *Agadir Affair.*

Again, war was avoided, but the nations of the world could hear Germany grumble. France was successful in tightening its grip on Morocco, which was made a protectorate of France. Germany was given a strip of land in the French Congo as compensation.

How Crises Developed in the Balkan Area

North Africa was not the only place where trouble was brewing. In the Balkan states of southeast Europe crises arose which brought Russia and Austria near war. (See map, p. 491.)

In 1908, Austria tried to add the provinces of Bosnia [boz'nē ə] and Herzegovina [her'tsə gō vē'nə] to its own territory. Because nationalism was very strong in this area, Austria's efforts were met with violent opposition. Russia came to the help of Serbia; Germany came to the help of Austria. Again, luckily for everyone, fighting did not break out. The Serbians gave in.

Serbia did not expect that the setback in the crisis of 1908 would be permanent. It was determined to get seaports which it badly needed. During the years 1912 and 1913, two wars were fought in the

Balkans. In both of these wars, Serbia tried to get outlets to the sea. In the *First Balkan War*, Bulgaria, Serbia, and Greece defeated Turkey.

When Serbia was prevented by Austria from getting a seaport, it made war on its old friend, Bulgaria. The *Second Balkan War* followed. This war ended in 1913. Serbia was the winner. Again, Austria prevented Serbia from getting the seaport on the Adriatic Sea that it desperately wanted. World war did not follow because again Serbia backed down.

How World War I Began

In the preceding paragraphs we outlined four main crises in North Africa and southeastern Europe. The frequent crises led nations to believe that they must be strong lest they be conquered by a stronger neighbor. As a result, an arms race developed. It was not long before a crisis came from which no nation would back down. Each of the little wars and each of the crises of the late nineteenth century and the early twentieth century had created a climate that was ripe for the outbreak of a major war.

On June 28, 1914, the Archduke Francis Ferdinand—who would have been the next king of Austria—was killed in Sarajevo [sar′ə yä′vō], a city in Bosnia. Austria was sure that it was a Serbian who had killed its prince. Austrian leaders made up their minds to make war on Serbia. Austria asked Germany for help. Serbia asked Russia for help. This made it almost impossible to settle the argument without fighting. When Serbia refused to accept all of Austria's harsh terms in settling the conflict, Austria declared war on Serbia.

The nations of Europe began to take opposing sides. Since France seemed ready to help Russia, Russia supported Serbia and went to war against Austria. Germany declared war on Russia. No one knew what Great Britain would do. The British minister of foreign affairs tried to work for peace. He was unsuccessful in getting any of the nations to back down. When Germany marched into neutral Belgium, it showed that Germany was ready to fight to the finish. France, in turn, hurried to help Russia. Great Britain finally joined Russia and France, and World War I was on. Italy deserted the Triple Alliance and joined Great Britain and France. In 1917, the United States went to the aid of Great Britain and France.

The Strengths of the Fighting Nations

In World War I the *Allies* fought the *Central Powers*. The major Allies were Russia, France, Great Britain, Italy, and the

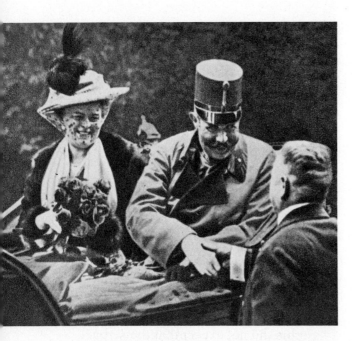

On June 28, 1914, the Archduke Ferdinand and Sophie, his wife, greeted a well-wisher. One hour later they were assassinated. What step did Austria take against Serbia as a result?

494

United States. The Central Powers were Germany, Austria, Turkey, and Bulgaria.

The Central Powers had many advantages and had reason to hope for victory. The German army was the best trained in the world. The German navy was also strong, although not as strong as Great Britain's. The Central Powers were close to each other and could work together more readily. A unified command was established early in the war. This made it easy for the Central Powers to organize their activities.

The Allies had more people and more money to spend on the war effort. The British navy, the best in the world, gave the Allies command of the seas. Supremacy on the sea meant that they could stop ships going to Germany or to Germany's friends. The naval blockade which the Allies put into effect early in the war helped them win. The French army was the best on the Allied side. The Russian army, though large in size, was weak. The Allies had no unified command, and it was not until later in the war that they were really united.

Check in Here

1. Indicate the importance of each of the following in contributing to World War I: (**a**) Algeciras Conference; (**b**) Agadir Affair.

2. Why has the Balkan Peninsula been described as the "powder keg" of Europe?

3. How did the First and Second Balkan Wars contribute to the outbreak of World War I?

4. Why was the assassination of Archduke Ferdinand the spark that ignited World War I?

5. Compare the strengths and weaknesses of the Allies and Central Powers.

A BITTER WAR IS FOUGHT AT HOME, ON LAND, AND AT SEA

How World War I Was Fought on the Home Front

World War I was a *total war*. It included soldiers and civilians, factory workers and farm workers, and all kinds of materials that had never been found useful in former wars. The farm, the factory, and the science laboratory were used by each side to help fight and win the war. All the tools and inventions of the Industrial Revolution were used. Machinery, railroads, telephones, and airplanes were used as a means to destroy the enemy.

In most former wars—except for the wars which grew out of the French Revolution—the fighting was done by professional soldiers. Not so in World War I. The men in the armies of all nations were made up of citizens who had, for the most part, been drafted. The success of the war was dependent upon the loyalty and enthusiasm of these soldiers. Success also depended upon those who remained at home to run the factories and the farms that turned out products needed to wage the war. As a result, *propaganda* became an important weapon of war.

Propaganda is used to influence people's minds. Those who use propaganda try to make others see the fairness of the cause for which they are fighting. Propaganda is also used to influence the people of the enemy. It tries to prove to them that the cause for which their country is fighting is worthless and one they cannot achieve.

In World War I the news media, to a far greater degree than in any other previous war, was used to win the war. At that time, the news media included newspapers, magazines, telephone, telegraph, and cable. The Allied governments were successful in gaining control of the news media. They convinced the British and American people that the Germans were demons who were committing grave crimes, including the killing of women and children. While some of this was true, it is important to see the way the information was used. It was used to whip up hatred for the enemy. Propaganda helped create uncritical enthusiasm and patriotism for one's own country. Even the theater and the music industries were called upon to stir up support for the war effort.

During World War I, the economic resources of each side were as important as the military resources. Among the Allies and the Central Powers industrial production was speeded up. On both sides the economy came under the control of the government. Owners of industry could keep the profits they made in wartime. However, what they made, how much they could charge, and the profits they could keep were largely determined by government. In Russia, a free economy was overthrown and replaced by a Communist system. In the other countries, free economies were restored immediately after the war.

At first, both sides thought that the war would be over quickly. They were clearly wrong. As they began to dig in for a long war, they took control of their nations' railroads. The countries of both sides depended upon the railroads to shift armies and equipment from one frontier to another. The amount of goods and the number of soldiers shifted from one battlefield to another was staggering. Britain, for example, sent its first army to France two weeks after war had been declared. To do so required the use of 1,500 trains. In one day, 104 trains entered Southhampton, the port of departure for France. The trains carried 25,000 men, 6,000 horses, and more than 1,000 tons of baggage.

Food and fuel were strictly controlled during the war. In every European country taking part in the war, a *rationing* system was introduced. Under rationing people were allowed only a certain amount of food and fuel. As the Allied naval blockade of the Central Powers tightened, the food and fuel shortages in those countries got much worse. Raw materials were carefully shared between the armed services and the large civilian population.

Paying for the war was a severe problem for the *belligerents* [bə lij'ər ents], or fighting countries. Only two methods were available: taxation and borrowing. At first, countries borrowed more than they taxed. They believed that the war would be a short one. Later, as the war dragged on, they had to increase taxes. No country could have paid for the war through taxation alone.

One form of borrowing involves the selling of *bonds* to the citizens of the country. Bonds are pieces of paper which represent money loaned to the government. Citizens receive interest on the money their government has borrowed from them. In World War I this proved to be a popular way of raising money.

Another form of borrowing is to issue paper money through the central banks of a country. This was also done. In the course of the war too much paper money was printed and put into the economy. Excessively high, or inflated, prices were the result. In most countries the government tried to *fix* prices to prevent high inflation. This measure was only partly successful. Inflation became a very serious problem among the Central Powers, especially as it became evident that they were going to lose the war.

Another problem the fighting countries had was how to replace the men who left the factories and farms for the armed services. There were labor shortages on the home front because many men had been drafted. The widespread and successful employment of women in factories was one way in which the labor shortage was eased. But in those days it was difficult for women to work outside the home.

Machines were developed to replace the men who went to war. Nevertheless, it became necessary for the belligerents to allow men with technical skills to return to the factories and shipyards. This policy caused a good deal of discontent. Some parts of the economy—farmers for example—thought that their sons were bearing a heavier burden of the war effort. They were asked to risk their lives in battle for the low pay of a soldier. Skilled workers, on the other hand, were safe from the battlefield and worked for the high wages their skills commanded. To prevent strikes, boards of workers and managers were set up. They discussed and settled differences and agreed on the terms and conditions of labor.

How World War I Was Fought on Land

German plans to win the war called for the quick defeat of France in the West before Russian troops could gather in the East. Thus, the German army went through Belgium in an effort to encircle Paris. For a time, it looked as if the Germans would reach their goal. But at the First Battle of the Marne [märn] (September 5-12, 1914), the French, under General Joffre [zhôf′rə], successfully defeated the Germans. Paris was never taken by the Germans during World War I. The Germans tried to capture the French seaports of Dunkirk, Calais, and Boulogne in order to destroy communications between England and France.

Both the Allies and Central Powers used words and pictures to help create patriotism on the home front. This German poster shows submarine warfare and reads, "Boats out."

They were prevented from doing so by the British at Ypres [ē′prə].

By the end of 1914 the *Western Front* had been stabilized. The Western Front went from the North Sea to the Swiss frontier for about 600 miles. The commanders on both sides dug deep trenches along the Western Front. Soldiers lived and fought in the trenches. They often had to share their quarters with rats, and death from enemy fire was never far away. Both sides in the conflict tried to kill as many enemy soldiers as they could. They did this by throwing troops, often recklessly, against the enemy. The death wrought by this terrible approach to battle reached a scale never before seen in wartime.

On the *Eastern Front*, the German armies of General Paul von Hindenburg [von hin'dən burg'] met the Russians at Tannenberg [tän'ən berkh'] (August 26-30, 1914) and defeated them. (See map p. 499.) The victory was so great that von Hindenburg became a German national hero. Because they were successful in the East, the Germans changed their plans. They decided to try to knock Russia out of the war. While the Russians fought gallantly, they lacked equipment. The British and French sought to help the Russians. They fought their way to the Dardanelles and captured Constantinople. At the eight-month Battle of Gallipoli [gə lip'ə lē], which was fought to control the Dardanelles and open the Black Sea for Allied equipment, the Allies suffered a humiliating disaster. Costly blunders

meant that 145,000 men were killed and wounded. Russia would never provide the military help England and France had hoped and expected. Nevertheless, the German plan to knock Russia out of the war was not easily achieved.

In 1915, the Western Front was manned by French and British soldiers. The fortress of Verdun [vär dun'], its strongest point, became the objective of the German effort. The Battle of Verdun, which began in February 1916, lasted for nearly six months. It was responsible for the death of half a million men. The French, under General Henri Pétain [pā tan'], were determined to defeat the Germans. It was here that General Pétain earned the gratitude of the French nation. Verdun held out and put the German army up against a wall as a result.

The year 1917 was a turning point in the war for the Allies. In March, 1917, the Allies were given a lift when the United States entered the war the very same

Canadian soldiers leap from their trenches to engage in battle.

World War I

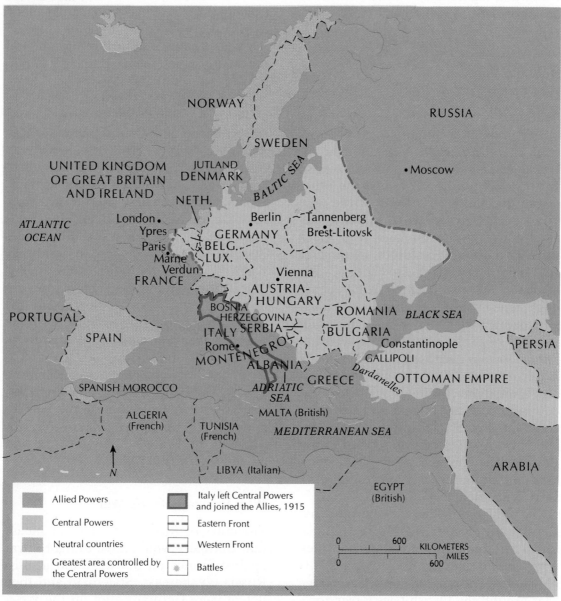

■ Allied Powers	■ Italy left Central Powers and joined the Allies, 1915
■ Central Powers	—·—·— Eastern Front
■ Neutral countries	—·—·— Western Front
■ Greatest area controlled by the Central Powers	✳ Battles

- According to the map key, which country changed alliances?
- In what country was the Eastern Front located?
- What is the approximate distance in kilometers between Berlin and Paris?
- Locate the country in which each of the following battles took place: Verdun, Tannenberg, Gallipoli.
- Locate two countries that were neutral during World War I.

year. The United States entered the war on April 6, 1917, on the side of the Allies. It made victory certain for the Allies. An American army, led by General John J. Pershing [pur'shing], landed in France in 1918. In France the American *doughboy*, or soldier, made a name for himself as a fighter. The Central Powers began to give up one by one, and on November 11, 1918, Germany surrendered and signed an *armistice,* which is an agreement to stop hostilities.

How the War Was Fought at Sea

Food and raw materials are very important in making a military victory possible. Therefore, both sides sought to blockade each other's supply shipments. In this way, each side hoped the other would tire and urge the end of the war. The Central Powers were initially successful in fighting on land; the Allies were initially successful in fighting at sea. The Allies were able to capture, sink, or drive into port all ships flying enemy flags. Great Britain declared all enemy territory in a state of blockade and began to try to seize all *contraband,* or war materials. Britain increased the list of goods it felt it could take from the enemy. It also limited the amount of goods neutral countries such as Holland and Denmark could import. The fear was that those goods would then be sold to the Central Powers. The United States joined other neutral countries in protesting the British position.

So tight did the blockade become that Germany decided to fight back. It did so mainly by mounting a campaign which used submarines to try to crack the blockade. The Germans declared the seas around the British Isles a *war zone.* Merchant ships of the Allies could be torpedoed without warning. On May 7, 1915, the British ship *Lusitania* was torpedoed. Over one thousand lives were lost, including one hundred Americans. The German campaign of *unrestricted submarine warfare,* as this was called, was only partially successful. It enraged public opinion against Germany. Great Britain made good use of its control over the news media. It described the tragedy as the heartless and needless destruction of innocent people who happened to be traveling at sea. This propaganda made the British practice of searching ships on the high seas and capturing cargo bound for enemy ports seem humane by comparison.

In general, the Germans sought to avoid a major fight with the British navy. At the Battle of Jutland [jut′lənd] (May 31, 1916), however, the British were almost successful in destroying the bulk of the German fleet. Superior German naval tactics saved that fleet from destruction. The Germans in turn caused serious losses to the British navy. Both sides claimed victory. The Germans said they had inflicted greater losses on the enemy. The British said they had chased, but not destroyed, the German fleet from the seas. Throughout the war, the British were never again challenged directly at sea by the Germans.

The German policy of submarine warfare had the effect of casting Germany in a bad light among the world's peoples. It was also responsible for drawing the United States into the war on the side of the Allies.

Why Russia Left the War

The entry of Russia into the war meant that Germany would have to fight a war against France on the west and against Russia on the east. Stalemate and then defeat were Germany's lot on the Western Front. It was far more successful on the Eastern Front.

The ease with which Russia was defeated was due in part to the weakness of the czar's government. The Russian army suffered greatly from its first defeat by the Germans. Lack of munitions and supplies added further to the discouragement among the Russian troops. To make matters worse, a revolution broke out in Russia and brought the Communists to power in 1917.

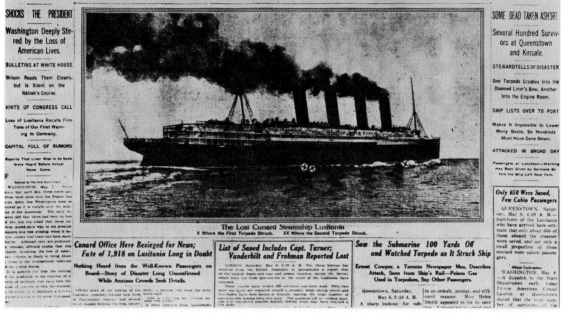

The *New York Times* reports the sinking of the *Lusitania.* How did German submarine warfare influence America's entry into the war?

The people wanted peace and, under the leadership of Nikolai Lenin [len'in], Russia left the war. It signed a separate peace treaty, which was favorable to the Central Powers. You will read about the Russian Revolution in some detail in Chapter 25. It is enough to note that the *Treaty of Brest-Litovsk* [brest' li tôfsk'], which Germany forced upon Russia, took away much of Russia's industry and resources.

Why the United States Entered World War I

The United States watched the war "over there" with interest, but it was determined to keep out of it. President Woodrow Wilson promised to keep America

out of the European war. He was elected to a second term as United States president. As the months passed and the Allied cause became increasingly desperate, Wilson was unable to keep his promise.

Both the Allied and the Central Powers looked to the United States as a neutral nation that could supply them with the things they needed. The United States was eager to trade with them. It felt that it could sell anything to either side, except weapons of war. But World War I, however, became a total war in which everything from food to guns was considered to be war goods. Rubber, oil, cotton, coal, and food were all war materials. The British as well as the Germans

Thomas Woodrow Wilson (1856–1924)

Thomas Woodrow Wilson was a southerner by birth. Although he was only a child when the American Civil War broke out, he recalled with pride having seen Jefferson Davis, president of the Confederacy, and having stood beside Robert E. Lee, the Confederacy's greatest general. As a youth, Wilson was a rather slow student. His father, a minister, would read to him from the popular books of the day, but they made little impression on the young boy. He was nearly nine before he learned the alphabet and by age eleven he was still a slow reader.

Physically, Wilson was slightly built, and his health was frail. As a result, he was a poor athlete. Nevertheless, his interest in athletics was great. With boys his own age he organized a baseball club and became its president and coach. The club won victories and earned local fame.

Although neither athlete nor scholar, Woodrow Wilson managed to enter Princeton in 1875. His scholarship improved, but it was still far from outstanding. Then in his senior year he surprised teachers, parents, and fellow students by writing a brilliant essay. It was called *Cabinet Government in the United States*. The article was published, and public affairs became Wilson's chosen field. He became a professor of political economy, president of Princeton University, governor of New Jersey, and president of the United States.

As a person, Wilson often seemed cold and distant. On shaking hands with him, one reporter complained that "the hand he gave me to shake felt like a ten-cent pickled mackerel in brown paper—irresponsive and lifeless." But personal criticism never seemed to bother Wilson. In fact, he was quite able to laugh at himself.

This same man was able to arouse the enthusiasm of masses of people by his moving speeches. His speeches revealed Wilson's sincere belief that he worked for the best interests of the people. In many ways, Wilson proved his care and compassion for people.

As president, Wilson led the nation through World War I. He believed strongly in the necessity for world peace. In the last stages of the war, Wilson proposed an organization to prevent future wars. This organization was the League of Nations. The Senate's failure to approve the entry of the United States into the League was a serious blow to Wilson. It contributed to his illness and death.

were determined that the other side would not get the things it needed. They stopped and searched American ships.

President Woodrow Wilson hoped to keep America out of the war. However, he believed that a world in which the German kaiser was strong would not be a safe world for American democracy. England and France were also democracies and they were our friends. He thought that the United States should help them. The people of the United States began to think so too.

American entry into World War I was a sign that the world was getting smaller, in the sense that it was impossible not to be concerned about events that happened in far-off places. American entry into World War I helped make the Allied victory possible. An Allied victory was necessary for the continuation of America's security and prosperity.

What World War I Cost

On November 11, 1918, an armistice was signed between the Allies and Germany. An armistice is a temporary agreement to stop fighting. It is replaced by a *peace treaty,* which outlines the conditions for permanent settlement and peace. Germany and its friends were defeated, but for winner and loser alike World War I had been costly.

Before World War I ended, over thirty nations had been involved in the war. No part of the earth was unaffected by it. Eight million young soldiers died. Nearly three times that many had been wounded, gassed, blinded, crippled, or paralyzed. Loss of life among civilians from submarine attacks, air raids, and shell fire is almost impossible to estimate in money. The grief, however, that such people must have sustained and the shock of enduring such a destructive war is beyond imagination.

Forests and mines were destroyed, factories ruined, and lands laid waste. There was much sickness, starvation, and demoralization. Modern methods of fighting were more costly in dollars than anyone had believed possible. Sixty-five million men had been drafted for military service. So great did the costs of supporting these soldiers become that at one point the war was costing ten million dollars an hour. By November, 1918, the cost was about 186 billion dollars.

New weapons such as poisoned gas, submarines, tanks (which were invented by the British), and the airplane were used in this war. The war ended in November, and a long, cold, hungry winter lay ahead for many people. These conditions made time ripe for change.

A dawn patrol flies over the countryside of France. At first, airplanes were used for surveying an area in preparation for battle. By 1915, the belligerents were using airplanes in combat.

How Peace Was Made

Although World War I was grim, it had one bright spot—hope for the future. Such complete destruction gave an opportunity to the living to make a fresh start. Leaders who met at Versailles, a city in France not far from Paris, sought to agree upon terms to end the war. They hoped to write a treaty that would end the war and make a peaceful future possible. The officials who met to prepare the peace treaty were faced with many questions: Who started the war? Should the guilty country be punished? Should the treaty be harsh or should it be generous? And finally, how could future wars be prevented?

One answer to all these questions came from President Woodrow Wilson. Wilson wanted "Peace Without Victory." The *Fourteen Points* is the name given to the program which he hoped would bring peace and future security to the nations of the world.

You need not study each of the fourteen items he suggested point by point, but the main ones are summarized here:

1. There should be no secret treaties.
2. There should be freedom of the seas for all.
3. Trade between nations should flow more freely.
4. Armaments should be reduced.
5. The boundaries between nations should be drawn according to the wishes of the people, that is, self-determination.
6. Rights of peoples not living in their own lands should be respected.
7. Foreign troops should be taken out of places where they were not wanted.
8. A League of Nations must be formed to keep peace among nations.

These were very high goals—too high to be acceptable to most nations.

The representatives of the victorious nations, known as the *Big Four*, met at Versailles in France. They were Woodrow Wilson of the United States, Georges Clemenceau [klem′ən sō′] of France, David Lloyd George of England, and Vittorio Orlando of Italy.

These men, without consulting any of the four defeated countries, wrote the *Versailles Treaty*. The Central Powers found it extremely difficult to accept the terms of this treaty. The Germans did not want to return the province of Alsace-Lorraine to France. They were stunned by that part of the treaty which blamed Germany for starting the war. Germany, as the guilty nation, was ordered to pay for most of the costs of the war. Until these payments were made, Allied armies were to stay in Germany.

Terms such as these were used in making separate treaties with the other countries. By these treaties, Austria, Bulgaria, and Turkey lost large parts of their former land areas.

The Versailles Treaty was a disappointment to President Wilson. He gave in on many points in order to save his proposal for a "league of nations." Only a few of the Fourteen Points found their way into the Treaty of Versailles. Part of the Versailles Treaty included a section that called for the establishment of the *League of Nations*, whose work was to try to keep peace in Europe. This provision was the only attempt to insure peace by means of an international organization.

However, the United States Senate, at that time, did not feel that it was wise for the United States to take part in world affairs. It was disappointed with the results of World War I and thought that, in the future, Americans should avoid getting mixed up in matters that did not concern them. Generally speaking, the American people agreed with this point of view. As a result of this feeling, the United States never signed the Versailles

The "Big Four" meet at Versailles, France, to hammer out the terms of the Versailles Treaty. How was this treaty received by the defeated countries? From left to right front are Orlando, Lloyd George, Clemenceau, and Wilson.

Treaty. It also never joined the League of Nations. A later agreement between the United States and Germany ended the war between those two countries. The League of Nations brought new hope to the world of the 1920s, but what kind of a world was it?

Check in Here

1. Explain each of the following terms: **(a)** propaganda; **(b)** unrestricted submarine warfare; **(c)** armistice; **(d)** trench warfare.

2. Why was the home front as important as the fighting front in achieving Allied victory in World War I?

3. Indicate the significance of each of the following battles of World War I: **(a)** First Battle of the Marne; **(b)** Battle of Tannenberg; **(c)** Battle of Jutland; **(d)** Battle of Verdun.

4. Explain why **(a)** Russia left the war;

and **(b)** the United States entered the war.

5. Choose two of the Fourteen Points and explain why Wilson included them in his plan for peace. Consider the causes of World War I when answering.

THE POSTWAR WORLD SEARCHES IN VAIN FOR PEACE

The Various Peace Efforts Made in History

Peace has been a goal which wise men and women everywhere have tried to reach. The League of Nations was not the first effort to bring law and order to a disordered world. The Pax Romana, or Roman Peace, was a 200-year period in which the Roman world saw little fighting. Rome's rule was not questioned, and the "god of war" had few worshippers.

Europe After World War I

The political map of Europe was changed after World War I.

- Locate four countries that were partly or entirely made from areas lost by Austria-Hungary.
- Locate three countries that were partly or entirely made up from areas lost by Russia.
- What country gained control of each of the following parts of the Ottoman Empire after World War I: Lebanon, Palestine, Syria?

During the Middle Ages, wars were frequent, but the Church tried to limit war by the Truce of God. According to this plan, the bishops would not allow the nobles to fight between Saturday and Wednesday. This plan was often ignored.

When nations became influential, they often tried to defend themselves by forming alliances with others. Unfortunately, such alliances were frequently made to wage war successfully against a common enemy. There were some people who said that alliances of this type would not be the answer to world peace. Something more permanent was needed. The Italian poet Dante spoke of a world organization that could stop wars. In 1625, Hugo Grotius [grō'shē əs] in his book *The Law of War and Peace* wrote about the need for laws which could rule nations as they do people.

In 1713, the Abbé de St. Pierre [pē er'] suggested that an organization made up of all countries be established. He said that such countries should have a court to hear and settle problems as they arose. He wanted member nations to help pay for an army made up of soldiers of all nations. Their job would be to keep peace in the world. This idea was a good one, but the individual nations of the world were not ready for it. In fact, they would not be ready for it for another 250 years.

Following the Napoleonic Wars in the nineteenth century, Czar Alexander I of Russia formed what he called a Holy Alliance. Members of this alliance agreed that they would let justice and Christian charity govern them in their relations with one another. While several European nations signed this agreement, few took it seriously.

After 1850, a number of organizations worked to establish a world in which wars would be unnecessary. The rights of neutral nations or those not taking part in wars were explained and written down. A further step in decreasing the brutality in wars was the formation of the International Red Cross.

In 1899, war clouds began to gather. Czar Nicholas II of Russia asked for a meeting which was held at The Hague [hāg], a city in the Netherlands. At this peace conference, twenty-six nations met to talk about reducing the dangers of war. One plan they approved was the establishment of an *International Court of Arbitration*. To this world court, nations could bring their disagreements in the hope of having them settled peacefully and fairly by a neutral third party. Unfortunately, the court had no power. An American, Andrew Carnegie, built a beautiful building in which the court might meet. Alfred Nobel, the Swedish chemist who invented dynamite, offered a prize to the person who had done most in the cause of peace. In 1907, a second peace conference was held at The Hague, but little came of this effort. The people "prayed for peace and prepared for war." World War I followed.

How the League of Nations Was Organized

With the end of World War I, there were many who felt that the time was ripe to prepare for future peace. Let us build, they said, an organization whose job is to police the *combative*, or those eager to fight, nations of the world and so stop future wars. The League of Nations, suggested by Woodrow Wilson, was the hope of stopping future wars. The basis of the League of Nations was a *Covenant* [kəv'ə nənt], or constitution, which asked that nations avoid war and deal frankly with one another.

The membership of the League grew from twenty-nine nations in the beginning to a maximum of sixty-two, each of which had one vote in the League's *Assembly*. This body could investigate and debate on disputes. It also admitted new states into the League.

The League's *Council*, made up of permanent and nonpermanent members, had whatever real power existed in the international organization. The Council met at least once a year and dealt with any matter affecting world peace.

There was a *Court of International Justice* (World Court) of fifteen judges who were chosen by the Council and Assembly for nine-year terms. The World Court handed down decisions on cases that were turned over to it. The judges could be chosen from any nation, whether or not it was a League member. A number of Americans served as judges of the World Court, although the United States was neither a League nor a World Court member. The World Court met at The Hague, the Netherlands. The chief meeting place of the League was in Geneva, Switzerland.

Since imperialism had been an important cause of war, the League of Nations was faced with the problem of what to do with the colonies taken from the defeated nations. Its answer to this problem was a *mandate system.* By this system a big nation was placed in charge of one or more colonies until such colonies could rule themselves.

The League of Nations tried to get at the causes of war. It studied labor and living conditions all over the world. It felt that better working and living conditions would make war less likely to occur. It studied health conditions the world over, cared for refugees, and sought to abolish slavery, which still lingered in some parts of the world.

Hope for Peace Through the League of Nations

The League of Nations was able to prevent war among small nations a number of times. However, it was not able to keep peace among the large nations. Why was this so? That the United States was not a member and that Russia became a member late made the League less effective than it might have been in dealing with international disputes.

More important, however, was the fact that the League of Nations had no power to force member nations to obey its decisions. The League did not punish aggressive nations by military action. Members could drop out of the League when they wanted to. Many countries did not take their membership in the League seriously, nor did they live up to its high ideals. Germany, Italy, and Japan were among those who did not give full support to the League. Their violations of League ideals helped set the stage for World War II.

It would not be fair to leave the discussion of the League of Nations on a note of failure. In a sense, it was a pioneer in that it set the stage for the United Nations. The United Nations profited from some of the League's mistakes. It owes much to the League of Nations. The United Nations is modeled upon it. The United Nations has bodies similar to the World Court and the International Labor Organization, which were once part of the League. Much of the work done by special committees of the League has been used by the United Nations as it tries to build a world free of war.

Other Efforts Made to Keep Peace

There was little respect and support for the League of Nations. The nations of the world looked for other ways in which to solve the problems of world peace. An arms race had been a cause of World War I. The League therefore tried during this postwar period to limit the production of land and sea arms. Most of these efforts were not successful.

After World War I, China again became a "happy hunting ground" for the big world powers. Since conflict over China was a possible cause of war, the United States, England, France, and Japan agreed to respect China's independence. They also agreed to respect each other's trade rights in that area. This agreement was short-lived. In the 1930s,

A League of Nations procession in London. Each member nation is represented by people in national costume. The world hoped for peace.

Japan grew more imperialistic and tried to conquer China. The Chinese suffered much for the world's indifference.

Germany still made many nations in the world uneasy. In 1925, in the *Locarno* [lô kär'nô] *Pacts*, Germany agreed to accept its boundaries with France and Belgium. It agreed that all future agreements would be peacefully settled. These agreements seemed to satisfy the people and the nations of the world.

For a time, during the 1920s, the air was cleared of thoughts and talk of war. Contributing to this feeling was the *Kellogg-Briand* [kel'ôg brē änd'] *Peace Pact* of 1928. It made war "as an instrument of national policy" illegal. It called upon all nations to agree to settle disputes peacefully. The pact was signed by most of the countries of the world. Germany, Japan, Italy, and Russia were

soon to ignore it. There was no way to enforce the terms of the pact. Let us now look at the problems of the twentieth century that were brought about largely by these nations.

Check in Here

1. Why has the search for enduring peace been unsuccessful?

2. Identify three efforts to achieve such a goal that were made before World War I. Why were they unsuccessful?

3. Describe the organization of the League of Nations.

4. Why was the League of Nations unable to stop wars?

5. How did each of the following contribute to a more peaceful world: (**a**) Locarno Pact; (**b**) Kellogg-Briand Pact?

World War I's major causes may be summarized as excessive nationalism, imperialism, militarism, secret alliances, and international lawlessness. The immediate causes were many small crises. These were the struggles between France and Germany over Morocco and the Balkan Wars, in which the Serbs sought to gain a port on the Adriatic. The most immediate cause was the assassination of Archduke Francis Ferdinand. Although Serbia gave in to most of Austria's demands, Austria was eager for battle. Eventually, over thirty countries would take part in the war.

The first World War was a total war. It was fought with a citizens' army made up of men who were drafted for military service. The home front had to be readied for war as never before. So great was this war effort that the economies of the participating nations were disrupted, never again to return to what they had once been. Food and raw materials had to be rationed, and women replaced men in the factories. On land, the Germans were successful at first, although they failed in their effort to take Paris. Stopped in the West, they were more successful in the East and eventually forced Russia to drop out of the war. A blockade of the Central Powers forced Germany to declare unrestricted submarine warfare. They destroyed many tons of supplies that were going to the Allies. However, such an arrogant step aroused public opinion against Germany. In due course, this was an important factor in bringing the United States into the war against Germany. Once Russia left the war the United States could enter the war "to make the world safe for democracy."

At the meeting to establish peace, the Big Four—Clemenceau, Lloyd George, Orlando, and Wilson—redrew the political map of Europe. Wilson sought "peace without victory." This was based on his Fourteen Points in which there was special emphasis on the League of Nations. His colleagues were more bitter and sought the spoils of victory. The United States made a separate peace treaty with Germany. Despite the urging of the president, the Senate refused to ratify the League of Nations. Because the United States was not a member, the League was greatly weakened. Like those peace efforts that came before it, such as the Truce of God, or the International Court, the League of Nations functioned for a time. However, it could not prevent the outbreak of World War II.

REVIEWING THE HIGHLIGHTS

People to Identify			
	Woodrow Wilson	Henri Pétain	Vittorio Orlando
	Paul von Hindenburg	John J. Pershing	Hugo Grotius
	Archduke Ferdinand	David Lloyd George	Abbé de St. Pierre
	Joseph Joffre	Georges Clemenceau	Alfred Nobel

Places to Locate	Morocco	Belgium	Adriatic Sea
	Agadir	Verdun	Sarajevo
	Bosnia	Serbia	Algeciras
	Bulgaria	Geneva	Balkan States
	Gallipoli	Versailles	Herzegovina
	The Hague	Dardanelles	Jutland

Terms to Understand	Triple Entente	the draft	Big Four
	Triple Alliance	World Court	mandate system
	international lawlessness	propaganda	Holy Alliance
		contraband	League of Nations
	Central Powers	blockade	Western Front
	Fourteen Points	total war	armistice
	nationalism	militarism	Locarno Pacts
	unrestricted submarine warfare	secret alliances	Pact of Paris
		Allies	

Events to Describe	Battle of the Marne	Battle of Gallipoli	Moroccan Crises
	Balkan Wars	Battle of Verdun	signing of the Versailles Treaty
	Battle of Jutland	sinking of the *Lusitania*	

Mastering the Fundamentals

1. How was an arms race a cause of World War I?
2. Germany's military and economic growth upset the balance of power in Europe. Why was this a factor that lead to war?
3. Why did Germany choose the year 1905 to make demands on Morocco?
4. Why did France want to have control over Morocco?
5. How did crises in the Balkan states lead to war?
6. Why was Austria unwilling to let Serbia get the seaport it wanted?
7. What was an *immediate* cause of World War I?
8. Why was Russia eager to help Serbia?
9. What was the importance of Germany's invasion of Belgium?
10. How was the home front made ready for war?
11. Why was Russia easily beaten? Why did Russia leave the war?
12. What reasons best explain why America entered World War I?
13. What part did the news media play in World War I?
14. What were President Wilson's peace plans? Why was he unable to realize his goals fully?
15. What problems faced the leaders who met at Versailles?
16. Why did the United States fail to approve the Versailles Treaty and join the League of Nations?

17. By what methods did the League of Nations hope to establish a peaceful world?
18. Why did the League of Nations study labor, health, slavery, and living conditions?
19. What did the United Nations learn from the League of Nations?
20. What were some of the costs of World War I?

THINGS TO DO

1. Prepare a report on Women in Wartime using as your sources the documents reproduced in part on pages 512 and 513 of this textbook.
2. Read *All Quiet on the Western Front,* which is now a classic story about trench warfare through the eyes of a German soldier. Report on your reading to the class.
3. Write an editorial for an American newspaper commenting upon the sinking of the *Lusitania.* You will have to decide for yourself whether yours will be an editorial designed to arouse passions to join the war or a calming influence.

YOU ARE THE HISTORIAN

Women in Wartime

Reading 1:

Given the rigidities* of the Edwardian (England) class structure, there are difficulties in the way of summing up the consequences of the war for women as an entire sex. In the business, medical, and military functions . . . the women concerned were very largely women of the middle and upper classes. Yet the major section of these women had been in pre-war years a depressed* class, tied to the apron-strings of their mothers or chaperons, or the purse-strings of their fathers or husbands. Now that they were earning on their own account, they had economic independence; now that they were working away from home, . . . they had social independence.

Obviously, then, women of all classes shared in a similar kind of emancipation.* The suffragette movement before the war had . . . aimed simply at the same limited franchise* for some women as was enjoyed by some men. The Women's Movement from 1915 onwards is a more unified movement than ever it had been previously.†

Vocabulary

rigidities—fixed customs
depressed—lowered in position

emancipation—freedom
limited franchise—the vote, in this case, given to people over a certain age

†A. Marwick, *The Deluge: British Society and the First World War* (New York: Norton, 1970), pp. 91–94

Reading 2

During the War women passed rapidly into trades hitherto considered unsuitable for them. . . . Because of this increase in numbers, as well as owing to the efficiency shown by women in every type of occupation, the Women's Employment Committee foresaw* an extension of openings for women not only in industry, but in the higher branches of commerce, and believed that employers would gladly continue to use them after the War in the work formerly done by men in shops, such as managing, buying and travelling. . . . These sanguine* hopes were doomed to disappointment. The War had certainly given the world an object lesson in women's achievement, but men in general showed a disturbing tendency to be appalled* rather than encouraged by this demonstration of unexpected ability. . . . While employers were quite ready to offer "equal pay by results" in trades to which women were not well adapted, they were most opposed to it in such industries as engineering and aircraft woodworking, in the light of the processes at which women notoriously* excelled men. . . . By the autumn of 1919 three-quarters of a million of the women employed at the time of the Armistice had been dismissed, and the position of women in general could certainly not be described as enviable.*†

Vocabulary

foresaw—saw ahead *notoriously*—widely
sanguine—optimistic *enviable*—worthy of envy
appalled—shocked

1. What are the different viewpoints of women's employment after World War I in these two readings? How do you account for the different viewpoints?

2. According to *Reading 2,* in which trades did women appear to excel? Why did employers *not* want to hire women in these trades?

3. According to *Reading 1,* how did work during World War I help to make women more independent?

4. In *Reading 1,* it says that the suffragette movement was aimed only at providing women with the same limited franchise as men had. How did World War I change this?

5. Why does *Reading 2* maintain that in 1919 women's position in general was not "enviable"?

†V. Brittain, *Women's Work in Modern England* (London: Nogel Douglas, 1928), pp. 8–15, as quoted in W. C. Langsam, ed. *Documents and Readings in the History of Europe Since 1918* (New York: Harcourt Brace Jovanovich, Inc., 1979), pp. 275–277.

Queen Victoria near the end of her reign

The Decline of Empire: Prelude to Global Conflict

The period between the end of World War I and the outbreak of World War II (1919–1939) may be described as a period of confusion. Democracies were being challenged everywhere by dictatorships and by their own colonies. Yet, this was a period of great material, cultural, and technical advances that brought enormous benefits to the people of the world. One would think that progress would lead to peace, but instead the years between the world wars were filled with anxiety and uncertainty. Fascism and communism were major threats. The sleeping giants of India and China were hoping that their turn would come to strike out for independence and freedom from colonial rule. They thought it was time for the democracies to make good on the promises that had been made, but postponed until after World War I. The very inventions that could make life so much more pleasant also meant that the problems of one part of the world touched every other part. As a result, the world was in ferment.

THE BRITISH EMPIRE BECOMES THE COMMONWEALTH OF NATIONS

How the British Family of Nations Is Organized

The Commonwealth countries were once colonies in the old British Empire. Today, each makes its own laws, decides its own taxes, conducts its own foreign affairs, maintains its own armies, and is responsible for its own debts and finances. In every way the Commonwealth nations are both completely independent and self-governing. Membership in the Commonwealth is by choice rather than by necessity.

These rights and duties were not given all at once. In 1931, in the *Statute of Westminster*, England said that its *dominions*, or the self-governing parts of the empire, were equal to it in every way. The association in the Commonwealth is a voluntary one. The member countries owe loyalty to one another. However, when any country wishes to leave the Commonwealth, it may do so. In 1949, Ireland withdrew from the Commonwealth. The Union of South Africa left in 1961 and became the Republic of South Africa.

Canada, New Zealand, Australia, and the Union of South Africa were the first of the British family of nations to become Commonwealth countries. These nations remained loyal to the parent country out of a common loyalty to the crown, a common language, and similar laws. Later, some of the non-English-speaking parts of the British Empire also became self-governing, independent, and members of the Commonwealth.

Ties that bind the nations of the Commonwealth together are strong. Among the practical ties are those which make it possible for Commonwealth nations to help one another. They have favorable tariff laws and trade agreements. Among the sentimental ties are those of loyalty, language, and common history. It is interesting that the sentimental ties are probably more effective in keeping these nations in the Commonwealth than the practical ones. Queen Elizabeth II seeks to preserve the Commonwealth on the foundations of friendship, loyalty, freedom, and peace. So different has the British Empire become that Empire Day, celebrated once a year, was renamed Commonwealth Day.

The colonies of the British Empire did not become members of the Commonwealth all at once. Britain's English-speaking colonies were the first to do so, and a review of their background and relations with Britain will help us to understand the changing role of empire.

The British Empire, 1920

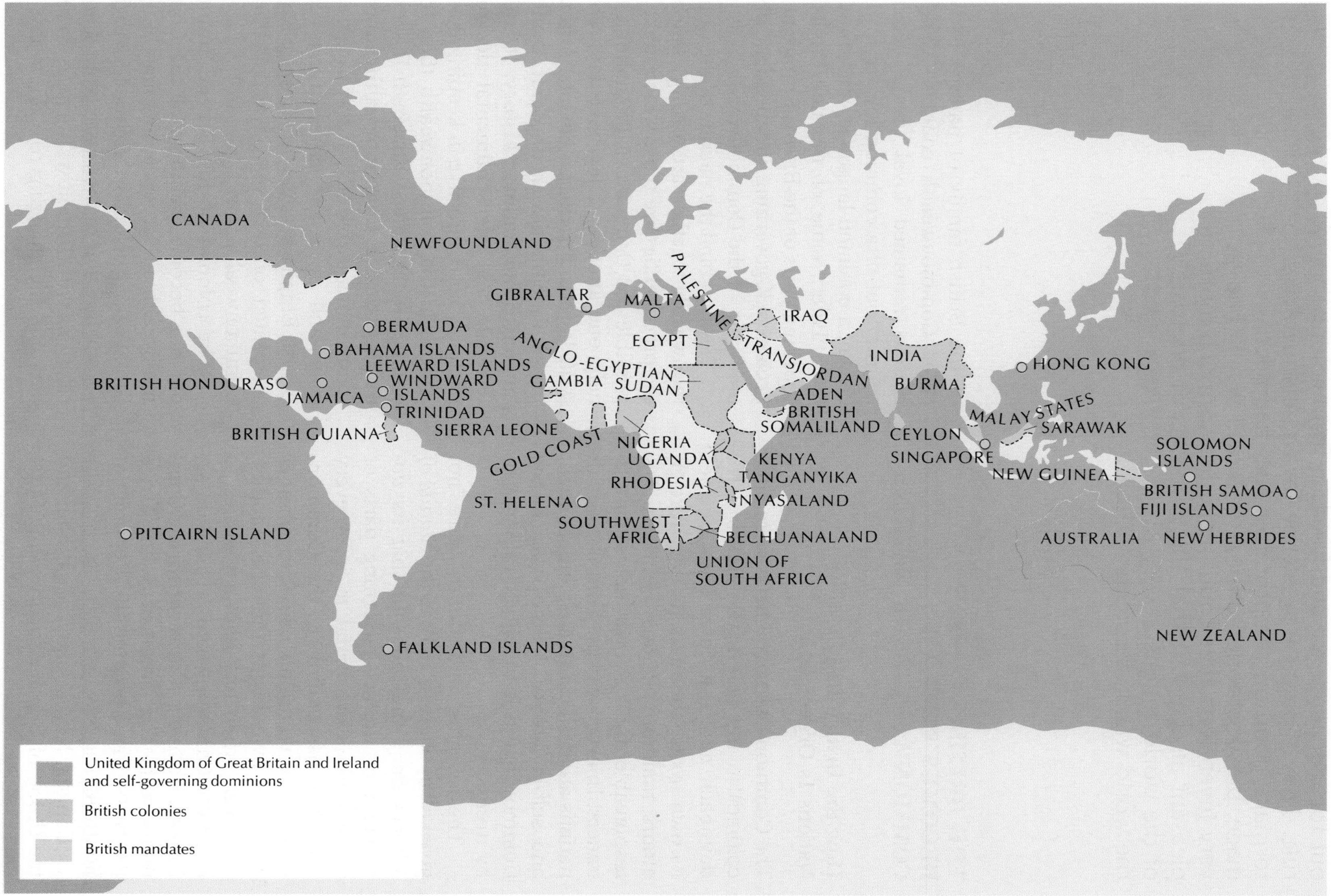

CANADA

NEWFOUNDLAND

BERMUDA
BAHAMA ISLANDS
LEEWARD ISLANDS
JAMAICA
WINDWARD ISLANDS
TRINIDAD
BRITISH HONDURAS
BRITISH GUIANA

GIBRALTAR

PITCAIRN ISLAND

FALKLAND ISLANDS

ST. HELENA

GOLD COAST
SIERRA LEONE
GAMBIA
ANGLO-EGYPTIAN SUDAN
NIGERIA
EGYPT
UGANDA
RHODESIA
SOUTHWEST AFRICA
BECHUANALAND
UNION OF SOUTH AFRICA

PALESTINE
MALTA
IRAQ
TRANSJORDAN
ADEN
BRITISH SOMALILAND
KENYA
TANGANYIKA
NYASALAND

INDIA
BURMA
CEYLON

HONG KONG

MALAY STATES
SARAWAK
SINGAPORE

NEW GUINEA

SOLOMON ISLANDS
BRITISH SAMOA
FIJI ISLANDS
NEW HEBRIDES

AUSTRALIA

NEW ZEALAND

	United Kingdom of Great Britain and Ireland and self-governing dominions
	British colonies
	British mandates

1. How did Great Britain respond to the demands of its colonies for their independence?

2. What are the ties that keep the Commonwealth together?

3. Why are the sentimental ties among the Commonwealth countries perhaps more important than the practical ones?

SATISFACTION AND DISCONTENT AMONG COMMONWEALTH COUNTRIES

Why Anglo-Irish Relations Were Unhappy Ones

The far-flung countries of the Commonwealth generally developed friendly relations with Great Britain. This was not so of England's neighbor, Ireland. The relations between these two countries are hostile to this day. A look into the past will help us understand the problem somewhat better.

During the twelfth century, England invaded Ireland, and for hundreds of years thereafter the Irish suffered under the heavy hand of English rule. Religious, economic, and political questions sowed the seeds of hate between the two nations. As a result of the Reformation, England became Protestant while Ireland remained Catholic. It was not until 1793 that Catholics in England were allowed to vote for members of Parliament, and it was not until 1829 that English Catholics were allowed to hold public office. As a result, the Irish deeply resented being forced to pay taxes to support the Anglican (English) Church in Ireland.

To make matters worse, most of the land in Ireland was owned by *absentee* English landlords. Absentee landlords were landowners who did not live in Ireland. They were concerned only with collecting high rents, and they sent harsh rent collectors to gather the rents from the Irish tenants. The Irish—already quite poor because of poor soil, small farms, and ancient farming methods—were made even poorer. Starvation was sometimes widespread, as in 1848. Many Irish came to America in the nineteenth century to find better living conditions.

In matters of government, Ireland was ruled entirely from Great Britain. By the *Act of Union* (1801), the Irish Parliament was dissolved, and the English gave the Irish the right to send representatives to the British Parliament instead. In the British Parliament, Irish representatives had few opportunities to make needed changes. They were always outvoted by British members who were often landowners in Ireland. These members of Parliament wanted no changes which would limit or interfere with their power and profits in Ireland.

According to the map on page 516, the British Empire extended around the world by 1920. Some of the British-controlled areas were colonies.
• Locate and name two British colonies in the Americas.
Other British-controlled areas were mandates given to Great Britain after World War I. (For mandate, see page 508.)
• Locate and name four of those mandates.
Still other regions with a connection to Great Britain were the self-governing dominions.
• Indicate whether or not the following were self-governing dominions: Canada, Nigeria, Union of South Africa, and Palestine.

Irish families receive a blessing from the parish priest before their long, hard journey to the United States. What were some of the reasons the Irish left their homeland in the nineteenth century?

A Solution to the Irish Question

As a result of these complaints, the Irish decided to fight for a law which would help them. In 1869, when William Gladstone was prime minister, Parliament passed a law which made it unnecessary for the Irish to pay taxes to the Church of England. The *disestablishment* (taking away of government support) of the Anglican Church in Ireland was a good start in solving the religious problem.

The Irish also had a land problem in that they wanted to be able to buy back more of their own land. Again, under Gladstone, the British government passed a law for lending money to Irish farmers. They could borrow money to buy land at low interest rates.

In response to the Irish demand for more self-government, Gladstone sup-

ported, without success, a number of parliamentary bills which would have given home rule to the Irish. In 1914, a bill providing for *home rule* (power to make their own laws on domestic affairs) was passed. But due in part to World War I in Europe, it did not go into effect at that time.

"England's difficulties were Ireland's opportunities," was the cry of the *Sinn Fein* [shin fān] during World War I. Sinn Fein meant "we ourselves." Led by Eamon De Valera [dev′ə lär′ə], the Sinn Fein took matters into its own hands. It decided to fight for independence. The idea of home rule was no longer enough to satisfy the Irish.

The methods of the Sinn Feiners were violent, and they brought results. In 1921, Ireland was partitioned (divided). Twenty-six counties became the *Irish Free State* and won the right of self-government. The six counties of Ulster became *Northern Ireland* and remained under British rule. Even self-government failed to satisfy the Irish in the Free State. In 1937, a new constitution was written, and the government of Ireland declared itself a sovereign (independent) state. Its new name was the Irish word *Eire*. Many Irish wished to be further separated from England by withdrawing from the Commonwealth. In 1948, Ireland adopted a republican form of government. It was no longer a dominion, and became, in 1949, the *Republic of Ireland*.

How Canada Became a British Colony

In about the year 1000, the Viking Leif Ericson sailed from Norway to Greenland. From there he sailed to Vinland, which may have been Canada. In 1497, Spain and Portugal were busy looking for a short southerly route to the wealth of the East. John Cabot, sailing for England, looked for a short northern route and in so doing reached Canada. In 1534, a French sailor, Jacques Cartier, was sent by King Francis I to stake a claim in the New World. He found the Gulf of the St. Lawrence River, but it was not until 1608 that Samuel de Champlain established the first permanent French settlement at Quebec.

Champlain gave his life to the government and welfare of the people of *New France*, as French Canada came to be called. France had great plans for an empire in the New World. Under Louis XIV these plans were partly realized. However, Great Britain, too, had plans for an empire in the New World. And Britain's plans were successful.

Britain and France had fought each other in Europe and India. They fought each other in America as well. In 1713, Nova Scotia and the lands around Hud-

The Republic of Ireland and the Kingdom of Great Britain and Northern Ireland

• Locate and name the countries that are part of the Kingdom of Great Britain and Northern Ireland.

son Bay were won by Great Britain. During the French and Indian War (1755–63), in a battle on the Plains of Abraham above the city of Quebec, the British General James Wolfe [wŭlf] surprised and defeated the Marquis de Montcalm [də mänt käm′]. Wolfe won all of Canada for the British.

Why Canada Avoided a Revolution

The history of Great Britain's relations with Canada is a good example of what relations between a colony and a parent country should be. After their victory over the French, the British began to trade with Canada and to settle there. Since the French were already located in Montreal and Quebec (Lower Canada), the British settled farther west in Ontario (Upper Canada).

By 1763, however, the French had already established their own way of life. They had their own language and their own laws, and they were Roman Catholics. Many of the British authorities felt that the French Canadians, having been defeated, should be made to give up their ways and accept British ways. For many years this question was debated. In 1774, the British came to a decision.

In the *Quebec Act* of 1774, the French Canadians were given the right to worship in the Catholic Church. They were allowed to follow their own laws and language. To satisfy the French, the Province of Quebec was increased in size so that it included lands around the Ohio River.

The Quebec Act of 1774 gave more land to the French Canadians, but it proved to be bad for the American colonies. The Americans were already angry with Great Britain for many reasons. Now they were further irritated because some of their western lands had been taken from them. Although the British held on to Canada, it was partly because of the provisions in the Quebec Act that they lost the American colonies.

How Canada Won Self-Government

By 1837, Canada had many complaints of its own against Great Britain. Canadians wanted to govern themselves. At the very least, they wanted a greater voice in their government. Led by William Mackenzie and Louis Joseph Papineau [pä′pē nō], a new revolution seemed to be on the way. But the Canadian rebels were not strong enough to impose their will on the British government.

The Canadians were not successful in gaining independence. The British, however, thought about their former American colonies and of the successful American Revolution. The American Revolution had cost them thirteen good colonies. Would a Canadian revolution cost them all of Canada? The British were not going to take chances.

They sent Lord Durham to Canada to see what needed to be done. His 1839 report said that Canada should have a democratic government, including a lawmaking body in which the people and the provinces would be represented. He pointed out that French Canadians should have a chance to rule themselves. The *Durham Report* became a model which the British used when they had problems with their other colonies. The ideas of Lord Durham gave rise to the Commonwealth of Nations.

Change did not come to Canada all at once. The British wisely, but slowly, put Lord Durham's suggestions into practice. By the *Union Act* of 1840, Upper and Lower Canada were united. This act combined the French and English settlements into one government, but it did not work out successfully because of differences among the settlers.

Finally, the question of Canadian government was settled by a law for self-government. In 1867, the British *North American Act* was passed. It united nearly all of the provinces in Canada. Thus, the Dominion of Canada was formed. Gradually, the government of Canada was given the right to make its own laws. In foreign affairs, however, Great Britain spoke for Canada. The Canadians, for a time, were glad that they had self-government. But Canada held closely to its British ties because it

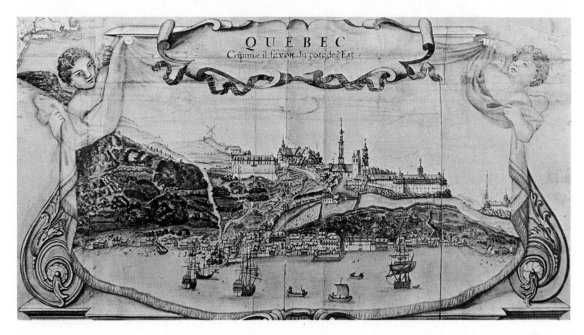

The settlement of Quebec in the seventeenth century. Quebec was the first French settlement in the New World. It eventually became part of the British Empire.

feared the growing power of the United States. It did not wish to be taken over by the United States. In time, even in foreign affairs, Canada spoke its own mind.

A new Canadian army and navy saw service in World War I. When the war was over, the cry for even greater freedom in foreign and domestic affairs grew louder. Canada became a separate member of the League of Nations and signed its own peace treaty ending the war with Germany. A series of Imperial Conferences in which the dominions talked over their problems with the British government was held. The British Parliament passed the *Statute of Westminster* (1931), which gave Canada and other dominions equality and independence.

How Australia and New Zealand Won Self-Government

At about the same time that gold was discovered in California (1848), gold was also discovered in Australia. The Australian gold rush that followed helped open up Australia to settlement. By 1875, most of Australia had been explored, but relatively little of it had been found good for settlement. The better parts attracted British settlers, who made it a vigorous colony.

In time, the first colony of New South Wales in southeast Australia was joined by the other colonies of Queensland, Victoria, South, West, and Northern Australia, and the nearby island of Tasmania. As early as the 1850s, there were those who believed that a union of these colonies would be a good thing. However, this good idea was not realized until many years later. By 1860, nearly all of the separate colonies had won a measure of self-government.

It was Sir Henry Parkes who gave his time and energy to the plan of uniting the provinces. In 1897, a constitution for all of Australia was drawn up which provided for a union of the six states and Tasmania under a central government. In 1900, this constitution was approved by the British Parliament. On January 1, 1901, the Commonwealth of Australia came into being.

New Zealand. When did this island become part of the British Empire? Locate New Zealand on the map on page 516.

It was not until 1839 that New Zealand, 1,200 miles to the east of Australia, became a part of the British Empire. The native New Zealanders, called *Maoris* [mou'rēz], fought against the British, but these uprisings were put down. Later the Maoris were given equal status with the rest of the population of New Zealand. In 1907, New Zealand became a dominion in the British Empire.

Check in Here

1. List three grievances that the Irish had against the English.

2. What were England's reasons for not giving Ireland home rule?

3. Why did Canada win independence from England without having a revolution?

4. What is the significance of each of the following: **(a)** Durham Report; **(b)** Statute of Westminster?

5. Why were Australia and New Zealand able to achieve commonwealth status rather quickly?

WORLD WAR II SLOWS INDIA'S MARCH TO INDEPENDENCE FROM BRITAIN

How India Changed Under British Rule

You have read that Great Britain both helped and hurt India. (See p. 472.) Under British rule, many changes took place in the way Indians lived. These changes paved the way for increased demands for independence.

The growth of commerce and the building of factories changed the Indian way of life greatly. The family began to weaken as some of its members worked in factories and other members still worked as farmers. As people went to the cities, the orderly life of the villages slowly broke down. Machine-made goods began to replace handmade goods.

The caste system also came into question. Members of different castes found it difficult to work with one another in the factory. Their traditional laws did not allow them to eat with one another. They could not work at the same machine, nor could they easily get used to riding with one another on crowded buses or trains.

The coming of factories also meant the beginning of the end of hand labor. Cotton goods from England took the place of cotton goods which were handmade in the villages. The manufactured metal goods of England replaced the handmade metal goods of India. The skills of carving, weaving, and painting were being lost. Those who lost their jobs and places in society found themselves without a way of life. Furthermore, most of the factories were British owned. Indians did the work, but the British profited. After accumulating wealth, the British business owners and executives left India to live out the rest of their days in comfort in England.

Improved sanitation, the building of hospitals, and an improved food supply increased Indian life expectancy. This increased population. There were many more mouths to feed and many more people to employ and educate. The increase in population added to India's poverty. These problems also made trouble for the British in India.

Why the Demands
for Indian Independence Grew

The British, on the whole, allowed freedom of the press, freedom of speech, and freedom of religion in India. People could discuss their problems rather freely among themselves. Indian leaders and scholars had their own books and newspapers in which they could express ideas as to what was wrong in India and how the wrongs could be made right. Also, the British school system in India educated Indian leaders who could see realistically what was wrong. These people were willing to devote their lives to making things better for their people. As a result, the British found themselves training leaders who would use their training to drive the British out of India.

Furthermore, each year hundreds of Indians went to study in England. There, they learned about democracy and freedom which had developed in other parts of the world. When these foreign-educated Indians returned home, they saw that democratic ideas were not always being applied in their own country. They were determined to remedy this situation and gain independence for all Indians. A struggle followed that focused worldwide attention and interest on the British Empire.

The British influence aroused an intense feeling of patriotism among the Indians. The British did not live in India for very long before they became impressed with Indian culture, beauty, and resources. The carvings of the Hindu gods, the Sanskrit of the Vedas, the beauty of the temples and other buildings, such as the Taj Mahal, were studied and admired. By observing this foreign interest shown in Indian culture, Indians began to appreciate their own history as one nation and realize their own national contributions to the world.

As a result of this new national self-consciousness, there arose Indian leaders who became well known in science, literature, and politics. Among the better known Indian scholars was Rabindranath Tagore [tä′gôr] (1861–1941). Tagore was awarded the Nobel Prize for Literature in 1913 and was knighted by the English Crown for his fine poetry. Another great leader was Mohandas Gandhi, who helped unify the people and lead them to independence.

How India
Fought for Independence

In 1885, the *Indian National Congress* was established to give some government representation to Indians. The congress devoted itself to the task of winning independence for India.

In response to the demand of the Indian National Congress for *swaraj* [swə räj'] (self-government) in domestic affairs, the British agreed to the Morley-Minto Reforms of 1909. These reforms called for giving Indians more representation in the government of India. They satisfied some leaders, but failed to stop the cry for independence. Further changes were not to come until after World War I. These changes were brought about by the work of Mohandas Gandhi [gan'dē].

Gandhi felt the best way to gain independence was through cooperation between educated Indians and the British government. He became the leader of the Indian nationalist movement. When World War I was over, he led the fight for greater changes.

During World War I, Indians were loyal to Britain. They served in the army and paid part of the costs of the war through taxes. When the war was over, Indians expected more independence. The Montagu-Chelmsford report promised the Indians an even greater voice in the government of India than they had had before. However, the British viceroy could still veto the work of the Indian lawmaking body which was set up. People were dissatisfied. Gandhi, too, was dissatisfied because he knew that the British still had control.

Gandhi was a fighter, but his weapons were not guns. Instead, he taught his people not to use violence. In dealing with the might of Great Britain, Gandhi believed new weapons had to be found. Gandhi urged his people to refuse to buy British goods, to make simple clothing for themselves, to pay no taxes, and to refuse to serve in the British army. If they were arrested, he wanted his people not to fight back, but to go to jail instead. Soon the jails would become overcrowded, and the British would have to set the Indians free. As a result of these methods Gandhi felt it would become impossible for the British to rule India. These teachings of *passive resistance, nonviolence,* and *civil disobedience* proved effective.

Gandhi was called *Mahatma* (great soul) by Indians. The Mahatma's methods disturbed the British, who knew how to meet force with force. But could force be used against people who did not resist? The British made the mistake of trying this. In April, 1919, the *Amritsar* [əm rit'sər] *Massacre* took place, in which several hundred Indians were killed while holding a peaceful demonstration. Gandhi urged peaceful resistance to the British in response to this outrage, but some Indians fought back. The result was that bloody rioting followed. Gandhi called off his campaign of peaceful resistance and took the blame for the violence that followed. In 1922, he went to prison, where he remained for two years. When he was released, he became an even greater hero. People were willing to follow wherever he led. He eventually led them to independence.

How India Continued Its Fight for Independence

In 1929, *Round-Table Conferences* on India were announced by the British government. The objective of the conferences was to give self-government to India. Gandhi wanted complete independence and led his people on a campaign of civil disobedience. The Indians showed their displeasure at the British by disobeying tax laws.

The salt tax was especially annoying to them. Salt was a necessity and the British monopolized it. Gandhi and some of his followers marched to the sea. There they boiled salt water to show that they would rather use the salt from the sea than pay Britain the tax it demanded. The British again arrested Gandhi for his

Mohandas K. Gandhi

(1869–1948)

Mohandas Karamchand Gandhi, like many other Hindus of his day, was engaged at eight and married at twelve. Unlike most Hindus, Gandhi was prosperous enough to go through school and college. At the age of nineteen, he went to the University of London. There he said he "wasted time trying to become an Englishman." His years in England were not, however, entirely wasted. They enabled him to become a lawyer and to build up a law practice.

Eventually, Gandhi's law practice took him to Africa where he saw other Hindus treated in the most humiliating manner. He was so moved by their plight that he gave up his practice to lead them in their fight for justice. In this fight Gandhi was spat upon, kicked, refused food in restaurants, and refused rides on trains. He was determined to fight back. The weapons were to be passive resistance, nonviolence, and noncooperation. Hindus were neither to fight nor to obey their employers. They were to prove that while they could be killed, they could not be provoked to attack or forced to obey. Be kind to the enemy when he is hurt, but "disobey him when he tries to hurt you," Gandhi said.

Using these practices, Gandhi was able to obtain some justice for the Hindus of South Africa. Having been successful in Africa, would his methods work against the British in India? They did, but during his long fight for Indian independence of British rule Gandhi was often much misunderstood, even by his own people. Once, for example, he delivered a lecture to rich Indian maharajahs urging them to give up their money, jewels, and arrogance. As he spoke, his audience gradually vanished, until, as Gandhi said, no one was left "but God, the Chairman, and myself." Soon the chairman left too. "Poor fellow," said Gandhi, "he must have felt very uncomfortable in that strange company."

In 1931, Gandhi was in London fighting for his people. Times were difficult: the world was in the grip of an economic depression. People did not have enough food to eat, and many had to be content to wear old clothing. Gandhi arrived in London in his usual dress consisting of only a loincloth. His costume aroused considerable laughter. "The only difference in our dress," laughed Gandhi, "is that you wear plus fours [knickers] and I wear minus fours." Then Gandhi added, "If this depression keeps up much longer, I shall be the best-dressed man in England."

Gandhi's methods were as successful in India as they had been in Africa.

Not long after Indian independence had been won (1947), Gandhi was killed by an assassin who rejected the philosophy of nonviolence that Gandhi preached. Gandhi's work in India is finished, but many of the problems for which he gave his life remain. Other people will have to help solve them. Gandhi's place in history is assured. Although not the founder of a great religion, he is truly one of the saintly ones in history.

disobedience. The campaign of civil disobedience aroused sympathy for the Indian cause in most parts of the world.

In 1931, Gandhi went to other Round-Table Conferences on India. While they did not give full self-government to India, the results of the conferences were used to pass the *Government of India Act* of 1935. The provinces established by the act were to be governed entirely by Indians. Moreover, the nation's lawmaking body was given more power. An attempt was also made to include the princely states in the government of India. The Government of India Act of 1935, while a step in the right direction, left many problems unsolved. These problems had to wait until World War II was over before they were solved.

Check in Here

1. How did Britain itself contribute to India's struggle for independence?

2. List three grievances India had against Britain.

3. What weapons in the fight for independence did Gandhi use? Were they successful?

4. Describe how each of the following contributed toward independence: (**a**) Montagu-Chelmsford Report; (**b**) Round-Table Conferences; (**c**) Government of India Act (1935).

5. Describe how each of the following contributed to India's independence: (**a**) Mohandas K. Gandhi; (**b**) Rabindranath Tagore.

CHINA AND JAPAN COME TO BLOWS

How China Became a Republic

China's Boxer Rebellion was the dying gasp of a dying system. (See p. 481.) The death of the powerful Empress Tzu Hsi and the puppet Emperor, Kuang Hsü, left the throne to a two-year-old child, Pu-yi. When China needed strong rulers most, it was in the hands of a mere child. The boy emperor, as he was called, was the last of the Manchus. Attempts to form a representative, constitutional government failed. By 1911, the time to overthrow the Manchu Dynasty had come.

The leader of the Chinese revolution, Sun Yat-sen [sü yät'sen'], was born in 1867 in southern China. As a teenager he was taken to Hawaii. There he learned English and became acquainted with the Christian religion, which he adopted. Later, he became a doctor, but the political problems of his people interested him more than medicine. When the Sino-Japanese War broke out in 1895, Sun thought the time had come for revolution. However, his attempt to overthrow the government was uncovered, and he was forced to flee. For years he wandered from country to country arousing the sympathy of Americans and Europeans for change in China. His goal in wanting to overthrow the Manchu Dynasty was to give China a democratic government.

526

Rebellion broke out in China in 1911. Sun Yat-sen hurried home to assume leadership of the forces of revolution. In 1912, Sun became the first president of the Republic of China.

Yüan Shih-k'ai [yü än' shē'kī'], a Manchu general, was called upon to crush the rebellion of Sun Yat-sen. This capable officer controlled fine armies. He would bring needed unity and strength to the new republic—if he could be won over. His price for supporting the republic was nothing less than the presidency itself. Sun Yat-sen stepped down and resigned, hoping that by this move the nation he loved would be unified.

Why Problems Burdened the New Republic of China

Sun Yat-sen wanted to be sure that his voice would be heard in the government of Yüan. He formed the Nationalist People's Party, better known as the *Kuomintang* [kwō min tang]. This party was to play an influential role in the history of China. Unfortunately for China, Yüan was not content to be merely president. Instead, he dreamed that he might become emperor and the founder of a new dynasty. It was the task of Sun Yat-sen and of the Kuomintang Party to stop Yüan from realizing this ambition. In 1913, a revolt against Yüan proved unsuccessful. Sun Yat-sen was forced to flee China, leaving Yüan in charge.

For China, problems of revolutions and counterrevolutions increased. During World War I, when the nations of the world were fighting each other, Yüan made an unsuccessful move to become emperor. His humiliation hastened his death in 1916.

China's lack of a strong leader gave Japan the opportunity to present China with the infamous *Twenty-one Demands.* If fully carried out, these would have

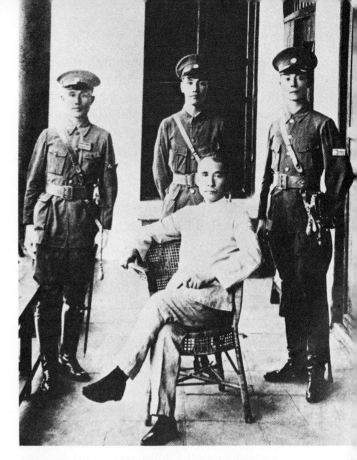

Sun Yat-sen, seated, became the first president of the Republic of China in 1912. Directly behind him is Chiang Kai-shek, who assumed leadership after Sun Yat-sen's death.

put China at the mercy of Japan. China was forced to give Japan special privileges in Manchuria and Inner Mongolia. However, American protests kept Japan from getting all that it demanded.

After the death of Yüan, China was more divided than ever. The central government was at Peking, and Sun Yat-sen set up a revolutionary government at Canton. War lords, with armies of their own, fought against the central government and among themselves for control of various portions of China. A new government declared war on Germany, hoping in this way to take advantage of the troubles of the world. China hoped to get rid of extraterritorial rights and payments for the Boxer Rebellion. Perhaps

527

the world's difficulties would prove to be China's opportunities. At Versailles, however, where the big powers met to write a peace treaty with Germany, China gained nothing. Civil war raged in China between 1920 and 1926, and the government was left with no real power.

How the Kuomintang Tried to Rebuild China

All this time, Sun Yat-sen was not idle. He spent his time trying to rebuild the Kuomintang Party. He hoped to make it the instrument by which China would become a democratic nation. The weakening of China, the strengthening of Japan, China's humiliation at Versailles, and the lack of unity at home were signs that for China time was running out. Under Sun Yat-sen's leadership, the Kuomintang pledged itself to fight for the removal of foreigners from China. It agreed to build democracy and to raise living standards. Its slogan became "Nationalism, Democracy, and Social Progress." This message of hope was carried to the people. They listened, liked what they heard, and gave their support to the Kuomintang, which had its first National Congress in Canton (1924).

The road ahead for the Kuomintang was a long, hard one. China needed help if it was to become a strong and unified nation. Russia, where the Communist Revolution had taken place, looked for an opportunity to embarrass the Western democracies. It posed as a friend of China. Russia gave up its rights of extraterritoriality, helped rebuild China's armies, and sent advisers to help reorganize the Kuomintang.

The Kuomintang government's heavy burden was increased when, in 1925, Sun Yat-sen died. To the Chinese, he had become an idol to be worshiped. His writings and his teachings spread over the land. He was buried in an elaborate tomb with great ceremony. Sun Yat-sen became a spiritual symbol of China and of the Kuomintang.

The nation was strengthened by Sun's inspiration. The Kuomintang Party, however, became so powerful that China turned into a one-party nation. Democracy is not likely to work well with a one-party system. The leaders have no competition for the elective offices. In a one-party system the leaders are in a strong position to take dictatorial powers.

How Chiang Kai-shek Continued Dr. Sun's Work

In the fight for power that followed the death of Sun, Chiang Kai-shek [chäng kī shek'] was successful. He was well prepared for the task of leading the Kuomintang Party. Chiang was born in 1887 to a middle-class family. His father died when Chiang was young, and his mother sent him to school in Japan, where he learned about modern ways of living. When he was twenty, Chiang cut off his *queue* (hair customarily worn in a pigtail by the Chinese) as a sign that he intended to learn Western ways. In Japan and in China, Chiang learned to become a soldier, a leader, and a gentleman.

A turning point in Chiang's life came when he met Dr. Sun Yat-sen in Japan. When revolution broke out in China in 1911, Chiang listened to Sun-Yat-sen. It was Sun's wish that Chiang go to Russia to study its methods and its ways. This Chiang was glad to do. When he returned to China in 1924, he organized the Whampoa Military Academy in Canton. At this academy, he used German and Russian military instructors. It was not long before the control of the Kuomintang Party fell into Chiang's hands.

After Sun Yat-sen's death, Chiang's first task was to unite the nation under democratic leadership. To gain order, he had to fight the warlords, who thought the revolution had gone too far. He also had to fight the Communists, who thought the revolution had not gone far enough. Chiang tried to unite China by military force. From his base at Canton in the south, Chiang was determined to fight people who stood in the way of his march to the capital at Peking. In 1928, Chiang's troops marched into Peking. It had taken three years of fighting to bring him this far. He defeated both the warlords and the Communists and, thus, united the nation. The new *Nationalist* government, as it was called, set up a capital at Nanking. This was about midway between the old capital at Peking and the revolutionary capital at Canton. From this central location, Chiang prepared China for the future.

Under Chiang, the nation was united. Foreign nations gave up special rights and privileges. Extraterritoriality was likewise gradually abandoned. Modern machines and factories began to manufacture goods, and modern cities with business centers grew. In old China there had been a large poor class and a tiny rich class. Under Chiang, a middle class was growing with the increase in trade and manufacturing.

These advantages were balanced by certain setbacks in the government. As leader of the Nationalist government, Chiang was expected to give China a democratic government, but under him, China was a dictatorship in which the Kuomintang was the only party. Chiang was the head of the Kuomintang Party. He was also the head of the government. Therefore, he had complete control. Chiang promised more democracy when the people proved that they knew what to do with it. However, there were many people who thought that Chiang was too slow in making changes.

In the course of events, Chiang had married well and had become rich. There were people who felt that he was too interested in the problems of landlords, business owners, and executives in the new middle class, and not interested enough in the old problems of the farmers. Most Chinese were still poor farmers who found life under Chiang nearly as hard as it had been under the emperors. The poor farmers had hoped for land redistribution and lower taxes, but Chiang's government was too slow in instituting these reforms. In fact, the government of Chiang appeared unwilling or unable to do very much in making changes.

How China and Japan Came to Blows

To make matters worse for China, a new enemy appeared in the form of its neighbor, Japan. Industrialized at home, Japan began expanding overseas. Wars against

In 1931, Japan invaded Manchuria, China. These Japanese soldiers enter the main gate of a Chinese walled city.

China (1894–1895) and Russia (1904–1905) brought success to Japan. Japan owned the South Manchurian railroad, which it had won as a result of the Russo-Japanese War. Because of its victory, Japan also controlled Formosa and Korea. During World War I, Japan played a small role. Nevertheless, it was awarded the Pacific colonies that had once belonged to Germany. These included the Caroline Islands, the Marshall Islands, and the Marianas Islands (except for Guam).

During the years after World War I, Japan played an increasingly important part in world affairs. It took part in peace conferences and disarmament meetings and was a member of the League of Nations. It remained sensitive to the custom of saving face in dealing with foreign nations. Saving face was particularly important when the United States, in 1907, greatly slowed Japanese immigration. The Japanese regarded this restriction on immigration as an insult, and they did not soon forget it.

During the 1930s, economic depression

After the Japanese invaded Manchuria, many Chinese became refugees.

came to Japan, as it did to the rest of the world. Japan's problems increased. Japanese military experts thought than an answer to these problems was to expand into China. Under the leadership of army and navy officers who sought opportunities for power, prestige, and promotion, Japan sent troops to northern China, or Manchuria.

In the year 1931, Japan undertook the conquest of China. Japan moved its troops to Manchuria and set up the independent state of Manchukuo [man chü'kwō]. The Japanese placed the Chinese boy emperor, Pu-yi, now a man, as ruler. As a puppet controlled by Japan, Pu-yi had no real power of his own. Instead, he took orders from his overlords in Japan.

Japan was not satisfied with controlling only Manchuria. In 1937, its armies sought to capture all of China. Japan was nearly successful. However, in the face of a common enemy the Chinese Nationalists and the Chinese Communists united to resist the Japanese invasion. China appealed to the League of Nations for help against Japan. The League sent a commission to China and reported to the world that Japanese attacks were inexcusable. This report was of little help, for China needed arms, money, and food—not words. China's failure to stop Japan helped bring on World War II.

Check in Here

1. Why is Sun Yat-sen important in modern Chinese history?

2. Why was China disappointed with the results of World War I?

3. How did Chiang Kai-shek contribute to the growth of the Chinese nation after Dr. Sun's death?

4. Why did China fail to achieve democracy under Chiang?

5. Why did China and Japan come to blows?

Left: An elaborately carved statue guards a temple in Thailand. Right: A Buddhist monastery in Burma.

COLONIALISM DECLINES IN OTHER PARTS OF THE WORLD

How Imperialism Began Its Retreat from Southeast Asia

In Burma, the forces that encouraged the end to imperialism in India and China were also at work. In 1935, Great Britain separated Burma from India, thus giving in to the demand of Burma for the Burmese. Great Britain granted Burma the beginnings of self-government and democracy. Later on, this led to a demand that all foreigners leave Burma and that control of the country be returned to the Burmese. Despite independence, Indian and Chinese business people dominated Burma's economy. Because they earned huge profits from their activities, they were disliked in Burma. The Japanese, too, recognized the wealth of Burma in rice, timber, and oil. They were not long in seeking control over Burma.

In their colony of Indochina, the French also experienced demands for self-rule. The French were active in Indochina. They built air fields and an important naval base at the colony's capital, Saigon [sī gən']. What upset the French was the rapidly growing influence of the Communist Party. Communism was to demonstrate its full force after World War II.

In the independent country of Siam (Thailand) educated groups sought a voice in government. After a bloodless uprising in 1932, some of the upper classes gained more power at the expense of royal authority. However, this was not a democratic move. Two facts about Thailand at this time are worth noting. First, that country enjoyed a measure of stability because much of the land was peasant owned. Second, the business life of the country was dominated by the Chinese who made a great deal of money and were disliked for their wealth.

531

The British colony of Malaya, about the size of New York state, appeared content to remain a colony because nationalism was not very strong among the Malay. The British island of Singapore, which was linked to the mainland by a causeway, was an especially strategically located colony. Here, in a port that ranked among the ten most important and busiest in the world, the Chinese were clearly in evidence. They dominated the economy. It was the conquest of Singapore that the Japanese sought in their expansion in Asia.

In Indonesia, the Dutch began to loosen their grip on this island country. In 1916, a People's Council had been established. While half its members were Indonesians, the word of the Dutch governor general was the law of the land. In 1927, a National Indonesian Party was established. It was led by an engineer from the Island of Java, Achmed Sukarno [sü kär′nō]. After World War II Sukarno assumed a leadership role in ending Dutch rule of the country.

Reza Pahlavi succeeded his father Reza Khan as Shah of Iran in 1941. He continued the modernization of Iran. In 1979, he was forced to flee, opposed by conservative Muslims who disliked Western ways.

How Imperialism Retreated from the Middle East

Persia (Iran), strategically located in the Middle East, has long been a prize sought by Western powers. Russia and Great Britain were the two foreign countries whose influence was greatest in Persia. When Russia fell to Communist rule during World War I, it was Great Britain's concern that this oil-rich land not be conquered. The British sought to retain control of the vast Anglo-Iranian Oil Company in which the British government owned most of the shares.

In 1925, in an elaborate ceremony, a military man, Reza Khan, became *Shah* (king) of Persia. He urged modernization upon that country. The Shah invited foreign investments and foreign engineers to build new roads and new industry. He placed the Muslim religion firmly under state control and sought to develop a stronger sense of nationalism in Persian nomads. In 1935, by royal decree, the ancient name of Persia was changed to Iran.

Modernization was underway in Turkey under the leadership of Mustafa Kemal, later known as Atatürk. (See page 379.) Turkey paid dearly for being on the losing side of World War I. Although Constantinople and the Dardanelles remained Turkish, they were not to be fortified. They were placed under the control of an international commission. Since some of Turkish territory in Anatolia [an′ə tō′lē ə] (in Asia Minor) was given to Greece, the long-standing hostility between those two countries grew worse.

The Turks were angry at these harsh terms. The Young Turks, a group of Turkish nationalists, were intent on modernizing their country. The group, aided by the French and led by Mustafa Kemal, drove Greek troops off the Turkish mainland and negotiated another peace settlement with the Allies. The *Treaty of Lau-*

The year is 1936. The British Royal Horse Artillery gallop across an Egyptian desert during military training. Heavy guns are drawn by three pairs of horses, each pair controlled by a soldier. In the shifting sands of the desert, horses were more practical than motorized equipment.

sanne (1923) was more generous. The lands in Anatolia were returned, and the Turks obtained full control over Constantinople, which was now called Istanbul. In 1922, Kemal and his followers overthrew the sultan, and the Republic of Turkey was established.

After World War I, the Arab countries of southwestern Asia became strategically important. They were vital for their large deposits of oil, which were necessary to the economy of industrial countries. Among the Arabs, British influence was dominant, with that of France second place. In response to Iraq's demands for independence, the British called upon King Feisal [fī'səl], of Arabia, to rule. Attempts were made to improve agriculture through modernization. A group of police and able administrators were trained to govern. Bagdad in Iraq became the capital and center for the British, French, and American oil companies that tapped the source of the nation's wealth.

In Saudi [sou'dē] Arabia, Ibn Saud [ib'ən sä üd'] conquered the Holy Cities of Islam along the Red Sea. In 1933, American companies agreed to develop the oil of the region. The money from the oil made Saudi Arabia and its rulers immensely wealthy and gave them an important role in world affairs.

In Egypt, the desire to throw off British influence grew after World War I. None was more aggressive in demanding the end to British influence than the *Wafd* [wäfd] *Party*. Before World War I, Lord Kitchener completed the conquest of the Sudan. This was set up as Anglo-Egyptian Sudan. During the first World War, when Turkey joined the Central Powers, Great Britain made Egypt a British protectorate. After the war, in 1922, the Wafd Party was successful in winning independence for Egypt. The country was ruled by King Faud [foud] I. In 1936, the British agreed to withdrawal of British troops. Faud was followed by his son, Farouk [fä rük'] I.

Much of Egypt's history between the world wars was a struggle for power between the Wafd Party and the Egyptian monarchy. Despite the increase in independence, the Wafd Party was dissatisfied. The party wanted to control the

Two refugees from Nazi Europe farm land in Palestine.

Suez Canal, but the British were not willing to grant this. Egyptian control of the Suez Canal did not come until after World War II.

After World War I, the idea of a Jewish national state in Palestine grew. When Great Britain took over Palestine, there were 650,000 people living in Palestine, most of whom were Muslims. There were some Christians, but there were also about 85,000 Jews. In the *Balfour Declaration* of 1917, Britain encouraged the idea of a national homeland for Jews in Palestine. This was to be done without violating the religious or civil rights of the Arabs living there.

During the 1930s, the Nazi threat grew in Europe and larger numbers of Jews sought refuge in Palestine. Over 400,000 Jews settled in Palestine. The Jews believed this was the homeland God had promised them. Of those who settled in Palestine some were very poor and some were well-to-do. All Jews, however,

seemed a threat to the Arabs of the region. In 1939, World War II broke out, and the Nazi threat to Jews became worse. At this time, Great Britain severely reduced the number of Jews who were allowed to enter Palestine. This increased tension among the Jews, the Arabs, and the British. It simmered among these groups all through World War II and then exploded.

The Nature of the American Empire

Until 1898, imperialism in the United States took the form of pushing the frontier farther and farther west. The desire of settlers to reach the Pacific resulted in many wars with the Native Americans. All territories that were settled were admitted as states into the federal union as states on an equal basis with the original states.

When the Latin American countries successfully undertook separation from Spain, President Monroe issued the famous *Monroe Doctrine* (1823). The Monroe Doctrine said that the Americas were no longer open to European colonization and conquest. It suggested that the United States would enforce this policy if need be. Fortunately, the Monroe Doctrine was not immediately challenged. In 1823, the United States was not able to defend it. Since then American influence in Latin America has grown. At different times that area has been the scene of some of the United States' most imperialistic goals.

Gradually, during the nineteenth century, the United States began to build an empire. Alaska became a territory of the United States in 1867, and in 1898, Hawaii became a territory. As a result of the Spanish-American War in 1898 and the Treaty of Paris, the United States obtained Puerto Rico, Guam, and the Philippine Islands. In 1904, through a treaty, the United States obtained the use of the Panama Canal Zone. During the early twentieth century, the Caribbean was turned into an American "lake." While Cuba was allowed to become independent after the Spanish-American War, it was basically under the influence of the United States. A naval base at Guantanamo was established there.

President Theodore Roosevelt believed it was the right and duty of the United States to *intervene* (step in) in Latin America. According to Roosevelt,

President Monroe and his advisors formulate the Monroe Doctrine in 1823. The doctrine warned European countries against interfering in the Americas. Although the doctrine was not recognized in international law, the United States used it as a guide in its relations with Latin America.

intervention was necessary when Latin American countries could not manage their foreign affairs or pay back their debts. This attitude encouraged the United States to intervene many times in Latin American affairs. This was greatly resented by Latin Americans. In 1903, the United States acquired land on which to build the Panama Canal. Colombia, as a result, lost the land that became Panama. The United States intervened with the marines in such places as Santo Domingo (1905, 1916), Nicaragua (1912), and Haiti (1915). America seemed to be the colossus (giant) of the north. In 1917, the United States bought the Danish West Indies, known as the Virgin Islands.

Beginning in 1910 relations between Mexico and the United States were difficult. "Chronic [constant] friction between the United States and the southern neighbor resembled the standing quarrel of Austria and Serbia in Europe. Revolutionary disturbances took American lives, imperiled [endangered] Yankee investments . . . and wounded the Yankee sense of honor."* Pressure grew to

*Harold King, Arthur J. May, Arnold Fletcher, *A History of Civilization* (New York: Charles Scribner's Sons, 1969), p. 912.

The United States as a World Power, 1917

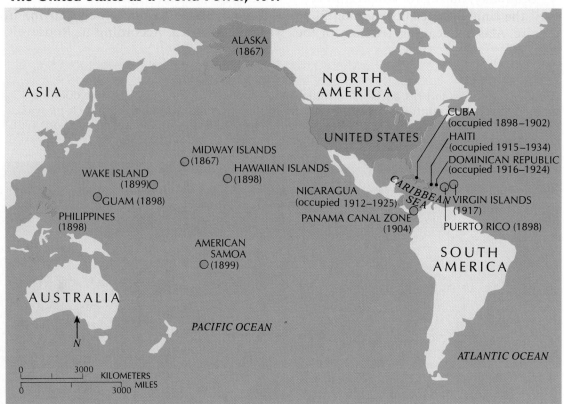

- In what year did the United States gain control of the Philippines and Puerto Rico?
- According to the map, what areas did the United States gain control of first?
- What territory controlled by the United States was farthest from the mainland of the United States?
- In what area was the United States most active, either in owning or occupying territory?

Tourists examine the Culebra Cut during the building of the Panama Canal in 1912. The canal has been a link between the United States and Latin America and also a source of tension. In the year 2000 the canal will be returned to Panama.

intervene militarily in Mexico. President Wilson adopted a policy of watchful waiting instead. When this policy failed, United States troops in 1914 occupied the port of Vera Cruz. Little was settled, and troops once more invaded Mexico in 1916. Because relations with Latin America were poor, only Brazil, of the major Latin American countries, followed the United States into World War I. It was not until World War II that the United States sought to improve relations with its neighbors in this hemisphere.

The United States took control of the Philippine islands from Spain and inherited substantial problems. There were great differences in wealth between absentee landowners and farm workers who farmed the huge estates (haciendas). The farm workers were very poor and the owners very rich. Under the leadership of Emilio Aguinaldo [ä′gē näl′dô], revolt was widespread. The United States found that it had inherited a problem with which it could not deal.

Before long, the United States agreed to grant the Philippines full independence by 1946. A legislature was set up and a democratic government was established under Manuel Quezon [kā′sôn]. The granting of independence to the Philippines showed that a retreat from imperialism had begun for the United States.

Check in Here

1. What reasons explain the retreat from imperialism in each of the following areas: **(a)** Southeast Asia; **(b)** the Middle East?

2. Why were the Chinese often hated in Southeast Asia?

3. How do you explain what stability there was in Thailand?

4. How did the Caribbean become an American "lake"?

The British boasted that their colonial empire was one upon which the sun never set. Yet when colonialism began to decline the British were also the first to set up an orderly way for former colonies to become self-governing and then independent. Canada, Australia, and New Zealand were among the first to become members of the Commonwealth, as the British family of nations was called. The British were quick to give most of the English-speaking colonies commonwealth status. They were less quick in giving such a privilege to non-English-speaking and, in their view, less well-developed countries.

As a result, the fight for freedom in India was a long and slow one. Using nonviolent ways, Gandhi gradually achieved self-rule and later independence for India. The Irish sought home rule and independence. Violence was the usual outcome of their struggle. It was not until after World War I that self-rule was achieved by the southern counties, where the Republic of Ireland was set up. The Protestant counties, known as Ulster, remained under British rule.

During World War I, China fought on the side of the victors. China did not obtain, it felt, a fair share of the spoils of victory. Under China's revolutionary leader, Sun Yat-sen, a stable, democratic government was sought. However, China remained weak while Japan grew strong. When Chiang Kai-shek assumed power upon the death of Sun Yat-sen, it seemed as if China had a leader worthy of a great nation. Unfortunately, that leadership was not a match for the growing might of Japan which sought to dominate Manchuria. Nor was Sun Yat-sen a match for the growing Communist Party inside China.

In the Middle East and in Southeast Asia, imperialism made a gradual retreat. It would not take definite form until after World War II. Jews continued to settle in Palestine in growing numbers. As the Nazi persecution continued in Europe, the growing Jewish population caused friction between Jews, Arabs, and the British.

America too developed an empire. The United States took Panama from Colombia, as Theodore Roosevelt boasted, built the Panama Canal, and converted the Caribbean into an American "lake." When the Philippines achieved independence, it was a sign that for the United States, too, imperialism, was in retreat.

REVIEWING THE HIGHLIGHTS

People to Identify

William Gladstone
Eamon de Valera
William Mackenzie
Louis Joseph Papineau
Lord Durham

Sir Henry Parkes
Maoris
Mohandas Gandhi
Rabindranath Tagore
Theodore Roosevelt
Achmed Sukarno

Sun Yat-sen
Chiang Kai-shek
Yüan Shih-k'ai
Riza Pahlavi
Emilio Aquinaldo

Places to Locate

Republic of Ireland
Ulster
United Kingdom
Canada
Australia
New Zealand
India

China
Indochina
Japan
Middle East
Palestine
Suez Canal
Panama Canal

Caribbean
Latin America
Panama Canal
Burma
Thailand
Iran
Quebec

Events to Describe

Amritsar Massacre

Japanese invasion of China

Terms to Understand

Statute of
  Westminster
Commonwealth of Nations
civil disobedience
Balfour Declaration
Wafd Party
Twenty-One
  Demands

Union Act (1840)
home rule
Quebec Act
Durham Report
Round Table
  Conferences
Government of
  India Act (1935)

Sinn Fein Party
swaraj
Kuomintang
Nationalists
nonviolence
Young Turks
Maoris

Mastering the Fundamentals

1. What were the major threats to the democracies following World War I?
2. What four countries were the first to become Commonwealth countries?
3. What are the responsibilities of each Commonwealth country in terms of governing themselves?
4. Summarize Ireland's complaints against Britain.
5. How did Canada achieve independence from Britain without a revolution?
6. Why was the Durham Report influential in establishing a new policy for the British Empire?

7. What is the significance of the Statute of Westminster?
8. What were the major grievances of India against Britain?
9. Why was Gandhi successful with his policies of civil disobedience and nonviolence?
10. Why was China dissatisfied with the results of World War I?
11. How did China fight each of the following: (**a**) warlords; (**b**) Communists; (**c**) Japan.
12. Why was Chiang unsuccessful in establishing a strong democracy in China?
13. Why did a one-party state develop in China?
14. Why did Japan seek to conquer China?
15. How did Japan become a major power in the Far East?
16. Give an example of colonialism in retreat during the period between the world wars for each of the following: (**a**) Middle East; (**b**) Southeast Asia; (**c**) the American empire.
17. Why did Arabs, Jews, and British come into conflict over the area of Palestine?
18. Why did Persia want to become a modern state? Why were the major powers interested in Persia?
19. How did Egypt regain a substantial measure of self-government? Why was the Wafd Party still dissatisfied with its gains?
20. Why was the United States viewed as the colossus of the north?

THINGS TO DO

1. Using the map on page 516 as a guide, draw comparative maps showing the extent of imperialism before 1914, at the outbreak of World War I, and in 1939, just before World War II.
2. Debate. *Resolved:* The English are blameless in their dealings with Ireland.
3. Conduct a "Meet the Press" conference in which you and several of your classmates form a news or television panel interviewing Gandhi on the eve of his departure for one of the Round Table Conferences.

Study the cartoon below, and on the basis of your interpretation of it, discuss the questions that follow. Draw your own cartoon on a separate sheet of paper selecting another theme from this chapter and discuss it with the class. Remember, cartoons are to be judged on the basis of the thought they attempt to convey and how successfully they convey it. They are to be judged less upon artistic excellence.

1. What is the subject matter of the cartoon? How can you tell?
2. What is the central figure being measured for? How can you tell?
3. In your view, what appears to be the attitude of the figures surrounding the central one? How can you tell?
4. When do you think such a cartoon may have appeared?
5. Make up one or more titles for the cartoon.

German poster of Adolf Hitler, 1938

The Rise of Dictatorships: Communism, Fascism, Nazism

In playing follow the leader one child is chosen to lead, and the others must do exactly what the leader does or leave the game. Everyone enjoys being leader because it gives one a sense of control and power. Many enjoy being followers because it relieves them of the responsibility of thinking for themselves, since they are told what to do.

When the game of follow the leader is played by children, it is amusing. When it is played by nations and their people, it becomes very serious. The years following World War I saw people and nations faced with many problems. When leaders arose who said that they had the answers, the people were often willing to follow them.

Such leaders rose in Russia, Italy, Germany, and in many smaller countries as well. Usually, they came to power through revolution, violence, and force.

They were responsible to no one and had absolute power of life and death over their people. This new form of absolutism, called *dictatorship*, was more ruthless than the absolutism of monarchs had ever been.

The years following World War I saw the growth of this enemy of democracy. Later, dictatorship became a mighty force that threatened the world.

IN RUSSIA, THE DICTATORSHIP OF THE PROLETARIAT REPLACES THE CZAR

How Revolution Began in Russia

The Russian Revolution of 1917 was one of the turning points in history. In the English, American, and French Revolutions, liberty was won. In the Russian Revolution old absolute rulers—czars—were only exchanged for new absolute masters—dictators. A study of that revolution and the government to which it gave birth is important because the Soviet Union plays a leading role in world affairs. It also poses the most serious threat of any nation to the United States.

When you studied the French Revolution, you read of the harsh conditions that existed in France under the Old Regime. The French Revolution was an attempt to do away with the Old Regime. Other revolutions that followed in the nineteenth century were also attempts to get rid of those features of the Old Regime that remained.

Features of the Old Regime could still be found in Russia in 1917. Russian czars ruled as absolute kings. Russia had privileged and unprivileged classes. The Russian Orthodox Church had vast wealth and power and a voice in government. There were serfs who belonged to the land and who worked without pay for their landlords. Taxes were unfair, in that the poor paid more than the rich. There was corruption in government and the ruling classes preferred luxurious living to wise governing.

During the course of the nineteenth century, many Russians wanted reform or change. It was difficult for them to communicate their ideas because most of the Russian people could neither read nor write. Newspapers and magazines opposing the government or even suggesting the mildest reforms were not allowed. Yet, despite these difficulties, Alexander II (1818–81) was called upon to make some needed changes. Hoping to be regarded as a forward looking czar, he allowed limited self-government in local communities, jury trial, and improvements in schooling.

Czar Alexander II is remembered most for having freed the serfs in 1861. Freeing the serfs proved to be only a halfway measure, however, because freedom did not mean much without opportunity. Freed serfs needed land of their own, and Alexander did not give them any. Instead, land was given to a local unit of government known as the *mir* [mēr]. The land would belong to the serfs after they had paid their dues or taxes to the mir for almost fifty years. This arrangement, of course, failed to satisfy the serfs.

Alexander II and the czars who followed him refused to make further improvements in the serfs' living conditions. To many people it seemed as if war and violence were the only means to a better way of life. Alexander II was assassinated in 1881. Because they were in constant fear for their lives, the czars who followed Alexander II were absolute and ruthless.

Underground (illegal) movements to overthrow the czars grew. To make matters worse, people began to realize that their government was weak when it failed to defeat Japan in the Russo-Japanese War of 1904. To some, this defeat was a signal that the government was weak enough to be overthrown by a revolution.

Strikes and revolts among soldiers and sailors became common. Father Gapon [gu pôn'] led a group of people to the palace with a petition (paper) asking Czar Nicholas II (1868–1917) for reforms. Soldiers fired on the group, and hundreds of Russians were killed on that day known as *Bloody Sunday* in January, 1905.

The events of 1905 sufficiently frightened the czar and his ministers to make them realize that they would have to give in. Although Nicholas II granted the people a representative lawmaking body, known as the *Duma* [dü'mə], he did not let it make laws. When the Duma did something he did not like, he dismissed it. Several Dumas met and, for the most part, tried to make some needed changes in the government. The czar would have been wise to listen to the demand for changes. He would have saved his throne and his life.

How the Communists Rose to Power in Russia

"Peace, Land, and Bread" were the things the Communists promised the people. Peace, land, and bread were the things the war-weary Russian people wanted. This simple slogan appealed to the Russian people. It goes a long way to explain the rise of the Communists and their later control of the government. The Russian Revolution of 1917 brought many changes to Russia.

The Russians had complaints against their government. In 1917, they had little freedom; they still lived under feudal conditions; they had not much land; and they had little food. Industry was growing, but the middle class remained small, and workers were restless. The government was weak, corrupt, and inefficient.

Russia's entry into World War I aggravated its problems. The soldiers were brave, but they were poorly fed, poorly clothed, poorly armed, and poorly led. The railroads could not bring war supplies to the fighting front on time. On the home front, prices were high. The wages of workers and of peasants could not buy what the people needed. Starvation stalked the home front, and defeat stalked the fighting front.

The czar felt that everyone was against him. He sought advice from Gregory Rasputin [ras pyü'tun], the evil-minded adviser of the *czarina* (the wife of the czar). Rasputin was feared and hated by the nobles at court. They believed that he was responsible for their country's plight. When they became aware of his growing power and influence with the czar as well as with the czarina, the nobles assassinated Rasputin in December, 1916.

Nicholas II hoped that his presence on the battle front would stiffen the spirit of his soldiers. Although he was not a soldier, he insisted on taking charge of his armies, with the hope that the sight of their czar among them would encourage the troops to strive for victory. The results, however, proved disastrous, and his absence from the capital at Petrograd only made matters worse at home. He hurried back, but it was too late.

Riot, revolt, and strikes broke out in Petrograd, and the troops mutinied to signal the end of the Old Regime in Russia. The Duma, taking power into its own hands, captured the czar and insisted that he resign. Czar Nicholas II was the last of the Romanov dynasty, which had ruled for 300 years. Now its rule came to an end.

When the czar resigned, a *provisional* (temporary) government was formed by Prince George Lvov [lə vôf'] (1861–1925), a Russian statesman. He promised to make changes for the better and to see the war with Germany through to a Russian victory. However, his program did not satisfy many, and Prince Lvov was forced to resign after a few months.

Lvov's place was taken by the revolutionary leader, Alexander Kerenski [kə ren'skē] (1881–1970), who promised more far-reaching reforms. But he, too, wanted to continue the war and keep Russia on the side of the Allies. His proposals did not satisfy those who thought the revolution had gone too far and did not satisfy those who thought the revolution had not gone far enough. Kerenski was unable to give the people at home what they wanted.

There were those who felt that the Duma and its leaders would not go far enough or fast enough in ending the war or in bringing about needed changes. They established a *soviet* (council) of peasants, workers, and soldiers, which for a time worked with the Duma. But much of the history of the Russian Revolution is the story of a test of strength between the members of the Duma and the leaders of the soviet. The soviet,

Lenin addressing the Bolsheviks. What were some of the effects of Lenin's Communist policies for Russia in the early twentieth century?

under the direction of its Communist leader, Vladimir Ilyich Lenin [len'in] (1870–1924), became supreme. The dictatorship of the *proletariat* [prō'li ter'ē ət], or of the workers, was begun.

How Lenin Became the Dictator of Russia

Lenin had been getting ready for revolution for years. He was a follower of Karl Marx, whose life and works he carefully studied. Lenin believed that the time would come when the workers would overthrow the capitalists and replace them as the world's rulers. He studied methods of revolution and believed that a few disciplined and dedicated leaders could overthrow a government.

For his views and for his revolutionary activities, Lenin was jailed and exiled many times. When Russia entered World War I, Lenin was living in Switzerland. He was preparing to return home when the time for revolution came. Lenin promised the Germans that he would take Russia out of World War I. The Germans sealed him in a railroad car and sent him across the borders of Germany and into Russia in the spring of 1917. In Russia, a hero's reception—prepared by the members of the soviet—awaited Lenin. In the following words, Lenin called on the people to support him:

The Communists used propaganda to create a feeling of unity among the Russian people. What do you think this poster tries to communicate?

Dear comrades, soldiers, sailors, and workers! I am happy to greet in your persons the victorious Russian revolution, and greet you as the vanguard [the lead] of the world-wide proletarian army. . . . The piratical [thieving] imperialist war is the beginning of civil war throughout Europe. . . . The world-wide Socialist Revolution has already dawned. . . . Any day now the whole of European capitalism may crash. . . . Long live the world-wide Socialist Revolution!*

Lenin convinced the soviet to follow him and his extreme ideas. At first, they were reluctant to do so. However, as Lenin and his *Bolshevik* [bōl'shə vik] supporters (the Communists) gained in strength, the people followed. The Bolsheviks used terror and a secret police, which Lenin organized. In November of 1917, the Communists seized the capital, Petrograd. Kerenski, who had led the temporary government, left the country. Other members of his government were arrested. The Russian Revolution had been captured by a well organized, disciplined, and aggressive minority.

It is one thing to seize power; it is another thing to keep it. Lenin's early government was not very strong. To strengthen it, he agreed to end the war. A harsh peace treaty, which took Russia out of the war, was signed with Germany. To defeat his opposition in Russia, Lenin used the secret police. People who were against the revolution were killed. A Bolshevik Red army, under the able leadership of Leon Trotsky, [trot'skē] (1879–1940), defeated the White army. These were anti-Bolshevik forces loyal to the czar.

Lenin tried to introduce communism quickly in Russia. The Russian Orthodox

*N. N. Sukhanov, *The Russian Revolution 1917*, abridged and translated by Joel Carmichael. (London: Oxford University Press), 1955.

Church, long a supporter of the czar, was all but destroyed. The observance of religion was totally discouraged. Private industry was taken over by the government. Thus, private business was abolished. Small farms were joined together to form government-owned farms. Lenin hoped that through government ownership of property, the classless society would be quickly established. Lenin, however, moved too quickly. The results were disastrous for Russia.

In 1919, Russia faced starvation. The Communist drive to *nationalize* (place under government ownership) all land reduced the amount of food farmers were able to grow. Industrial production had dropped. Lenin would need help before Russia could have the kind of government and economy that he wanted. He decided that the change was too quick and that it would be wise to retreat. In the New Economic Policy, known as the *NEP* (1921), he returned some farms and factories to private owners. This temporary measure helped matters somewhat, but as soon as it seemed possible, farms and factories were placed under government ownership once again.

By 1924, when Lenin died, the Communist government was in complete control of Russia. His position as leader was taken by Joseph Stalin [stä'lin], a ruthless and dedicated Communist. Stalin, who had served the revolution from the very beginning, was to hold the Union of Soviet Socialist Republics in his grip for an entire generation.

Check in Here

1. What were some of the major grievances of the Russians under the czars?

2. Why were the reforms of Alexander II inadequate?

3. How did Russia's entry into World War I make its problems worse?

4. What was the role of each of the following in the Russian Revolution: (a) Duma; (b) soviet; (c) Lvov; (d) Kerenski; (e) Lenin; (f) Trotsky?

5. Why did Lenin resort to the New Economic Policy? Why was this policy short-lived?

THE RUSSIANS LIVE UNDER COMMUNISM

How the Soviet Government Works

The government built by the Communists grew over a period of time. However, in the following paragraphs you will read about the government of Russia as it is today.

The area controlled by the Communists is called the *Union of Soviet Socialist Republics*. This name, often shortened to the Soviet Union or the USSR, gives us a number of clues about the kind of government in the Soviet Union. First, the government is a federal union of fifteen states. These states are bound together by constitutional agreement. The United States, you remember, has a federal system with power divided between the states and the national government. The Soviet Union, too, is a federation, in which power is shared with the fifteen republics.

The word *soviet* means council. The Chairman of the Council of Ministers is the most powerful post in the government of the Soviet Union. The chairman is the premier of the nation.

The word *socialism* means a system of government in which the farms and factories are owned by the state. Private ownership and private profit, except on a very limited scale, are not allowed in a socialist state like the Soviet Union.

The capital of the Soviet Union is

(turn to page 549)

Joseph Stalin (1879–1953)

Stalin means "steel" in Georgian. It is the adopted and better known name of Joseph Vissarionovich Djugashvili [dzhü gäsh'vil ē]. Stalin was born to poor but hard working parents in the southern Russian province of Georgia. Georgians are known for their quick tempers, daring horsemanship, and physical strength. These qualities helped make Joseph Djugashvili a man of steel and the eventual dictator of the Union of Soviet Socialists Republics, also referred to as the USSR.

Stalin's parents wanted him to be a priest. They sent him to a religious school. But the priestly life was not at all to his liking. He wanted to be a revolutionary instead. Between 1898 and 1917, Stalin worked for the cause he thought was right. He read Marx, followed Lenin (the leader of the Russian Communists), and by constant labor helped build a Communist revolutionary organization. During these years, he was arrested, exiled, imprisoned, and sent to Siberia. But prison walls could not hold Stalin. Each time he was arrested he managed to escape. When the Russian Revolution of 1917 began, Stalin was in Siberia and from there he was freed by his Bolshevik comrades.

Stalin proved he was a man of steel during the years he was preparing for revolution. If the party needed money, Stalin became a thief and robbed banks to get it. On one occasion, news came of a huge shipment of money being transported by coach from one bank to another. The coach was under Cossack guard (soldiers of the czar). Leading a group of men, Stalin bombed the coach and killed the twenty Cossacks who guarded it. Then, on fast horses, Stalin and his men made off with the funds. The death of the twenty men seemed to outrage Lenin, who had Stalin thrown out of the party—at least temporarily. During this period, Stalin found time to edit a newspaper, write books, and deliver fiery speeches at mass meetings to arouse enthusiasm for his cause.

In 1917, the Bolsheviks seized power and became masters of Russia. Despite his activities for the Communist revolution, Stalin was relatively little known. However, upon Lenin's death, Stalin was ready to seize power as head of the Communist Party and dictator of the Soviet Union. This power he held ruthlessly until his death in 1953.

Years later, his daughter, Svetlana Alliluyeva [ä lēl ü yā'və], exiled herself from the Soviet Union. She now lives in the United States, and uses her mother's name rather than her father's. Alliluyeva wrote that while alive her father had absolute power. He became "the most complete personification [person representing an idea] of power without democracy, built on the suppression [putting down] of millions of human lives."*

Moscow. The government leaders with executive control over the republics are in the *Kremlin* [krem'lin]. While the republics have self-government in local affairs, the Kremlin is the home of the Soviet government and seat of Soviet power.

Earlier in this book you read about the difference between a republic and a democracy. (See pp. 57–58.) Each state in the Soviet Union is called a *republic* because each state has an elected legislature and executive officials. There is no democracy in the Soviet Union. Freedom of speech, freedom of the press, and the right of assembly are guaranteed in the Soviet constitution. These rights are severely limited in practice. The Soviet Union has only one political party—the Communist Party—which selects candidates for political offices. Therefore, the people elect officials only from a list of Communist Party candidates.

Since the Communist Party selects the candidates for office, the few leaders of the Communist Party are the government of the Soviet Union. Power in the Soviet Union is in the hands of the leader of the Communist Party, who is not chosen by the people. In a democracy any citizen can join a political party, but in the Soviet Union this is not true. The Communist Party is all-powerful, but most Soviet citizens are not admitted to party membership. Less than 6 percent of the total population of the nation are Communist Party members. Only those specially trained and recommended may

*Svetlana Alliluyeva, *Only One Year* (New York: Harper and Row, 1969), p. 173.

join the Party. Usually, it is only through membership in the Party that one can rise to the highest ranks of the Soviet government.

If the government of the Soviet Union is to be understood, the relationship of the Communist Party to the government must be understood. The lawmaking body of the Soviet Union is the *Supreme Soviet*. The Supreme Soviet is a "rubber stamp" for the decisions made by those at the head of the government, and for those made by the leaders of the Party. The Supreme Soviet chooses the members of the *Presidium* [pri sid'ē əm] of the Supreme Soviet. The Presidium acts when the Supreme Soviet is not in session. The head of the Presidium is the president of the Soviet Union. This job is largely ceremonial. At the very head of the government is the *premier*, who is Chairman of the Council of Ministers. The decisions of the premier and of the presidium of the Council of Ministers are rarely questioned.

The organization of the Communist Party parallels that of the Soviet government. The Party is headed by the First Secretary and a *Politburo* [pol'it byür'ō], which control the *Central Committee* and the *Party Congress*. The most powerful group in the Party is the Party Congress. This group meets at least once every five years. The Party Congress elects another group called the Central Committee. The Central Committee does the government work when the Party Congress is not meeting. The Communist Party controls both these groups. Local units of the Communist Party send representatives to the Party Congress. When

USSR

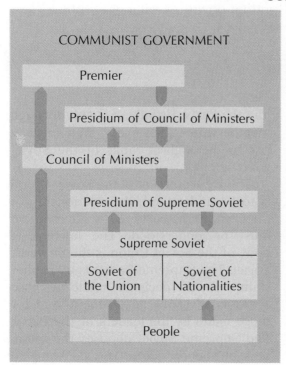

COMMUNIST GOVERNMENT

Premier

Presidium of Council of Ministers

Council of Ministers

Presidium of Supreme Soviet

Supreme Soviet

| Soviet of the Union | Soviet of Nationalities |

People

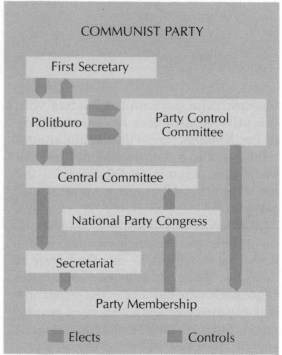

COMMUNIST PARTY

First Secretary

Politburo

Party Control Committee

Central Committee

National Party Congress

Secretariat

Party Membership

Elects   Controls

Which is more powerful, the government or the Communist Party?

the posts of First Secretary of the Party and Chairman of the Council of Ministers are held by one person, he or she has a great deal of power, indeed. It is in the Politburo of the Communist Party that important decisions are hammered out and where the party plans are made. Those who oppose the Party may be punished for having gone against either the government or the Party.

How Communism Controls Industry

In the Soviet Union there is neither private ownership nor private profit in industry. Almost all industry is owned by the government. Nearly all workers are government workers. Therefore, industry and labor are under the supervision of the government.

The Soviet economy is a *planned economy*. Decisions about production,

distribution, and wages in capitalistic countries are made by individual business owners and corporations. In the Soviet Union such decisions are made by a central planning agency. This body decides how much shall be produced in farming, transportation, communication, mining, electric power, and other industries. Usually, such plans are made on a five-year basis. Goals to be reached by the end of five years are established, but these may change with changing conditions. Since there is almost no private profit, the Communists say that the goals set in the Soviet Five-Year Plans give managers and workers a reason to do better. Through these plans, the Soviet Union hopes to grow and manufacture more goods and improve living conditions. The goal is to achieve prosperity and outstrip the United States.

By government planning, the Russians have changed their economy from a very backward one to a more highly developed one. For this progress the Soviet people have paid a high price. While the Soviet people would like washers, refrigerators, cars, and other conveniences, the plans of the Soviet Union have called for heavy machinery, airplanes, and rockets. In the Soviet Union, what mechanical conveniences the people will have are pretty much determined by government planners.

Most workers in the Union of Soviet Socialist Republics are government workers. Their wages, hours, and working conditions are decided upon by the government. The government permits labor unions, but it does not allow them to strike. The unions serve as tools and organizations of the Communist Party, rather than as workers' organizations. Since the government is the chief employer, workers cannot easily look for another job if they dislike the one they have. Ordinary workers cannot hope to improve themselves by going from one job to another. Success for the workers comes from meeting production quotas and thus becoming heroes in the ranks of labor.

In the Soviet Union, private business is discouraged. As long as the owner of a business does not employ others, he or she may stay in business. In other words, the business must be run entirely by the owner. Limited savings and individual ownership of homes and personal property such as furniture and television sets are permitted.

How Farming Is Organized in the Soviet Union

The *collective farm* is the basic unit of Soviet farming. On a collective farm a group of farmers and their families live and work the land owned by the collective. According to government plans, they must produce a certain amount of grain, meat, eggs, and butter. Farmers are paid on the basis of the number of days they work. Farm machinery is owned and operated by the collective farm. The products grown on the farm are bought by the government at fixed prices. The collective farms have managers appointed by the government.

At the beginning of the Communist state, the organization of collective farms caused starvation and death for millions. Lenin had promised the peasants land. The collective farms did not satisfy the land needs of the peasants. The result

The Kremlin was once a Russian fortress. It was used by the Communists as their government center until 1955, when it became a national museum. The term "Kremlin" is still used when referring to the government of the Soviet Union.

was that not enough food was grown. The government was forced to give in to the capitalist leanings of the peasants by giving them land and perhaps a few farm animals. The produce from this land belongs to the peasants, which helps them to have more to eat. By selling some of the food they grow on the open market, the peasants can get the money with which to buy the few luxuries that are available to them. The peasants are still expected to spend most of their time on land the collective owns. But their small land holdings have made them happier and have also increased the amount of food.

In addition to collective farms, there are large *state farms*. These may be thought of as farm factories, on which experiments in scientific farming are carried out. Farmers work for wages on the state farms, as workers do in the factories. The state farms are entirely owned by the government and are run by a manager who hires the necessary labor. Despite great improvements, Soviet farming has not lived up to the great production that was expected of it. Perhaps poor management, lack of incentive to grow more than private ownership might provide, and poor growing seasons are reasons why the Soviet Union has not reached its goals.

Check in Here

1. Why is it said that in the Soviet Union the Party is more important than the government?

2. Define each of the following: **(a)** Supreme Soviet; **(b)** Presidium; **(c)** Central Committee; **(d)** Politburo.

3. Explain how the USSR plans its economy for each of the following: **(a)** industry; **(b)** agriculture.

4. Distinguish between a collective farm and a state farm.

MUSSOLINI AS *IL DUCE* FORCES FASCISM ON ITALY

How Fascism Was Born in Italy

After unification in the nineteenth century, one of Italy's problems was lack of experience in democracy. Italy was a victorious nation in World War I. However, the war had taxed its resources heavily. The Treaty of Versailles gave little in repayment to Italy. Italy's postwar problems were grave. It could not reorganize its industry, nor could it put its soldiers back to work. Farm production fell, workers rioted, and farmers demanded land of their own. Some Italians saw in communism an answer to the problems that they faced. Many felt a sense of disgrace because Italy was not playing a big role in world affairs. The Italians needed a government that would bring order out of chaos.

Benito Mussolini [müs′sô lē′nē] (1883–1945) at one time had been a Socialist. As a journalist, he wrote articles favoring the overthrow of capitalism. He was very outspoken in urging Italy to join World War I on the side of the Allies. After the war, his socialist views began to change, and he wrote about the need of Italy to become a great nation.

In 1919, Mussolini organized the Fascist Party, which undertook the task of restoring Italy to a glorious position in the world. The Fascist Party urged its members to obey the rules of the party and to fight those parties that had different ideas. The Fascists chose a Roman battle-ax wrapped in reeds, known as *fasces*, [fas′ēz], as a sign of power. Its members began to wear a special uniform made up largely of a black shirt and military trousers. They rallied newcomers to their cause with inspiring songs and with exaggerated promises of a better life.

Fascism seemed to offer something to every Italian. It offered visions of greater glory for Italy. It promised jobs to the unemployed, land to the peasants, and security from communism to business owners. Workers and property owners alike thought they found something of value in fascism. With cries of *"Viva il duce!"* ("Long live the leader!"), the huge crowds cheered Mussolini's fiery speeches. He lured people to his program. Those he could not attract, he had his strong men beat into submission.

Soon Mussolini felt strong enough to challenge the government. In October, 1922, the *March on Rome* took place. From all parts of Italy, Fascists began to make their way to Rome, and civil war seemed on the way. King Victor Emmanuel III gave in before the threat and appointed Mussolini as premier. Soon the Fascists controlled the Italian parliament. With Mussolini as premier and with his followers in parliament, the march of fascism could not be stopped. Democracy, which the patriots of Italy had worked so hard to build, fell. Dictatorship took its place.

How Fascists Governed Italy

In a short time, Italy became a dictatorship under the direction and control of the Fascist Party and of its leader, Mussolini. As a result, Italy became a one-party nation. The press was censored, and personal rights crushed. Voting rights were severely restricted. Mussolini held all the power in his own hands. He controlled both king and parliament, neither of whom dared oppose him. Italians, under Fascist teachers, were taught to believe, obey, and fight. They were told that they were better than other nations and that they should build their military to defeat the "corrupt democracies."

Mussolini was not satisfied with complete control over Italy's political life. He wanted control over its industrial life as well. He wanted to combine the political

Benito Mussolini, Fascist leader of Italy, considered himself an heir of Julius Caesar. Fascism attracted Italy's middle class, which feared communism as a threat to private property.

life with the industrial life by creating the *corporate state*. Mussolini organized industrial units called *corporations*. Owners, workers, and Fascist Party members decided together on what factories would manufacture and what profits would be made. Labor unions were not allowed, and strikes were forbidden. Although there were also some restrictions on owners, Italian business prospered under the corporate state.

For a time, fascism seemed to be successful. There were many who envied a nation free of strikes. The government made attempts to create more farmland. Some marshland was reclaimed, that is, it was made good for farming once again. The government also started public works projects which put unemployed people back to work. Mussolini was proud of the efficiency he brought to the government. He even boasted that the trains, which were often late under the democratic government, now ran on time. In 1929, he made peace with the Church. He signed a treaty which recognized the pope as ruler of Vatican City and made Catholicism the religion of the nation.

The first ten years or so of Fascist rule were its honeymoon period. Everything seemed to go well. The second ten years were to prove stormy, as you will see. Success encouraged Mussolini, but his ambition was to prove a bad thing for Italy and for the world as well.

Check in Here

1. Why did fascism and Mussolini appeal to the Italians?

2. Describe how Mussolini came to power in Italy.

3. Describe how Mussolini governed Italy.

4. How did Mussolini make peace with the Vatican?

HITLER AS *DER FÜHRER* BRINGS NAZISM TO GERMANY AND DOMINATES EUROPE

How Fascism Came to Germany

Earlier you learned that democratic traditions never took deep root in Germany. Bismarck frowned upon democracy and helped establish a strong monarchy. When World War I ended, Kaiser Wil-

liam II was forced to flee. As a result of the war, a republic was born. Germany under the Weimar [vī'mär] Republic had a democratic government for the first time. However, democracy calls for more than a democratic constitution. It needs people who are willing to cooperate so that democracy might live. Unfortunately, the Germans had not been taught to believe in democracy.

The Weimar Republic faced what must have seemed like insurmountable problems. Jobs were scarce and industry needed to be rebuilt. Prices skyrocketed and the value of the money went down. Runaway inflation gripped the country. The government could not solve these problems at once. People were impatient. They feared communism and felt humiliated because Germany had been made to accept a distasteful peace treaty. Then, the *National Socialist Party*, of which Adolf Hitler became the leader, offered a program to save the country.

Adolf Hitler (1889–1945) was born in Austria. He believed himself destined to lead Germany to greatness. His book, *Mein Kampf* [mīn kämpf'] (*My Battle*), was written while he was in prison for trying to overthrow the Weimar republic in 1923. The book expresses some of Hitler's chief ideas: his passionate German nationalism, his hatred of the Jews, and his ideas about a super race of people who were meant to rule the world.

Hitler learned a great deal from Italian fascism. He learned how to draw people to his ideas through fiery speeches. He saw the importance of a uniformed, disciplined political party. The *Nazi* [nät'sē] (National Socialist) Party, which was led by Hitler, was made up of those who wanted to see a greater Germany. They also wanted to avenge the defeat in World War I. In this party could be found those who feared communism, as well as workers who wanted jobs, soldiers who wanted uniforms, and officers who wanted promotion. Many were flattered when Hitler called them a master race.

By 1932, although Hitler's Nazi Party was not in the majority, it was the largest single party in the *Reichstag* [rīks'täg'] (the lawmaking body) of the Weimar Republic. Field Marshal von Hindenburg, hero of World War I, was president of the Weimar Republic. Real power, however, was in the hands of a chancellor (prime minister), who had the support of a majority of the Reichstag (parliament). No party leader except Hitler could command such a majority. Hindenburg was forced to call upon Hitler to accept the post of chancellor. As chancellor, Hitler dissolved the Reichstag and, in 1933, called for a new election.

Before the election, Hitler and the Nazis used every trick to make sure that they would win. They held huge rallies, and shouted the words *"Heil Hitler!"* throughout the land. Opponents of the Nazis were in danger; opposition newspapers were abolished; Jews were imprisoned; and finally, the Communists were blamed for starting a fire which destroyed the Reichstag building. Fear of Communists drove many Germans into the Nazi camp. In the election called by Hitler in 1933, the Nazis tried to get a big majority. They failed. But they did get enough votes to leave all power to Hitler. The Reichstag adjourned, leaving Hitler supreme in Germany. He soon tried to become supreme in Europe. To do this, he turned Europe into a battlefield.

The charred remains of the Reichstag building. How was Hitler able to use the burning of the Reichstag to gain support for the Nazi Party?

How Hitler
Governed Germany

The Nazi Party became the only legal party in Germany. Its members wore special uniforms, and an elite group, known as the *Storm Troopers,* or *S.S.,* went about destroying opposition to the party. Mass meetings were held in which *Der Führer* [fyür'ər] (the leader, Hitler) and the idea of a greater Germany were hailed. Books which opposed Nazi ideas were burned with great ceremony. The *Gestapo* [gə stä'pō], a secret police, was organized to put down opposition to Hitler. Many great German writers and scientists, such as Thomas Mann and Albert Einstein, fled to the United States.

Hitler relied heavily on *propaganda* (a deliberate plan for spreading ideas) as a weapon in achieving his domestic and foreign goals. He held that the *big lie,* if told often enough, would in time be believed. That is, he said that the most distorted interpretations of history would be believed if they were repeated often in speeches and books and on the radio. With this idea in mind, he had textbooks rewritten and teachers were told what to teach. The radio was used to tell the Germans whom to believe, what to expect, and how to behave.

No sooner had he obtained power than Hitler prepared for war. The Treaty of Versailles limited the size of the German army. To Hitler, the Treaty of Versailles could be violated because it was a "blot on German honor." German industry was turned over to war production. Important business people who had supported him had hoped that Hitler would be a mere puppet in their hands. But Hitler controlled industry as well as government, and while many business people would have preferred to do away with this monster, it was too late. Hitler brought Germany and the world to the brink of ruin.

How Hitler Persecuted
Religious Groups

Hitler was responsible for the deaths of six million Jews, both in Germany and in the lands he conquered. He was determined to drive the Jews out of Germany and to wipe them out as a people as well. In concentration camps, where they were imprisoned, serial numbers were tatooed on their bodies. Murder, torture, pseudo-scientific (false science) experimenting, cremation (burning), and the gas chamber were used in an effort to exterminate them. The *New York Times* quoted an eyewitness to these atrocities as follows: "He saw his family battered to death with Nazi rifle butts and he saw countless other Jewish men, women, and children shot, clubbed, drowned, gassed, burned, and turned into fertilizer and laundry soap."

One of Hitler's lieutenants, Adolf Eichmann [īch'män] (1906–1962), was given the responsibility of providing for a final solution to the "Jewish Question." This was a vague term that meant the Jews were to be destroyed as a people.

Holocaust is the word historians use to describe the destruction of the Jews by the Nazis. In the Holocaust of European Jews the world has never seen such inhuman, barbaric, and fantastic methods of killing and torture as Hitler devised. The enormity of his crime was beyond any description. A new word, *genocide* [jen'ə sīd'], was coined to describe it. Genocide is the deliberate attempt to wipe out an entire religious or racial group, as Hitler attempted to do to the Jews.

The Nazis persecuted Protestants and Catholics as well as Jews, but only the Jews were singled out for extermination. The Protestant Pastor, Martin Niemoller [nē mô lər], was arrested and sent to a concentration camp for opposing Hitler. Priests found it difficult and, at times, impossible to hold church services or to perform the rites of the Catholic Church. Many of them were arrested for what Hitler called "meddling in political affairs." Increasingly, Christianity itself came under attack, since it taught kindness, mercy, humility, and self-sacrifice—virtues scorned by the Nazis.

Check in Here

1. List the major problems facing the Weimar Republic. Why was the Weimar Republic unable to solve these problems democratically?

2. Why were Germans attracted to the promises of the National Socialists?

3. Describe the way in which the Nazis came to power in Germany.

4. How did Hitler make use of the big lie technique to strengthen his position in Germany?

COMMUNISM AND FASCISM FIGHT FOR CONTROL OF OTHER EUROPEAN COUNTRIES

What Conditions Were Like in Other Countries

In the smaller countries of Europe, democracy, fascism, and communism waged a three-cornered fight for power. Those governments with strong democratic traditions such as the Netherlands, Belgium, Norway, Denmark, and Sweden were able to defeat those who proposed either fascism or communism.

Other countries were less fortunate. Spain, at the end of World War I, was a backward, poverty stricken monarchy. In 1931, King Alfonso left the country and was not allowed to return. In new elections the people established a republic. The Spanish tried many reforms, but there were many who wanted to go back to the old ways and old privileges of the

Francisco Franco ruled Spain until 1975. What event in 1936 helped this dictator rise to power?

monarchy. The wealthy wanted to hold onto their property. They thought that General Francisco Franco [frang'kō] (1892–1975), a Fascist, could help them.

In 1936, the *Spanish Civil War* began. It soon came to be called a "dress rehearsal" for World War II. The Fascist countries of Italy and Germany supported Franco and his rebels, while Russia supported the *loyalists* (the armies of the republic). The democratic countries might have supported the loyalists, too, but fear of being on the same side as the Communists kept them from doing so. Franco defeated the loyalists. In 1938, he became dictator of Spain. As *El Caudillo* [el kou dē lyō] (the Leader), Franco ruled Spain until his death in 1975. He was succeeded by Prince Juan Carlos of Bourbon. In 1969, Franco had named him to be king and head of state upon Franco's death.

In Hungary, there was much poverty and unrest because of the harsh terms of the Versailles Treaty that ended World War I. Monarchists, Communists, and

The Twentieth Century

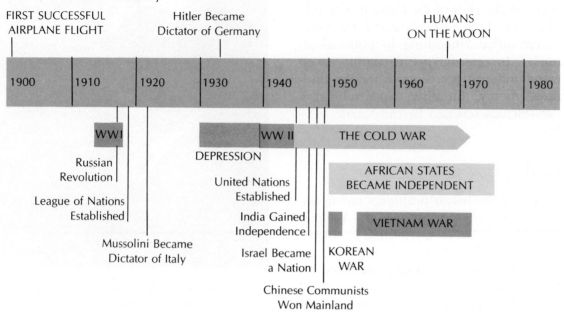

FIRST SUCCESSFUL AIRPLANE FLIGHT

Hitler Became Dictator of Germany

HUMANS ON THE MOON

1900 | 1910 | 1920 | 1930 | 1940 | 1950 | 1960 | 1970 | 1980

WWI

Russian Revolution

League of Nations Established

Mussolini Became Dictator of Italy

DEPRESSION

WW II

THE COLD WAR

AFRICAN STATES BECAME INDEPENDENT

VIETNAM WAR

United Nations Established

India Gained Independence

Israel Became a Nation

KOREAN WAR

Chinese Communists Won Mainland

Many dictatorships appear in the twentieth century. Which ones are indicated here?

Fascists tried to rule, but the Fascists, under Admiral Nicholas Horthy [hôr′tē], won out in 1919. Horthy eventually became a puppet of Hitler.

In Poland, a similar fight for control took place between Communists and Fascists. Hitler tried to make Poland a German puppet state. This struggle was a contributing cause of World War II.

The Nature of Totalitarianism

To win a war it is necessary to know your enemy. In much of the twentieth century, that enemy has been *totalitarianism*. What do totalitarian governments have in common? Whether the government is of the Communist or Fascist variety, one leader becomes the symbol of power and prestige. Such a leader has nearly unlimited power, and the leader's party has total political control. In all totalitarian governments, the leader relies heavily on propaganda and control of the press and radio to bend the people to his or her will. Such propaganda plays

on ignorance, distorts the truth, and paints exaggerated pictures of greatness.

In all totalitarian governments, those who do not bend readily to the demands of the leader or the government are killed or imprisoned. Secret police usually stamp out opposition, and spies report any suspicious people to the government. Totalitarianism depends on military force, exaggerated feelings of nationalism, and war as a means of achieving what it wants.

Totalitarian governments have certain weaknesses. When the all-powerful leader makes bad decisions, those mistakes are costly to the nation and its people. For example, Germany and its people suffered as a result of Hitler's mistakes. Totalitarianism seems to encourage conspiracy, since no one can be sure of another. No one knows when he or she will be the next one reported to the secret police. As a result, totalitarian governments, despite their boasts to the contrary, are often inefficient. Moreover, totalitarian governments use war in order to demand a great many sacrifices from their people. This in itself makes for discontent and grumbling among people.

Although fascism and communism are both based on totalitarian governments, there are differences between them. Fascism is highly nationalistic. Communism teaches the need for international or worldwide revolution. Under fascism, private profit and private ownership continue to exist, although they are under direct control of the government. Communism abolishes the idea of private profit and private ownership except on a very small scale. Fascism glorifies the state. Communism claims that after worldwide revolution has been accomplished, "the state will wither away."

Totalitarian governments can be formidable enemies. In war, they are able to move quickly, take chances, and risk lives as no democracy would dare. As a result, World War II lasted six years before a final Allied victory was achieved. The causes, events, and results of World War II will be the subject of the next chapter.

Check in Here

1. Why was the Spanish Civil War called a dress rehearsal for World War II?

2. Why were countries like the Netherlands, Belgium, Sweden, Denmark, and Norway able to resist totalitarianism?

3. What do totalitarian countries have in common?

4. How do Fascist and Communist dictatorships differ in the principles upon which they are based?

5. What advantages and disadvantages may be claimed for totalitarianism?

REVIEWING THE BASICS

World War I was a turning point in the world's history. In Europe, Russia turned to communism, the czar was overthrown, and a dictatorship of the proletariat was set up under Nicholai Lenin. The Union of Soviet Socialist Republics, established in 1917, remains the government of the Soviet Union today. The central feature of its government is the domination of the nation's political structure by the Communist Party. The Soviet Union is a Communist state in which private ownership of factories, mines, shops, and farms has been eliminated, except in small, individually owned enterprises.

In Italy, Mussolini established the Fascist Party which overthrew the monarchy, made peace with the pope, and established a Fascist dictatorship. For the first decade, Mussolini was widely credited for the efficiency and effectiveness of his government. He tried to bring industrial peace through corporations made up of owners, workers, and Fascist Party members. During the second ten years of his rule, when Hitler became the dominant European dictator, Mussolini copied some of the worst aspects of the Nazi system. Freedom of speech and press were eliminated by him, as were other political parties and other sources of opposition.

Hitler came to power through legal means. Although in the election of 1933 he did not get a clear majority, he did get enough support to force von Hindenburg to appoint him chancellor. The National Socialist Party (Nazi) dominated Europe until it was destroyed in World War II. It preached racial superiority, hatred for the Versailles Treaty and democracy, and extermination of Jews and other peoples.

Among the smaller countries of Europe, democracy survived in Belgium, Holland, Switzerland, and in the Scandinavian countries. In Hungary, a fascist dictatorship was set up. In Poland, the Soviet Union and Germany competed for control. It would be over Poland that the two countries would come to blows and start World War II. In Spain, a bitter Civil War broke out from which Francisco Franco, with the help of Germany and Italy, emerged victorious.

Communism and fascism are alike in that they are both totalitarian forms of government. But they are more different than alike. Fascism encourages private profit, capitalism, and nationalism. Communism is based on government ownership of the means of production and the abolition of capitalism. Communists believe that ultimately the whole world will become Communist. At that point, the state will wither away.

REVIEWING THE HIGHLIGHTS

People to Identify		
Alexander II	Alexander Kerenski	Adolf Hitler
Father Gapon	Lenin	Francisco Franco
Nicholas II	Leon Trotsky	Nicholas Horthy
Rasputin	Joseph Stalin	Spanish rebels
George Lvov	Benito Mussolini	Spanish loyalists

Places to Locate		
Petrograd	Moscow	Vatican City

Terms to Understand		
dictatorship	Gestapo	corporate state
totalitarianism	Supreme Soviet	National Socialist Party
mir	Presidium	state farm
Duma	proletariat	fascism
"Peace, Land, and Bread"	Kremlin	Nazism
soviet	Politburo	Reichstag
to nationalize	Council of Ministers	propoganda
NEP	socialism	Holocaust
Bolshevik	Party Congress	Weimar Republic
Storm Troopers	planned economy	totalitarianism
Central Committee	collective farm	
	genocide	

Spanish Civil War   Russian Revolution   March on Rome (1922)
Bloody Sunday   of 1917

**Mastering
the Fundamentals**

1. In what ways are modern dictators similar to the absolute monarchs of old? How are they different?
2. List the causes for dissatisfaction that existed in Russia in the early 1900s.
3. Why did the reforms of Alexander II fail to satisfy the Russian people?
4. Why was the Russo-Japanese War of 1904 a signal for revolt in Russia?
5. Why was it unwise for the czar to refuse to listen to the Duma?
6. Why was the slogan "Peace, Land, and Bread" a good one for the Communists in 1917?
7. What problems faced the Russian people and government in 1917?
8. Why did the governments of Prince Lvov and Alexander Kerenski fail?
9. How did Lenin and the Bolsheviks gradually gain power?
10. Why was Lenin unsuccessful in establishing communism quickly in Russia?
11. What is the relationship between the Soviet government and the Communist Party?
12. Why is the Soviet economy called a planned economy?
13. What rights did the individual have under Mussolini's rule?
14. Why was Italy under fascism called the corporate state?
15. Why were the first ten years of Italian fascism called the honeymoon period?
16. What did Hitler learn from Italian fascism?
17. What are some of the ideas contained in Hitler's book, *Mein Kampf?*
18. Why was the Nazi Party popular with many Germans?
19. How did fascism, communism, and democracy fight one another in other countries of Europe? Who won? Why?

THINGS TO DO

1. Prepare a biographical sketch of one of the following dictators: (a) Lenin; (b) Stalin; (c) Hitler; (d) Mussolini; (e) Franco. Try in your biographies to get at the qualities of the individual that seemed to attract supporters.
2. Prepare a report on the Spanish Civil War under the general heading of "Dress Rehearsal for World War II."

3. Draw a cartoon illustrating what happens to such freedoms as freedom of speech and press, fair trials, civil liberties, and civil rights under a totalitarian form of government.

YOU ARE THE HISTORIAN

On November 9, 1938, the Nazis attacked Jews and Jewish-owned property and synagogues throughout Germany and Austria. The action was in retaliation for the assassination of Ernst Von Rath. He was an official of the German Embassy in Paris. Rath was killed by Herschel Grynszpan, the son of Polish Jews who had been deported from Germany. The Nazis swept through the Jewish quarters, arresting and sending victims to Buchenwald, Sachsenhausen, and Dachau (concentration camps). They left a trail of broken windows in the streets. Hence, this night was called *Kristallnacht* (Crystal Night). Here is what one man remembered, forty years later, about that night. Read the selection and discuss the questions that follow it.

Kristallnacht
by Frederick Morton

The day began with a thudding through my pillow. Jolts waked me. Then, like an alarm clock, the doorbell rang. It was six in the morning. My father, my mother, my little brother and I all met in the foyer, all in our robes. We did not know yet exactly what. But we *knew*. We were Jews in Vienna in 1938. Everything in our lives, including our beds, stood on a cliff.

My father opened the door on Frau Eckel, the janitress.

"They are down there . . . they are throwing things." She turned away. Went on with her morning sweep. Her broom trembled.

We looked down into the courtyard. Pink-cheeked storm troopers chatted and whistled. Chopped-up furniture flew through the window. The troopers fielded the pieces sportively, piled them into heaps. One hummed something from "The Merry Widow."

"Franz! Run somewhere!" my mother said to my father.

By that time we'd gone to the window facing the street. At the house entrance two storm troopers lit cigarettes for each other. Their comrades were smashing the synagogue on the floor below us, tossing out a debris* of Torahs and pews.

"Oh, my God!" my mother said.

Something overwhelming wanted to melt down my eyes. I couldn't let it. All this might not be real as long as real tears did not touch my face. A crazy last-resort bargain with fate.

"All right," my father said. "Meanwhile we get dressed."

Meanwhile meant *until they come up here.* No other Jews lived in the building. It had no back door. But as long as I could keep my tears down, I could keep *them* down. While they were destroying down there, they would not come up here. As long as the shaking of the floor continued, the axe blows, the sledgehammer thuds, we might live.

I had gym for my first class. I laced on my sneakers. I knew I never would see school that morning. I didn't care that I knew. I only cared not to cry. I tried to pour my entire mind into the lacing of my sneakers.

We met in the living room. We saw each other dressed with a normality made grotesque* by the crashing of the perdition* downstairs. It stopped. The shaking and the thudding stopped. Silence. A different sound. Heavy, booted steps ascending. I relaced my sneakers.

My father had put on his hat.

"Everybody come close to me," he said. "My two sons, you put your hands on top of your heads."

We put our hands on top of our heads, as hats. My father put his arms around all our shoulders, my mother's, my brother's, mine.

"Shema Yisroel," my father said. "Repeat after me: Shema Yisroel Adonoy Elohenu Adonoy Echod. . . ." ["Hear, O Israel: the Lord our God, the Lord is One. . . ."]

The doorbell rang. Once. Ever since the Anschluss*, we'd rung our doorbell twice in succession to signal that this was a harmless ringing, not the dreaded one. Now the dreaded ring had come.

"Hansi, you go," my father said.

"No!" my mother said.

"Hansi is the only one they might not hurt on sight," my father said. "Hansi, go."

My brother, a tiny blond eight-year-old, an Aryan-looking doll, went.

A minute later he returned. Behind him towered some 10 storm troopers with heavy pickaxes. They were young and bright-faced with excitement. Ten bridegrooms on their wedding day. One had freckles. How could a freckle-faced man kill us? The freckles kept me from crying.

"House search," the leader said. "Don't move."

We all stood against the wall, except my father. He placed himself, hat still on, a foot in front of us.

They yanked out every drawer in every one of our chests and cupboards, and tossed each in the air. They let the cutlery jangle across the floor, the clothes scatter, and stepped over the mess to fling the next drawer. Their exuberance* was amazing. Amazing, that none of them raised an axe to split our skulls.

"We might be back," the leader said. On the way out he threw our mother-of-pearl ashtray over his shoulder, like confetti. We did not speak or move or breathe until we heard their boots against the pavement.

"I am going to the office," my father said. "Breitel might help."

Breitel, the Reich commissar in my father's costume-jewelry factory, was a "good" Nazi. Once he'd said we should come to him if there was trouble. My father left. My mother was crying, with relief, with terror; she cradled against herself my little stunned brother. I turned away from her. I swore I would do something other than cry.

I began to pick up clothes when the doorbell rang again. It was my father.

"I have two minutes."

"What?" my mother said. But she knew. His eyes had become glass.

"There was another crew waiting for me downstairs. They gave me two minutes."

Now I broke down. Now my father was the only one not crying. His eyes were blue glass, relentlessly dry. His kiss felt stubbly. He had not shaved this morning. After one more embrace with my mother he marched to the door, turned on his heel, called out.

"Fritz!"

I went to him, sobbing.

"Stop!"

I couldn't stop.

Harshly his hands came down on my shoulders.

"If I don't come back—avenge me!"

He was gone. The fury of his fingers stung. It burned into my skin a sense of continuity* against all odds. I stopped.

Four months later he rang our doorbell twice, skull shaven, skeletal, released from Dachau, somehow alive.

Forty years later, today, he is practicing the tango with my mother in Miami Beach. My little brother Hansi is chairman of the political science department at Queens College. I am a writer in America with an American family. We are atypically lucky. But to this day we all ring our American doorbells twice.†

Vocabulary

debris—fragments	*Anschluss*—when Germany took over Austria, in 1938
grotesque—bizarrely ugly	*exuberance*—enthusiasm
perdition—utter destruction	*continuity*—being connected

1. It is only during the past ten years or so that the Holocaust is being studied in some depth. Why do you think it has taken so long?
2. The author describes the scene above from his memory. Do you think that memory can be trusted for accuracy? Why or why not?
3. If the memory is not accurate about some things, does the selection have any value to the historian? Explain the value it may have.
4. Look up additional details on Crystal Night and see if other descriptions are seriously different from the one above. Report on your findings to the class.

†The *New York Times, November 10, 1978.* © 1978 by the New York Times Company. Reprinted by permission.

United States army equipment at Anzio, Italy

The Second World War: The War to Save Civilization

Sunday, December 7, 1941, was a warm December day, just right for taking a drive in the country. Many families were enjoying the beauty of the day and the music on the car radio when suddenly the music stopped. "We interrupt this program to bring you. . . ."

By 1941, these familiar words had interrupted many a radio news broadcast. Reports told of Hitler's invasion of neighboring European countries, of Mussolini's invasion of Ethiopia in 1936, of the Japanese bombing of the American gunboat *Panay* in 1937. Then, in September, 1939, came England's declaration of war against Germany.

The announcement of December 7 brought the war even closer to citizens of the United States. The news report told of the surprise Japanese bombing attack on the United States naval base at Pearl Harbor, in the Hawaiian Islands. Ninety-two United States naval vessels were anchored there. As a result of the attack, 5 of America's battleships and 13 other American ships were sunk or badly damaged; about 170 planes were destroyed; and many American lives were lost. The next day, December 8, President Franklin D. Roosevelt went before Congress. In a stirring speech he said that December 7, 1941 was a day that would "live in infamy." He asked the Congress for a declaration of war against Japan. Congress quickly granted the president's request.

AN UNEASY PEACE ENDS AND WORLD WAR II BEGINS

The Basic Causes of World War II

The period from the end of World War I to the start of World War II has often been called the "long armistice." This period of peace was only temporary. For twenty years, some people had expected another world war. They believed that causes similar to those that started World War I would start another war.

Beginning in 1934, Germany began to rearm. This was in violation of the Versailles Treaty. A year later, Japan began to rebuild its navy. This was in violation of the Washington Agreement of 1922 to limit the number of naval vessels. The alliance between Germany and Italy in 1936, known as the *Rome-Berlin Axis*, was an agreement in which Hitler and Mussolini agreed to help one another in their ambitions for power and conquest. In 1940, this alliance was joined by Japan. Thus, the *Rome-Berlin-Tokyo Axis* was formed. The Axis nations demanded more power and influence.

They looked upon themselves as a group of have-not nations. That is, they believed they did not have a fair share of the world's natural resources and that the democracies had too much. Hitler, especially, complained that Germany lacked *lebensraum* [lā'bəns room'], or living space, and needed to expand. The Axis maintained that too much soft living had made the democracies weak. The time had come for a new order in Europe and Asia.

Extreme nationalism played a part in bringing on World War II. Worship of the emperor in Japan and idolization of Hitler and Mussolini in Europe encouraged the birth of a dangerous form of patriotism. The Germans were told the falsehood that, as true *Nordics* (a division of the white race), they were better than other people and were meant to rule the world. The Japanese proclaimed Asia for the Asiatics and preached a crusade to drive out all non-Asiatics. Thinking of this kind fanned the flames of war and inspired violence and ultra-nationalism. Humanity and civilization were soon to become the victims of such thinking.

Closely tied to excessive nationalism as a cause of World War II was *imperialism,* or the desire to rule foreign lands. Germany wanted more land in Europe; Italy wanted colonies in Africa and in southeastern Europe; and Japan wanted to extend its influence throughout Asia, especially in China. The *Axis powers* (Germany, Italy, and Japan) tried to divide and rule the world and were nearly successful. While the Axis countries sought more colonies, the democracies were gradually being forced to give up some of theirs. This, too, contributed to instability. A climate was being created in which another world war could start.

Events That Led to World War II

Japan was a member of the League of Nations, but that did not stop Japan from making war on China. In Manchuria, in 1931, it set up the state of Manchukuo, with the boy-emperor, Pu-yi, as puppet ruler. With the vast resources of Manchuria, Japan built factories whose products fed the Japanese war machine. Pu-yi had to do Japan's bidding. China and the Chinese people were exploited for the benefit of their harsh Japanese conquerors.

The League of Nations took steps to stop the Japanese invasion of the Chinese mainland. The League of Nations sent the *Lytton Commission* to look into conditions in China. The commission reported that Japan was guilty of aggression. It had violated its pledge as a League member. The Lytton Commission condemned Japan's action and urged Japan to withdraw its troops from China. Japan refused to leave China. Instead, it quit the League in 1933. This proved that the League of Nations was not strong enough to stop a strong country bent on aggression.

Hitler saw that the League of Nations had not been able to stop Japan and knew that it would not stop Germany either. In October of 1933, Germany withdrew from the League. It began to violate the terms of the Treaty of Versailles. The Versailles Treaty said that Germany could not have a large army. Hitler startled the world by building a vast army. In 1936, he sent his troops into the Rhineland. This area between France and Germany was supposed to be a buffer (a neutral area which separates nations) between the two nations. The buffer was to reduce the tension and the possibility of war. The League tried to stop Hitler but was unable to do so. In 1938, Hitler sent his troops into Austria. The *anschluss,* as the annexation of Austria was called, was also a violation of the Versailles Treaty. In annexing Austria Hitler achieved one of his most important aims.

Italy felt that it too should grab what it could before it was too late. In 1935,

German troops occupy the Rhineland. This was in direct violation of the Versailles Treaty. Locate the Rhineland on the map on page 569.

Mussolini sent his new Italian army into Ethiopia, a backward but independent nation in Africa. Mussolini wanted Ethiopia to be an Italian colony. Mussolini's son, who flew with the Italian air force, reported what a "glorious thing" it was to drop bombs on helpless people. He enjoyed seeing their huts burn and the people scatter as they ran for shelter. The League of Nations proved unable to stop Mussolini's Ethiopian "adventure."

How the Failure to Stop the Dictators Led to War

The democracies watched all these events with horror. Leaders of the large nations thought that if they gave in a little to Germany's demands, perhaps Germany would be satisfied. But Hitler was never satisfied. It was his aim to occupy and rule Europe. This he nearly did. Part of the reason for his success was that the democracies were willing to give in and let Hitler do as he wanted.

This policy of giving in to a strong power in hopes of avoiding trouble is called *appeasement*. The democracies were not ready for war and hoped that they would not have to fight. They seemed willing to give up moral principles to avoid another war, even though they knew Germany's demands were not right and just. Appeasement seemed the right course to take because the 1930s were years of depression. The democracies did not want to burden their people with the costs of big armies or high taxes.

Among democratic leaders, the fear of rising communism complicated matters. Some diplomats in Europe and America hoped that, in time, the Nazi dictatorship and the Communist dictatorship would come to blows and bleed each other to death. You will see later that this was wishful thinking.

Hitler's system for taking over a country was well planned. A so-called *fifth column* was made up of specially trained citizens of a nation which Hitler wanted to conquer. Members of the fifth column were supporters of the Nazis. They would try to blow up important bridges and buildings. In public meetings, Nazi-trained speakers would tell the people what to think. They encouraged them to act in ways that would be good for Germany. In short, the fifth column was used to soften the enemy before the German troops moved in. Such people often posed as tourists. With their cameras they took innocent-looking pictures of the country and its military defenses. The Nazis were able to use these photos when they invaded the country.

Not long after occupying the Rhineland and taking over Austria, Hitler announced that he had only "one last demand" to make. He wanted the Sudetenland of Czechoslovakia. This was an area bordering Germany, where many Czechs of German descent lived. Hitler sent Nazis into the Sudetenland to act as spies and to tell people to join Germany.

Czechoslovakia mobilized (prepared) for war, but alone it was no match for Germany. Earlier, in 1935, England, France, and the Soviet Union had agreed by treaty to help Czechoslovakia. Czechoslovakia looked to England and France for help, but received no support. Only the USSR was willing to help, but it was not invited to the conference in Munich in 1938. Prime Minister Neville Chamberlain of England, Premier Édouard Daladier [dä lä dyā'] of France, and Mussolini of Italy met with Hitler in the German city of Munich. There, the democracies gave in to Hitler's demands and allowed Germany to annex the Sudetenland. Again the democracies had given in. Munich came to mean appeasement and humiliation. Chamberlain, not knowing how wrong he was, returned to England proud that he had brought his people "peace in our time."

Europe and North Africa, 1939

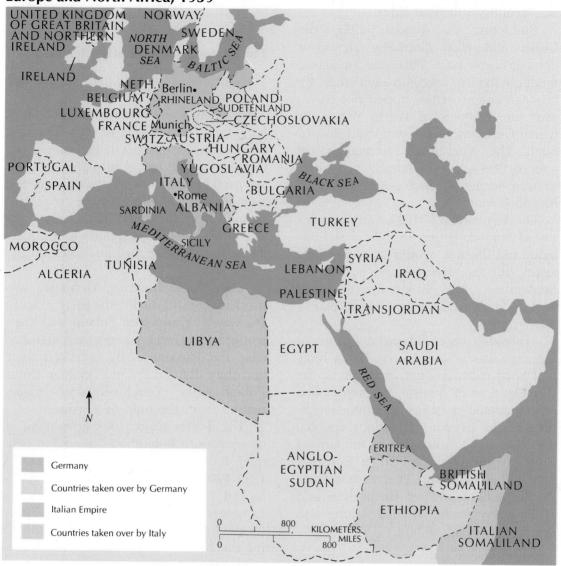

By 1939, Germany and Italy had extended their power over many countries and areas.
- Which country, Germany or Italy, had taken over the following: Albania, Czechoslovakia, Ethiopia, Austria?
- Locate the country in which each of these cities is found: Munich, Berlin, Rome.

In 1938, the Sudetenland became part of Germany. A year later, Hitler broke his promise, took nearly all the rest of Czechoslovakia, and in effect removed that country from the map.

The dictators were still not satisfied. They had promised to demand no more, but dictators' promises are made to be broken. In April, 1939, Italy grabbed Albania. The countries of England and France were now really worried and looked to the Soviet Union as a friend.

But the Soviet dictator, Joseph Stalin, was dealing with both sides.

Suddenly, in August, 1939, the USSR and Nazi Germany signed a *nonaggression pact*. This was an agreement not to go to war with each other. By this agreement, Hitler hoped not to repeat the mistakes of World War I, in which Germany had a two-front war to fight. The Nazi-Soviet nonaggression pact of 1939 assured Germany of a quiet eastern border. It encouraged Hitler to invade Poland.

On September 1, 1939, Germany invaded Poland. Hitler thought that England and France would appease him again, but this time he was wrong. On September 3, 1939, England and France declared war on Germany. World War II had begun.

Hitler felt he could win a European war and was willing to try. If his bluff had been called sooner, perhaps in the Rhineland or in Austria, he might have been defeated more easily. But the weakness of the League of Nations encouraged him. The reluctance of the United States to become involved in Europe's affairs helped him. The democracies were unwilling to arm themselves and Hitler grew strong. It took a long and costly war to defeat him.

Check in Here

1. List three underlying causes of World War II.

2. How did each of the following lead to World War II: (**a**) Japanese aggression in China; (**b**) Italy's aggression in Ethiopia; (**c**) Germany's aggression in Austria?

3. Define each of the following terms: (**a**) appeasement; (**b**) fifth column; (**c**) buffer; (**d**) *anschluss*.

4. Why was Chamberlain wrong when he declared that he had achieved "peace in our time?"

THE AXIS POWERS SCORE EARLY VICTORIES AS THE WAR WIDENS

The Dictators Won Early Victories

The Germans had been getting ready for this war for a long time. They had developed a new method of fighting known as *blitzkrieg*, [blits'krēg'], or lightning war. It was a sudden, swift, overpowering attack that made use of airplanes in ways not used before. Cities were bombed, and soldiers and civilians were machine-gunned from the air. It made use of war machines and armored tanks in numbers never used before and put soldiers into battle quickly.

Using the blitzkrieg, Germany was most successful during the early years of the war. It conquered Poland with little trouble. The German army then marched east, the Russian army marched west, and they divided Poland between them. Poland, like Czechoslovakia, disappeared from the map of Europe.

The Soviet Union took advantage of its success in Poland and moved to conquer Estonia, Latvia, and Lithuania in 1939–1940. When the Soviet Union attacked Finland, it was expelled from the League of Nations. Although the Finns fought back bravely, they were no match for the forces of the Soviet Union. Finland negotiated a peace settlement and gave up a number of vital seaports and airfields.

Hitler's armies advanced into Denmark, Norway, the Netherlands, Belgium, and Luxembourg. By 1940, all these nations had fallen under the Nazi blitzkrieg. Germany was now ready to apply lightning warfare to France.

Why France Fell to the Nazis

For many years (1930–1934), France had developed a defense line, the *Maginot* [mazh'ə nō'] *Line*, along her eastern border. It was the pride of the French army. The line gave the French people a false sense of security because they were sure that it could never be crossed. All at once, the Nazi armies were on the move. They did not cross the Maginot Line. They went around the northern end instead. The poorly prepared French saw their first line of defense crumble. Then Paris was taken.

On June 10, 1940, Italy stabbed France in the back. It declared war on France and England and invaded southern France. Hitler was extremely elated when, on June 22, 1940, France signed an armistice at Compiègne. It was signed in the same railway car and in the same place where Germany had been forced to surrender to France in 1918, at the end of World War I.

According to the terms of the agreement ending the war with France, most of France was to be occupied by Nazi forces. The resources and factories of France were to be placed at the disposal of Germany. A government that agreed to collaborate (work with) with the Nazis was set up under French Marshall Henri Pétain [pā tan′]. Vichy [vish′ē] became the new capital of the totalitarian government, and France became a puppet of Germany.

A few brave French leaders flew to England where they set up a *Free French* government under General Charles de Gaulle [də gôl′]. This government called for French patriots to join them. It raised an underground army which later contributed to the German defeat. In France, the Free French waged *underground resistance* (secret action) against the Germans in their homeland.

How the Battle of Britain Was Fought

After the French were defeated, England stood alone against Germany. Poorly

Londoners prepare to spend the night in a bomb shelter. Brave cheerfulness was characteristic of the English during the war.

armed, the English people tried to prepare for the worst, and the worst was not long in coming. In the Battle of Britain, England was nearly brought to its knees. England was bombed without pity by the infamous Nazi air force, the *Luftwaffe*. English families spent hours at a time in hurriedly-built air raid shelters. British pilots in Spitfires (fighter planes) successfully answered the German challenge and gave England the time it needed to get ready to fight.

Hitler was not able to defeat Great Britain. The English people courageously faced the worst that Hitler could offer. They were greatly inspired by their prime minister, Winston Churchill. The *British Royal Air Force* (*RAF*) fought back valiantly. It destroyed many of Hitler's bombers and so large a portion of his invasion fleet that he was unable to carry out his plan to invade the nation of Great Britain.

Why Hitler Went to War Against Russia

A dictator needs victories to stay in power. Hitler had not defeated Great Britain, and it now appeared that the war would be a longer one than he had expected. To make matters worse, a number of Germany's most famous battleships had been destroyed. The sinking of the battleship *Bismarck* was the greatest German naval disaster of the war.

Finding that the war was growing longer, Hitler felt that he would need Soviet resources if the British blockade of Germany proved successful. He would need Soviet oil for his war machinery and Soviet wheat for his troops. With these thoughts in mind, Hitler turned on his former ally, the Soviet Union, in hopes of winning a quick victory.

On June 22, 1941, using his well-known blitzkrieg methods, Hitler invaded the USSR. This attack proved to be a costly mistake. Hitler failed to achieve a quick victory. Instead, he opened his nation to the two-front war he had tried to avoid. Joseph Stalin, the Soviet dictator, was by no means ready to fight the Germans. The Soviet armies fell back in a retreat that drew the Germans farther into the Soviet Union. This advance proved to be a net from which Germany could not emerge victorious.

A common enemy made the Soviet Union and England friends. Soon they were joined by many more countries in an effort to bring about the downfall of the German Reich.

How the Nazis Exterminated Six Million Jews

It had long been Hitler's plan to destroy the Jews of Europe. During World War II, the Nazis set up *concentration camps* in Germany and in the countries Germany conquered. Freight cars of Jews were sent to these concentration camps. In some of the camps Jews were forced into slave labor for the large German corporations that helped supply Germany

A German army infantry column in Russia. Why did Germany invade the USSR?

Dachau, a German concentration camp and extermination center.

with what it needed for the war. The slave laborers worked long hours, with little food or medical attention, until they died. Then they were promptly replaced by new freightloads of slave laborers brought from all over Europe.

The program to destroy the Jews took many forms. Special Nazi troops were sent into conquered territory. They rounded up all the Jews, had them dig mass graves, then machine gunned them into the pits. Trucks equipped with poison gas were also used to kill the victims. Most horrible of all, many of the concentration camps were turned into huge extermination camps. There, Jewish men, women, children, and infants were herded into vast rooms and gassed to death. Their bodies were burned in giant ovens called crematoria. Millions of people were destroyed in this way. Six million Jews died in the Holocaust.

How the United States Entered World War II

In the beginning, the United States tried to stay out of World War II. Because it did not want war, laws were passed by the Congress to keep the United States neutral. American businesses were not allowed to sell goods to the fighting nations, and American travelers were not allowed to visit those countries.

Soon the United States began to realize that a victory for Hitler would not be in its best interests. American industry began to supply war materials to the nations fighting Germany. Laws that made it easier for England and France to get the war materials they needed were passed by Congress. One of these laws was the *cash-and-carry* law, which said that the United States would sell war materials to those nations that would pay cash and carry the goods away in their own ships. England, for a time, was able to take advantage of this cash-and-carry law. However, war materials are expensive, and in time England found that it did not have enough cash.

The United States passed another law which made it possible for the country to lend or lease war materials to England and its allies. Under this *lend-lease* arrangement, those nations fighting against Germany could pay back the United States after the war. The cash-and-carry law and the lend-lease law helped England carry on when it was in great need of food and supplies.

The people of the United States could see their nation getting involved in war. As much as the nation dreaded the prospect of war, it began to get ready. The first peacetime draft of soldiers was put into effect, and young men from all parts of the country began to report to army camps.

In August, 1941, Winston Churchill, the British prime minister, and Franklin D. Roosevelt, the American president, held an historic meeting on a cruiser in the North Atlantic, near Newfoundland. Because they knew that soon they would be fighting as allies, they drew up the *Atlantic Charter*. This outlined a number of postwar peace aims. It dealt with problems on a worldwide scale. It said that neither England nor the United States wanted any more land. It gave assurance that the United States and England believed that people the world over should be able to choose the kinds of government they wished. It favored an improvement in living conditions, a reduction in arms and armies, and the restoration of self-government to all conquered nations. The Atlantic Charter declared that freedom from fear and from want should be guaranteed to all people.

The fighting went on in Europe, but the United States was drawn into World War II by events in the Far East. While Hitler was grabbing more and more land in Europe, Japan was doing the same in Asia. It grabbed French Indochina and was getting ready to grab the rich islands of the Dutch East Indies. Since 1898 America had followed the Open Door policy. (See p. 479.) According to that policy, all nations had the right to trade equally in China and in the Far East. Americans were not ready to let Japan close the open door of the Far East. Moreover, America needed the tin and rubber of the East Indies and did not want these rich lands to fall into Japanese hands.

America urged Japan to stop its expansion and aggression in the Far East. Japan sent a special ambassador to the United States to confer on these problems. He met with the American secretary of state, Cordell Hull, and President Roosevelt.

While these talks were going on, the Japanese attacked the United States naval base at Pearl Harbor on December 7, 1941. On the following day, the United States declared war on Japan. On December 11, Germany and Italy and their puppet countries declared war on the United States, and the United States declared war on them the same day.

Check in Here

1. Why was Hitler's Germany victorious during the early days of World War II?

2. Distinguish between the roles of Pétain and de Gaulle following the fall of France.

3. Why was Hitler's invasion of the Soviet Union a mistake?

4. How did the United States try to stay out of World War II?

5. What is the significance of the Atlantic Charter?

THE ALLIES TRIUMPH AND BRING THE WAR TO AN END

How World War II Was Fought

World War II was global in preparation, but it was fought in four main areas, or *theaters of war*. In Europe, North Africa, Asia, and the Islands of the Pacific, nations were fighting or getting ready to fight. The United States and its friends soon called themselves the *Allies* and, sometimes, the United Nations. They were supported by many of the Latin American countries. These countries agreed with the ideas of the Atlantic Charter and declared that they would cut off relations with the Axis nations.

The Far Eastern theater was opened by Japanese aggression on United States and British possessions. The surprise attack by the Japanese on Pearl Harbor caused a serious loss for the United States. This loss included many large naval ships, over a hundred aircraft, and about 300 casualties. Within a few days, Guam and Wake Island were captured by Japan, and landings were made on the Phillippine Islands. The Japanese took the British port at Hong Kong and invaded British Malaya. In the early

- Which of the following fell under Japanese control either before or during World War II: Australia, Dutch East Indies, Philippine Islands?
- About how far in kilometers (or miles) is the distance between Tokyo and Pearl Harbor?
- Judging from the pattern of Allied advances, can you tell what the objective of the Allies was in winning the war in the Pacific?

The Pacific and Asia During World War II

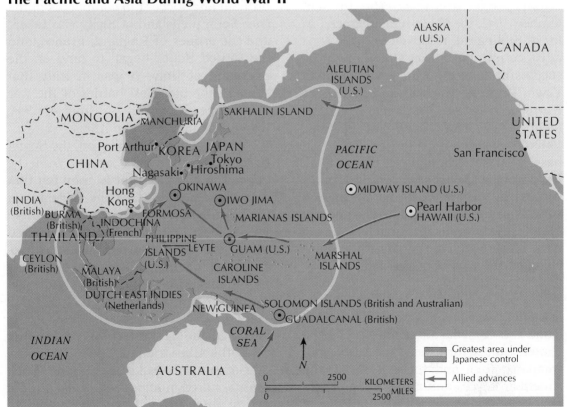

In the fighting in North Africa, the Allies used camouflage nets to conceal themselves from the enemy. This is from a 1942 British poster.

months of 1942, the Philippines and the Dutch East Indies fell to the Japanese.

The early years of the war were discouraging for the Allies. Although the Soviets fought well in Europe, by September, 1942, the Nazis had advanced as far as Stalingrad. It looked as if the Nazi advance into the Soviet Union might be successful. In North Africa, Nazi General Erwin Rommel [rom'əl] and his *Afrika Korps* [af'ri kə kôrz'] had reached El Alamein [el ä'lä mān'] in Egypt in May, 1942. They threatened the British naval base at Alexandria and the Suez Canal. For a time, it almost seemed that Japan's success in the Far East and Germany's success in Europe, North Africa, and the Middle East would bring victory to the Axis. Fortunately, the efforts of the Allies changed the course of the war.

How World War II Was Won

With lend-lease the United States became the "arsenal of democracy." The United States furnished the Allies with weapons, fuel, and food. By 1942, the American forces and arms began to win victories. On April 18, 1942, Colonel James Doolittle made a surprise air attack on Tokyo from a secret starting place which Roosevelt would describe only as "Shangri-la." Actually, in this daring raid Doolittle and his fliers took off from the aircraft carrier *Hornet*. They bombed Tokyo, and then landed in China because lack of fuel prevented them from returning to the aircraft carrier. One of the more crucial victories was in the Battle of the Coral Sea, where the threat of a Japanese invasion of Australia was halted. Another major naval defeat for the Japanese was at Midway Island. Three months later the United States Marines captured Japanese airfields on Guadalcanal [gwä'dəl kə nal'].

In Europe, the Soviet armies, aided by a bitter cold winter, made a heroic stand at Stalingrad and stopped the Nazi advance. In North Africa, the British General Bernard Montgomery stopped the Nazi advance and drove the Germans from the continent in one of the most brilliant and successful campaigns of the war. Soon the island of Sicily was taken, and the armies of England, France, and the United States began to land on the mainland of Italy. It was in Italy that some of the bloodiest battles of the war took place. However, on June 4, 1944, Rome was taken by the Allies.

While all this was going on, the Soviet Union insisted that a *second front* be opened in Europe. That is, they felt that the Allies should attack the Germans in the west, while the Soviets fought them in the east. England and the United States promised that they would do so. It took a long time, however, to get ready. In the meantime, a series of round-the-clock bombings of German factories and cities took place. Through these air attacks, including thousands of bomber raids, the Allies tried to reduce the ability of Germany to make war goods. Such raids resulted in high death tolls, but did not do much to halt Germany's ability to

Europe During World War II

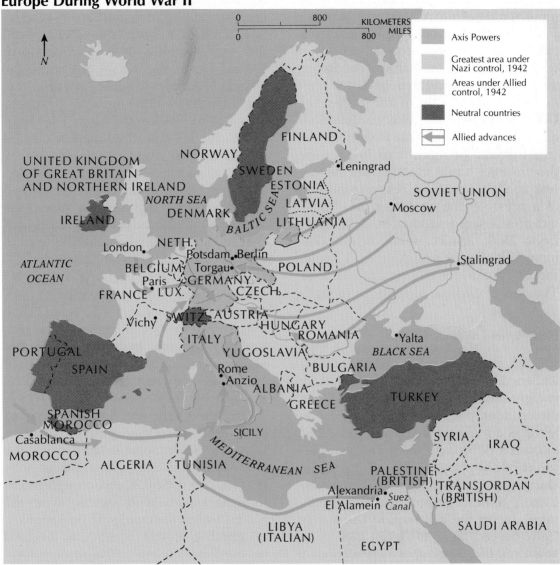

- Locate at least five countries that were under Nazi control by 1942.
- Where was the French capital located during Nazi occupation?
- How close, approximately, had Germany advanced toward Moscow by 1942?

manufacture weapons. The raids made the German people realize how terrible war could be and what Der Führer, Hitler, had done to Germany as well as the world.

After Germany had been thoroughly bombed, England and the United States felt ready to invade what Hitler had called the European Fortress. On June 6, 1944, British and American troops, under the command of General Dwight D. Eisenhower, invaded Normandy, France. There, the Allies began the offensive that took them through France to Germany and victory. During the remaining months of 1944, the Allies fought through France to the German border. The Germans made a last counter-offensive, which brought on the Battle of the Bulge, in Belgium, in December 1944.

During the Battle of the Bulge, the Germans fought well and hard and almost defeated American troops. At the frightful cost of more than 76,000 men, the costliest battle in American history was finally won. The Allies were assured of success on the western front. Soviet victories assured success on the eastern front. Both armies drove across Germany. The Soviet and American armies met at Torgau [tôr gō'] on April 25, 1945. The end of Nazi Germany was in sight.

How World War II Ended

In 1945, the war ended. Three wartime leaders died that same year. With victory in sight, President Franklin D. Roosevelt died suddenly on April 12, 1945. He was listed as a war victim. It was said he died of overwork brought on by the heavy responsibilities he had. Vice President Harry Truman became president of the United States. Benito Mussolini, captured during the last days of the war in Italy, begged his anti-Fascist captors to spare his life. They shot him without a formal trial in April, 1945. They hung his body up by its heels and, for days, his dead body was kicked and battered by an angry people. Hidden in an underground bunker (bombproof shelter), Hitler passed his last days. The Germany that he boasted would last for a thousand years was near collapse. On April 30, 1945, Hitler killed himself as the Soviet army was entering Berlin. On the day of Hitler's death, the fighting ended in Italy. On May 8, 1945, victory in Europe was proclaimed by President Truman. The day is known as *V-E Day*.

The Japanese were near defeat when the war ended in Europe. General Douglas MacArthur, who had sworn that he would return and retake the Philippines, did so in October, 1944. Moving north toward Japan, the marines captured the island of Okinawa in June, 1945, after several months of bitter fighting. The next step was to land on the home islands of Japan. By this time, the Japanese wanted to end the war. But the only terms they could get were unconditional surrender.

During the war, the United States had developed a terrible weapon. It was the atomic bomb. President Truman decided that the atomic bomb should be used to end the war quickly and decisively.

The first atomic bomb was dropped on Hiroshima, Japan on August 6, 1945. It was many, many times the force of the most powerful bomb known until that time. The atomic bomb destroyed life and property on a vast scale. More than 160,000 people were killed or injured by this one bomb.

Until this time, the Soviet Union had done little more than promise to enter the war against Japan. It seemed as if the war would now end without Soviet help, despite the USSR's earlier agreement to fight Japan. With victory near, the Soviet Union declared war on Japan.

Another atomic bomb was dropped on the Japanese city of Nagasaki on August 9. The next day the Japanese offered to surrender. Victory over Japan was declared on August 14, 1945. On September 2, 1945, aboard the U.S.S. *Missouri*, the Japanese signed the agreement ending the war. Japan was occupied by American troops, and World War II was over.

How the Allies
Got Ready for Peace

In World War I, little effort was made to plan for the postwar world. During the earliest and darkest days of World War

The devastation of Hiroshima shortly after the explosion of the first atomic bomb dropped on Japan. Why did President Truman decide to use this terrible weapon?

II, the leaders of the Allies met to plan not only how they might win the war but also how they might win the peace.

The meeting which produced the Atlantic Charter was followed by other meetings and conferences among the leaders of the allied nations. One of the big problems in the conferences was the mutual distrust between the Soviet Union and the other Allies. Only the war against a common enemy was able to bring together the Soviet Union and the democracies in a common cause.

In 1943, Roosevelt let the world know that unconditional surrender was the only basis upon which fighting would stop. In the same year, Roosevelt and Churchill met with Chiang Kai-shek of China and agreed that Japan's conquests would be taken from her.

In November, 1943, the leaders of the *Big Three*—Roosevelt, Churchill, and Stalin—met at Teheran, Iran, where Stalin asked that a second front be opened. The Big Three promised to "work together in war and in the peace that will follow." In Moscow, in 1943, the foreign ministers of the Big Three (the Soviet Union, Great Britain, and the United States) agreed to work together until the war had been won. They agreed that Austria should regain independence. The Germans who were guilty of starting the war and killing innocent people should be tried in a special court for their crimes. The Big Three agreed that they would build an organization which would take the place of the League of Nations. In later conferences, the leaders of the Allies made plans for conducting the war.

In the later years of the war, the conferences dealt with terms of the peace settlement. In 1944, the American, Soviet, Chinese, and British officials met near Washington, D.C., and drew up suggestions for the form of the *United Nations*. In 1945, at the *Yalta Conference*, Great Britain, the United States, and the Soviet Union agreed to invite all those governments that had fought on their side to meet at San Francisco. There they would form the United Nations. This big meeting was held on April 25, 1945, shortly after the death of President Roosevelt.

579

Winston Churchill
(1874–1965)

"The naughtiest boy in the class," they used to call him. Although not quite at the bottom of the class, young Winston Spencer Churchill found school days and studies difficult. He did poorly in Latin and math but brilliantly in English literature. His mastery of the English language was to prove decisive in his political career. It would inspire much of the English-speaking world.

When he was old enough, Churchill took the examinations for Sandhurst, the English military college. After failing three times, he was finally admitted. Success seemed to smile upon him. He enjoyed the military life and became an excellent horseman. He eventually graduated near the top of his class.

This was but the beginning of Churchill's military career. Where the fighting raged most widely, there Winston Churchill could be found. In India, where he took part in a battle against the ferocious Mamuds, Churchill remained behind to help a wounded comrade, who had lost an eye to an enemy dagger. Churchill and his wounded friend found themselves surrounded on every side and shot at from behind every tree. Churchill tried to shoot his way out. His pistol failed. He grabbed a revolver, fired numerous salvos in rapid succession, and was able to clear a path to safety.

In his youth, Winston was an excellent athlete as well as soldier. While stationed at Hyderabad, India, his polo team was challenged by the Golcondas, the polo champions of India. Everyone was sure that Churchill's Hussars would lose, everyone, that is, but Churchill. In the game that followed Winston led his team to victory by a score of 9 to 3. When it was all over, Churchill nearly fell from his horse. He had led his team to victory despite a broken shoulder.

In 1900, Winston Churchill was elected to Parliament for the first time. His political career had its ups and downs. It never shone more brilliantly, however, than when he led his nation to victory in World War II as his country's courageous prime minister. His famous "V," made with his middle finger and index finger, was his sign for victory in war. The "V" sign became popularized. It is used today by many people to indicate their desire for peace. After the war, Churchill worked to build a strong peace. He suggested a Council of Europe and Anglo-American postwar cooperation.

In 1900, Churchill was on a speaking tour of the United States. He was introduced to the audience by Mark Twain as follows, "Ladies and gentlemen. I give you the son of an American mother and an English father—the perfect man!"*

*Henry Thomas and Dana Lee Thomas, *Great Modern Lives* (Garden City, N.Y.: Hanover House, 1956), p. 366.

It was at the Yalta Conference, also, that the Big Three agreed to divide Germany into four *zones,* or parts, for military occupation. One part was to be occupied by each of the Big Three and one part by France. The city of Berlin, in the Soviet part of Germany, was also divided into four zones. German factories were to be turned over to the Allies. The Soviet Union got most of these because of heavy Russian losses during the Nazi invasion. War criminals were to be punished. The German puppet states were to be made independent. In free elections, they were to decide upon the kind of government they wanted. Special provision was made for Poland; it was given German land on the west in exchange for Polish land on the east taken by Russia. At Yalta, Russia promised to fight Japan. This was in exchange for the southern part of the island of Sakhalin and a lease on Port Arthur.

There are many people who felt that American leaders had given in too much to Russian demands at the Yalta Conference. At the time of the conference, however, the Americans did not know that Japan could be defeated without an invasion of the islands. Nor did they know that the atomic bomb would be ready in time to make victory possible. Above all, they did not know that the Soviet Union would not honor its agreements.

In July, 1945, the *Potsdam Conference* was held. Harry Truman, who succeeded Roosevelt, and Clement Atlee, who suc-ceeded Churchill, met with Stalin. They agreed on the peace settlement with Germany. They drew up plans for Japan's surrender and occupation, although Russia was not yet at war with Japan.

At Potsdam, Truman hinted to Stalin that America had an atomic bomb. States one author, "Very few turning points of history can be specified precisely . . . when Rome began to decline . . . when the Renaissance began . . . [but] here is one turning point that can be dated with extraordinary precision [accuracy]: the twentieth-century nuclear arms race began at Cecilienhof Palace [site of the conference] at 7:30 p.m., on July 24, 1945,"* when Stalin took Truman's hint.

Check in Here

1. Why was the United States described as the arsenal of democracy?

2. Why was Stalin eager for the Allies to open a second front?

3. What were the similarities and differences between the Atlantic Charter and Woodrow Wilson's Fourteen Points?

4. Explain the significance of each of the following conferences in preparing for peace: (**a**) Casablanca; (**b**) Teheran; (**c**) Yalta; (**d**) Potsdam.

5. Why does the text say that the twentieth-century nuclear arms race began exactly at 7:30 p.m. on July 24, 1945?

*Charles L. Mee, Jr., *Meeting at Potsdam* (New York: M. Evans and Company, 1975), pp. 222–3.

THE PEACE-KEEPING MACHINERY OF THE UNITED NATIONS IS ESTABLISHED

How the United Nations Is Organized

During World War II, there was high hope that a new organization of nations could be created that would be strong enough to prevent war. The United Nations was the result of plans to form such an organization. Just as they had joined in a common effort to win the war, the allied nations met in April, 1945, and worked out a plan called the Charter of the United Nations. In June, 1945, fifty nations signed the charter to preserve peace.

The preamble to the UN Charter contains the aims and purposes of the organization. It states in part:

We the people of the United Nations determined

TO SAVE succeeding generations from the scourge of war, . . .

TO REAFFIRM FAITH in fundamental human rights,

TO ESTABLISH conditions under which justice and respect for the obligations arising from . . . international law can be maintained, . . .

TO PROMOTE social progress . . . and for these ends

TO PRACTICE tolerance. . .

TO UNITE our strength to maintain international peace. . .

TO ENSURE . . . that armed force shall not be used, save in the common interest. . .

TO EMPLOY international machinery for the promotion of economic and social advancement of peoples,

have resolved to combine our efforts to accomplish these aims.

The Twentieth Century

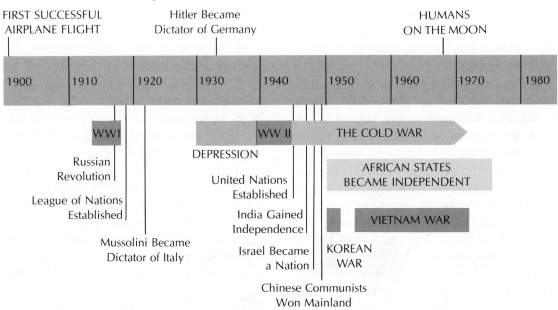

FIRST SUCCESSFUL AIRPLANE FLIGHT

Hitler Became Dictator of Germany

HUMANS ON THE MOON

1900 1910 1920 1930 1940 1950 1960 1970 1980

WWI

DEPRESSION

WW II

THE COLD WAR

Russian Revolution

League of Nations Established

United Nations Established

AFRICAN STATES BECAME INDEPENDENT

India Gained Independence

VIETNAM WAR

Mussolini Became Dictator of Italy

Israel Became a Nation

KOREAN WAR

Chinese Communists Won Mainland

Structure of the United Nations

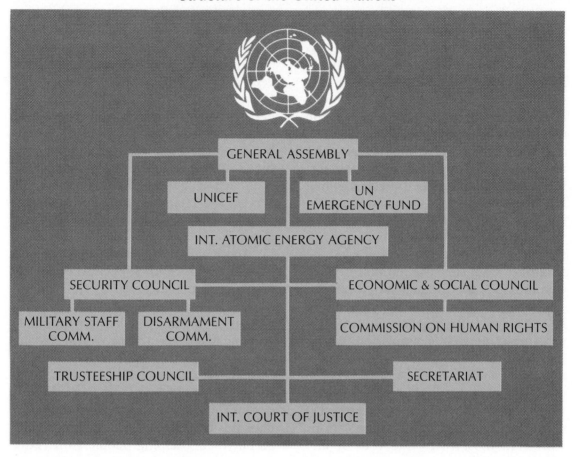

GENERAL ASSEMBLY

UNICEF

UN EMERGENCY FUND

INT. ATOMIC ENERGY AGENCY

SECURITY COUNCIL

ECONOMIC & SOCIAL COUNCIL

MILITARY STAFF COMM.

DISARMAMENT COMM.

COMMISSION ON HUMAN RIGHTS

TRUSTEESHIP COUNCIL

SECRETARIAT

INT. COURT OF JUSTICE

To carry out its plans and reach its goals, the United Nations set up various bodies and organizations, each with specific jobs. The United Nations has six main parts: the *General Assembly*, the *Security Council*, the *Economic and Social Council*, the *Trusteeship Council*, the *Secretariat*, and the *International Court of Justice*.

In the General Assembly, each member nation has one vote. The General Assembly meets once a year and can be called into a special meeting if this is necessary. It is in the General Assembly where problems of the world may be brought into the open. Here, in the town meeting of the world, member nations can freely discuss world problems in hopes of finding solutions. The General Assembly cannot pass laws, but it can make decisions about what action the nations should take.

Upon the recommendation of the Security Council, the General Assembly chooses the secretary-general of the United Nations. It decides on the admission of new members and chooses the non-permanent members of the Security Council. A two-thirds vote is needed to make a decision on important matters. One such matter is the decision to send troops to troubled areas.

The Security Council has fifteen member nations. There are five permanent members—the United States, the Soviet Union, France, Great Britain, and the People's Republic of China. In addition to the five permanent members, the

Security Council is made up of ten other member nations. These are elected every two years by the General Assembly.

The Council meets regularly. It is always in a position to take up world problems as they arise, because its members can be called into meeting at a moment's notice. The Security Council has the main job of keeping the peace. It looks into the problems that may cause wars and urges nations to talk over their differences and settle them. The Council has the authority to use armed forces to keep a member nation from being attacked. There is a Military Staff Committee which works at the direction of the Security Council. The Military Staff Committee of the United Nations has the job of directing troops that are put under its control in an emergency. There is also an Atomic Energy Commission whose job it is to develop international control of atomic energy.

The voting method of the Security Council should be clearly understood if one is to know how the United Nations works. In most cases, the vote of any nine of the fifteen members is all that is needed for a decision to be made. However, on important questions, every one of the permanent members must agree. If any permanent member votes "No," no decision can be reached and no action can be taken by the Security Council. This is the well-known veto power which belongs to all of the permanent members of the council.

The UN was able to send troops to Korea because the representative of the Soviet Union had walked out of the meeting. If he had been there, his "No" would have been enough to stop UN action. (See p. 682.) Russia's use of its veto power makes it difficult for the United Nations to have all the power it needs to stop wars. Although the veto may be considered a weakness of the United Nations, both the Soviet Union and the United States wanted this veto power included in the UN Charter. They felt it was important.

Sometimes a matter which has been vetoed by one member of the Security Council can be turned over to the General Assembly in which there is no veto. By a two-thirds vote, the General Assembly can urge members to take the step that was vetoed in the Security Council. This action by the General Assembly serves as a check on the veto power of the permanent nations of the Security Council.

Another body in the United Nations, the Economic and Social Council, has fifty-four nations elected by the General Assembly for three-year terms. Since hunger, sickness, poor living conditions, and low wages are among the underlying causes of war, this branch of the United Nations studies these problems. The United Nations tries to eliminate the reasons for which wars have been fought. It does this by studying ways of improving employment, helping people gain better employment, helping people gain better health, and raising wages. The Commission on Human Rights is one of the most significant bodies of the Economic and Social Council. It wrote the Universal Declaration of Human Rights which, states that human beings the world over are entitled to certain rights, including the right to choose their own government and to enjoy good living standards.

The Trusteeship Council of the UN looks after the interests of those lands placed under its trusteeship system. These colonies, taken from defeated nations, were given to certain UN members to hold in trust until the colony could rule itself. The only trust territory left is that of the trust territory of the Pacific Islands, administered by the United States.

The United Nations in New York City symbolizes hope for world peace.

The Secretariat is the organization that does the necessary day-to-day recording, filing, and corresponding. Papers have to be typed; information must be filed; languages must be translated; printed matter must be distributed. An international civil service staff is responsible for the everyday work of the organization of the United Nations. The Secretariat is headed by a *secretary-general,* who is chosen by the General Assembly for five years. The first secretary-general was Trygve Lie of Norway. He was followed in 1953 by Dag Hammarskjold of Sweden, who was killed in a plane crash in 1961. U Thant of Burma replaced him. In 1971, Kurt Waldheim of Austria became secretary-general. A Peruvian, Javier Pérez de Cuellar replaced him in 1981.

The secretary-general is a highly qualified diplomat. This person may have much influence on world affairs through the authority given the office by the UN Charter. The secretary-general spends much time traveling from one trouble spot to another, hoping to get the nations of the world to solve their problems without using force. The secretary-general is really a citizen of the world. He or she cannot be a citizen of any of the permanent nations in the Security Council. The secretary-general lives in an apartment on the grounds of the United Nations.

The United Nations' territory in New York City belongs to no country. It has special police officers and workers who come from all parts of the world and who, like the secretary-general, are citizens of the world. For these people, the interests of the United Nations are supposed to come before the interests of any country.

Another body of the UN, the International Court of Justice, has fifteen judges. The United Nations meets in the United Nations buildings in New York. The International Court of Justice meets at The Hague in the Netherlands. The judges are chosen by the General Assembly and Security Council for a term of nine years. No nation can have more than one judge at a time on the bench of the court.

The International Court of Justice tries to settle disagreements among nations on the basis of international law. It is possible for a nation to be a member of the Court without being a member of the United Nations. Furthermore, all nations who signed the Court Statute are subject to decisions of the Court. The Court also gives opinions on cases put before it by organizations of the UN.

There are a number of points which should be kept in mind about the United Nations. It is not a government or a confederation of nations. Within the limits of the constitution the government of the United States may tell the fifty states what to do. The United Nations has no power to tell its members what to do. Each nation retains the right to do as it wishes because the government of each nation is completely independent. No nation can be ordered about by the United Nations. The idea is that member nations are interested in world peace and progress. They have, therefore, volunteered to support the plans of the UN Charter.

The United Nations was founded in 1945. Since that time it has gained much experience by facing many problems.

How successful has the United Nations been? It is not easy to keep score. Much of the work of the United Nations deals with problems of improving living conditions, education, and health. These jobs do not often make headlines. In the long run, however, they are most important because they try to solve the underlying causes of war. As you study the postwar world in the next unit, you will be able to judge for yourself how successful the UN has been.

Check in Here

1. What are the aims and purposes of the United Nations?

2. Name the major agencies of the United Nations.

3. Why is the secretary-general of the United Nations described as a citizen of the world?

4. Explain the differences between the General Assembly and the Security Council.

5. Explain how the veto power in the Security Council works.

REVIEWING THE BASICS

In the Far East, Japan's aggression on Manchuria went unchecked by the League of Nations. This contributed to Hitler's aggression on the Rhineland and his *anschluss* (annexation) of Austria. The Allies, thinking that perhaps the terms of the Versailles Treaty had been too harsh, tried to appease Hitler. This was especially true at Munich when the Allies gave in to Hitler's invasion of the Sudetenland of Czechoslovakia. However, when Germany invaded Poland, the end of appeasement was at hand; and World War II began.

Hitler, using *blitzkrieg* tactics, invaded Poland, which was divided up with the Soviet Union. The Soviet Union also moved to conquer Latvia, Estonia, and Lithuania. The Soviet Union defeated Finland, while Hitler's armies advanced into and defeated Denmark, Norway, Belgium, and Luxembourg. Hitler's armies invaded France, which fell to Hitler in June 1940. A new, Nazi government was set up at Vichy, France. Charles de Gaulle escaped to England where he organized the resistance fighters. England, however, now stood alone. Its air force was successful in turning back the worst air raids Hitler could send against England's cities. Failing to bring England to its knees, Hitler ordered an invasion of the Soviet Union. He thus brought upon himself the two-front war he had hoped to avoid.

The United States became the arsenal of democracy. It sent lend-lease arms and military equipment to the Allies. On December 7, 1941, Japan made a surprise attack at Pearl Harbor, in the Hawaiian Islands. The next day, upon President Roosevelt's urging, Congress declared war on Japan. Thus, the United States entered World War II.

America's contributions to victory were both in the Pacific area and in Europe. By the time the war ended, atomic bombs had been dropped on Hiroshima and Nagasaki. This probably shortened the war, but unleashed a new order of destruction. The war in the Pacific ended in September, 1945, with the formal signing of the peace treaty. Japan had surrendered to the United States. During the war, a number of conferences were held to prepare the way for peace. The Atlantic Charter was drawn up even before the United States was at war. The charter came out of talks between Roosevelt and Hitler. At Teheran the Big Three,—Roosevelt, Churchill, and Stalin—agreed to set up a new organization to replace the League of Nations. At Yalta, in 1945, the terms of the peace settlement were agreed upon, as was the idea for a United Nations.

REVIEWING THE HIGHLIGHTS

People to Identify		
Franklin D. Roosevelt	James Doolittle	Bernard
Winston Churchill	Édouard Daladier	Montgomery
Adolf Hitler	Neville	Dag Hammarskjold
Dwight D.	Chamberlain	Clement Atlee
Eisenhower	Benito Mussolini	Douglas MacArthur
Erwin Rommel	Joseph Stalin	Kurt Waldheim
Chiang Kai-shek	Henri Pétain	

Places to Locate		
Manchuria	The Hague	Nagasaki
Poland	El Alamein	Teheran
Rhineland	Philippines	Yalta
Ethiopia	Midway Island	Potsdam
Sudetenland	Stalingrad	Sakhalin
Pearl Harbor	Torgau	Port Arthur
Munich	Okinawa	New York City
Albania	Hiroshima	The Hague

UN Charter
Lytton Commission
zone
Maginot Line
lebensraum
appeasement
United Nations
Security Council
Axis powers
Allies

fifth column
blitzkrieg
Maginot Line
RAF
Luftwaffe
cash-and-carry
General Assembly
Nazi-Soviet
  nonaggression
  pact

anschluss
Vichy
secretary-general
lend-lease
arsenal of democracy
Atlantic Charter
Big Three
second front
Free French
  government

Battle of the Coral
  Sea
Battle of Stalingrad

Battle of the
  Bulge
Yalta Conference

Potsdam Conference
Casablanca Conference
Battle of Britain

1. Why did President Roosevelt say that December 7, 1941, was a day that would "live in infamy"?
2. Why is the period between World War I and World War II called the "long armistice"?
3. Was the Munich Conference a disgrace for the democracies? Why or why not?
4. Why did Hitler and Stalin sign a nonaggression agreement?
5. How was Czechoslovakia removed from the map of Europe?
6. How was Poland removed from the map of Europe?
7. Why did Hitler attack Russia?
8. How did America help Great Britain and France fight Hitler?
9. Why was the United States fearful of Japanese aggression in the Far East?
10. Why did the Axis powers win early victories?
11. State four aims of the United Nations as expressed in the preamble of the Charter.
12. Why did the Allies begin to win victories?
13. How did the Allies prepare for peace?
14. How was the way prepared for the formation of the United Nations?
15. Why was Germany divided into four zones?
16. Is the United Nations a world government? Why or why not?
17. Name the main parts of the United Nations and give the chief tasks of each.
18. Describe the voting procedure in the General Assembly. In the Security Council.
19. Who are the permanent members of the Security Council?
20. How may the success of the United Nations be judged?

THINGS TO DO

1. Debate. *Resolved:* Dropping the atomic bomb on Hiroshima and Nagasaki was necessary to end the war quickly.
2. Draw a map showing Asia and/or Europe in 1939 and 1945.
3. Draw a cartoon illustrating one of the following: **(a)** The Battle of Britain; **(b)** The Fall of France; and **(c)** The Surrender of Japan.

YOU ARE THE HISTORIAN

Read the selection below. With your class **(a)** make a list of the questions you would ask based upon your understanding of the document; and **(b)** make a list of questions you would ask as a citizen interested in world peace.

The Effects of the Atomic Bomb on Hiroshima

The morning of 6 August 1945 began bright and clear. At about 0700 there was an air-raid alarm and a few planes appeared over the city. Many people within the city went to prepared air-raid shelters, but since alarms were heard almost every day the general population did not seem to have been greatly concerned. About 0800 an all-clear was sounded. . . .

After the all-clear sounded, persons began emerging from air-raid shelters and within the next few minutes the city began to resume its usual mode of life for that time of day. It is related by some survivors that they had watched planes fly over the city. At about 0815 there was a blinding flash. Some describe it as brighter than the sun. . . . Following the flash there was a blast of heat and wind. The large majority of people within 3,000 feet of ground zero were killed immediately. Within a radius of about 7,000 feet almost every Japanese house collapsed. Beyond this range and up to 15,000–20,000 feet many of them collapsed and others received serious structural damage. Persons in the open were burned on exposed surfaces, and within 3,000–5,000 feet many were burned to death while others received severe burns through their clothes. In many instances clothing burst into spontaneous flame and had to be beaten out. Thousands of people were pinned beneath collapsed buildings or injured by flying debris*. . . .

Shortly after, the blast fires began to spring up over the city. Those who were able made a mass exodus* from the city into the outlying hills. There was no organized activity. The people appeared stunned by the catastrophe and rushed about as jungle animals suddenly released from a cage. Some few apparently attempted to help others from the wreckage, particularly members of their family or friends. Others assisted those who were unable to walk alone. However, many of the injured were left trapped beneath collapsed buildings as people fled by them in the streets. Pandemonium* reigned as the uninjured and slightly injured fled the city in fearful panic.†

Vocabulary

debris—rubble

exodus—departure

pandemonium—wild confusion

†From "The Effects of the Atomic Bombs on Health and Medical Services in Hiroshima and Nagasaki, "in *The United States Strategic Bombing Survey* (Washington, D.C.). Department of the Air Force, 1947.

1. Invite someone to your class who took part in World War II. The person may have been a soldier, a nurse, or a worker in a war plant. Ask him or her to give the class a brief talk about his or her wartime experiences. Allow time for questions and discussion.

2. Prepare an oral report on one of the following topics: The Red Cross during World War I and World War II; The Use of Poison Gas; Life in the Trenches; Life on the Home Front during World Wars I and II.

3. Write a term paper on the events that led Franklin D. Roosevelt to support research that led to the atomic bomb.

4. Have a "Round Table Discussion" on one of the following: Appeasement Was the Principal Cause of World War II; Unconditional Surrender Lengthened the War Unnecessarily.

5. Debate. *Resolved:* the dropping of the atomic bomb on Hiroshima and Nagasaki was a war crime.

6. Prepare a class newspaper for the day December 7, 1941.

7. Prepare a class newspaper for the day June 28, 1914.

8. Select a World War II leader, such as Churchill, Eisenhower, MacArthur, or Montgomery, and prepare a report in which you describe the highlights of his life since 1945.

9. Prepare reports on the subject of Women in War. Each group of three students might investigate the role of women on the home front, and on the fighting front in each of five Allied or Axis power countries.

10. List in your notebook five of the most stirring quotations of Winston Churchill and Franklin D. Roosevelt.

11. Dramatize an interview with the secretary-general of the United Nations in which you raise questions concerning the power of the United Nations to resolve disputes.

12. Prepare a score card for the United Nations in which you identify the successes and failures of the UN.

13. Prepare an oral report on "The Blitzkrieg as a War Tactic."

14. Prepare a program for your class entitled, "The Year of the Woman." In the program indicate the achievements of women before 1945 comparing them with women's achievements after that date.

15. Prepare a "Meeting of Minds" program in which the following groups meet to discuss the problems they experienced. **Group A:** Churchill, Napoleon, Catherine the Great, Woodrow Wilson; **Group B:** Roosevelt, Hitler, Gandhi, Sun Yat-sen; **Group C:** Stalin, Mussolini, Lord Durham, Pu-yi.

BIBLIOGRAPHY

Forbath, Peter. *The River Congo.* Harper & Row. The legend and the history of a great river vividly told.

Frank, Anne. *Diary of a Young Girl.* Doubleday & Co. An account of a Jewish family's persecution by the Nazis.

Green, Gerald. *Holocaust.* Bantum. A moving, fictionalized account of slaughter of six million Jews in Nazi concentration camps. Story has been televised.

Irving, David. *The Trail of the Fox.* Dutton. A thrilling biography of Field Marshal Erwin Rommel.

Koehn, Isse. *Mischling, Second Degree.* Greenwillow Books. Hitler's Germany as seen through the eyes of a member of the Hitler Youth.

Lord, Walter. *Lonely Vigil.* Viking. The incredible achievements of those who spied upon the enemy when Japan swept the South Pacific in 1942.

Manchester, William. *American Caesar: Douglas MacArthur.* Little, Brown. A splendid biography of Douglas MacArthur, who led American forces to victory in the Pacific during World War II.

Mee, Charles L. *Meeting at Potsdam.* Evans. A well-written reinterpretation of what took place at the decisive meeting at Potsdam in 1945.

Reynolds, Quentin. *Battle of Britain.* Random House. A thrilling account of Great Britain's "finest hour."

Ryan, Cornelius. *The Last Battle.* Simon & Schuster. A highly readable and exciting account of the fall of Berlin during World War II.

Ryan, Cornelius. *The Longest Day.* Simon & Schuster. A vivid retelling of D-Day.

Salisbury, Harrison E. *Russia's Revolutions: 1905–1917.* Doubleday. A vivid and readable account of the event that gave birth to the Soviet Union.

Shirer, William. *Berlin Diary.* Alfred A. Knopf. A reporter's rise to power and America's entry into World War II.

Shirer, William. *The Rise and Fall of the Third Reich.* Simon & Schuster. A history of Nazi Germany told as only a first-rate reporter can. Research based on captured German documents.

Speer, Albert. *Inside the Third Reich.* Avon. An account of Hitler and his associates as told by a surviving war criminal.

Taylor, Edmond. *The Fall of the Dynasties.* Doubleday. A scholarly and readable treatment of the fall of the ruling houses of Europe between 1905 and 1922.

Trevor-Roper, Hugh. *Final Entries, 1945.* The fall of Nazi Germany as told in the diaries of Joseph Goebbels, Hitler's chief propagandist.

Tuchman, Barbara. *The Guns of August.* The Macmillan Co. An account that recaptures the circumstances surrounding the opening of World War I.

Toward
Global Peace

Celebrating the end of World War II in Times Square, New York City, May 7, 1945

From Cold War to Detente: Europe Since 1945

On August 15, 1945, the news headline of the day was, "Japanese War Ends!" World War II was over and people everywhere could hope for a peaceful world.

In 1952, President Eisenhower urged Americans to join the forces of light against the forces of darkness. European unity was tested. America and the Soviet Union competed with each other for worldwide power and prestige. The cold war grew out of that struggle and cast deep shadows over the free world. In this chapter, we will examine the problems of Europe during the postwar years. In the next chapter, we will look at the problems of the Americans following World War II.

THE COLD WAR
AND POSTWAR BRITAIN

The Nature of the Cold War

World War II had made uneasy partners of the Communist and the non-Communist countries. Suspicion, mistrust, tension, and competition took the place of unity created by war. The Communist countries were dictatorships. They sought to take advantage of the war's end and to expand their power and influence. The non-Communist countries thought that any expansion of communism had to be stopped. They felt that unless it was stopped, both democracy and capitalism would fall.

As soon as the war with Germany and Japan ended, the so-called *cold war* began. The cold war is the name given to the struggle between the Soviet Union and other Communist countries on one side and the United States, Great Britain, France, and other Western nations on the other. It is called a cold war because there is, generally speaking, no shooting among the big powers engaged in the struggle. The cold war takes many forms. It is a war of brain power, of money power, and of propaganda. It is fought inside and outside the United Nations.

Joseph Stalin, the Soviet dictator and war leader, died in 1953. There were hopes that the cold war would end with his death. But it did not. It continued under Nikita Khrushchev [krüs'chev], who followed Stalin, and under Leonid Brezhnev [brezh'nef] and Aleksei Kosygin [kə sē'gin], who followed Khruschev.

The cold war is not just a war of words. It is fought by scientists as well as by politicians. The Soviet Union and the United States are in scientific competition. In this struggle each side has sent people into space. The United States and the Soviet Union each hope that, among other things, success will convince the rest of the world that their kind of government and their way of life are best. In this area of the cold war, the battlefields are classrooms and laboratories.

One weapon in the cold war is *propaganda*. Propaganda is word and picture power. Each side tries—through newspapers, radio, television, and speeches—to spread its ideas and to convince people that it is right and that the other side is wrong.

The cold war is fought with money where people and nations are poor. The United States has tried to help the poor countries of the world. The *Truman Doctrine* was a plan to give aid to countries threatened by communism. It gave military and economic help to Greece and Turkey in 1947. This help enabled those nations to remain free. The *Marshall Plan* gave aid to sixteen European countries trying to recover from the effects of the war. Because the European nations agreed to help themselves, the United States gave them financial aid. As a result, Western Europe resisted the threat of communism.

A freight train carries goods to needy Greeks after World War II. Why was the Marshall Plan established?

What Postwar
Great Britain Was Like

Great Britain was America's ally in two big wars. Its people have a strong attachment to democratic customs and traditions. Great Britain faced many big postwar problems, as did most of the countries of Europe after World War II.

Many of Great Britain's buildings were destroyed in the war. In the cities, whole blocks lay in shambles. The war cut Great Britain off from the colonies that had helped supply the raw materials

Britons line up for supplies of vitamins, which are available through the National Health Service. How is this program financed?

Great Britain lacked. The few available raw materials were given to the armed forces. There were shortages of food and clothing.

Winston Churchill was the leader of the Conservative Party. He had the cooperation of other parties during the trying and difficult days of the war. However, he and his party were defeated by the Labour Party in the election of 1945. The British felt that the time had come to make a change. The Conservative Party had been successful in fighting the enemy. Nevertheless, people were not sure the Conservative Party wanted the social reforms that they hoped for in peace time. So the Labour Party was voted into power. People believed that the Labour Party would raise living and health standards.

Under the leadership of the Labour Party, Parliament passed many laws. The government became the owners of the Bank of England, the coal mines, the railroads, and the iron and steel factories. The taking over of industry by government is called *nationalization*. For most people, nationalization meant few changes in their daily lives. They went to work as usual; they got their pay envelopes in the same way; their supervisor and immediate boss remained the same. In addition to nationalizing some industries, the Labour Party also started a *National Health Service*. In this plan, called *socialized medicine*, doctors and dentists are paid by the government for their work. Such things as eyeglasses and false teeth are available from the National Health Service.

Although the Labour Party brought about many social changes aimed at improving life for the working classes, disagreements within the party helped the Conservatives to win in 1951. For the next thirteen years, the Conservatives, led by such prime ministers as Winston Churchill, Anthony Eden, Harold Macmillan, and Alec Douglas-Home, directed the nation.

The Labour Party was returned to power in 1964 with a very slim majority. Harold Wilson, as leader of the majority party, became the new prime minister. The Labour Party continued Great Britain's strong ties with its Western allies. At home, the Labour government improved social and economic programs.

In 1970, British voters returned a majority of Conservatives to the House of Commons. Labour was stunned at its defeat. Edward Heath, leader of the Conservative Party and the new prime minister, moved into 10 Downing Street. Heath served as prime minister until 1974. In the election that took place that year, Labour candidate Harold Wilson defeated him to become prime minister once again. Inflation, troubles with Northern Ireland, and continued participation in the Common Market (see p. 614) were among the most important issues facing Great Britain and the Labour Party, which remained in office until 1979.

Circumstances were once again ripe for a new election and a victory for the Conservative Party. Conservative Party candidate Margaret Thatcher [tha'chûr] became the first woman to be elected prime minister of Great Britain.

In 1982, dissatisfied members of the Labour Party formed the *Social Democratic Party*. If this new party grows, it too may have a chance to govern Great Britain.

How Problems Grew in Ireland

Margaret Thatcher must work to solve the problems of inflation and the need to develop a more modern industrial system. She is also faced with continuing problems in Northern Ireland. When the Republic of Ireland was established in 1949, the six Protestant counties of Ulster, which made up Northern Ireland, remained under British rule. In 1969, the Catholics of Ulster pressed for greater freedom and greater voice in political matters. They also felt that in times of economic stress, jobs were open to Protestants but closed to Catholics. Catholics and Protestants fought violently. Great Britain sent troops to try to restore peace, but the fighting only increased. Since 1969, many hundreds of persons have died as a result of this religious, economic, and political struggle.

In 1972, Great Britain did away with the Northern Ireland Parliament. The British tried to rule Northern Ireland directly. On the eve of Thatcher's election, one of her future cabinet officers was killed by a terrorist. In 1979, Great Britain's war hero, Lord Louis Mountbatten, and members of his family were killed by a bomb planted by the Irish Republican Army (IRA).

In Scotland a spirit of nationalism appears to be rising. The Scottish National Party has urged independence. However, in a 1978 election, Scotland chose to remain part of the United Kingdom.

Check in Here

1. Define the term *cold war* and explain how such a "war" is carried out.

2. What were Great Britain's problems immediately after World War II?

3. What reforms did the Labour Party bring to postwar Great Britain?

4. What problems exist between Great Britain and (**a**) Scotland (**b**) Northern Ireland?

5. What continuing problems does Margaret Thatcher face?

Margaret Thatcher

(1926–   )

"What Britain needs is an iron lady." Margaret Thatcher said this during the parliamentary campaign in 1979. It is by the nickname of "iron lady" that she has become known throughout her country. Thatcher is the kind of person who rarely takes a vacation. She seldom seems to need more than five hours sleep a night. This workaholic, as she has been described, was born in a two-room flat above the family grocery store in a small town sixty kilometers (100 mi.) north of London. The apartment had neither hot running water nor an indoor toilet. Thatcher's father, Alfred Roberts, was also a Methodist minister who was active in the Tory (Conservative) Party.

In grammar school Thatcher was a bright pupil. At Oxford University, when she wasn't studying chemistry, she was reading religious books. Or, she was working for the Oxford University Conservative Association. This debating society elected her chairperson in 1946. In those days the popularity of the Labour Party was high among students. But Margaret Roberts took a different view and expressed strong sympathy for the Tory (Conservative) Party.

In 1950 and 1951, Roberts ran for political office and lost the election both times. She married Denis Thatcher, an army major and owner of a paint factory. Staying out of politics for eight years, she devoted her time to twin sons and studying law. A devoted follower of Winston Churchill, Thatcher was finally elected to the House of Commons in 1959.

As a party worker, Thatcher became noted for her attention to detail and her great supply of energy. She never tired of calling for tax cuts. She attacked the labor unions which, she felt, were largely responsible for Great Britain's inefficient industry.

In 1970, Conservative leader Edward Heath became prime minister in a surprising victory over Harold Wilson. Thatcher became minister of education. She aroused much bitterness by abolishing free milk for school children. She was called "Mrs. Thatcher the milk-snatcher." Thatcher regretted her decision, but it taught her how active the opposition can be. She learned the need to go slowly in making changes.

In 1974, the Labour Party again defeated the Conservatives. At this time, Margaret Thatcher and her supporters successfully took the leadership of the Conservative Party away from Edward Heath. This prepared the way for her eventual choice as prime minister of England in 1979.

In one of her speeches to a woman's group, Thatcher quoted the Greek philosopher Sophocles: "Once a woman is made equal to a man, she becomes his superior." Despite this statement, Thatcher has been criticized by women for not being militant enough in the feminist cause. No woman serves in a major post in the new prime minister's cabinet.

Margaret Thatcher lives at 10 Downing street, the traditional home of the British prime minister. People wonder how far she will be able to turn England to the right. "It is time," she is quoted as saying, "for Great Britain to become a leader, not a straggler."

EUROPEANS MAKE POSTWAR RECOVERIES

What Postwar France Was Like

Five years of war and enemy occupation left their mark on France. Over one million homes had been destroyed. About eighteen hundred cities, some quite large, needed to be rebuilt. And French industry had to be restored.

France faced loss of trade and inflation (very high prices). There was not enough money due to the government's inability to collect taxes. The French Empire acted as a drain upon France's small resources. French machinery was out of date. Inefficient factory methods pushed the prices of goods sky high. As a result, France was unable to compete in the world market.

Like the government of Great Britain, the government of France tried to solve its problems by taking over some of the important industries. These included banking, insurance, and public utilities. Today, French industry is being modernized. Workers are getting better pay. Most French people have some form of protection against the problems of sickness, accident, and loss of jobs. People who are ill get money to pay for medical care. Those who are out of work get money to take care of themselves and their families until they can find new jobs.

In 1958, Charles de Gaulle [də gôl'] (1890–1970) was elected president of the Fifth Republic. He promised to restore French glory and was quite successful. Under the earlier republics, power had been in the hands of a premier. The president was only a figurehead, a position without real power. The premier, however, kept his power only as long as he had a majority in the lawmaking body. Because there were many political parties in France, it was hard to have a majority for a long period of time. As a result, during the Fourth French Republic (1945–1958), French premiers rose and fell quickly. This gave France an unstable government. In times of crisis, the French government was weak.

The government of Charles de Gaulle was different in many ways from the previous governments. For one thing, de Gaulle was a strong president, not a weak one. Indeed, he had more power than the premiers of the previous republics. As a strong president, de Gaulle kept his powers independent of the legislature. The French president is elected for a seven-year term. Originally, he was elected by an electoral college made up of prominent French people. But, in 1962, the constitution was changed so that the president of France would be elected directly by the people. The premier, who has limited powers, is now appointed by the president and is not chosen by the legislature.

The president, on the other hand, may dissolve the French legislative body. In a national emergency the president

599

Charles de Gaulle, former president of France. Why was his presidency stronger than previous ones?

This time, however, the French people did not support the proposals of their president. Defeated in the referendum, Charles de Gaulle resigned. An era ended simply and suddenly when De Gaulle said, "I am ceasing to exercise my functions as President of the Republic." He died on November 10, 1970.

The new president, Georges Pompidou [pôm pē'dü'], was as concerned with domestic affairs as de Gaulle had been with foreign affairs. Pompidou tried to raise the French standard of living by improving French industry.

When Pompidou died in 1974, Valéry Giscard d'Estaing [də stang'] became president. Although not a Gaullist (follower of de Gaulle), Giscard favored a moderate program of economic, social, and educational reforms. In the local elections of 1976 and 1977, the large French Communist Party, with help from the Socialists, won many offices. It was feared that France would be headed by a Communist as a result of victory in the national election of 1978. This did not happen, and Giscard retained his position as president of the French Republic. In 1981, a Socialist, François Mitterand [mē'tėr an], was elected president of France.

Postwar Developments That Shook the French Empire

At one time, France ruled the second largest empire in the world. Since the end of World War II, however, France has lost much of its empire. France hoped its colonies would join the *French Union* and stay within the French family of nations. The French Union was patterned after the British Commonwealth of Nations. The French Union, however, was not as successful as the British Commonwealth of Nations.

The colonies in the French Union were called *associated states*. The associ-

can assume full powers. The president can call upon the people to vote on specific issues in a *referendum* (a vote by the people).

In 1966, the women of France gained the right to open checking accounts and to own their own businesses. This seemingly small step was, however, a great advance over the legal rights of women as provided in the Code Napoleon of 1804.

In May, 1968, widespread rioting almost ended in a revolution when both workers and students demanded government reform. Charles de Gaulle placed a proposal to change the French constitution before the voters of France. The change he wanted to make was not a very great one, but De Gaulle insisted on a referendum. He wanted to measure his support among the people. He told the French people that unless they approved the change, he would leave office. He had said this a number of times before.

ated states felt that they did not have enough freedom and they become dissatisfied. They began to fight for independence. In 1956, Morocco won its independence, as did Tunisia in 1957. In 1954, Arabs in Algeria demanded independence. France refused, and a brutal civil war broke out. This helped bring about the downfall of the Fourth French Republic. Algeria was granted independence in 1962.

As a result of these problems with the associated states, the French Union has become the *Community of Free Peoples.* The right to vote has been given to all men and women, and all lands overseas may choose their own kinds of government. They may choose to become part of France itself or be self-governing within the French Community. Charles de Gaulle promised that those countries that chose membership in the French Community might leave it at any time they wished.

Why Postwar Germany Became a Divided Land

At the postwar Yalta and Potsdam conferences, Germany was divided into four zones. One zone went to each of the Big Four (the USSR, France, Great Britain, and the United States). The former capital city of Berlin lay in the Soviet part of Germany. It, too, was divided and governed separately by the four powers.

The Yalta agreement (1945) gave the Soviet Union, France, Great Britain, and

Postwar Germany

- In 1945, what Allied power controlled the area surrounding the divided city of Berlin?
- In which country are each of the following cities located: Potsdam, Bonn, Nuremburg, Berlin?

the United States the right to govern Germany on a temporary basis. In 1949, the Western powers (France, Great Britain, and the United States) set up the *German Federal Republic* (West Germany) with the capital at Bonn. The so-called *German Democratic Republic* of East Germany became a *satellite* [sat′ə līt′] of the Soviet Union.

A satellite country is a country that is independent in name only. The term satellite is borrowed from science. It is used in science to describe a body (such as the moon) that depends on a larger planet (such as the earth). Those countries that are controlled by the USSR are called satellites.

Under Allied occupation, important German Nazis were tried for their war crimes in a Four Power military court. The military court proceedings were called the *Nuremberg Trials.* The Nazi leaders were made responsible for having broken world peace and for having committed crimes against humanity. Eleven former high-ranking Nazis were condemned to death. Others were given prison sentences.

Under Konrad Adenauer [ad′nou ər] (1876–1967), West Germany established a democratic government and prospered. Adenauer was chancellor of the German Federal Republic when it was formed in 1949. He remained its chancellor until 1963. Industry was rebuilt, and people once again enjoyed a high standard of living. West Germany has begun to play a leading part in plans for defending Western Europe. Communist-controlled East Germany, on the other hand, is an agricultural state whose people have a rather low standard of living.

In 1969, Willy Brandt [brant] (1913–) became the chancellor of West Germany. In foreign policy he worked toward a better understanding between the German Federal Republic (West Germany) and the German Democratic Republic (East Germany). This was a change in West German foreign policy. It was based on an understanding that East Germany and West Germany would not be united soon. Willy Brandt urged that the two nations establish closer economic and political ties.

Progress Made By Postwar Germany

The postwar division of Germany into two nations has had a great influence on the lives of the German people. In East Germany, for example, the Soviets took much of the country's resources and industries. This has made economic recovery difficult. While most people in West Germany work in manufacturing, most people in East Germany are farmers. The guiding hand of the Soviet Union is heavy. When they can, many East Germans leave their friends, their homes, and their possessions behind and they cross the border to West Germany. In West Germany, they have to start new lives, but they seem to believe that West Germany offers them greater economic opportunity and political freedom.

Berlin is located entirely within East Germany. After World War II, Berlin was divided among the Allies, with the Soviet Union controlling East Berlin, and France, Britain, and the United States controlling West Berlin. In time, East Berlin became the capital of the German Democratic Republic, and West Berlin became a state within the German Federal Republic. Relations between the Soviet Union and the Allies have been troubled over West Berlin. East Germany and the Soviet Union can pressure West Berlin and the Allies by blockading goods going into and out of the city.

West Berlin, which is controlled by the Allies, is a refuge for dissatisfied people from East Berlin and East Germany. Its very existence is a threat to the Soviet

Union. Friction over divided Berlin has created international crises and fear of a new war. In the summer of 1961, the East German government stopped East Germans from going to West Berlin by building a concrete wall. This wall is known as the *Berlin Wall*. The division of Berlin became one of the chief causes of tension between the West and the Soviet Union.

On May 23, 1979, West Germany celebrated its 30th anniversary as a nation. Despite its defeat in World War II, West Germany has had much to celebrate. Democracy is strong in that country. Its economy is strong. As a nation, West Germany is sorry about the many atrocities committed under Hitler. Helmut Schmidt [shmit], Willy Brandt's successor, was an able leader. As chancellor, he understood the problems created by nuclear weapons and the need for greater European unity.

There are still, however, unsolved problems in West Germany. From time to time, new Nazi parties appear. There is evidence of government spying on youth to detect those who may have communist tendencies. At one time, German political and business leaders were the targets of terrorism. Many of the young people in West Germany are not active in the political life of the nation. Even though these problems exist, the recovery of West Germany has been very impressive.

What Postwar Italy Was Like

Although politically unstable, Italy has made good economic recovery in the postwar years. In part, its recovery was made possible by its membership in the Common Market. (See p. 614.) There are, however, great economic differences within the nation. The southern part of Italy is largely agricultural and very

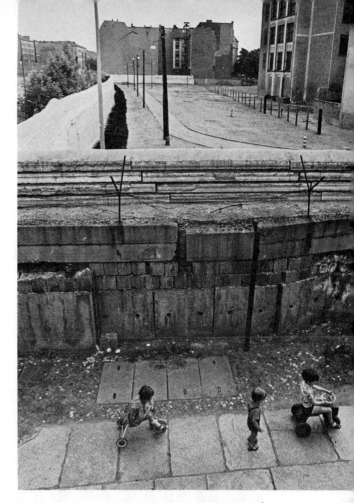

Children play on the western side of the Berlin Wall.

poor. The northern part of Italy is mostly industrial and quite rich. The workers in the northern factories are often members of the Communist Party. In their view, their wages have not kept up with the growing rate of Italian inflation.

In 1974, Italian voters decided to keep a three-year-old law permitting divorce. This law was bitterly opposed by the Catholic Church. The Christian Democrats favored repeal (withdrawal) of the divorce law. When the law was kept, the Christian Democrats lost a good deal of support. The Communists, on the other hand, did not favor the repeal and therefore gained support. In time, the Communists won important elections in such major cities as Rome, Turin, Naples, and Florence. In 1976, the Vatican agreed to change its 1929 agreement with Mussolini. (See p. 554.) According to the new agreement, Roman Catholicism is no longer the state religion of Italy.

Terrorism has added to Italy's serious problems. In May, 1978, Aldo Moro [mo'rō], a former Italian premier, was kidnapped by the Red Brigades, a terrorist organization. He was eventually killed. Italy and the world were shocked. It was the Red Brigades' boldest act to date. Other political and industrial leaders have been also kidnapped. Terrorists seek to take advantage of Italy's political instability and to establish their own political views throughout Italy.

How Spain and Portugal Fared During the Postwar Period

After Francisco Franco died on November 20, 1975, Juan Carlos de Borbón y Borbón [bôr bôn'] became king of Spain. Juan Carlos set up a constitutional monarchy in place of Franco's dictatorship. Free elections were held in 1975. Moderate parties were elected to the Cortes, the legislature of Spain. Spain is rapidly becoming a more industrialized country. However, it continues to have problems with *separatist* groups. These are groups that want to break away from Spain. These include the Basques [basks] and the Catalans [kat'ə lanz']. These groups are seeking self-rule. In fighting for their cause they at times use terror.

Two Italian newspapers, appearing on the same day, express doubt about the fate of former premier Aldo Moro. The headline on the left says Moro lives; the headline on the right raises the fear that he might have been assassinated.

From 1932 to 1968, Portugal was under the dictatorial rule of a strongman: Premier Oliveira Salazar [sal′ə zär′]. For over thirty years Salazar had control over the Portuguese. In 1968, illness forced him from power. However, he was succeeded by another dictator, Marcello Caetano [ca tä′nō]. In 1974, a military group seized power. In elections that followed, Soviet-supported Communist parties were voted into office, but they were forced out by anti-Communist groups.

In 1976, a new constitution was written, and free elections were held. The moderate Socialist party gained a majority of the votes. However, it has needed the cooperation of other parties to remain in power. Therefore, the government of Portugal has been unstable.

Portugal held on to its vast colonial empire longer than most countries. During the postwar years, Portugal was forced to give many of its colonies their independence. Guinea-Bissau [gin′ē bi sou′], Mozambique [mō′zəm bēk′], Cape Verde [vėrd] Islands, Angola [ang gō′lə], São Tomé [soun′ tô me′], and Principe [prin′sə pē] were among them. Portugal has agreed to allow the United States to use the Azores [ā zōrz′] as a military base. The Azores, the islands of Macao [mə kou′] off the China coast, and the island of Madeira [mə dēr′ə] off the northwest coast of Africa are all that remain of the once great Portuguese empire. Portugal, like Spain, was an Axis sympathizer. Its postwar recovery has been slow. However, aid from the United States has contributed to Portugal's continuing economic progress.

Postwar Problems That Faced Greece and Turkey

The postwar period was a difficult time for Greece and Turkey. The deep bitterness between the two countries may be traced back to 1821-1829. Then Greece won its war of independence from Turkey. (See p. 377.) During World War II, Greece was occupied by German, Italian, and Bulgarian troops. In 1944, the invading forces left Greece, and the Communist forces inside the country were defeated. George I was recalled to the throne and reigned until his death in 1947. He was followed by his brother, Paul I.

With the support of the Truman Doctrine (see p. 595) Communist uprisings in Greece between 1947 and 1949 were put down. In 1967, a military dictatorship took power. King Constantine [kon′stən tēn′], who had come to the throne in 1964, was forced to flee the country.

Cyprus achieved independence in 1959, but hostility between *Turkish Cypriots* [si′prē uts] and *Greek Cypriots* remained great. The Greek Cypriots were in the majority. They favored union with Greece. The Turkish Cypriots wanted the island divided between the two groups. Despite the efforts of a UN peace-keeping force, war between Greeks and Turks on Cyprus was never far away. Archbishop Makarios [mə kar′ē əs], president of Cyprus, sought an independent country that was not tied either to Greece or to Turkey. Greece's military dictatorship fell because it could not unite the island of Cyprus with Greece. In 1974, a civilian government under Constantine Caramanlis [kärə man′lis] took power. In 1981, Andreas Papandreou became president. In his campaign he spoke against Greek participation in NATO and EEC.

The postwar years were harsh on Turkey. A series of governments has been unable to solve Turkey's basic political and economic problems. Hopes were high that Turkey would make important gains. However, unemployment remains high and industrial production low. High prices keep the people poor.

Archbishop Makarios of Cyprus (right) is welcomed by President John F. Kennedy on a visit to Washington in 1962.

There is continuing political violence in Turkey. There are disagreements between the Shiite and Sunni Moslems. The Kurds want independence. Left and right wing terrorist political groups clash violently.

Because of Turkey's role in the Cyprus dispute, the United States stopped aid to Turkey. With the fall of the Shah of Iran in 1979, Turkey has become important to the West. Because of its location, the major Western nations have agreed to help Turkey.

Check in Here

1. Why did France, Germany, and Italy recover from the war faster than Spain, Portugal, Turkey, or Greece?

2. How did the French and Portuguese colonial empires change during the postwar period?

3. Why did the Soviet Union order the Berlin Wall to be built?

4. How do economic and political conditions in East Germany differ from those in West Germany?

5. Why is Turkey important to the defense of the free world?

THE USSR DOMINATES EASTERN EUROPE AND CLASHES WITH WESTERN EUROPE

How Russia Profited from World War II

During World War II, Nazi armies caused much damage to the Soviet Union before they were pushed back. Soviet losses amounted to about twelve million dead, more than the total losses of all other Allies combined. Property damage amounted to many billions of dollars.

In March, 1953, Joseph Stalin died. He had led his nation to victory in World War II. In the postwar world he continued to be a tough dictator. Georgi Malenkov [mä'lən kəf'] became dictator soon after Stalin's death. It seemed for a while as if there would be no fighting about who the next Soviet ruler would be. However, Laurentia Beria [ber'ē ə], who had been chief of the secret police under Stalin, wanted power. His unsuccessful attempt to become Soviet dictator resulted in his death. In the meantime, there were others who opposed Malenkov and some of his ideas. Nikita Khrushchev [krüs'chev] was one of those. He was able to force Malenkov to give up his post. Khrushchev became premier in 1958. In an important speech, Khrushchev made Stalin appear less of a hero in order to prepare people for the changes in the government and economy. In doing so, Khrushchev tried to give himself a clean slate to make the changes he thought necessary.

In October, 1964, Khrushchev was driven from power. He was replaced as general secretary of the Party by Leonid Brezhnev [brezh'nef] and by Aleksei Kosygin as premier. One of the most important reasons for Krushchev's fall from power was his failure to increase Soviet food production.

As general secretary of the Communist Party, Leonid Brezhnev soon became the most important leader in the Soviet Union. In 1977, Brezhnev took the additional position of president of the Supreme Soviet. In this way, he emphasized the tradition of one person rule in the USSR.

At home the Soviet Union is faced with a number of severe problems that are not easy to solve. The Soviet government, for example, is worried about the growing rate of divorce. Most Soviet women must work in order to provide for their families. However, their position is inferior to that of Soviet men. There are far fewer opportunities open to Soviet women than to Soviet men.

There is also concern that Soviet industry is inefficient and does not use its labor force well. Some fear that there will be a shortage of workers during the 1980s. The heads of major industries in the Soviet Union complain that they cannot get the workers they need. The growing labor shortages are partly due to lower birth rates.

The limits on personal freedoms are less severe than they once were for many Soviet intellectuals. Nevertheless, life is still controlled. There is a growing group of Soviet *dissidents* [dis'ə dənts], (Dissidents are people who disagree with

Russian writer and dissident Alexander Solzhenitsyn.

the policies of the government.) These are mainly scientists and writers who want the freedom to do research or to write as openly as do their friends in the United States and in other free countries. The most outstanding dissident is Alexander Solzhenitsyn [sōl zhə nēt'sin], the author of *Gulag Archipelago* [gü'läg är'kə pel'ə gō]. In this book the author describes the slave labor camps that are scattered throughout the Soviet Union. Solzhenitsyn was exiled (sent away) from the Soviet Union and is now living in the United States. One of the more outspoken dissidents on human rights (basic freedoms) is Andrei Sakharov [säk'ə rof]. He has been arrested for his activities.

607

In 1979, an attempt was made to improve relations between the United States and the Soviet Union. The two countries exchanged prisoners: five well-known Soviet dissidents for two Soviet spies in American jails. The Russians released Aleksander Ginsburg [ginz′bərg], one of its most important spokespersons on human rights.

Communist Control of Eastern Europe After World War II

Soviet Union

Other Communist countries of Eastern Europe

- Locate and name five Communist countries of Eastern Europe.
- What Eastern European countries have borders with the Soviet Union?
- What Communist countries besides the Soviet Union have coastlines on the Black Sea?

Soviet Jews have had a particularly difficult time. However, the Soviet Union at times listens to pressures for greater freedom. The United States has asked the Soviet Union to allow more Jews to leave. In 1979, the rate of Soviet Jewish emigration (leaving one country for another) was at 50,000 per year.

Why the Soviet Union Dominates the Countries of Eastern Europe

After World War II, the Soviet Union made satellites (dependents) of many of its neighbors. Poland, Czechoslovakia, Yugoslavia, Hungary, Romania, Bulgaria, and Albania became satellites of the Soviet Union. All established Communist governments, and all were dependent upon the Soviet Union to some degree. After Stalin died in 1953, there were new but less powerful leaders in the Soviet Union. Some of the satellite nations were encouraged to become more independent.

Of the Soviet satellites none was more independent of the Soviet Union than Yugoslavia. That country was ruled by Marshal Tito [tē′tō] (1892–1980). He controlled the government from 1945 to 1980. Tito tried to keep his ties to the Soviet Union loose. This did not please the Soviet Union at all. The Soviet Union tried to turn the people against Tito. It limited trade to make it difficult for the people of Yugoslavia to buy the things they needed. In 1963, Yugoslavia adopted a new constitution. It provided that Tito was to be president for life. Yugoslavia showed it intended to follow an independent role in world affairs. President Tito died in May, 1980. It remains to be seen whether Yugoslavia can remain free and independent of the Soviet Union.

Beginning in 1956 in Poland, there were many strikes and much street fighting. Wadislaw Gomulka [gə mül′kə]

In 1979, Pope John Paul II visited Poland, his homeland. Thousands of Poles greeted him on his motorcade.

became the Polish premier. He had once been put into prison for not following Soviet communism strictly enough.

In 1968, Poland joined other Communist-bloc nations in sending troops to put down the revolt in Czechoslovakia. In December, 1970, workers in a number of Polish cities rioted. Gomulka resigned. His place as general secretary of the Communist Party was taken by Edward Gierek [ger′ək]. A new five-year plan (a program for running the country) was adopted. It provided for new housing and consumer goods. Poland was the first Communist state to get most-favored-nation status in trade with the United States. In 1980 and 1981, strikes of workers and farmers nearly brought an invasion of Soviet troops. Whether a Communist state can have free and strong labor unions is an important question for the countries dominated by the USSR.

Although it is controlled by Communists, Poland is a Catholic country. Under two Catholic church officials, Stefan Wyszynski [wi zin′skē] of Warsaw and Krol Wojtyla [wō ti′lə] of Cracow, the Roman Catholic Church continued to be an important influence in the daily lives of the people. In 1978, Cardinal Wojtyla became the new pope and took the name John Paul II.

In Hungary, Soviet communism has shown its power. In 1956, open fighting broke out in Hungary. The Soviet Union was faced with a widespread and popular uprising. Hungarians demanded that Imre Nagy [nog′yə], who had been thrown out of the Communist Party, become prime minister. Hungarians also wanted Soviet troops withdrawn from Hungary. When Nagy became head of the government in 1953, he promised to improve conditions in Hungary by allowing greater freedom in business and

609

farming. He also pulled Hungary out of the Warsaw Pact (see p. 615), which greatly alarmed the Soviet Union.

Shortly after Nagy took office, Soviet troops invaded Hungary. In the bloody fight that followed, thousands of Hungarians were killed. Many were captured and sent to slave labor camps in Siberia; and thousands escaped to the United States and Canada. The Hungarian fight for freedom was lost. Imre Nagy was later arrested and killed. He was replaced by Janos Kadar [kä′där], who was willing to be a Soviet puppet ruler.

Soviet action in Hungary shocked the world. The United Nations condemned Soviet actions, but Soviet troops remained in Hungary. Since the revolution, conditions in Hungary have continued to improve.

In 1944, Soviet troops entered eastern Czechoslovakia, and in May of 1945, they reached the capital, Prague. Eduard Beneš [ben′esh] became president in the May, 1946, elections. In 1948, the Communists seized power. They wrote a new constitution, which Beneš refused to sign. Beneš resigned and died soon after. A period of censorship and suppression followed.

The world was shocked again in 1968 by Soviet actions in Czechoslovakia. During the mid-1960s, the Czechs had been enjoying some freedom in their personal, artistic, and cultural growth. In January, 1968, Antonin Novotny [nə vot′nē] was removed as First Secretary of the Communist Party. He was replaced with the more forward-looking Alexander Dubcek [düb′chek] (1921–). Dubcek tried to democratize his country. The taste of democracy encouraged the Czechs to demand even more. Non-Communist political parties were beginning to form.

All this, however, was far too much for the Soviet Union. It pressed Dubcek to limit the freedom of his people. The pressure mounted. Then in August, 1968, hundreds of thousands of Soviet troops, including troops from the Communist countries of Eastern Europe, poured into Czechoslovakia. The Czech people resisted the Soviet troops nonviolently. One young man even burned himself to death to protest the presence of foreign troops. In March, 1969, Dubcek was forced to resign. Gradually but surely, hope for a freer Czechoslovakia was snuffed out.

The Soviet Union depends upon the enormous quantities of raw materials available in the countries of Eastern Europe. Eastern European countries sell their agricultural and manufactured goods to the Soviet Union. The six countries of Eastern Europe and the Soviet Union together form the Council for Mutual Economic Assistance, or *Comecon*. Some Eastern European countries are more economically dependent than others on the Soviet Union. The more dependent they are the more they accept Soviet political views. It is not surprising that the two freest countries of Eastern Europe, Hungary and Romania, do more business with the West than they do with the Soviet Union.

How the Soviet Union Clashed with Western Europe

After World War II, the Soviet Union extended its power and influence. When the United States, Great Britain, and France set up the German Federal Republic in 1948, the Soviet Union tried to force these countries out of Berlin. The Soviets stopped British and American trucks and trains from bringing goods into the British and American parts of Berlin, but giant cargo planes were able to supply the British and Americans with the goods they needed.

In the spring of 1959, the foreign ministers of the United States, the Soviet

A busy street in Budapest, the capital of Hungary. Since the end of World War II, the Hungarian standard of living has been rising.

Union, Great Britain and France met at Geneva to see if they could settle their differences. They were unsuccessful.

Unable to drive the Western powers from Berlin, Khrushchev thought he could divide them by becoming friendlier with the United States. Vice President Nixon visited the Soviet Union, and Khrushchev visited the United States. Plans were made for a *summit* (top level) meeting, that is, a meeting of the heads of states of the United States. This included President Eisenhower (United States), Premier Khrushchev (Soviet Union), Prime Minister Macmillan (Great Britain), and President de Gaulle (France). This summit meeting was to be held in Paris in May, 1960.

The summit plans collapsed. The So-

viet Union captured an unarmed American U-2 plane that was flying over the Soviet Union. Khrushchev used the incident to destroy the summit meeting. He accused the United States of aggression. He withdrew the invitation that had been made to President Eisenhower to visit the Soviet Union, and thus brought an end to the thaw that had been developing in the cold war.

In 1961, President Kennedy of the United States met with Premier Khrushchev in Vienna. Here, Khrushchev warned that he had not given up his plan to place Berlin under East German control. Kennedy, on the other hand, warned that the United States would not sacrifice the freedom of the people who live in West Berlin.

The Possibility
for Ending the Cold War

There has been concrete evidence that the nations of the world have been trying to end the cold war by cooperation. The most important show of such cooperation came in 1963. The United States, Great Britain, and the Soviet Union signed a limited nuclear test ban treaty. These nations agreed to halt all tests of nuclear bombs, except those tests that could be conducted underground. However, other nations who have also become nuclear powers have not signed the test ban treaty.

In 1968, the United States and the Soviet Union agreed to sponsor a *nuclear nonproliferation* [non'prō lif'ə rā'shən] treaty. The purpose of this treaty is to get the nations of the world to agree to stop the proliferation (spread) of nuclear weapons. One part of the treaty provides that the nations with atomic materials use them for peaceful purposes only. Another part of the treaty provides that nonnuclear powers, such as Japan and West Germany, do not get or make nuclear weapons. A third part states that the members of the "nuclear club" (United States, the Union of Soviet Socialist Republics, China, and France) must not arm their neighbors and allies with nuclear weapons. There is nothing in the treaty, however, to prevent the club members themselves from continuing to make such weapons. In March, 1969, the nuclear nonproliferation treaty was ratified (approved) by the Senate of the United States.

In August, 1972, the United States ratified a treaty that limits the United States and the Soviet Union to two defensive missile sites (locations) each. This agreement grew out of the *Strategic Arms Limitation Talks* (*SALT I*). These talks were held in Helsinki [hel syn'kē], Finland. Here, the two world giants were able to agree on the ground rules upon which future talks would be based.

In 1979, the United States and the Soviet Union signed the *Strategic Arms Limitation Treaty II* (*SALT II*). This agreement took seven years to accomplish. SALT II limits the amount, the quality, and the types of nuclear weapons that the United States and the Soviet Union can make. Although the treaty was signed in Vienna by President Carter and Soviet President Leonid Brezhnev, it was not approved by the United States Senate.

The United States and the Soviet Union have sought to substitute *detente* [dā tänt'] for cold war. Detente means that two countries understand each other, although they recognize that there is disagreement between them. Detente may be said to mean agreeing to disagree. If there is a better understanding between the two world giants, perhaps a climate more favorable to world peace can be achieved.

Check in Here

1. What changes in the Soviet Union did the death of Stalin bring about?

2. Identify three domestic problems the Soviet Union faces.

3. How did the Soviet Union bring the countries of Eastern Europe under its control?

4. How did the Soviet Union and the Western countries clash over Berlin?

A NEW EUROPE
IN THE MAKING

The Outlook for
Cooperation in Europe

Today, European nations are not as strong as they once were. All of them are concerned nevertheless about their own position in world affairs. The two most powerful countries of the world are the

The Twentieth Century

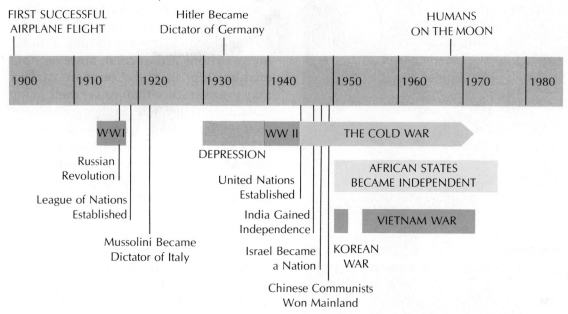

Identify four events that occurred in the beginning of the cold war.

United States and the Soviet Union. The nations of Europe do not wish to be caught in an atomic and space war between these two strong countries or between groups of countries. As a result, they have tried to think in terms of cooperative organizations called *blocs*. Despite difficulties, the countries of Western Europe are working toward their goal.

How Europeans Are Cooperating in Trade

The cold war forced the countries of Western Europe to unite for security. The countries of Western Europe have been encouraged to do so by the United States and the United Nations. The *Marshall Plan* set up by the United States helped them unite. George C. Marshall, American Chief of Staff in World War II and later United States Secretary of State, was largely responsible for the Marshall Plan. He knew that communism seemed most appealing to poor people. Therefore, in 1947, he suggested a plan in which America promised to help the countries of Europe. Help was offered to the Soviet Union and its satellites but was refused. A condition for aid was that European countries were to get together and decide what help they could give one another. Sixteen nations met at Paris, France, to establish the *Organization of European Economic Cooperation* (*OEEC*). This agency would carry out the Marshall Plan. OEEC was an early and important step toward economic cooperation in Europe.

The struggle for greater unity among the countries of Western Europe is far from over. It is being considered by more and more nations. An example of this interest is the *Organization for Economic Cooperation and Development* (*OECD*). Austria, Belgium, Canada, Denmark, France, Germany, Greece, Iceland, Ireland, Italy, Luxembourg, the Netherlands, Norway, Portugal, Spain, Sweden, Switzerland, Turkey, Great Britain, and the United States have signed the OECD agreement.

Top: Shoppers enjoy a variety of fresh produce as a result of free trade among Common Market countries. Bottom: Officials from Common Market member countries meet in Brussels, Belgium.

As results of cooperation are seen, European nations are encouraged to work together even more. In 1957, the leaders of six European nations met and planned what was called a *Common Market*. Its members—Belgium, the Netherlands, Luxembourg, France, Italy, and West Germany—planned to allow goods to move freely among the member nations without tariffs. On the other hand, they agreed to tax goods of nations who were not members. Thus, the goods of the Common Market members would be cheaper among members.

In 1973, after years of discussion, Great Britain joined the Common Market. Ireland and Denmark also joined, raising the membership to nine nations. Many Britons are worried, however, that membership in the Common Market may lower (rather than raise) their living standards. They fear higher prices and competition from workers willing to work for lower wages. But with the Empire and Commonwealth mostly gone, Great Britain's membership in the Common Market ties that country to Europe's future.

In addition to trade agreements, there is an agreement among some European countries to pool atomic energy resources. *Euratom* is the name given to the European Atomic Energy Community. This community includes Belgium, the Netherlands, Luxembourg, West Germany, France, and Italy. The United States has lent money to Euratom and has also given it some uranium.

How Europeans Are Cooperating in Defense

In 1949, a group of European leaders met in The Hague, the Netherlands, to form the *Council of Europe*. Some of them had high hopes that a United States of Europe would soon be established. They were mistaken. The Council of Europe had little power. But it did show that prominent people were thinking about plans for a European union.

European leaders were more successful in forming an organization that united Western Europe militarily. This was the *North Atlantic Treaty Organization (NATO)*. NATO was formed in 1949. It is made up of Great Britain, France, Belgium, Luxembourg, the Netherlands, Denmark, Iceland, Italy, Norway, and Portugal. It also includes two non-European nations: Canada and the United States. Later, West Germany, Greece, and Turkey joined. Each member of this

Military Alliances in Europe

Legend:
- North Atlantic Treaty Organization (NATO) countries in Europe
- Warsaw Treaty Organization (Warsaw Pact) countries
- Communist countries not belonging to the Warsaw Pact

ICELAND

ATLANTIC OCEAN

UNITED KINGDOM OF GREAT BRITAIN AND NORTHERN IRELAND

NORWAY

SWEDEN

FINLAND

U.S.S.R. (Soviet Union)

BALTIC SEA

IRELAND

NORTH SEA

DENMARK

DEMOCRATIC REPUBLIC OF GERMANY (East Germany)

FEDERAL REPUBLIC OF GERMANY (West Germany)

NETH.

BELG.

LUX.

Berlin

POLAND

Warsaw

FRANCE

CZECHOSLOVAKIA

SWITZ.

AUSTRIA

HUNGARY

ROMANIA

BLACK SEA

PORTUGAL

SPAIN

ITALY

YUGOSLAVIA

BULGARIA

ALBANIA

GREECE

TURKEY

MEDITERRANEAN SEA

NORTH AFRICA

0 500 KILOMETERS
0 500 MILES

- Name the Warsaw Pact members that have borders touching members of the NATO alliance.
- What alliance controls the water route between the Black Sea and the Mediterranean?
- Name the European countries that do not belong to either the Warsaw Pact or NATO.

group promises to come to the help of the others in case of attack. A council of foreign ministers makes the big decisions and has troops available. These are troops that each member nation has set aside for the use of NATO. In a sense, this is a European army that, in the event of war, would be led by a single commander. There is a unique feature in the NATO agreement. Member nations have given up a measure of independence and control over their own armed forces for the security and peace of all.

In 1955, Russia signed a defense pact with its satellite nations. The *Warsaw Pact*, as this is called, is Russia's answer to NATO's challenge. Member nations are Albania, Bulgaria, Czechoslovakia, East Germany, Hungary, Poland, Romania, and the USSR.

In June of 1979, the people of the Common Market countries went to the polls. In an historic vote, Europeans elected members of the first European parliament. The European parliament opened in Strasbourg, France, in July 1979. It chose Simone Weil [wīl], a Jewish Frenchwoman who survived the Auschwitz death camp, as the first president. The parliament of Europe will have relatively little power. The election is significant, however. For the first time representatives of Germany, Great Britain, Italy, France, the Netherlands, Belgium, Denmark, Ireland, and Luxembourg will have a place where they can discuss and reach agreement on European issues. Perhaps such cooperation among the countries of Western Europe can overcome old rivalries and bring in a new era.

Check in Here

1. Give some examples of how the free nations of Western Europe are cooperating in trade and defense.

2. On a map be able to identify the following: **(a)** Common Market Countries; **(b)** NATO Countries; **(c)** Warsaw Pact Countries.

3. What was the importance of the Marshall Plan?

4. What is the importance of the SALT agreements?

5. What significance may be attached to the vote for a European parliament?

REVIEWING THE BASICS

Immediately after World War II the countries of the world were plunged into the cold war. The cold war weapons are competition and tension. The cold war is between the free countries of the world led by the United States on the one hand and the Soviet Union and its satellite countries on the other.

More than most countries, postwar recovery for Great Britain has been very difficult. Great Britain is no longer the great power it used to be. Its governments have alternated between Labour and Conservative, with the Labour Party in power most of the time. In 1979, Margaret Thatcher became the first woman to become British prime minister. She has tried to limit the powers of the unions and to lower taxes.

The greatest postwar recoveries took place in France, Germany, and Italy. Destroyed by war, these countries recovered economically and politically.

The Soviet Union suffered the greatest casualties during World War II. Under Stalin, that country experienced severe oppression. When Stalin died and Khrushchev replaced him, there was an attempt to provide greater freedom. But this did not really develop. Oppression continued at home, and the cold war continued abroad. After World War II, the countries of Eastern Europe became satellites of the Soviet Union. In many countries of Eastern Europe, standards of living are higher than that in the Soviet Union itself.

The attempt to end the cold war is called detente. The relationship has different periods of friendship and cooperation. Tensions and conflict remain, however, between the Soviet Union, the United States, and the countries of Western Europe.

To help European nations recover from the war, the United States began a program of economic help known as the Marshall Plan. The Western European countries set up NATO, or the North Atlantic Treaty Organization, as a means of mutual defense. The Soviet Union and the countries of Eastern Europe responded with the Warsaw Pact. The most notable achievements among the Western European nations were the establishment of the European Common Market and the beginnings of the establishment of a European parliament. In June of 1979, the people of these countries went to the polls to vote on the membership of this unique and as yet untried organization.

REVIEWING THE HIGHLIGHTS

People to Identify

Konrad Adenauer
Willy Brandt
Helmut Schmidt
Aleksei Kosygin
Janos Kadar
Leonid Brezhnev
Nikita Khrushchev
Alexander Dubcek
Archbishop
  Makarios

Charles de Gaulle
Georges Pompidou
Giscard d'Estaing
Aldo Moro
Margaret Thatcher
Harold Wilson
Alexander
  Solzhenitsyn
King Juan Carlos de
  Borbón y Borbón
Eduard Beneš

Constantine Caramanlis
Simone Weil
Karol Wojtyla
Wadislaw Gomulka
Edward Gierek
Marshal Tito
Imre Nagy
Andrei Sakharov
Aleksander
  Ginsburg

Places to Locate

Berlin
East Germany
Poland
Hungary

Romania
Czechoslovakia
Helsinki
Bonn

Azores
Cape Verde Island
Macao
Bulgaria

Terms to Understand

satellite
socialized medicine
Labour Party
Common Market
NATO
Cypriots
propaganda
Berlin Wall
Yalta agreement
nationalization

postwar
Tory Party
detente
Warsaw Pact
Nuremberg Trials
Community of
  Free Peoples
summit meeting
cold war
SALT I

SALT II
dissidents
nuclear
  nonproliferation
OECD
Marshall Plan
Council of Europe
Christian
  Democrats
Comecon

Events to Describe

U-2 incident

Soviet Invasion
  of Hungary

1. Explain why a cold war replaced the shooting war of World War II.
2. Describe the cold war uses of: (**a**) propaganda; (**b**) money; (**c**) brain power.
3. How did the Truman Doctrine help countries threatened by communism?
4. Why did the British prefer the Labour Party to the Conservative Party after the war?
5. How did postwar conditions in Great Britain compare with those in France?
6. Why was Germany divided?
7. How do you explain Germany's postwar recovery?
8. How is France indebted to President Charles de Gaulle for political stability?
9. What is terrorism? What terrorist acts have the Italian Red Brigades committed?
10. What were the postwar problems of the following: Spain, Portugal, Greece, Turkey?
11. Why was a divided Berlin created in East Germany? Was this a wise decision? Why or why not?
12. Are the countries of the Eastern bloc still USSR satellites? Why or why not?
13. How did the Soviet Union put down rebellions in Poland, Hungary, and Czechoslovakia?
14. Explain the significance of the nuclear nonproliferation treaty signed by the United States and the Soviet Union.
15. What is the purpose of the North Atlantic Treaty Organization (NATO)?
16. Would a reunited Germany be desirable? Why or why not? Is such reunification likely within the next generation? Why or why not?
17. What is the importance of the election of representatives to the European Parliament?

THINGS TO DO

1. Debate. *Resolved:* The satellite countries of Eastern Europe are satellites no longer.
2. Prepare a "Meet the Press" program in which a group of students holds a mock interview with Margaret Thatcher on the occasion of her moving into 10 Downing Street.
3. Prepare a report using information from newspapers and journals on the problems of being a dissident in the Soviet Union.

Study the pie chart below. It divides the world's 165 countries as free, partly free, and not free. On the basis of your understanding of the chart, indicate whether the statements that follow it are true, false, or not shown in the chart. Give an explanation of your point of view.

A World Divided: Free, Partly Free and Not Free†

A total of 1.6 billion people in 51 countries—37 percent of the world's population—enjoy almost full political and civil rights. With the exception of India, most are in North America or Western Europe.

Another 1.8 billion people, 41.7 percent or more than 4 persons in every 10, exist under dictatorships or governments which deny many or all of their political and personal liberties.

The remaining 21.3 percent of the population—921.2 million people living in 55 countries—are allowed only partial political and civil freedom.

1. A majority of the world's population live in countries that are not free.
2. Most people live in free countries.
3. The number of people living in free countries is increasing.
4. The number of people living in free countries is decreasing.
5. Most people live in free or partly free countries.
6. A total of 1.6 billion people in 51 countries live in free countries.
7. Four-tenths of the world's population live under dictatorship.

†Basic Data from Freedom House from *U.S. News and World Report*, February 4, 1980.

Peruvian village, Andes Mountains

The Western Hemisphere Today: North, South, and Central America

The United States, Canada, and Latin America are distant neighbors. They share the continents of North and South America, which make up most of what is generally called the *Western Hemisphere.*

Canada, the United States, and nearly all the countries of Latin America were allies during World War II. During the postwar period they needed each other as much as they did during wartime. But a spirit of cooperation among these countries has not always been easy to achieve. As more is understood about postwar developments in these countries, better relationships among them should be possible.

POSTWAR UNITED STATES

The Nature of Postwar United States

Vice President Harry S Truman [trü'mən] (1884–1972) became president when President Roosevelt died in 1945. He then won the presidential election in 1948. Truman said his victory was a vote of confidence in his plan, the *Fair Deal*, a program that provided aid to schools, to the housing industry, to the sick, and to the aged. President Truman also fought for higher social security benefits and higher minimum wages. While he was unsuccessful in getting much of his program passed, Congress did pass a new *Minimum Wage Act*. For some workers, this raised minimum wages from forty to seventy-five cents an hour.

In 1952, Dwight Eisenhower, the Republican candidate for the presidency, defeated Adlai Stevenson, the Democratic candidate. With the election of Eisenhower, a Republican controlled the White House for the first time since 1932. In a program of conservatism, Eisenhower tried to turn gradually away from the Fair Deal.

During the Eisenhower years, the United States Supreme Court heard the now famous case of *Brown* v. *Board of Education of Topeka* (1954). The court ruled unanimously that *segregated* (separation of blacks and whites) schools were illegal. Blacks and whites were to attend public schools together. *Desegregation* (doing away with the separation of races) proceeded slowly, however. President Eisenhower had to send federal troops to enforce the *integration* (bringing together) of blacks and whites in schools in Little Rock, Arkansas. In 1979, when the nation observed the twenty-fifth anniversary of this important decision, it was clear that total desegregation still had

White students look on as heavily guarded black students approach Central High School in Little Rock, Arkansas in 1957.

not been achieved. To the surprise of some, more progress had been made in the South than in the North.

The United States During the Post-Eisenhower Years

In 1960, John Fitzgerald Kennedy (1917–1963) became president of the United States. Under Kennedy, the nation took some new directions in foreign affairs. In his inaugural address Kennedy said, "Let us begin anew, remembering on both sides [United States and Soviet Union] that civility is not a sign of weakness, and sincerity is always subject to proof." In

621

Chou En lai and Richard Nixon (center) enjoy a farewell banquet at the end of Nixon's goodwill trip to mainland China in 1972.

June of 1961, in Vienna, Kennedy had a chance to test both civility and sincerity during his meeting with Nikita Khrushchev, leader of the Soviet Union. The meeting was historical as well as important. It gave each of the world leaders a chance to learn about the other as well as to discuss issues.

The Kennedy administration established the *Peace Corps.* In this organization, Americans help people in developing nations to improve their agricultural, industrial, and educational skills.

On November 22, 1963, Kennedy was assassinated in Dallas, Texas, while on a political trip. His vice president, Lyndon B. Johnson (1908–1973), became president. Under Johnson, great strides were made in *civil rights.* (Civil rights refers to those rights guaranteed by various amendments to the Constitution and by acts of Congress.) By the time his administration was over, however, Johnson and his programs for the Great Society had been destroyed by conflict over the war in Vietnam.

In 1968, two other great American leaders were assassinated. Martin Luther King (1929–1968) was killed in Memphis, Tennessee. Dr. King had been America's most important fighter for black Americans. In the same year, Senator Robert F. Kennedy (1926–1968), brother of the assassinated President Kennedy, was shot and killed in Los Angeles.

In 1968, Richard Nixon again ran for president (1913–   ). Nixon had been defeated in the 1960 presidential race by John F. Kennedy. This time, amid demonstrations against the war in Vietnam, Nixon successfully defeated Hubert Humphrey. Nixon's administration was largely devoted to foreign affairs. Perhaps his most notable achievement was the establishment of better relations with the People's Republic of China.

Nixon's second term in office was destroyed by corruption. During the presidential campaign of 1972, five men were caught and arrested for breaking into the Democratic National Committee headquarters in the Watergate building in Washington, D.C. The president tried to deny any role in these events and other illegal activities. White House tapes of his conversations proved otherwise. Further corruption followed. Nixon's vice president, Spiro T. Agnew [ag'nü], had to resign because of income tax evasion. Gerald Ford replaced him as vice president. When Richard Nixon became the only president forced to resign from office, Gerald Ford became the president. In 1976, Ford was defeated for the presidency by Jimmy Carter, former governor of Georgia.

Carter's administration began with the problem of unemployment, which was especially high among young blacks and other minority groups. His administration ended in 1981 with the problem of skyrocketing inflation and an energy shortage. The American supply of gasoline began to dwindle in 1973. The gasoline shortage became even more serious when the government of Iran fell and an important source of oil was abruptly cut off. (See p. 659.)

In foreign affairs Carter made progress in bringing about a peace agreement between Israel and Egypt. As a result, peace in the Middle East came somewhat closer. (See p. 655.) Carter recognized the People's Republic of China as the official government of China. (See p. 680.) With Senate approval Carter agreed to give the Panama Canal to Panama by the year 2000. (See p. 634.) In addition, Carter negotiated the SALT II treaty with the Soviet Union. The SALT agreements limited the testing and manufacture of some nuclear weapons. (See p. 612.) However, many voters questioned Carter's policies, and the Senate refused to ratify SALT II. Jimmy Carter lost the presidential election of 1980 to Ronald Reagan.

President Reagan took the oath of office on January 20, 1981. He promised to balance the Federal budget and to achieve other economies. He also said he would restore America's military might.

Check in Here

1. What things did Truman's Fair Deal provide for people?

2. List one achievement of each of the following presidents: (**a**) Kennedy; (**b**) Johnson; (**c**) Nixon; (**d**) Carter.

3. What were two major achievements of the Carter administration in foreign affairs?

CANADA STRIVES FOR UNITY

Canada in the Postwar World

In the early history of Canada, the French and the British fought for control of this vast and rich land. By the terms of the Treaty of Paris in 1763, France gave England all its North American possessions except Louisiana. There are three important facts central to the history and government of Canada. First, Canada is a nation of about twenty-three and a half million people, twenty-eight percent of whom are of French descent. It is a bilingual nation (French-English), with French mostly spoken in Quebec. Second, early in Canadian history England gave Canada the right to govern itself. (See p. 520.) Later, Canada became a Commonwealth. It enjoys full independence in every way. Last, but important, Canada is America's neighbor and shares with the United States a border of 6,415 kilometers (3,987 mi.). This is the longest undefended international boundary in the world.

The government of Canada is a federation. This means that Canada is made up of ten provinces and two territories. Each province has its own government which handles local concerns. The territories have some self-government. National issues are controlled by a central government which acts for the whole country. The central government meets in Ottowa, the Canadian capital, in the province of Ontario. The Canadian provinces are Newfoundland, Nova Scotia, New Brunswick, Prince Edward Island, Quebec, Ontario, Manitoba, Saskatchewan, Alberta and British Columbia. The two territories are the Northwest Territory and the Yukon Territory.

The Canadian provinces send representatives to the central government in Ottowa. Provincial government in Canada is very strong and national unity is hard to achieve. The Canadian prime

North America in the 1980s

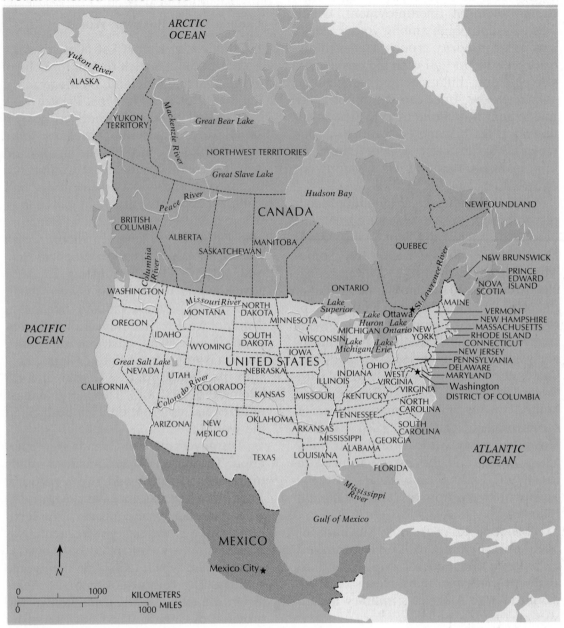

- Which is longer, the Canadian-United States border or the Mexican-United States border?

minister and the cabinet members are members of the House of Commons. The House of Commons has the highest governmental authority in Canada. Its members are elected by the Canadian people. The symbolic head of Canada is the British monarch, Queen Elizabeth II. However, she has no real power.

Although Canada is a member of the British Commonwealth of Nations, Quebec Province and Montreal, Canada's second largest city, are French-speaking.

A French restaurant in Quebec is a reminder of the province's cultural heritage.

For twelve years after World War II, Canadian politics were dominated by the Liberal Party. This party sought to establish good relationships with the large French community of Canada. In this they were partly successful. Under the Liberal Party, farmers were given price supports so that they could get a fair price and earn a fair profit for their crops. A number of social reforms were passed. In 1940, an Unemployment Insurance Act was passed. This was followed in 1944, with a Family Allowances Act to help large families. An Old Age Security Act was passed in 1951. Mackenzie King and Louis St. Laurent [san' lô rän'] were the leaders of the Liberal Party during these years. In 1957, John Diefenbaker [dē fen bā'kər], a Conservative, became prime minister of Canada; but his support in Parliament was not strong. Diefenbaker was defeated for office in 1963.

Relations with the United States were especially friendly under Prime Minister Lester Pearson. He was followed in 1968 by Pierre Elliot Trudeau [trü dō'], a popular leader. Trudeau served until 1979 when he was defeated by Joe Clark. To the surprise of many Clark failed to win a vote of confidence in the Canadian Parliament. Pierre Trudeau was promptly reelected in 1980.

In 1981, the heads of the major democratic nations met in Ottowa, Canada. Trudeau, as Canada's prime minister, served as host to President Ronald Reagan of the United States, and to the heads of West Germany, France, Great Britain, Italy, and Japan. The meeting may be said to demonstrate Canada's growing importance in world affairs. At home, the major problem continues to be the threat that French-speaking Quebec may try to break away from Canada.

Quebec's Relationship with Canada

The chief domestic problem in Canada is maintaining national unity. The French-speaking province of Quebec has threatened to form a separate government of its own. In November, 1976, the *Partis Quebecois* [pär′tē kā′be kwä′] (PQ) won election in the local government of Quebec. Under the leadership of Quebec Premier René Levesque [lə vek′], the party has made clear its aim of separating from Canada. If this should happen, the political and economic consequences for Canada would be grave.

Quebec is the country's largest province. It is second largest in population, with twenty-seven percent of the nation's total population. Quebec is second in industry and third in the production of energy. The separation of Quebec from Canada would isolate, or cut off, the Maritime Provinces. It is questionable whether the rest of Canada could survive. The separation of Quebec might lead to the break-up of Canada into separate independent states. Most of the French-speaking people, it appears, do not want total separation, but they are tired of second-class citizenship. In Quebec, French has replaced English as the language of schools and business. In this way, the French-speaking population hope to have equality with English-speaking Canadians in both political and economic matters.

Check in Here

1. What is Canada's chief domestic problem?

2. List the ten provinces of Canada.

3. What is the relationship of Canada to Great Britain?

4. Why is the city of Quebec important to Canada?

THE STRUGGLES OF MEXICO AND THE ISLANDS OF THE CARIBBEAN

Mexico Between the World Wars

In 1910, a revolution led by Francisco Madero [mä der′ō] began in Mexico. It would not end until 1940. By the time it ended, Mexican government was made more stable. Education for the masses was improved. Peasants were helped to own farms of their own. Railroads were placed under national control. Oil leases held by foreign countries, especially the United States, were taken from them. Mexico's vast wealth would be used to improve living standards of Mexicans.

Madero proved to be an inept leader. He was assassinated and replaced by Victoriano Huerta [ü er′tə]. In 1914, in a revolt led by Venustiano Carranza [kä rän′zə] and Francisco Villa [vē′ä]. Huerta was overthrown. Both men wanted to become leader of Mexico. Carranza won. In part, this was a result of United States support of Carranza and pressure on Huerta to resign. Mexicans were resentful of American interference in their affairs.

Under Carranza, a new constitution was written. It provided for separation of church and state and for economic and land reforms. Due to the outbreak of World War I in 1914 and disagreements among Mexicans, the new constitution was not put into effect right away.

In 1916, the United States sent troops, led by General John J. Pershing, into Mexico. They pursued Francisco Villa, also known as Pancho Villa. He was believed to have killed some Americans in a border city of New Mexico. Relations between the United States and Mexico were bitter for years because of this.

In 1920, Carranza was overthrown by General Álvaro Obregón [ô′bre gôn′]. Under him, illiteracy among Mexicans was somewhat reduced. Artists such as

José Clemente Orozco [ô rôs′kô], Diego Rivera [ri ver′ə], and David Siqueros [sē kä′rôs] were encouraged to use their talents to paint giant murals, showing the revolution and the struggle of the Mexican people for a better life.

The troubled Obregón regime was followed in 1924 by that of Plutarco Elías Calles [kä′yes]. Under Calles, Mexico was torn by conflict with the United States on the one hand, and with the Catholic Church on the other. Calles tried to regain Mexican control over oil and land rights owned by United States companies in Mexico. This brought the two countries close to war. The United States ambassador, Dwight W. Morrow [mo′rō], helped to improve relations and to settle the oil and land disputes—at least for a time.

Calles also tried to keep strict separation of church and state, as provided in the 1917 constitution. He sent foreign priests out of the country and closed the churches. In protest, the Mexican priests refused to conduct services. The struggle with the Church lasted for three years. Many people, including revolutionaries, worshiped privately. In 1929, a settlement was reached with the Church and better relations were attempted.

In 1928, Obregón was reelected to the presidency, but Calles held the real power of the government. Obregón was assassinated before he could take office. Because he held total power, Calles was able to choose the new presidents for a period of six years. This period is often described as the low point in the modern history of Mexico.

Mexico During and After World War II

In 1938, President Lázaro Cardenas [kär dä′näs] *expropriated*, or took over, the control and ownership of the prop-

The oil shortages of the 1970s encouraged the development of Mexico's oil resources.

627

erty of seventeen foreign oil companies in Mexico. It was an act that made Cardenas popular with the Mexican people. It is often seen as Mexico's declaration of economic independence. Mexico became an important world power and a neighbor that the United States had to regard seriously.

Taking over such vast properties was in some ways like a revolution. It was successful because the United States accepted the situation. Fortunately, at this time the United States was well represented by its ambassador, Josephus Daniels [dan′yəls]. Under President Franklin Roosevelt, the United States tried to give meaning to its *Good Neighbor Policy*. According to this policy, the United States would work more closely and cooperatively with the countries of Latin America. Over a ten-year period, Mexico agreed to pay foreign oil companies, including American companies, for their losses. The United States agreed to recognize the Mexican takeover of oil companies as legal.

Manuel Ávila Camacho [kä mä′chō] governed Mexico from 1940 to 1946. Mexico quickly joined the United States in the war against the Axis powers in World War II. Although state and church remained strictly separated during this period, the Catholic Church won back much of its earlier influence.

Although it is a one-party state, Mexico has freedom of speech, press, religion, and assembly. The development of agriculture is being encouraged. The state petroleum monopoly, *Pemex*, was made more efficient. A new University City was built near the edge of Mexico City. Under President Adolfo Ruiz Cortines (kôr tē′nəs), Mexico continued to grow economically. Organized labor became stronger, but it remained non-Communist.

Mexico has long been considered an oil-rich country. Mexico could become second only to Saudi Arabia among the major oil-producing nations of the world. Under President López Portillo [pôr tē′yō], Mexico's oil wealth was further developed. Pemex is using its own knowledge and skills to do this. With oil as a source of income and with a stable government, Mexico is rapidly becoming a major world power.

Why Cuba Became a Communist Country

As a result of the Spanish-American War (1898), Cuba became free from Spain. During much of its history after the war, and until 1959, Cuba was under the influence of the United States.

This control was made possible by an amendment to the Cuban constitution that was written by the United States and known as the *Platt Amendment*. When adopted by the Cubans, the amendment provided that (1) Cuba would never make a treaty by which it would lose its independence to a foreign power; (2) Cuba would not go into debt greater than its ability to pay; (3) the United States could intervene to preserve law and order and preserve the independence of Cuba; (4) Cuba would provide the United States with military bases through lease or sale. Although the terms of the amendment ended in 1934, its humiliating provisions marred the relations between the two countries.

In 1954, Cuba fell under the dictatorship of General Fulgencio Batista [bä tēs tə]. The Batista regime was both tyrannical and corrupt. Rich Cubans enjoyed luxurious living and many privileges. Cuba became a place for pleasure-seeking Americans and for many other foreigners.

Batista's opponents were led by Fidel Castro [kas′trō] (1926–   ). Castro and his followers, known as the *26th of July*

Movement, conducted a guerilla war from the Sierra Maestra mountains in eastern Cuba. They were helped by the professional revolutionary Ernesto Che Guevara [shā′ gwə vär′ə].

On January 1, 1959, Batista and his followers were driven from Cuba. Castro became premier. He began to make many changes in Cuba. When Castro was fighting in the mountains, his political ideas were not well known. Although many recognized the need for drastic reform in Cuba, few people expected Castro to become a Communist. When he did, he lost friends in the United States and gained the friendship of the Soviet Union. The Soviet Union wished to take advantage of a Communist ally so close to the United States. Because Cuba is only 144 kilometers (90 mi.) from Florida, the cold war was brought closer to the United States than ever before.

Castro's Cuba became a Communist dictatorship. Freedom of speech and freedom of the press were denied. Enemies of the state and even suspects were killed without trial. Agriculture was nationalized, that is, taken over by the government. Private business all but ceased to exist. Property that was owned by the United States was taken over by the Cuban government without compensation (payment).

Under Castro, Cuba experienced many changes. More children went to school. Many who could not read or write before, could now learn to do so. Many people of the upper class and middle class left Cuba when their wealth was taken from them. The poor worked in the fields and in factories. They hoped that they would be better off than before. However, shortages of food, clothing, and shelter made life hard. Castro blamed Cuba's troubles on the United States. He openly sought Soviet help and openly placed himself in the Soviet *bloc* (group of nations).

Cuban leader, Fidel Castro (seated, wearing white shirt and straw hat) talks to sugar cane workers in 1965.

The United States broke off relations with Cuba in 1961. In 1962, Cuba was ousted from the Organization of American States (OAS). Cuban refugees began to organize themselves in an effort to regain Cuba and overthrow Castro. They were secretly helped by the Central Intelligence Agency (CIA) of the United States. In April, 1961, about 1,400 Cuban exiles landed in the Bay of Pigs on Cuba's southern coast. Here they met with disaster. Many were killed and more were imprisoned. The *Bay of Pigs incident* brought Cuba and the United States close to war. It also brought the Soviet Union and the United States close to war.

Following the Bay of Pigs episode, the Soviet Union began arming Cuba with nuclear missiles. Since Cuba is so close to the United States, this was a clear threat. In October, 1962, President Kennedy took a daring step. He ordered a blockade of Cuba. He said that any missile launched from Cuba would be regarded as an attack by the Soviet Union on the United States. Kennedy demanded that the Soviet missiles be removed. At that moment, Soviet ships were streaming toward Cuba. If they did not turn back, war was possible. Khrushchev ordered the ships to return. He ordered that the nuclear missile bases be

A state department official shows newswriters an airview of missile bases being constructed by the USSR in Cuba in 1962. World tension was intense when President John F. Kennedy ordered a blockade of Cuba until the missiles were removed.

taken down. Khrushchev's decisions were seen as a victory for the United States.

In 1979, Cuba was accused of having Soviet troops on its territory. The United States, under President Carter, failed to have them removed. However, their activities are being carefully watched. President Reagan has taken an even more aggressive attitude toward Cuba.

The Postwar Problems of Other Caribbean Islands

Following World War II, Puerto Rico [pwer'tə rē'kō], another Caribbean island, had to decide whether it wanted independence or statehood. If Puerto Ricans voted for independence, they would no longer have the protection of the United States. They would lose the financial and tariff protections that helped the Puerto Rican economy. Statehood, on the other hand, would allow the Puerto Ricans to elect representatives to the United States Congress.

According to a constitution adopted in 1952, Puerto Rico became a commonwealth of the United States. As a commonwealth, its people have control over their internal affairs. Puerto Ricans do not pay income taxes to the United States government. Duties on imported goods go to the government of the island, not to the government of the United States. Puerto Ricans are citizens of the United States, but they cannot vote in a presidential election or have representation in Congress.

At one time, Puerto Rico was called the "poorhouse of the Caribbean." As governor of Puerto Rico between 1948 and 1964, Luis Muñoz Marin (1898–   ) raised living standards. In "operation bootstrap," industry and business were attracted to the island. Jobs and educational opportunities improved. As a result, the people of the island enjoy the highest *per capita* (for each person) income in Latin America. Although conditions are improving, Puerto Rico is divided between those who urge statehood and those who urge complete independence for the island.

Haiti [hā′tē] and the Dominican Republic are the two countries that share the island of Hispaniola [his′pən yō′lə]. This island was the first discovered by Columbus. In the seventeenth century, France took control of the western part of the island. In 1804, under Toussaint L'Ouverture [tü san′ lü ver tür′], this part of the island won its independence from France. Forty years later, the eastern two-thirds of the island won independence from Spain and became the Dominican Republic. Haiti and the Dominican Republic had weak governments, and in the early part of the twentieth century they were controlled by the United States, which had sent marines to maintain order.

Haiti has some major problems. One is a growing population that remains largely uneducated, and another is a declining supply of natural resources. Haiti has also had an unstable government. Between December 1956 and May 1957, for example, there were four governments in Haiti. In 1957, Dr. François Duvalier [dü′väl yā′] (1907–1971) became president. In 1964, Papa Doc, as he was sometimes called, was made president for life. He attempted to achieve stability, but the people of Haiti were cruelly treated in the effort. Duvalier died in 1971. His place was taken by his son, Jean-Claude Duvalier, called Baby Doc. A less violent government had been promised.

After the United States marines left the Dominican Republic in 1955, Rafael L. Trujillo [trü hē′ō] (1890–1961) became dictator. During his time in power, advances were made in public health and

transportation. Illiteracy was reduced. The Trujillo budgets were balanced and foreign and domestic debts were paid.

Much of the progress made in the Dominican Republic, however, was made at the expense of democracy. No opposition was allowed. The press was under strict government censorship. The Dominican Republic was largely a police state, and many members of the dictator's family became rich at government expense. Trujillo was assassinated in 1961. After him, Juan Bosch [bosh] was elected president in the first free election in thirty-six years.

Bosch, however, was overthrown in 1963, by the military. He fled, and the United States withheld economic aid and broke off diplomatic relations. The generals ruled until 1965, when forces favorable to Bosch sought to oust them from power. They were unsuccessful and the United States sent marines who intervened against Bosch. The marines were sent to protect American lives. A truce was arranged through the Organization of American States. An Inter-American Armed Force made up of military from Brazil, Paraguay, Honduras, and Costa Rica sought to keep the peace. In June, 1966, an election was held in which Juan Balaguer [ba lä ger′] was elected over Bosch. Foreign troops were withdrawn. Balaguer was reelected in 1970 and 1974. In 1978, the presidency was won by Antonia Guzman Fernandez [fer nän′dās].

Check in Here

1. Why was the period between World War I and World War II a period of turmoil for Mexico?

2. How did Cardenas help Mexico on its way toward becoming a world power?

3. What common problems seem to face Puerto Rico, Haiti, and the Dominican Republic?

CENTRAL AMERICA, COLOMBIA, AND VENEZUELA SEEK FREEDOM AND PROSPERITY

Postwar Problems in Central America

Central America lies between Mexico and South America. It is a subcontinent that is made up of six countries: Costa Rica [kos'tə rē'kə], El Salvador [el sal'və dôr'], Guatemala [gwä'tə mä'lə], Honduras [hon dür'əs], Nicaragua [nik'ə rä'gwə], and Panama [pan'ə mä']. All of these countries were once part of the Spanish Empire in America. All, except Panama, achieved independence from Spain in 1821.

In Guatemala, in 1944, dictator General Jorge Ubico [ü bē'kō] was overthrown after a thirteen-year rule of little accomplishment. He was followed by many dictators. Some of the dictators tried to make reforms to improve life in Guatemala. Today, this northernmost country of Central America is being destroyed by warfare between groups that want reform and a government that wants little if any change.

El Salvador is the smallest and most crowded country in Central America. In El Salvador there is violence between those who want immediate reform and those who support the government. In May, 1979, the leaders of the *Popular Revolutionary Bloc* (*PRB*) kidnapped the foreign ambassadors of France and Costa Rica. They hoped to force the release of five of their group who were held prisoner by the government. A demonstration took place in front of the cathedral of San Salvador, the nation's capital. Soldiers from the government fired into the crowd, killing and wounding many people. As a result, two PRB revolutionaries were released. Since then, violence in El Salvador has worsened. Hundreds of people are killed every week.

As in other Central American countries, the revolutionary movement in El Salvador is often led by Catholic priests. The priests feel deeply about the poverty of their people. In El Salvador, for example, eighty-five percent of the best land is owned by fourteen families. How to achieve government reform and avoid communism in Central America is no small problem.

In many ways, Honduras is typical of the countries of Central America. It has been ruled by unstable dictators. These people, for the most part, did little to help their country. When countries are governed in this way, people may join revolutionary groups, some of which may be Communist.

From 1909 to 1933, Nicaragua was dominated by the United States. United States marines kept some measure of political stability. In 1936, when the marines left, Anastasio Somoza [sə mô'sə] quickly rose to power. Using dictatorial methods Somoza made some surprising economic gains. He boasted that under his rule, Nicaragua had more teachers than soldiers, that health had improved, and that roads and electric power were more widely available. Despite these advances, Somoza was assassinated in 1956.

Until overthrown by the *Sandinistas* [san'də nēs'təs], the Nicaraguan government remained in the hands of Somoza's sons. Civil war in Nicaragua, led by the Sandinista guerillas, began in May, 1979. The Sandinistas were victorious, and in July, 1979, Somoza went into exile in the United States. The Sandinist National Liberation Front, or Sandinistas, is named after General Augusto César Sandino [sän dē'nō] who fought against United States intervention in the late 1920s. The Sandinistas seek land and economic reform. Fidel Castro of Cuba supplies them with money and weapons. The country is led by a five-man Sandinista *junta* [hün'tə] (ruling group).

A banana plantation in Honduras. Bananas are the chief economic asset of this small Central American country. Plantations like this one dot the northern coast.

In the small country of Costa Rica nearly all the people have European rather than Indian backgrounds. Costa Rica's literacy rate is high, its standing army small, its history peaceful, and its presidents mostly civilians. Costa Rica, however, has many problems. There is widespread poverty and malnutrition. Women have second-class citizenship, as do women in many societies of Central and South America. While literacy is widespread, there are few children in the upper grades. Very few children have the opportunity or money to go on to higher education.

In 1901, the United States and England agreed that the United States could build a canal in Central America, if such a canal would be open to all nations. The canal was to provide a short route between the Pacific and Atlantic Oceans. Theodore Roosevelt was determined to build the canal. There was debate in Congress as to whether a route through Nicaragua was better than a route through Panama. Congress finally voted to build the canal through the Isthmus of Panama. The Colombian Senate (Panama was then a part of Colombia) refused to accept the terms that had been negotiated between Colombia and the United States. Thereupon, Theodore Roosevelt encouraged the Panamanian leaders to revolt. As soon as the revolt took place, Panama was recognized by the United States. "While Congress debated," boasted Theodore Roosevelt, "I took Panama."

The Panama Canal was built between 1904 and 1914. In 1922, Colombia accepted 25 million dollars from the United States for the loss of its territory. In 1903, Panama gave the United States the right to use forever a 16 kilometer- (10 mi.) wide zone surrounding the Canal construction area. Panama was paid 10 million dollars for this land. It was to receive an annual yearly payment as well. These terms have been reviewed many times since then. At the end of World War II, Panama thought that the terms were unfair. Some Panamanians felt that Panama should own the canal.

In 1964, a minor incident happened in Panama that led to a major riot. The Panamanians could not agree on whether the American flag should be flown there. Twenty-six people were killed, among them four Americans. President Johnson agreed to review all parts of the old treaty again.

Under President Carter's urging, the United States Senate reluctantly approved a treaty that gave the Panama Canal to Panama, but not until the year 2000. Some Americans feel that giving up the canal was a mistake. They point out that revenues (monies) from the canal are increasing all the time. The canal has played an important part in every war. The United States can also be counted on to operate the canal efficiently for the benefit of all countries of the world.

There are also Americans who favor returning the canal. They say that the treaty requires the United States to continue to protect the canal if it is threatened, even after the year 2000. They point out, also, that because the United States now has a two-ocean navy, the canal is no longer really needed in case of war. Supertankers and aircraft carriers are too big for the canal. The canal can be bombed easily and it would be hard to defend. Furthermore, by signing the treaty the United States has perhaps gained friends in Latin America.

The Postwar Problems of Colombia and Venezuela

Colombia and Venezuela [ven'ə zwā'lə] are among Latin America's more important nations. This is due to their size, their agricultural products, their raw materials, and their strategic location on the Caribbean.

Colombia became independent in 1910. Its history for years after that was a

The Gatun Locks, Panama Canal Zone. Compare this photo with the one on page 537. What are the arguments for returning the Panama Canal to Panama?

Latin America in the 1980s

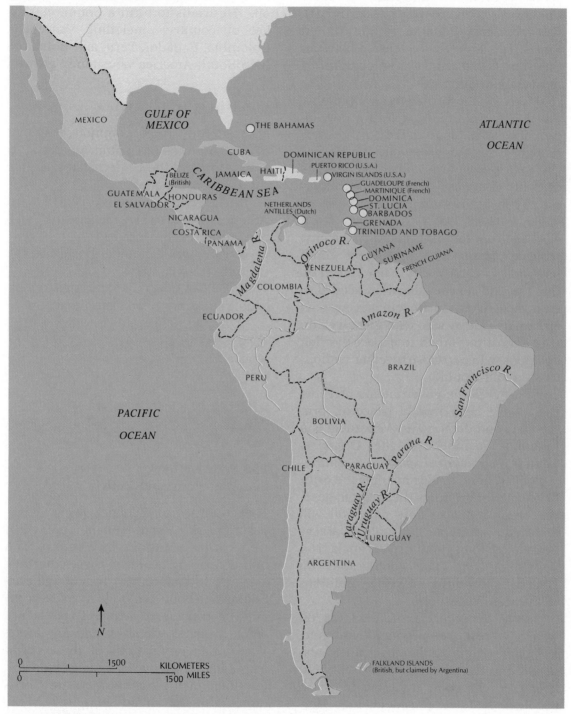

- Which Latin American country has the largest area?
- Locate and name the islands off the coast of Latin America that are owned by the United States or European countries.

series of revolutions and wars that made Colombia's economy very shaky. In 1903, Colombia lost Panama to the United States. This loss created tension between the United States and Colombia that was not easily overcome.

Many of the problems of Colombia are due to its rapidly growing population. They are also related to the overcrowding of the great city of Bogotá [bō′gə tä′]. Bogotá is called the "Athens of South America," and is the fifth largest city in Latin America. Nine years of violence (1948–1957) drew many farm workers from the countryside to the city. However, many of these people could not find work in the city. They lacked either the skills or the education needed to earn their living. In Bogotá, severe poverty exists side by side with great wealth. It is almost too much to expect the rich and poor to live so close together without tension and trouble.

Since 1959 the governments of Venezuela have been mostly peaceful, progressive, and democratic. Venezuela is a founding member of the *Organization of Petroleum Exporting Countries (OPEC)*. It helps decide not only the price of oil and oil products (heating oil, gasoline, etc.), but also how much oil will be made available for sale. Caracas [kə rä′kəs], the capital of Venezuela, is a flourishing city. The photographs on page 637 show different living conditions in Caracas, Venezuela.

While Venezuela is in debt, its oil wealth is real. Yet problems continue. Politicians get rich at government expense, and the government does little to help the very poor. Inflation, too, is a problem. The new president, Luis Herrera Campins [kam pēnz′] a father of five children, hopes to bring a tone of morality and family life to Venezuela. "Venezuela," said the new president, "should aspire [try] to be known as a land of work, sacrifices, and discipline, instead of a guzzler [drinker] of whiskey and oil.* He wants to form a Common Market of countries including Venezuela, Colombia, Ecuador, Peru, and Bolivia to help South America's economic growth.

Check in Here

1. Identify three common problems of the countries of Central America.
2. How did the United States acquire the Panama Canal?
3. Give two arguments for and against America's treaty to give the Panama Canal to Panama in the year 2000.
4. Why was Colombia hostile to the United States in 1903?
5. Explain how oil contributes to Venezuela's prosperity and problems.

RICH NATIONS AND POOR NATIONS OF LATIN AMERICA

The Poor Nations: Ecuador, Peru, and Bolivia

The countries of Ecuador [ek′wə dôr′], Peru [pə rü′], and Bolivia [bō liv′ē ə] were carved out of the Inca empire. The majority of the people in these countries are pure Indian, or part Indian and part Spanish. About ten to fifteen percent may be considered white. The rest are black, mulatto, Chinese, and Japanese. The Indian populations of these countries speak their own languages and follow their own religions. Few are Christians. Although many in number, the Indians have little power. Power remains with the small number of whites.

Ecuador's longtime dictator was José María Velasco Ibarra [i bär′ə], who

* *The New York Times*, March 18, 1979.

Caracas, the capital of Venezuela is a study in contrasts. Gradually, hill shacks are being replaced by modern housing.

served at different times from 1933 to 1978. During his years in office, he tried to steer a course between communism and fascism. Ibarra was unable to solve any of Ecuador's problems. These include widespread poverty and ill health among the people. There are undeveloped areas in Ecuador where few people live and that have not developed industry and agriculture. In August, 1972, oil began to flow through a 504 kilometer- (313 mi.) pipeline across the Andes from the wells in the Amazon basin to the port of Esmeraldas [ez'mə ral'däs].

Despite Ecuador's newly found oil wealth, the people were dissatisfied. Ibarra was removed from power and a new president was elected in 1978. In the past, Ecuador has been ruled by civilian and military dictatorships. The election of Jaime Roldos Aguilera [ä gē lēr ə] was significant because it was the first election in eleven years in Ecuador. Aguilera declared, "I am not going to overlook a single citizen, but I am going to put the principal emphasis on those who need the most."* Ecuador joined OPEC in 1974, and is that group's smallest oil exporter.

Peru is a country five times the size of Ecuador. Because of Peru's geography, transportation has been a problem since the days of the Incas. Most of the people are Indian. The government and the economy, however, are dominated by the people of European background, most of whom live in the mountain capital of Lima [lē'mə]. Here live the so-called "forty families" that control the nation's wealth.

Peru has many continuing problems. One of them is the need to make Indians a part of the general culture, another is how to gain control of the country from wealthy landowners. It is also necessary to limit the power of the Church in Peru.

*The New York Times, May 1, 1979.

637

Bolivia has sometimes been described as a beggar sitting on a chair of gold. This is so because the Bolivian land is rich and varied, while most of the people are poor. Bolivia includes enormously valuable silver mines. It also has equally valuable tin mines. The wealth from the mines, however, goes either outside the country or to the few ruling whites. Of all the Indian people of Latin America, those of Bolivia have been the most exploited. Their health has been ruined by years of overwork in the mines and on the farms of the rich.

The Postwar Problems of Argentina

During the post-World War II years, Juan Domingo Perón [pe rōn'] (1895–1973) and his wife Evita Duarte Perón (1919–1952) brought worldwide attention to Argentina [är'jən tē'nə]. For the decade between 1945 and 1955, Argentina was ruled by Perón. The influence of Perón remains an important part of Argentina's life and politics even to this day.

Juan Perón was the great-grandson of Italian immigrants. His great sources of strength were the army and the poor. Between 1943 and 1945, as head of the Department of Labor in Argentina, he made many reforms. As a result, the very poor and unskilled workers, who were called the "shirtless ones," voted Perón into power in February, 1946. Evita and Juan Perón were very powerful for ten years. *Peronistas*, followers of Juan Perón, believed in land reform and the taking over of industry by the nation. There was press censorship and no public criticism of Perón. Perón claimed that he was offering a better alternative to either communism or capitalism.

Perón tried to improve the Argentinian economy. He built new industry and bought out foreign-owned industry. In 1949, a new constitution gave him still greater power. Perón became even more dictatorial. He interfered with the academic freedom of universities. In 1951, he seized Argentina's world-famous newspaper, *La Prensa* [pren'sə]. This

Juan and Evita Perón salute Argentina's military guard as they ride in an open motorcade in Buenos Aires. What people voted Juan Perón into power?

was an attempt to suppress freedom of the press. In 1952, Evita died. Perón and the nation mourned deeply. Juan Perón had lost an important political ally, and the shirtless ones had lost someone they believed loved them.

Perón's plans to improve the economy began to collapse. Meat became scarce and people began to grumble. Because he had built up a cult of personality for himself and his wife, Perón lost the support of the Church. The Church disliked the worship of Perón at the expense, the Church believed, of the worship of God. Even the army turned against him.

In 1955, the armed forces rose against Perón and drove him from the country. He spent his years of exile in Venezuela, the Dominican Republic, and Spain. He enjoyed the enormous wealth his corrupt government had helped him obtain. Argentina spent years trying to clean up the economic and political problems Perón had created. After a period of turmoil, Arturo Frondizi [fron dē'sē], was elected in 1958. Argentina began a slow recovery.

But Perón's days were not entirely over. The popularity of Perón among the poor was enough to bring him back to power. He was reelected president in a national election held in 1973. He returned to power after eighteen years of exile, but his triumph was short-lived. Perón failed to gain real support from the army or from the young Peronistas. The Peronistas demanded more radical reforms than Perón was prepared to give. Violence spread even among the Peronists themselves. They disagreed about the kind of the reforms, if any, that were to be sought. In the midst of the turmoil, Perón died in 1974. Power went to his second wife, Isabel Martínez de Perón.

In 1976, a military coup ousted Isabel Perón, and kept her prisoner. She was released in 1981, and she left Argentina for Spain. In Europe and elsewhere there are Peronistas who still have a following in Argentina. The chances of their return to power are, however, remote.

The Argentine government rules by dictatorial means. Citizens suddenly disappear without a trace. Government authorities are unwilling or unable to say what has happened to them. When some reappear, it is clear that they have been tortured. As a result, there is considerable concern about human rights in Argentina. In 1977, Jacobo Timmerman [tim'mer mun], a Jewish editor of a leading newspaper, was arrested and tortured. His imprisonment concerned many who felt it meant a possible growth of anti-Jewish feeling among Argentinians. The OAS Commission on Human Rights won Timmerman's release in 1979.

What Brazil Was Like in the Postwar World

Unlike Argentina, Brazil [brə zil'] has a long history of friendship with the United States. When in 1941 the United States declared war on Germany and Japan, Brazil was not long in following. It let the United States use important naval bases located on its territory. When World War II ended, Brazil was under the mild dictatorship of Getulio Vargas [vär'gəs]. In 1945, however, under pressure from the military, Vargas was forced out. His place was taken by his hand-picked successor, General Eurico Gaspar Dutra [dü'trə]. Vargas remained active in Brazilian life. In 1950, he was reelected president. He committed suicide in August 1954, shamed by the discovery of scandals in his administration.

Between 1956 and 1964, Brazil had a democratic government. Under President Juscelino Kubitchek [kü'bi chek], a new capital was established in 1960. Brasília, [brä'zil yä] as it is known, is a

A modern building in Brasília, the capital city of Brazil.

beautiful city near the center of the country. Here, in the middle of an undeveloped area of Brazil, is the capital of South America's largest nation. It is a symbol of how Brazil hopes to develop its vast resources.

In 1964, the military overthrew the elected government of president Jõao Goulart [gü lär']. The "March Revolution," as the military takeover has been called, had wide civilian support. It was partly brought about by runaway inflation, by an attempt to save Brazil from corruption in government, by fear of total economic collapse, and by the fear of communism.

Chile's Troubles During the Postwar Period

By the time World War II ended, Chile [chil'ē] was well on its way toward developing a welfare state. It had a program of social security and unemployment and health benefits that was ahead of those found in most countries of the world at that time. However, such a program was not enough to overcome the great problems Chile faced. It did not get rid of the system which allowed poor farm workers to toil for long hours and little pay for rich landowners.

In 1970, Salvador Allende [ä yen'dā'] (1908–1973), a Communist, was elected president of Chile. This was the first time a Communist had been chosen head of state in a democratic election. Although Allende did not get most of the votes, he got more than any other candidate. As a Communist, Allende tried to get rid of American businesses in Chile. He wanted to change Chile's economy to one in which the government owned most large farms and factories. His policies, however, lowered the living standards of the middle class. Their protest was enough to bring about a crisis in Chile's government. His narrow victory was not enough to give him the political strength to ride out the crisis. Moreover, his program led to financial trouble and declines in production.

Gabriela Mistral

(1889–1957)

Lucila Godoy Alcayaga [äl kā ä′gə], was born in a small village in Chile. She took the name Gabriela Mistral [mē stral′] from the two writers she most admired. The first was the Italian poet and revolutionary Gabriele d′Annunzio [də nun′zē ō]; the other, a French Nobel Prize winner, Frédéric Mistral. The climax of her career came in 1945 when she, too, won the Nobel prize for literature.

Mistral's father was a village school teacher, who was well known in his community for the children's verses he wrote. It was her father who helped Mistral with her early schooling. Because of him, she became interested in both poetry and education. After teaching both history and Spanish, she began to make her reputation as a poet. She entered and won a poetry contest held by a writer's society in Santiago. At this time, she adopted the name by which she is generally known to this day. She rapidly took her place among the foremost poets of Latin America.

In addition to her work as a poet, Mistral helped the governments of Mexico and Chile establish schools and libraries, especially in rural areas. She represented Chile in the Institute of Intellectual Cooperation of the League of Nations. She taught in the United States for a short time, and was appointed by the Chilean government to important diplomatic posts in Madrid, Lisbon, Genoa, and Nice. When she contributed the money from some of her writings to help orphans of the Spanish Civil War, she displeased the Spanish dictator, Franco.

Gabriela Mistral believed that racial prejudice was among the leading causes in preventing a better understanding among the countries of Latin America and between those countries and the United States. "We of North and South America," she said, ". . . should find a three-fold fulfillment on our continent in an adequate standard of living and perfect and ample liberty."

Gabriela Mistral served as a member of the United Nations Sub-Commission on the Status of Women. She resigned when she could not agree about its goals. She felt that the commission should not seek special protection for women, but instead should be concerned about all people. Only in this way, she felt, would women achieve the full equality they wanted and deserved.

In September, 1973, the military toppled the Communist government. Salvador Allende was found dead. Some people believe that he killed himself. Some say the United States Central Intelligence Agency (CIA) had a hand in Allende's death.

Chile is now under the rule of a military group headed by President Augusto Pinochet Ugarte [ü gär'tā]. There have been accounts of imprisonment, torture, and murder of "enemies of the state." In 1976, relations between Chile and the United States were strained when Orlando Letelier [lə tel'yā'] was killed by a bomb that exploded under his car. Letelier had been a cabinet officer under Allende. He was against the Ugarte government. The United States suspected that Chile's government had ordered his assassination. Almost three years of investigation showed that American suspicions were correct. The Chilean secret police had ordered the execution. The United States wanted those who were accused of committing the crime sent to the United States to stand trial. Chile refused.

Chile and Argentina have been near war over the ownership and control of the area around the Tierra del Fuego [tē er'ə del fwā'gō], which is at the extreme southern tip of South America. The dispute involves the Beagle Channel and three tiny islands. Oil, in as yet unknown amounts, has been discovered on these islands. "These mountains will crumble into dust before the peoples of Argentina and Chile break the peace sworn at the feet of Christ the Redeemer." These words are carved on the pedestal of the statue of the Christ of the Andes that stands on the Argentina-Chile border. The statue was made in honor of the settlement of the 1896 border disputes between the two countries. Regrettably, the words on the pedestal were not enough to prevent renewed conflict between the two countries over the area.

How Latin America Faces Its Foreign Problems

During the early years of independence, the new nations of Latin America had problems establishing stable governments. This led some European countries to think they could move into Latin America and take over some of the countries. But, in 1823, President James Monroe of the United States warned the nations of Europe not to interfere with the new republics of Latin America.

Monroe's warning is known as the *Monroe Doctrine*. By it, the United States tried to give independence and freedom a chance to develop in Latin America. Then the United States irritated Latin Americans in the Mexican-American War (1846–1848). They felt that the United States was wrong in fighting Mexico, and in taking away a large part of its lands. In the hands of President Theodore Roosevelt, the Monroe Doctrine became a part of his Big Stick policy. Roosevelt wanted to keep foreign nations out of Latin America and to promote American interests in that area.

Roosevelt also encouraged Panama to break away from Colombia so that the Panama Canal might be built. The Panama Canal has helped bring Latin America, the United States, and other nations of the world closer together. However, the United States' impatience in getting the right of way for the canal was a source of concern to Latin Americans.

In time, the Monroe Doctrine became the basis for *Pan-Americanism*. This refers to the political, economic, and cultural cooperation among the countries of North, Central, and South America. In 1881, the American secretary of state suggested calling a conference of all the American states to meet in Washington. The first Pan-American Congress finally met in 1889. The conference established the *Pan-American Union*, which served as a bureau of information for all the

Left: The Pan American Highway in Mexico. Right: Part of the Trans-American Highway under construction in Brazil. Highways are necessary to the economic development of Latin American countries. They link cities and are essential for the transporting of goods.

member countries. The Pan-American Union encouraged an exchange of scientific and cultural information among its members.

In later years, other conferences were held in other countries of Latin America. A greater feeling of understanding grew among the Latin American countries. A Pan-American highway between Latin America and the United States was built. The new highway increased travel between the United States and the nations of Latin America.

In 1933, President Franklin D. Roosevelt of the United States declared that in its relations with Latin America the United States would observe the *Good Neighbor Policy*. According to this, the United States agreed not to intervene in the affairs of the countries of Latin America. Intervention, in the form of sending marines to Cuba, Nicaragua, and elsewhere, had been a hindrance in the development of good relations between the United States and the countries of

Central and South America and the island countries of the Caribbean. In the Pan-American conferences the United States agreed to consult with other members if the peace of North or South America were threatened.

As a result of the Pan-American conferences the United States found many friends in Latin America when World War II began. In the *Declaration of Panama* (1939), the American states declared neutrality in the war in Europe. In 1942, all of the Latin American countries except Chile and Argentina broke off diplomatic relations with Germany, Japan, and Italy. Chile broke off diplomatic relations with Germany in 1943, and Argentina did the same in 1944. In March, 1945, Argentina, after much urging by the United States, declared war on Germany.

When World War II ended, the people of North and South America continued to be good neighbors. The *Act of Chapultepec* [chə pül'tə pek'] (1945) said that an attack on any country in North America or South America would be met by all the countries that had signed the agreement. Again, Argentina had to be pushed into signing the agreement. At the *Caracas Conference* of 1954, the countries of North America and South America agreed to fully cooperate to hold back communism.

In 1948, the *Organization of American States (OAS)* was formed at a meeting in Bogotá, Colombia. The main headquarters of the organization was set up in Washington, D.C., where its major committees and councils meet. The Permanent Council can call the OAS into session to deal with emergencies. The OAS may be likened to a mini-United Nations because its aims are similar. It tries to keep the peace and to improve the economic relationship of Latin America and the United States. This relationship of Latin America and the United States is fragile. However, with goodwill on both sides, it can be carefully cultivated.

Check in Here

1. Why are Ecuador, Peru, and Colombia poor countries despite their rich resources?
2. Why did Peron appeal so strongly to Argentinians?
3. Why did the election of Allende, as president of Chile, worry the United States?
4. Why was Brasília built?
5. What was the importance of the Good Neighbor Policy?

In 1948, the OAS was founded. What other important events happened in the 1940s?

The Twentieth Century

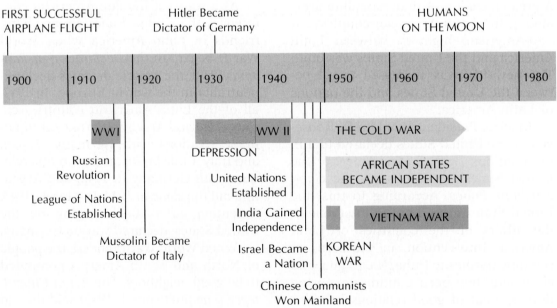

This chapter was about post-World War II developments among neighbors: the United States, Canada, and the countries of Latin America. The United States emerged from World War II as the leader of the free world. That country enjoyed a period of stability under President Eisenhower. Some progress was made in civil rights and in school desegregation. Yet, assassination was also part of the picture as President Kennedy, his brother, Robert Kennedy, and civil-rights leader Martin Luther King, Jr., were all slain. Under Nixon, an opening to improved relations with China was begun. Nixon became the only United States president to resign. He did so because of the Watergate scandal and cover-up. Under President Carter, new attempts to achieve world peace were made. He recognized the People's Republic of China and negotiated arms reductions with the Soviet Union. In 1981, President Reagan replaced Carter as president.

Canada emerged from World War II a much stronger country, and a more independent one. Its major problem has been that of trying to keep the nation together. In French-speaking Quebec, there is a movement to try to set up a separate nation.

There are many common postwar problems in Latin America. With some exceptions, as in Mexico, these countries are dominated by dictators who usually have the support of the military. There are many pressures on Latin American governments. Mostly, they involve the great gap that exists between the very rich and the very poor. In most countries of Latin America, there are also great differences in wealth between the cities and the countryside. Despite the slums of the larger cities, the urban areas continue to lure people from the farms. People hope to find jobs in the cities and to make more money than they can on the farms. Inflation is a threat to most of the countries of Latin America, where the price of food, clothing, and shelter can, in some cases, double each year.

The newly discovered oil resources of Mexico make that country especially important to the United States. Mexico and other Latin American countries do not trust the United States. These countries view the United States as having dominated the economies of Latin America without giving a great deal in return. The actions of the United States in taking Panama to build the canal, or sending marines to Nicaragua, were very much resented. However, through a growing interest in inter-American affairs, a Good Neighbor Policy begun by Franklin Roosevelt, and the Organization of American States, this resentment is beginning to fade.

REVIEWING THE HIGHLIGHTS

Persons to Identify

Harry Truman	Josephus Daniels	Francisco Villa
Dwight Eisenhower	López Portillo	René Levesque
John Kennedy	Fulgencio Batista	Pierre Trudeau
Robert Kennedy	Fidel Castro	Francisco Madero
Martin Luther King, Jr.	Papa Doc Duvalier	Rafael Trujillo
	Luis Campins	Anastasio Somoza
Richard Nixon	Gabriela Mistral	Álvaro Obregón
Jimmy Carter	Getulio Vargas	Diego Rivera
Plutarco Calles	Salvador Allende	Juan Perón
Dwight Morrow	Venustiano Carranza	Evita Duarte Perón
Ronald Reagan	Augusto Ugarte	

Places to Locate

Panama Canal	Sierra Maestra	Beagle Channel
Quebec	Bay of Pigs	Caribbean
Maritime Provinces	Brasília	Central America
Montreal	Amazon Basin	South America
Toronto	Chaco	Canada
St. Lawrence Seaway	Tierra del Fuego	

Terms to Understand

Great Society	Sandinistas	*Brown* v. *Board of Education of Topeka Kansas* (1954)
New Frontier	Monroe Doctrine	
Parti Quebecois	Pan-Americanism	
Peace Corps	shirtless ones	Organization of American States
26th of July Movement	Declaration of Panama	Act of Chapultepec
forty families	desegration	Fair Deal
Pan American Union	OPEC	Good Neighbor Policy
	Caracas Conference	
	PRB	

Events to Describe

Bay of Pigs

Mastering the Fundamentals

1. Do the assassinations of John and Robert Kennedy and Martin Luther King, Jr., reveal anything about our society? Why or why not?
2. Why was the Supreme Court decision in *Brown* v. *Board of Education of Topeka, Kansas,* a significant one in society generally, as well as in education?
3. Why does Quebec want to separate from Canada? What problems for Canada would such a separation cause?
4. Why has Mexico become more important as a world power?

5. How could Mexico be called a democracy if it is also a one-party state?
6. Why was Batista overthrown in Cuba?
7. What serious dangers to America does a Communist regime in Cuba pose?
8. Why is Puerto Rico a commonwealth rather than a state? Why do some Puerto Ricans prefer independence?
9. What economic problems face Haiti? What economic problems face the Dominican Republic?
10. What common political problems are shared by the Central American countries?
11. Why did the Sandinistas want to overthrow Somoza? If the Sandinistas retain power, what problems for Central America and the United States might develop?
12. Why do the Panamanians feel justified in taking back the Panama Canal?
13. Why did the United States agree to give up the Panama Canal?
14. Of what significance is the fact that Venezuela is an OPEC member?
15. How may oil help the economy of Ecuador?
16. What were the causes of the "March Revolution" in Brazil?
17. Why was Perón both loved and hated?
18. Why did Brazil set up a new capital, Brasília, in its interior?
19. Why was Allende overthrown?
20. How has the United States tried to improve its relations with Latin America?

THINGS TO DO

1. Do a map study of North, South, and Central America. On your map locate the following: (a) the countries of North America; (b) the countries of South America; (c) the countries of Central America; (d) the island countries of the Caribbean; (e) the important topographic features (rivers, mountains, deserts, etc.) of North and South America; (f) the provinces of Canada.
2. Prepare a report on The Role of Women—Past, Present, and Future in Latin America.
3. Debate. Resolved: The United States should intervene in Latin America to prevent the spread of communism.

Study the cartoon below and on the basis of your understanding of it, discuss the answers to the questions that follow it.

Mexican standoff

The Christian Science Monitor

1. In your own words, what is the "Mexican Standoff" to which the cartoonist is referring?
2. What does the attitude of Mexico appear to be? How can you tell?
3. What is the problem of the United States, as the cartoonist sees it?
4. What has happened to the "clout" of the United States? How can you tell?
5. Draw your own cartoon depicting the Mexican Standoff.

An oil field on the Persian Gulf

The Middle East and Africa: Peril and Promise

If the nineteenth century belonged to Europe, then it can certainly be said that the twentieth century belongs to America. What does the future hold? Perhaps the twenty-first century will belong to the countries and people of Africa and the Middle East.

Africa is a vast continent made up of mostly new countries. Many seek membership in the world community of nations. Growing Soviet influence in Africa concerns free nations. The Middle East is an important area; it is a strategic geographic region. In addition, the industrialized nations of the world depend on oil from the Middle East.

In earlier chapters we explored Africa and the Middle East in terms of their ancient past. Now we turn to the problems they face today and their prospects for tommorrow.

CHAPTER FOCUS

Taking Risks for Peace in the Middle East

The Troubled Lands of North Africa

Peril and Promise in Sub-Saharan Africa

TAKING RISKS
FOR PEACE
IN THE MIDDLE EAST

Why the Middle East Is Important

The Middle East is a vital area because of its oil and its location. It is situated between the continents of Asia, Europe, and Africa. Here Iran and Afghanistan share common borders with the Soviet Union. Here also are the important Straits of the Dardanelles that connect the Black Sea and the Mediterranean. Although Egypt has no oil, Egypt has the Suez [sü ez'] Canal, an important shortcut between Europe and the Far East.

The Middle East is oil rich but water poor. Water is urgently needed to produce food in the Middle East. Because rain is scarce, expensive irrigation projects must be built. The Nile, Jordan, Tigris, and Euphrates rivers may be used to bring water to the Middle East. Building dams on these rivers, however, takes a great deal of money and engineering skill. Irrigation systems are difficult to develop because the countries are so poor. Through oil, the Middle East may soon have the money to develop water supplies and other resources. Most Arab countries have joined the Organization of Petroleum Exporting Countries (OPEC)* to keep world oil prices high.

The Arab-Israeli conflict is one of the most serious of modern times. The bitter dispute continues to upset the peace in the Middle East and even threatens the peace of the entire world. The Middle East is the site of a power struggle between the West and the Soviet Union, with the Soviet Union supporting the Arab nations. The United States seeks to curb the influence of the Soviet Union in the Middle East and to achieve peace and stability there.

*OPEC was formed at the suggestion of Venezuela in 1960. Its members include: Algeria, Ecuador, Gabon, Indonesia, Iran, Iraq, Kuwait, Libya, Nigeria, Qatar, and Saudi Arabia.

How Israel Became a Jewish Nation

In 1917, Chaim Weizmann [wīz'man] took up the cause of a homeland for the Jews. He had escaped from Russia and had become a British subject. He was a chemist and contributed greatly to British science, particularly during World War I. Weizmann encouraged Lord Balfour to issue the *Balfour* [bal'fúr] *Declaration*. In it, the British promised that when the war was over, they would favor the building of a Jewish country in Palestine.

When World War I ended, Palestine became a British *mandate*. This meant that Britain was to be in charge of Palestine. Hopes were high that a Jewish homeland would not be far away. Many were disappointed when this did not happen.

In the 1930s, when Hitler started to persecute German Jews, many fled to Palestine. The Jewish population there began to grow. Palestine seemed to be the only place for Jewish refugees to go. The Arabs, however, opposed the idea of a Jewish nation in Palestine. They did not wish to see Jerusalem—a holy city to Muslims and Christians as well as Jews—fall into Jewish hands. They did not want to give up any land on which they had lived for over a thousand years. They tried unsuccessfully to stop the Jews from coming to Palestine.

In 1947, the British left Palestine. The United Nations divided Palestine into Arab and Jewish states. The name of the part of Palestine that became Jewish was changed to *Israel* [iz'rē əl]. Its citizens are called *Israelis* [iz rā'lēz] and their official language is *Hebrew* [hē'brü]. David Ben-Gurion [ben'gü ry ôn'] (1886–1973) became Israel's first prime minister. Israel insisted that its capital was Jerusalem. That city, however, was divided between Jordan and Israel. As a result, the government of Israel remained at Tel Aviv [tel' ä vēv'].

Israel and Its Neighbors, 1919–1981

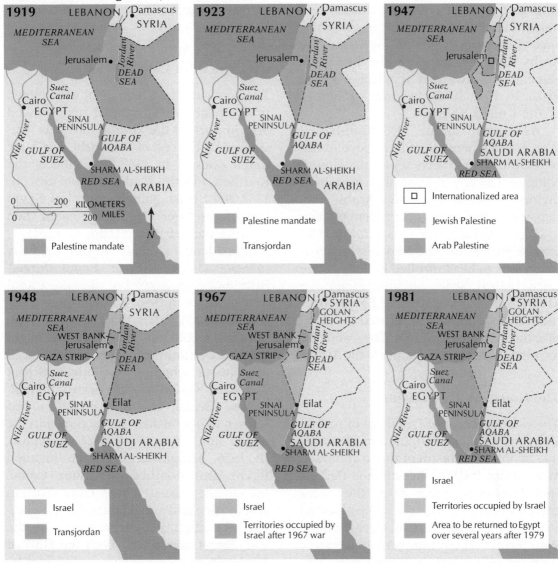

- When was Palestine divided between the Arabs and Jews?
- What territory did Israel gain after the 1967 war?
- What territory (according to the Arab-Israeli peace agreement) would be returned to Egypt after 1979?
- Judging from the map, why do you think the Golan Heights and the West Bank are still disputed areas?

When the nation of Israel became independent, its Arab neighbors attacked it hoping to defeat Israel at once. The Arabs argued that Palestine had been an Arab land for centuries and that it had been taken from them. In the *Arab-Israeli War* of 1948 the Arabs had many more soldiers than the Israelis, but they could not destroy Israel.

After much fighting and terrorism, the United Nations sent a truce commission to the Middle East. It was headed by Count Folke Bernadotte [bur'nə dōt'] of Sweden and Dr. Ralph Bunche [bunch] of the United States. These men tried to stop the fighting. Bernadotte was assassinated, and Bunche negotiated the *armistice* (temporary peace) between the Arabs and the Israelis. For his work Bunche was awarded the Nobel Peace Prize. In 1949, Israel became a member of the United Nations.

As a result of the 1948 Arab-Israeli War, Israel extended its land beyond the borders that had been set by the United Nations. The city of Jerusalem remained divided between Jews and Arabs. Jordan, which had been given independence in 1946 by Britain, was to control the Old City of Jerusalem. The New City of Jerusalem was to be controlled by Israel. The Gaza [gä'zə] Strip, an area along the Mediterranean, was given to Egypt. After the war, the Arab states refused to recognize the existence of Israel. They were determined to restore Palestine to the Arabs.

The Homeless Palestinians

The establishment of Israel out of part of Palestine created a population of homeless people. As a result of the Arab-Israeli War, about 900,000 Palestinians fled Israel. Having no place to go they were forced to settle in *refugee camps* located in Lebanon, Syria, Jordan, Gaza, and the West Bank. Their numbers grew after each Israeli victory over the Arabs. The camps are overcrowded and squalid. The main source of assistance for the refugees has been the United Nations and other Arab countries.

Some of the homeless Palestinians have vowed to establish a land of their own and to fight Israel. In 1964, the *Palestine Liberation Organization (PLO)* was formed. It is led by Yasir Arafat [a'rə fat] (1926–   ). The PLO often resorts to raids against Israeli settlements. The Israelis fight back to prevent terrorist raids and to retaliate against the attacks they can not prevent. This nearly constant violence makes the Middle East a dangerous place. War never seems far away.

Why a War Was Fought Over the Suez Canal

The war over the Suez Canal was related to the Arab-Israeli conflict and showed how important the Middle East was considered by the rest of the world. The Suez Canal opened in 1869. It connects the Red Sea and the Mediterranean Sea. In 1882, the British gained control of Egypt and of the Suez Canal. The canal then became part of their lifeline to India.

President Gamal Abdul Nasser [nä'sər] (1918–1970) of Egypt forced Britain to turn control of the Suez Canal over to Egypt in 1956. This alarmed many countries. They felt that, under Egypt, the canal would not be well run and might fall into Communist hands. Israel feared that Nasser, who had been buying Soviet weapons, would try to destroy Israel.

The British and the French urged Nasser to reconsider his action, but he would not return control of the canal. In 1956, Britain and France invaded Egypt and bombed the Suez Canal. Meanwhile, Israel joined Great Britain and France and attacked the Sinai Peninsula. Through its participation in the war, Israel hoped that both the Gulf of Aqaba [ä'kä bä'], which was blocked by Egypt to prevent Israeli shipping, and the Suez Canal would be opened to Israeli use.

The British, French, and Israelis might have been successful in the war to take the canal. The United Nations, however, sent troops to Egypt to restore peace. When the fighting ended, a 6,000-person United Nations Emergency Force was stationed in Egypt. Part of its job was to keep the Gulf of Aqaba open to Israel. However, Israeli forces were forced to leave the Sinai Peninsula, and the Suez Canal remained closed to Israeli ships.

Nasser was successful in his attempt to control the canal. Despite fears and doubts, the Egyptians were able to operate the canal well. All nations except Israel were allowed to use it. The income the Egyptian government received from the canal was to be used to help raise the living standards of the Egyptian people. Failure to allow Israel to use the Suez Canal made it hard to achieve peace in the area. It took two more wars before the canal was open to Israel.

The Causes and Results of the Six-Day War

Eleven years after the conflict over Suez, war again broke out (1967) between Israel and the Arab states. Those years had not been peaceful ones. Israel's Sinai campaign during the war over the Suez was successful, but Israel had not been allowed to keep what it had won. For years Israel had guarded its borders from the raids and sudden attacks of the Arab countries. Israel was determined not to let such attacks go unchallenged. In 1966, Arab attacks on Israel began to mount. These came particularly from Syria and Jordan.

Nasser saw an opportunity to show his leadership and influence in the Arab world. In May, 1967, the Arab countries of Syria and Egypt began to move their troops toward Israel. Nasser then demanded that the seven-nation United Nations Emergency Force pull out of Egypt. Since Israel had never allowed a similar force within its borders, Secretary-General U Thant [ü' thont'] believed he had no choice but to pull UN troops out of Egypt. For years, this force had safeguarded the peace of the Middle East. Now it was gone.

When the UN troops left, Nasser again stopped Israeli ships from going through the Gulf of Aqaba to the Israeli port of Eilat [ā'lät']. This is Israel's only

Each year, visitors flock to the ancient city of Jerusalem, a holy place for Jews, Moslems, and Christians.

port for trade to the south and east, particularly to Africa and Southeast Asia. Eilat is also the chief port for Israeli oil imports. The Aqaba blockade was therefore seen as an act of war. It was a violation of the idea that freedom of the seas exists for all nations in international waters. But Israel hesitated to strike back, or so it seemed. Although not a particular friend of Nasser, Jordan's King Hussein [hü sän'] went to Cairo where he announced that he supported Nasser. Saudi Arabia also supported Egypt. Never before had the Arab world seemed so well armed. The Soviet Union strongly supported the Arab cause.

In the *Six-Day War*, Israeli troops were led by General Yitzhak Rabin [ra bēn'] and Defense Minister Moshe Dayan [dä yän'], hero of the Sinai campaign of 1956. They planned well and struck suddenly. On the morning of June 5, 1967, Israeli jet fighters attacked. In one day they destroyed the Egyptian air force. Israeli tanks struck deep into the Sinai Peninsula. Egyptian troops were pushed back across the Suez Canal.

Israeli soldiers captured East Jerusalem and all of the West Bank of the Jordan River. Israel destroyed the Egyptian forces in the Gaza Strip and those at Sharm El-Sheik. Those forces had guarded the Gulf of Aqaba and had prevented Israeli ships from entering. And, in the north, Israeli soldiers stormed from the Syrian heights and pushed the Syrians back from where they had attacked Israeli border settlements.

As a result of the Six-Day War, Israel won a united Jerusalem and control of the holy places. It gained secure borders, having pushed Egypt to beyond the Suez Canal. It also won the Gaza Strip, over which there had been much fighting in the past. Jordanian forces were pushed back beyond the Jordan River. The Syrian heights, from which Arab attacks had been launched, was also captured.

Bullet-riddled pieces of military equipment from the 1967 Six-Day War litter a roadside in the Sinai Desert.

The Causes and Results of the October War

In October, 1973, Egypt and Syria attacked Israel. The fourth Arab-Israeli war, the *October War,* in twenty-five years had broken out. Israel had known that war would come soon. This time Israel did not strike first. It was under United States pressure not to, and it hoped to win support from other nations. Egyptian troops crossed the Suez Canal and went deeply into the Sinai Peninsula. After much fighting and loss of life on both sides, Israel's troops began to win. They crossed the Suez Canal. They conquered Egyptian territory on the west bank of the canal. Then on October 24, 1973, a cease-fire was arranged between Israel and Egypt.

In January, 1974, a troop withdrawal agreement was negotiated through Henry Kissinger, the American Secretary of State. By March, a buffer zone (an area of land that neither side could invade) was established between Israeli and Egyptian forces in the Sinai.

The Arab countries felt they won the 1973 war. They had shown unity during the war. The Arab oil-producing nations stopped exporting oil. Thus, Arab control of much of the world oil supplies became a political weapon. Through it, they tried to win friends among nations that might otherwise be sympathetic to Israel. This action threw the world into confusion. Countries sympathetic to Israel thought twice before giving that country aid. As a result, Israel found itself almost alone. It could count only upon the United States, which was also urging Israel to agree to a troop withdrawal.

During the October War, it appeared that the Soviet Union might join in on the side of Egypt and Syria. The United States then went on a worldwide military alert. The Middle East seemed to be the fuse that could start another world war. Golda Meir [mī'ər] (1891–1979) was premier of Israel during the October War. Some Israelis felt that too many had lost their lives during the war. They also felt that Israel had not used its military forces to best advantage. As a result, Golda Meir resigned. A new government under Yitzhak Rabin [räb ēn'] was elected.

In April, 1975, Kissinger succeeded in arranging another peace agreement. In addition to other terms, Egypt and Israel agreed that conflict in the Middle East should not be resolved by military force. The United States would provide aid to Israel and would place an observer team between Egyptian and Israeli forces to enforce the terms of the agreement. The agreement was not what either side wanted, but it was an encouraging step toward peace in the Middle East.

How Israel and Egypt Made a Peace That Is Threatened

In November, 1977, Anwar El-Sadat [el sä'dät], President of Egypt, made a historic visit to Jerusalem. In a speech to the *Knesset* [knes'et], the Israeli parliament, he urged that the two nations make peace. Although these talks began with high hopes, they nearly failed to achieve an agreement. Each side wanted to give up as little as it could. With the aid of Jimmy Carter, president of the United States, an agreement between the two countries was finally reached. Prime Minister Begin [bā'gin] of Israel, President Sadat of Egypt, and President Carter met in September, 1978, at Camp David, Maryland. There, in a long meeting, the terms of the agreement were hammered out. Although an agreement had been reached, it appeared to unravel just a few weeks later. Through the fall of 1978 there was concern that Carter had failed to bring the two sides together.

(turn to p. 658)

Menachem Begin

(1913–   )

Menachem Begin became the sixth prime minister of Israel in 1977. He is one of the few remaining leaders of Israel's early struggle for a Jewish nation. Born in Poland, he was well-educated in Judaism and went on to a Polish gymnasium (high school). There he acquired an interest in Greek and Latin classics. He went to the University of Warsaw where he studied law and became a lawyer.

Menachem Begin went to Israel under harsh circumstances. In early 1939, just before the outbreak of World War II, Great Britain limited the number of Jews who could enter Palestine. Begin led a mass protest in front of the British embassy in Warsaw. He was arrested by the Polish police and spent several months in jail. Upon release from prison he fled Warsaw, just as the Nazi troops began to invade that city. Mostly on foot, he and his family made their way to Vilna in Lithuania. When the Soviet Union divided that country in 1949, Begin was arrested and sentenced to eight years as a slave laborer in Siberia.

In 1941, Germany attacked the USSR. Begin, along with thousands of other Polish prisoners, was released in order to help the Soviet Union fight. It was Begin's good fortune to be assigned to a Polish Army unit that was sent to the Middle East in May, 1942. At this time, he entered Palestine. His father, mother, and only brother were all killed during the Nazi Holocaust of European Jews. His sister survived. She now lives in Israel.

These experiences may explain why, as a fighter for Israel, he joined Jewish terrorist groups. The underground *Irgun* [ir gün'] started a program of sabotage and terror. It would force Great Britain, which controlled Palestine, to agree to a homeland for the Jewish people. The British had said they would "view with favor" the establishment of such a homeland in Palestine. When the Jewish state of Israel was established, members of the Irgun joined the Israeli army. It fought the war that broke out between Jews and Arabs in 1948.

Perhaps only a man whose loyalty to Israel had been so tested could have responded to Egyptian President Sadat's peace overtures. For his role in helping bring peace to the Middle East, Begin was awarded the Nobel Peace Prize in 1978. He shared this prize with Anwar El-Sadat of Egypt.

Anwar El-Sadat

(1918–1981)

In October, 1970, Anwar El-Sadat was sworn into office as President of the United Arab Republic. It seemed that he would follow in the footsteps of Egypt's beloved leader, Gamal Abdul Nasser.

Anwar El-Sadat was born to a poor family of Muslims in a village in the Nile delta. Sadat received a thorough teaching in the traditions of his faith, and was a deeply religious man throughout his life. In 1936, the Egyptian military academy was opened to members of the lower and middle classes. Sadat was admitted and was graduated two years later. At the academy, he worked with Nasser and other officers in plotting the overthrow of the monarchy of King Farouk [fä rük'].

While Begin fought the British to release their grip on Palestine, Sadat fought the British to release their grip on Egypt. For his struggles against the British, Sadat was imprisoned for two years. Sadat escaped from prison and went into hiding. After another series of terrorist attacks against the British, Sadat was captured and imprisoned for three years.

Later, Sadat joined other officers led by Nasser in a bloodless overthrow of King Farouk in 1952. There is a story about this incident. Sadat was summoned to Cairo by Nasser, but when he arrived he received no further instructions. While waiting to hear from Nasser, he took his family to the movies. He did not know that the revolution was beginning without him. Nevertheless, it was Sadat who was asked by Nasser to announce the revolution to the world. It was Sadat who was given the responsibility of seeing to it that Farouk left Egypt.

Sadat held several posts under Nasser. There was a feeling of personal trust between the two men. There were few who were more loyal both to Nasser and to Egypt than Sadat. As a result, Sadat succeeded Nasser.

During his early career, Sadat was intensely hostile to Israel. In the 1967 War, he regretted Nasser's agreement to a settlement with Israel. He vowed never to make peace with Israel unless every inch of Egyptian soil that Israel had taken was given up. In flying to Jerusalem and starting direct talks with Israel, Sadat showed great courage. Sadat knew that prosperity could not come to his poverty-stricken land if it had to be always prepared for war. For his efforts for peace, Sadat shared the Nobel Peace Prize with Begin in 1978. He died in 1981 believing he had achieved what God had wanted him to do.

In March, 1979, President Carter made a dramatic trip to the Middle East. He visited Begin and Sadat. The leaders of the two countries reached new compromises in March, 1979. Finally, an agreement was made between two countries that had been officially at war for over thirty years.

The provisions of the agreement may be summarized as follows: 1) Israel is to give up the Sinai Peninsula over a three-year period, remove its military forces, and give up its settlements; 2) the UN and the United States are to help establish security on both sides of the Israeli-Egyptian border; 3) the state of war between the two countries is to end; 4) Israeli ships are free to use the Suez Canal; 5) Israel is to give up developed oil wells in the Sinai but may buy oil from Egypt; 6) Egypt and Israel are to begin negotiations for Palestinian self-rule on the West Bank and in the Gaza Strip.

The agreement is a milestone in Egyptian-Israeli relations, although it is not the complete one that has long been sought. Egypt hoped that other Arab states would follow its lead. Thus far, they have not done so. Instead, they have isolated Egypt and have become hostile to it.

What to do about such contested areas as the West Bank and the Gaza Strip remain grave problems. Some Israelis have insisted on establishing settlements on the West Bank. They do so in part because they believe the land was theirs in biblical times. They are also afraid that unless Israelis are settled there, the West Bank may become a home exclusively for Palestinians. The Palestinians living on the West Bank, on the other hand, are bitter about being ruled by the Israeli military. They also claim to own land on the West Bank, which they say is being increasingly taken over by the Israelis.

Many Palestinian terrorist raids against Israel are launched from southern Lebanon. Unlike other countries of the Middle East, which are mostly Muslim, Lebanon was formed in 1946 as a nation with a Christian majority. Christians also have a great deal of power in government. As the Muslim population grew in Lebanon, these people demanded a greater share in the government. Civil war between Christians and Muslims began in 1975. Israel helps the Christians. Arab peoples, including Syria and the PLO (Palestine Liberation Organization), provide support to some Muslim groups.

In the spring of 1981, Israel said it would destroy Soviet missiles placed in Syria. Syria said these missiles were needed to protect Lebanon. President Reagan of the United States sent a representative to try to work out a peaceful settlement of the problem. In June, 1981, however, Israeli bombers totally destroyed the Osirak nuclear reactor in Bagdad, Iraq. Israelis said they were defending themselves against the Iraqis. There was evidence that the Iraqis were building an atom bomb to use against Israel.

The United States, in 1981, decided to sell advanced aircraft to Saudi Arabia. It did so with the hope that Saudi Arabia would help keep peace in the Middle East. Saudi Arabia did put forth a proposal for peace that seemed to suggest Arab recognition of Israel. The proposal was totally turned down by all other Arab states.

In October, 1981, Anwar El Sadat was assassinated. He was murdered by Muslim fanatics who opposed his attempts at peace with Israel. He was succeeded by his vice president, Hosni Murabak [mùr'ə bek']. Murabak promised to follow in Sadat's footsteps. The peace of the Middle East may depend on his promise.

How the Shah Was Toppled from the Throne of Iran

One of the major events of 1979 was the fall of the Shah of Iran. He was toppled by an aging Islamic holy man, the Ayatollah Khomeini [ī ə tō′lə kō mā′nē]. The fall of the Shah was as unexpected as it was swift. The United States lost an important ally in the Shah. It lost a vital listening post on the borders of the Soviet Union. Israel lost an important source of oil. Oil-rich Iran fell to a religious leader whose views go back to the roots of the Muslim faith.

Mohammed Reza Pahlavi [pä′lə vē′] (1919–1980) became Shah in 1941, when his father, the founder of the ruling dynasty, stepped down. Under Premier Mohammed Mossadegh [mō′sä deh′], an attempt was made in 1951 to nationalize the oil industry. In a test of strength with Mossadegh, the Shah lost and fled the country. In 1953, Mossadegh was over-

- Locate and name the countries along the Persian Gulf.
- Locate and name the countries that border Iran.

The Middle East in the 1980s

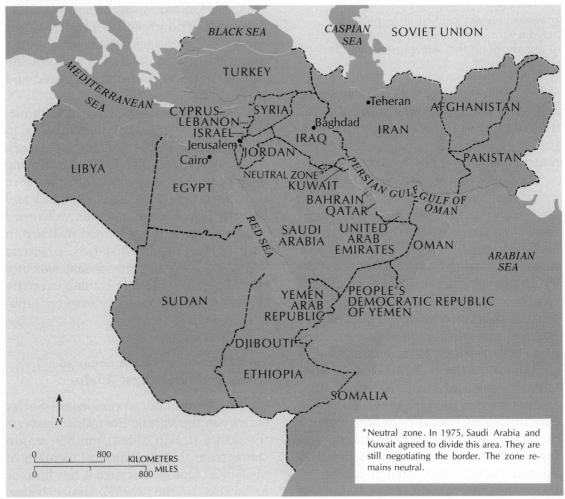

*Neutral zone. In 1975, Saudi Arabia and Kuwait agreed to divide this area. They are still negotiating the border. The zone remains neutral.

Louise Kennedy, wife of an American hostage in Iran. She wears a yellow ribbon to signify hope that the captives will be returned safely.

thrown with the help of the United States and other foreign countries. These countries did not want their oil industries in Iran taken away from them. The Shah returned and took power.

By the 1960s, the plan to make Iran a modern nation was underway. Those who watched closely, however, knew there was no true reform. Land remained in the hands of the rich. The benefits of modernization did not reach the majority of the population. Iranian traditions were not valued much by the Shah. There was little creativity in the fields of art, music, or architecture. Instead, "culture" was imported from abroad.

Schools and universities were set up, but with scant academic freedom. Discontent among Iranians grew. The presence of *SAVAK* [sä'väk], the secret police of the Shah, became more harsh and more evident. Modernization seemed to be doing away with Muslim teachings. Frustrated, the people turned to their

ayatollahs, or holy men. The Ayatollah Khomeini was only one of a group of religious leaders who listened to the discontent among Iranians.

The Ayatollah Khomeini had been exiled by the Shah for activities threatening his rule. It was widely believed that the Ayatollah's son may have been killed by the SAVAK. From a village in France the Ayatollah Khomeini won support from Iranians who hailed him as their leader. First the people, then even the Iranian army, supported the Ayatollah. When this happened, the Shah fled.

Homeless, the Shah lived in Egypt, the Bahamas, Morocco, and Mexico. President Carter was told that the Shah was incurably ill with cancer and needed medical treatment. The Shah was admitted to the United States. This angered the Ayatollah, who urged his people to "expand . . . their attacks against the United States and Israel, so they may force the United States to return the deposed and cruel shah."

In November, 1979, Iranian militants stormed the United States embassy in Teheran, Iran. They took fifty-two Americans as hostages. The Shah, after being operated upon, was encouraged to leave the United States. He fled to Panama and then to Egypt where he was welcomed by President Sadat. He died in Cairo in July, 1980. For the fifty-two American hostages, however, the ordeal was not over. They were held in Iranian captivity for 444 days until their release on January 20, 1981.

How the Soviet Union Seeks to Influence Middle East Affairs

There are a number of reasons for Soviet activity in the Middle East. One reason is the desire to win allies. Another reason stems from the geographical location of the Soviet Union. Because it has little or no access to the world's major water-

660

ways, the Soviet Union has always tried to extend its influence and control in the Mediterranean area.

Just how far the Communist interest in the Middle East will go remains to be seen. In 1958, American troops were sent to Lebanon, and British troops were sent to Jordan in order to keep those countries free from Communist influence. The Soviet Union once had substantial influence in Iraq. But in 1978, twenty-one Communists were executed and Iraq took a neutral position. Iraq has had many political upheavels as one regime forces its way to power, only to be overthrown by another. Its government has been ultra-nationalistic and has supported the PLO. Iraq and Iran went to war in 1981.

The unrest in the Middle East plays into the hands of the Soviet Union. After its success in seizing the Suez Canal, Egypt became the leader of the Arab world. In 1958, Egypt united with Yemen to form the United Arab States and with Syria to form the *United Arab Republic (UAR)*. But in 1961, Syria revolted against Egyptian rule and withdrew from the United Arab Republic. Today, the Arab Republic of Egypt consists only of Egypt.

The Soviet Union has encouraged Egypt's ambitions to dominate the Middle East. It has supplied Egypt with both ammunition and money. In the 1960s, the Soviet Union also provided Egypt with skilled engineers and aid in building the Aswan [as'wän] High Dam on the Nile River. This dam, officially opened in 1971, is providing Egypt with water for irrigating farm land. It generates electric power for factories. In July, 1972, fearful of excessive Communist control, Sadat ordered the Soviet Union to remove its troops.

Nowhere else in the Arab world has the Soviet Union succeeded as well as in South Yemen (People's Democratic Republic). Here, the Soviet Union has been gaining control not only over the nation's economy, but over its educational and cultural affairs as well. Cubans, Russians, and East Germans who are Communists run the government of South Yemen. South Yemen and its neighbor, Yemen (Yemen Arab Republic) are poor countries; yet their location is very important to the free world.

Check in Here

1. What is the strategic importance of the Middle East?

2. What are the major causes of hostility between Arabs and Israelis?

3. Explain the political and economic reasons for the fall of the Shah of Iran.

4. List two reasons behind the Soviet Union's activities in the Middle East.

THE TROUBLED LANDS OF NORTH AFRICA

North Africa: Land in Turmoil

Following World War II, there was much unrest in North Africa, where Moroccans, Tunisians, and Algerians were fighting the French. Since 1830, France had had special privileges in these areas. Under French domination many improvements in the quality of life were made. Thousands of French people went to live in North Africa. There they became owners of stores, factories, and fertile farms. Tunisia and Morocco were ruled by native princes who took orders from France. But Algeria was regarded as a part of France.

After World War II, the people of the North African colonies decided that the time had come to rule themselves. The French, especially those who lived in the colonies, did not agree. There was a good deal of angry talk and fighting. Finally, Morocco, in 1956, and Tunisia, in 1957, were given their independence.

President Muammar el-Qaddafi (right) of Libya is host to PLO leader Yasir Arafat (left) during Libyan festivities.

It seemed as if Algeria would be the next to win independence. Instead, a war followed. To the one million French living in Algeria, separation would have meant living in a foreign nation of nine million Algerians. The French in Algeria feared that an independent Algeria would pass laws to take away their good living conditions. In addition, oil had been discovered in Algeria. This made Algeria even more valuable to France, since the oil of the Middle East was becoming more difficult to get. To make matters worse, France had lost other colonies. It did not want to lose Algeria.

Each succeeding premier of France failed to solve this problem. Then Charles de Gaulle was called to power in 1958 by the French people and by the so-called *Committees of Public Safety*. These committees were first formed in Algeria and later spread to France. They demanded that the French government take a strong stand against the Algerian rebels. President de Gaulle refused to suppress the rebels. Instead, he presented a plan for Algerian self-government. In January, 1961, after years of bloody fighting, the French people (in France and in Algeria) approved de Gaulle's plan for Algerian self-government and eventual independence.

In January, 1952, Libya [lib′ē ə] became a constitutional monarchy under King Idris I [ī′dris]. Libya is essentially a poor land with a fertile area along the coast where fruits are grown. Since oil was discovered in Libya, however, its prosperity and power now depends on oil.

In 1969, the military led by Colonel Muammar el-Qaddafi [el kä dä′fē] (1942–19) overthrew the monarchy. Under Qaddafi's leadership, Libya took over most foreign holdings of Libyan oil. Libya has played an important role in Middle Eastern affairs. Qaddafi has sought to stir up Arab nationalism. In North Africa, among such nations as Mauretania [môr′i tā′nē ə], Morocco, and Algeria, as well as in the territory of former Spanish Sahara, Qaddafi has sought a Saharan Confederation. He has also tried to unite Egypt and Libya. While this project at first appealed to Sadat, it was finally rejected. Libya gives money to terrorist organizations around the world.

The political stability of Northwest Africa is in danger because of a dispute over the area formerly called Spanish Sahara. Western Sahara, as this area is also called, was divided in 1975 between Mauretania, which took one-third of it, and Morocco, which took two-thirds. This settlement did not please Libya and Algeria.

Under President-for-Life Habib Bour-

662

Africa in 1950

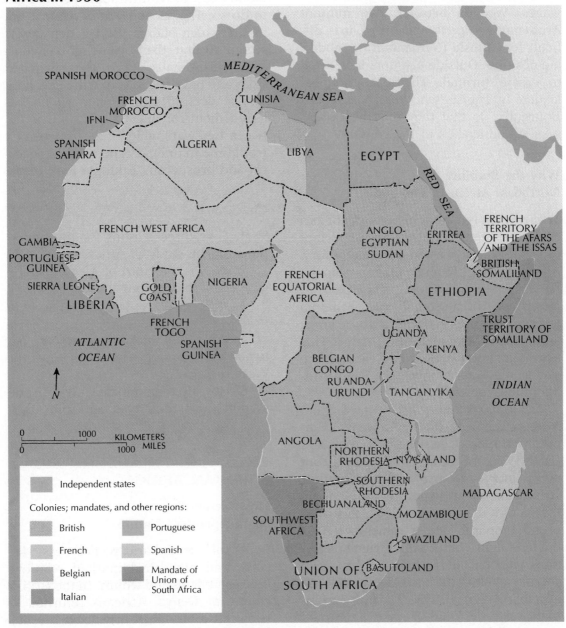

SPANISH MOROCCO
FRENCH MOROCCO
IFNI
SPANISH SAHARA
ALGERIA
TUNISIA
LIBYA
EGYPT
MEDITERRANEAN SEA
RED SEA
FRENCH WEST AFRICA
GAMBIA
PORTUGUESE GUINEA
SIERRA LEONE
LIBERIA
GOLD COAST
NIGERIA
FRENCH TOGO
SPANISH GUINEA
FRENCH EQUATORIAL AFRICA
ANGLO-EGYPTIAN SUDAN
ERITREA
FRENCH TERRITORY OF THE AFARS AND THE ISSAS
BRITISH SOMALILAND
ETHIOPIA
UGANDA
KENYA
TRUST TERRITORY OF SOMALILAND
BELGIAN CONGO
RUANDA-URUNDI
TANGANYIKA
ATLANTIC OCEAN
INDIAN OCEAN
N
ANGOLA
NORTHERN RHODESIA
NYASALAND
SOUTHERN RHODESIA
MADAGASCAR
BECHUANALAND
MOZAMBIQUE
SOUTHWEST AFRICA
SWAZILAND
UNION OF SOUTH AFRICA
BASUTOLAND

0   1000   KILOMETERS
0   1000   MILES

Independent states

Colonies; mandates, and other regions:

British

French

Belgian

Italian

Portuguese

Spanish

Mandate of Union of South Africa

- What two European countries controlled the largest areas in Africa in 1950?
- Locate and name three independent countries of Africa in 1950.

guiba [bûr gē bə] (1903–   ), Tunisia took a more peaceful course. Tunisia is a Muslim state in which modernization has gone forward. Women have achieved notable gains in the political and educational life of the nation. Foreign investments have been encouraged as tourists pour large sums into the economy. Bourguiba has been sympathetic to Israel. He has urged the Arabs to negotiate with Israel. However, Bourguiba is an aging man and his coun-

663

try is torn by strife. Workers want better wages. Wedged between two militant Arab states, Algeria and Libya, it is difficult for Tunisia to maintain its moderate position. Outside agitators have tried to create turmoil. There are political leaders in Tunisia who hope to succeed Bourguiba so that they may have their turn as the leaders of the country.

Why the Stability of Northeast Africa Is Threatened

While Egypt is commonly thought of as a Middle Eastern country, it is important to think of it also as an African country. Along with Ethiopia, Libya, Somalia [sō mä′lē ə], and Chad, it is part of Northeast Africa. Somalia and Ethiopia are two countries in a region whose lands are in the strategic Horn of Africa. This area is just across the Red Sea from the important Arab countries of Saudi Arabia and Yemen.

Ethiopia is today a disrupted land. After a reign of fifty-eight years, Emperor Haile Selassie [hī′lē sə las′ē] (1891–1975) of Ethiopia was pushed from power in 1974 by army officers. Famine, strikes, and an army mutiny were among the factors that brought down this once proud monarch. He is remembered as the lone figure before the League of Nations who called for help for his weak country against the merciless attacks of Mussolini's Italy in 1936. The army group that overthrew Haile Selassie attempted to bring about land and economic reforms. While the army's approach to the economic improvement of Ethiopians was sound, progress was halted because of a two-front war.

One war was against Eritrea [er′ə trē′ə]. A former Italian colony, it was joined to Ethiopia in 1952 and sought separation from Ethiopia for years. Encouraged by Arab states, it tried to set up an independent country of its own. It fought bloody battles with Ethiopia for its right to do so. The second war is against Somalia, which claims the Ogaden desert region. At first, the Soviet Union encouraged the Somalis. Later, they switched sides and have been arming the new military leadership of Ethiopia, which has asked them for aid. Caught as it is between two wars which flare up violently from time to time, prospects for a peaceful and prosperous Ethiopia look bleak.

Check in Here

1. Give three reasons for the importance of the study of Africa.

2. Why is the Horn of Africa a strategic geographic region?

3. Why is Ethiopia fighting a two-front war?

4. Why is there disagreement between Morocco and Mauretania over the Western Sahara?

5. How do the political views of Tunisia differ from those of Algeria and Libya?

PERIL AND PROMISE IN SUB-SAHARAN AFRICA

How Kenya Became an Independent Nation

South of the Sahara, restlessness, discord, and bloodshed marked relations between blacks and whites. In the British colony of Kenya, Africans returned to tribal customs. They organized a rebellion against the British. The *Mau Mau* [mou′ mou′], as the rebellion was called, let loose a reign of terror against the Europeans. Not only were Europeans killed, but tribes that refused to cooperate with the Mau Mau were also slaughtered. It took much bloodshed before the Mau Mau rebellion was put down. The rebellion lasted from 1953 until 1961. The people of Kenya had many fair complaints. These included demands for a

Prince Philip of Great Britain and Premier Jomo Kenyatta take part in ceremonies that mark Kenya's independence after seventy years of British rule.

greater share of the more fertile lands in their country which were taken by the Europeans. The Mau Mau rebellion showed the depths to which Africans were moved to do something to reestablish their own ways of living.

Ten years after the rebellion, Kenya was granted its independence within the British Commonwealth of Nations. In 1964, it became a sovereign republic.

Jomo Kenyatta [ken yä′tə] (1893–1978), the grandson of a Kikuyu [ki kü′yü] medicine man led the Mau Mau rebellion against whites. This English-educated African leader was successful in restoring stability to his land. In a policy known in the Swahili language as *Harambee* [hä räm′bē] (Let us all pull together) he sought to unite his nation and did so. With Tanzania and Uganda,

Kenya set up the East African Community to encourage trade among members. This effort was a failure. The three nations could not live peacefully with one another. Relations between Tanzania and Kenya remain strained. The bloody and harsh dictatorship of Idi Amin Dada [e dē′ ä min′ dä′dä] of Uganda was brought down by invading troops from Tanzania. Jomo Kenyatta died in 1978; whether those who follow will be as successful as he was remains to be seen.

What the Future Holds for Nigeria

Nigeria is a large country, more than twice the size of the state of California. It is made up of four self-governing regions, each of which seems to have the natural resources and people required for the

665

The harbor of Lagos, capital of Nigeria. One of Africa's richest nations, Nigeria has used money from oil sales to build its economy.

development of a rich life. Oil, coal, iron, limestone, and natural gas are abundant. About one-fifth of all the population of Africa live in this former British colony. It became an independent nation in 1960 and a republic within the British Commonwealth in 1963. It is a member of the United Nations. Its constitution assures personal liberties and provides the independent regions with self-government.

In 1964, a national election took place which almost divided Nigeria. Tribal loyalties are very strong. Because people are not used to self-government, let alone democracy, violence resulted. Charges of dishonesty in the election added to the turmoil. So sharp did the differences become that some tribes living in the eastern regions of the country threatened to break away.

The threat made in 1964 became a reality in 1967. The Eastern Region of Nigeria is made up mainly of Ibos [ē'bōz].

They are members of the Christian church. They are well-educated and think along modern lines. Because of their effort and education, many Ibos gained high jobs in the central government of Nigeria. The other tribes of Nigeria have resented the rise of the Ibos. This is particularly true of the Hausa [hou'sə] tribe. These people live in the Northern Region. They are mainly Muslim. They are not as well-educated as the Ibos, and are less progressive.

After an army takeover in 1966, an Ibo headed the first military government. This enraged many of the northern Hausas. In July of 1966, a slaughter of thousands of Ibos took place. Ibos living in the north fled to their homeland in the Eastern Region. Badly outnumbered, the Ibos were fearful that they might be totally destroyed.

Led by college-educated Odumegwu Ojukwu [ō jü'kwü], the Ibos of the East-

666

ern Region decided to try to break away from Nigeria. In 1967, they declared their independence from Nigeria. They took the name *Biafra* [bē ä'frä], from the waters on which their ports are located. Ojukwu felt that the government at Lagos, Nigeria's capital, was not giving the eastern region enough money to resettle the refugees from the north. He felt that the oil of the Eastern Region would see the Ibos through financially. If the income from oil did not have to be shared with the central government, the Eastern Region could become rich. Ojukwu thought that it was unfair for the Ibos of the eastern region to pay taxes to the central government because that government did not protect the Ibos from assassination.

Biafran resistance collapsed in January 1970. In a ceremony in Lagos, Major General Yakubu Gowon [gə'wôn], head of Nigeria, joyously announced the end of the struggle. "We have been reunited with our brothers," he said. The struggle that had just ended was costly. More than a million Biafrans, many of them children, had died of starvation. About two million soldiers and civilians on both sides had died.

Nigeria today, thanks to vast oil reserves, is a wealthy country. General Gowon wisely settled the war with Biafra without trying to get even with the Ibos. The result is that even the former state of Biafra is enjoying prosperity. Children are in school, and the shops are busy with men and women who have money to spend. After thirteen years of military rule, Nigeria peacefully returned to civilian government in October, 1979.

Why Zaïre Is a Troubled Land

When the Congo, now called *Zaïre* [zī'er], won independence from Belgium in June, 1960, chaos followed. The Congo was a colony nearly eighty times larger than Belgium, the parent country. Although the Africans had fairly good jobs, they were good only by African standards. Most earned less than $150 a month. They resented the fact that most businesses were owned by Belgians. Belgium provided elementary schooling, but did not provide higher education of any kind for the Africans. Unlike Britain, which often encouraged brilliant young men and women from its colonies to study at the great universities of Oxford and Cambridge, Belgium made it almost impossible for bright students to study in Belgium.

One of the most serious grievances was that Africans were not allowed to vote. The white governor, sent by Belgium, together with the white owners of businesses ruled the country. This meant the blacks were without either a voice in or control in the government.

Eventually, these grievances led to a clamor for independence. Belgium, realizing that nationalism could not be resisted, gave in. It left the Congo to shift for itself. Belgium pulled out of the Congo so fast, however, that it left a vacuum. The Congolese, lacking education and skills, were unable to fill it.

After the Belgian government withdrew, several black leaders took control of the Congo. Patrice Lumumba [lü mum'bə], the first premier of the Congo, was unsuccessful in putting down the violence that followed. He was removed from office by President Kasavubu [kas'ə vü'bü]. While attempting to return to power in 1961, Kasavubu was assassinated.

Immediately following independence, the province of Katanga [kə täng'gə], under the leadership of Moise Tshombe [chom'bā], broke away. Katanga is a rich mining area in the southeast. It set up an independent government that lasted until 1963. This division in the new nation and the confusion that followed

667

caused the United Nations to send in military troops to restore order and unity to the Congo. In some measure the UN did help restore order. While on a peace mission to the Congo, Dag Hammarskjold [häm'är shüld'], the Secretary-General of the United Nations, was killed in a plane crash. After the collapse of the Katanga rebellion in 1963, the Congo was unified.

In 1971, the Congo changed its name to the Republic of Zaïre. The famous Congo River was changed to the Zaïre River. In 1972, all people in Zaïre were forced to use African names. In 1974, most foreign-owned businesses were forced to sell to Zaïre citizens. However, when this did not work, the government invited the original owners to return. While there was a period of stability under Joseph Mobutu [mō bü tü], Zaïre is still a troubled land under his rule. Katanga remains a problem area. Since so much of Zaïre's economy is based on copper, the living standards of the people rise and fall with the price of this important product. An uneasy peace may be said to summarize the state of affairs in Zaïre today.

Why Ghana and Zimbabwe Are a Study in Contrasts

Events in Ghana [gä'nə] and those in Zimbabwe [zim bä'bwā] are a study in contrasts for many reasons. Ghana is the name of a proud and ancient land. It is also the name of a modern country, one of the first to receive its independence following World War II. Kwame Nkrumah [ənkrü'mə] (1909–1972), who became prime minister, was hailed as a great hero. He built schools and hospitals. He made it possible for more people to learn to read and write. Ghana has a great university and a comparatively large number of college students. However, in the process of building,

Nkrumah plunged his country into debt. The democracy he said he would build became instead a one-person rule.

In 1962, Nkrumah was voted president-for-life. In 1964, he was granted dictatorial power. Those who opposed him were jailed. Only one party was allowed to exist. Ghana is an illustration of a country that began its life as an independent state on a note of hope, but which became debt-ridden instead of prosperous. Its educated people can find few opportunities. And its democratic beginning was twisted into a dictatorship. Nkrumah was overthrown by a military coup in 1966.

Following the fall of the Nkrumah regime, Ghana's government was made up of a succession of civilian and military leaders. These governments were unsuccessful in bringing Ghana's major problems under control. However, strong measures are being taken to wipe out corruption, reduce inflation, and maintain human rights.

While Ghana was being given independence by Great Britain, Rhodesia [rō dē'zhə] declared itself independent. (Today, Rhodesia is called Zimbabwe.) These countries took different roads to independence. Britain refused to grant Rhodesia independence unless that country gave the right to vote to its black population. The whites who controlled the government refused to do this. They insisted on cutting off their relations with Britain and in setting up a racist government. They wanted to copy the Union of South Africa and keep the black population separate second-class citizens who had no say in running the government.

The white prime minister, Ian Smith (1919–), declared his country independent in 1965. To the disappointment of some African nations, Britain was reluctant to use force against Rhodesia. Instead, Britain refused to sell Rhodesia the oil and gasoline that it desperately

Africa in the 1980s

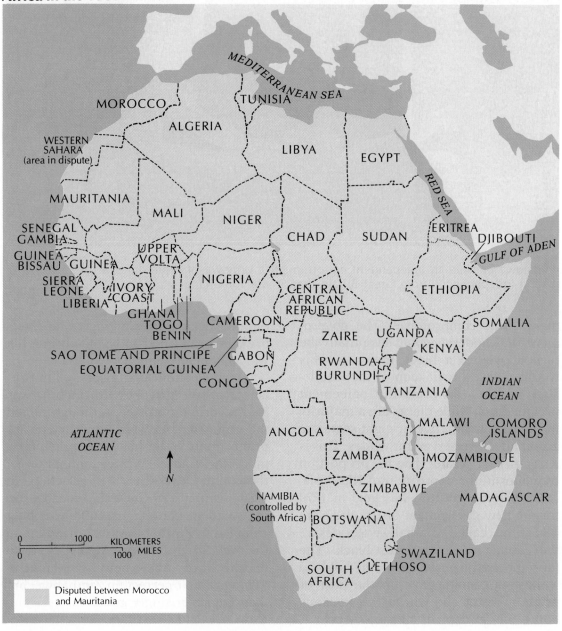

Compare this map with the map on page 665.
• What major change took place in Africa between 1950 and 1980?

needed. Many other countries followed Britain's example. However, the Rhodesians hoped that countries would continue to buy the Rhodesian tobacco crop. With the money earned from selling tobacco, they hoped to buy goods from countries who would be willing to sell to them.

Rhodesia's white-supremacy policy was unsuccessful. Ian Smith had to

Zimbabwe became an independent nation in 1980. Why was it more difficult for Zimbabwe to gain independence from Great Britain than it was for Ghana?

make some compromises. The government of Rhodesia would eventually be turned over to a black majority. This would reflect the makeup of the Rhodesian people. However, the agreement provided that while blacks are a majority in the parliament, twenty-eight seats are automatically reserved for whites. This is a number far greater than the proportion of whites in the population of Rhodesia.

In the election that was held in 1979 for the new government of Rhodesia (at that time called Zimbabwe-Rhodesia), the cabinet was two-thirds black. The most powerful posts were still held by whites. Ian Smith gave up the post of prime minister and with it the spacious home he occupied. Bishop Abel T. Muzorewa [mü zôr ē′wə] moved in when he became the new prime minister.

The government of Bishop Muzorewa was unsuccessful. Violence continued. It was felt that the new prime minister had been chosen in an election that was dominated by whites. The election did not really reflect the wishes of the black majority. The British government of Margaret Thatcher set out to try to bring some peace to the country. Under the skillful

diplomacy of Lord Carrington, a cease-fire was established and a bloody guerilla war was finally ended.

In an election supervised by the British, Robert Mugabe [mü gä′bē] was elected prime minister. Although he led the group that favored communism, as prime minister he has been pursuing a moderate course. White domination of the country ended with his election. In 1980, Zimbabwe-Rhodesia became an independent nation. (Its name was later changed to Zimbabwe.) As a headline in the *Wall Street Journal* (August 14, 1980) declared of the new government, "Things aren't perfect, in Zimbabwe, but they are surprisingly good."

Apartheid Hurts the Republic of South Africa

In the Republic of South Africa, Afrikaners [af′rə kä′nərz] control the government. Afrikaners are descendants of the early Dutch settlers. They follow the racial policy of *apartheid* [ə pärt′tīd], which totally segregates blacks from whites. The blacks must live and work in special

670

areas. They need passes to go from one place to another. They have few economic opportunities and no political privileges. The British who lived in South Africa did not believe that apartheid or strict segregation was the right course to follow.

In 1961, as a result of racial troubles and British opposition to apartheid, the Union of South Africa withdrew from the Commonwealth of Nations. It became the Republic of South Africa. In 1966, an assassin shot and killed the South African prime minister, Dr. Henrik Verwoerd [fər vürt']. He was succeeded by Balthasar J. Vorster [vôr'stər], who also strongly supported apartheid.

South Africa is rich in gold and other minerals, but has a serious shortage of skilled workers. This is largely because of apartheid. South Africa's need for skilled workers may yet cause the country to change its apartheid policy.

The policy of apartheid in South Africa has not been meekly accepted by blacks. The most notable example of resistance took place in the huge black ghetto called Soweto [sō wā'tō], a black suburb of Johannesburg, South Africa's capital. Here, students repeatedly challenged police. Violence has flared up many times. In 1977, South Africa's police reportedly beat to death Steven Bantu Biko [bē'kō]. Biko fought for his people by trying to end apartheid. His funeral was attended by over 20,000 blacks, something they would not have dared to do twenty years earlier.

Lands controlled by the Republic of South Africa have become independent. This is true for Botswana [bät'swa nə]. Southwest Africa, called Namibia

Mourners display a photograph of black South African leader Stephen Biko, who died in a government prison.

The Twentieth Century

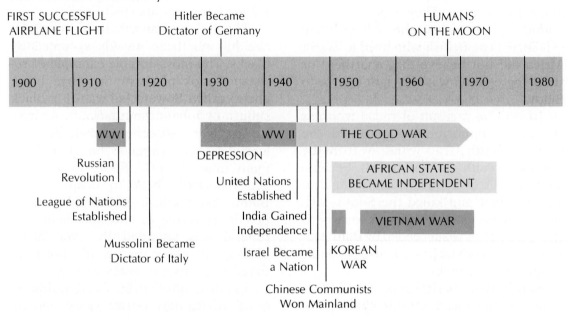

FIRST SUCCESSFUL
AIRPLANE FLIGHT

Hitler Became
Dictator of Germany

HUMANS
ON THE MOON

| 1900 | 1910 | 1920 | 1930 | 1940 | 1950 | 1960 | 1970 | 1980 |

WW I

Russian
Revolution

League of Nations
Established

Mussolini Became
Dictator of Italy

DEPRESSION

WW II

United Nations
Established

India Gained
Independence

Israel Became
a Nation

Chinese Communists
Won Mainland

THE COLD WAR

AFRICAN STATES
BECAME INDEPENDENT

VIETNAM WAR

KOREAN
WAR

Be able to place the following events on the time line:

1917	Balfour Declaration	1979	Arab-Israeli peace agreement
1948	Arab-Israeli War	1979	Islamic revolution in Iran toppled Shah
1967–70	civil war in Nigeria		

[nä mib′ē ə], is an especially rich land that came under South African control during World War I. Under pressure from blacks and from the United Nations, South Africa reluctantly agreed to give this land its independence. It has not done so yet. *SWAPO* (South-West Africa People's Organization) is a guerrilla group that fights for Namibian independence.

How the Soviet Union Takes Advantage of Turmoil in Africa

In 1975, when Portugal left Angola, civil war followed. The Soviet Union, with Cuban aid, sought to extend Communist influence. The situation in Angola is a good example of how the Soviet Union has tried to take advantage of trouble in Africa for its own ends. It seeks to make Communist nations out of those who have overthrown their former colonial masters. Since the end of colonial rule in Africa, at least twenty wars and other

conflicts have taken place. There is fighting from the Western Sahara to the Horn of Africa. These wars are increasingly drawing in Cuban and Soviet troops.

In Ethiopia, for example, there are up to 15,000 Soviet and Cuban troops. They are training to fight in any part of Africa where they believe communism can gain an advantage. Africa has become both the prize and the battleground between the Communist and non-Communist forces of the world.

There is fear in Africa that unending turmoil will drain the resources of any nation drawn into these conflicts. There are conflicts over who will rule now that self-government has been achieved in these areas. Tribalism is very much alive, and many political parties are based on tribal loyalties. Out of these stresses and strains, the Soviet Union, Cuba, and the nations of Eastern Europe hope to win new converts to communism.

672

1. On a map, locate the nations of Sub-Saharan Africa. For each, indicate the date it achieved independence.

2. Why did Rhodesia try to retain its policy of white supremacy? Why did the policy fail?

3. What attacks on apartheid have occurred in the Union of South Africa?

4. How do the Soviet Union and Cuba seek to take advantage of the problems of Sub-Saharan Africa?

REVIEWING THE BASICS

In this chapter we examined the perils and the promise that may be found in the Middle East and Africa. The Middle East is made up partly of North Africa, where the important country of Egypt is located. In the Middle East the problems center around the Arab-Israeli dispute and oil. Israel was established by the United Nations out of Palestine. It has not been recognized by any Arab country except Egypt. Israel fought many wars to try to protect its right to exist. It has reclaimed the desert and brought farming to lands that were once considered useless.

The Arab countries, for their part, see Israel as an intruder in their land. They want the Palestinians, who had been removed from the land when Israel was created, to be relocated. They believe that relocation should be the responsibility of Israel. Most of the Arab countries are oil-rich members of OPEC. Since 1973, they have used oil as a means to get what they want. They have raised prices and have withheld oil from the markets of industrialized nations. Under the Shah, Iran was friendly to the United States. It was both an important source of oil and a place from which to watch the activities of the Soviet Union. When the Shah was overthrown, both these advantages were lost. A hopeful sign for peace in the area may be the agreement between Egypt and Israel that was achieved with the help of the United States. Sadat's assassination in 1981 endangers that agreement.

After World War II, the North African colonies of Algeria, Morocco, and Tunisia won independence from France. In the case of Algeria there was a costly war, which ended when Charles de Gaulle granted that country self-government. The stability of North Africa is threatened by Qaddafi, the leader of Libya, who supports Arab nationalism. In Northeast Africa, war is a constant threat between Ethiopia and Eritrea and Ethiopia and Somolia.

Nations in Sub-Saharan Africa have also experienced turmoil.

Under the leadership of Jomo Kenyatta, the colony won independence from Great Britain. From 1967 to 1970, a tragic civil war was fought in Nigeria between the Ibos and the Hausas. The Ibos formed the nation of Biafra, which was eventually defeated by Nigeria. Today, Nigeria is united. Belgian rule of the Congo ended in 1960. The province of Katanga made an unsuccessful attempt to break away from the Congo. The Congo was renamed Zaïre in 1971. Ghana has witnessed many civilian and military governments since its independence from Great Britain. In Zimbabwe (formerly Rhodesia) the election of Robert Mugabe finally ended white control. In South Africa there is rising opposition among blacks to the policy of apartheid. South Africa resists full independence for Namibia. Instability in many countries of Africa helps the Soviet Union to spread communism in that continent.

REVIEWING THE HIGHLIGHTS

People to Identify		
Gamal Abdul Nasser	Kwame Nkrumah	Mau Mau
King Farouk	Colonel Qaddafi	Robert Mugabe
Count Bernadotte	Moise Tshombe	Steven Biko
Dr. Ralph Bunche	Kasavubu	Yakubu Gowon
David Ben-Gurion	Joseph Mobutu	Anwar El-Sadat
King Hussein	Golda Meir	Abel Muzorewa
Habib Bourguiba	Haile Selassie	Riza Pahlavi
Ian Smith	Menachem Begin	Ayatollah Khomeini
Jomo Kenyatta	Palestinians	
	Yitzhak Rabin	

Places to Locate		
Sinai Peninsula	Cairo	Soweto
Jerusalem	Gulf of Aqaba	South Africa
Zaïre	Suez Canal	Nigeria
Angola	Algeria	Jordan
Kenya	Namibia	Zimbabwe
Libya	Tunisia	

Terms to Understand		
Balfour Declaration	Ibos	Harambee
Hausas	refugee camps	SAVAK
Biafrans	apartheid	tribalism
	PLO	Mau Mau

Events to Describe		
1948 Arab-Israeli War	war over the Suez Canal	Civil War in Nigeria
Six-Day War	the fall of the Shah of Iran	

1. How has oil become a political weapon in the Middle East?
2. Why did Egypt deny Israel the right to use the Suez Canal?
3. Why was the blockade of the Gulf of Aqaba an act of war?
4. Why was a Jewish homeland established in Israel?
5. What financial support do the Middle East countries have in developing their resources?
6. What were the results of the Six-Day War?
7. What is the significance of the 1979 agreement between Israel and Egypt?
8. Give three reasons for the fall of the Shah of Iran.
9. Why is unity within African states difficult to achieve?
10. Why was Rhodesia's declaration of independence an illegal act?
11. Why were blacks still not satisfied with the new black majority government of Zimbabwe-Rhodesia?
12. What problems will the new nation of Namibia probably have?
13. Can apartheid succeed? Give reasons for your answer.
14. How does the Soviet Union often take advantage of turmoil in Africa?
15. Explain the role tribalism plays in contributing to African instability?
16. Is there peril or promise or both in Africa? Justify your point of view.
17. Is there peril or promise or both in the Middle East? Justify your point of view.
18. Why has the text described Africa as both the prize and the battleground between Communist and non-Communist forces? Why may the same be said for the Middle East?

THINGS TO DO

1. Prepare a map using different colors to show when each country of Africa achieved independence.
2. Prepare a graph showing the increasing dependence of the industrialized countries on OPEC oil.
3. Prepare a Meet the Press program in which a group of student reporters interviews students playing the role of one of the following: Anwar El-Sadat; Menachem Begin; Jomo Kenyatta; Abel Muzorewa

Low-Cost Technology Spreads to Developing Countries

Developing countries are those that are using their limited resources to develop industry. They have some industry, but most people are employed in agriculture. Many developing countries are in Africa, the Middle East, Southeast Asia, and South America. Instead of relying on the technology of highly industrialized countries, the developing countries are being encouraged to devise technology that suits their needs. They are using smaller machines that are low in cost, simple to operate, and do not disturb the way of life of the people.

Examine the pictures below and discuss with your teacher and class the questions that follow.

Many inventors, scientists, and engineers in developing countries believe that technology should meet people's needs in practical ways. They are therefore coming up with simple low-cost inventions for use in developing countries.

The Ferrumbu
Sealed grain storage bins help farmers to preserve the 20 to 40 percent of grain that is often lost to pests.

Small Turbine
A turbine is an engine driven by the pressure of water or some other energy source. A turbine powered by a country stream can generate 1,000 watts of electricity for a farm family. The family can use the energy for many purposes, such as running farm equipment. The turbine costs $150 and needs little repair.

Yucca Grinder
The yucca is a plant found in South America that has many uses, including the making of soap. A pedal-powered yucca grinder does two months' work in a day. This allows South American farmers to raise and export the root of the yucca in greater quantities.

Art by David Suter

1. Is it correct to apply the word "technology" to the equipment shown? Why or why not?

2. Explain how these pieces of equipment are practical.

3. Why are they suited to people's way of life in developing countries?

Text in illustration adapted from *The New York Times*. © 1979 by The New York Times Company. Reprinted by permission.

Tokyo, Japan

Asia in Today's World: Sleeping Giants Awakened

Glance through your newspaper any day of the week and you will see that news about Asia is increasing. It was in Asia that America was involved in two major wars. Since World War II ended, American soldiers have fought and died in Korea and in Vietnam. Japan, our enemy in World War II, is today both our ally and our most powerful competitor in commerce and industry. The countries of Asia include China, India, Japan, Pakistan, Indonesia, Vietnam, the Philippines, Korea, Malaysia, as well as Australia and New Zealand. Most of these countries are establishing themselves as strong and stable nations.

In 1972, President Richard Nixon visited the People's Republic of China, and a new era of Chinese-American relations began. In 1979, under President Carter, full recognition was given to the People's Republic of China. From this, trade between China and the United States may develop. However, such recognition is not without risk. There has been, in the United States and elsewhere, serious debate as to whether such recognition was the wisest course. The risks in China are matched by risks elsewhere in Asia. A study of the area will help you prepare for the expected, as well as for the unexpected changes that are likely to take place in that area.

CHINA RUSHES TO REENTER WORLD POLITICS

How the Communists Won Control of China

When the Communists were defeated by Chiang Kai-shek [kī-shek'] in 1928, they faced a setback, but they were not discouraged. For a time, they tried to regain their strength in southeastern China, but they were pushed out by Chiang. Later, from southeastern China, the Communists made the *Long March* north. Traveling several hundred miles out of their way to avoid Chiang's armies, they made their way to north China. They made the Shensi [shen'sē'] province their stronghold. While there, they studied communism and prepared to take power.

The Chinese Communists asked the Soviet Union for help. The Soviet Communists advised them. In north China, Chinese Communists were taught to read and write and to understand the meaning and methods of communism. These new ideas were spread far and wide. They prepared the people for a Communist victory.

The Communists were quick to recognize that the Chinese wanted peace more than freedom, land more than liberty, bread more than justice. Under the *Kuomintang* [kwō'min'tang'] (the party of Sun Yat-sen and Chiang Kai-shek) there had been much talk. But there was little progress in breaking up large estates and giving land to the poor farmers. The Kuomintang had appealed to the rich and middle classes. The Communists appealed to the great masses of people who were peasants. It was among the peasants that the Communists gained their greatest strength.

Between 1945 and 1949, China was torn by civil war. Fighting between Chiang Kai-shek and the Kuomintang and Mao Tse-tung [mow' dzu' tüng'] and the Chinese Communists ended in victory for the Communists. The United States had strongly supported Chiang. Chiang's forces were driven from the mainland of China to the island of Taiwan, [tī'wän'], also called Formosa [fôr mō'sə]. There, the *Republic of China* was set up. In October 1949, the *People's Republic of China* was established on the mainland.

The Problems of the People's Republic of China

Between 1958 and 1960, the People's Republic was determined to achieve progress. It wanted to start an economic program, in order to catch up with the United States and the Soviet Union. China needed to modernize its production of agricultural and industrial goods. This was called the *Great Leap Forward.* Forced labor in *communes* (state-run farms or factories) was the answer the Chinese Communists believed would help them catch up.

By 1967, the People's Republic of China was almost torn apart by civil war. Two main causes may have brought it about. First, there was some doubt about leader Mao Tse-tung's physical and mental health. Those near the seat of power were eager to gain a position of power should Mao die. The second reason may have grown out of the failure of the so-called Great Leap Forward. This was an attempt by the government to raise living standards by improving industry and agriculture. On the contrary, it brought chaos and hardship for many.

In many ways, Mao Tse-tung himself brought on the crisis. In 1966, he had begun a *Cultural Revolution.* Bands of young Communists—mostly teenagers—under the leadership of Mao were determined to prevent any setback in Communist zeal for revolution. They were known as the *Red Guards.* They wanted a Chinese, non-Western brand of communism. In Peking, thousands of young Red Guards, apparently with the approval of Mao, took over the city. They sought to

A young Red Guard puts a revolutionary slogan on a wall in Peking during Mao Tse-tung's Cultural Revolution.

rid the city of whatever was left to remind them of Western ways. Streets were renamed and churches were robbed. Many young people beat up men and women of the older generation. Young people wanted no compromise with the revolution. A reign of terror gripped Peking. From there, terror spread to other Chinese cities. By 1969, because the excesses of the Red Guards appeared to be hurting even him, Mao brought these activities to an end.

Mao's Cultural Revolution was an indirect attack on and criticism of the Soviet Union. Mao felt that the Soviet Union had abandoned revolutionary ways. He was determined that China would not do so. As a result, Communist China and the Soviet Union became bitter enemies.

How Better Relations Began to Develop Between the United States and China

In April of 1971, the United States' table tennis team was allowed to visit the People's Republic of China. The match was a sign that relations between the United States and China might be easing a little.

In August of 1971, *New York Times* correspondent James Reston visited China. He had a long interview with Premier Chou En-lai [jō en'lī']. It was a further sign that both China and the United States were seeking better relations with each other.

At the same time that Reston was in China, Henry Kissinger was there also, but his visit was secret. Dr. Kissinger, President Nixon's foreign policy adviser, was making plans for a presidential visit to China. The visit took place in February, 1972. It came after the United States withdrew its opposition to the admission of the People's Republic of China to the United Nations.

On his visit, Nixon met with Chairman Mao and with Premier Chou. It was a highly publicized trip and it caught the imagination of Americans as few other events have. The visit was fully televised. It seemed a great success. A beginning

had been made toward friendlier and more normal diplomatic relations between the two countries.

In 1976, both Chou En-lai and Mao Tse-tung died. Mao's widow and three associates tried to take power. They failed and were arrested. This *"gang of four,"* as they have been called, attempted to continue Mao's policies. The new group that assumed power wanted to modernize China more quickly. Under the leadership of Teng Hsiao-ping [teng' shou'ping'], friendlier relationships were sought with the West, especially with the United States.

In January, 1979, President Carter extended full recognition to the People's Republic of China. Many Americans applauded this move. Many other Americans strongly opposed it. In the same year, Deputy Prime Minister Teng visited the United States. Teng was interested in getting for China the newest technology America had to offer. Teng also tried to win America's support for any war that might develop between the People's Republic of China and the Union of Soviet Socialist Republics. There is great hostility between these two Communist countries. Each feels that it has been wronged by the other. Each seeks control of Asia for itself.

In February, 1979, China and Vietnam went to war. Deputy Prime Minister Teng felt that Vietnam was too close politically to the Soviet Union. Another reason for the Chinese attack on Vietnam was to make up for the defeat of Pol Pot [pol' pot'], the leader of Kampuchea (Cambodia). Pol Pot was supported by the Chinese but opposed by the Vietnamese. There is a long history of hatred between Kampuchea and Vietnam that goes as far back as the third century B.C. There was no clear-cut victory and no clear-cut defeat for either side. The war seemed to demonstrate the willingness of the People's Republic of China to chal-

Fishing boats in Taiwan. In 1979, the United States recognized the People's Republic of China, not Taiwan, as the official government of China.

lenge, by force of arms if necessary, Soviet-supported nations.

The United States has been trying to use its new friendship with China to maintain peace in Asia, and between China and the Soviet Union. China hopes to improve the living standards of its people. The United States hopes to sell its products to the large, important, and hopefully prosperous nation of China.

The Problems of the Republic of China

When the Kuomintang was defeated by the Chinese Communists, two million Chinese nationalists led by Chiang Kai-shek fled to Formosa (Taiwan). There, they set up the Republic of China. They wanted to be recognized as the seat of the Chinese government. They hoped, in time, to overthrow the Communists and to restore their rule to all of China. This hope has vanished.

The United States has given help to the Republic of China, and was one of the few nations to retain formal ties with it. America did this because of its own disappointment that the Communists had won control of the mainland. Recognizing the Republic of China and withholding recognition of the much larger nation, the People's Republic of China, was a difficult position to hold for very long. For a time, the United States hoped this *"two-China policy"* might be possible. It did not work out. The United States did, however, ask Chiang Kai-shek to give up the idea of returning to the mainland of China by force. Chiang reluctantly agreed to this. In 1975, Chiang Kai-shek died at the age of eighty-seven. Those who fled to Taiwan with him are now quite old.

In 1972, the Republic of China was forced from the United Nations. As a founding nation of the United Nations, the Republic of China held a permanent seat on the Security Council. During the UN debates on the admission of the People's Republic of China, the United States hoped that both the Republic of China and the People's Republic of China would be accepted as members. The United Nations voted to admit the People's Republic of China as the only representative of the Chinese people. This weakened the claim of the Republic of China to the Chinese mainland.

When the United States extended full recognition to the People's Republic of China, it had to give up diplomatic recognition of the Republic of China (Taiwan). This was a bitter moment for the people and the government of Taiwan. It was also difficult for many Americans to accept. However, giving up diplomatic relationships did not mean that commerce and trade between the United States and the Republic of China had to end. The United States removed its troops from the island, but business relationships continued. The people of Taiwan are prosperous. There are many American industries there which bring money to the island. This can be expected to continue, despite the diplomatic break.

Check in Here

1. Describe the differences between the People's Republic of China and the Republic of China.

2. How did the Communists win control of China?

3. What was the significance of the Cultural Revolution?

4. How have relations between the United States and the People's Republic of China improved?

WAR AND PEACE IN OTHER COUNTRIES OF ASIA

How War Came to Korea

Independence came to Korea after World War II ended and Japan was defeated. The Soviet Union insisted that Korea be divided along the *38th parallel.* United States troops remained in the south and Soviet troops in the north. Both countries were to withdraw their troops when Korea was able to rule itself. What was to be a temporary division of Korea proved to be a permanent one.

In 1948, the *Republic of Korea* was born in the south. A Communist *People's Republic* was formed in the north. The troops of both nations were to remain under United Nations supervision until a government for Korea could be established. The Soviets, however, established a permanent Communist government in the north. In South Korea, elections were held and Syngman Rhee [rē] became president. In 1949, American troops left Korea.

In June, 1950, well-armed Communist troops of North Korea suddenly attacked South Korea. President Truman ordered American aircraft and soldiers to the scene. A few hours later, the American action was approved by the Security Council of the United Nations. It urged its members to supply additional troops. The UN asked President Truman to name Douglas MacArthur as supreme commander of the troops. Most of the troops were from South Korea and the United States. The United States also provided most of the money and materials. The significance of the Korean War was that for the first time an international (UN)

General Douglas MacArthur in Korea. Why did President Truman "fire" General MacArthur as supreme commander in Korea?

army was trying to stop one nation from attacking another.

The Communists almost defeated South Korea. They were not able to do so because of the skillful leadership of General MacArthur. Although the UN forces drove the North Koreans back to the 38th parallel, MacArthur was not satisfied. He wanted to drive the Communists back to the Yalu [yä'lü'] River which separates Korea from China. China was supplying the Communists of Korea with weapons. MacArthur brought UN troops to the Chinese border of North Korea. This led to an attack by 200,000 Chinese Communist troops. They drove the UN forces back, and thereby caused the war to drag on. President Truman feared that MacArthur's words and deeds would result in an all-out war with the Communists of China and the Soviet Union. So he replaced MacArthur as commander-in-chief of the United Nations forces in Korea.

In July, 1951, the Communists agreed to talk about ending the war. Truce talks, held at Panmunjon [pän'mün'jon'] in Korea, dragged on for two years. The Communists demanded that all prisoners be returned, whether or not they wished to return to a Communist nation. The UN refused to return prisoners who did not want to go back. In time, the Communists gave in enough to make a cease-fire possible. The terms of the settlement ending the shooting in Korea were finally signed in July, 1953. The Communists in North Korea—Soviet and Chinese—were to remain north of the 38th parallel. The people of South Korea felt that they had been cheated because Korea remained a divided land. The people of America were glad that the shooting was over.

Why North and South Korea Remain Troubled Lands

After the Korean War, Korea was a troubled area. In South Korea widespread

Asia and the Pacific Region in the 1980s

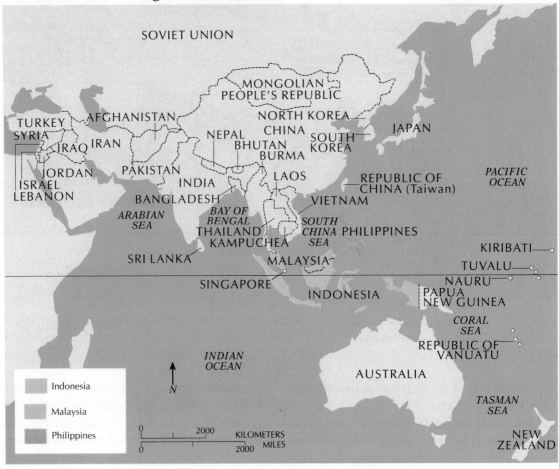

- Name two Southeast Asian countries that share borders with China.
- With what country does China share its longest border?
- Name three countries with coastlines on the South China Sea.

corruption in government helped end the rule of Dr. Syngman Rhee [rē]. He was driven from power. General Chung Hee Park [pärk'] in time became chairman of the ruling party. He later became president of Korea. In 1979, Park was assassinated by another member of his government. General Chun Doo Hwan [wän] became the new president in 1980. In the early 1980s, South Korea continued to achieve a good deal of prosperity. The country is fast becoming a modern, industrialized power. It produces textiles, steel, and electronic equipment.

North Korea is a Communist dictatorship and has friendly relations with the Soviet Union. The Soviet Union has made every effort to keep it from joining Communist China. Its occasional attacks along the 38th parallel have contributed to keeping the peace in Korea uncertain.

In 1967, North Koreans captured the American vessel *Pueblo* [pweb'lō] and its crew off their coast. North Korea refused to release the crew unless the United States agreed to admit that it had entered North Korea's territorial waters illegally, for the purpose of spying. The United

States refused. Eventually, however, the United States did sign a statement admitting that the *Pueblo* had penetrated North Korea's waters. But while signing, the United States labeled the statement as false. Such was the price the United States was willing to pay to avoid war and rescue the crew.

President Kim Il Sung [il' sung'] dominates the political life of North Korea. This Communist country has managed to keep relations with both the USSR and with the People's Republic of China. Since the Soviet Union and the People's Republic of China are enemies, it remains to be seen how long North Korea will be able to work with both countries. Prosperity in North Korea lags behind that of South Korea.

Why Japan Makes Progress

In the fall of 1945, the American Army of Occupation under General MacArthur began teaching the Japanese a democratic way of life. American occupation was expected to last a long time. However, the Japanese were very cooperative. The occupation took less time than had originally been planned. A democratic constitution, modeled after the American Constitution, was written. Labor unions were allowed, and a supreme court similar to the American one was established. Above all, the emperor was no longer considered divine. He was no longer worshipped as a god. Those Japanese who were guilty of committing acts of war against the United States were executed or imprisoned. The army and *zaibatsu* [zī'bät sü'] (powerful business families) lost power too.

As conflict between the United States and the USSR grew, the search for allies by both nations became more intense. The United States looked to Japan as a friend. In 1951, a peace treaty with Japan was signed by the United States and forty-eight other nations. The treaty was a generous one. It abolished further *reparations* (payment for damage done during the war) and allowed Japan to rearm in self-defense. Most American troops

After World War II, the Japanese quickly rebuilt their industries. These women work on a knitting machine assembly line.

occupying Japan left. In 1956, Japan was admitted to the United Nations.

In 1960, President Eisenhower planned a good-will trip to Japan. He hoped Japan would sign a treaty strengthening the alliance between itself and the United States. However, despite generous treatment by the United States, riots were staged by young Japanese Socialists and university students. These riots reached such proportions that Eisenhower's trip had to be canceled. The treaty was approved, but the riots were evidence that Japan had many unsolved problems.

In May, 1972, the United States returned Okinawa [ō'kə nou'wə] to Japan. This important island had been occupied by the United States since World War II. Conquering it had taken a heavy toll on American life. Yet growing national pride in Japan seemed to make the return of Okinawa a wise move. Perhaps its return will help to improve relations between the United States and Japan. Both countries realize the importance of achieving and maintaining good relations.

From crushing defeat in 1945, Japan has become one of the world's leading industrial nations. Its products may be found all over the globe. Its living standards are high. In 1974, when the Arabs stopped shipping oil for a time, Japan, totally dependent on imported oil, was hard hit. Conditions worsened when prices for imported oil rose dramatically. Japan is faced with grave problems of air and water pollution. Inflation (excessively high prices)—a problem for all industrial countries—is particularly severe in Japan. The problems of modern Japan are similar to those of the other rich countries.

Why Indonesia Achieved Stability

Indonesia [in'də nē'zhə] is a country of over 13,000 islands and over 140 million people. It become independent in 1945. Dr. Achmed Sukarno [sü kär'nō] (1901–1970) became its first president in 1949. He governed for nearly twenty-eight years, but his government brought terror rather than peace or prosperity to Indonesia.

Hunger, unemployment, and political unrest troubled Indonesia. These problems were used as excuses by which Sukarno could take almost unlimited power for himself. In May, 1963, he became president-for-life. Thereafter, Sukarno became bolder and sought aid from the Soviet Union. With support from the Soviet Union, Sukarno threatened Malaysia [mə lā'zhə], a new nation of southeast Asia whose formation he opposed. In January, 1965, Sukarno dramatically withdrew Indonesia from the United Nations and the World Bank. He dreamed of sharing with Mao Tse-tung the control of Asia. A large Communist Party was organized in Indonesia, much of it with the encouragement of Sukarno. This party was allied with that of Mao Tse-tung in China.

Early in September, 1965, Sukarno was near death. The Communist Party attempted to take over the government. On the night of September 30, gangs of Communists roamed through the streets of Jakarta [jə kär'tə], the capital of Indonesia. They stopped in front of the houses of seven of the highest ranking officers of Indonesia. One general, sensing a plot, escaped. Another refused to do the bidding of the Communists, and was shot on the spot. The remaining five were taken to an airforce base and killed. Despite the torture and death of these men, the Communist plot to take over the government of Indonesia failed.

When the fate of these generals was known to the people, the non-Communists of Indonesia fought back. Known and even suspected Communists were hunted down, and in their turn tortured and killed. An ugly mood prevailed in Indonesia. By the time it ended, over 500,000 supposed Communists had been killed. General Suharto [sü här'tō] became the new president in March, 1966, when Sukarno was forced to turn over all the powers of government to him.

How the Philippines and Malaysia Fared in the Postwar World

In 1934, the Congress of the United States agreed to the independence of the Philippines. However, freedom did not come until the end of World War II. In 1946, the Republic of the Philippines was established. The United States and the Philippines have signed treaties of mutual defense. The United States has a number of military bases in the Philippine islands. Originally, the United States was to keep control of these bases for ninety-nine years. In 1966, however, the two countries agreed to a twenty-five-year lease on these bases.

In 1954, Communist fighters called *Huks* [huks] sought to lead a rebellion in the Philippines. The attempt was put down by the government. Another source of hostility to the government comes from Muslims, mostly from the island of Mindanao [min'dä nä'ō]. The *Moros* [mōr'ōz], as the Muslim groups are known, seek independence from the Philippines.

President Ferdinand Marcos [mär'kōs] (1917–   ) became president of the Philippines in 1945. During the 1970s, however, he was confronted with widespread riots. The riots were led by those who felt that the United States had too much power in the Philippines. The rioters also believed that their government was corrupt. In 1975, the Philippines opened trade relations with China, and in 1976, with the Soviet Union. Imelda Marcos, the wife of the president, was given wide powers in 1978. She is responsible for

Leaders of Africa and Asia at the United Nations in 1960. President Nkrumah of Ghana (left) shakes hands with President Sukarno (right) of Indonesia.

planning the economic development of the islands.

After the defeat of Communist rebels, Malaya became independent in 1957. In 1963, it joined with Singapore, Sarawak [sə rä'wäk] (Northwest Borneo), and Sabah [sä'bä] (North Borneo) to become the *Federation of Malaysia.* However, this union did not last. Differences grew between the Chinese, who dominated Singapore, and the Malays. The Chinese were well-educated and in control of the business life of the country. They tended to dominate the Federation.

In 1965, the Malays forced Singapore to leave the Federation. Singapore became an independent nation. Singapore, the world's fourth largest port, prospers. Manufacturing has become more important than shipping as the nation's leading industry. Next to Japan, the people of Singapore enjoy the highest *per capita* (per person) income in Asia. There are high standards in education, housing, and health care. Singapore has become an important outpost of capitalism. It has demonstrated what a free economy can do to raise living standards.

How Australia and New Zealand Fared in the Postwar Period

Although thousands of miles from the Asian mainland, Australia and New Zealand were fearful of Japanese attack during World War II. After the war, New Zealand and Australia joined Britain in a pact to defend Singapore and Malaysia. At the present time Australia and New Zealand carry on considerable export and import business with Japan, further linking them with the fortunes of Asia.

Australia and New Zealand have been called "social laboratories" because these countries have tried new ways of governing. In these countries the *Australian ballot* (secret ballot) was started. In them too, the right of all men and women to vote was granted as early as 1893.

Australia and New Zealand experimented with government ownership of some industries, such as the railroads, telephone, and telegraph. They were among the first (by 1900) to have old-age insurance, as well as insurance in case of accident or unemployment. Under these plans, those too old to work, or those who are hurt or are unemployed through no fault of their own are taken care of by insurance payments. Labor disputes are settled by a neutral third party. Decisions are accepted by both workers and owners. This method of settling labor disputes is known as *binding arbitration* (forced settlement).

New Zealand, like Australia, is a commonwealth. A governor-general represents the Crown in New Zealand, as in Australia. The head of government and the real authority of this country of about 3 million is the prime minister. The Maori [mä'ō rē] population of New Zealand came to the island from Polynesia around the fourteenth century. Origi-

Australia's outback is a sparsely populated area of great natural beauty.

nally, they were persecuted by the whites, but in more recent years they have been included in the government where they are represented in Parliament. Australia tried to keep nonwhites out through a strict immigration policy. In New Zealand many Samoans, Tongans, and other South Pacific islanders come to work and live.

Because of their importance in World War II, Australia and New Zealand seem to be closer to the United States than they are to Great Britain. They are tied to Britain by loyalty and culture. They are tied to the United States by shared interests in the Pacific.

Check in Here

1. What reasons explain the clashes between North and South Korea?

2. Why did the Huks and the Moros oppose the government of the Philippines?

3. Why are Australia and New Zealand often called "social laboratories"?

4. With regard to Japan, what reasons explain: (**a**) the relatively short American occupation; and (**b**) Japan's prosperity?

WARS IN SOUTHEAST ASIA

Why There Is War in Southeast Asia

We have briefly studied the island countries of Southeast Asia such as Malaysia, Singapore, Indonesia, and the Philippines. Continental Southeast Asia is made up of Burma and Thailand, and the countries of Indochina that include Vietnam, Laos, and Cambodia.

Burma became independent of Great Britain in 1948. The people agreed that the British should be driven out. They could not agree among themselves about the kind of a government to have. U Nu [ü nü'], the hero of independence, became the first premier of the country.

Of the countries of Southeast Asia, only Thailand was never governed by a foreign power. In World War II, Thailand was on the side of Germany and Japan. It was the first Axis partner to be admitted to the UN. Thailand's chief political problems are with its neighbor, the People's Republic of China. There is also fear that the wars in Laos and Kampuchea (Cambodia) may spill over into Thailand. Thailand unwillingly provides a haven for the victims of war in Kampuchea.

During World War II, in the area once known as French Indochina, the Japanese set up three kingdoms: Laos, Cambodia, and Vietnam. These nations were supposed to be independent, but in fact they were subject to the wishes of Japan. When World War II ended and Japan was defeated, the French returned. They tried to reestablish their power and influence in the area, but failed. Resistance to French plans came from the League for the Independence of Vietnam, or the *Vietminh* [vē'et min']. It was led by the Communist-trained leader Ho Chi Minh [hō' chē' min'].

In 1946, in an attempt to hold their influence in Indochina, the French bombed the harbor of Haiphong [hī fäng]. About 6,000 people were killed. This may be said to be the start of a long, drawn-out war in Indochina. In 1949, the French recognized former emperor Bao Dai [bou dī'] as the government of Vietnam. His non-Communist government was also recognized by the United States and Great Britain. Ho Chi Minh set up an opposing Communist government. It was recognized by the People's Republic of China and by the Soviet Union.

War between the French, who sought to keep Indochina, and the Communists, who sought independence, grew more bitter. At Dien Bien Phu [dyen' byen' fü'] where the French built a military camp, the forces of Ho Chi Minh decisively defeated the French. The French sought

American help. President Eisenhower, though sympathetic to France, refused to allow American troops to fight in Southeast Asia.

After the French were finally driven out of Indochina, a conference was held in Geneva in 1954. It was made up of delegates from France, Great Britain, the United States, the Soviet Union, Vietnam, Laos, Cambodia, and the People's Republic of China. There was much hope that the *Geneva Conference* would lead to peace. Far from ending, the war in Vietnam grew. So did America's participation in it.

How the United States Involvement in the Vietnam War Increased

Participation in the Geneva Conference led to the United States involvement in what eventually became a major war. In 1954, at the Geneva Conference, it was agreed to divide Vietnam into North and South at the *17th parallel.* Neither the United States nor South Vietnam signed the Geneva agreement. South Vietnam opposed the idea of the permanent division of Vietnam. The United States felt that since North Vietnam was the richer part of the country, the agreement was really a victory for the Communists.

North Vietnam came under control of Ho Chi Minh. In South Vietnam, Bao Dai was removed. A republic under control of Ngo Dinh Diem [dē'em] was set up. He was supported by the United States. The Communists of North Vietnam were bent on conquering South Vietnam. They would fight for a united Vietnam dominated by Communists. Armed Communist sympathizers were hiding throughout South Vietnam. They were prepared to use terror to achieve a Communist government in Vietnam.

To stop the threat of a Communist takeover in Southeast Asia the United States organized the *Southeast Asia Treaty Organization (SEATO).* SEATO was organized for the purpose of trying to stop Communist advances in Asia. Because the United States never signed the Geneva agreement, the members of the SEATO alliance were given the job of protecting the independence of South Vietnam.

In 1954, under President Eisenhower, the United States began to give military assistance to South Vietnam. It was felt that unless communism were stopped here, all of Southeast Asia might fall. This was the so-called *"domino theory."*

In 1956, according to the Geneva agreement, free elections were to be held in both North and South Vietnam. South Vietnam, then under Ngo Dinh Diem refused to hold elections. Diem felt that North Vietnam would not permit the free expression of opinion.

When President Kennedy came into office in January, 1961, America was deeply committed to preserving South Vietnam's independence. By the fall of 1961, there was an increase in guerrilla attacks by North Vietnam. It became clear that the United States would have to offer even more help if South Vietnam were to remain independent. In November, 1963, Diem was overthrown and killed.

For a year and a half, there was chaos in South Vietnam. South Vietnam Communists, known as the *Viet Cong,* sought to undermine the government. Religious differences existed between the Buddhist majority and the rulers, mainly Catholic. This contributed to political and social unrest and to Diem's fall. Generals Ngugen Van Thieu [van' tyü] and Nguyen Cao Ky [kē] managed to restore some order and government by June, 1965.

In the summer of 1964, President Johnson asked Congress to approve his policies in Vietnam and to expand his powers. On August 7, 1964, Congress voted for the now famous *Tonkin Gulf Resolution.* This resolution stated that ". . . the United States is . . . prepared and determined to take all necessary steps, including the use of armed force . . ." to assist any Southeast Asia Treaty Organization member. This included South Vietnam. The Tonkin Gulf Resolution gave the president power to commit troops and planes in increasing numbers. This he did in accordance with his judgment of the danger to South Vietnam.

The Nature of the Vietnam War

Although the Vietnam War was the longest war in American history, the American people were not called upon to make unusual sacrifices. It is true that soldiers were drafted for an unpopular war, and that families and careers were disrupted. However, unlike World War II, there was no rationing, no price fixing, and no price or wage ceilings. There were no unusual taxes imposed to pay the costs of the war.

On the battlefield, battle lines were unclear. The war front was everywhere. Guerrilla and terrorist tactics, as well as those of conventional warfare were used. The Communists claimed to be fighting to help free the Vietnamese from Western influence. The Communists hoped to win by wearing down the enemy's will to fight. Because of the nature of the fighting, the words "victory" and "defeat" and "enemy" seemed to have little meaning. It was a frustrating war.

President Johnson gave a speech in which he promised that once the war was over, the United States would assist in a massive development program in all of Vietnam. This program was to provide river and flood control, generate electric-ity, irrigate the land, and help Vietnam move into the industrial era.

The United States tried to encourage South Vietnam to be democratic. In 1967, Generals Nguyen van Thieu and Nguyen Cao Ky were elected president and vice-president respectively. While the elections left much to be desired, there was hope that a stable democratic government had been established. This hope was dashed, however, when Thieu ran a one-man race in the 1971 election. His reelection was never in doubt.

The Vietnam War, 1964–1973

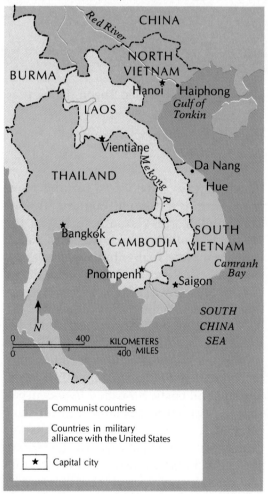

- Name the capital of North Vietnam.
- What countries had a military alliance with the United States during the war?

Vietnamese families flee Saigon during the Tet offensive in 1968.

How the Vietnam War Ended

In many ways, 1968 was a turning point in the war. At the end of January, the Viet Cong and North Vietnamese began the *Tet* [tet] *offensive,* which was also called the Lunar New Year Offensive. The strategy was effective. The great Vietnamese city of Hué [hwā] was held for twenty-five days and Saigon was attacked.

The Tet offensive was spectacular for its effect on the American public. An unpopular war was made more unpopular. So-called *doves* urged that the war be ended at all costs. So-called *hawks* urged that the United States launch a full-scale offensive to win. President Johnson's popularity reached a new low. In March, 1968, President Johnson withdrew from the presidential race. He withdrew, he said, so that he would be in a position to work for peace.

A limited bombing halt made it possible for peace talks to be held in Paris. The United States, North Vietnam, South Vietnam, and the *National Liberation Front* (the Viet Cong) began peace talks in January, 1969.

The American people went to the polls to vote for a new president. By the narrowest of margins they chose the Republican candidate, Richard Nixon. He said he had a plan for ending the Vietnam war. His plan was based on a gradual withdrawal of American fighting forces in Vietnam. The South Vietnamese would become responsible for fighting the war. In 1969, Ho Chi Minh died. The war, however, continued.

In Paris, peace talks dragged on fruitlessly for years. The United States invaded Cambodia in 1970. In November, 1972, President Nixon ran for reelection. Henry Kissinger, the president's adviser on foreign affairs and chief American negotiator in the secret peace talks, held a news conference. Kissinger said that he had been talking with Le Duc Tho [lu′ duk′ tō′] of North Vietnam

Ho Chi Minh (1890–1969)

The first president of North Vietnam was born in Annam in what was then French Indochina. Few things are known about his birth, and Ho preferred it that way. It suited his purposes to keep his origins secret. Throughout a long life he was known by many names, and this too served to add to the air of mystery.

Early in life, Ho Chi Minh acquired a hatred for the French who dominated the nation in which he was born. The Vietnamese made many attempts to drive the French out. It was not long before Ho was part of those efforts. Under the name of Ba [bä], Ho Chi Minh fled Annam and served as a cabin boy on a ship bound for France. After some years, during which he visited Boston and New York among other places, he settled in London. There he made a bare living as a dishwasher. He then left London, where he felt he could accomplish little in his attempt to win freedom from the French for his people. His next stop was Paris, where he lived for six years. It was in Paris that he became a Marxist and got to know Communist revolutionaries. In 1924, Ho left Paris for the first of several trips to the Soviet Union.

Ho's life was devoted to the cause of Marxism and to the independence of his people. More than anything else, Ho Chi Minh sought to make communism a national cause for the Vietnamese. He felt this movement could liberate his people from the French. Ho Chi Minh was a man of action rather than one who created new ideas. For over fifty years, he fought for the cause he believed just. This fragile little man inspired genuine love among the people he led. He also won the grudging respect of his enemies.

and that they were close to an agreement. But the peace that Kissinger thought he had reached, came apart.

By December, President Nixon was frustrated by what he considered to be a build-up of the war by North Vietnam. He ordered that negotiations be broken off and that a heavy bombing of North Vietnam begin. Behind the scenes negotiators were still in touch with one another. Finally, President Nixon went on television to announce that on January 27, 1973, at 7:00 p.m., a cease-fire agreement would go into effect.

The agreement was a complex one. The United States agreed to withdraw all its troops from Vietnam. All American prisoners were to be released. The cease-fire itself was to be supervised by a team from Canada, Hungary, Indonesia, and Poland. Thieu held power, but there was to be a supervised election.

The Twentieth Century

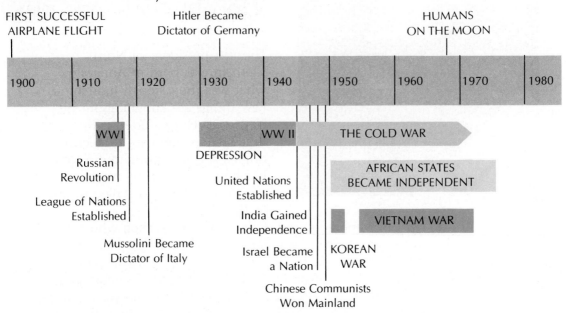

FIRST SUCCESSFUL AIRPLANE FLIGHT

Hitler Became Dictator of Germany

HUMANS ON THE MOON

1900 | 1910 | 1920 | 1930 | 1940 | 1950 | 1960 | 1970 | 1980

WWI

WW II

THE COLD WAR

DEPRESSION

Russian Revolution

League of Nations Established

Mussolini Became Dictator of Italy

United Nations Established

India Gained Independence

Israel Became a Nation

Chinese Communists Won Mainland

AFRICAN STATES BECAME INDEPENDENT

VIETNAM WAR

KOREAN WAR

Be able to place the following events on the time line:

1945–49	civil war in China	1973	Cease-fire agreement (Vietnam War)
1959	Great Leap Forward	1978	Socialist Republic of Vietnam established
1950–53	Korean War		
1964	Gulf of Tonkin Resolution	1979	U.S. recognizes Communist China as official government of China
1966–69	Cultural Revolution		

Although America withdrew its troops from Vietnam, peace did not follow. In April, 1975, after careful preparation, the armies of North Vietnam struck. President Thieu of South Vietnam, without consulting the American president, and to the surprise of nearly everyone, ordered a retreat. As his armies fled south, they left behind over a billion dollars worth of American military equipment. South Vietnamese refugees by the millions sought to flee by boat or plane to escape the rapidly approaching North Vietnamese army. South Vietnamese soldiers deserted fleeing women and children. Rarely in military history was a defeat and retreat so disorderly and so shameful.

In April, 1975, President Thieu resigned. His place was taken by General Duong Van Minh [van' min'], the only one in South Vietnam with whom the North Vietnamese were willing to talk. The noose around Saigon tightened. Foreign embassies closed their buildings. It was clear that the final victory of North Vietnam over South Vietnam could not be long postponed.

In Cambodia things were no better. Under Prince Norodom Sihanouk [sē'ə nouk], Cambodia had been at peace. Sihanouk looked the other way when North Vietnam used Cambodia as a base for preparing troops to send to South Vietnam. He was unsuccessful at keeping peace. The Cambodian Communists, the *Khmer Rouge* [kmer′ rüj′], began to make guerrilla attacks against non-Communists. The United States and South Vietnam tried to destroy the *sanctuaries* (places of safety) from which the North Vietnamese prepared to fight.

In March, 1970, when Sihanouk was on a visit to Moscow, he was removed by Lon Nol [lon nōl′]. Because Lon Nol supported both the Americans and the South Vietnamese, his country was rapidly drawn into war. A peaceful nation, whose people had rarely known extreme poverty or hunger, was plunged into chaos. The Khmer Rouge took the offensive, and in April 1975, they captured Phnom Penh [nom′ pen′], Cambodia's capital. Lon Nol fled.

The collapse of Cambodia and of Vietnam marked the end of the road for American involvement in Southeast Asia. Americans were quick to respond to the needs of the Vietnamese refugees. The United States immediately began a giant airlift of orphans. Plans were made to provide humanitarian aid and help for thousands of refugees. Yet, as President Gerald Ford remarked in a speech in New Orleans on April 23, 1975, "The war [in Vietnam] is finished as far as America is concerned." A week later, General Duong Van Minh unconditionally surrendered to the Provisional Revolutionary Government of South Vietnam (the Communists) who were in control.

There Is No Peace in Indochina

On July 2, 1978, a united Vietnam was established. The Socialist Republic of Vietnam, as it is officially called, adopted Hanoi as its capital. Its flag, currency, and national anthem became that of North Vietnam. Thus, the Communists achieved a final triumph in all of Vietnam. In 1977, Vietnam became a member of the United Nations.

In 1975, Lon Nol was overthrown by the Khmer Rouge. They conquered Cambodia and converted it into a Communist state. They renamed the country Kampuchea [käm pü chē′ə], from Cambodia's ancient history. The government, headed by Pol Pot, emptied the Kampuchean cities. He sent almost the entire population into the countryside to plant and to clear the forest. Nearly all relationships with the outside world ceased.

Little was known about the policies of Pol Pot nor what plans were made, if any, for the nation's economy. It is known, however, that several million Kampucheans were murdered or starved to death because of Pol Pot's policies. Vietnam, supported by the Soviet Union, overthrew the Pol Pot regime that was supported by China. Despite China's brief war with Vietnam over Cambodia, Vietnam remains in control of Kampuchea.

The government of Laos also fell to the Communists of that country, the *Pathet Lao* [pä′thet′ lou′]. It has close ties with Vietnam. The fall of Vietnam, Cambodia, and Laos to communism reflects the worst fears of the United States, namely, that once one country fell to communism the others would follow.

Check in Here

1. What reasons explain the division of Vietnam into North and South?

2. How did the United States involvement in the Vietnam War begin?

3. Why did the United States refuse to sign the Geneva agreement of 1954?

4. What reasons explain the success of North Vietnam?

5. How was Vietnam reunited?

A business district in Bombay, India.

PROGRESS AND POVERTY IN INDIA AND PAKISTAN

Why India Was Divided

By the outbreak of World War II, good progress toward independence had been made. From 1935 to 1945, India and its people made gains both politically and economically. The Indian voice in government was increasing. Indians of all castes could serve in the Indian Civil Service. The lot of the Untouchables (see page 86) was improving slowly. Jawaharlal Nehru [nä′rü] (1889–1964) became Gandhi's most important supporter. He was second in command of government. Later, Nehru became India's first prime minister.

In the early days of World War II there was a three-way conflict among the Hindus, the Muslims, and the British. It threatened India's progress toward independence. In 1941, when the Japanese threat grew more serious, the three groups worked together temporarily. India also took advantage of Great Britain's difficulties to press for a promise of absolute independence.

By 1947, the Indian economy was increasingly returning to Indian hands. Indians got more opportunity for self-rule. British business owners gradually sold their investments in India to Indians and left. As the British economic investment in India fell, Britain became more willing to give India its independence.

The solution of lingering problems between Muslims and Hindus in India was the last stumbling block to complete independence. As early as 1885, Hindus and Muslims had met together to talk over and work out their differences in the *First Indian National Congress*. However, the Muslims soon found it difficult to get along with the large Hindu majority.

Under Mohammed Ali Jinnah [ä lē′ zhē′nə], the *Muslim League*, founded in 1906, demanded the establishment of a separate Muslim state. It was to be called *Pakistan*. As time went on, and as victory for Indian independence appeared closer, hostility between the Muslims and the Hindus grew.

In 1947, independence, which had been so slow in coming, was finally granted to India. All that remained to be done was to set up a new Indian government. The differences between the Hindus and Muslims also had to be solved. This was easier said than done. The two states of India and Pakistan were formed from the country of India. The purpose of the division was to put Hindus in India and Muslims in Pakistan.

The division of the nation into India and Pakistan aroused strong feelings. Boundaries were established around the sections where Hindus and Muslims were living. Thus, Pakistan itself was divided into East and West Pakistan. Many fled their homes and sought new ones in Hindu India or Muslim Pakistan. In 1948, Gandhi was killed by a Hindu who opposed the division of India.

Foreign Problems Face India and Pakistan

India is said to be the pivot of Asia because many Asian countries follow India's lead. In the continuing cold war between the Soviet Union and Western nations, India is trying to remain neutral. The West would like to have India on its side. Its people, resources, and location would make it a desirable friend. But because India was so long under the control of Western powers, today it is reluctant to support the West.

India has involved itself in world affairs by working for international peace. However, an incident in December of 1961 marred India's record of neutrality. India invaded and took over the Portuguese trading posts of Goa, Damao, and Diu located along the west coast of India. These trading posts had been owned by Portugal for 450 years. The continued possession of these ports by Portugal was a thorn in the side of the Indian government. They were symbols of a past India wanted to forget.

India's foreign policy has been referred to as one of neutrality. India seeks to maintain friendly relations with the People's Republic of China as well as with the Soviet Union and United States. This is difficult to do. In 1959, when the Chinese conquered Tibet, a revolt took place. As a result, the Dalai Lama [da lī′ lä′mə] of Tibet fled to India. This put Communist China even closer to India's borders. In 1960, fighting broke out between the two countries when China invaded northeastern India. The Chinese demonstrated their power by invading India. However, they retreated.

In 1947 the Muslim population of India became self-governing as the nation of Pakistan. Because large Muslim populations lived in the northern regions of India, Pakistan was divided between East and West Pakistan. The two sections were a thousand miles apart. There was and is a great deal of hostility between Hindu India and Muslim Pakistan. But religion is not the only source of friction. Both countries claim Kashmir [kash′mēr], which lies between them. Kashmir was one of British India's largest princely states. There a Hindu prince ruled a Muslim people. Since the majority in Kashmir was Hindu, the state probably should have gone to Pakistan. However, since the ruler was Hindu, he preferred to see Kashmir join India.

Armed conflict between India and Pakistan broke out over Kashmir in the summer of 1965. The United Nations intervened to demand a cease-fire between them. Both India and Pakistan agreed. In January, 1966, the leaders of the two countries signed the so-called *Tashkent* [täsh kent′] *Declaration.* They agreed to withdraw their armed forces behind the established cease-fire line. Prime Minister Lal Bahadur Shastri [shäs′trē] signed for India. Pakistan's president, Ayub Khan [a ub′ kän′], signed for his country.

From the beginning of its existence, Pakistan was dominated by the West Pakistanis. East Pakistanis felt they lacked control over their own affairs. In 1970, they won enough votes in the national elections to have their party leader become prime minister. West Pakistanis refused to accept this and sent an army to arrest the East Pakistani leaders. A massacre followed and thousands were killed. India invaded East Pakistan to help defeat West Pakistan and to establish an independent country in East Pakistan, which is now called *Bangladesh* [bang′lä desh′]. Zulfikar Ali Bhutto [ä′lē bü′tō] became the new president of Pakistan. Sheik Mujibur Rahman [rä′mən] became the leader of Bangladesh.

Domestic Progress in India and Pakistan

India's free elections prove that people who can neither read nor write can vote intelligently. India continues to teach its people to read and write. India also seeks to increase life expectancy at birth, which is now forty-two years for men and even less for women.

Jawaharlal Nehru, India's first prime minister, sought to unite India. But the problems created by different language, separate castes, and local rather than national interests had to be overcome. Nehru wanted to free the government of India from religious influences. Most importantly, he wanted a democratic government that would encourage business and industry. Under Nehru, some private industries were built while others were built, owned, and operated by the government. Such a mixed economy helped India develop, but it was not enough.

Nehru's daughter, Indira Gandhi (1911–   ), became India's prime minister in 1966. She knew India and Indian politics at first hand, having often helped her father. In March 1971, she ran for reelection and was determined to make a showing at the polls great enough to be a political force in her own right. She was successful. She had campaigned on the slogan "Abolish Poverty," but failed to do this.

There were some who felt that Mrs. Gandhi did not deal harshly enough with corruption in her own political party. In 1975, she herself was charged by the courts of having engaged in corrupt practices in the 1971 campaign. She then used her emergency authority to assume dictatorial powers. She imprisoned polit-ical opponents and abolished freedom of speech, press, and assembly. She sought to control prices, protect small farmers, and raise productivity. She enforced birth control measures. Her own son, Sonjay [son′jā], was accused of making unfair and unjustified profits.

These activities strengthened the opposition against Mrs. Gandhi. In 1977, the Congress Party that she headed was turned out of power. Moraji R. Desai [də sī′] represented several groups that shared hostility toward Mrs. Gandhi. Desai was chosen as prime minister. He restored democracy, imprisoned Mrs. Gandhi, and went about the task of trying to solve India's continuing problems. Political trouble led to Desai's resignation in 1979. In the election that followed, members of Indira Gandhi's New Congress Party won enough seats in Parliament to enable her to become prime minister once again in 1980.

While great poverty is typical of much of rural India, it is in striking contrast to some of the real progress that is being made. India has an economy that is largely self-sufficient. It has modern industry and has developed, with American help, nuclear power plants. India has many technically trained people and is especially proud of its capability in nuclear technology. India has an atomic bomb. In 1977, the value of the steel and engineering goods that India exported was greater than the value of its traditional exports such as sugar and textiles. As a result of these developments, aid to India is less necessary than it once was.

In Pakistan there is less hope for the economy. Zulfikar Ali Bhutto (1928–1979) became president of Pakistan in December of 1972. He sought to give land to the poor and to nationalize a number of key industries. In doing this, he angered a number of wealthy Pakistanis who felt that he was interfering with their right to conduct business as they wished. In 1973, a new constitution was adopted. Since the presidency was largely ceremonial, Bhutto became prime minister instead. The new constitution provided for an Islamic republic. With one out of every four children dying before the age of five because of malnutrition, Pakistan under Bhutto sought to rebuild the nation's economy. He was, for a time, very popular. People were eager to follow him. However, Ali Bhutto was never able to achieve economic change in a major way.

In July of 1977, Ali Bhutto was overthrown. He was replaced by Mohammad Zia ul Hag [zia ul hak]. In 1979, Ali Bhutto was executed despite pleas from many nations to save his life. Bhutto left behind a weak country, yet one that had developed an atomic bomb. Bhutto declared it was the only atomic bomb in the Muslim world. Would a country that is economically desperate risk using an atomic bomb? It is a question for the world to ponder.

Check in Here

1. Why was India divided into India and Pakistan? Why was Pakistan in turn separated into East and West Pakistan?

2. How did India and Pakistan clash over the following: (**a**) the Kashmir; (**b**) Bangladesh?

3. What were Nehru's goals for India?

4. Why did Indiri Gandhi assume dictatorial powers?

REVIEWING THE BASICS

In today's world, Asia is more important than ever because among its many nations is the People's Republic of China. The United States sought for thirty years to maintain a two China policy; that policy was unsuccessful. In 1979, seven years after Nixon's visit to China, the Carter administration recognized the People's Republic as the only government of China.

In Korea, World War II ended with that land being divided into North and South Korea. When American troops left South Korea, it was invaded by Communist forces of North Korea. A long war followed, in which the Communists almost won. However, while led by the United States, the Korean War was really fought to carry out the vote of the United Nations.

Although defeated in World War II, Japan made a quick recovery. It adopted a democratic constitution modeled after that of the United States, and proceeded to build its economy. This it did so well that today Japan's economy is the third strongest in the world (after those of the United States and the Soviet Union).

The island countries of Southeast Asia, including the Philippines, Malaysia, and Indonesia, have had troubled times. The Philippines were granted independence by the United States, but actual freedom was delayed until after World War II. Although faced with problems of Muslims who wish to secede (Moros) and Communists (Huks), the government of the Philippines appears stable. In Indonesia, a Communist takeover was narrowly avoided.

Suharto soon replaced Sukarno as the leader of Indonesia. Economic progress is being made. Malaysia, after removing Singapore from the Malaysian Federation, continues to struggle to maintain a strong economy and a stable political system. Singapore, however, remains an example of a capitalist, free enterprise system that is raising living standards for large numbers of people.

The war in Vietnam began in 1946, when the French tried to regain the role they once had in the area. The French were driven out by the forces of Ho Chi Minh. Then an attempt was made through the Geneva Conference to arrive at a political solution. This failed, war resumed, and the United States became more and more involved. When the war was finally brought to a close, it was clear that the Communists had won all of Vietnam. Cambodia and Laos too fell under Communist rule.

After World War II, separate nations of Hindu India and Muslim Pakistan were created. East Pakistan separated from West Pakistan and became the country of Bangladesh. The economy of India shows some signs of correcting its problems of malnutrition and poor health. The economies of Pakistan and Bangladesh, on the other hand, have been less successful in improving the living standards of their people.

REVIEWING THE HIGHLIGHTS

People to Identify		
Mao Tse-tung	Norodom Sihanouk	Pol Pot
Ho Chi Minh	Jawaharlal Nehru	Nguyen Van Thieu
Chiang Kai-shek	Lon Nol	Nguyen Cao Ky
Ayub Khan	General Suharto	Zulfikar Ali
Indira Gandhi	Lyndon Johnson	Bhutto
General MacArthur	UNU	Ferdinand Marcos
Moraji Desai	Ngo Dinh Diem	Teng Hsiao-ping
Dr. Achmed Sukarno	Bao Dai	Richard Nixon

Places to Locate		
Indochina	Hanoi	Korea
Laos	Saigon	Bangladesh
Kampuchea (Cambodia)	Peking	Kashmir
Thailand	Geneva	Goa
Indonesia	Haiphong	Pakistan
Nationalist China	Formosa	Malaysia
Philippines	Okinawa	Pammunjon
	Vietnam	

Terms to Understand		
Great Leap Forward	Geneva Agreement	two-China policy
Tonkin Gulf Resolution	Kuomintang	17th parallel
	Republic of China	38th parallel

Tashkent Declaration	Cultural Revolution	People's Republic of China
domino theory	Red Guards	Huks
SEATO	Viet-Cong	Moros
	"gang of four"	

Events to Describe

Long March   Pueblo incident   Tet offensive

Mastering the Fundamentals

1. How did Mao Tse-tung come to power?
2. Why was Chiang unsuccessful in keeping power in China?
3. Why did the United States refuse to recognize the People's Republic of China?
4. Why did President Carter finally recognize the People's Republic of China?
5. To what extent was America's policy in breaking diplomatic ties with Taiwan wise or unwise?
6. Why did the Great Leap Forward fail?
7. How did Teng Hsiao-ping change the policies of Mao Tse-tung?
8. Why was Korea divided?
9. What evidence exists to show that Japan has made a quick postwar recovery?
10. Why did the Japanese oppose Eisenhower's trip to Japan?
11. Why was Sukarno overthrown in Indonesia?
12. Why was France defeated in Indochina?
13. What is the significance of the Geneva Conference?
14. Why did the United States feel that it had to get involved in Indochina?
15. Why was the Vietnam war called a frustrating war?
16. How did the views of the hawks differ from those of the doves on Vietnam?
17. Why did India and Pakistan come to blows over Kashmir?
18. Why did Indira Gandhi suspend the constitution?
19. Identify two foreign problems that face India.

THINGS TO DO

1. Debate. *Resolved:* The United States participation in the Vietnam War was entirely justified.
2. Hold a Meet the Press program in which a group of students acting as reporters hold a group interview of Teng Hsiao-ping upon his visit to this country.
3. Prepare a Report on "Indira Gandhi: Her Life and Times." An especially important and interesting part of such a report could center around her relationship with her father, Nehru, whom she served in a number of official capacities.

Read the selection below and answer the questions that follow it.

On Guerrilla Warfare

by Mao Tse-tung

What is basic guerrilla* strategy*? Guerrilla strategy must be based primarily on alertness, mobility*, and attack. It must be adjusted to the enemy situation, the terrain*, the existing lines of communication, the relative strengths, the weather, and the situation of the people.

In guerrilla warfare, select the tactic* of seeming to come from the east and attacking from the west; avoid the solid, attack the hollow; attack; withdraw; deliver a lightning blow, seek a lightning decision. When guerrillas engage a stronger enemy, they withdraw when he advances; harass him when he stops; strike him when he is weary; pursue him when he withdraws. In guerrilla strategy, the enemy's rear, flanks and other vulnerable* spots are his vital points, and there he must be harassed, attacked, dispersed*, exhausted and annihilated*. Only in this way can guerrillas carry out their mission of independent guerrilla action and coordination with effort of the regular armies. But in spite of the most complete preparation, there can be no victory if mistakes are made in the matter of command. Guerrilla warfare, based on the principles we have mentioned and carried on over a vast extent of territory in which communications are inconvenient, will contribute tremendously towards ultimate* defeat of the Japanese and consequent* emancipation* of the Chinese people.

Vocabulary

guerrilla—refers to military force that fights a superior
strategy—plan
mobility—ability to move
terrain—land
tactic—plan

vulnerable—weak
dispersed—scattered
annihilated—destroyed completely
ultimate—final
consequent—resulting
emancipation—freedom

1. When might Mao have written the above? How can you tell?
2. To what extent did Mao have the opportunity to test his ideas?
3. On what occasions in American history, might the United States have resorted to similar tactics?
4. Besides China, what other countries and leaders have tried to fight a war based on the principles of Mao?
5. What does Mao mean when he says, "Attack the hollow"?
6. Can these tactics prevail against a country such as the United States?

UNIT ACTIVITIES

1. Make a line graph showing the growth of United States participation in the Vietnam War.
2. Debate. Resolved: The Cold War Has Ended.
   Debate. Resolved: Salt II adequately provides for American Security.
3. Prepare a report on the European Parliament, which met for the first time in 1979, describing the following: **(a)** Membership; **(b)** Election Procedures; **(c)** Powers; **(d)** Future Prospects.
4. Dramatize an interview with the secretary-general of the United Nations, in which you raise questions concerning the power of the United Nations to resolve disputes.
5. Prepare a mural for your classroom entitled: "The Pageant of World History." On it, include the major turning points in world history. Explain why you regard each as a major turning point.
6. Make a survey of the number of students in your high school from Asia, Africa, or Latin America. Invite a panel of these students to speak to your class on America and the world.
7. Prepare a Round Table Discussion on the subject: "The Separation of Quebec: What it Means for Canada."
8. Pretend you are a newspaper reporter covering the Yom Kippur War. Prepare an objective account on the causes and results of that war.
9. Prepare a report describing how the energy crisis is affecting each of the following countries, and how each country is trying to meet the crisis. **(a)** Japan; **(b)** Germany; **(c)** Italy
10. Draw maps of Africa for each of the following dates. **(a)** 1914; **(b)** 1919; **(c)** 1939; **(d)** 1945; **(e)** 1979. Summarize the changes that took place.
11. Prepare a Meeting of Minds program in which the following people meet to talk about world affairs from their respective vantage points. **(a)** Franklin Roosevelt; **(b)** Harry Truman; **(c)** Winston Churchill; **(d)** Joseph Stalin; **(e)** Charles De Gaulle
12. Draw one or more cartoons explaining the fall of the following leaders. **(a)** The Shah of Iran; **(b)** Somoza of Nicaragua; **(c)** Idi Amin of Uganda
13. Debate. *Resolved:* The Palestine Liberation Organization (PLO) deserves to be recognized as a nation.
14. Debate. *Resolved:* Apartheid serves the people of the Union of South Africa well.
15. Research and prepare a report showing some of the conditions of the boat people of Vietnam.
16. Hold a Town Meeting of the Air on the subject "Tomorrow Will Be Better than Today."

Caputo, Philip. *A Rumor of War*. Ballantine. A first-hand account of the fighting in Vietnam as experienced by a marine.

Dawson, Alan. *55 Days*. Prentice Hall. A vivid account of the fall of South Vietnam to the Communist.

Eban, Abba. *Abba Eban: An Autobiography*. Random House. The founding of Israel as it was experienced by one of its founders.

Epstein, Helen. *Children of the Holocaust*. Putnam. The impact of the holocaust upon the children of those who survived.

Herr, Michael. *Dispatches*. Knopf. One of the best books on the Vietnam War.

Horne, Alistair. *Algeria 1954–1962*. Viking. An account of the fighting in Algeria that led to its separation from France.

Lacoutre, Jean. *Arabs and Israelis*. Holmes & Meier. An unusual dialogue between two Arabs and one Israeli about the prospects of working together for peace.

Lewis, Bernard (ed.). *Islam and the Arab World*. Knopf. A beautifully illustrated book on the faith, the culture, and the people of Islam.

Leys, Simon. *Chinese Shadows*. Viking. A brilliant attack on the China of Mao Tse-tung.

Mehta, Ved. *Mahatma Gandhi and His Apostles*. Viking. A short but fast-paced account of the Indian leader and his followers.

Mehta, Ved. *The New India*. Viking Press. An account of the overthrow of the government of Indira Gandhi.

Meisner, Maurice. *A History of the People's Republic*. Free Press. A fair-minded account of developings in China under Mao Tse-tung.

Naipaul, V.S. *India, a Wounded Civilization*. Knopf. A well-done book of essays about the torments of a vast subcontinent.

Payne, Robert. *A Rage for China*. Holt, Rinehart & Winston. Written by one who lived in China throughout World War II, the book eloquently describes emerging China.

Peretz, Don. *The Middle East*. Houghton Mifflin. A fine survey of the origins of today's Middle Eastern problems.

Reischauer, Edwin O. *The Japanese*. Harvard University Press. This volume contributes enormously to an understanding of the people of Japan. It was written by America's leading scholar on the subject.

Sachar, Howard M. *A History of Israel*. Knopf. An account of the development of Israel from the earliest days until our own time.

Sadat, Anwar Al. *In Search of Identity*. Harper & Row. An interpretation of Egypt's long history by the country's president.

Schama, Simon. *Two Rothschilds and the Land of Israel*. Knopf. This is a moving account of the earliest days of Zionism and the role of Baron Edmond de Rothschild.

Shawcross, William. *Sideshow*. Simon & Schuster. A very critical account of America's role in the destruction of Kampuchea.

Yglesias, Jose. *The Franco Years*. Bobbs-Merrill. Profiles of Spaniards, some great, some not so great, who lived through the Franco years.

The space shuttle Columbia, launched in 1981

Epilogue:
Toward the Twenty-First Century

In ancient Greece and Rome no emperor would dare start any important political or military activity without having a seer (wise person) predict its outcome. The oracles at Delphi in Greece studied the entrails (intestines) of dead animals. The oracles thought that such entrails gave clues to the future. Distinguished visitors were offered predictions about what they could expect to happen. When the oracles said that omens were bad, people put off decisions until more favorable signs appeared.

Today, people continue to be concerned about the future. We no longer examine the entrails of dead animals in order to make predictions. However, we do identify major developments happening in our time. We try to see how these developments may continue and affect the future. In this way, we hope to get ready for what may take place in the twenty-first century. St. Augustine (354–430) wrote, "Time is a three-fold present, the present as we experience it, the past as present memory, the future as present expectation." We can well ask: What does the future hold?

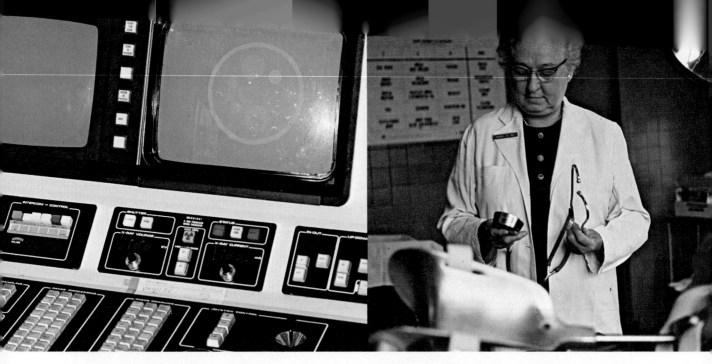

Atomic energy is being used to advance medical technology. For example, a device known as a CAT scanner enables physicians to see detailed pictures of the brain and other internal organs of a patient. The scanner shoots X-rays through a patient's body from many angles. An X-ray detector measures the rays that come through. A computer (right) reads information from the detector and constructs an image on a television screen. That information is then used by doctors (left) to diagnose a patient's condition.

Why Atomic Energy Is a Double-edged Sword

At the end of World War II, atomic bombs destroyed the Japanese cities of Hiroshima and Nagasaki. These bombs had the force of twenty thousand tons of ordinary explosives. The manufacture of atomic bombs was made possible by the work of scientists, not soldiers or politicians. In 1905, Albert Einstein, a theoretical physicist, said that an object could be changed into energy. This energy would be greater than anything the world had ever seen. Einstein was a peaceful man. However, in World War II, when Einstein thought his adopted country, the United States, was in danger, he made a decision. He wrote President Roosevelt to tell him how atomic energy could be used to make atomic bombs. The president acted at once. Scientific research was hurried, and the atomic bomb was created. The use of the atomic bomb may have shortened World War II considerably.

The same scientific work that made an atomic bomb possible is also used for peaceful purposes. Atomic energy is used in medicine. It may also be used as fuel in place of coal, oil, or natural gas to run factories, heat homes, light cities, and drive ships. A single pound of atomic fuel can heat as many homes as 1,500 tons of coal.

In 1973, OPEC, the Organization of Petroleum Exporting Countries, raised the price of oil. The United States and other countries began to think of ways to become independent of foreign oil and solve the energy problem. Nuclear power plants are one possible answer. However, many people think that nuclear energy and nuclear power plants are unsafe. They urge new approaches to the question of energy. They say coal should be more widely used. There is great interest in further research into solar energy. Energy from the sun would be of great help to all of humankind to run industry, to provide light, and to heat homes.

Top: A close-up of moon rocks on the surface of the moon.
Bottom: A scientist cuts a lunar (moon) sample.

Adventures in Space Exploration

For hundreds of years people have dreamed about traveling from the earth to the moon and back. Today that dream is reality.

The Soviet Union developed the first successful satellite. It circled the earth, much the way the moon circles the earth. The satellite sent back signals telling about conditions in outer space. In 1961, Yuri Gagarin, a Soviet cosmonaut, became the first person to make a successful orbit around the earth in a Soviet satellite. Early in 1962, John Glenn circled the world three times in a United States satellite. He became the first American to complete an around-the-world space flight. These early American flights were followed by many others.

In July, 1969, Neil A. Armstrong and Edwin E. Aldrin, Jr., became the first human beings to land on the moon. Their spacecraft, also piloted by astronaut Michael Collins, was called *Apollo II*. Armstrong and Aldrin collected samples of the surface of the moon. They brought these lunar samples back to earth for scientific study. The first two United States astronauts to land on the moon left a

plaque there. It said, "We came in peace for all mankind."

Distant space probes have been directed at the moon and at planets. In 1965, the United States sent *Mariner 4* deep into space. From there, it sent back rare pictures of Mars. In 1980, the United States sent *Voyager I* into the outer solar system. There it took pictures of the rings of the planet Saturn. In 1981, the United States sent a space shuttle aloft. The space shuttle was called *Columbia*. After circling earth three times, the *Columbia* landed safely. The *Columbia* is the first reusable spacecraft. It will be used often in scientific and military space experiments.

In July, 1975, *Soyuz* (Soviet) and *Apollo 18* (United States) spacecrafts left launching pads thousands of miles apart. The two vehicles linked up in space. Astronauts of the Soviet Union and the United States exchanged handshakes, greetings, and flags. They dined together in space. This was the first cooperative space experiment of their two countries.

The exploring spirit that drove people to cross the dangerous Atlantic Ocean during the fifteenth century continues to drive modern space explorers. Extending human knowledge into the reaches of outer space will bring many changes and discoveries not even dreamed of today.

The Magic of Chemistry

At our fingertips today there is a kind of magic made possible by science. Chemists have developed synthetic (artificial) fabrics such as rayon, nylon, and orlon. The science of chemistry has also increased the strength of metals. For example, steel has made possible the building of skyscrapers. Strong, light metals such as aluminum and magnesium are used in airplanes. On the ground, in homes and in factories, advances are made possible through the different uses of chemistry.

Progress in chemistry has freed people from some dependence on nature for the things they need. If natural rubber is hard to get, artificial rubber can be made in factories. If fuel from petroleum is unavailable, a synthetic fuel may be possible. If lumber is not plentiful, substitute products can be manufactured from plastic and metal. Wise use of chemicals has also helped people to grow more food and to keep it fresh longer.

The Revolutions of Our Time

In a book entitled *Rich Nations and Poor Nations,** Barbara Ward identified four revolutions that are in progress today. These revolutions will no doubt have a great affect on our future. They are revolutions in

1. The application of science to nearly all forms of human effort and reason
2. The biological revolution
3. The idea of progress
4. The idea of the equality of men, women, and of nations

Let us see what these revolutions may mean for us.

1. The Application of Science to Nearly All Forms of Human Effort When people think about life in the year 2000 and beyond, they may imagine plastic domes that cover whole cities. They may look forward to having mechanical robots to perform ordinary household tasks for them. Some foresee that after the year 2000 people will be living on space platforms. Others believe that people will be living entirely underground. Among the changes that science and technology may very likely bring in the twenty-first

*New York: W.W. Norton, Co. Inc., 1962

708

century are weapons that paralyze rather than kill, disease control, and weather control.

Scientific and technological wonders are always on the horizon. Such changes will surely make a difference in the way we live. Developments in nuclear energy, space travel, new communication techniques, personal and business computer technology, and plastic parts for body organs, are just a few of the advances of science. Everyday life is affected by what was science fiction just a generation ago.

2. The Biological Revolution From the dawn of history to about 1630, the total population of the world grew to half a billion people. By 1830, there were one billion people in the world. It had taken nearly 200 years for the population to double. In 1930, however, there were two billion people in the world. It had taken only 100 years—between 1830 and 1930—for world population to double. Today, the world's population is over four billion. It is estimated that by the year 2000 there will be nearly six and a half billion people on this planet.

The "population explosion," as it is called, has many results. Among these are overcrowding in city areas of the world and the growing differences between rich and poor nations. Such problems encourage international conflict.

3. The Idea of Progress Throughout most of human history, leaders and governments did little to improve conditions for the masses of people. Most people, from the earliest days of ancient Egypt, Greece, and Rome, and through the Middle Ages, worked hard just to stay alive. They had very little time or energy left over to think about changing their lives. The struggle to live was difficult all over the world.

Today, there are still hunger and poverty in many parts of the world. How-

An earth station for a communications satellite. The station is able to transmit messages and pictures via satellite around the world.

ever, people expect decent housing, food, and health care. Many people also measure progress by consumer goods and labor-saving devices—refrigerators, washing machines and dishwashers, microwave ovens, and video-cassette recorders. Nations measure progress by the industries they develop and some by the weapons they stockpile. Few people on earth are content to do without the things that civilization can provide.

4. The Idea of Equality The idea of human equality is based on one of the most revolutionary principles of the Declaration of Independence, "that all men are created equal." This statement has been the subject of much debate. What does it mean? When the statement was first written, equality existed in neither the American colonies nor in any other country in the world. At first, the

709

Sandra Day O'Connor (center) on the day she assumed office as the first woman justice of the Supreme Court. With her, from left to right, are Mrs. Reagan, President Reagan, Chief Justice Warren Burger, and members of Justice O'Connor's family.

statement meant equality for only a small group of people. For them (adult white males who owned property), it meant equality before the law.

Later on, the statement came to mean more than merely equal legal rights. It meant that all men and women should have equal opportunity to develop and use their capabilities. Today, this meaning is probably the most accepted one.

The idea of equality of opportunity has by no means been fully achieved. Equality of opportunity means that all men and women should be given an equal chance without regard to class, country of origin, race, wealth, intellectual or physical abilities. Politically, this means one person, one vote. In the UN General Assembly it means one nation, one vote.

At a meeting in Helsinki, Finland, in 1975, thirty-five Communist and non-Communist countries stated their support for basic human rights. These include freedom of speech and freedom to move from one country to another. The

struggle for human rights around the world is part of the revolution for human equality.

Today, all these revolutions are taking place all at the same time and very rapidly. What used to take centuries to achieve now takes only decades. The Agricultural Revolution, which may be said to have begun about 25,000 B.C., took thousands of years to unfold. The Industrial Revolution, which may be said to have begun about 1750, took only a couple of hundred years. Today, a major revolution completes its cycle within the lifetime of an individual. The late Charles Frankel, a Columbia University professor, called this phenomenon the "telescoping of revolutions." A person living today might have been born in the age of steam. That same person may live to see the revolution in humankind's conquest of space. As the great anthropologist Margaret Meade put it, "The most vivid truth of our age is that no one will live all his life in the world in which he was born, and no one will die in the world in which he worked in his maturity."

Tommorrow's Agenda

In view of these developments, what will the twenty-first century bring? The *Global 2000 Report* was prepared for President Jimmy Carter of the United States. Its authors declared, "If present trends continue, the world in 2000 will be more crowded, more polluted, less stable . . . and more vulnerable to disruption than the world we live in now." The report said that if present trends continue, the world's population would grow to over six billion people from the present four billion. This report says that there may not be enough food to feed the world's people. Farmland may not increase fast enough. Shortages may develop in fuel resources such as coal, oil, gas, and uranium. We may not have enough water or forest resources. Some animals and plants may disappear.

This description of what the future may be like is a gloomy one. However, these developments will take place only "if present trends continue." The disasters of the *Global 2000 Report* may be avoided by careful use of resources. New resources may be found. Hunger is widespread, but world food output is continuing to grow. One problem is how to get food from areas where there is plenty, to places where there is not enough. It is encouraging that China and India have practically conquered hunger.

The world is already learning to rely less on fossil fuels, oil, coal, and natural gas, and is conserving them. The chances are good for finding additional natural resources people never thought were available. The forests of such continents as South America and Asia have been rapidly used up. Nevertheless, there are successful programs for the planting of new forests in India, North Africa, and China. These efforts at reforestation mean that the forests of the world need not disappear.

Some people fear the rapidly changing nature of modern society. They feel that a global catastrophe is likely to happen. Yet if disaster overtakes the world by the year 2000, it will not be because of science and technology. It will not be because we have run out of food, fuel, or forests. It will be because we have not responded effectively enough to such questons as:

Will we learn to live peacefully with one another?

Will we finally control the spread of nuclear weapons?

Will we organize a system of law throughout the world?

Will we safeguard human rights?

Will we strengthen the family?

Will we help more people to learn to read and write?

Will we provide health care and nutrition for all people?

Will we improve living standards around the world?

Will the people of the world learn to live in freedom?

In his book *The History of the Idea of Progress,** the scholar Robert Nisbet writes that the history of civilization shows that there has been a steady advance in knowledge. He contends that there has been spiritual and moral improvement as well. He expresses the hope that such progress can continue. The future of civilization depends on the wise use of knowledge. Through your study of world history you are in a better position to use your knowledge. You can help find answers to the problems people face. Your contributions can make your generation the greatest period of human history. You will create the future by your dreams and by your deeds today.

*New York: Basic Books, 1980

GLOSSARY

A.D. – the period of time since the birth of Christ. The letters stand for Anno Domini which is Latin for "in the year of the Lord."

absolutism – a theory of government which gives all power to the monarch or dictator.

Age of Discovery – that period from about the fifteenth century to the seventeenth century in which the New World was found and much of the Far East and Sub-Saharan Africa was explored.

Age of Reason – a change in the ways of thinking which took place between 1650 and 1800. People began to rely on reason to solve their problems rather than on the accepted ways of thought.

aggression – an unfair attack by one nation upon another.

Agricultural Revolution – the change from the use of hand labor to machine labor in farming. It began about the beginning of the eighteenth century and brought many social and economic changes.

Allah – the name for God in the faith of Islam.

alliance – a group of nations joined temporarily for a common purpose.

allies – a term used to describe any group of nations working together, especially applied to the U.S., Britain, France, and their friends in World War I and World War II.

ancient history – that period of written history that began about 6000 B.C. and lasted to about the fall of Rome in A.D. 476.

apartheid – complete separation of white and black races in South Africa.

appeasement – a term which describes the policy of "giving in" to a possible enemy in the hope of preventing war.

Arabic numbers – the numbering system in use in the West today. It developed in India.

armistice – a temporary agreement between two sides to stop fighting.

arms race – a policy of building a nation's military might in order to keep up with or ahead of the military might of its neighbors.

Athenian democracy – a form of direct democracy in ancient Athens in which each citizen had a part. Since relatively few were citizens, Athenian democracy was not "democracy" as understood in the twentieth century.

Ausgleich – a compromise between Austria and Hungary in 1867 which set up the Dual Monarchy.

autonomy – the right of a nation to rule itself.

Axis Powers – the term applied to Fascist Italy, Nazi Germany, and Japan during World War II.

B.C. – the period of time before the birth of Christ.

balance of power – a condition in international affairs in which competing countries have equal or nearly equal strength. This condition supposedly prevents nations from dominating one another or going to war.

Balkans – the countries of the Balkan Peninsula. These include Turkey, Greece, Bulgaria, Albania, Romania, and Yugoslavia.

Baltic countries – those nations bordering the Baltic Sea. They are Estonia, Latvia, and Lithuania. They are now part of the Soviet Union.

barbarians – originally a word used to mean any "foreigner" in the sense of being non-Greek or non-Roman.

Later, it was applied to the German tribes who invaded Rome.

belligerents – nations fighting a war.

"benevolent despot" – a ruler who holds absolute power but who uses that power in ways he or she believes will help the people.

blitzkrieg – "lightning warfare" used by Nazi Germany. It involved rapid and fierce attacks intended to destroy the enemy totally or to force the surrender of the enemy.

bloc – a group of nations, people, or political parties with similar ideologies who join together at times in order to get the things they want.

"blood and iron policy" – a program followed by Bismarck to bring about the unification of Germany through war.

bourgeoisie – French name for the middle class.

boycott – an agreement to avoid doing business with a person or nation, usually for the purpose of forcing that person or nation to give in.

Brahman – the highest rank in the Hindu caste system.

British Isles – Great Britain (England, Scotland, Wales), Ireland, the Isle of Man, and other nearby islands in the North Atlantic.

Buddhism – the religion of Buddha, which stresses the need to strive for correct living in order to avoid suffering.

Byzantine Empire – the name given to the Eastern Roman Empire which lasted a thousand years after the fall of the Western Roman Empire. The Byzantine Empire fell in 1453.

capitalism – an economic system in which there is usually free enterprise, individual profit, and private ownership of property.

caste system – an unchanging social and religious order in which the people are divided into specific classes. Usually associated with the Hindu religion of India.

Central Powers – the name given to Germany, Austria, and their allies in World War I.

charter – a constitution, guarantee of rights.

chivalry – a code of courtesy and behavior of knights in medieval days.

chronology – the arrangement of events according to the dates on which they took place.

city-state – an independent self-governing political unit on a small scale.

civil disobedience – the refusal to obey the laws of the land. It is used as a peaceful method of forcing reform.

civil rights – the rights of personal liberty such as speech, press and assembly which a democratic nation gives its people.

civilization – a term applied to a people who have reached a certain level of culture.

coalition – an alliance of nations or other groups with similar aims.

cold war – strong economic and political competition between the Soviet Union and the West. There is no actual shooting.

common law – a system of law based on accepted customs, traditions, and past decisions. It is used in most English-speaking countries.

Commonwealth of Nations – the voluntary association of Great Britain and its former dominions and colonies on the basis of absolute equality, one with the other.

commune – the organization of workers and farmers in Communist societies into industrial and farming communities. Those in the commune live, eat, and work together. There is no private ownership of goods.

communism – as an economic system it is based on government ownership of industry and the near absence of all private profit. As a political system its theory calls for a "dictatorship of the people" leading to an eventual democratic "classless society." In practice it has most often developed into a dictatorship of the Communist Party.

concession – that which one nation (or person) allows another to do. Usually this involves the rights to do business in an area or the grant of land for this purpose.

confidence vote – a vote taken in a law-making body to find out if there is a majority in support of the premier or prime minister.

Confucianism – a belief in a way of life based on the teachings of Confucius. The teachings stress morality and correct manners.

conquistadors – the name given to the Spanish explorers in the New World.

Copernican theory – a theory that the earth rotates on its axis and that the planets revolve around the sun. This belief was advanced in the sixteenth and seventeenth centuries and is accepted today.

coup d'etat – "a stroke of state," a palace revolution. A forceful seizure of government by a small group.

confederation – the loose association of states under a weak central government.

cradles of civilization – areas of the Middle East, China, India, and Central America in which civilizations were born. The locations are favorable to the development of civilization.

Crusades – religious wars. Historically, they were unsuccessful attempts of European Christians to take the Holy Land from the Muslims. They took place during the eleventh, twelfth and thirteenth centuries.

culture – the sum total of the artistic, scientific, and educational contributions of a people.

cuneiform – the writing of ancient Babylonians. The marks were made by a wedge-shaped reed on damp clay and then baked.

democracy – a government based on the consent of the governed. Each citizen has a voice in the government, by his or her vote and by his or her right to run for office. Democracy is based on majority rule. In a direct democracy all citizens may participate directly in the government. In a representative democracy, such as the United States, elected officials act on behalf of the voters.

detente – a temporary thaw in the cold war.

despot – a monarch or dictator who holds complete power over his or her subjects. The despot may be brutal in the use of power.

dictatorship – a government based on the will of one person who has usually taken power by force.

disarmament – a policy of reducing the size of a nation's military might. This may be voluntary or involuntary.

"divine right" theory – the explanation that the monarch received his or her right to rule from God rather than from the people.

domestic system – the manufacturing method of the sixteenth and seventeenth centuries in which workers were given raw materials from which they made products—usually textiles—at home.

dominion – a British colony which has become completely self-governing and independent within the Commonwealth of Nations. May also be called a Commonwealth country.

domino theory – the idea that if one country (especially in Southeast Asia) falls to communism, the others will follow.

Duma – a form of lawmaking body established in Russia in 1905.

dynasty – a group of kings or queens with the same family name. It is also used as a measure of time in India, Egypt, and China.

Early Middle Ages – a term applied to Western Europe from about A.D. 476–1000. It was a period of growth that helped make the flowering of the medieval period possible.

economics – the study of how people make a living and the financial relationships of countries.

economy – the way people make a living.

"enlightened despot" – a term applied to some of the eighteenth century absolute monarchs (Catherine and Frederick the Great) who "toyed" with advanced ideas of liberty. (Also called a "benevolent despot.")

Estates-General – ancient French lawmaking body made up of three estates, which had little power. Before the French Revolution the Third Estate declared itself the national Assembly.

executive – that person or branch of government that enforces or carries out the laws.

exploitation – the selfish use of people, wealth, and natural resources by a person or nation.

extraterritoriality – the right of foreigners not to obey the laws of the nation in which they live. Instead, they are subject to the laws of their own land.

factory system – a way of making things in which machines and workers are brought together in one building for the purpose of manufacturing goods.

fascism – a dictatorship in which there are one party, strict censorship, glorification of the nation, and complete control of the people by the government. Private ownership of property is allowed, but is closely watched and regulated by the government.

federation – a union between two or more states or nations in which each gives up power to a central government which is superior to both.

Fertile Crescent – a crescent-shaped area in the Middle East that extends the Tigris-Euphrates rivers to the Nile. Civilization began here because the land was able to support human life.

feudalism – a government based on a system of landholding. In return for protection and the use of a fief (gift of land), a vassal (one who receives the land) promises to faithfully serve his or her lord and lady (those who give the land). As a social system it is one in which each person occupies a fixed place in society. Feudalism was characteristic of the Middle Ages in Europe.

fief – that portion of land over which a lord in a feudal system rules but which he does not own. The lord is usually vassal of a greater lord.

free enterprise – a term used to describe an economy in which there is little government control of business.

free trade – commerce between two or more nations without tariff restrictions.

fundamental cause – one that has deep roots in the past.

"geographical expression" – a scornful term used to describe disunited lands, such as Italy before unification in 1870.

government – the study of the laws by which people live and how those laws are carried out.

Great Britain – England, Scotland, and Wales.

Great Leap Forward – the attempt by the People's Republic of China to modernize and raise living standards quickly.

guild – an economic, political, and social union of persons doing the same kind of work. Usually associated with Medieval Europe. The guild set standards for members and was for mutual aid and protection.

Hegira – the flight of Mohammed in 622 from Mecca to Medina. For Moslems it marks the beginning of the religion of Islam.

Hellenic – pertaining to the civilization and culture of Greece.

Hellenistic – a term used to describe a mixture of Greek and Near Eastern cultures. This mixture was made possible through the conquests of Alexander the Great.

heretic – one who holds beliefs which are different from accepted ones. Most often used to describe one whose ideas differ from those of an established church.

hieroglyphics – Egyptian picture writing.

Hindu – an ancient religion associated with India and characterized by a caste system.

historic – the name given to that period of time since the first written records.

history – the study of the past.

Holocaust – the destruction of European Jews by the Nazis during World War II.

Holy Roman Empire – a loose organization of German-speaking peoples usually under the king of Austria. It no longer exists.

House of Commons – the lawmaking branch of the British Parliament. It is more powerful than the House of Lords.

House of Lords – the branch of the British Parliament in which members are seated on the basis of inherited titles of nobilty.

immediate cause – one that leads directly to action and change.

imperialism – a policy of strong countries owning colonies or dominating less powerful areas of the world. The motives behind imperialism are desire for resources, international prestige, greed, and nationalism.

Industrial Revolution – the change from hand to machine labor and all the social, political, and economic changes that resulted. It began in England about 1750.

inflation – excessively high and rapidly rising prices.

"iron curtain" – an expression used by Churchill to describe the difficulty of the West in getting people, materials, and ideas across an imaginary line that divides Soviet countries from Western countries.

irrigation – a method by which water is channeled to dry places to water crops.

Islam – the religion founded by Mohammed.

isolation – a policy of having as little as possible to do with other nations.

jihad – a holy war by which Mohammedans were to gain converts.

judiciary – that part of government that interprets the meaning of the laws.

jury – a group of persons called in to hear evidence and reach a decision about a case in court.

Koran – the bible of the Islamic faith.

kowtow – the act of touching the floor with one's forehead. A gesture once used in China as a sign of respect for authority.

Kuomintang – a political party in China first organized by Sun Yat-sen and later known as the Nationalists under Chiang Kai-shek.

laissez faire – "Leave alone." It was an idea developed by Adam Smith in his book *Wealth of Nations* in which he said government should not interfere with business.

Latin America – the name given to those countries in the Western Hemisphere once owned by Spain and Portugal. It includes Mexico, Central America, South America, and the islands of the Caribbean.

legislature – that branch of government that makes laws. Congress and Parliament are lawmaking or legislative bodies.

lend-lease – a plan used by the U.S. to help Great Britain and those who were fighting Germany in World War II by "lending" or "leasing" goods rather than by selling.

"Liberty, Equality, Fraternity" – a rallying cry of the French Revolution. By "Liberty" was meant freedom. By "Equality" was meant the abolition of special privleges and three Estates. By "Fraternity" was meant love of country and the brotherhood of people.

limited monarchy – a government in which the rule of the monarch is held in check by a constitution.

living standards – a term used to indicate the luxuries, comforts and necessities a people are able to enjoy.

Long March – the temporary retreat of the Chinese Communists to Shensi province where they prepared for eventual victory.

Magna Carta – a document King John of England signed in 1215 guaranteeing such rights as jury trial, freedom from unjust arrest, and the protection of life and property.

majority – more than half.

mandate – an area or country under one administration of another country, especially those determined by The League of Nations after World War I.

manor – the lord's castle and the farm land around it. The manor was the economic basis of Medieval Europe.

Mau Mau – a group of revolutionaries who ousted the British from Kenya by resorting to tribal terrorist acts.

Medieval history – that period of history that begins about A.D. 476 and lasts until the close of the fifteenth century. It begins with the "fall" of Rome and ends with the "Age of Exploration."

mercantilism – an economic theory in which government closely regulated business and in which colonies existed in order to increase the wealth of the "parent" country.

militarism – the spirit or policy of maintaining a large army and navy.

mobilization – the last step in the gathering of soldiers and materials in preparation for war.

modern history – that period of time that begins about the beginning of the sixteenth century and continues to the present.

monarchy – a form of government in which a king or a queen rules.

Moslems – the followers of Mohammed.

nation – a union of people having complete control over their own domestic and foreign affairs. It has self-government and independence.

nationalism – a feeling of belonging and loyalty which causes people to think of themselves as a nation.

nazism – a philosophy of dictatorship followed by Germany under Hitler. It was somewhat modeled after Fascism, but also taught racial superiority.

Nazi – the short form for Hitler's *National Socialist Party.*

neutrality – the refusal to take sides in an argument or war among nations. It is very often a difficult position to maintain. Switzerland is a neutral nation.

new imperialism – imperialism associated with nations in the nineteenth and twentieth centuries, in which overseas colonies were sought for markets, raw materials, and investments.

New World – a term used to describe North, Central, and South America, together with the islands of the Western Hemisphere.

nonviolence – an attempt to oppose a law by any means short of acts which cause bodily harm or bloodshed. Advocated by Mohandas Gandhi of India in the fight to win independence from Great Britain.

old imperialism – imperialism marked by the search for "Gold, God, Glory" and the settlement of new lands. It is associated with European nations in the fifteenth and sixteenth centuries.

Old Regime – a term used to describe feudal conditions which existed in Europe before the French Revolution.

OPEC – Organization of Petroleum Exporting countries (mostly Arab) whose members seek to protect oil prices.

Open Door – an American policy of insisting upon equal rights in China for all nations.

PLO – Palestine Liberation Organization, an organization seeking to establish a Palestinian homeland.

papyrus – Egyptian writing material. A word from which we get "paper."

Parliament – the lawmaking body of Great Britain. Used also to describe lawmaking bodies modeled after the British Parliament.

parliamentary government – a government in which there is no separation of powers between the legislative and executive branches of government. The best example is the government of Great Britain.

passive resistance – efforts to oppose a law by nonviolent means such as fasting and demonstrations.

patrician – a member of a noble family in ancient Rome.

Pax Romana – Roman peace. A 200-year period in Roman history beginning in A.D. 27 during which there were no major wars.

pharaoh – the title of the all-powerful ruler of ancient Egypt.

philosophers – people who study life to gain wisdom about the best ways to live. In France, before 1789, they were critics of the Old Regime and were called *philosophes.*

plebeian – a member of a humble family in ancient Rome.

pocket borough – a borough (or town) whose election to the House of Commons in the nineteenth century was controlled by a wealthy person or family.

police state – a nation whose government stays in power by the force of a secret police and military power.

polytheism – a religious belief based on the worship of many gods.

prehistoric times – the time before written records began.

prejudice – an unfavorable opinion formed without examination of the facts.

premier – another name for prime minister.

primary source – a first or original source of information. An "eyewitness" account of an event.

proletariat – the working class.

propaganda – an attempt to influence the minds of people through words and pictures—speeches, newspapers, magazines, radio, and television.

protectorate – a weaker nation under the control of, and protected by, a stronger nation.

Ptolemaic theory – a theory which held that the earth was the center of the universe. It was generally accepted until the sixteenth and seventeenth centuries when the Copernican theory was accepted.

puppet state – a government whose decisions are made by a stronger nation.

purge – the killing or dismissal of members of a party who disagree with its leaders.

pyramid – an Egyptian pharaoh's tomb.

ratification – giving official approval to an agreement.

reign – a term used to indicate the number of years a king or queen was head of a nation. It is also used to mean the absence of any real power. The queen of England "reigns but does not rule."

Renaissance – a "rebirth" of Greek and Roman learning. It began in Italy and is usually applied to the period from the fifteenth to the seventeenth centuries in Europe.

reparations – a payment of a sum of money imposed upon a defeated nation to pay for the cost of the war or as a punishment for starting the war.

republic – a government in which the people choose representatives to govern them.

repudiation – an announcement that a nation does not intend to pay its debts. Or it may be an announcement that a nation will not live up to the terms of a treaty.

Restoration – took place in 1660 when Charles II of England returned to the throne a few years after the death of Cromwell.

rotten borough – a borough (or town) which in early nineteenth century Britain was sparsely populated but which sent more than its share of representatives to Parliament; i.e., it was overrepresented.

sanctions – refusal to sell goods to another country.

Sandinistas – revolutionaries of Nicaragua who overthrew the Somoza regime in 1979.

satellite – a rocket that circles the earth. A nation whose decisions are made by a stronger nation. A state controlled by the Soviet Union.

scientific method – an approach to a problem based on available facts which have been determined by observation and experimentation.

Scientific Revolution – a term which describes the great scientific advancements of the twentieth century made possible by use of the scientific method.

secondary source – an account of an event that is not based on original or primary sources. A "second-hand" account of what happened.

self-sufficiency – a condition in which a person or nation is not dependent on others for important products.

sepoys – Indian soldiers in the British army when Britain controlled India.

serf – a peasant who was not allowed to leave the land. A part of the feudal system of medieval Europe and of Russia until 1861.

Shintoism – a Japanese religion in which devotion to ancestors, state, and emperor is encouraged.

socialism – a form of economy in which large industries are partly or completely owned and operated by the government.

sovereignty – the state of full independence of a nation.

Spartan – a term used to mean a person who is able to get along with few comforts. The people of ancient Sparta were required to live with few comforts.

sphere of influence – an area in a country in which a foreign nation holds special trading privileges and builds and controls industry.

Tao – "the way of God." Included in the teachings of Lao-tze.

tariff – a tax on goods coming into or leaving a nation.

tolerance – respect for the beliefs of others. Absence of religious or racial prejudice.

totalitarianism – a government in which the individual is less important than the state and in which all parts of society are made to serve the state rather than the individual.

treaty – an agreement among two or more nations to do or not do something.

trusteeship – a method in which the UN "trusts" a larger nation to look after a colony or developing area and to report back to it.

two-party system – a form of government based on the activities of two main parties competing for offices.

tyranny – harsh rule by an absolute monarch or dictator.

ultimatum – a final warning made by one nation to another that war will come unless certain conditions are met.

United Kingdom – Great Britain and Northern Ireland.

unwritten constitution – those traditions and practices which, although not written down, have the force of law.

Utopia – a perfect society. The subject and title of a book by Sir Thomas More in the sixteenth century.

utopian socialism – a form of socialism which aims at achieving a perfect society.

vassal – a person who agrees to perform military service for his lord in exchange for a portion of the lord's land.

vernacular – the language of the people of a region as opposed to a language whose formal use is widely accepted beyond that region. Latin was the formal written language of medieval Europe. Spanish, French, etc., were vernacular languages.

veto – the power of one of the Big Five (U.S., USSR, China, France, Great Britain) of the Security Council to block action it dislikes. The power of the president of the U.S. to block laws he dislikes.

ATLAS

The World

—— International Boundaries

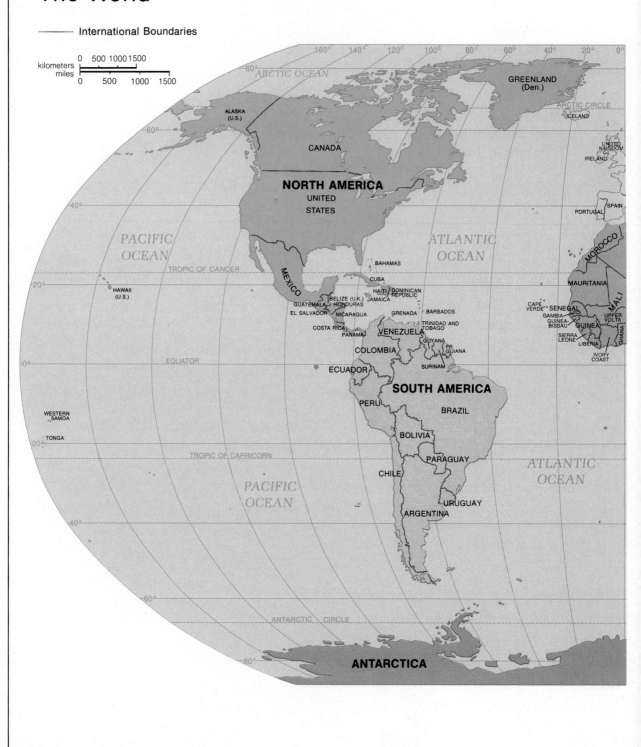

kilometers
miles

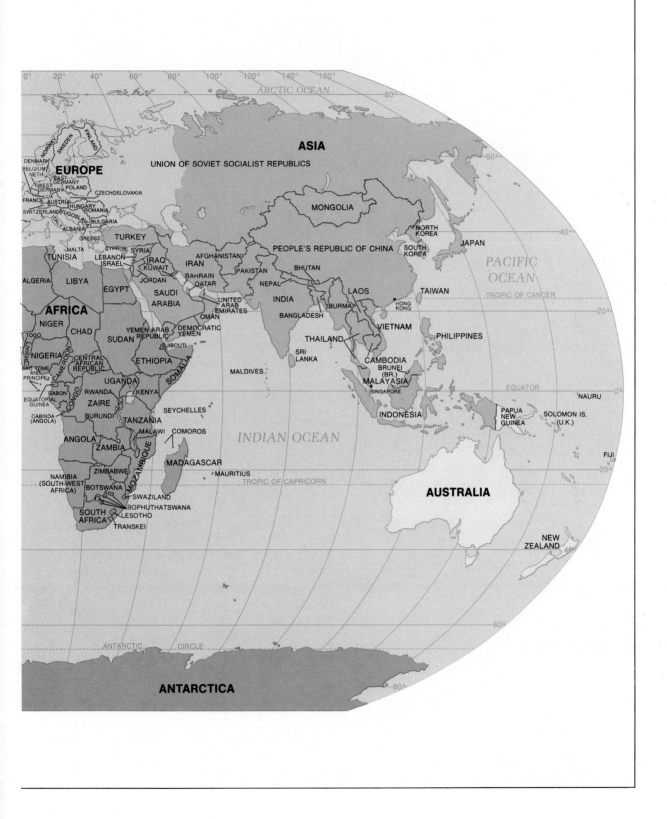

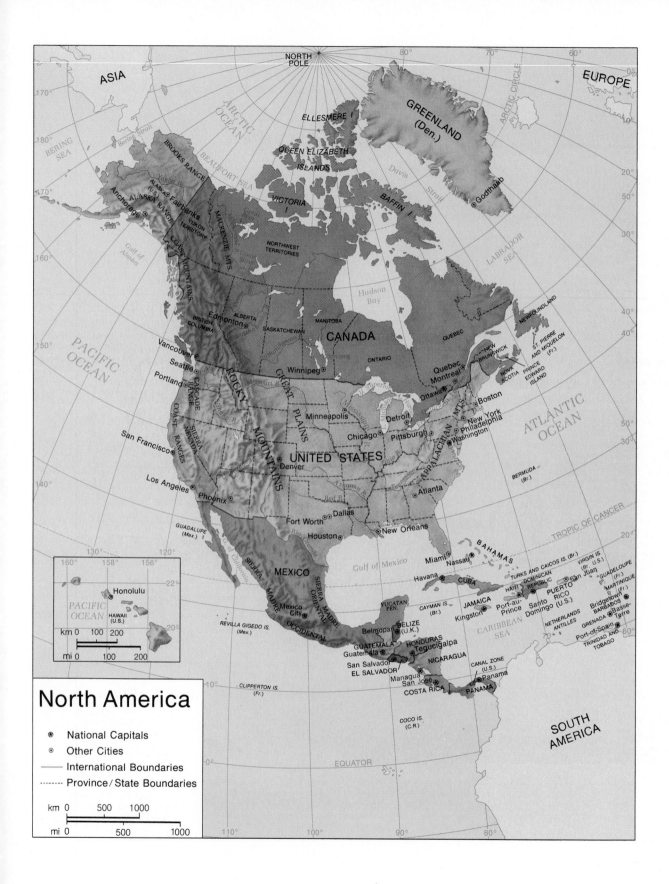

North America

⊛ National Capitals
⊙ Other Cities
— International Boundaries
------- Province/State Boundaries

km 0 — 500 — 1000
mi 0 — 500 — 1000

CENTRAL
AMERICA

CARIBBEAN SEA

Barranquilla
Maracaibo
Caracas

Medellín

GUYANA
Georgetown
SURINAM
Paramaribo
FRENCH GUIANA
Cayenne

VENEZUELA

LLANOS

Bogotá

GUIANA

HIGHLANDS

MALPELO
(Colombia)

Cali

COLOMBIA

GALÁPAGOS ISLANDS
(Ecuador)

Quito

ECUADOR

SELVAS

Manaus

Belém

EQUATOR

ROCAS
(Brazil)

Guayaquil

Iquitos

Amazon R.

AMAZON   BASIN

FERNANDO DE
NORONHA
(Brazil)

Marañón R.

Negro R.

Recife

ANDES

PERU

BRAZIL

Callao
Lima

Cuzco

La Paz

Madeira R.

MATO
GROSSO
PLATEAU

Brasília

Salvador

BRAZILIAN   HIGHLANDS

PACIFIC
OCEAN

MOUNTAINS

BOLIVIA

Sucre

Belo
Horizonte

TROPIC OF CAPRICORN

SAN FÉLIX
(Chile)

SAN AMBROSIO
(Chile)

Antofagasta

GRAN

CHACO

PARAGUAY

Asunción

São
Paulo

Rio de
Janeiro

Tucumán

JUAN
FERNÁNDEZ
(Chile)

Valparaíso

ARGENTINA

Porto
Alegre

Santiago

Córdoba

Buenos Aires

URUGUAY

Montevideo

CHILE
ANDES

PAMPAS

Bahía
Blanca

ATLANTIC
OCEAN

Valdivia

MOUNTAINS

PATAGONIA

FALKLAND ISLANDS
(U.K.)

Strait of
Magellan

CAPE
HORN

SOUTH GEORGIA
(Falkland Is.)

South America

⊗ National Capitals

⊙ Other Cities

— International Boundaries

km 0   350   700

mi 0   350   700

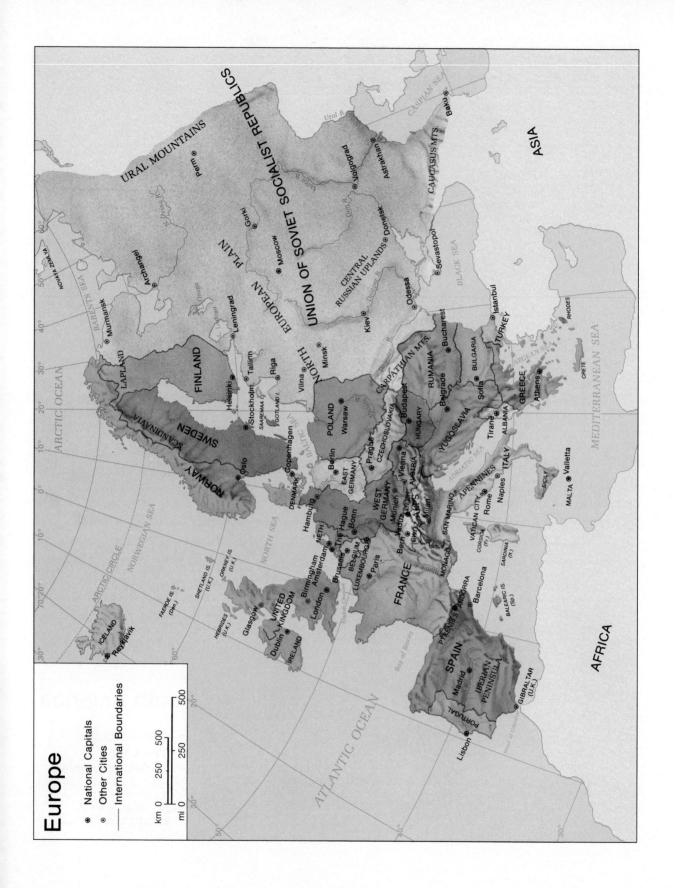

Europe

⊛ National Capitals
⊙ Other Cities
— International Boundaries

km 0   250   500
mi 0   250   500

URAL MOUNTAINS

UNION OF SOVIET SOCIALIST REPUBLICS

NORTH EUROPEAN PLAIN

CENTRAL RUSSIAN UPLANDS

Ural R.

CASPIAN SEA

ASIA

CAUCASUS MTS.

Baku ⊛

Perm ⊙

Gorki ⊙

Moscow ⊛

Volgograd ⊙

Astrakhan ⊙

Archangel ⊙

Murmansk ⊙

NOVAYA ZEMLYA

BARENTS SEA

Leningrad ⊙

Onega L.

Ladoga L.

Helsinki ⊛

FINLAND

LAPLAND

SWEDEN

SCANDINAVIA

NORWAY

Oslo ⊛

Stockholm ⊛

Tallinn ⊙

Riga ⊙

Vilna ⊙

Minsk ⊙

Kiev ⊛

Odessa ⊙

Donetsk ⊙

Sevastopol ⊙

BLACK SEA

Istanbul ⊛

TURKEY

RHODES

CRETE

MEDITERRANEAN SEA

AEGEAN SEA

Athens ⊛

GREECE

Bucharest ⊛

RUMANIA

CARPATHIAN MTS.

BULGARIA

Sofia ⊛

Belgrade ⊛

YUGOSLAVIA

Budapest ⊛

HUNGARY

Vienna ⊛

Tirane ⊛

ALBANIA

ADRIATIC SEA

Rome ⊛

VATICAN CITY

SAN MARINO

APENNINES

ITALY

Naples ⊙

SARDINIA (It.)

CORSICA (Fr.)

SICILY

MALTA

Valletta ⊛

Warsaw ⊛

POLAND

Berlin ⊛

EAST GERMANY

Prague ⊛

CZECHOSLOVAKIA

Milan ⊙

Bern ⊛

SWITZ.

ALPS

Vaduz ⊛

LIECH.

MONACO

Munich ⊙

WEST GERMANY

Copenhagen ⊛

DENMARK

Hamburg ⊙

Bonn ⊛

NETH.

The Hague ⊙

Amsterdam ⊛

Brussels ⊛

BELGIUM

LUXEMBOURG

Paris ⊛

FRANCE

Barcelona ⊙

Madrid ⊛

SPAIN

IBERIAN PENINSULA

PORTUGAL

Lisbon ⊛

GIBRALTAR (U.K.)

Strait of Gibraltar

ANDORRA

PYRENEES

BALEARIC IS. (Sp.)

Bay of Biscay

London ⊛

Birmingham ⊙

UNITED KINGDOM

Glasgow ⊙

Dublin ⊛

IRELAND

HEBRIDES (U.K.)

SHETLAND IS. (U.K.)

ORKNEY IS. (U.K.)

FAEROE IS. (Den.)

ICELAND

Reykjavik ⊛

ARCTIC OCEAN

ARCTIC CIRCLE

NORWEGIAN SEA

NORTH SEA

ATLANTIC OCEAN

BALTIC SEA

GOTLAND I.

SAAREMAA I.

Rhine R.

Seine R.

Rhône R.

Danube R.

Elbe R.

Volga R.

Don R.

Dnieper R.

AFRICA

726

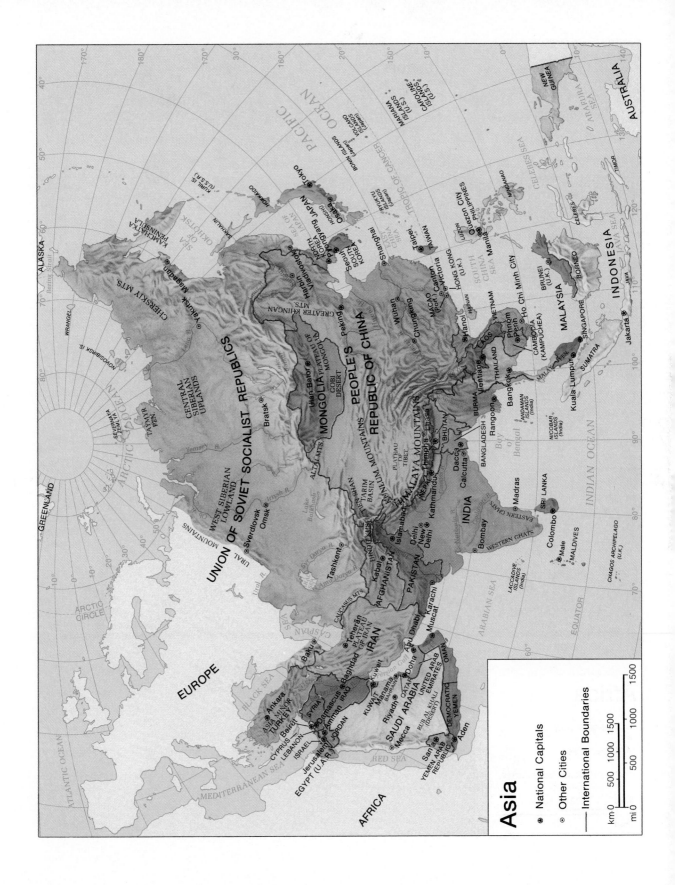

Asia

* National Capitals
◉ Other Cities
— International Boundaries

km 0   500   1000   1500
mi 0   500 1000 1500

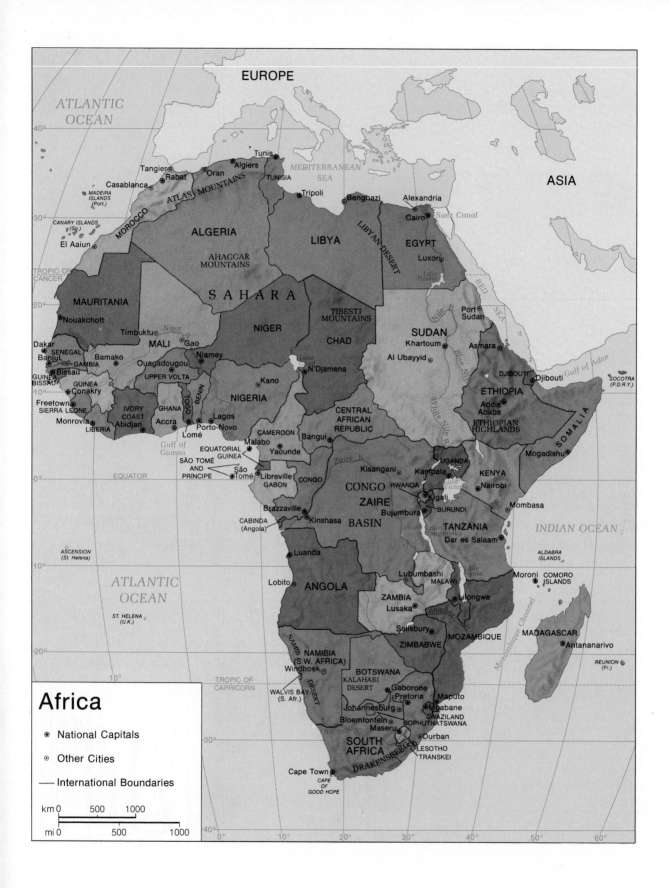

Africa

⊛ National Capitals

⊙ Other Cities

— International Boundaries

km 0   500   1000

mi 0   500   1000

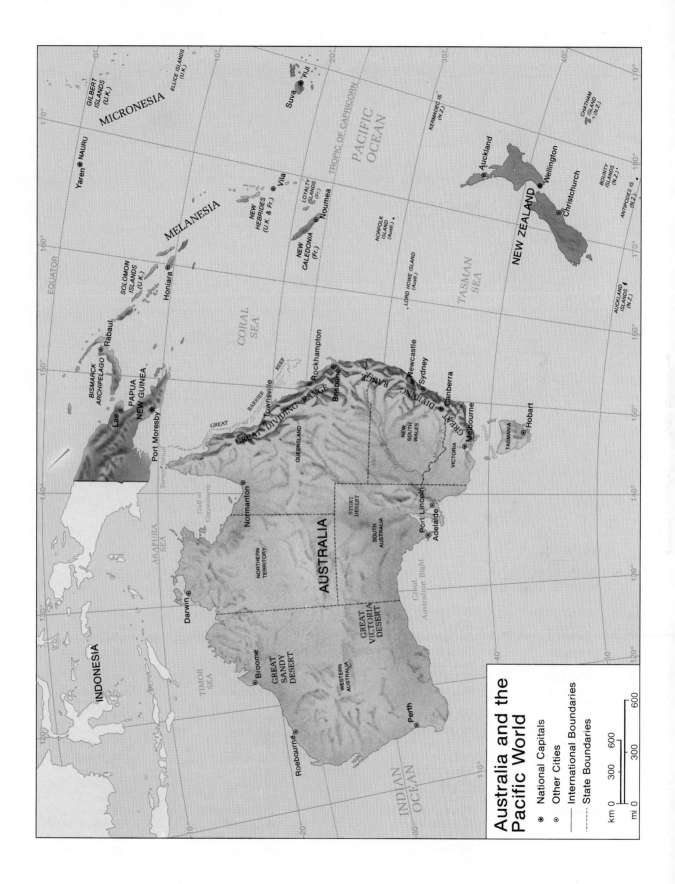

Australia and the Pacific World

⊛ National Capitals
◉ Other Cities
—— International Boundaries
---- State Boundaries

km 0   300   600
mi 0   300   600

Freedom in Today's World

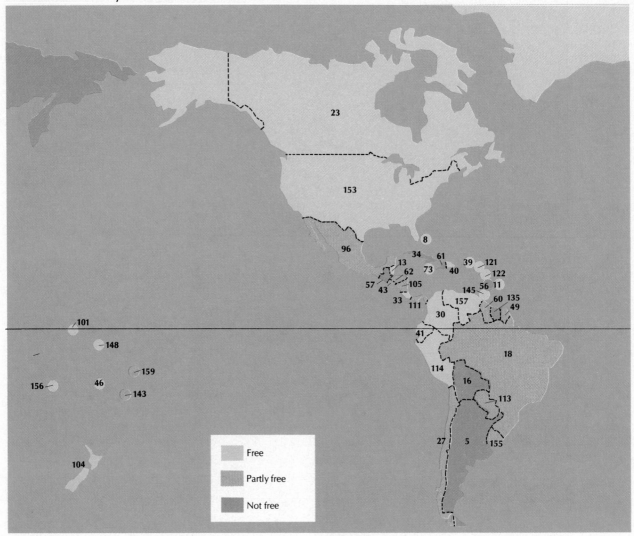

Free

Partly free

Not free

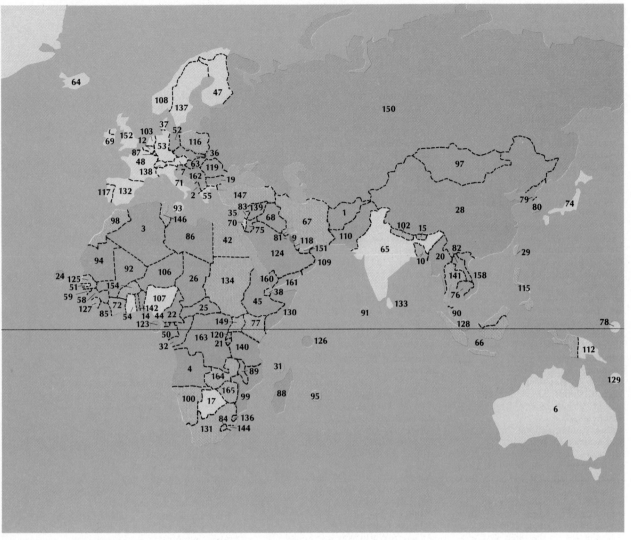

INDEX

Italicized page numbers indicate illustration.

China (cont.)
111, 112; unification of, 111–117; under Shih Huang Ti, 111–113; Han Empire in, 113–114, 128; barbarian invasions of, 114; T'ang and Sui Dynasties, 115, 128; later dynasties, 115–117, 128; life in, 117–121; culture of, 121–123, 126, 128, 212; Europeans in, 474–481; under Manchus, 474–478, 481, 485, 526; Opium Wars, 477–478, 485; T'ai P'ing Rebellion, 478; U.S. and, 478–481, 485, 574, 622–623, 678; Sino-Japanese War, 479, 484, 526, 567; Boxer Rebellion, 481, 526, 527; and Japan, 492, 509, 526–530, 579; and World War I, 508, 527, 528, 538; becomes a republic, 514, 526–527, 538; Kuomintang Party in, 527, 528, 529; Nationalist government in, 529; Japan's conquest of, 530, 567; Communists in, 530, 538, 678–679; People's Republic established, 679; Republic of Taiwan established, 679; relations with Soviet Union, 528, 530, 678, 680; relations with U.S., 678, 680–681, 699; Cultural Revolution, 679–680; and Southeast Asia, 689; and India, 697

China, People's Republic of. See China

China, Republic of. See Taiwan

Ch'in Dynasty, 109, 113, *120*

chivalry, 182, 197

Chopin, Frederic, 440

Chou Dynasty, 108–109, 114, 117, 128

Chou En-lai, 680

Christ. See Jesus Christ

Christianity, 26; rise of, 55–56, 76; and Roman Empire, 73, 74–76; in India, 93, 467, 472, 474; in China, 121; in Ethiopia, 144, 145; in Middle Ages, 170, 172; in New World, 348, 350; in Africa, 453, 455, 462

Christians: Roman persecution of, 69, 74; and Muslims, 170–171, 234–235; Luther and, 218

Christian Socialism, 401, 403

Churchill, Winston, 428, 458; and World War II, 571, 574, 579, *580*–581, 587, 596

Cicero, 73

Circus Maximus, 70, 75

circuses, 62, 70

cities: Industrial Revolution and, 395, 402, 407, 420; in nineteenth century Europe, 424–425. See also urbanization

Citizenship: in Athens, 40, 46–47, 52; in Rome, 69, 72

city-states, 40; origin of, 35–36, 52; Athens, 36, 41; Sparta, 36, 41–42; wars between, 40–42; African, 144; Italian, 205, 210, 222, 238

Civil Constitution of the Clergy, 326

civil disobedience concept, 524, 526

civil rights, 622

Civil War, in U.S., 380–381, 382, 417, 502

clan, 126

class struggle, 399

Claudius, Roman Emperor, 67

Cleisthenes, 38, 39

Clemenceau, Georges, 504, *505*, 510

Cleopatra, 65–66

Clive, Robert, *469*–470

cloth, 391

Clovis, king of the Franks, 178

Cnossus, Crete, 33, *34*

coal, 389–390, 391, 402

Code of Manu, 95

Co-hong, 476–477

Colbert, Jean Baptiste, 270–271

Cold War, 594, 595, 611, 612, 616, 697

Coleridge, Samuel Taylor, 439

collective farm, 551–552

Colombia: Spain and, 347, 351, 352; independence, 353; and Panama Canal, 536, 538, 633, 642; after World War II, 634–636

colonial system, 452

colonies, 253, 452, 462, 466. See also imperialism

Colosseum, 55, 70, *72*, 73, 75, 453

Colossus of Rhodes, 50

Columbus, Christopher, 131, 144, 240, *241*, 631

combine, 393

Comecon, 610

commerce. See trade

Committee of Public Safety, 329, 331, 662

common lands, 396

common law, 229

Common Market, 597, 603, 614, 616, 617

Common Sense (Paine), 311

Commonwealth of Nations, 414, 458; members of, 515–*516*, 520, 538, 623; discontent in, 516–522, 623, 625–626, 665, 671

communications, Industrial Revolution and, 391, 426

communes, 679

communism, 514, 559, 560; Marx and, 400–401, 403; in China, 530, 538; in Russia, 532, 544–545, 546–547; in Italy, 552, 603–604; in Eastern Europe, 555, 601–603, 608–610; and World War II, 568, 595; in Greece, 605; in Cuba, 628–630; in Central America, 632; in South America, 640; in the Middle East, 661; in Africa, 672; in Korea, 682; in Indonesia, 686, 690, 691, 695, 700

Communist Party: in Russia, 500, 549–550, 559, 607–608; in China, 530, 538, 678–680; in France, 600; in Italy, 603–604; in Portugal, 605

Communist Manifesto (Marx), 399, 400

Community of Free Peoples, 601

compass, 122, 242

concentration camps, 572

Condorcet, Madame de, 330

Concordat, 334, 604

Concordat of Worms, 189

confederation, 372

Confederation of the Rhine, 334, 372

Confucianism, 212, 127

Confucius: philosophy of, 109, 110–*111*, 112, 118; and the Han rulers, 114; influence of, 120–121, 127, 128

Congregational religion, 220

Congress, U.S., 415, 416

Congress of Berlin, 378

Congress of Vienna, *343, 344;* purpose of, 336, 341–345, 346, 358; effect of, 344–345, 355–356, 371, 372, 458

conquistadores, 245

Conservative Party, in Britain, 596–597

Constantine, king of Greece, 605

Constantine, Roman emperor, 74, 157, 160

Constantinople: in Byzantine Empire, 157, 158, 163; Turkish invasion of, 165, 236; Crusades and, 187; in Ottoman Empire, 376–378; becomes Istanbul, 379, 533; in World War I, 498, 532

constitutions: in Britain, 415, 420; in France, 326, 327, 331. See also Constitution, U.S.

Constitution, U.S., 314, 316, 380, 415, 420, 438

Consulate, in France, 332

consuls, 58, 75

Continental System, 336

contraband, 500

Cook, James, 451

coolies, 119

cooperatives, 398–399

Copernicus, Nicolas, 213, 223, 286

Coptic Church, 144

Cordova, Francisco de, 245

Cordova, Spain, 170, 171

Corinth, 36

Corneille, 272

Corn Laws, 396, 402

Cornwallis, Charles, 470

Coronado, Francisco, 247

corporation, 394, 402, 553

Corsica, 333

Cortés, Hernando, 137, 240, 245

Cortes, in Spain, 236

Cortinès, Adolfo Ruiz, 628

Costa Rica, 632, 633

cotton gin, 391

Council of Chalcedon, 161

Council of Europe, 614

Council of Trent, 221

Counter Reformation, 221, 223

coup d'etat, 332, 338

Court of International Justice (World Court), 508

Court of Star Chamber, 305, 315

craft guilds, 192–194

Kuang Hsü, emperor of China, 480, 481, 526
Kubitchek, Juscelino, 639
Kublai Khan, 100, 115, 116–117, 128
Kuomintang Party, 527, 528, 529, 678, 681
Kurds, 606
Kushans, 90
Kutbuddin, Aibak, Muslim ruler, 92
Ky, Nguyen Cao, 690, 691

labor unions: in England, 401, 425, 426; in Soviet Union, 551; in Italy, 553
Labour Party, Britain, 412–413, 596–597, 598, 616
Lahore, India, 92
Lacombe, Claire, 330
Lafayette, Marquis de, 356
La Fontaine, 272
laissez faire, 293, 396–398, 402
Laocoön, 51
Laos, 83, 100, 101, 689, 695, 700
Lao-tze, 109, 110, 111
Las Casas, 247
Latin America: defined, 132; countries of, 132–134; geography of, 132–133; Native Americans in, 133–134, 149; Spaniards in, 136, 149; Columbus' discovery of, 144; under Spain and Portugal, 346–350; independence in, 350–355, 354, 359, 535; U.S. and, 535–536, 628, 630–636, 640–644; in the 1980s, 635. See also Central America; Mexico; South America
Latin language, 73, 132, 164, 204
Latins, 56, 57
Lausanne, Treaty of, 532–533
Lavoisier, Antoine, 288
laws: Greek, 38, 43, 50; Roman, 58, 71, 73, 164; English, 228–229, 265–266, 309; French, 332. See also constitutions; Constitution, U.S.
laws of gravity, 287
League of Nations: organization of, 502, 507–508, 510; U.S. and, 502, 504, 508; members of, 508, 510, 521; and Japanese invasion of China, 530, 567; power of, 567, 570; and Hitler's invasion of Poland, 570, 586; and attack on Finland, 570
Lebanon, 658, 661
Lee, Robert E., 502
Leeuwenhoek, Anton van, 289
legions, 59
leisure time, in Victorian Age, 426, 428
lend-lease law, 574, 576
Lenin, Nikolai, 501, 545–547, 551
Leo I, pope, 76, 161, 162
Leo III, Byzantine emperor, 157
Leo III, pope, 162
Leo X, pope, 215, 217
Leo XIII, pope, 437
Leopold II, king of Belgium, 459

Lespinasse, Julie de, 295
Latelier, Orlando, 642
Levesque, René, 626
Lhôte, Henri, 140
Liberal Party, Canada, 625
Liberal Party, Great Britain, 411, 414
Libya, 662, 664
Lie, Trygve, 585
limited monarchy, 309, 327–328, 414, 419
Lincoln, Abraham, 381
Linnaeus, Carl, 289
Lin Tse-Lsu, 477
Li Po, 122
Lister, Joseph, 428–429
Liszt, Franz, 440
literature: Greek, 47–48; Roman, 73; Indian, 97, 98–99, 523; Chinese, 121; African, 148; Muslim, 170; in Middle Ages, 197–198; French, 197, 271–272, 277, 439; German, 197, 290; of the Renaissance, 211; English, 265, 289–290, 307, 308, 309, 439; in Age of Reason, 289–290, 296; Spanish, 290; American, 311; in nineteenth century, 439; Russian, 439
Livingston, David, 455, 456–457, 462
Liu Pang, 114
Locarno Pacts, 509
Locke, John, 292–293, 311, 316
Lombards, 178
Lombardy, 367, 369
Long March, 678
Long Parliament, 305–306, 315
Lon Nol, 695
Louis VII, king of France, 196
Louis XI, king of France, 234
Louis XIII, king of France, 266, 268
Louis XIV, king of France: absolutism of, 266, 268, 273, 280; and War of Spanish Succession, 268; life at Versailles, 268–270, 280; economy under, 270–271, 272, 308, 322; cultural growth under, 271–272; and India, 468; and Canada, 519
Louis XV, king of France, 272, 320
Louis XVI, king of France, 336; and French Revolution, 272, 324; problems of, 320, 322–323; death of, 328, 356
Louis XVIII, king of France, 336, 342, 355
Louis Napoleon. See Napoleon III
Louis Philippe, king of France, 356, 359, 416
L'Ouverture, Toussaint, 631
Loyola, Ignatius, 221
Lucretius, 73
Lumumba, Patrice, 667
Lusitania, 500, 501
Luther, Martin, 216–218, 217, 223, 262–263
Lutheranism, 218, 220
Luthuli, Albert John, 147–148
Lvov, George, Russian prince, 545
Luxembourg, 570, 586

Luxor, Egypt, 11, 13, 16
Lycurgus, ruler of Sparta, 37
Lydia, 26–28, 29
Lyell, Charles, 436
Luzon, Philippines, 100

McAdam, John, 391
Macao, China, 467, 474, 605
MacArthur, Douglas, 578, 682–683, 685
McCormick, Cyrus, 393
Macedonia: conquers Greece, 35, 42–43; conquers Persia, 42; Roman conquest of, 61
Macedonian Wars, 61
Machiavelli, Niccolo, 211, 261, 367
Mackenzie, William, 520
Macmillan, Harold, 596, 611
Madeira, 605
Madero, Francisco, 626
Madison, James, 351
Madjaphit Empire, 102
Magellan, Fernando, 240, 474
Maginot Line, 570–571
magistrates, 58
Magna Carta, 229, 230, 415
Mahabharata, 98–99
Mahavira, 87
Mahmud of Ghazni, 91–92
maize, 136
Makarios, president of Cyprus, 605
Malaya, 532, 575, 687
Malay Peninsula, 101, 474, 484, 485
Malaysia, 83, 100; after World War II, 687–688; Federation formed, 687, 699, 700
Malenkov, Georgi, 606
Mali, Kingdom of, 142, 143, 145, 149
Mali, Republic of, 142
Malta, 343
Malthus, Thomas, 397–398, 433
Manchu Dynasty, 107; rise to power, 117; armies of, 474–475; Europeans and, 475–478, 485; and Opium Wars, 477–478, 485; and Boxer rebellion, 481, 526
Manchuria: early history, 117; Japan and, 527, 530, 538, 567, 586
mandate system, 508
Manet, Édouard, 441
maniples, 59
Mann, Horace, 430
manor, 182, 192
Mansa Musa, king of Mali, 142, 149
manufacturing. See industry
Maoris, 522, 688–689
Mao Tse-tung, 678, 679–680, 686, 702
marathon, 40
Marathon, Battle of, 40
Marcos, Ferdinand, 687
Marcus Aurelius, Roman emperor, 68–69
Marduk, Babylonian god, 21
Marianas Islands, 530
Maria Theresa, empress of Austria, 275, 278, 279, 280
Marin, Luis Muños, 630

Marius, Gaius, 63, 79
Marne, Battle of, 497
marriage: in India, 95; in China, 118; of the Mayas, 136; Muslim, 168; in Middle Ages, 195
Marshall, George C., 613
Marshall Islands, 530
Marshall Plan, 595, 613, 617
Martel, Charles, Frank leader, 168, 178
Martineau, Harriet, *433–434*
Marx, Karl, 399–401, *400*, 403, 545
Mary I, queen of England, 264, 266, 267
Mary II, queen of England, 308–309, *310*, 316
Mary, queen of Scotland, 264–265
Mason, Lowell, 440
Massachusetts, 430
mathematics: in Egypt, 17, 50; in Babylonia, 23–24; in Greece, 50; in India, 97; of the Mayas, 134; in the Middle Ages, 198; in the Renaissance, 287
Mau Mau rebellion, 664–665
Mauretania, 662
Maurice, Denison, 401
Maurya Empire, 89–90
Maximilian, emperor of Mexico, 417
Mayas, 134–136, 149, 245
Mazarin, 268, 271
Mazzini, Giuseppe, 368, 382
Mead, Margaret, 710
Mecca, 166, 167, 168, 170, 172
medicine, 18; in Greece, 50; in Rome, 73; in India, 98; Muslims and, 170; medieval, 192; Renaissance and, 213; Enlightenment and, 289; socialized, 596
Medici, Lorenzo de, 208, *210–211*
Medeci, Marie de', 209, 266
Medieval Period. *See* Middle Ages
Medina, 168
Mediterranean area: Phoenician traders in, *26;* Persian Empire in, 27; Minoan traders in, 34; Crusades in, 191. *See also* Middle East; trade
Mein Kampf (Hitler), 554
Meir, Golda, 655
Memphis, Egypt, 12, 13, 14
Mencius, 110,111
Mendelssohn, Felix, 440
Menes, Egyptian pharoah, 12
mercantilism, 252, 253, 270–271, 311
merchant guilds, 192–194
Mesopotamia, *19*, 82; early civilizations in, 18–21, *22*
mestizos, 350
metics, 47
metric system, 331
Metternich, Prince Klemens von, 367; and Congress of Vienna, 342; resignation of, 358, 359; influence of, 361
Metternich System, 343, 346, 356, 359
Mexican War, 355, 642

Mexico: oil in, 132, 627, 628, 645; Native Americans in, 133–137; Spaniards in, 136, 240, 245, 347; Aztecs in, 136; fight for independence, 351, 353, 417; under Maximilian, 417; U.S. and, 536–537, 626, 628, 642, 645; after World War I, 626–627; in World War II, 628; after World War II, 627–628. *See also* Latin America
Michelangelo Buonarroti, *208*, 211, 223
microscope, 286
Middle Ages: defined, 156; Feudal Period in, 156; in Byzantium, 157–165, 171; schism of Eastern and Roman Catholic Church, 160–163, 172; power of the pope, 162, 172; the Crusades, 165, *166*, 171; spread of Islam, 166–168, 172, 175; Muslim Empire, 168–171, 172; Christianity in, 172; in Western Europe, 175–199; early period, 176, 180–181, 228; later period, 181; culture of, 194–199; religion in, 204; rise of nationalism, 226, 228
middle class: in England, 390, 410; Industrial Revolution and, 394, 395, 402, 408; in Victorian Age, 427
Middle East: influence in Greece, 33, 51–52; Roman conquest of, 61; defined, 82, 673; and World War II, 576; after World War II, 649–674; in 1980s, *659*, 673. *See also names of individual countries*
Milan, Italy, 191, 212
Milan Decree, 335
militarism, and World War I, 492
Militiades, Athenian leader, 40
Milton, John, 308, *309*
minerals: in Egypt, 17; in Greece, 45; in Latin America, 136
Ming Dynasty, 117, *118*, 123, 128, 474
Ming Huang, 115
Minh, Duong Van, 694, 695
Minimum Wage Act, 621
mining methods, 17, 391
Minoan civilization, 33–34
Minos, king of Crete, 33
Minos, Palace of, 33, *34*
miracle plays, 198
Miranda, Francisco, 351
Mirandola, Picodella, 211
missionaries, 350; in Africa, 451, 453, 462; in India, 467, 472
Mistral, Gabriela, *641*
Mitterand, François, 600
Mobutu, 668
Model Parliament, 229–230
Modigliani, Amedeo, 146
Mogul Empire, *91*, 93–94, 471
Mohammed, prophet, 92, 166–168, 172
Mohenjo-Daro, *84–85*, 102
Molière, *272*
Molza, Tarquinia, 209
Monarchists, 416

monarchy, 64, 89
Monet, Claude, *441*
money systems: in Babylonia, 22; in Lydia, 26–27, *28*, 29; under Louis XIV, 271; in France, 326; in India, 84, 97; in Feudal Period, 191
Mongolia, 527
Mongols: in India, *91*, 92, 93; in China, 107, 115–116, 117, *119*; in Korea, 123; in Russia, 236. *See* Mogul Empire
Monophysites, 160–161, 162
monotheism, 15, 16, 26
Monroe, James, 353, 535, 642
Monroe Doctrine, 353, 417, 535, 642
Montagu-Chelmsford report, 524
Montaigne, 271
Montcalm, Marquis de, 519
Montenegro, 378, 383
Montesquieu, Baron de, 292, 293
Montessori, Maria, 431
Monteverdi, Claudio, 291
Montezuma, Aztec king, 137, 245
Montgomery, Bernard, 576
moon, landing on, 707–708
Moors, 144, 264, 272
morality plays, 198
More, Thomas, 204, *205*, 220
Morehead, Scipio, 146
Morelos, José, 351
Morley-Minto Reforms, 524
Moro, Aldo, *604*
Morocco: and World War I, 492, 493, 510; independence, 601, 661, 662
Moros, 687
Morrow, Dwight W., 627
Morse, Samuel F. B., 392
Moscow, Soviet Union, 132, 236, 547
Moses, 24, *25*
Mossadegh, Mohammed, 659
Mountbatten, Louis, 597
movies, 426
Mozambique, 453, 605
Mozart, Wolfgang Amadeus, 291
Mugabe, Robert, 670
mullahs, 167
Murabak, Hosni, **658**
Murillo, Bartolomé, 291
music: African, 146–*148;* in Age of Reason, 291; in nineteenth century, 440
Muslim Empire, 168–171, 172, 175; extent of, *169*
Muslim League, 696
Muslims, 101; in India, 91–94, 102, 471, 474, 696–697; in Africa, 142, 144, 149; in Middle Ages, 166–171, 172, 177, 185–187, 191; in Spain, 177, 234; in Iran, 532. *See also* Islam
Mussolini, Benito, 438, 566, 568; rise of, 552–554, 559; invasion of Ethiopia, 565, 664; invasion of Albania, 569; death of, 578
Mutsuhito, emperor of Japan, 483
Muzorewa, Abel T., 670
Mycenae, 35

mystery plays, 198

Nagy, Imre, 609, 610
Namibia, 671–672
Nanking, China, 529
Napoleon I (Bonaparte): campaigns, 11–12, 333, 334, 336, 440; rise to power, 331–332, *333*, 336, 338; an Emperor, 333, *334*, *335*, 337, 352; defeat of, 335–336, 338, 377; effects of, 343, 351, 357, 358
Napoleon III (Louis Napoleon), king of France: and the Second Republic, 357, 416–418; and the Second French Empire, 357, 359, 416–418, 420; and Crimean War, 368–369, 417; and Franco-Prussian War, 374–375, 418
Napoleonic Law Code, 332, 372, 600
Napoleonic Wars, 507
Nasser, Gamal Abdul, 652–653, 657
National Assembly, 323–327, 330, 337
National Convention, 328, 329–331, 332
nationalism, 226–227, 366–383; in France, 336–337, 366; and imperialism, 452; and World War I, 491–492; in World War II, 566–567
Nationalists, in China, 529
nationality, 376
nationalization, 547, 596, 629
National Liberation Front. *See* Viet Cong
National Socialist Party, 554–557, 560. *See also* Nazi Party; Nazism
National Workshops, 399
Native Americans: in Latin America, 131–132, 134, 149, 636–637; origins of, 133; and U.S. frontier, 534
NATO (North Atlantic Treaty Organization), 614–615, 617
natural resources, 227
nature, worship of, 126
navigation, 242
Nazi Party, 419, 437, 602, 603
Nazism, 555–556, 562, 568
Nebuchadnezzar, king of Babylon, 20–21
Negritos, 100
Nehru, Jawaharlal, 696, 698
Nelson, Horatio, 334
Nepal, 83
Nero, Roman emperor, 67–68
Nerva, Roman emperor, 68
Netherlands, 301; democracy in, 301, 419; and World War I, 500; and World War II, 570, 586. *See also* Dutch; Holland
New Amsterdam, 248, *249*
New Economic Policy (NEP), 547
New France, 519
New Granada, 347, 352
New Lanark, Scotland, 398
New Mexico, 355
Newspapers, 392, 425
Newton, Isaac, 287, 288, 437
New York City, 248, *249*

New Zealand: in Commonwealth of Nations, 515, 538; self-government, 521–522; after World War II, 688–689
Nicaragua, 536, 632, 643, 645
Nicholas I, czar of Russia, 346, 376
Nicholas II, czar of Russia, 507, 544
Nigeria, 146, 665–667
Niger River, 454
Nightingale, Florence, *429*
Nika riot, 160, 161
Nile River: and ancient Egypt, 11, *12*, 13, 16, 17–18, 28; explorations of, 454–457; irrigation by, 650, 661
Ninety-Five Thesis (Luther), 216
nirvana, 88
Nisbet, Robert, 711
Nixon, Richard M.: and relations with China, 622, 645, 678, 680, 699; resignation of, 622; and Vietnam War, 692, 693
Nkrumah, Kwame, 668
Nobel, Alfred, 507
nobles: in Egypt, 13, 14, 16; in Babylonia, 23; in China, 109; in feudal system, 181, 182, 187, 190, 278
nonviolence concept, 524, 525
Norman, 180
North Africa: Romans in, 141; Phoenicians in, 141; Muslims in, 168; World War II in, 576; after World War II, 661–664, 673; countries of, 664, 673. *See also* Africa
North America: Native Americans in, 133, 149; in 1980's, *624. See also* Canada; United States
Northern Ireland, 569, 597
North German Confederation, 374
Norway, 343, 419, 570, 586
Novotny, Antonia, 610
Nubia, 17
nuclear weapons, 612, 623, 630
nuclear non-proliferation treaty, 612
Nuremberg Trials, 602

obelisks, 13
Obregón, Alvara, 626–627
Octavian. *See* Augustus, Roman emperor
Odovacar, German general, 76
Odyssey, the (Homer), 35, 52
O'Higgins, Bernardo, 351, 355
oil, 642; in Iran, 532, 623, 659; in Middle East, 533, 628, 649, 650, 655, 662, 673; in Mexico, 132, 627, 628, 645; in Venezuela, 636; in Ecuador, 636; in Africa, 667
Ojukwu, Odumegwu, 666–667
Okinawa, 686
Oklahoma, 247
Old Regime, France, 320, 358, 543
Olympic games, 32
Omar, caliph, 169
On the Origin of Species (Darwin), 436
Open Door policy, 479–481, 485, 574
open field system, 392

open-hearth process, 391
opium, 477
Opium Wars, 477–478, 485
oracles, 45, 705
Orange Free State, 458. *See also* South Africa, Union of
Orders in Council, Britain, 336
Organization for Economic Cooperation and development (OECD), 613
Organization of American States (OAS), 629, 631, 644
Organization of European Economic Cooperation (OOEC), 613
Organization of Petroleum Exporting Countries (Opec), 636, 637, 650, 673, 707
Orlando, Vittorio, 504, *505*, 510
Orleans, Battle of, 232–233
Orozco, José Clemente, 627
Osiris, Egyptian god, 15
ostracism, 39
Ostrogoths, 178
Othman, caliph, 169
Otto I, Holy Roman Emperor, 185
Ottoman Empire, 376–*378*
Ottoman Turks, 165
Ovid, 73
Owen, Robert, 398

Pacific Ocean, 83
Pahlavi, Reza, Shah of Iran, 532, 606: fall from power, 659, 660, 673
Paine, Thomas, 311, 316
Pakistan, 82, 99, 696–699, 700; establishment of, 696; division of, 697
Palestine, 13, 20, 24, 185, 534, 650, 651. *See also* Israel
Palestine Liberation Organization (PLO), 652, 658
Palestinians, 652, 658, 673
pampas, 133
Panama: under Viceroyalty of New Granada, 347, 351, 632; independence of, 351; Colombia loses, 536, 538, 633, 642, 645; given control of Canal, 623
Panama Canal: U.S. and building of, 535, 536, 538, 633–634, 642, 645; control given to Panama, 623
Pan-Americanism, 642
Pan-American Union, 642–643
Panchatantra, 99
Pankhurst, Emmeline, 432
Pantheon, 73
papal infallibility, 437
Papal States, 178, 185, 238; and unification of Italy, 367, 370, 371, 438
Papandreou, Andreas, 605
paper, 122
Papineau, Louis Joseph, 520
papyrus, 16, 17
Paraguay, 347
Paris, France, 272
Paris, Treaty of: in 1763, 623; in 1856, 377–378
Park, Chung Hee, 684

Park, Mungo, 454
Parkes, Henry, 521
Parliament, Great Britain: Great Council, 229–230; Elizabeth I and, 265; Stuarts and, 302–306, 315; reforms in, 407–412; role of, today, 412–416; Irish question, 517, 518, and Canada, 521
Parliament Act of 1911, 411–412
parliaments: in Germany, 373, 375; in Austria and Hungary, 376; in Ireland, 518, 597; in Canada, 520–521, 623–625. *See also* Estates-General; Parliament, Great Britain
Parthenon, *39*, 47
Partis Quebecois (PQ), 626
Pascal, Blaise, 288
passive resistance concept, 524, 525
Pasteur, Louis, 428, 429
pasteurization, 428
Pathet Lao, 695
patriarchs, 162
patricians, 58, 62
patriotism, 226, 227, 366, 452, 566
Paul, St., 74
Paul I, king of Greece, 605
Pax Romana, 66, 69, 505
Peace Corps, 622
Peace of Augsburg, 217
Peace of Westphalia, 238–*239*
peace treaty, 503
Pearl Harbor, 565, 574, 575, 587
Pearson, Lester, 625
Peasants' War 218
Pedro I, emperor of Brazil, *353*, 355
Pedro II, emperor of Brazil, 355
Peel, Robert, 435
Peking, China, 115, 116, 527, 529, 679
Peloponnesian Wars, 41, 49, 50, 52
Pemex, 628
Pennsylvania, 380
Pepin the Short, Frank leader, 178
Pericles, Athenian leader, 41, 47
Perón, Evita Duarté, 638–639
Perón, Isabel, 639
Perón, Juan Domingo, 638–639
Peronistas, 638, 639
Perry, Matthew, *482*, 485
Persia: conquers Egypt, 13; empire of, 13, 21, 24, 27–29; wars with Greece, 40, 52; under Roman Empire, 28, 165, 168; during World War I, 532. *See also* Iran
Persian Wars, 40, 52
Peru, 133; early civilization in, 133; Incas in, 138–140, 247, 347, 636; viceroyalty in, 347; independence of, 351; after World War II, 637–638
Pescadores islands, 479
Pestalozzi, Johann, 430
Pétain, Henri, 498, 571
Peter I (the Great), czar of Russia, 273–274, 275, 280
petition, 309
Petition of right, 305, 315
petit jury, 228

Petrarch, 204, 207
phalanstérès, 398
phalanxes, 59
pharoahs, 12–13, 14–15, 16, 18, 25, 28
Philip II, king of Spain, 93, 262, 263, 264, 265, 279, 280
Philip II of Macedon, *42*
Philip V of Macedon, 61
Philip Augustus, king of France, 187, 230
Philip the Fair, king of France, 230, 231
Philippi, Battle of, 65
Philippines, 83; early history of, 100, 474; U.S. and, 479, 535; independence of, 537, 538, 687; in World War II, 575–576, 578, 687
philosophes, 292, 293, 295, 296
philosophy: in Greece, 48–50; in India, 98; in China, 109–111, 112; Medieval, 198; in France, 292–293; in England, 292–293
Phnom Penh, 695
Phoenicia, 20, *26*, *27*, 29; explorations and trade, 61, 141
Picasso, Pablo, 146
pictographs, 33–34
Pilgrims, 303
Pinzon, 244
Pisa, Italy, 191, 205, 212
Pius IX, pope, 437
Pizzaro, Francisco, 247
Plato, 48, 49, 50, 109, 204, 207
Platt Amendment, 628
plebeians, 58, 61, 62, 63
Pliny the Elder, 73
Pluto, Greek god, 44
pocket borough, 407
Poland: division of, 274, 277, 278, 283; Russia and, 343, 560; Hitler and, 558, 560, 570, 586; after World War II, 581, 608–609; Soviet Union and, 608–609
Politburo, 549
Politics (Aristotle), 50
Polo, Marco, 115, 474, *475*
Pol Pot, 680, 695
Polybius, 59
polygamy, 95, 168
polytheism, 21
Pompeii, 136
Pompey, Gnaeus, 63, 64, 79
Pompidou, Georges, 600
Ponce de León, Juan, 240, 245
Pondicherry, India, 468, 469
Pope, Alexander, 289–290
popes, 74; in Byzantine Empire, 160, 162; political power, in the Middle Ages, 178, 185, 188, 238; French and Italian rivalry, 215–216. *See also* Papal States; Roman Catholic Church
Popular Revolutionary Bloc (PRB), in El Salvador, 632
population growth: in Middle Ages, 192; in nineteenth century, 424, 442; in India, 523

Po River, 367, 368
Portales, Diego, 355
Portillo, López, 628
Portugal: Muslims and, 168; becomes a nation, 234–236, 252; overseas empire, 240, 243–249, 253, 347–355, 605, 697; under Spain, 263; imperialism in Africa, 453; and slave trade, 454; and India, 466–467, 468; and China, 474; after World War II, 604–605
Poseidon, Greek god, 44
postal service, 391–392
Potsdam Conference, 581
poverty, urbanization and, 425
power loom, 391
praetors, 58
Pragmatic Sanction of Bourges, 234
Prakrit, 98
Pre-Columbian civilizations, 132–140
premier, 549
Presbyterian faith, 220, 303
president, in the U.S., 414–415, 416, 420
Presidium, 549
Priestley, Joseph, 288
priests, in India, 86
prime minister, 412, 415–416, 420
Prince, The (Machiavelli), 211
Principe, 605
printing press, 212, *214*, 225
prison reform, 434–435
Procopius, 161, 174
proletariat, 545
propaganda: in World War I, 495–496; Hitler and, 556; and Cold War, 595
protectorate, 452
Protestants, 264–265; and theory of evolution, 437–438; in Ireland, 517, 597
Protestant Reformation, 214–215, 218–220, 228; results of, 212–222, 517
Proudhon, Pierre Joseph, 401
provinces, Roman, 68, 75
Prussia, 238, *239;* under Frederick the Great, 275–277; and Austria, 275–277; absolutism in, 275–278, 342; in Franco-Prussian War, 370, 375, 418; and unification of Germany, 371, 372, 373, 376, 382
Ptolemy, rulers of Egypt, 65–66
Ptolemy, scientist, 50, 141, 197, 213
Pueblo incident, 684–685
Puerto Rico, 535, 630–631
Punic Wars, 61, 141
purdah, 95
Puritans, 220, 264, 303, 305, 306, 308
Pu-yi, ruler of China, 567, 526, 567
Pygmies, 140
pyramids: in Egypt, 12, 13, 16, 17, 29, 134, 453; of the Mayas, 134, 136
Pythagorean theorem, 98

Qaddafi, Muammar, 662

San Martín, José de, 133, 351
Sanskrit, 87, 91
Santa Anna, ruler of Mexico, 353, 355, 417
Santo Domingo, 536
São Tomé, 605
Sappho, 48
Sarawak, 687
Sardinia, 368, 369, 370, 376, 377
Sargon I, Sumerian king, 19
Sarharov, Andrei, 607
Saudi Arabia, 664; after World War I, 533; oil in, 628; and the Six-Day War, 653; U.S. and, 658
SAVAK, in Iran, 660
Scandinavian countries: development of nations in, 236–237, 253; democracy in, 419
Schiller, Friedrich von, 290
schism, 162, 163
Schliemann, Heinrich, 35
Schmidt, Helmut, 603
scholasticism, 198, 199
Schweitzer, Albert, 456
science: in Babylonia, 23–24; in Greece, 50–51; in Rome, 73; in India, 97–98; in China, 122; in Middle Ages, 197; during Renaissance, 212–214, 223; in Age of Reason, 286–289, 296; in nineteenth century, 435–437; and religion, 437–438; in twentieth century, 708. See also astronomy
scientific method, 223, 285–289
Scotland, 264–265, 302, 305, 597
scribes, 14, 15, 17, 21
sculpture: Greek, 47–48, 51; African, 146
Sea of Marmara, 157
segregation, 621
Selassie, Haile, 664
Seljuk Turks, 165, 170, 186
Senate: in Sparta, 37; in Rome, 58, 63
Seneca, 73
Seoul, Korea, 123–124
separation of powers, 416
separatists: in Spain, 604–605: in Quebec, 625–626
Sepoy Mutiny, 471, 485
sepoys, 470–471
Serbia, 378, 383, 492, 494, 510
serfs, 182, 183, 191, 192, 321, 544
Seven Years' War, 275–277
Shah Jahan, Mogul emperor, 93–94
Shakespeare, William, 261, 265
Shang Dynasty, 107–108
Shastri, Lel Bahadur, 697
Sheba, queen of, 144
Shelley, Percy Bysshe, 439
Shensi province, China, 678
Shih Huang Ti, 109, 111–113, 128
Shiite Moslems, 606
Shintoism, 126, 127
Shogun, 126, 128
shogunate system, 483, 485
Shrivijaya, Kingdom of, 102
Shudras, 86

Sicily, 370–371, 576
Sierre Leone, 141
Sihanouk, Norodom, 694, 695
silk, 163, 266
Sinai Penninsula, 652, 654, 655, 658
Singapore, 532, 687–688, 700
Sinn Fein, 518
Sino-Japanese War, 479, 484, 526
Si River, 107
Six-Day War, 653–654
slave factories, 454
slavery: in Egypt, 16, 24, 25, 453; in Babylonia, 21, 23; in Athens, 40, 47, 52; in Rome, 61, 70, 72, 141, 453; in Africa, 141, 146, 453–454; in New World, 251, 347, 348, 454; in U.S., 434; defined, 453
slave trade, 251–252, 345, 347, 348; in nineteenth century, 434, 453–454, 462
Slavic language, 236
slums, 395, 396, 402, 426
Smith, Adam, 293, 296, 397, 433
Smith, Ian, 668, 669
social class: in ancient Greece, 46–47, 52; and the Aztecs, 138; and the Incas, 139–140; in the Victorian Age, 427–428
Social Darwinism, 436–437
Social Democratic Party, England, 597
socialism: in Germany, 375; Marx and, 400–401; defined, 549; in Russia, 549; in France, 600; in Portugal, 605
socialized medicine, 596
Socrates, 47, 48–49, 50, 109, 110, 204
Socratic method, 48
Soga clan, 126
Solomon, Hebrew king, 24
Solon, 38–39
Solzhenitsyn, Alexander, 607
Somalia, 144, 664
Somoza, Anastasio, 632
Songhay, 142, 143–144, 145
Sophocles, 48
Sophonisba of Cremona, 209
South Africa, Republic of, 147, 248, 515, 670–672
South Africa, Union of, 458, 515, 525
South America, 132–133; Native Americans in, 133–134, 138–140, 149; Spaniards in, 240, 244–247. See also Latin America; names of individual countries
South Asia: defined, 82; countries of, 82–83
South Carolina, 381
South China Sea, 83
Southeast Asia, 82–84; countries of, 83, 100–102; people of, 99–100, 102; history of, 100–102; European domination of, 474, 484; imperialism in, 531–532, 538; wars in, 689–695, 699. See also names of individual countries

Southeast Asia Treaty Organization (SEATO), 690
Southwest Africa. See Namibia
South-West Africa People's Organization (SWAPO), 672
South Yemen, 661
sovereignty, 227
soviet, 545, 547
Soviet Union: formation of, 545–547, 559; rise of communism, 532, 544, 545–547, 559; government of, 547–552, 607; economy of, 550–551, 607; agriculture in, 551–552; in World War II, 570, 572, 576, 578–579, 581, 586–587, 606; and Cold War, 595, 611–612, 629; and U.S. 595, 608, 612, 622; and East Germany, 601–602, 610–611; after World War II, 606–611; and Poland, 609; and Czechoslovakia, 609, 610; and Hungary, 609–610; in Eastern Europe, 608–610; and SALT talks, 612; and Cuba, 629–630; and Middle East, 650, 655, 658, 660–661; and Africa, 664, 672; and China, 528, 678, 680; and Korean War, 682, 684; space exploration, 707–708. See also Russia
Soweto, 671
space exploration, 707–708
Spain: Romans in, 61; and Latin America, 133, 136; and Mexico, 136; Muslims in, 168, 170, 177, 234; Visigoths in, 177; kingdoms of, 236; becomes a nation, 234–236, 252; overseas empire, 240–249, 253, 263, 312, 346–355, 359, 453, 632; absolutism in, 261–264, 280, 342; in Holy Roman Empire, 261–264; defeat of Armada, 265, 267; culture of, 291; and China, 474, 479; in Spanish-American War, 479–480; Civil War in, 557; after World War II, 557, 604–605, 641; separatists in, 604–605
Spanish-American War, 479–480, 535, 628
Spanish Main, 346
Spanish Sahara, 662
Sparta, 36; political power in, 37; life in, 37–38, 46, 52; wars with Athens, 41–42
Speke, John, 454–455
Spencer, Herbert, 436
sphere of influence, 452
Sphinx, 12
spices, 97
spinning jenny, 390–391
spinning mule, 391
Sri Lanka (Ceylon), 83, 343
stadtholder, 301
Stalin, Joseph: rise of, 547, 548–549; dictatorship, 570, 607, 616; and World War II, 572, 579, 581, 587; death of, 595, 606, 608, 616
Stanley, Henry M., 455, 456–457, 459, 462

ACKNOWLEDGMENTS AND READINGS

Photos

1 Dr. George Gerster/Photo Researchers, Inc.; **3** George Holton/Photo Researchers, Inc.; **4** The Bettmann Archive, Inc. (T); **4** The Bettmann Archive, Inc. (C); **4** The Bettmann Archive, Inc. (B); **6** Allyn & Bacon Inc. (L); **6** Allyn & Bacon Inc. (R); **9** Lee Boltin; **10** The Metropolitan Museum of Art; **12** PROPIX/Monkmeyer Press Photo Service; **14** DRYFOOS/Monkmeyer Press Photo Service; **15** Editorial Photocolor Archives, Inc.; **17** The Metropolitan Museum of Art, Rogers Fund, 1912; **20** Alinari/Editorial Photocolor Archives, Inc.; **22** The Metropolitan Museum of Art, Harris Brisbane Dick Fund, 1959; **23** D. Rawson/Photo Researchers, Inc.; 11 **25** THE GRANGER COLLECTION, New York; **26** The Bettmann Archive, Inc.; **28** Culver Pictures, Inc.; **32** The Metropolitan Museum of Art, Purchase 1947, Joseph J. Pulitzer bequest; **34** Michael Tzovaras/Editorial Photocolor Archives, Inc.; **38** The Bettmann Archive, Inc.; **39** James Theologos/Monkmeyer Press Photo Service; **42** The Bettmann Archive, Inc.; **43** The Metropolitan Museum of Art, gift of Alexander Smith Cochran, 1913; **45** Alinari/Editorial Photocolor Archives, Inc.; **48** Scala/Editorial Photocolor Archives, Inc.; **49** The Bettmann Archive, Inc.; **51** Scala/Editorial Photocolor Archives, Inc.; **55** Adam Woolfitt/Woodfin Camp & Associates; **57** The Bettmann Archive, Inc.; **59** The Bettmann Archive, Inc.; **61** The Bettmann Archive, Inc.; **63** Alinari/Editorial Photocolor Archives, Inc.; **65** Culver Pictures, Inc.; **68** John G. Ross/Photo Researchers, Inc.; **70** Courtesy New York Public Library; **72** William Hubbell/Woodfin Camp & Associates; **75** THE GRANGER COLLECTION, New York; **81** The Bettmann Archive, Inc.; **83** Chris Bonnington/Woodfin Camp & Associates; **84** Paolo Koch/Photo Researchers, Inc.; **87** Marc Bernheim/Woodfin Camp & Associates; **88** The Metropolitan Museum of Art, purchase Enid A. Haupt gift, 1979; **89** Scala/Editorial Photocolor Archives, Inc.; **93** Herbert Lanks/Monkmeyer Press Photo Service; **95** Paolo Koch/Photo Researchers, Inc.; **96** Borromeo/Editorial Photocolor Archives, Inc.; **98** Lynn McLaren/Photo Researchers, Inc.; **99** Joan Lebold Cohen/Photo Researchers, Inc.; **101** Bernard Silberstein/Monkmeyer Press Photo Service (L); **101** Bumiller/Monkmeyer Press Photo Service (R); **106** The Metropolitan Museum of Art, anonymous gift, 1942; **108** The Metropolitan Museum of Art, Munsey Bequest, 1924; **111** The Bettmann Archive, Inc.; **112** DRYFOOS/Monkmeyer Press Photo Service; **115** Sotheby Parke-Bernet/Editorial Photocolor Archives, Inc.; **116** Courtesy New York Public Library (T); **116** Culver Pictures, Inc. (B); **118** The Metropolitan Museum of Art, gift of Mr. and Mrs. John S. Menke, 1972; **120** The Metropolitan Museum of Art, bequest of John D. Rockefeller, Jr. 1960; **121** The Bettmann Archive, Inc.; **123** The Metropolitan Museum of Art, gift of the Dillon Fund, 1973; **124** The Metropolitan Museum of Art, gift of R.H. Macy & Co., 1919; **126** Mike Yamashita/Woodfin Camp & Associates; **127** The Metropolitan Museum of Art, the Rogers Fund, 1912; **131** Scala/Editorial Photocolor Archives, Inc.; **133** Loren McIntyre/Woodfin Camp & Associates; **134** Marc Bernheim/Woodfin Camp & Associates; **137** Scala/Editorial Photocolor Archives, Inc.; **138** Culver Pictures, Inc.; **139** Allyn Baum/Monkmeyer Press Photo Service; **141** The Brooklyn Museum; **144** Courtesy New York Public Library; **146** The Metropolitan Museum of Art, Michael C. Rockefeller Memorial Collection of Primitive Art, gift of Nelson A. Rockefeller, 1972; **147** United Press International; **148** Else Sackler/American Museum of Natural History; **155** THE GRANGER COLLECTION, New York; **156** THE GRANGER COLLECTION, New York; **158** Scala/Editorial Photocolor Archives, Inc.; **160** The Bettmann Archive, Inc.; **161** Alinari/Editorial Photocolor Archives, Inc.; **165** Roland and Sabrina Michaud/Woodfin Camp & Associates (L); **165** Roland and Sabrina Michaud/Woodfin Camp & Associates (R); **166** The Bettmann Archive, Inc.; **167** Robert Azzi/Woodfin Camp & Associates; **171** Sotheby Parke-Bernet/Editorial Photocolor Archives, Inc.; **175** Scala/Editorial Photocolor Archives, Inc.; **176** Courtesy New York Public Library; **178** Scala/Editorial Photocolor Archives, Inc.; **181** THE GRANGER COLLECTION, New York; **183** Editorial Photocolor Archives, Inc. (BL); **183** Scala/Editorial Photocolor Archives, Inc. (TR); **183** Editorial Photocolor Archives, Inc. (TL); **185** Alinari/Editorial Photocolor Archives, Inc.; **187** Editorial Photocolor Archives, Inc.; **192** Scala/Editorial Photocolor Archives, Inc.; **194** The Bettmann Archives, Inc.; **196** THE GRANGER COLLECTION, New York; **198** Courtesy New York Public Library; **203** Scala/Editorial Photocolor Archives, Inc.; **205** Courtesy New York Public Library; **208** The Bettmann Archive, Inc.; **209** Courtesy New York Public Library; **210** The Bettmann Archive, Inc.; **211** Alinari/Editorial Photocolor Archives, Inc. **213** Scala/Editorial Photocolor Archives, Inc.; **214** Courtesy New York Public Library (T); **214** The Bettmann Archive, Inc. (B); **217** Courtesy New York Public Library; **220** Scala/Editorial Photocolor Archives, Inc.; **222** The Bettmann Archive, Inc.; **226** THE GRANGER COLLECTION, New York; **229** Scala/Editorial Photocolor Archives, Inc.; **230** The Bettmann Archive, Inc.; **233** The Bettmann Archive,

Inc.; **238** The Bettmann Archive, Inc.; **241** The Bettmann Archive, Inc.; **244** Scala/Editorial Photocolor Archives, Inc.; **245** The Bettmann Archive, Inc.; **247** Porterfield-Chickering/Photo Researchers, Inc.; **249** Culver Pictures, Inc.; **252** The Bettmann Archive, Inc.; **259** THE GRANGER COLLECTION, New York; **260** THE GRANGER COLLECTION, New York; **262** The Bettmann Archive, Inc.; **263** The Bettmann Archive, Inc.; **265** THE GRANGER COLLECTION, New York; **267** THE GRANGER COLLECTION, New York; **270** THE GRANGER COLLECTION, New York; **272** Courtesy of French Cultural Services; **274** THE GRANGER COLLECTION, New York; **277** The Bettmann Archive, Inc.; **279** Editorial Photocolor Archives, Inc.; **284** THE GRANGER COLLECTION, New York; **286** THE GRANGER COLLECTION, New York; **288** The Bettmann Archive, Inc.; **290** The Bettmann Archive, Inc.; **291** THE GRANGER COLLECTION, New York; **293** THE GRANGER COLLECTION, New York; **294** THE GRANGER COLLECTION, New York; **295** THE GRANGER COLLECTION, New York; **299** The Bettmann Archive, Inc.; **301** THE GRANGER COLLECTION, New York; **303** The Bettmann Archive, Inc.; **304** THE GRANGER COLLECTION, New York; **306** The Bettmann Archive, Inc.; **307** Culver Pictures, Inc.; **309** THE GRANGER COLLECTION, New York; **310** THE GRANGER COLLECTION, New York; **314** The Library of Congress; **319** THE GRANGER COLLECTION, New York; **321** THE GRANGER COLLECTION, New York; **322** THE GRANGER COLLECTION, New York; **324** THE GRANGER COLLECTION, New York; **325** THE GRANGER COLLECTION, New York; **327** THE GRANGER COLLECTION, New York; **328** THE GRANGER COLLECTION, New York; **329** THE GRANGER COLLECTION, New York; **331** The Bettmann Archive, Inc.; **333** THE GRANGER COLLECTION, New York; **334** THE GRANGER COLLECTION, New York; **340** The Bettmann Archive, Inc. (L); **340** Culver Pictures, Inc. (R); **341** The Bettmann Archive, Inc.; **343** THE GRANGER COLLECTION, New York; **345** THE GRANGER COLLECTION, New York; **347** The American Museum of Natural History; **350** The American Museum of Natural History; **352** THE GRANGER COLLECTION, New York; **353** The Bettmann Archive, Inc.; **357** The Bettmann Archive, Inc.; **365** THE GRANGER COLLECTION, New York; **366** THE GRANGER COLLECTION, New York; **368** Editorial Photocolor Archives, Inc.; **370** THE GRANGER COLLECTION, New York; **372** THE GRANGER COLLECTION, New York; **374** THE GRANGER COLLECTION, New York; **379** The Bettmann Archive, Inc.; **381** The Bettmann Archive, Inc.; **385** Culver Pictures, Inc.; **386** THE GRANGER COLLECTION, New York; **389** THE GRANGER COLLECTION, New York; **390** THE GRANGER COLLECTION, New York; **392** THE GRANGER COLLECTION, New York; **393** THE GRANGER COLLECTION, New York; **395** THE GRANGER COLLECTION, New York; **399** The Bettmann Archive, Inc.; **400** THE GRANGER COLLECTION, New York; **406** THE GRANGER COLLECTION, New York; **409** THE GRANGER COLLECTION, New York; **410** THE GRANGER COLLECTION, New York; **413** THE GRANGER COLLECTION, New York (L); **413** THE GRANGER COLLECTION, New York (R); **415** Fred J. Maroon/Photo Researchers, Inc.; **417** The Bettmann Archive, Inc.; **423** THE GRANGER COLLECTION, New York; **425** The Bettmann Archive, Inc.; **426** The Bettmann Archive, Inc.; **427** THE GRANGER COLLECTION, New York; **428** The Bettmann Archive, Inc.; **429** THE GRANGER COLLECTION, New York; **430** The Bettmann Archive, Inc.; **431** The Bettmann Archive, Inc.; **433** The Bettmann Archive, Inc.; **435** THE GRANGER COLLECTION, New York; **436** THE GRANGER COLLECTION, New York; **439** THE GRANGER COLLECTION, New York; **441** THE GRANGER COLLECTION, New York; **449** Peabody Museum, Salem, Massachusetts; **450** THE GRANGER COLLECTION, New York; **452** THE GRANGER COLLECTION, New York; **454** THE GRANGER COLLECTION, New York; **455** Wallace Kirkland/Photo Researchers, Inc.; **456** THE GRANGER COLLECTION, New York; **457** THE GRANGER COLLECTION, New York; **458** The Bettmann Archive, Inc.; **464** THE GRANGER COLLECTION, New York; **465** The Bettmann Archive, Inc.; **467** THE GRANGER COLLECTION, New York; **469** THE GRANGER COLLECTION, New York; **473** The Bettmann Archive, Inc.; **475** The Bettmann Archive, Inc.; **476** The Bettmann Archive, Inc.; **480** THE GRANGER COLLECTION, New York; **481** THE GRANGER COLLECTION, New York; **482** The Bettmann Archive, Inc.; **489** The Bettmann Archive, Inc.; **492** THE GRANGER COLLECTION, New York; **494** The Bettmann Archive, Inc.; **497** THE GRANGER COLLECTION, New York; **498** United Press International; **501** WIDE WORLD PHOTOS; **502** THE GRANGER COLLECTION, New York; **503** THE GRANGER COLLECTION, New York; **505** The Bettmann Archive, Inc.; **509** The Bettmann Archive, Inc.; **514** THE GRANGER COLLECTION, New York; **518** THE GRANGER COLLECTION, New York; **521** THE GRANGER COLLECTION, New York; **522** Robert Frerck/Woodfin Camp & Associates; **525** THE GRANGER COLLECTION, New York; **527** The Bettmann Archive, Inc.; **529** WIDE WORLD PHOTOS; **530** FPG; **531** Carl Purcel/Photo Researchers, Inc. (L); **531** George Holton/Photo Researchers, Inc. (R); **532** Gerry Granham/Photo Researchers, Inc.; **533** United Press International; **534** WIDE WORLD PHOTOS; **535** The Bettmann Archive, Inc.; **537** The Bettmann Archive, Inc.; **541** The Bettmann Archive, Inc.; **542** THE GRANGER COLLECTION, New York; **545** The Bettmann Archive, Inc.; **546** The Bettmann Archive, Inc.; **548** The Bettmann Archive, Inc.; **551** Julian Calder/Woodfin Camp & Associates; **553** The Bettmann Archive, Inc.; **555** The Bettmann Archive, Inc.; **557** Sabine Weiss/Photo Researchers, Inc.; **565** United Press International; **567** WIDE WORLD PHOTOS; **571** United Press International; **572** THE GRANGER COLLECTION, New York; **573** Patricia Hollander Gross/Stock Boston; **576** THE GRANGER COLLECTION, New York; **579** THE GRANGER COLLECTION, New York; **580** THE GRANGER COLLECTION, New York; **585** Richard Choy/Peter Arnold, Inc.; **593** THE GRANGER COLLECTION, New York; **594** THE GRANGER COLLECTION, New York; **595** WIDE WORLD PHOTOS; **596** WIDE WORLD PHOTOS; **598** Malcolm J. Gilson/Black Star; **600** John Launois/Black Star; **603** United Press International; **604** WIDE WORLD PHOTOS; **606** WIDE WORLD PHOTOS; **607** Rey—Rapho/Photo Researchers, Inc.; **609** United Press International; **611** Paolo Koch/Photo Researchers, Inc.; **614** Lynn Karlin/ FPG (T); **614** United Press International (B); **620** Victor Engelbert/Black Star; **621** United Press International; **622** United Press International; **625** E. Nagele/Alpha Photo Associates; **627** Steve Northup/Black Star; **629** Black Star; **630** Ross/Pictorial Parade; **633** Carl Frank/Photo Researchers, Inc.; **634** Sepp Seitz/Woodfin Camp & Associates; **637** John Bryson/Photo Researchers, Inc. (L); **637** Gerhard Gscheidle/Peter Arnold, Inc. (R); **638** United Press International; **640** Claus Meyer/Black Star; **641** United Press International; **643** Toby Molenaar/Woodfin Camp & Associates (R); **643** Monkmeyer Press Photo Service (L); **648** Guernsey LePelley/ Christian Science Monitor; **649** John G. Ross/ Photo Researchers, Inc.; **653** E. Cromwell/Monkmeyer Press Photo Service; **654** George Gerster/ Photo Researchers, Inc.; **656** Ricardo Watson/ Pictorial Parade; **657** Photographers International/Pictorial Parade; **660** Diego Goldberg/ Sygma; **662** Sipa Press/Black Star; **665** AFP Photo/Pictorial Parade; **666** George Gerster/ Photo Researchers, Inc.; **670** Sipa Press/Black Star; **671** Peter Jordan/Sygma; **676** David Suter/The New York Times; **677** Mike Yamashita/Woodfin Camp & Associates; **679** Harry Redl/Black Star; **681** Susan McCartney/Photo Researchers, Inc.; **683** WIDE WORLD PHOTOS; **685** Courtesy of Japan Trade Center; **687** THE GRANGER COLLECTION, New York; **688** Robert Frerck/Woodfin Camp & Associates; **692** WIDE WORLD PHOTOS; **693** Charles Bonnay/Black Star; **696** John de Nissen/Black Star; **705** WIDE WORLD PHOTOS; **706** S.J. Mirabella/FPG (TL); **706** J. Baker/FPG (TR); **707** WIDE WORLD PHOTOS (T); **707** Martin Rogers/Woodfin Camp & Associates (B); **709** John Blaustein/Woodfin Camp & Associates; **710** O. Franken/Sygma

Readings

p. 54 From a translation of the *Apology* by Plato, c. 399 B.C.

p. 130 From the travels of *Marco Polo* by Manuel Komroff, ed. (New York: Liveright Publishers, 1953).

p. 225 Chart from *Engineers and Engineering in the Renaissance* by William Barclay Parsons (Cambridge: Mass.: The MIT Press, 1968). Used by permission of The Wiliams & Wilkins Co., Baltimore.

p. 405 From *First Report from Commissioners appointed to collect Information in the Manufacturing Districts, relative to Employment of Children in Factories; and as to the property and means of curtailing the Hours of their Labour; with Minutes of Evidence and Reports of District Commissioners.* Published for Parliament as a Sessional Paper, 1833 (450).

pp. 730–31 Maps based on data from *Freedom House*